The
Diversity
Machine

The
Diversity
Machine
The Drive to Change the
"White Male Workplace"

With a new preface by the author
Frederick R. Lynch

Transaction Publishers
New Brunswick (U.S.A.) and London (U.K.)

Second printing 2005

New material this edition copyright © 2002 by Transaction Publishers, New Brunswick, New Jersey. Originally published in 1997 by The Free Press.

The author acknowledges with thanks, permission to reprint material from the following sources: Lewis Griggs, *Valuing Diversity* (videotape series), Griggs Productions, San Francisco; George F. Simons, "Diversophy" (game cards), ©1995 Multus Inc., all rights reserved; Sondra Thiederman, "Cultural Diversity Quiz: How's Your 'Cultural I.Q.'?" in *Profiting in America's Multicultural Marketplace: How to Do Business Across Cultural Lines*, copyright ©1991 Sondra Thiederman, all rights resrved [first published by Lexington Books—all correspondence should be sent to Jossey-Bass Inc., Publishers, San Francisco]; R. Roosevelt Thomas, Jr., "From Affirmative Action to Affirming Diversity"; R. Roosevelt Thomas, Jr., *Beyond Race and Gender: Unleashing the Power of Your Total Workforce by Managing Diversity*.

Library of Congress Catalog Number: 00-062923
ISBN: 0-7658-0731-9
Printed in the United States of America

Library of Congress Cataloging-in-Publication Data

Lynch, Frederick R.
    The diversity machine : the drive to change the "white male workplace" / Frederick R. Lynch ; with a new preface by the author.
        p. cm.
    Includes bibliographical references and index.
    ISBN 0-7658-0731-9 (pbk.: alk. paper)
    1. Diversity in the workplace—United States. I. Title.

HF5549.5.M5 L96 2000
331.13'3'0973—dc21   00-062923

For my sister, Peg
And the memory of Mother and Dad

Contents

Acknowledgments

This book could not have been written without the support of the Boards of Trustees of the Sarah Scaife Foundation and the Carthage Foundation. Special thanks are due to Richard Larry, president and treasurer, respectively, of those foundations. Claremont McKenna College (CMC) president Jack Stark and two faculty deans, Ralph Rossum and Tony Fucaloro, also proved to be fearless champions of academic freedom. They sheltered a maverick sociologist in a first-rate teaching and research environment. The John Olin Foundation provided crucial support. A summer fellowship from the Benjamin Z. Gould Center sustained much rewriting, as did summer research grants from the Office of the Dean of Faculty.

CMC colleagues Jack Pitney, Joe Cardoza, Riccardo Quinones, Langdon Ellsbree, Steve Davis, Bob Faggen, and Judith Merkle always provided lively exchanges on this topic. *Forbes* magazine senior editor Peter Brimelow gave my research and spirits an early and vital boost.

Free Press senior editor Adam Bellow took a chance on a controversial author and topic. My editor at Free Press, David Bernstein, and my copy editor, Beverly Miller, were tireless—and above all patient—in rereading and continually providing valuable insight and feedback. My agents, Laurie Fox and Linda Chester, listened and listened to my prepublication ramblings. Monica Morris gave feedback on a first draft way back. Long-time friends Jan Allard and Gary Jason never tired of talking about these issues. The increasing number of friendly notes and telephone calls from people who read my first book were more encouraging than they realize.

Finally, I must credit most diversity consultants for practicing what they preached by providing a welcoming environment for a researcher they might have had reason to suspect. Pam Fomalont and I had many spirited exchanges, and Anita Rowe, an accomplished author in her own right, was always candid and helpful, as were Lewis Griggs, Sondra Thiederman, and many others.

Preface to the Transaction Edition

The new Transaction edition of *The Diversity Machine* may be even more relevant today than was the original text in 1997. In the past three years, the social policy movement that sought to move multiculturalism from academe to the American workplace has increased its influence. As the nation enters the new millenium, the words "diversity" and "inclusion" are everywhere. Powerful CEOs and politicians (from Bill Clinton and Al Gore to George W. Bush) chant the bipartisan mantra that "diversity is our strength." Major magazines, newspapers, and business and professional journals have run cover stories or feature articles on the new diversity, particularly the rising visibility of Hispanics.

Since 1997, then, the nation's leaders and most of its citizens have become much more aware of demographic change—as correctly heralded a decade ago by the diversity machine. It remains to be seen how the nation will respond to such changes. The diversity machine's menu of "valuing diversity" policies remains seductive, yet questionable. Still lacking is systematic social science evidence that emphasizing collective identities in the workplace increases productivity, creativity, and harmony. And for every enthusiastic testimonial, there are accounts which claim that diversity policies inflame, rather than reduce, inter-group tensions. But no corporate or political leader dares question publicly the call to celebrate diversity.

The Diversity Machine remains the only sociological study of how a relatively small coalition of consultants (and their allies in business, government, foundations, and universities) built a social policy machine which rhetorically recast much of American life into a multicultural mold.[1] Indeed, I am impressed anew with both the insight and foresight of some of the diversity machine's chief architects.

The Diversity Machine is actually two books. The first half outlines the evolution of workplace diversity theories which linked multiculturalism to demographic change and global capitalism. Through books, articles, lectures, workshops, networking, and conferences, policy proponents replaced shopworn, moralistic affirmative action arguments with a practical, business-friendly rationale.

The new "dollars and demographics" prescription was basically this: savvy employers should create "diversity-friendly," multi-ethnic workplaces to capitalize upon a world of globalizing markets and Third World immigration. Rising numbers of Third World employees and customers will allegedly gravitate towards organizations where others resemble them. Greater minority and female representation at all organizational levels will also provide a measure of legal insurance against expensive discrimination lawsuits. Altering workplace cultures designed by and for white men will break the seen-but-unnoticed "glass ceiling" barrier of discrimination. Women and minority employees will be freed to "be themselves," and avoid forced assimilation to white male norms.

The second half of *The Diversity Machine* provides a literature review and in-depth case studies. The case studies demonstrate how the many types of workforce diversity programs merged with other trends and events in actual organizational settings. Diversity programs were initiated for a variety of reasons and percolated through organizational structures in many ways, which produced a multiplicity of intended and unintended results. In the realm of diversity policy, as in few others, the difference between rhetoric and reality was often difficult to discern.

A central theme in *The Diversity Machine* is the passage of this social policy juggernaut through the stages typical of social movements. The initial theories, journal publications, and conferences began in the late 1980s climate of urgency created by forecasts of major demographic changes. Writer-consultants such as Lewis Griggs, Roosevelt Thomas, Jr., Sondra Thiederman, and Tom Kochman (all profiled in *The Diversity Machine*) emerged as theoreticians and spokespersons who, along with several others, defined the problem, articulated solutions, organized continuing conferences and research institutes, and published books, articles, newsletters and journals. During the 1990s, these valuing and managing diversity theories were mainstreamed into textbook chapters and meetings of professional and business associations. Corporations appointed vice presidents devoted to diversity issues. Sections on respecting cultural differences were woven into the core-values or mission statements of many corporations and government agencies.

The saga of this successful policy movement has continued to unfold on a weekly, and sometimes daily, basis. It was difficult, therefore, to "close the book" on the 1997 edition of *The Diversity Machine*. Indeed, two late-breaking events were included in the book's conclusion only because the publisher kindly "held the presses" for last-minute additions. In late October 1996, secretly recorded audiotapes of high-level Texaco executives' intemperate, if not racist, remarks were leaked to the major news media. Texaco's CEO, Peter Bijur, immediately ordered company-wide sensitivity training as well as other expensive diversity initiatives prescribed by consultants. A few days later, a powerful counter-trend asserted itself: the passage of California's Proposition 209, which banned the use of ethnic and gender preferences by the state's public agencies. That capstone of a gathering public rebellion against real and alleged quotas in the workplace and college admissions followed a federal appeals court decision earlier that year banning ethnic preferences in student admissions in Texas, Louisiana and Arkansas.

In this preface, I wish to update the never-ending story of the drive to implement and expand various multicultural workforce initiatives. It is a movement that both shapes and is shaped by important societal trends and historical events. Many trends observed in the first edition of *Diversity Machine* have continued. But there have been significant new developments, especially the advent of long-predicted tight labor markets. In conjunction with changing labor demographics-especially among younger workers—white employers and managers today interact with increasing numbers of minority and female employees. In addition, the longest economic boom in American history has accelerated the expansion of global labor and customer markets, thereby further strengthening the emphasis within the diversity machine on studying international cultural differences. And the advent of the "new economy industries" has created what I earlier termed preference-free "diversity laboratories" which have brewed a demographic mix that is overwhelmingly male, white and Asian, and immigrant—with few women, African-Americans, or American Hispanics. These new economy demographics were not what diversity machine theorists had in mind.

Nor have diversity proponents been pleased to see the spread of ballot propositions restricting the use of ethnic and gender criteria in hiring and college admissions. (Versions of California's Proposition

209 have migrated to Washington, Florida, and Houston.) In December, 2000 the University of Michigan (the focus of Chapter 9) in federal court successfully defended racial preferences in undergraduate admissions by arguing that ethnic diversity provided educational benefits; two months later, however, another federal judge struck down preferential admissions at the U-M law school. These conflicting decisions (along with those involving universities elsewhere) will likely be appealed to the U.S. Supreme Court.

The diversity machine's effort to supplant emotional affirmative action rhetoric with cooler, business-friendly rationales for valuing workforce diversity was a fundamental thesis of *The Diversity Machine*— an important theme missed by some reviewers. How and why this crucial transition took place bears brief restatement.

"Dollars and Demographics" Replaces "Do the Right Thing"

"Valuing diversity" and "managing diversity" theories emerged in the 1980s as the result of four factors: (1) the forecast of major ethnic changes in the nation's workforce, as well as immanent labor shortages, by the 1987 Hudson Institute's *Workforce 2000* report. (2) The beginning of "glass ceiling" audits of government contractors' female and minority promotion rates by the Department of Labor's Office of Federal Contract Compliance. (3) Large-scale Third World immigration. (4) The increased globalization of labor and consumer markets, especially after communism's collapse.

By the late 1980s, most consultants reluctantly recognized that both CEOs and the general public viewed affirmative action as tarnished, strident, and legally enforced "social work." Thus, the new dollars and demographics diversity rationales were a godsend to legions of weary affirmative action officers who knew that "eyes glazed over" when they tried to present the case for using race, ethnicity, and gender as factors in personnel processes.

The expansion of the movement also wrought internal divisions. Different schools of thought emerged around the question of how to achieve "diversity-friendly" workplaces.

One difference in emphasis concerned the extent of organizational change needed to accommodate minority and female employees. As seen in Chapter 3, the movement's enthusiastic "evangelist," Lewis Griggs, outlined his expansive "valuing diversity" philosophy and practice in books, articles, and videotapes. Griggs and early partner Lennie Copeland emphasized the need for long-term sensitivity training, the transformation of organizational values, and sincere, individual "conversion" to the value of diversity. Former Harvard Business School professor, R. Roosevelt Thomas, Jr. (also profiled in Chapter 3) was more cerebral in his "managing diversity" approach. Given the inevitability of demographic change and the hiring of more women and minority employees, Thomas saw his task as educating white managers on how to change their organizations' values and management styles to "manage people who are not like them." Effective management of diversity would require creation of a multicultural workplace where women and minorities could "be themselves" rather than assimilate to white-male standards. Thomas and Griggs were both "change masters" who prescribed long-term and deep organizational change, especially to encourage retention and promotion of culturally different talent.

On the other hand, Sondra Thiederman and Tom Kochman, both social science Ph.Ds, focused more on intensive short-term cross-cultural training. They offered mini-sociology courses in order to educate high and mid-level managers about cultural traits and habits of diverse customers and newer employees (see "Cross-Cultural Consultant Profiles II and III"). Wider organizational change was implied rather than explicitly prescribed.

Divergent emphases on organizational change v. cross-cultural training were more of a continuum of difference than a sharp division. Indeed, in actual practice, the more ambitious diversity proponents found plans for long-term organizational overhaul frustrated by the employers' tendency to favor short-term and inexpensive "quick fix" solutions such as half- or one-day training sessions.

A sharper debate among consultants and other participants within the diversity machine arose over the definition of diversity and its relationship to affirmative action. Older, African-American proponents wanted the new valuing diversity theories to continue affirmative action's emphasis on race and gender discrimination. They posed a direct link between affirmative action recruitment efforts and new federal and state enforcement of "glass ceiling" initiatives to foster minority/female retention and promotion. These "traditionalists" vigorously defended the former against the rising tide of criticism. They resisted, to varying degrees, the effort by more forward-looking, business-savvy consultants to expand the definition of diversity "beyond race and gender" (in Roosevelt Thomas' phrasing) to other personnel management arenas—including generational differences, work-family issues, class issues, differences among occupational subcultures, etc.

The trend in diversity management unquestionably has been a move toward the expanded definition of diversity. Yet diversity prescriptions for organizational change still often incorporate three assumptions rooted in affirmative action theory and legal enforcement. First, it is often assumed that the absence of some sort of proportional representation of women and minorities at all organizational levels is *ipso facto* evidence of hidden, "institutional racism"—taken-for-granted values and practices that exclude culturally-different employees. (This belief finds legal expression in the "disparate impact" standard of statistical proof of discrimination, whereby organizational patterns and practices are held to be discriminatory if they disproportionately exclude specific ethnic or gender groups.)

Second, workforce diversity theories imply a version of ethnic and gender determinism popularly termed "identity politics." Put simply,: an individual's views are assumed to reflect or represent those of his or her entire racial or gender group. Skin color and gender are seen as indicating special sensitivity or set of "cultural assets." That is, a woman on the board of directors will provide "the woman's point of view," or Hispanic managers will more "naturally understand" Hispanic employees and customers, etc.

Third, workforce diversity theories are premised upon cultural relativism, a doctrine derived from both affirmative action and from campus multiculturalism. Prevailing organizational values and standards are held to be arbitrarily designed by and for white men and inherently biased in their favor. The popular consultant slogan, "equal treatment is not fair treatment," encapsulates the concept that the evaluation of women and minorities according to criteria created by the dominant white male caste is unfair. The work world cannot be truly equal or just until the values and cultural styles of all groups are incorporated into organizational life.

Recent Developments: Views From Within The Diversity Machine

Four noted author-consultants were profiled in depth in *The Diversity Machine*: Lewis Griggs, R. Roosevelt Thomas, Jr., Thomas Kochman, and Sondra Thiederman. In mid-March of 1999, I re-interviewed each of them by telephone. By and large, the views of these consultant-authors seemed primarily rooted in their day-to-day consulting activities. Overall, they were less concerned with the impact of wider historical and societal events—events which I discuss in the next section.

Kochman, Thomas, and Thiederman viewed progress towards a diversity-friendly workplace as slow and incremental. Thiederman, Kochman and Thomas perceived in CEOs more interest in long-term change and increased recognition of the benefits of understanding cultural differences. However, employer interest in diversity was primarily driven by concerns of customer sales and service. (In response to increased variations in domestic ethnic markets, Kochman's consulting firm had added new instructional modules on East Asian, Middle Eastern, Russian-Jewish, and Native American cultures.) The characteristically ebullient Griggs saw "great progress" being made.

All four consultants agreed that flush economic times and (more importantly,) tightened labor markets had furthered employer concerns over worker retention and satisfaction, which led to the creation of "diversity friendly" workplaces. Thiederman felt there was more money available for training (except in health services, where managed care pressures had taken a toll on training budgets). Kochman suggested that training budgets were the same, but that diversity had become a higher priority.

On the other hand, consultants admitted that employers still tended to favor the one-day workshop and inexpensive quick fix. (Employers' desire is to "take a pill," said Kochman; or for "the silver bullet," as Thomas put it.) All four consultants grumbled about the lack of top-level corporate patience and long-term commitment required to achieve full understanding and management of cultural differences. Instead, said Thiederman, organizations often took short cuts via quotas and attempts to "match" employees stereotypically with same-ethnicity customers.

The author of *Beyond Race and Gender,* R. Roosevelt Thomas, Jr., was especially dissatisfied that broader and more complex diversity frameworks were only acknowledged theoretically. In practice, most programs were affirmative-action throwbacks to numbers-driven "representation" within an assimilationist framework. Race remained the primary focus, followed by gender. Thiederman, Kochman and Griggs concurred, and added the related dimension of "ethnicity" or immigrant cultures. Griggs emphasized a growing awareness of and interest in international diversity (a theme in consultant journals and newsletters); the other three consultants said little about this.

Age and generational conflict, a growing concern in social policy circles and the mass media, had not yet registered as a major workforce diversity issue. (Thiederman and Griggs cited some employer concerns over the work habits of Generation X. Thomas mentioned that generational issues sometimes arose in largely white male workplaces.)

Thiederman, Thomas, and Kochman reluctantly admitted that the "business case" for managing diversity in the workforce was still not deeply accepted among corporate leaders. Thiederman stated that there was "perpetual talk about the business case," but little else. Lack of systematic proof of diversity management's effectiveness was still a roadblock. Thomas admitted that diversity management's case rested, to some extent, on logic and faith, while Kochman admitted as a fact of life that varying economic conditions might limit organizations' abilities to fund diversity initiatives.

Yet the consultants detected signs that there was a growing awareness of the business case for effectively managing workforce diversity. Kochman felt that some employers, initially interested only in addressing customer diversity, subsequently developed an interest in "workforce equity." But that course inevitably raised touchy issues of sharing power and benefits as well as arguments over smaller shares of the pie. Thomas observed that more clients were coming to him in the wake of legal problems—indicating that employers may be thinking more in terms of long-term, fundamental change rather than quick, one-day fixes. Those corporations that had been working towards fuller diversity management for several years, said Thomas, were now pausing to re-evaluate progress and directions. He could think of no corporation that had made the transition to full diversity management. "They're at the river and wondering how to cross it," he said. Thomas compared the ambivalence around the transition from numbers-driven formulae to full diversity to the wider societal resistance to segregation-integration. Much work had been done on dismantling segregation, but successful integration was another matter.

Griggs and Thiederman saw glimmerings of one of the fondest hopes of diversity consultants: that diversity issues were being woven into general management. Griggs went further than the others in maintaining that an increasing number of CEO's "get it." They differentiate between affirmative action and valuing diversity. And they are more willing to see diversity issues as systemic and requiring long-term nurturing. (Griggs was hesitant to offer examples. He was enthusiastic about the vigorous presentation offered at a recent convention by the new CEO of the embattled Denny's restaurant chain. Beyond that, Griggs could name no exemplar.)

All consultants felt that white male backlash remained a problem to be dealt with through greater "inclusion" of white men in the diversity management dialogue. Griggs suggested that the strength of reaction to diversity by white men was an indicator of real change and progress. Kochman admitted that previous diversity efforts had often targeted white males, and thereby increased polarization. The impact of the Clinton sex scandals, offered Kochman, could be seen within the context of national polarization over diversity issues. Women and minorities who doggedly defended Clinton appreciated his pro-diversity record and saw attempts to "get" Clinton as part of a white-male-led effort not only to terminate Clinton's presidency, but his pro-diversity policies as well. (Griggs was pleased that he had anticipated the Clinton scandal with a new instructional videotape, "Sexual Dynamics.")

Only Griggs felt that the notorious Texaco controversy had had much impact. Thomas dismissed the episode as a lesson in short-term crisis management. Nor were any of the consultants familiar with Texaco's current efforts. Few other societal or political events were cited as shaping the diversity machine. Thomas felt that the passage of Proposition 209 had caused debate to regress into race-and-gender representation, which he termed, "the door we came through" but should have moved beyond.

The views of these four consultants were echoed and elaborated by more than 30 consultants and other experts interviewed by Barbara Deane for her 2000 survey report on "New Frontiers for Diversity."[2] By and large, they, too, viewed diversity issues from the more pragmatic realm of consulting. Diversity definitions and practices were seen as increasing in complexity. Globalization was seen as a primary force, moving diversity away from generalized training and towards more specific areas of "cultural competence." (I was somewhat surprised that none my subjects nor Deane's mentioned the major revision of *Workforce 2000*, the new *Workforce 2020*. Nor did any refer to William Bowen and Derek Bok's widely heralded 1998 book, *The Shape of the River*, one of the first to use social science data to argue the educational benefits of diversity.[3] The consultants also ignored President Clinton's *One America* racial initiative.)[4]

Other Indicators: Conferences and Associations

Conference and professional association indicators of interest in diversity appear to have "plateaued," according to an information officer for the American Society for Training and Development. On that organization's main website, there are no references to diversity. The 1999 index for the ASTD's *Training and Development* magazine has no entries on diversity or related topics; and the 1998 index has one. An editorial assistant remarked that diversity was a topic "that has come and gone for us." On the ASTD website there is no "community group" on diversity nor any subgroup within the "management development community." The ASTD's *Buyer's Guide* to consulting also indicates a fall-off in interest. In 1996, there were 73 consultants or firms listed under the "diversity" heading; by 2001, there were 29 under the "diversity training" section and another 3 under a new category, "diversity training/measurement." Yet the rising interest in global diversity was signaled at the ASTD 2001 annual conference which featured a keynote address by Robert Rosen and Patricia Digh, authors of a new book on *Global Literacy.* (The authors were also featured on the organizational development community group website and global-multicultural issues were hailed on the "emerging trends" webpage.)[5]

The Society for Human Resource Management, located in the same city as ASTD (Alexandria, Virginia), is more enthusiastic about workforce diversity programs. It still partners with Lewis Griggs (who founded the National Annual Diversity Conferences) in hosting an annual conference on diversity. At those gatherings, consultants Anita Rowe and Lee Gardenswartz (profiled in *The Diversity Machine*) have established a series of "train-the-trainer" certificate seminars. SHRM's own workplace diversity initiative is featured on its website, and the initiative has its own monthly publication, *Mosaics.* The organization sponsors an annual 25-page supplement on diversity in *Fortune* magazine. As at ASTD, however, there is no "professional emphasis group" on diversity. Two recent articles in SHRM's own monthly publication, *HR Magazine*, help to explain why.[6]

Robert Grossman's "Race in the Workplace" and "Is Diversity Working?" contradict SHRM's glowing endorsement of workforce diversity, while confirming findings in the 1997 edition of *The Diversity Machine* and in this new preface. In "Is Diversity Working?," Grossman highlights the division between consultants who wish to expand the definition of diversity and those who resent the focus being taken off race. There are the usual consultant complaints about the employers' penchant for short, "quick fix" workshops.

Grossman's questions about the effectiveness of diversity training were surprisingly sharp. Neither he nor anyone else could find evidence of diversity programs' effectiveness. Grossman cited Arizona State University management professor Carol Kulik: "'If rigorous assessments were conducted, the results might be disturbing.'" According to Grossman, Kulik believes that diversity training does little to change day-to-day relations at work. "'How would you feel if you invested all this money and found out that it had no effect?,' she asked." A Columbia University psychology professor suggested, "'there's disincentives to do evaluations. You might find out the programs are costly and not very effective.'"[7] In both articles, Grossman found widespread complaints that diversity programs are instituted only to help avoid lawsuits and for public relations purposes. In both articles, black consultants complained about lack of progress behind the veneer of diversity programs.

The New York-based Conference Board sponsored "Diversity 2000 Conference: A Change Lever for Organizational Success." But the organization has shown very little interest in the topic in its other publications and seminars.

Recent Development: External Trends and Events

Placing the diversity machine in wider societal contexts, I would agree with the consultants about the importance of increased high-level CEO awareness of workforce diversity issues and the tightening of labor markets. I might emphasize more than they did the continued volume and magnitude of discrimination and harassment lawsuits and the resultant public relations campaigns by corporations such as Texaco and Denny's. Paradoxically, the lawsuits have spurred diversity training, but in many instances they have also checked more extensive efforts by holding initiatives to the "legal minimum." Thomas properly appreciated that efforts to widen the scope of diversity and to provide a more sophisticated theoretical framework have been complicated by the revival of debates over ethnicity and preferences, as well as by renewed efforts to provide data that "diversity works."

Tight Labor Markets and Continued Discrimination Lawsuits:

As consultants and others quickly recognized, the most important impetus to workforce diversity awareness has been the advent of tight labor markets and outright labor shortages in the U.S. during the final years of the twentieth century. Though corporate layoffs continued apace in the late 1990s, millions of jobs were also created. Debates continue about the quality and compensation of the new jobs compared to those eliminated in downsizing. But official unemployment levels have dropped and remain low. The need for skilled workers in urban areas is now quite strong, as indicated by press reports like "Builders and Unions Court New Workers."[8] More than half the chief financial officers at U.S. companies cited in a quarterly survey by Duke University reported problems finding qualified employees.[9] In some regions of the nation, McDonalds has been forced to offer signing bonuses and pay above the minimum wage. In California, Disneyland has dropped its "no facial hair" requirement in order to permit recruitment of men with moustaches. Demand for technically skilled and computer-savvy workers is very strong. In other words, the labor shortages forecast a decade ago in *Workforce 2000* have appeared at last. And, according to a front-page report in the *Wall Street Journal*, these labor shortages are likely to persist. [10] These developments strengthen the bargaining position of employees who wish to promote workplace changes on cultural diversity and other matters.

Workplace discrimination lawsuits continue to focus corporate and public awareness on diversity controversies.[11] Resolution of several cases has produced expanded diversity efforts. For example, the settlement of the Texaco lawsuit mandated diversity training for all employees and a task force was assembled to revise personnel procedures. The former head of the U.S. Justice Department's Civil Rights Division, Deval Patrick, has been made a Texaco Vice President. Texaco, IBM, and Mobil Oil have run full-page advertisements extolling workforce diversity in business-oriented publications.

Discrimination complaints at Denny's forced major management changes, extensive diversity training, and an increase in the number of minority members of the board of directors. Complaints also spurred greater efforts to expand minority ownership of franchises. In addition, Denny's sponsored a series of television messages on the topics of anti-discrimination and diversity. In July 1998, the giant financial services firm, Salomon Smith Barney, agreed to settle a class action bias case brought by female employees. The company promised to spend more than $15 million over four years on programs to recruit and promote women and minorities. In 1999, aircraft manufacturer Boeing Co., paid $15 million dollars to settle class action lawsuits by African-American employees alleging workplace discrimination. The company promised programs to enhance retention and promotion of minorities.

In early 2000, Ford Motor Company followed the example of Boeing and other corporations by settling discrimination charges out of court with the Labor Department's Office of Federal Contract Compliance. Rather than face the costs and uncertainties of protracted litigation—as well as the bad publicity—Ford agreed to pay $3.8 million in back wages to women and minorities not hired at seven of the company's plants. Ford further agreed to modify hiring procedures throughout the company by hiring women and minorities in proportion to the percentage that apply. The statement by a Ford spokesperson typified corporate talk on diversity. "We want to reestablish a good working relationship with the agency," said a Ford spokesperson. "We fully share the same goals regarding diversity in the workforce."[12] And on May 31, 2001, a federal judge approved the largest corporate employee racial discrimination settlement to date when Coca-Cola agreed to pay a record $192.5 million to end a class action lawsuit. Individual black plaintiffs receive an average $40,000 back pay package and—following the Texaco example—Coca-Cola is establishing a diversity task force to monitor personnel practices. (In a subsequent action, Coca-Cola donated $1.5 million to establish a Diversity Academy—to be developed and administered by star consultant R. Roosevelt Thomas, Jr.)

Sagging sales or shrinking market share led other corporations to expand minority outreach. In 1998, Nissan Motor Co. set a goal of expanding its minority dealerships by twenty-five percent, and tied compensation of high-level executives to achieving that goal. General Motors also announced plans to expand the number of minority-owned dealerships.

Views of White and Minority Business Executives:

Recent attitude surveys of business executives reinforce those cited in *The Diversity Machine*. Among executives, there remains a general theoretical support for workplace diversity; affirmative action is viewed less favorably. Typical was a December 1997 survey for the television program "Nightly Business Report." Eighty-five percent of business executives (for large and medium-sized firms) thought "workplace diversity" was extremely or very important. Between seventy-five and eighty percent felt that "diversity is essential to their on-going success." Yet though a majority of all executives surveyed reported the existence of company-wide policies against discrimination, less than half indicated that their organizations actively recruit women or minorities. Only thirty percent had affirmative action programs in place, and less than twenty-five percent provided diversity training. Larger firms were more pro-active. More than seventy percent actively recruited minorities and women, and half of the larger firms offered diversity training.[13]

On the other hand, the term "affirmative action" garnered mixed or negative support. Only half of large company executives (thirty-nine percent of all executives) deeply believed in affirmative action and nearly sixty percent would favor its abolition. Nearly forty percent felt that affirmative action was not necessary to produce diversity, and nearly double that percentage indicated that business has been forced to hire and promote less than qualified individuals. These findings reinforced those of a Time/CNN poll in which only thirty-three percent of executives favored university scholarships reserved for women and minorities and only twelve percent favored hiring goals for African-Americans. (Somewhat paradoxically, nearly ninety percent of respondents to the Nightly Business Report survey thought that discrimination was not a problem in the workplace, yet sixty-three percent of business executives in the Time/CNN poll thought racism was a problem for the wider society.)[14]

Not unexpectedly, minority executives have a more favorable view of affirmative action and diversity efforts. A 1998 Korn Ferry/Columbia Business School surveyed two hundred eighty minority executives. The majority reported various forms of workplace discrimination. Fifty-five percent reported seeing harsh or unfair treatment of minorities by whites, fifty-nine percent reported double standards in delegation of assignments, and forty-five percent had been the victim of racial or cultural jokes. The findings reinforced the importance of diversity policy proposals such as establishing supportive networks of co-workers and superiors and, especially, finding mentors to promote upward mobility. Only twenty percent of executives in the Korn-Ferry/Columbia study had formal mentors; but nearly seventy-one percent indicated the importance of an informal (usually white male) mentor. Timely and accurate feedback from superiors was deemed important—as were direct responses to superiors regarding instances of perceived discrimination.[15]

Renewed Efforts to Prove "Diversity Works:"

A glaring dilemma for proponents of workforce diversity policies has been the lack of systematic social science evidence that the programs deliver the promised results of increased productivity, and improved intergroup relations. Efforts to prove the effectiveness of diversity policies were redoubled in the wake of popular referenda and court decisions limiting the use of ethnic-gender preferences in higher education admissions.

To try and provide social science justification for both affirmative action and institutional diversity, William Bowen and Derek Bok, former presidents of Princeton and Harvard, respectively, researched and wrote *The Shape of the River: Long Term Consequences of Considering Race in College and University Admissions.*[16] As testimony to the power of the diversity machine and its high-level allies, the book was accorded extensive professional and mass media attention.

The Shape of the River is largely based on the study of two groups of students who graduated from highly selective colleges and universities in 1976 and 1989. The book's main conclusion is that an ethnically diverse educational environment is an important institutional goal benefiting both higher education and the wider society. The use of "race sensitive" admissions policies, the authors argue, is a legitimate and legally defensible means to that end.

Bok and Bowen maintain that minority access to elite institutions has been vital in fostering subsequent minority occupational mobility and racial integration of the professions and middle classes. Black graduates were more likely than white peers to attend graduate or professional schools, and blacks were also more likely to participate in civic and community activities. As many blacks as whites majored in sciences and engineering—contradicting the popular perception that black students were majoring disproportionately in softer curriculums such as "black studies." Black students at selective schools did have somewhat higher dropout rates than white peers, but also graduated at higher rates than blacks with similar SATs at non-selective schools. Blacks didn't feel stigmatized by affirmative action, although "at almost every college in our sample, black students are not only performing less well academically than whites, but also performing below the levels predicted by their SAT scores."[17]

As for societal benefits, Bok and Bowen argued that a diverse educational setting helped erode wider segregation patterns and promoted greater integration in students' lives after graduation. Graduates acknowledged that inter-racial experiences in education helped them deal with race relations in work and the wider world. Among graduates, majorities of all races approved the emphasis placed on diversity by their alma maters.

In an invited article for the *Harvard Business Review*, "Lessons for Business from Higher Education," Bok and Bowen (with co-author Glenda Burkhart) repeated justifications for using racial criteria in college admissions to foster ethnic diversity, emphasizing that educating people to work across the lines of race, class, religion, and background were goals highly relevant to modern global businesses. The authors merged merit and diversity by contending that the selection of individuals must be based not only on individual merit, but also according to the organization's goals and societal responsibilities. Ethnic diversity is just such a worthwhile organizational goal—for universities, for businesses, and for society.[18]

Ultimately, Bok, Bowen, and Burkhart echoed the warning of many elites cited in *The Diversity Machine*: affirmative action and diversity measures are necessary to maintain social control and societal stability. Without "race-sensitive" selection criteria in colleges and workplaces, American society will be racially polarized. "Corporations will not be healthy unless the society is healthy."[19]

The University of Michigan subsequently released a study of its undergraduate students that reinforced Bok and Bowen's findings.[20] The Harvard Civil Rights Project more recently published similar findings based upon a Gallup survey of law school students at Harvard and Michigan.[21] The methods and findings of these studies have been subjected to severe criticisms, most notably by Steve and Abigail Thernstrom. With specific regard to the Bok and Bowen study, the Thernstroms pointed out a crucial flaw: in the surveys sent out by Bok and Bowen: the key term "diversity" was left undefined. If, for example, survey subjects had been told that their alma maters' pursuit of "diversity" included dual admissions criteria, the subjects might not have been so approving. The "proof" that "diversity works" was that subjects simply said they felt positively about it. Nor were Bok and Bowen's upbeat findings from elite college graduates compared with similar race relations data in the general population. [22]

Ironically, studies like Bok and Bowen's constituted something of a throwback for the ambitious architects of diversity machine. As Roosevelt Thomas indicated in his 1999 re-interview (and on pp., 199-202 in *Diversity Machine*), he and other consultants are frustrated by the regression to affirmative action "representation" battles within an assimilationist framework. Basically, that is the thrust of Bok and Bowen's book and others like it. They seek to justify overt ethnic preferences and ethnic "numbers games," or the use of proportionalism to achieve social stability through greater assimilation of minorities. The expanded definition of diversity, as well as any fundamental change of white male organizational values and managerial styles are ignored.

Workforce 2020, a substantial revision of *Workforce 2000*, received far less attention than *The Shape of the River*. [23] The new report's authors, Richard Judy and Carol D'Amico, immediately disowned the "diversity craze" launched by the earlier *Workforce 2000*. They corrected exaggerated predictions about the decline of white male workers, and took issue with diversity proponents' claims that minority and female workers must be regarded as "differently qualified." Instead, *Workforce 2020* concluded that " what the new workers principally need—whether they are white and male or female and minority—are the skills that education must provide, not managers trained in diversity and sensitivity."[24] The chief problems for the twenty-first century workforce will be the maturation of the Baby Boomers (the "graying" of America, not its "browning") and the threat of a society polarized along multiple dimensions of age, class, education, and ethnicity. [25]

Though economists Harry Holzer and David Neumark could not prove that affirmative action/diversity improves organizational efficiency, they gamely argued that, at least, the policies do no harm. Their literature review in *The Journal of Economic Literature* (September 2000) found that female affirmative action beneficiaries have the same educational qualifications and job performance ratings as males. Minorities tend to have weaker qualifications, but there is little evidence of weaker performance in labor markets. Data on effectiveness of preferential contracting and procurement programs for women and minorities were limited, mixed and compromised by inclusion of data from bogus, "minority-front" businesses whose success and failure rates are mixed in with those of valid minority business enterprises.

The *New York Times* quickly hailed the Holzer-Neumark report, but the economists' review actually contains many highly qualified, mixed verdicts and inconclusive evidence. Several cited studies indicate obvious reverse discrimination and Holzer-Neumark caution that "the potential effects of affirmative action on performance, at least in the labor market, appear to depend on how it is implemented." In higher education, they found limited and mixed data. However, one dramatic contradiction of the Bok and Bowen education-diversity thesis—ignored by social scientists and news media—emerged from Holzer and Neumark's conclusions: "there is no evidence of positive (or negative) effects of a diverse student body on educational quality."[26]

Immigration and "Demographic Divides"

In the early 1990s, the architects of the diversity machine were pleased to announce that "the future is now L.A."—implying that the ethnic transformation of Los Angeles (and California) was the harbinger of similar changes throughout the nation. But several demographers, notably the Milken Institute's William Frey, now suggest that multi-ethnic diversity has been and will remain largely concentrated in a few states, and that even within those states, diversity will be heavily confined to large, urbanized areas. The rest of the nation will be more homogeneous and largely white, especially insofar as areas like the Rocky Mountain States and Pacific Northwest take in the "diversity flight" of whites from California and other areas favored by non-white immigrants. Frey sees a "demographic divide" emerging. [27]

Recent U.S. Census data and an increasing number of investigative reports published in newspapers such as the *Washington Post*, indicate greater dispersion of Third World immigrants to urban areas and small towns in the south and Midwest.[28] (Chicago recently displaced Houston as having the second largest concentration of Hispanics of Mexican origin in the nation; Los Angeles has the largest.) The new census data and news media accounts suggest Frey's anticipated "demographic divide" may be a transitional phase.

Debates over the distribution of immigrants have implications for more delicate conversations over how immigration-driven diversity will affect the nation's unity and stability. Will large numbers of culturally distinct immigrants, in combination with multicultural policies advocated by the diversity machine, fragment and polarize American society?

Most political liberals and most social scientists seem to welcome the new multiculturalism and discount dangers of polarization. Many political conservatives, as well as some social scientists, contend that the forces for cultural assimilation remain strong, comparing current immigration to that of Eastern Europeans one hundred years ago. Today's immigrants are anxious to learn English and American values. Immigrants allegedly reinforce traditional American emphases on family cohesion, and bring needed job skills, industriousness and creativity. Cross-ethnic intermarriage rates are increasing.[29] On the other hand, the geographical clustering of ethnic minorities discerned by Frey can be seen as more conducive to the separatism and ethnic "balkanization" vividly portrayed in such anti-utopian films as "Blade Runner.[30]

Recent forecasts from Rand Corporation and the Public Policy Institute of California suggest a demographic future wherein ethnic and class divisions may reinforce one another.[31] These projections indicate that a smaller group of older Anglos and some Asian groups will retain a disproportionate share of wealth and higher education degrees, while a larger population of Hispanics, blacks, and other Third World immigrants will remain disproportionately poor and undereducated. The formation of this triple ethnic-age-class "sociological San Andreas Faultline"—as I termed it in *The Diversity Machine* —has become manifest in voting patterns. Most notably, in March, 2000, older, wealthier white voters defeated California's Proposition 26 which would have substituted a simple majority vote for the older two-thirds required to authorize bonds for local schools. Younger, poorer, minority voters—whose children would have benefited—overwhelmingly supported Proposition 26. [32]

The Diversity Machine, The Law, and "Higher Lawlessness"

Affirmative action preferences and diversity programs often have been instituted in the wake of discrimination or harassment lawsuits. (This remedial format is what I termed "diversity penance" in the 1997 edition of *The Diversity Machine*. It has done much to tarnish the image of diversity programs.)More widespread reasons for affirmative action and other diversity measures are so-called "voluntary" hiring preferences and other programs which are self-imposed by both private and public organizations to ward off future lawsuits or to blunt possible penalties by state or federal regulatory agencies. (Corporations with federal contracts must maintain affirmative action plans.) The legality of voluntary affirmative action to achieve "diversity" in the public sector has become increasingly suspect.

The idea that states have a "compelling interest" in ensuring diversity in public institutions has hung by the slender thread of a few sentences in Justice Lewis Powell's opinion in the famous 1978 decision in *Alan Bakke v. the Regents of the U. of California*. Powell's was the deciding opinion for a very divided court, and he briefly suggested that racial diversity was one consideration justifying the use of preferences.

A decade later in another landmark case, *Richmond v. Croson (1989)*, Justice Sandra Day O'Connor emphasized instead the doctrine "strict scrutiny" in evaluating use of ethnic or gender preferences by state and local governments in the awarding of public contracts. Laws favoring minorities would be studied with the same intensity as laws that might disfavor them. Thus, O'Connor held that government agencies must demonstrate a proven history of discriminatory behavior in order to justify use of "MWBE" (minority-business-enterprise or women-business-enterprise) set-asides. Efforts to revive state and local MWBE preferences through use of bogus "disparity studies" designed to prove discrimination have not fared well when challenged. In early 2000, a notice from the Project on Civil Rights and Public Contracts at the University of Maryland, Baltimore County, declared: "Through a variety of legal actions from Mississippi to New Jersey, MWBE programs have been ended."[33]

In 1994, the Supreme Court found unconstitutional the overly broad use of ethnic classifications in federal set-aside programs in *Adarand Constructors, Inc., v. Pena*. This led to President Clinton's response to "mend, not end" federal affirmative action. One response has been to promote diversity through reviving advantages for minority-owned businesses in bidding for federal government contracts. Though still subject to considerable debate, preferences are to be awarded in industry sectors where there is a disparity between percentage of "available" minority-owned firms and the percentage of dollars awarded such enterprises.[34]

That the alleged benefits of organizational diversity constitute a "compelling state interest" in justifying ethnic or gender preferences has been rejected by many lower courts and federal appellate courts.

Chief among these was the Fifth Circuit Court of Appeals's 1996 *Hopwood* decision forbidding the use of ethnic preferences at the University of Texas Law School.

On March 21, 2000, the Supreme Court sent another strong, though tacit, signal that maintaining ethnic diversity could not be used as a justification in assigning pupils to public schools. The court did so by refusing to hear an appeal from the Fourth Circuit Court of Appeals against Montgomery County's use of racial criteria in limiting student transfers within a school district—a policy largely designed to inhibit white flight. Though not binding in other federal appellate jurisdictions, the court's action likely will be carefully noted throughout the nation.

The trend of decisions by the Supreme Court and many lower courts towards strict scrutiny regarding the use of ethnic categories in allocation of occupational or educational opportunities could be reversed by the 2000 presidential election. Most of the court's decisions on affirmative action and the "compelling state interest " diversity rationale have been narrow 5-4 or 6-3 decisions. Therefore, affirmative action and diversity will be among key "litmus tests" administered to any new Supreme Court nominees.

And yet, as repeatedly noted in *The Diversity Machine*, the law has often been seen as a minor impediment in the top-down drive to achieve more "representative" workplaces. The contempt for legal restraints that I have termed "higher lawlessness" was apparent among many people in leadership positions whom I interviewed for *The Diversity Machine*. Higher lawlessness was notably present at the University of Michigan, which recently won a federal court challenge to its preferential admissions for undergraduates but lost a similar case regarding law school admissions.

Though U-M's workforce diversity, not student admissions, was the primary focus of the 1997 edition, I find that the drive for student diversity there and elsewhere often mirrors preferential pressures for faculty and staff. The plaintiffs in the undergraduate admissions case charge that U-M used different admissions formulae for Asians and whites, on the one hand, and blacks and Hispanics, on the other. While not admitting guilt, U-M has subsequently developed a single index for all applicants in which grades, test scores, extra-curricular activities, and membership in an under-represented group receive numerical weights. The attempt to maintain ethnic preferences, however, was made manifest in how weights were allocated. For example, being a member of an ethnic minority (black or Hispanic) received the same weighting as having perfect college admissions test scores.

(In December 2000 the federal district court judge ruled that the separate admissions grids were unconstitutional but sustained the weights used for ethnicity in the newer index.)[35]

In a similar fashion, racial and ethnic criteria for faculty hiring have become less explicit as they once were under the Targets of Opportunity Program. Such criteria are currently combined with others (such as "intellectual focus") under a more general program called the Provost's Faculty Initiative. Regardless of these programs, the percentage of blacks and Hispanics in upper middle and higher occupational ranks at U-M remains small, and the percentage of black men in faculty ranks has actually fallen (from 3.0 percent in 1995 to 2.6 percent in 1999). Nearly 17.5 percent of the total faculty is "minority," but more than half (10 percent) of that total figure is "Asian." In addition, "Asian" and other categories often include substantial numbers who are foreign-born and non-citizens.[36]

There is general agreement that U-M's diversity blueprint, the Michigan Mandate, is now more than ever seen as the creature of its creator, former U-M president James Duderstadt. (An employee in the Office of Equity and Diversity had heard the Mandate mentioned only once.) Some high-level administrators insisted that the spirit and most of the programs of the Mandate continue; but one high-level administrator remarked that the lawsuits have produced a "different atmosphere" about such matters on campus just as Proposition 209 did for the entire nation. Another administrator reported that questions are now raised more often about the legality of some diversity measures.

U-M has put considerable time, effort and expense into the two reverse discrimination cases, marshalling data and legal arguments to prove alleged benefits of a diverse student body.[37] Pro-diversity themes are trumpeted loudly in the campus alumni literature and other U-M publications.[38] A panel on diversity was featured during U-M's most recent California Rose Bowl tour. Former President Gerald Ford published an editorial extolling diversity and defending his alma mater in the *New York Times*.[39] Two U-M social scientists published a study attributing opposition to affirmative action to racial prejudice.[40]

One might expect higher education in California to be developing new alternatives to achieve or manage diversity in the wake of the 1996 passage of Proposition 209, which prohibited state agencies' use of ethnic or gender preferences in admissions, hiring, or contracting. Indeed, there has been much more talk and effort by the University of California improve outreach efforts and better prepare students in secondary schools. The proportion of black and Hispanic undergraduate students admitted initially fell. By the fall of 2000, however, black, Hispanic, and Native American enrollments rebounded throughout the UC system to levels above those when preferences were in place. Minority enrollments did not do so at highly-competitive UC Berkeley and UCLA; gains were most impressive at UC Riverside—a campus that also has long had a vigorous outreach effort.[41]

Besides outreach efforts, there has been legal tinkering. To be eligible for the eight-campus UC system, California high school students must graduate in the top 12.5 percent of students statewide and take the requisite curriculum. In the wake of Proposition 209, the UC Board of Regents tried to ensure diversity by enacting a "4 percent solution." Those graduating in the top 4 percent at each high school class are UC eligible.

Behind legal tinkering, however, there has been outright subterfuge. In a long, revealing *New York Times Magazine* article on the University of California System after Proposition 209 (May 19, 1999), James Traub revealed that the UC system was boosting minority enrollments through some "deft fiddling with admissions criteria."[42] At UC Berkeley, undergraduate admissions evaluators were sent a profile of each applicant's high school so that they might review the applicant's grades and test scores "in light of each applicant's history and circumstances." Approximately half of the freshman class is admitted primarily on the basis of grades and test scores alone. For the remainder, other factors are counted including "likely contribution to the intellectual and cultural vitality of the campus" and " "the opportunities the applicant has had and the way in which he or she has responded to them."[43] The percentage of blacks and Hispanics admitted jumped from ten in 1998 to thirteen percent in 1999. [44]

Less than covert ethnic selection criteria are evident in admissions to UC's graduate and professional schools, as seen in data obtained and analyzed by Jerry and Ellen Cook. At the UCLA Medical School, for example, the Cooks calculate that being black or Hispanic triples an applicant's chances of being admitted. According to the Cooks, "admissions to the UC medical schools at San Francisco, Davis and Los Angeles are more race based now than they were before California voters approved the ban on racial preferences! It appears that enforcement of the amendment to the State Constitution will have to be done through the courts."[45]

The second-tier California State University system continues to fund a "forgivable loan program" whereby the system provides up to $30,000 for selected undergraduates who were members of "underrepresented groups" to obtain Ph.D.'s. The loans are forgiven if the recipient returns to teach in the Cal State system. (Since Cal State does not confer the Ph.D., the program has been seen as a means of "growing our own" minority faculty—in the words of the program's founder, former system chancellor Ann Reynolds.) The program has provided support for more than 1200 persons—nearly all women or minorities. For the 1999-2000 year, official ethnic classifications have been omitted from application forms, though, according to one of the program's administrators, proxies for race such as membership in associations, biographical and other background data will be used. ("Some things are obvious," she said.)

Behind-the-scenes pressures for ethnic preferences in faculty hiring reportedly remain strong.[46] Just how strong was suggested in April, 1999, when the a CSU San Francisco part-time lecturer won $2.75 million in a reverse discrimination lawsuit when a jury decided that he'd been denied a full-time position because of his race. (One reason for this rare victory is that a full-time faculty member testified that he had heard a dean state that no white male would be hired for the position.)[47]

Revisiting Two Key Case Studies:

The California Community Colleges system, the focus of Chapter 8 in *The Diversity Machine,* has continued to struggle with lingering effects from budget starvation wrought by the state's long recession. Though it remains the largest community college system in the world, its campuses are, according to the *Los Angeles Times,* the "ugly ducklings of higher education." The system remains tied to an outmoded reimbursement system that links funding levels to early-semester class enrollment. [48]

Nevertheless, without expensive affirmative action or diversity efforts, the ethnic composition of the students continues to mirror the changing demographics of the state. Efforts to change the ethnic make-up of the faculty continue to be hampered by budget constraints and the heavy reliance on part-time faculty. (Though the system has tried to mandate that the percentage of credit courses taught by part-time faculty be limited to 25 percent, most campuses remain far from compliance.[49])

According to Tosh Shikasho, Specialist for Faculty Staff Diversity, the early emphasis on faculty/staff diversity has languished for a variety of reasons. The full-time staff devoted to diversity in the system's main headquarters in Sacramento has dwindled from seven to one, and the level of funding for faculty/staff diversity projects at the campuses has stagnated. There is worry—though no systematic evidence—that the passage of Proposition 209 slowed the diversity bandwagon. The Chancellor's Megaconference for 2000 had the theme of "Celebrating the Pursuit of Excellence"—but there was little emphasis on diversity, which was once trumpeted as synonymous with excellence. On the other hand, the State Personnel Board continues to contest a lawsuit launched by former Governor Wilson against the section of the education code which mandates that the Community Colleges system have a faculty that ethnically mirrors the adult population of the state of California by 2005. [50]

The Los Angeles County Sheriff's Department, the focus of Chapter 7, remains embroiled in diversity dilemmas. The entire department completed cultural awareness training. After Sheriff Sherman Block died in 1998, Lee Baca was elected sheriff and became the organization's first Hispanic leader. But lawyers and other officials monitoring the terms of the 1992 *Bouman* decree, which settled a court case involving charges of gender discrimination and sexual harassment, are pressing for greater progress in female and minority representation. A "goal" has been set in the LASD that 25 percent of all new sergeants should be women. Though there are as of yet no formal goals for minorities, there is heightened sensitivity to improving promotions percentages.[51] In late 1999, a jury found that an Asian American sheriff had been the victim of harassment and discrimination;the county is appealing the $60,000 damage award.[52]

Officers in the LASD's training unit are pondering another round of cultural awareness training on the assumption that "something more" must be done. Thus far, however, official or court-ordered quotas have been avoided,unlike in the city's other major law enforcement agency, the Los Angeles Police Department. The LASD's official core values statement remains committed to equal treatment and universal standards. The more separatist, multicultural call of the diversity machine to "celebrate differences" is not yet officially enshrined. All this may not last.

On March 29, 2000, a front-page story in the *Los Angeles Times* Metro section carried the story, "Harassment in Sheriff's Department Decried."[53] The Southern California chapter of the American Civil Liberties Union released a report by a private consulting firm commissioned by the LASD. The consultant found that "the department does not value diversity and resists change. A wall of silence...certainly exists with respect to gender and racial equity."[54] Based on six months of focus groups, interviews, document reviews, and observations at work stations, the report's authors concluded that the top brass deny "'that the department has a serious problem related to workplace equity.'" [55]

The LASD is now considering adopting recommendations in a report formulated by the County's Office of Affirmative Action Compliance, entitled "Guide for a Model Diversity Plan." The plan draws heavily on the diversity machine's professional literature. The plan is a comprehensive design for changing workplace culture through emphasizing affirmative action and valuing diversity in order to recruit, retain and promote a workforce that better represents the county's changing demographics.

The New Diversity Laboratories: From High Tech to Auto Sales

At the close of the 1997 edition of *The Diversity Machine*, I suggested that California and the states under the Fifth Circuit Court of Appeals *Hopwood* ban on higher education preferences might become preference-free "diversity laboratories." Though there is resistance to abandoning ethnic preferences in California's public sector, in the private sector, preference-free diversity laboratories have arisen.

Without preferences or even much planning, California's Silicon Valley and other high tech enclaves around the nation have created a somewhat unique "natural" diversity mix. Especially in the small business and managerial realms of the high tech world, the demographics are overwhelmingly male, most of them white or from immigrant groups, especially men from India, China and other Asian regions. Journalist James Fallows worked in a high tech firm to research an article for *The New York Times Magazine*.[56] Fallows noted the emergence of a "post racial meritocracy" that is emotionally detached from the nation's social problems, especially those of inequality and poverty:

> The tech establishment has solved, in a fashion, a problem that vexes the rest of America—and therefore thinks about it in a way that seems to prefigure a larger shift. The hallway traffic in any major technology firm is more racially varied than in other institutions in the country. (It is also overwhelmingly male.) But the very numerous black and brown faces belong overwhelmingly to immigrants, notably from India, rather than to members of American minority groups. The percentage of African-Americans and Latinos in professional positions in the booming tech businesses is extremely low, nearing zero at many firms.
>
> People in the tech world inhabit what they know to be a basically post-racial meritocracy. I would sit at a lunch table in the software firm with an ethnic Chinese from Malaysia on one side of me, a Pole on the other, a man from Colombia across the table and a man born in India but reared in America next to him. This seems, to those inside it, the way the rest of the world should

work, and makes the entrenched racial problems of black-and-white America seem like some Balkan rivalry one is grateful to know is on the other side of the world. [57]

In a long article in *Cultural Diversity at Work*, Kimberlee Jensen also analyzed the lack of blacks, Hispanics, and people with disabilities in the high tech world. She observed that, "diversity has not permeated the industry as a priority...In Silicon Valley, where millionaires appear overnight, the business case for diversity may fall on deaf ears."[58] A major reason for the lack of female, black, and Hispanic representation is that among all scientists and engineers in the U.S., only 2.8 percent are Hispanics, 3.5 percent are black, and 22.4 percent are women. Robert Suro pointed out the role of well-educated immigrants in the nation's high tech regions in an article for *American Demographics*.[59] The Gates Millennium Scholars program is a foundation established by Microsoft founder, Bill Gates in an attempt to use ethnic preferences to redress the lack of American minorities in high tech industries.[60]

Another model of this preference-free workforce diversity has emerged—again without legal mandates or planning— on the sales lot of the largest Toyota dealership in the world: the giant Longo Toyota facility, just outside of Los Angeles. In a 1998 *Los Angeles Times* case study of Longo, reporter Peter Hong found that an individual's ability to sell cars to the area's rapidly changing demographics was largely unrelated to race or ethnicity—though the sales force was heavily male. Successful salespersons simply developed cultural sensitivities in dealing with the increasingly multicultural customer base; those who could not adapt, departed. The only cultural "matching" of salesperson and customers was in cases where the customer did not speak English. (Evidently, this was not an insurmountable problem for whites: Longo's top salesman was Jewish.)[61]

The Diversity Machine: Victory by Default?

Workforce and consumer diversity is increasing and will continue to do so. To paraphrase Karl Marx, the forces of international capitalism, immigration, and ethnic heterogenicity may indeed burst asunder the cultural boundaries of nation states. Yet, as Roosevelt Thomas once told me, "diversity in itself isn't bad, or good. It just is." What is important is how this diversity is conceptualized, emphasized, and managed within the workplace and the wider society.

It's always been good common sense to know your customer. Mushrooming global markets mandate a certain degree of cross-cultural understanding. Thus, as cross-cultural educator Tom Kochman is fond of pointing out, "when you're buying, you need one language; when you're selling, many." Given today's tight U.S. labor markets, a measure of cultural sensitivity is also relevant in hiring and retaining employees and in avoiding discrimination lawsuits.

But does demographic change mandate fundamental cultural change, the "celebration of differences," and the quest for ethnic gender proportionalism in "workplaces that look like America"? Will the dynamic assimilation of cultures that characterized much of the twentieth century continue into the twenty-first? Will the spirit of *E Pluribus Unum*, equal opportunity, and universal equal-treatment standards prevail?

It is worth pointing out that the much-derided melting pot model of assimilation that structured much of race and ethnic relations in twentieth century America was always "multicultural," insofar as that term is synonymous with pluralism. Behind a public veneer of Anglo-WASP behavioral uniformity, the U.S. has *always* had neighborhood, friendship, and marriage patterns structured by religion and ethnicity. The other sources of diversity have also long been present. The "cultural mosaic" that is thought to be so new today has been a reality in places such as New York City for generations.

For the twenty-first century, the diversity machine endorses a more group-based, collectivist outlook with its hallmark slogans of "celebrating differences," and "equal treatment is not fair treatment." The version of multiculturalism from which many of today's workplace diversity policies are derived is more critical, egalitarian, and separatist. To some extent this has been refreshing and socially beneficial. But in the background lurk the premises of ethnic and gender proportionalism, identity politics, and cultural relativism. Assimilation is viewed as a mask for imposing white male oppression. Calls for mutual tolerance and accommodation of cultures can veer into "politically correct" censorship.

Those committed to free markets and/or global capitalism appear quite blasé about accepting diversity management techniques and the diversity machine's broader ideology. This seemingly odd alliance between global capitalism and multiculturalism was noted in the 1997 edition of *The Diversity Machine*—as were the obvious attempts to celebrate diversity at the Republican Party's national conventions in 1996 and, especially, in 2000.

Indeed, the Republican Party may provide a window into the corporate boardroom's view of the changing demographic landscape. The GOP has increasingly adopted the rhetoric of the diversity machine.

As predicted by *The Diversity Machine*, the source of this shift was demographic: The GOP's multicultural makeover took on special urgency after the party's disastrous defeat in the 1998 elections in vote-rich California, where burgeoning numbers of Hispanic voters emerged as a formidable anti-GOP bloc. Republican leaders in California are vigorously searching for minority and female candidates—even if it means the exclusion of white males.

The 2000 presidential election revealed sharp ethnic and cultural divisions. Newly elected George W. Bush obtained one-tenth of the black vote and only one-third of the Hispanic vote. In response, White House strategists redoubled diversity efforts. The new cabinet was ostentatiously designed as the most diverse ever and weekly presidential radio addresses to the nation are bilingual. An Hispanic is favored as the next Supreme Court nominee. Bush has avoided polarized debates over diversity and affirmative action by speaking vaguely of "diversity without differences," and "affirmative access." But his new justice department appointees will have to take more explicit positions in pending Supreme Court cases and in maintaining or revising government regulations.

Rhetoric to Reality?

Paradoxically, the insensitivity of business elites to cultural and political issues both frustrates and empowers the diversity machine. Diversity advocates are correct when they fume that diversity issues have a low priority with most American businessmen. And, I think, they are partly correct that white males can be remarkably insensitive to diversity issues. But this has to do with a broader "American" value system that encompasses both "businessmen" and "white males"—and likely includes many "businesswomen." It's a capitalist worldview that emphasizes markets, individuals, rationality, technology, and what sociologists call "task orientation." Due to its emphases, this viewpoint gives short shrift to collective, cultural, sociological and political phenomena.

Preoccupied with matters of markets and individuals, America's business leaders don't have the time or inclination to think about such soft topics as personnel and "people issues." Most have little background in the social sciences, least of all sociology. Therefore, diversity issues are left, by default, to the diversity machine. "You handle it," the CEOs seem to say, "and if it isn't too expensive, we'll go along."

In this regard, hitching the wagon of workforce diversity to immigration and globalization was truly a stroke of fortune, if not genius.

Immigration and globalization have become unquestioned assumptions not only among America's business elites but by its political and cultural establishments as well. Acceptance of the diversity machine's rhetoric and policies follows naturally.

Yet diversity issues are too important to be left to the diversity machine. The incessant, high-level chanting of diversity rhetoric can be self-fulfilling, producing intentional and unintentional results. There is a symbiotic relationship between social policy and societal realities. Diversity policies, even pragmatic multicultural marketing, can mold the way people think and act.

In the conclusion to the 1997 edition of *The Diversity Machine*, I suggested that the nation is at a turning point. It still is. Racism and sexism still exist. A host of new ethnic cultures must be recognized and dealt with due to the continuing high level of Third World immigration and the integration of the global economy. But this must be done within the law and *without making things worse*. Or, as the best diversity consultants wisely note: Do no harm. This is difficult to accomplish. Group and cultural differences exist, and it is most appropriate to recognize and manage them in many situations—in health care delivery for example.

I must again conclude that the western ideals of individual liberty and equal treatment under law and policy "without regard to race, color, or creed" provide the best basis for cohesion in a truly multi-ethnic, multi-cultural society. These ideals are the direct opposite of the more radical assumptions of the diversity machine: group proportionalism ("equity"), identity politics, and cultural relativism.

The top-down campaign by America's elites to value and manage diversity may have had rhetorical utility for public relations, political campaigns, lawsuit avoidance, and societal stability. But it is doubtful that a social scientist will statistically prove the "business case" for having a workforce that looks like its customer base.

In the meantime, some of the more sophisticated diversity consultants have recommended that we should emphasize cultural similarities as well as differences. Perhaps America's corporate, political, and cultural leaders should speak more about transcending cultural differences, or, at least, should worry less about categorizing and managing diversity and simply let it happen.

Notes

1. In a long article in *The American Behavioral Scientist*, Erin Kelly and Frank Dobbin—generously footnoting *The Diversity Machine*—have offered a

slightly different interpretation of how affirmative action became diversity management. They stress the "invention" of diversity management as a response by EEO/AA officers to enforcement cutbacks by the Reagan administration. But, I would submit, it was a far broader social movement than this. See Erin Kelly and Frank Dobbin, "How Affirmative Action Became Diversity Management," *American Behavioral Scientist* 41 (April, 1998): 960-984.

2. Barbara R. Deane, "New Frontiers for Diversity." (Seattle, Washington: The Gildeane Group, 2000).
3. Richard Judy and Carol D'Amico, *Workforce 2020: Work and Workers in the 21st Century* (Indianapolis: Hudson Institute, 1997). William G. Bowen and Derek Bok, *The Shape of the River: Long-Term Consequences of Considering Race in College and University Admissions* (Princeton, New Jersey: Princeton University Press, 1998).
4. The Advisory Board's Report: President's Initiative on Race. *One America in the 21st Century: Forging a New Future.* (Washington, D.C. U.S. Government Printing Office, 1998).
5. http://www.astd.expoventure.com/ASTDBuyerGuidenoreg/Booths/Booths.html. See also Robert Rosen, Patricia Digh, Marshall Singer and Carl Phillips, *Global Literacies* (New York: Simon and Schuster, 2000).
6. Robert J. Grossman, "Race in the Workplace," HR Magazine, 45 (March, 2000; and Robert Grossman, "Is Diversity Working?" HR Magazine 25 (March), http://www.shrm.org/hrmagazine/articles/0300grossman.htm
7. Robert J. Grossman, "Is Diversity Working?" op. cit.
8. "Builders and Unions Court New Workers," *New York Times*, March 12, 1999. See also, Patrick O'Driscoll, "Mayors 'Lack of Skilled Workers Hurting Cities,'" *USA Today*, September 23, 1999; and James P. Miller, "Worker Shortage Stays Widespred, Hiring Study Says," *Wall Street Journal*, February 28, 2000.
9. *Los Angeles Times*, July 7, 1998.
10. *Wall Street Journal*, March 22, 1999.
11. Michael J. Sniffen, "Workplace Bias Suits Soared in the 1990s," *USA Today*, January 17, 2000.
12. Catherine Strong, "Ford Pays $3.8 Million in Employment Discrimination Settlement," *The Detroit News* (February 19, 2000).
13. "Nightly Business Report Diversity Survey." 1997. http://www.nightlybusiness.org/divtext.htm.
14. *Ibid.*
15. Korn/Ferry International and Columbia Business School. "Diversity in the Executive Suite: Creating Successful Career Paths and Strategies" (New York: Korn Ferry, 1998).
16. William G. Bowen and Derek Bok, *op. cit.*
17. *Ibid.*, 88.
18. Howard Bowen, Derek Bok and Glenda Burkhart, "A Report Card on Diversity: Lessons for Business from Higher Education," *Harvard Business Review* 77 (January/February, 1999): 139-149.
19. *Ibid.*, 141.
20. Patricia Gurin, "Expert Report of Patricia Gurin," http://www.umich.edu/newsinfo/Admission/Expert/gurintoc.html
21. Gary Orfield, "Affirmative Action Works: But Judges and Policy Makers Need to Hear That," *Chronicle of Higher Education, December 10, 1999.*
22. Stephan Thernstrom and Abilgail Thernstrom, "Racial Preferences: What We Now Know," *Commentary* (February, 1999); Stephan Thernstrom and Abigail Thernstrom, "Reflections on the Shape of the River," *UCLA Law Review* (June, 1999): 1589-1631. For more recent and thorough critiques see Thomas E. Wood and Malcolm J. Sherman, "Is Campus Racial Diversity Correlated with Educational Benefits?" Washington, D.C., National Asso-

ciation of Scholars, 2001. (Available online at http://www.nas.org; and, "Robert Lerner and Althea Nagai, "A Critique of the Expert Report of Patricia Gurin in *Gratz v. Bollinger.*" Washington, D.C., Center for Equal Opportunity, 2001.

23. Richard W. Judy and Carol D'Amico, *Workforce 2020: Work and Workers in the 21st Century* (Indianapolis: The Hudson Institute, 1997).

24. *Ibid.*, xiv-xv.

25. *Ibid.*

26. Harry Holzer and David Neumark, "Assessing Affirmative Action," *Journal of Economic Literature*, Vol. 38 (September 2000): 559.

27. See William Frey and Ross C. Devol, "America's Demography in the New Century: Aging Baby Boomers and New Immigrants as Major Players." Santa Monica, California: Milken Institute, March 8, 2000. See also, "The Diversity Myth," *American Demographics*, June, 1998.

28. Some of these articles include: Toni Lepeska and Ron Maxey, "Hispanics Changing the Face of Memphis," *The Commercial Appeal* (Memphis), January 1, 2000; Teresa Puente, "Wave of Hispanic Immigrants Alters Demographics in the Heartland," *Chicago Tribune*, January 16, 2000; Hector Tobar, "Illegal Migrants Take Interstates to Mid-America," *Los Angeles Times*, January 16, 2000; Sylvia Moreno and Scott Wilson, "Latino Newcomers Struggle to Adapt and Excel," *Wahington Post*, January 21, 2000; Paulette Thomas, "In the Land of Bratwurst, a New Hispanic Boom," *Wall Street Journal*, March 16, 2000; Mary Edwards and Jeff Ortega, "The Land of Plenty: Latinos Make Strides in Job-Rich Central Ohio," *Columbus Dispatch*, March 19, 2000.

29. For example, see Gregory Rodriguez, "The Power in Forgetting: As Latinos Become the Largest Minority, They Are Creating a New Racial Paradigm," *Los Angeles Times*, April 2, 2000.

30. See, for example, an analysis by "Stuart Silverstein, "Ethnic Clustering Seen as Future in Much of Nation," *Los Angeles Times*, March 23, 2000.

31. Gerges Vernez, Richard A. Krop, C. Peter Rydell, *Closing the Education Gap: Benefits and Costs.* (Santa Monica, California: Rand Corporation, 1999); Deborah Reed, *California's Rising Income Inequality: Causes and Concerns* (San Francisco: Public Policy Institute of California, 1999).

32. See analysis in Dan Morain and Martha Grove, "California Election Issues Brought Out Conservatives," *Los Angeles Times*, March 9, 2000.

33. "New Legal Developments," Project on Civil Rights and Public Contracts at the University of Maryland, Baltimore County, February, 2000.

34. See John Sullivan and Roger Clegg, "New Year's Resolution: No More Racial Preferences in Public Contracting," *Washington Times*, January 16, 2000; also George LaNoue, "To the 'Disadvantaged' Go the Spoils?" *The Public Interest*, Winter, 2000: 91-98. The U.S. Supreme Court will revisit revised government guidelines stemming from the *Adarand* case in its fall 2001 term.

35. For a recent analysis of Michigan's formula and other admissions systems see Kenneth Cooper, "Deciding Who Gets In and Who Doesn't," *Washington Post*, April 2, 2000; and Kenneth J. Cooper, "Colleges Testing New Diversity Initiatives," *Washington Post*, April 2, 2000.

36. Data supplied by Office of Equity and Diversity, University of Michigan, Ann Arbor.

37. See Steven A. Holmes, "Diverse U. of Michigan Tries New Legal Tack," *New York Times*, May 11, 1999.

38. Somewhat to my surprise, the chapter on U-M in *The Diversity Machine* was selected to be extensively excerpted in the widely-distributed alumni journal, *Michigan Today*. The editor, a U-M veteran and an African American, considered the chapter "one of the best anthropological studies" he'd ever seen of the institution. Alas, when the lawsuits were filed, the excerpt

became too politically radioactive and, instead, a brief review of the book was published.

39. Gerald R. Ford, "Inclusive America, Under Attack," *New York Times*, August 8, 1999.
40. "Affirmative Action: Major Source of White Opposition Is Racial Prejudice," *University Record, March 6, 2000.*
41. Barbara Whitaker, "Admissions of Minorities Rebounding in California," *New York Times*, April 7, 2000.
42. James Traub, "The Class of Prop. 209," *New York Times Magazine*, May 2, 1999, 46.
43. http://www.ucop.edu/pathways/infotr/qr/qrucbsel.html
44. *Ibid.,* 78.
45. (http://www.acusd.edu/~e_cook/index.html)
46. On p. 244 of *The Diversity Machine* , I quoted the remarks of the President of Cal State Chico to a conference of community college administrators about policies requiring Cal State campus presidents to cancelsearches when insufficient numbers of minorities were finalists and to implement a "two-for-one" bonus option in faculty searches. Evidently, these policies are still in operation. In the academic year 1999-2000, the campus diversity director threatened to cancel a job search in San Diego State University's math department when the finalist list contained an insufficient number of minorities—even though 5 of the last 7 hires in the math department had been women, while another was an Asian male. Eventually, two white males (the department's top choices) were hired while a black female (further down the list) was awarded a bonus, "opportunity hire."
47. Jonathan Curiel, "White Lecturer Wins Bias Suit Against SFSU: Jury Awards $2.75 Million," *San Francisco Chronicle*, March 31, 1999.
48. "Not Making the Grade," *Los Angeles Times*, April 1, 2000.
49. Jennifer Kerr, "Community Colleges Keep Part-Time Teachers on the Road," *Inland Valley Daily Bulletin* (AP Story), October 22, 1999.
50. Interview with Tosh Shikaso, April 3, 2000.
51. Stephanie Cain, "Sheriff's Department Struggles to Fill 180 Vacancies by 2001," *Inland Valley Daily Bulletin,* October 30, 1999. Three members of the L.A. Sheriff's Training Staff were also interviewed for this section—they wished to remain anonymous.
52. Nicholas Riccardi, "Sheriff's Staffer Wins Bias Trial," *Los Angeles Times*, December 8, 1999.
53. Edward J. Boyer, "Harassment in Sheriff's Department Decried," *Los Angeles Times*, March 28, 2000.
54. *Ibid.*
55. *Ibid*
56. James Fallows, "The Invisible Poor," *New York Times Magazine*, March 19, 2000.
57. *Ibid.,* 95
58. Kimberlee Jensen, "Wanted: Diversity in High Tech Industry," *Cultural Diversity at Work*, 10.
59. Robert Suro, "Crossing the High Tech Divide," *American Demographics*, July, 1999.
60. See the website, http://ww.www.gmsp.org/about_prog.html;see also, Rene Sanchez, "Gates to Give $1 Billion for Minority Scholarships," *Washington Post*, September 17, 1999.
61. Peter Y. Hong, "Diversity Driven by the Dollar," *Los Angeles Times*, May 26, 1998. See also, Kevin Wallsten, "Diversity Pays Off In Big Sales for Toyota Dealership," *Workforce* (September, 1998): 91-92.

Prologue: A Taste of Diversity Training

"You're trying to get us to label and classify one another!" The middle-aged white male who offered this snort of protest was one of fifty California middle managers compelled to attend a one-day diversity workshop on a sunny morning in November 1991. About 50 percent of the participants were white males, most of them over forty-five years old. Another 20 percent were white females, and the rest were an ethnic mix. I was an invited (white male), participant-observer.

We had just completed the Name Five exercise. Successively, in two-minute intervals, we each were asked to write down names of five famous male Americans, female Americans, white Americans, Asian Americans, Catholic Americans, Hispanic Americans, African Americans, and disabled Americans. Predictably, most people did well with white Americans, but lists got markedly shorter for Asian Americans, Hispanic Americans, and the disabled. ("Mentally disabled?" came an inevitable snicker.)

Sue Schmidt and Carmen Hidalgo (pseudonyms) were billed as the ethnically diverse teaching team from the Anti-Defamation League's (ADL) Workplace of Difference program. Sue patiently took up the complaint of the white male (termed "white male resistance" by diversity pros) that the session was encouraging ethnic labeling.

"I'm trying," she began steadily and firmly, "to get you to see that some people are alive and well and that they didn't melt into the melting pot. I'm trying to illustrate the salad bowl of people who don't blend. The melting pot ignores the advantages of diversity and difference."

Resistance faded for the time being, but it would be a long day in this large meeting room of a public library. The reason for the workshop was not stated openly. An ADL handout cheerfully stated that the session would "allow participants to examine the concepts of stereotypes and assumptions, provide participants an opportunity to examine ways they perceive others—and others perceive them, invite participants to explore the idea of culture, and, most important, teach participants how diversity in the workplace enhances the environment and translates to a higher level of satisfaction and a better overall working environment."

The real reason for the workshop, I was told during the coffee breaks, was that two city government officials had made intemperate remarks about minorities in the local press. This was taken as evidence of widespread racism in city government. Penance was called for—and possibly defensive legal maneuvering. Hence, the workshop for 150 middle managers, at a cost to the city of approximately $33,000.

Carmen and Sue launched the diversity workshop by describing their personal backgrounds. Both, it turned out, had been teachers. (There are a lot of ex-educators in the diversity business.) They then explained the mission of the ADL (to combat prejudice, discrimination, and stereotyping). Sue offered the standard rationale for diversity training: the ethnic composition of the United States is changing rapidly, and southern California is changing faster than anywhere else. Sue quickly cited the Hudson Institute's *Workforce 2000* report, which forecast that two-thirds of the people entering the workforce by the year 2000 will be female or minority.

To remove any threatening sting to the figures, Sue calmly emphasized, "It's what's there; it's what's true. But it doesn't mean you have to give up who you are." Nevertheless, she said, the new demographics would mean that "corporate communities should create environments that will ensure positive interaction between members of a rapidly changing workforce." Therefore, "we should look at what differences have to offer us. Look at differences in a different way."

We formed a line around the room and counted off in order to form discussion groups of five or six people. (This mixing tactic prevented people from gravitating to friends and others like themselves for a "taste of home" in a strange setting.) Seated in our new groups, we were given the ground rules: (1) respect one another, (2) say anything, but do not be insulting, (3) be open, (4) participate, and (5) keep comments within the workshop. Then we were asked to write down one-word descriptors of ourselves as individuals. Five minutes later, we began discussing our answers. At the front of the conference room, Carmen listed our responses on a huge flip-pad of paper. The expected ethnic labels tumbled out—white, Anglo-Saxon, Russian-Jewish, African American, Lebanese, Swedish, German, woman, Caucasian—but a surprising number of people seemed confused or unconcerned about their ethnic heritage. In addition, there were other forms of self-identification that suggested rumblings of skepticism: large, old, overweight, bored, bald, multicultural, red-blooded. Nevertheless, Sue and Carmen were accommodating. The variety of labels, we were told, showed that "diversity was anything that made us different—not just race or gender."

Next came the Name Five game and the first open glimmer of revolt. Then we viewed a video on the dangers of ethnic humor. Sue advised us to use the "three-year-old rule": before telling a joke, consider whether a three-year-old child should hear such a joke or whether the child could tell it without being reprimanded. As we digested this in our focus groups, Sue joined mine—only to be outraged to hear Jake, a self-described jovial "large white male," describe how he routinely asked job applicants whether they could tolerate the rough humor used in his unit. She was less perturbed when Sam, an older Hispanic man, told of his unit's practice of hiring relatives of those already working for the city. He explained that this added an extra measure of workplace control by combining official and familial pressures.

After lunch, we were shown a video, *Eye of the Beholder,* which featured the experiments of Iowa elementary schoolteacher Jane Elliot. In the late 1960s, Elliot had divided her class of schoolchildren into arbitrarily assigned groups of "blue eyes" and "brown eyes." At first, blue-eyed students were labeled superior and described as having more positive attributes. They were given privileges and allowed to dominate those with brown eyes; then the eye color roles were reversed. The video showed Elliot later using this experiential exercise with police, correctional officers, and other adults. The object of this simulation, of course, was to have people experience the social-psychological effects of being labeled and treated as an oppressed group.

Eye of the Beholder illustrated the impact of the experiment's results. But the video also conveyed the preachy, political correctness of both Elliot and the filmmakers (e.g., they admonished, "Abraham Lincoln's grandmother was probably black—but you aren't taught that in white history"), and the guilt-mongering video proved counterproductive. When Sue and Carmen initially asked for comments, no one said anything. More repeated coaxing by the two consultants yielded one lame comment that the program was "interesting." The resumption of deep silence and noncooperation suggested simmering anger. What group purpose and cohesion had been generated was disintegrating.

Sue sensibly suggested a five-minute break followed by focus group discussions of the video. During the break the two consultants adjourned to a kitchen adjacent to the conference room. Their nervous peals of laughter escaped into the main meeting room as they talked about how to put the workshop back together.

After fifteen minutes, Sue and Carmen called us into an assembled group of fifty.

"What did you come up with?" Sue asked.

One white male, a captain in the fire department, flung down the gauntlet: "We got into a discussion of quotas, and that we'd like to hire by merit. But we are stuck with them."

A ripple of nervous laughter moved through the room. Ann McGuire, the city's training administrator, quickly intervened: "We don't have quotas. We have goals."

"At ADL," Sue offered helpfully, "we cast a wider net to hire a person of color to team with me. You must think of these things."

This exchange was followed by more silence and a few random comments.

"I'm glad I had brown eyes and would not have been the target," volunteered Sarah, an especially naive member of my focus group.

"I sympathized with the white southern lady in one of the experiments," said another white woman. "Jane Elliot assumed white southerners were prejudiced."

Sue cited social science experiments that illustrated the power of labeling. Then she asked, "What are you going to do to break that system? I'm not accusing you of being racist. Certain types of people do apply for certain types of jobs for historical and cultural reasons. What are five things we can do to stop prejudice?"

"You're teaching it!" shouted a white man at the back of the room. He was ignored, and we again formed our discussion groups. Then we once more reassembled as a committee of the whole, where spokespersons for each group read off lists of strategies to reduce prejudice. "Education, explanation, confronting inappropriate behavior, clarifying expectations, intervention, and top managers realizing the problem" were typical offerings.

Then the sniping began again on affirmative action and reverse discrimination.

"We discussed hiring practices where the city itself puts collars and labels on people," declared a white male.

Sue looked exasperated. "Diversity and affirmative action are not the same thing. Diversity goes beyond race. It goes to who you hire and why. Don't point the finger at quotas and have quotas be at fault. Don't scapegoat."

Training administrator McGuire again interjected: "Managing diversity and cultural diversity is not affirmative action. Read some of the articles we've distributed."

Sue drew a diagram. "Affirmative action is the law. We're getting caught up in hiring practices. But diversity goes beyond the law. It has to do with respect and tolerance."

The discussion limped into the final phase of the workshop and the final task of our discussion group: to formulate "action plans" to implement what we had learned. Here we were supposed to deal with on-the-job-behavior questions—for example, What are the strengths and weaknesses of our corporate culture in regard to valuing and effectively utilizing all employees? What diversity issues do we face in the work environment, and how have we dealt with them? What kinds of things can a manager do to create an environment conducive to valuing diversity? What steps can a supervisor take to effect change?

In general, the recommendations dealt with increased sensitivity toward race, gender, double standards, family stress, people who live in poor neighborhoods, and so forth. Two white males sharply challenged the city's training manager over the fact that the top administrators got a mini-version of the workshop while middle managers were getting the full treatment.

"Well, that's what they decided," snapped Ann McGuire. And that was the end of the diversity workshop.

Introduction

Beyond Affirmative Action

"We're at the point where we really understand that in order to be a competitive global company we are going to have to have diversity in our work force," says Emily Duncan, Hewlett-Packard's manager of affirmative action.

The potential political difficulty for such aggressive affirmative action efforts is that they often rely on racial preference that appears to be at odds with what most Americans consider equitable. Companies like Coca-Cola, Xerox, Kodak, IBM, Johnson and Johnson, du Pont, and Hewlett-Packard say their affirmative action efforts are based on assessment of what is good for them, not what government or the public expects of them.

Many corporations tie executives' bonuses and promotions to their affirmative action performance. "We would do it whether it was the law or not," says Wilfred D. Oliver, a director of minority business development at Kodak.

San Francisco Chronicle, August 4, 1991

Change is usually created with a small percentage of the population who can envision a better future.

Consultant-author Judith Katz, Cultural Diversity at Work

During the 1980s, neither business elites nor the highest officials of the Reagan and Bush administrations were aware that the cultural revolutions sweeping through universities and major foundations were also pulsing through the mass media, professional associations, the legal system, and into the workplace. Affirmative action programs, accommodated by corporations and government agencies since the 1970s, provided the beachhead for a more expansive "diversity machine." This policy engine has been constructed and

1

piloted by a host of egalitarian reformers: human resources directors, government bureaucrats, lawyers, academics, consultants, civil rights advocates, feminists, and young college-educated employees. By the mid-1990s, the field of diversity management had established itself as the business branch of multiculturalism, academe's policy export to the American workplace.

In *Illiberal Education,* Dinesh D'Souza observed that affirmative action did not stop at the admissions gate.[1] It necessitated the multicultural transformation of the university. So it would be in the world of work. Just as the changing ethnic composition of enrollments forced curricular reform and an altered campus climate, so changing workforce demographics were said to require the dismantling of white male workplace "monoculturalism." Merely hiring women and minorities was not enough. Their special needs and cultural identities should be productively "valued" or "managed" to gain the competitive edge in increasingly multicultural global markets. "Differences are assets," proclaims video training guru Lewis Griggs.

Diversity consultants argued that assimilation and the concept of the melting pot were out; the more separatist salad bowl was in. Women, immigrants, and American minorities now wished to "be themselves" and retain their cultural identities. Culturally diverse workers resisted conforming to the outmoded "one-size-fits-all" organizational cultures fashioned by and for white males. Consultants called on employers to adjust standards and practices to the cultures of women and minorities, not the other way around.

Diversity consultants anticipated new federal regulatory efforts to ensure that women and minorities were not just hired but also proportionately retained and promoted, regulations hinted at in the U.S. Department of Labor's 1991 *Report on the Glass Ceiling Initiative.*[2] Consultants offer to spur upward mobility of women and minorities by rooting out institutional racism and sexism hidden in organizational cultures. For fees ranging from $2,000 (for a one-day workshop) to well over $200,000 (for a complete cultural overhaul), diversity consultants claim they can create a workplace environment where women, minorities, older workers, disabled workers, and those with other lifestyle differences can "be themselves." More flexible management of organizational systems and cultures that "value differences" purportedly will offer a competitive edge in retaining and promoting talented workers as well as preventing ill will and expense generated by discrimination complaints.

Money magazine and *U.S. News and World Report* hailed diversity management as a hot profession for the 1990s. The July 8, 1991, *Business Week* blended affirmative action and managing diversity programs in its cover story, "Race in the Workplace." *Nation's Business* followed in September 1992 with the cover "Winning with Diversity," and CEOs began harkening to the call. "We've got to get right with the future!" proclaimed *Miami Herald* publisher David Lawrence.

In the early 1990s, pioneers in diversity management began to build a social policy machine to extend their reach into the American workplace, and by the mid-1990s, they had enjoyed considerable success. Besides the ubiquitous sensitivity workshops, diversity management programs had proliferated in many ways throughout several major corporations:

• **General Motors** recently reaffirmed its commitment to "press the envelope" on affirmative action while moving into the broader concept of managing diversity. Backed by CEO and President John Smith, GM's broadened diversity thrust covers four areas: marketing ("to increase market share in diverse markets"), human resource management ("to become an employer of choice among a diverse population"), minority supplier development ("to create a partnership relationship with minority suppliers . . . and to increase minority suppliers' share in . . . GM community" and community relations ("to become the automotive company of choice within the community").

William J. O'Neil, a former Cadillac spokesman who now handles public relations for GM's Chevrolet Division, says "There are now 36 million owners of Chevrolet/Geo cars and trucks. In the past, in our eyes, we probably would have classified all of those people as looking alike—essentially white and Midwestern.

"Well, we've changed. We've done research. We now realize that not only do those people not look alike, but they don't always speak the same language; nor do they shop for vehicles or look at products in the same way or have the same values . . . [but] . . . they all want cars and trucks and we want to be the people to sell them those cars and trucks."[3]

• **IBM's** global workforce diversity theme is "None of us is as strong as all of us," a theme that helps the company focus on the opportunities for employee and marketplace progress. Understanding that winning in the marketplace necessitates adopting management practices to maximize the productivity of diverse employees, IBM's global workforce diversity council identified five issues to be addressed by each of its geographic regions: cultural awareness and acceptance; multilingualism; diversity of the management team; the advancement of women; and workplace flexibility and balance. "These are issues that touch our day-to-day workplace, cross all borders, and have strategic impact on our business," says J. T. (Ted) Childs [director of workforce diversity].

Childs cites two recent tactical accomplishments. IBM participated with a group of its customers as one of the "champion" companies that led the American Business Collaboration for Quality Dependent Care. This team of companies led the investment of $25 million for dependent-care projects in 1992, and an additional $100 million for 1995 through the year 2000. The team played a significant role in redefining the work-family debate as a legitimate and strategic business issue.

Second, a "work in progress" involved the launching of eight task forces in 1995 representing constituencies that reflect IBM's work force and its customers. The task forces are: Women, Asian, Black, Hispanic, Native American, Gay and Lesbian, White Male, and People with Disabilities. Each was led by representative executives and had three objectives—to determine: (1) what is required for that constituency to feel welcomed and valued at IBM; (2) what IBM and the group can do to maximize their productivity, and (3) what IBM can do to maximize the pursuit of marketshare from the constituency's community.[4]

• In 1992, [**Merrill Lynch's**] CEO Daniel Tully called for the formation of a Diversity Task Force, made up of line and support professionals, to map out Merrill Lynch's strategy. The task force developed specific goals, objectives and monitoring systems, and formed the diversity office to implement the plan. Programs that advance accountability, training, recruiting, development, mentoring, networking, work-family policies, compensation and leadership reflect the firm's comprehensive approach to managing diversity. The diversity goals have, in fact, become critical objectives for the company's most senior executives, as well as a factor in their compensation.

Expanded sourcing efforts, development opportunities, and a focused retention program are some of the specific diversity initiatives of Merrill Lynch that have already seen positive results. A dramatic example is the full-time associate job class in the Corporate and Institutional Client Group, which has experienced a 37 percent increase in minority hires since 1992. Career Net, a job-posting system, was expanded in 1993 to include middle-management and revenue-producing positions. Since that time, more women and minorities are reporting increased satisfaction with their ability to find better jobs within the company.

Merrill Lynch is also the only securities industry company to have either a minority vendor program or membership in the National Minority Supplier Development Council. The recent emphasis on diversity has affected positively the amount of money spent on services from women- and minority-owned businesses—in 1995, the company spent $28 million as customers of such businesses.[5]

• "[**Ford**] must have a culture that values differences if we are to attract, develop, and retain the world's best and brightest employees to, in turn, ensure that Ford becomes the premier automaker," says Romeo McNairy, diversity and work-life planning manager. "So understanding diversity in the workplace is not only the right thing to do, it's also the best thing to do from a business perspective."

To address the new business issues, in March 1994 senior management formalized its commitment to diversity by establishing the Executive Council on diversity. Co-chaired by CEO Trotman, the council brings together 22 U.S. and European top managers to lead the company's global diversity efforts. All of the council's members have been through diversity awareness training, which will be rolled out to Ford's salaried and involved hourly employees starting 1996.

But diversity awareness is not new at Ford. More than 80,000 Ford-UAW hourly employees in the United States have already participated in an ongoing diversity program called "A Matter of Respect." Jointly developed by the UAW and Ford, it includes a video that illustrates age and sex discrimination situations, and addresses other diversity issues. In Britain, many plants and locations have joint hourly/salaried/Management Equal Opportunities Committees that deal with a wide range of diversity matters.

The commitment to diversity at Ford, however, means more than organizing training sessions and drafting policies, says Bob Kramer, vice president, human resources. "This is an evolutionary process—not a 'program' with a beginning and an ending. We're changing our culture. We have to."[6]

• **NYNEX Corporation**'s 60,000 employees are eligible to participate in a wide range of network and "affinity groups" including the Hispanic Support Organization, the Minority Multicultural Association, the Asian Focus Group, Gays and Lesbians Working for Culture Diversity, and the Disability Support Organization. They function as employee resource groups and some have their own community outreach programs.

Edwin Martinez, the staff director of corporate cultural initiatives, has pointed out how its affinity groups can contribute to marketing strategies. "The Asian Focus Group pointed out that the number four is bad luck to Koreans, and now whenever possible we try not to assign telephone numbers with that digit to our Korean customers." The group also encouraged the formation of multilingual marketing sales centers, which increased the Asian residential market base by 3.9 percent. The NYNEX Diversity Consortium sponsored "Survival Skill Workshops" to teach employees skills for managing their careers. NYNEX has conducted a cultural audit of all its employees to assess barriers that might inhibit advancement of women and minorities.

In 1994 NYNEX offered a dozen "Diversity Salute" awards to employees who help to foster a work environment that "practices inclusion and values its employees as assets."[7]

• **Hughes Aircraft** has long been a leader in institutionalizing diversity measures. The company has made commitment to affirmative action and diversity part of its overall corporate policy, not just a compliance measure. David Barclay has been Vice President for Workforce Diversity at Hughes Electronic subsidiary. The company began extensive diversity training of management and other employees in the late 1980s, nourished the formation of women's and minority support groups, rewards managers on the basis of their affirmative action records, and has even used race-and-gender criteria during massive layoffs in post–Cold War downsizing. Senior and mid-level managers mentor women and minorities to advance them up career ladders.

From 1970 to 1995, women's proportion of "supervisor and above" positions rose from 2 percent to 15.5 percent; minority representation in the same categories rose from 6.1 percent to 17 percent. Women are 10 percent of the 70 vice presidents; minorities, 12 percent.

Hughes also has minority outreach programs including a partnership with predominantly black engineering schools. The program includes helping the schools design curricula, donating surplus equipment, and faculty internships.[8]

• In August 1995, **Procter & Gamble** won the U.S. Department of Labor's Opportunity 2000 Award for outstanding equal employment opportunity. The award recognized the company's comprehensive affirmative action programs, which resulted in women obtaining 40 percent, and minorities 26 percent, of new management slots. P&G's Brand Managers' Program recruits large numbers of women and minorities to ensure a substantial pool of candidates for advancement into executive level positions. P&G also recruits heavily at minority and women's colleges and has donated millions of dollars to the United Negro College Fund, the National Hispanic Scholarship Fund, and colleges with high Native American enrollment.

In the same year, the Labor Department's Office of Federal Contract Compliance (OFCCP) conducted a "glass ceiling audit" of the company and praised P&G's efforts, "especially its strong recruitment, career planning, and careful monitoring of minority and female development." The OFCCP's audit followed P&G's own internal five-year diversity review that showed representation of women and minorities increasing at all levels.

P&G's CEO and President Edwin L. Artst argues that equal opportunity, at every level of the organization, is in the company's best interest. "It's not a matter of merely complying with government rules and regulations. It's a fundamental part of our corporate philosophy." The company has always set its own affirmative action goals higher than government mandates.

"Regardless of what government may do, we believe that we have a moral contract with all the women and minorities in our company—a moral contract to provide equal opportunity employment, equal opportunity for advancement, and equal opportunity for financial reward—and no change in law or regulation would cause us to turn back the clock. No matter what happens to affirmative action laws, we will keep this moral contract, and we will deliver."[9]

By 1995, a survey of the top Fortune 50 corporations by A. T. Kearney Executive Search found that 70 percent had formal diversity management programs in place, 8 percent were developing programs, and 8 percent had more scattered programs; 12 percent had no such programs in place.[10]

The diversity machine is likely here to stay. The leaders of this surprisingly fragile policy vehicle have bridged internal schisms and survived the sudden conservative counterrevolution of 1994. Indeed, diversity management has become deeply rooted in the federal government and has achieved bipartisan support among the leadership of both major political parties. Democratic party chieftains and the Clinton White House have long been committed to all manner of workforce diversity theory and practice. More recent has been the conversion of the Republican party's leadership, which imposed strong top-down themes of diversity and inclusiveness on the 1996 Republican National Convention program. "Diversity is our strength!" chirped Newt Gingrich on ABC's *Nightline.* The consultant gurus of the diversity machine could not have said it better.

Although there is still no systematic proof that diversity management programs decrease ethnic and gender tensions while increasing profits, productivity, and creativity, the policies nonetheless roll forward, changing and being changed by the wider society. A professional literature has evolved. Diversity management is becoming a recognized specialty in business and organizational behavior textbooks.[11] The early, unchecked proliferation of consultants has lately stabilized.[12] The prestigious Conference Board and the Society for Human Resource Management (SHRM) have begun sponsoring major diversity conferences, and SHRM offers a credentialing program for diversity consultants.

The basic questions now are what forms diversity management policies will assume in the future and how these controversial policies will intentionally and unintentionally change the allegedly "white male" workplace and the basic values of American society.

The Diversity Machine

Theories and techniques of diversity management have been developed, refined, packaged, and spread energetically by a loosely organized social change movement. The key personnel, ideas, and strategies driving this diversity machine come from preexisting, heavily female or minority networks in corporate, government, foundation, or university human resources departments, especially in affirmative action offices. Those still inside these institutions have linked up with an army of downsized colleagues-turned-consultants to form the core of the diversity machine. Leaders tend to be academically trained author-consultants, some of whom founded research institutes to study or promote diversity management. For example, R. Roosevelt Thomas founded the Atlanta-based American Institute for Managing Diversity, Ann Morrison helped form (but has since left) the Center for Creative Leadership in San Diego, and Lewis Griggs's many activities are based in Griggs Productions in San Francisco. (Catalyst, a nonprofit research and advisory organization promoting women's issues, is also active in the diversity machine.)

The diversity machine has powerful allies and resourceful CEO champions inside major corporations, universities, nonprofit organizations, government agencies, research institutes, foundations, and, of course, a Clinton administration that wants to "look like America" (a favorite phrase coined by the diversity machine). A potent outpost of the diversity machine within the federal government has been the Department of Labor's Glass Ceiling Commission, which issues fact-finding reports and policy recommendations. Although it is now officially out of business, the commission's recent studies are often cited by diversity proponents.

(Though the U.S. military is also a distant part of the diversity machine, their extensive race relations and social engineering programs are beyond the scope of this book. Few consultants and little of the developing diversity literature make any reference to the military's models. It is worth noting, however, that since the 1970s, the Defense Equal Opportunity Management

Institute at Patrick Air Force Base in Florida has trained equal opportunity officers with a variety of "shock treatment" sensitivity courses, elements of which have been incorporated into the military's basic training.[13] The military's rhetoric for handling equal opportunity and diversity has been echoed in the pronouncements of retired general Colin Powell.)

The diversity machine has lately become anchored in three mainline, business-based, research-and-education professional associations: the American Society for Training and Development (comprising both a national organization, in Alexandria, Virginia, and several regional associations, especially Los Angeles); the New York-based Conference Board, with twenty-five hundred membership organizations, including 75 percent of the Fortune 500; and SHRM, also in Alexandria, Virginia, the most prestigious human resources society with 53,000 professional and student members. Civic and religious groups, some of which pioneered tolerance and prejudice-reduction training, have become major centers of training, information, and personnel exchange within the diversity machine, especially the B'nai B'rith Anti-Defamation League's Workplace of Difference education and consulting unit, and the National Conference's (formerly the National Conference of Christians and Jews) Dialogue series and other more tailored education and consulting programs. The National Association for the Advancement of Colored People and its Legal Defense Fund, the Mexican American Legal Defense and Education Fund, the National Organization for Women, and the National Council of Churches are also organizations promoting programs to reduce prejudice and increase acceptance of cultural diversity.

Building the Diversity Machine

The diversity machine's construction has been a near-formulaic illustration of social movement building outlined in Ralph Turner and Lewis Killian's classic textbook, *Collective Behavior and Social Movements.*[14]

In the 1970s and 1980s, early individual pioneers incubated basic concepts and some techniques of what would become known as "valuing diversity" or "managing diversity." In the late 1980s, a sense of crisis, urgency, and purpose for the policies was provided by the Hudson Institute's *Workforce 2000* report, which projected rapid demographic change. Backward-looking affirmative action frameworks were retooled into new policy rationales aimed at matching the workplace ethnic and gender diversity with that of rapidly changing customer bases. By 1988, Lewis Griggs and Lennie Copeland's articles and "Valuing Diversity" training videos popularized a combined humanistic and business agenda. Three years later, former Harvard professor R. Roosevelt Thomas, Jr., commanded more professional attention with a 1990 *Harvard Business Review* article scripting a more purely business-oriented scenario for managing diversity. Both manifestos preached that workforce diversity was good for business.[15]

Conventions, workshops, newsletters, and journals arose as forums to debate approaches, refine techniques, and establish networks. Like other social movements, the growing diversity management movement branched out into various schools and leaders, with attendant tensions and rivalries. Movement leaders became concerned with diversity management's public image. Rumors of confrontational diversity training blow-ups began to circulate among professionals and the public. The policy movement's identity remained blurred: diversity management became caught up in the rising controversy over affirmative action. The drive nonetheless continued for professional recognition and acceptance of diversity policies as a business necessity, not just "social work."

The more ambitious, change-oriented diversity management systems incorporated a powerful ideology premised on three key concepts: proportional representation, cultural relativism, and identity politics. The presumptions that American society was deeply racist and sexist and that only ethnic and gender proportionalism was proof of such barriers' eradication were core ideas drawn from both the civil rights movement and affirmative action regulation. So was the doctrine of cultural relativism, which held that so-called universalistic standards, such as grades and test scores, were biased, "Eurocentric" measures that favored white males. The doctrine of so-called identity politics presumed that individual thought reflected or represented that of the groups in which each person is embedded. (An African American board director thus "represents" the interests and feelings of African American owners or customers; an Asian American manager will be more in tune with Asian American customers and employees; a woman reporter will be more sensitive and have greater insight with regard to women's concerns; and so on.) But diversity management also incorporated the trappings of organizational change theory, especially the need for strong CEO "change agents" and human potential "sensitivity" techniques (the "workshop," talk therapy, and the need for "inner work" on personal transformation).

Divisions and Frictions Within the Diversity Machine

Diversity management branched into two major approaches. Cross-cultural trainers tended to emphasize teaching managers basic cultural anthropology to understand and motivate minority and immigrant workers better; they did not necessarily promote broader organizational change. (Three such cross-cultural educators are profiled in this book: Lillian Roybal Rose, Sondra Thiederman, and Tom Kochman.) The more ambitious change masters prescribed not only training but extensive organizational changes, such as manager mentoring of minority and female subordinates, the formation of minority and female support associations, and accountability, or firmly tying managers' rewards and bonuses to their record of retaining and promoting women and minorities. Aside from competing for clients, however, this fault line was relatively minor.

The schism that has made it difficult for diversity consultants to manage their own differences has been the running battle between the moralists, who mirror the emotional civil rights heart of the movement, and the pragmatists, its cooler social engineers, who are the machine's business-oriented head.

Continuing homage to the civil rights tradition tends to give diversity management the mantle of a self-righteous, religious crusade, no matter how hard its key architects tried to stress the secular, business, and demographic rationales. Civil rights moralists are largely current and former affirmative action officers who view diversity efforts as an extension of affirmative action's mission of overcoming race and sex discrimination. They pepper their presentations with "do-the-right-thing" and "walking-the-talk" cadences and slogans of the civil rights movement and bristle at criticisms of affirmative action.

On the other hand, image-conscious pragmatists, such as R. Roosevelt Thomas, Jr., try to distance diversity management programs from civil rights moralism by portraying managing diversity as independent of affirmative action's legal mandates. Thomas has defined "managing diversity" as a strictly business necessity, with corporate culture change required by a wider and deeper range of cultural pluralism in employee and customer bases. The pragmatists wish to mute political rhetoric and widen the scope of diversity to other social differences based on age and generational cleavages, work-family tensions, and sexual orientation. Expanding the definition of diversity is not only a subtle means of distancing diversity policies from affirmative action's race and gender focus but an effort to escape increasingly public battles over affirmative action. The moralists sense this and resent it.

The clash between civil rights moralism and business-demography pragmatism has flared in books and articles as well as in keynote and panel presentations. Tensions sometimes crackle during question-and-answer periods. Conference participants are especially candid in formal and informal discussion groups. In these settings, conventioneers raise impolitic issues, argue, and talk freely about problems in specific organizations. In actual practice, however, many consultants mix civil rights rhetoric with business-based arguments. Nevertheless, the overall trend of diversity management has been away from moralism and toward strictly business arguments. As diversity evangelist-businessman Lewis Griggs told a workshop at the First Annual National Diversity Conference, "Stress dollars and demographics."

External challenges pose even greater obstacles to success. Diversity management programs gained initial popularity and optimistic momentum just as a host of societal headwinds began to build: the deep recession; continued downsizing and restructuring; competing management trends; continuing confusion of increasingly disreputable affirmative action policies with diversity management; and major political and intellectual reversals embodied in a rising white male rebellion, the success and controversy surrounding Richard Herrnstein and Charles Murray's *The Bell Curve,* and the 1994 elections. (Variations of this same cycle have occurred within organizations that implemented diversity programs.) The 1992 Los Angeles riots and the 1995 O. J. Simpson verdict and public response were major embarrassments to those trying to promote ethnic engineering.

Inside the Diversity Machine

I became aware of the initial stirrings of the diversity machine during prior research on the intended and unintended consequences of affirmative action programs. In 1989, as I completed *Invisible Victims: White Males and the Crisis of Affirmative Action,* I noted a sharp shift in affirmative action rhetoric. Affirmative action policy had quietly undergone a major transformation from equality of opportunity for individuals to proportional representation for women and minorities. As a consequence, the phrase "equality of opportunity" had all but disappeared. A new slogan, befitting equality of results, was replacing it: "access, equity, diversity." Measures of ethnic and gender diversity, in the form of organizational goals and timetables, were no longer merely a benchmark for assessing progress toward the goal of equal opportunity. Diversity was being hailed as an end in itself. Ethnic and gender diversity was morally good. It qualitatively changed and enriched an institution.

When I decided to continue studying the apparent transition from affirmative action to diversity, I found that the task was not difficult. Within the university world in which I worked, job advertisements extolling multicultural environments and cultural diversity multiplied rapidly. As never before, jobs and scholarships were blatantly set aside for minorities or women in the form of "targets of diversity" positions or "equity scholarships." Yet these brash preferences masked a certain desperation and sense of foreboding that the end might be near. Affirmative action advocates assumed that eight years of Ronald Reagan's presidency had paved the way for George Bush or the Supreme Court to ring down the final curtain on affirmative action. And yet it didn't happen. (Several Supreme Court decisions in the late 1980s did indeed shift the burden of proof in affirmative action cases from defendant to the plaintiff, in part by limiting the use of employment statistics, but some of these restrictive decisions were reversed in the 1991 Civil Rights Act, which, to the surprise of both Democrats and Republicans, President Bush signed.)

When presidential candidate Bill Clinton began to use phrases such as "a cabinet that looks like America" and "workplace fairness," I recognized—and was inside of—the new policy vehicle that was the source of these phrases. I had begun to interview independent and corporate diversity experts after even a conservative policy advocate, Clint Bolick, praised diversity training in his 1989 book, *Opportunities 2000.* In the spring of 1991, I attended a trio of conferences: UCLA's HR2000 Conference, Strategies for Managing the Multicultural Workforce; the first California Community Colleges Faculty/Staff Diversity Conference in San Diego; and in May, I attended the First Annual National Diversity Conference in San Francisco.

At these 1991 conferences, I sensed a powerful urgency and euphoria about the coming demographic transformation of California and, eventually, the rest of the nation. Indeed, I was very aware of being one of the few white males at these occasions and became increasingly leery of reaction to spreading publicity about my book on affirmative action's effects on white males and society. Instead, I was greeted not only as a rare white male specimen but as a valuable resource. The emerging top problem in the diversity industry was "white male backlash," which puzzled most politically correct consultants. By 1993, I had moved from being a more passive observer to a participant panelist on "white male blues." As I attended more conferences and read the growing popular and professional literature, I realized I had climbed aboard a policy bandwagon poised to transform the culture and structure of the American workplace. Or would it?

Basic Questions of the Study

The same basic dilemma that intrigued me about the nature of affirmative action programs drew me into researching the emerging diversity machine.

There is no question that racial and sexual discrimination persist in American society, in overt and more subtle, institutional forms. The major policy questions, often not openly debated, revolve around the following issues: What do we do about discrimination, within the law, without bashing white males and Western values, and *without making matters worse?*

Diversity management proponents have promised not only a more equitable society but a more harmonious one as well. But have these policies, in fact, delivered their intended results: increased productivity, creativity, and intercultural harmony? If so, will these policies become institutionalized as standard business and personnel practice? Will diversity management become a standard, or even required, part of management curriculum? To what extent will diversity programs be used as mere cosmetics or defenses for past or future discrimination complaints? To what extent have diversity policies mellowed from their early radical phase? Or is diversity management still a trojan horse to perpetuate affirmative action's underpinning ideology of ethnic-gender preferences and cultural relativism?

Just as important, what may be the unintended consequences of the proliferation of diversity management theory and practice? Will the policies spread with little criticism or public outcry—as affirmative action did? Or might conflict and resistance be brewing? Indeed, might diversity management's "celebration of differences" generate far more problems than they purportedly solve? Will these programs encourage a retribalization of American society?

The diversity machine is not a monolith. The amazing range of programs and participating personalities has not been fully explored. Nor has anyone explored the continuing dialectic of change between diversity management and American society. Neither is the same as it was in the late 1980s.

Popular business books on the topic have tended to be consultant testimonials and "how-to-do-it" cookbooks. Newspaper reports have tended to be descriptive and somewhat positive, accepting at face value the validity of diversity rationales and demographic predictions. Three articles in major opinion journals—and sections of one book—were far less positive. Heather MacDonald's 1993 *New Republic* cover story, "The Diversity Industry," tended to portray the movement as more monolithic and well-paid than it is.[16] Andrew Ferguson's jolly romp through a National Institute for Multiculturalism conference isolated the key elements of what he dubbed "diversity dogma" in the closed system of business jargon, left-wing politics, and the techniques of the human potential movement.[17] But Ferguson laughed so hard at some conference follies that he slighted the more seductive policy appeals of demographic change and possible government mandates to convince employers to mold their workforces to mirror their customer bases.

In *The Dictatorship of Virtue,* Richard Bernstein did note the demographic appeal (and its flaws), and he described two diversity workshops in his study of multiculturalism's slide into radical *derapage*.[18] The *New York Times* reporter observed with appropriate alarm that the "demagogues of diversity" had penetrated elite cultural institutions and also some businesses. Yet Bernstein focused primarily on cultural matters, especially curricular battles at educational institutions. He did not sufficiently credit the pragmatic appeal of diversity management for ambitious CEOs seeking to master global capitalism, racial polarization, burgeoning immigrant workforces, as well as the uses of diversity training in deflecting or warding off discrimination lawsuits. Bernstein also discounted diversity management's role in legitimizing and reinforcing affirmative action, corporate and government elites' original solution to the racial turmoil of the 1960s. (Indeed, the liberal Bernstein stated that he and "other reasonable people are willing to accept a degree of favoritism to black people and others who have been kept out in the past").[19]

Ruth Shalit's October 2, 1995, *New Republic* exploration of diversity management at the *Washington Post* raised interesting questions, but they were drowned out by shrill denunciations by the *Post*'s executives and the newspaper's liberal allies. (I will revisit Shalit's article and the response to it in the conclusion of the book.)

The Diversity Machine follows the path of diversity management from its enthusiastic beginnings to the current period of sober reassessment and renewed resolve. Throughout the book, I take readers inside a policy movement that both changed and has been changed by American economics and politics.

Chapter 1 provides a brief overview of the historical roots and policy predecessors of modern diversity management, as well as the efforts of "diversity pioneers" in the 1970s and 1980s. Chapter 2 outlines in detail two of the first major diversity blueprints: the "Valuing Diversity" article-and-videotape prescriptions produced by the team of Lennie Copeland and Lewis Griggs and the seminal definitional statements on "managing diversity" by academic consultant R. Roosevelt Thomas, Jr. Chapters 3, 4, and 5 show how such theories and practices of diversity management were debated, refined, and—increasingly—defended at workshops, conventions, and forums on both the national level and in southern California. These chapters are something of a "live tour" of the developing diversity machine. The primary focus is on the evolution of themes and moods at the First, Second, and Third National Annual Diversity Conferences with comparative glances at two other national conferences, each with different missions and audiences. These data are augmented with dozens of independent formal and informal interviews as well as observations and data gathered at regional workshops and panels (largely in Los Angeles, once hailed in the slogan, "The Future Is Now in L.A.!").

Chapter 6 has a triple focus. First is the diversity machine's somewhat belated union with two major business-sponsored professional associations: the Conference Board and the Society for Human Resource Management. (The latter, in addition to launching other diversity initiatives, has agreed to partner with Lewis Griggs's faltering National Annual Diversity Conference.) Second is the confirmation of many convention and workshop themes in survey data on the extensiveness, depth, and effectiveness of diversity initiatives. Third is a look at new reformulations of diversity theory by Lewis Griggs and R. Roosevelt Thomas, Jr., still two of the reigning leaders in the diversity machine.

Chapters 7 through 9 examine the implementation of different diversity management strategies in three organizational case studies. Chapter 7 chronicles primarily defensive diversity training in the L.A. Sheriff's Department. Chapter 8 looks at the ambitious diversity dreams formulated for the California Community Colleges system, dashed during the state's long budget nightmares of the early to mid-1990s. And Chapter 9 deals with one of the nation's most ambitious and expensive multicultural makeover attempts at the University of Michigan. (Though these are nominally public sector organizations, the findings in these studies closely mirror those on diversity initiatives in the private sector. When it comes to diversity transformations and other management trends, a workplace is a workplace is a workplace.) An overall assessment and forecast for diversity management is offered in Chapter 10.

The field that has become known as diversity management is beset with terminology differences. Griggs popularized his version of "valuing diversity" policies, while Roosevelt Thomas subsequently defined "managing diversity" somewhat differently. Throughout this book, I shall refer to the various "valuing diversity" or "managing diversity" policies by the more generic term of "diversity management" or, more broadly, "workforce diversity programs." (In actual practice, many of these programs were stalled at the level of one-day "diversity training" workshops.)

The dominant critical focus of the book is on the more ambitious aims of the change masters, who usually urged a full plate of diversity strategies on clients: initial cultural surveys or "audits," awareness or sensitivity training, minority and female support groups, mentoring programs, and rewarding managers for their records of hiring, retaining, and promoting women and minorities. The profiles of consultants Sondra Thiederman, Tom Kochman, and Lillian Roybal Rose are designed to help readers sample cross-cultural diversity training goals and styles.

Diversity Management: Useful, Less Useful, and Dangerous

The Diversity Machine is based on more than five years of field research, passive and active participation in workshops, panel discussions, and conventions, and more than a hundred interviews and reinterviews with consultants, personnel experts, and rank-and-file employees. (See the Methodological Appendix.)

Objective analysis of diversity management theory and practice is admittedly difficult. I found a mixture of valuable, silly, and dangerous diversity theories and techniques during my investigation of the diversity machine. Neutral, cross-cultural training oriented toward understanding an increasingly diverse mix of customers or employees is likely a sound and sensible practice; indeed, it seems unreasonable not to have such training for corporations or public agencies servicing New York, Los Angeles, or other urban centers with increasingly large immigrant populations. And it seems to me that the best diversity frameworks move beyond affirmative action's preoccupation with race and gender. Human behavior is structured by a variety of factors, such as: socioeconomic class, education, religion, regional influence, family background, personality styles.

On the other hand, I remain suspicious of massive efforts to transform "white male cultures" of organizations in order to "break glass ceilings" and do away with "institutional racism and sexism." The latter may (or may not) exist in varying degrees in organizations; but the modern workplace represents a convergence of economic, technological, political, and sociological forces that empower or ensnare individuals in complex ways. Indeed, white males in middle management have been the primary casualties of the downsizing campaigns of the 1990s—carried out by other white males.

In addition to mixing useful and dubious management and educational tools, the diversity machine indiscriminately blends social science and ideology, serious substance with silly platitudes. Often it is easy to tell the difference; sometimes it is not. Therein lies one of many dangers.

The Diversity Machine and Political Correctness

The greatest danger posed to American society by the diversity machine is its underlying ideology of ethnic-gender proportionalism, cultural relativism, and identity politics. Social classifications and policies tend to mold social reality. Affirmative action and some forms of diversity management strongly stimulate ethnic and gender group consciousness, even among white males. There is no way of predicting how such inherently irrational, sociological forces will develop.

In spite of repeated calls to move "beyond race and gender," diversity consultants slide back all too frequently into the dogma of ethnic-gender determinism, more popularly termed and enacted as "identity politics." Despite repeated caveats from more thoughtful diversity practitioners, many diversity management policies encourage the concept that an individual's thought and style can be deduced from his or her ethnic or gender identity. Indeed, this is the basis of ethnic-gender proportionalism and the call for workforces that "mirror" customer bases. Throughout much diversity rhetoric and literature it is assumed, for example, that a Hispanic manager may more effectively manage Hispanic subordinates because he comes from the same cultural background and "thinks Hispanic." (Internal group diversity is ignored. The "Hispanic" manager could be a fourth-generation Mexican-American with an Anglo mother and a Stanford M.B.A.; subordinates might be first-generation Guatemalans with a sixth-grade education.)

Sociological literature does demonstrate that individual self-concept and thought are structured to some degree by membership in a multiplicity of groups. Valid, though limited and qualified, empirical generalizations may sometimes be made about immigrant, ethnic, or gender cultures. But the race and gender determinism of identity politics ignores all group memberships save two: race and gender. Empirical generalizations about culture slide quickly into stereotypes. The contradiction between the consultant mantra to "discuss cultural differences" and the fervent desire to avoid negative group stereotypes I shall term the "diversity paradox."

Throughout my research, I was not very surprised to discover that consultant and CEO converts scorned or evaded nondiscrimination and due process constraints; what did shock me was that legal issues often weren't considered at all. So imperative was the cause of workforce diversity that the law appeared only as an afterthought. Perhaps as a consequence, there is an enormous amount of fear, silence, and intimidation surrounding these policies; since laws may be twisted and warped to implement these programs, critics know they'll have little protection.

With its outbursts of moral certitude and righteousness, with its quest for top-down policy implementation and contempt for dissent and constitutional law, with its emphasis on cultural relativism, egalitarian proportionalism, and identity politics, the diversity machine demonstrates its links not only to affirmative action but to the kindred censorship of political correctness.

I shall define and use the term "political correctness" throughout this book to refer to a radically egalitarian, intolerant ideology emphasizing race and gender determinism. At the heart of PC is not only mere censorship but, worse, the mobilization of social pressure to make individuals publicly praise and acknowledge falsehoods that privately they know not to be true. Economist Timur Kuran has aptly described this process as "preference falsification."[20] (Indeed, the term PC was originally coined during attempts to force adherence to 1930s Stalinist orthodoxy, in spite of massive contradictions and inconvenient facts, such as Stalin's prewar nonaggression pact with Adolf Hitler.)

Though sometimes dismissed or lampooned as a silly and purely academic movement to reform language, PC has been anything but funny. This race and gender radicalism has had profound consequences throughout American life. Like its 1930s namesake, PC confuses "ought" with "is," sometimes out of discretion or fear. Indeed, PC has become so pervasive among CEOs that even top diversity consultants cannot distinguish truth from PC. Author-consultant David Jamieson remarked to me in 1992 that "CEOs have learned to speak PC so well we can't tell if they're genuinely interested in diversity or not."

The impact of PC has been especially severe in the social sciences and mass media where investigation and study of major policies were long suppressed, including critical analyses of affirmative action and diversity management.

Chapter 1

From "American Dilemma" to
Affirmative Action and the Diversity Pioneers

The diversity machine is the latest in a series of social movements designed to transform American ethnic relations. As is the case today, prior efforts have always coupled moral suasion with more practical arguments and strategies—for example, business and store boycotts, political lobbying, bloc voting, civil disobedience, and carefully chosen court contests. Moral and practical impulses to change the nation's race relations have deep historical roots.

The moral tension underlying American race relations was bluntly identified by Swedish sociologist Gunnar Myrdal in his 1944 classic, *An American Dilemma:* the gap between egalitarian ideals versus blatantly unequal treatment of African Americans. Myrdal declared that black-white relations constituted the central moral dilemma in the United States:

> The American Negro problem is a problem in the heart of the American. . . . The "American Dilemma," referred to in the title of this book, is the ever-ranging conflict between, on the one hand, the valuations preserved on the general plane which we shall call the "American Creed," where the American thinks, talks, and acts under the influence of high national and Christian precepts, and, on the other hand, the valuations on specific planes of individual and group living, where personal and local interests; economic, social and sexual jealousies; considerations of community prestige and conformity; group prejudice against particular persons or types of people; and all sorts of miscellaneous wants, impulses, and habits dominate his outlook.[1]

The purely sociological urgency of managing U.S. ethnic relations was noted by Alexis de Tocqueville a century earlier in *Democracy in America.*

21

The French observer warned that conflict among the "three races" in the United States (blacks, whites, and Native Americans) might be the young nation's ultimate undoing. His grim managerial prophecy was that blacks would have to be kept rigidly subordinated or be made entirely equal to whites. As for the Indians, he wrote, "I believe that the Indian nations of North America are doomed to perish. . . . The Indians have only the alternative of war or civilization. They must either destroy the Europeans or become their equals."[2]

Tocqueville did not foresee another factor that would complicate American ethnic relations: the subsequent arrival of large numbers of immigrants who were ethnically or religiously different from the dominant Protestant, Western Europeans. The arrival of large numbers of Irish on the East Coast and Chinese and Japanese on the West Coast generated massive popular hostility. By the turn of the century, third wave of immigration was at high tide, with an annual peak of more than one and a quarter million persons in 1907. This time, a majority of the newcomers were from Eastern and Southern Europe and Russia, and their arrival was complicated by massive economic, demographic, and sociological changes accompanying the emergence of the United States as an industrial world superpower.

Then, as today, a new policy movement arose to tame America's changing ethnic landscape. Before dealing with the more obvious precursors of workforce diversity—civil rights regulations and affirmative action—it is worth noting how today's diversity machine resembles another movement of educated, moralistic, middle-class reformers: the early twentieth-century Progressives.

Progressivism: The First Drive to Manage Immigration and Social Change

Modern diversity management's uneasy mixture of social science, social engineering, and moralism first came together in turn-of-the-century progressivism. The largely urban, middle-class reformers were the first to promote rational management of problems wrought by immigration and economic polarization, primary goals in today's diversity industry. Admittedly progressivism was much more broadly conceived and did not focus on black-white relations, and early-twentieth-century reformers emphasized assimilation rather than modern diversity's militant pluralism. But both the Progressives and contemporary diversity consultants have been vigorous believers in government regulation of workplace practices, and leaders of both movements had faith that training, education, and manipulation of organizational environments could produce major attitudinal and behavioral changes.

Although most Progressives were white, they otherwise resembled diversity consultants in being middle class and well educated; many were women. Social activists and professional groups were actively involved in progressivism and the modern diversity machine. In *The Search for Order,* historian Robert Wiebe noted that the Progressives' ambition was to fashion a new social order and stability for an industrializing, dynamic, changing America. The impulse toward managerialism, futurism, social engineering, and social control was strong.[3] So it is today in diversity management.

Many diversity experts also warn of instability inherent in an emerging two-tiered class structure and polarized ethnic relations. Progressives too were alarmed by growing concentrations of great wealth and immigration-generated poverty. As Richard Hofstadter observed in *The Age of Reform,* "On one side, they feared the power of the plutocracy, on the other the poverty and restlessness of the masses."[4] Progressive reformers lobbied strongly for expanded and improved public services, especially in education, criminal justice, and workplace safety regulation. In attempts to forestall open class warfare, President Theodore Roosevelt (later the presidential candidate of the Progressive party) moved to institutionalize union-management bargaining.

Maintaining social control and societal stability have been underlying themes of both progressivism and the diversity machine, though through sharply differing approaches. The Progressives were adamant that immigrants assimilate and learn American culture. Progressives like Jane Addams founded settlement houses and other private charities to teach the new arrivals the American way of life. There was a nativist streak in some forms of progressivism, and nearly all the reformers loathed the corrupt, urban-ethnic political machines. (The establishment of the city manager form of government was an attempt to circumvent and rein in the machines. And as Anthony Platt observed in *The Child Savers,* control over unruly immigrant children was a primary source of Progressives' interest in establishing a juvenile justice system.)[5]

Contemporary diversity proponents, on the other hand, have stood assimilation on its head. Employers are admonished to adjust to immigrant and minority cultures, "celebrate differences," and permit women and minorities to "be themselves." Diversity change masters scorn calls for assimilation as a ruse for white male dominance. Massive immigration has become the engine for transforming Eurocentrism and generating a multicultural "beautiful mosaic."

The most intriguing parallel between progressivism and today's diversity machine is that both movements were propelled by a volatile mixture of righteous moralism and pragmatic social engineering. Progressivism was laced with militant Protestant moralism that eventually subverted the entire movement. Hofstadter argued that Progressives attempted to impose small-town, middle-class, Protestant values of individual responsibility, self-restraint, and civic duty on a new social order centered on large organizations and the impersonality of big city life. For example, the Progressive party's standard bearer, Theodore Roosevelt, waxed morally righteous on many issues, especially when railing against the evils of the corporate trusts as the "malefactors of great wealth." He concluded his fiery presidential nomination speech at the Progressive party convention with a memorable evangelical flourish: "We stand at Armageddon and we battle for the Lord!"

Progressivism's strident moralism eventually consumed more rational efforts for more limited, secular engineering. The movement's energies veered into grandiose, ill-fated moral reforms such as establishing the ill-fated prohibition and into pompous plans to establish world peace after World War I.

Whether business-savvy architects of today's diversity machine will be more successful in reining in shrill civil rights moralists will be tested during the coming months and years as legislative battles to repeal ethnic and gender preferences reach a climax. There is also the deeper question—and far greater doubt—as to whether the diversity machine can break free of collectivist ideological roots in race and gender identity politics and the "justice" of proportional representation.

World War II and the 1964 Civil Rights Act

World War I may have extinguished the Progressive impulse for rational management of change, but World War II rekindled the flame of racial, ethnic, and gender reform. The war's patriotic rhetoric highlighted the gap between attitudes and treatment of African Americans as noted in Myrdal's postwar *American Dilemma*. Meanwhile, domestic sociological changes unleashed by the war opened up new occupational vistas for blacks and women.

During World War II Franklin Delano Roosevelt issued executive order 8802, directing the federal government and defense contractors to be nondiscriminatory employers. Harry Truman desegregated the armed forces. Returning black veterans were less content to endure southern segregation, as were black civilians who experienced wartime employment in the industrial North. The war effort also moved thousands of women from home life into high-wage factory jobs. Although most returned to domesticity, the imagery of Rosie the Riveter would forever shatter the stereotype that women were unsuited for "masculine" blue-collar jobs. Indeed, in the 1960s, Rosie the Riveter's daughters surged into expanded higher education systems and then into the labor force, pursuing career objectives similar to those of men.[6]

But it was the gathering civil rights movement, the 1964 Civil Rights Act, and transformation of affirmative action theory and practice that paved the way for today's diversity machine. The dramatic, televised confrontations between nonviolent black demonstrators and southern officials enforcing segregation statutes have been etched into America's collective consciousness. "We shall overcome" dominated the nation's moral life well into the 1990s.

The civil rights movement culminated in the 1964 Civil Rights Act and the 1965 Voting Rights Act. Title VII of the 1964 Civil Rights Act prohibited employment discrimination on the basis of race, sex, national origin, or religion. The Equal Employment Opportunity Commission (EEOC) was established to investigate charges of such discrimination and solve such disputes through administrative action or through filing charges in federal court. In 1970, the agency won a $50 million consent decree against giant American Telephone and Telegraph for alleged gender and racial discrimination and imposed a strict court-imposed system of hiring and promotion quotas on the company. The lesson was not lost on other private and public employers.

The Transformation of Affirmative Action

By the late 1960s, the U.S. Labor Department's Office of Federal Contract Compliance (OFCCP) began to elaborate enforcement rules for Title VII and President Johnson's 1965 executive order 11246, which directed federal contractors to undertake "affirmative action" to overcome the effects of past discrimination.[7] The question for OFCCP officials was how to prove that employers were engaging in nondiscriminatory hiring and the vaguely defined affirmative action. The solution was the requirement that recipients of federal contracts establish affirmative action plans demonstrating that they were taking steps to remedy proportional imbalances between the composition of their workforce versus that of labor pools (or sometimes general population data was used). This resulted in goals-and-timetables formulas (sometimes criticized as quotas) to ensure that an increasing number of groups were not "underutilized": blacks, women, Native Americans, Hispanics, and Asian–Pacific Islanders.

The possibility of warding off negative regulatory or court judgments with affirmative action plans encouraged other employers to begin adopting pre-emptive voluntary affirmative action to achieve more proportional ethnic and gender workforce balances. The programs were understood by government agencies not to constitute admission of previous discrimination. Voluntary affirmative action programs that excluded white males were upheld by the Supreme Court in the case of *Weber v. Kaiser Aluminum and Chemical Corporation and United Steelworkers of America* (1979). Also by the late 1970s, the EEOC shielded employers taking voluntary affirmative action measures from reverse discrimination complaints.

In 1972, the Supreme Court ruled in *Griggs v. Duke Power* that general employment aptitude tests yielding racially disproportionate results are discriminatory unless such tests are directly related to job performance. This decision led many companies to abandon testing temporarily or adapt the secret practice of ensuring ethnically proportionate test results using a statistical format termed race norming. More technically termed "within-group scoring," race norming is a process whereby individual test scores are compared only with others of the same ethnicity: Hispanics with Hispanics, blacks with blacks, and so forth. Each individual score is compared to the appropriate ethnic group mean and then officially reported to employers as a percentile score based on that comparison. Thus, a Hispanic and an Asian with identical numerical employment test scores, say 300, would be reported with very different percentile scores if the Asian group mean were 275 and the Hispanic group mean were 175. The Hispanic individual would be reported as scoring significantly higher in percentile terms. But many employers and nearly all test applicants were never told about such statistical manipulations; the percentile scores were presented as if they were based on all of those taking the test.

For more than a decade, the federal government administered race-normed civil service exams, as did many state and private testing services, adversely affecting up to 12 million people. Following exposure in the press, the practice was outlawed in the 1991 Civil Rights Act. (Banding of test results—whereby individuals are grouped within broad test score ranges and then chosen by ethnic and gender criteria—continues but is being legally challenged.)

By the end of the 1970s, affirmative action theory and practice had undergone a major transformation. Originally designed to ensure equal opportunity for individuals through expanding the diversity of applicant pools (through outreach, advertising, and reasonable reexamination of employment criteria), affirmative action became entrenched as a system of ethnic and gender proportional preferences. This top-down transformation, powered in part by the civil rights movement, was made possible by a changing intellectual climate.

Blaming the System: Institutional Racism and Sexism

The transformation of affirmative action from equality of opportunity into equality of results was accompanied by what Charles Murray first termed a shift in "elite wisdom" and what Christopher Lasch later characterized as a "revolt of the elites."[8] This shift in thinking began in the 1960s among intellectuals, then spread to key leaders in government and corporations. The change represented the triumph of a sociological worldview that emphasized the operation of social systems and structural factors rather than the actions of individuals. To some extent this was a revival of the Progressives' faith in rational reform and the power of social engineering.

Middle-class Americans continued to adhere to conventional wisdom based around middle-class values of individual responsibility, the work ethic, the necessity to mold behavior through rewards and punishments, and a social justice in terms of "a hand, not a handout." But the elite wisdom took up the view that the system is to blame for social ills such as poverty, crime, and inequality. Top-down social engineering and redistribution, it was increasingly thought, would reduce, maybe even cure, many societal ills. The title of psychologist William Ryan's influential book stated a new taboo. *Blaming the Victim* was no longer acceptable, especially if the individual victim were black or female.[9]

The 1960s witnessed a surge of interest in the field of sociology that crested in the early 1970s. Sociology's emphasis on the importance of group forces in molding human behavior reinforced the drift in 1960s social policy thinking toward two key concepts: cultural relativism and institutional racism and sexism.

Cultural relativism simply means that values, customs, and norms vary by group, time, and place. (For example, during the 1920s, consumption of alcohol was prohibited throughout the United States; today it is not. Before 1973, the age of adulthood in most of the United States was twenty-one; today it is eighteen.) Ethnocentrism is the sin of the sociologist who presumes specific cultures to be "better" or "worse," or "right" or "wrong." But such cool scientific detachment has been transmuted politically into sustained verbal and legal attacks on universalistic, impersonal, objective standards. This has been most apparent in the challenges to standardized testing—ergo, the popular diversity dictum: "Differences do not mean deficiencies." The cultures and behaviors of women and minorities may differ from those of many white males, but they are not inferior.

That the cultural preferences and behaviors of many women and minorities are nonetheless judged deficient or unqualified is held by diversity consultants and many sociologists to be the result of institutional racism and sexism, or institutional discrimination. According to the sixth edition of Richard T. Schaefer's sociology text, *Racial and Ethnic Groups,* "institutional discrimination refers to the denial of opportunities and equal rights to individuals and groups that results from the normal operation of a society." Indeed, states Schaefer, "a consensus is growing today that this institutional discrimination is more significant than that committed by prejudiced individuals."[10]

It is axiomatic in the theory of institutional racism or discrimination that American society reflects the cultural biases and interests of European white males who have long occupied the highest positions of authority. The "Eurocentrism" inherent in traditional or established customs, laws, and routine practices such as standardized IQ and aptitude tests, criteria for mortgage applications and credit risks, and educational curricula penalizes groups and individuals who do not conform or who have not been socialized into Eurocentric culture. Theory veers into ideology and actual social policy with the corollary assumption that ethnic groups and women would be proportionally distributed throughout all levels of major social institutions but for widespread institutional racism and sexism.

Indeed, it is precisely this sort of thinking that has been incorporated in enforcing diversity management's parent policy, affirmative action. Patterns and practices of selection that result in disproportionate impact ("disparate impact") on minorities and women are likely to be viewed by regulators and many judges as evidence of institutional discrimination, however unintentional (hence the rush by employers and universities to establish goals and timetables, to demonstrate good-faith efforts in expunging purported institutional racism and sexism).

Institutional racism and sexism easily slide into race and gender determinism, which produced "identity politics"—the doctrine that an individual's thought patterns can be deduced from his or her membership in ethnic or gender categories. In fact, the role of race, ethnicity, and gender in human destinies is quite complex and difficult to determine. Among the host of known and unknown variables cutting across ethnic and gender boundaries are age, educational level, occupation, family size, generational cohort, and immigration cohort. Indeed, scholars who study social mobility (usually comparing the earnings and occupational attainments of fathers and sons) find they can predict only one-third to one-half of the results; the factors behind most intergenerational movement up and down career or income ladders remain "unexplained."[11]

This new sociologically based "system-is-to-blame" viewpoint found dramatic public expression in the 1968 National Commission on Civil Disorders report on the urban disorders of the mid-1960s (the so-called Kerner Report, named after the Illinois ex-governor who was the commission chair). The commission laid the blame for black rioting at the door of institutional white racism: societal-wide, often unintentional, social practices that excluded blacks. "What white Americans have never fully understood—but what the Negro can never forget—is that white society is deeply implicated in the ghetto. White institutions created it, white institutions maintain it, and white society condones it."[12] Though initially shocking—the Johnson White House was largely silent when the report was issued—the report's "white racism" conclusion nonetheless became part of the moral shield of the civil rights movement and a rationale for the increasing sweep and aggressiveness of affirmative action.

The urban disorders of the mid-1960s and the emergence of more militant and revolutionary black protest movements, such as the Black Panthers, lent added urgency to accelerated implementation of affirmative action for a quick and peaceful inclusion of minorities into the American mainstream.

Affirmative Action's Silent Revolution

Affirmative action and workforce diversity thus became part of American life because the nation's economic and political elites actively or passively accepted such programs as a means to forestall racial conflict and polarization.[13] And as Shelby Steele observed, the civil rights movement produced thirty years of guilt and shame regarding black-white relations. Compassion and compensatory treatment for blacks were difficult to dispute publicly:

> Social policymaking over the last 30 years was made by people and institutions lacking in moral authority to make principled decisions. Policy was made *defensively* to protect institutions from shame and the threat of legal action. . . . Racial quotas came in during the Nixon administration, not because Republicans believed in them, but because they lacked the moral authority to resist them.[14]

Sheer ignorance and indifference also played a significant role in the silent expansion of affirmative action. Throughout the 1980s, aside from fleeting, popular attention to occasional court cases, most CEOs, Republicans, conservatives, and popular business writers knew little and cared less about affirmative action and the movement toward a broader, more militant multiculturalism. They had little inkling of the coming diversity crusades. Many simply did not want to know what was happening. Affirmative action was not a priority issue for Beltway Republicans.

The Reagan–Bush Years

The white-male-dominated Republican party, in control of the White House for twelve years, might have been expected to end ethnic and gender proportionalism quickly. Given the huge public opinion majorities opposed to ethnic and gender preferences, the Republicans might have even used quotas as a political hammer, and antiquota language indeed was contained in Republican platforms. Yet all but a handful of Beltway conservatives and Republicans thought affirmative action policies were a minor matter, not worthy of debate.

Constitutional scholars Herman Belz, Robert Detlefsen, and Richard Epstein have provided a legal and administrative overview of various behind-the-scenes battles over affirmative action during the Reagan years.[15] Notes Belz, "Instead of consistently opposing race-conscious affirmative action throughout the government the administration tried to limit its excesses and make it more politically and administratively palatable."[16] A split within the policymaking establishment evolved. While the Reagan (and Bush) Justice Departments opposed quotas, the Department of Labor and its Office of Federal Contract Compliance enforcement arm merely routinized them. Some reforms were accomplished by informal policy processes. The EEOC finally took an antiquota position, though midlevel bureaucrats continued encouraging corporations to race-norm employment exams.

In 1985, Attorney General Edwin Meese set in motion an attempt to rewrite executive order 11241, the source of affirmative action programs, and make goals and timetables voluntary, but Meese met strong resistance from Labor Secretary William Brock and others in the administration.[17] (The ability of Meese and his allies to overcome opposition within the administration was undercut by negative responses from the business community, where affirmative action goals and timetables had become a way of life. In considering a revision of the executive order, the Reagan administration surveyed 127 chief executives of large corporations. Ninety-five percent responded yes to the question, "Do you plan to continue to use numerical objectives to track the progress of women and minorities in your corporation, regardless of government requirements?"[18]) Supreme Court decisions upholding some forms of quotas in 1986 and 1987 ended the matter in favor of the Labor Department's position.

Assistant Attorney General for Civil Rights Bradford Reynolds, U.S. Civil Rights Commission staff head Linda Chavez, and Bush White House counsel C. Boyden Gray bitterly noted lack of support. Few high-level conservatives or Republicans cared about affirmative action. "There was a strategic decision by conservatives not to oppose quotas," said current Heritage Foundation vice-president Adam Meyerson. "We felt we just couldn't win. Swing voters in the suburbs were too sensitive to the 'racist' label." Said Kenneth Cribb, an assistant counselor under Attorney General Meese, "People didn't want to use their political capital on this." In spite of Ronald Reagan's personal opposition to quotas, his administration maintained the machinery for goals and timetables and also expanded the Small Business Administration's system of minority set-aside loans. (Some Republican minority businessmen were so dependent on the loans that they were known as "8A Republicans," so-named for the section of the Small Business Administration code through which they obtained federal funds.)[19]

George Bush triggered the first popular outburst of anger against affirmative action when he signed the 1991 Civil Rights Act in the wake of the Clarence Thomas hearings. He also refused to sign a document crafted by White House counsel Boyden Gray ending preferential treatment in the federal government. Indeed, George Bush wanted to appoint more women and minorities to his administration than had any other president. To this end, the administration ran its own highly effective computerized diversity screening system. Race and gender criteria became a "prime consideration" in determining who got jobs in the Bush administration. Said Katja Bullock, in charge of the computerized system, "Bush was just very, very concerned about it. We had statistics coming out of our ears. In the end, his numbers surpassed any other administration."[20]

Writer Michael Crichton was stupefied to find that none of the corporate executives he interviewed for his best-selling novel on sexual harassment, *Disclosure,* knew anything about modern feminism. None had heard of Catherine MacKinnon, the University of Michigan's feminist law professor, and scoffed when they discovered she was a mere academic.[21] (Yet MacKinnon's successful efforts at redefining federal sexual harassment law as behavior "creating a hostile environment" will likely cost business billions in lawsuits and settlements.)

Gray finally stumbled on what he quickly realized was the "most significant silent policy revolution in American history" when he tried to oppose a coalition of corporate and government lawyers fashioning what became the 1991 Civil Rights Act.[22] Few high-level colleagues would join him in opposing the bipartisan coalition's efforts to overturn limits on affirmative action recently imposed by the Supreme Court and further cement ethnic and gender preferences into law.

Many conservatives and Republicans now profess stunned surprise at how they could have so misread the affirmative action revolution. By 1994, the conservative Claremont Institute's director, Larry Arnn, joined Gray in admitting affirmative action's revolutionary nature. "Affirmative action blindsided us. We just didn't see it coming. It's a major social revolution."[23]

Like many other Americans, they had assumed that affirmative action programs still served the early ideals of color-blind nondiscrimination and equality of opportunity for individuals. But they found that two decades of social engineering and legal subterfuge had subverted these principles. Increasingly the goal was outright ethnic and gender proportionalism at all organizational levels to produce President Clinton's "workplace that looks like America." How did this happen? And at whose expense?

Six Factors Behind the Affirmative Action Revolution

Six interrelated factors explain affirmative action's silent revolution and the subsequent foundation for subsequent workforce diversity initiatives.[24]

First, affirmative action was a redistributionist policy implemented by white corporate and government elites against younger, working- and middle-class white males. Judges, corporate human resources officers, and government bureaucrats unilaterally formulated the policies in a behind-the-scenes fashion. As we have just seen, remarkably few Republicans or businessmen wished to dissent from a growing, quiet consensus at the top of American society to do something about urban unrest. Sociologist John Skrentny has observed that affirmative action "had to happen incrementally, unintentionally, in behind-the-scenes meetings of White House officials and meetings of administrators, and in pragmatic, nickel-and-dime court decisions. It needed special circumstances, such as the crisis perceived in the cities, a Cold War moral struggle based on a global model of human rights, and a conservative President Nixon needing to confound a liberal establishment used to having its way."[25] (In 1972, the Nixon Justice Department had forced the first quota plan aimed at solidly Democratic trade unions in Philadelphia.)

Second, affirmative action has had a fluid, informal, oral character. Specific directives to hire by ethnicity or gender have usually been issued orally behind the cover of more general and vaguely phrased equal opportunity guidelines. Harvard political scientist Harvey Mansfield aptly characterized affirmative action: "Word comes down, but does not go out."[26]

A third factor reinforced the informal, ad hoc nature of affirmative action: the legality of the many forms of affirmative action remained largely unclear. The U.S. Supreme Court was indecisive and ambivalent, intimidated by the moral force wielded by proponents of affirmative action. Court action badly lagged policy practice, and legal decisions, when they came, were often deeply divided and narrowly construed. Justice Lewis Powell's controlling opinion in the landmark 1978 case of *Alan Bakke v. Regents of the University of California* permitted the use of race as a criterion in selecting university applicants so long as there were no "hard quotas." Justice William Brennan's majority opinion in the 1979 *Weber v. Kaiser Aluminum* case opened the door to private employers' use of "voluntary" affirmative action quotas to balance workforces, though "voluntary" might be one step ahead of regulatory sanction or a consent decree. Brennan opened the door even wider in *Johnson v. Santa Clara County Transportation Agency* (1987) by permitting a public agency to grant preferential treatment to correct statistical workforce imbalances so long as there was no "unnecessary trammeling" of the rights of white males. (After *Johnson,* however, a series of reverses in 1988 and 1989 made it harder for plaintiffs in discrimination cases to use "disparate impact" statistics to prove discrimination. In the 1989 case, *Richmond v. Croson,* Justice Sandra Day O'Connor authored a majority opinion limiting the use of voluntary minority contract set-asides by state and local governments. O'Connor found that state or local governments must be guilty of intentional discrimination before implementing any preferential or set-aside procedures. More ominously for champions of affirmative action, she wrote that in the future the Court would apply the same "strict scrutiny" to laws that favored blacks over whites as it did those that favored whites over blacks. O'Connor sharply signaled her suspicion of "benign" racial classifications: "Classifications based on race carry a danger of stigmatic harm. Unless they are strictly reserved for remedial settings, they may in fact promote notions of racial inferiority and lead to a politics of racial hostility.")

The fourth factor propelling affirmative action was a peculiar, powerful spiral of silence that suppressed public discussion of affirmative action, much less any politics of racial hostility.[27] Public opinion polls had long found 75 to 80 percent of Americans opposed to ethnic or gender preferences, especially when contrasted with "merit alone."[28] Yet the poll results remained largely unknown and unarticulated as misperception, fear, and silence fed one another in an escalating spiral. Affirmative action advocates appeared to be in the majority. They were more vocal and won considerable sympathy in the major news and entertainment media, wielded the collective guilt created by the civil rights movement, and brandished the hammer of the most lethal label of the past twenty years: "racist." In turn, guilt and fear of labeling fed rising "politically correct" censorship and suppressed embarrassing questions or data concerning racial realities or racial reforms: busing, affirmative action, the rising number of single-parent families, and increasing violence by urban youth gangs. Worse, as Timur Kuran has brilliantly demonstrated in his study of "preference falsification," under affirmative action, people felt compelled to justify programs in public that they deeply doubted in private.[29]

Fifth, the spiral of silence and political correctness quashed any form of class consciousness or organized complaint by the primary victims of affirmative action: young working- and middle-class white men seeking their first jobs or promotions. The public's reluctance to discuss the issue, coupled with lack of coverage by the mass media, made reverse discrimination accounts somewhat unbelievable. In addition, affirmative action did not affect whites equally. In a classic case of pluralistic ignorance, many groups of white males were unaware of what was happening because of educational, occupational, age, and geographical barriers. White males in engineering and other fields demanding a high level of mathematical or hard-science training were relatively unscathed by affirmative action quotas because of the lack of women and minorities with credentials in those fields. They had relatively little contact with those hit hard by affirmative action: younger white males in the public sector, in service or people-oriented professions, and in "progressive," multiethnic states, such as California and New York. When the subject did arise, white males untouched by affirmative action were likely to dismiss or jeer others' reverse discrimination complaints. In part, this was due to the manly code of silence. In silent John Wayne style, white men were expected to hurdle obstacles without whining or excuses. With the partial exception of the B'nai B'rith Anti-Defamation League, most civil liberties organizations—notably the American Civil Liberties Union (ACLU)—turned a deaf ear to white males. Rarely or never did they file friend-of-the court briefs in favor of white men; many times, they filed briefs in favor of preferences. Civil rights enforcement agencies largely ignored white males' discrimination complaints. And it bears repeating that white males found little relief from the U.S. Equal Employment Opportunity Commission, which shielded employers taking voluntary affirmative action from reverse discrimination complaints.

The sixth and final factor sustaining a quiet affirmative action revolution was that the liberal news and entertainment establishments simply could not cope with the topic. Critical coverage of affirmative action was politically incorrect. Civil rights moralism ruled without question, and polling of journalists indicated much stronger support for affirmative action than in the general public.[30] Because of the policy's backstage nature and the complicity of white male victims, it was hard to track. Supreme Court cases, especially *Bakke,* occasionally produced a brief spike of media interest. Otherwise, there were few paper trails and little organized protest. Since the media authenticate and prioritize social issues, as well as validate what opinions may be expressed about them, the relative absence of major media coverage until the mid-1990s made discussion in ordinary day-to-day settings difficult. (The social sciences, especially sociology, were similarly paralyzed. Concerning one of the most massive social engineering schemes of the twentieth century, few sociologists had anything to say publicly.)[31]

Without media or social science scrutiny, affirmative action was transformed into proportional representation. By 1990, Bush White House counsel C. Boyden Gray was appalled to find that affirmative action's forced proportionalism was permeating the workplace in many hidden ways. The powerful Business Roundtable winked at manipulating employment tests through race norming. (Indeed, so quietly was race norming implemented that the Reagan-appointed chair and vice-chair of the Equal Employment Opportunity Commission first learned in the newspapers that their own agency staff were pressuring employers to use race norming.)[32] Although the 1991 Civil Rights Act reversed several Supreme Court curbs on affirmative action, Gray claims to this day that his hard-fought battles produced a bill that did not further encourage employers' use of quotas to prevent lawsuits by women and minorities. Nearly no one else agreed. Most of the public and conservative press were outraged when Bush signed what he had earlier termed a "quota bill." And smaller and midsized businesses were groaning under the costs of regulatory paperwork and lawsuits. Horror stories became increasingly common as writer James Bovard gathered a partial list of court cases filed during the 1980s and early 1990s:

- The Internal Revenue Service was sued for discrimination after it fired a black secretary who refused to answer the telephone.
- Mobil Oil Corporation was sued for racial discrimination after it fired a black employee who had misappropriated company property, violated conflict-of-interest policies, and falsified expense reports.
- Kemper Life Insurance was sued for racial discrimination after it discharged a black employee who committed expense-account fraud and missed scheduled appointments with clients.
- An ex-employee sued Buckeye Cellulose Corporation of Georgia, claiming that the company's policy of terminating employees for "absence and tardiness" was racially biased because it had a disparate impact on blacks.
- The U.S. Postal Service was sued in 1990 by a job applicant whose driver's license had been suspended four times and who claimed that the agency's policy of not hiring individuals as mail carriers whose licenses had been suspected unfairly discriminated against blacks—even though carriers must drive government vehicles to deliver the mail.[33]

By 1992, *Forbes* reporters Peter Brimelow and Leslie Spencer estimated that affirmative action quotas constituted a 4 percent tax on the national gross national product.[34] Yet their measurements could not quantify the greatest of all tolls: worker demoralization, tension, cynicism, and duplicity.

The Crisis of Affirmative Action

Although corporate chieftains and high-level Republicans paid little heed to the increasing costs and unpopularity of affirmative action, the policy's chief proponents were well aware of rumbles of revolt, especially among long-silent white male workers. The first national outburst against quotas occurred in what was otherwise a triumph for affirmative action forces with the passage of the 1991 Civil Rights Act. Opposition to affirmative action was already emerging as a potent weapon in some local political contests. Louisiana voters hungry for any sort of referendum on affirmative action gave ex-Klansman David Duke more than 40 percent of the vote in a contest for a U.S. Senate seat. Two years later, North Carolina senator Jesse Helms won reelection with a television advertisement portraying a white factory worker crumpling a rejection letter, informing him that the company to which he had applied had "had to give the job to a minority."

Talk radio, especially the success of Rush Limbaugh, proved decisive in breaking the spiral of silence on affirmative action and other politically incorrect topics. Caught by surprise, mainstream liberal news organizations reacted quickly to neutralize or scorn both talk radio and white males' complaints against affirmative action. After the 1993 movie *Falling Down* portrayed an unemployed white male lashing out at minorities, *Newsweek* countered with the cover story "White Male Paranoia," and *Business Week* shortly followed with its cover story, "White, Male, Worried."[35]

On the other hand, the mainstream media were fragmenting on the question of egalitarian censorship in the name of political correctness. The simmering topic burst on the popular scene with a remarkable December 24, 1990, *Newsweek* cover story, "Thought Police—Watch What You Say." The debate on political correctness often spilled over into arguments about multiculturalism and affirmative action. "PC" became a popular topic for scorn and derision, despite frantic attempts to quash the term altogether. Ridicule of PC was another strong signal that affirmative action would need to be reformulated for the 1990s.

Paradoxically, the opening up of discussion on affirmative action brought to the surface complaints about the policies from women and minorities. Their achievements risked being stigmatized as the public became aware of widespread statistical race norming of employment exams, as well as growing use of set-aside contracts and positions. Women and minorities tried to resist being seen as an "affirmative action hires"—that is, as unqualified or less qualified than their peers. Furthermore, whatever the gains wrought by affirmative action hiring, there was rising dissatisfaction with the lack of minority or female employee retention and promotion through glass ceilings.

Although the promise of new federal rules was welcomed, worried affirmative action proponents knew that the coercive, legally mandated nature of the policy had been a potent source of its growing unpopularity. New multicultural policies could not be government imposed; they would have to be motivated by self-interest. The new programs would adhere to affirmative action's ironclad presumption that American society's inherent racism and sexism were the primary causes of occupational and educational inequalities. But mere assertion of politically correct dogma would not be as persuasive in business circles as it had been in universities, foundations, and the Equal Employment Opportunity Commission.

Winning hearts and minds in the crusade for workplace diversity would require a less moralistic and more bottom-line rationale. Ethnic and gender diversity would have to be portrayed as demographically inevitable and therefore an asset to be valued, managed, and championed. Efforts to establish a new policy machine to supplant and supplement affirmative action were already under way.

Diversity Pioneers

Racial awareness seminars and other group dialogue devices accompanied the civil rights movement and other campaigns for ethnic and gender liberation during the 1960s.[36] The basic idea behind these forums was to open up intergroup dialogue and to exchange varying viewpoints. The mere sharing of perspectives, it was assumed, would lead to greater interracial harmony and understanding.

Serious or superficial attempts to promote interracial peace became a concern in corporate America following the urban racial disorders of the mid- and late 1960s. For example, Connecticut General Life Insurance, under the leadership of Henry Roberts, identified itself as a progressive corporation during the late 1960s with the slogan, "We do things a little differently." Roberts initiated T-groups led by social psychologist Carl Rogers during the late 1960s and then introduced the first black-white workshop in 1972, "Intergroup Cooperation and Understanding." Also driving these changes was Frederick Miller, who would later become president of Kaleel Jamieson Consulting Group, which garnered a substantial share of the diversity business during the 1990s. According to consultant-historian Clare Swanger, the black-white seminar had a profound impact on whites:

> After the sessions, the participants formed problem-solving groups to address issues, such as performance appraisals, mentoring, and recruiting policies and to plan reunions and newsletters. . . . Many other interventions revolved around urban issues. One of the consultants in this field was Robert Terry, a white man who was involved with groups responding to the Detroit riots of 1967. He worked with Doug Fitch, an African American who pushed Terry to focus on what it meant to be white. Terry recalled, "I realized that I didn't have to think about what it means to be white, which is a paradox, because once I realized this, I *could* think about it." Terry wrote the book *For Whites Only*, a pioneering examination of whites' attitudes toward racism and the privilege and power whites enjoy because they are white.[37]

American Telephone and Telegraph became the locus of ethnic and gender engineering for a host of consultants in the wake of settling its class action lawsuit in 1972. One group of associates worked under Marilyn Loden, who would become a major diversity consultant and author during the 1990s, writing *Workforce America!* in 1991 with Judith Rosener and *Implementing Diversity* in 1995.[38] Loden found that AT&T's female employees already possessed managerial skills, but their limited self-perceptions hindered their access to new opportunities for advancement:

> Initially, we looked at the impact of bringing more women managers into the executive suite and at male attitudes toward this change. We ran programs for both men and women addressing competition, collusion, and gender bias and took a deeper look at socialization. Within two or three years after the programs began, women's progress accelerated in the company. Many realized they could be more successful if they joined with other women as allies, resources, networks, and support systems. In the awareness training, we asked participants to talk about their feelings regarding men and women working together as peers. Interestingly, we found it was harder for the men, many of whom focused on their loss of influence, whereas the women focused on the upside potential.[39]

Elsie Cross, who would become one of the most highly paid diversity consultants of the 1990s, also got a piece of the action at AT&T. Cross inaugurated a workshop on men and women in the work environment at Bell Laboratories but was frustrated when Bell officials refused to go beyond individual attitude change and confront what Cross felt was systemic racism.[40]

Cross's initial encounters with the business world were not pleasant. She had earned a bachelor's degree in business from Temple University in 1951 but claimed no corporation would hire her. Her interests in diversity were stimulated when she began teaching in inner-city schools in the 1960s. In 1968, she was appointed a "change agent" in the Philadelphia school system to increase community involvement; in 1970, she attended a summer internship program at the National Training Laboratory for Applied Behavioral Science, where she learned experiential learning techniques and the impact from gaining personal insights.[41] After using these small group and organizational development techniques in the Pennsylvania State College system, Cross began a six-year "intervention" at Exxon's Linden, New Jersey, refinery with a program titled "Managing and Working in a Diverse Workplace Environment." Unlike her experience with Bell Labs, Cross was pleased when Exxon's focus moved beyond changing individual attitudes to the study and reform of routine policies, practices, and organizational structures.[42]

University of Massachusetts graduate student activist Judith Katz also believed that the system was to blame for institutional racism and sexism. She began a twenty-year mission to educate whites about their complicity in such practices in the mid-1970s when she became a human resources coordinator for fourteen predominantly white residence halls. In 1978, she authored *White Awareness: A Handbook for Anti-Racism Training* (a paperback version is still in print). By the late 1980s, Katz had joined Kaleel Jamieson Consulting Group, a major force in the 1990s diversity movement.[43]

A University of Michigan sociologist since the 1960s, Mark Chesler became interested in diversity engineering through his specialty: race relations. In the 1960s, the Ford Foundation funded a series of organizational interventions to mitigate interracial and intergenerational conflicts in eight high schools. He became convinced that mere desegregation was not enough; the entire pedagogy and system had to be changed. (Chesler eventually authored several papers on diversity and was active in campus diversity efforts at Michigan during the 1990s.)

Loden, Cross, Katz, Chesler, and Tom Kochman, Lillian Roybal Rose, and psychiatrist Price Cobbs (coauthor of *Black Rage* and active in the diversity efforts at Digital Equipment, Hughes Aircraft, and other major corporations) acquired their fashionably liberal, blame-the-system perspectives through a combination of direct or indirect experiences in higher education, race relations, and the civil rights movement. Cross, Chesler, and Los Angeles consultant-authors Anita Rowe and Lee Gardenswartz specifically gained training in secondary school efforts to mitigate racial tensions. Others, such as "Valuing Diversity" videotape producers Lennie Copeland and Lewis Griggs, as well as consultant-authors David Jamieson and Julie O'Mara (*Managing Workforce 2000*), arrived at diversity consulting through adjoining consulting interests in cross-cultural communications or organizational development.

By the 1980s, then, there was a slow and growing institutional migration of consultants carrying blame-the-system liberalism from academe and a powerful civil rights establishment into business. Several of these consultants were establishing themselves on the corporate circuit during the financially flush days of the 1980s, before the massive lean-and-mean downsizings of the early 1990s. There, these consultants linked up with change advocates within business corporations—often with "progressive" CEOs responding to racially tinged crises. Several major businesses were making affirmative action and new "valuing differences" programs part of their corporate philosophies. These organizations served as the laboratories for the thesis statements and policy machine that began to take shape in the early 1990s.

The Diversity Machine's Corporate Incubators

Xerox Corporation

According to organizational psychologist Valerie I. Sessa, the commitment of Xerox Corporation to affirmative action and managing diversity reflected in part the personal philosophy of its founder, Joseph C. Wilson.[44] He was committed to fairness, social responsibility, and, during the 1960s, affirmative action. This all-important commitment from the top remained strong into the early 1990s. (Indeed, Xerox's CEO during the late 1980s and 1990s, David Kearns, was celebrated as a "champion of diversity" in Lewis Griggs and Lennie Copeland's landmark video training series, "Valuing Diversity.")

Xerox's initial interest in affirmative action and diversity arose out of a series of crises. There were race riots in Rochester in 1964 and again in 1967. Government pressures on hiring began to build with the passage of the 1964 Civil Rights Act and the 1965 White House executive order on affirmative action. Black caucus groups formed—against resistance from the company—and a class action discrimination suit resulted in 1971. The suit was settled out of court after David Kearns revised allegedly discriminatory policy practices and promoted three blacks into managerial positions.

Following the settlement, affirmative action was deemed an official business priority, and sensitivity seminars were instituted for management. In 1973, women's issues became an affirmative action concern, and in 1974 senior management formally recognized black caucus groups. In 1975 a series of management seminars that including listening and communication skills were instituted. That same year, managers' bonuses were linked to their affirmative action records (a practice that was later abandoned). Hispanic and women's caucus groups proliferated. "In making layoffs," writes Valerie Sessa, "senior management decided to maintain the representation it had built over the past ten years and possibly risk a reverse discrimination suit."[45] This increased "feelings" among white males that they were being neglected and hurt and that women and minorities who were promoted were less qualified.

In 1984 Xerox shifted to a Balanced Workforce Plan (BWF) to achieve "equitable representation" of all employee groups at all levels in the organization. U.S. Census data and internal Xerox head counts were used to calculate goals for each job category and grade. Resistance to the plan was dealt with sternly: "Xerox senior management used an interesting approach. It did not attempt to change attitudes; it changed behavior by saying, 'You *will* have a certain number of women managers by next year.' Managers who were unable to comply were held accountable."[46]

By the 1990s, Xerox's workforce was more diverse than that of the general population, and the corporation won the Malcolm Baldrige National Quality Award in 1989. But Xerox's diversity and affirmative action manager, Theodore Payne, was growing concerned that more general workforce diversity efforts might displace affirmative action gains made by women and minorities, an argument that would prove troublesome in trying to organize a united policy movement.

XYZ Corporation

Although he disguised the name of the corporation, the account of a ten-year diversity change program by consultant-professor Clayton P. Alderfer is noteworthy in several respects.[47] First, XYZ's efforts to change race relations date from 1976—relatively early. Second, there was a top-down-driven attempt to both educate and change the ethnic and gender composition of management. Third, if Alderfer's article reflects the spirit of the programs, there was a strong political and moral tone to this fifteen-year effort. Alderfer's intergroup theoretical framework assumed that group membership structures emotions, cognitions, and behavior. At times, his interpretations veered close to more politicized identity politics: "When the project began, corporate personnel committees were overwhelmingly populated by white men. No wonder, then . . . that it was difficult to find qualified black managers."[48] Alderfer also repeatedly and openly criticized the changing political climate, especially the policies of the Reagan and Bush administrations: "Some white male middle managers in the corporation used the ideology and practices of the Reagan administration to criticize corporate policy. . . . I think it is unlikely, for example, that Edwin Meese or William Bradford Reynolds would have approved of the XYZ race relations improvement program, if they had known about it."[49] Fourth, the experience of XYZ corporation provides a preview of what would happen in other organizations and in the effort to build a diversity policy machine in the 1990s: high initial expectations were difficult to sustain as XYZ ran into downsizing, new leadership, and changes in corporate mission.

Alderfer became the fourth member of a gender-balanced consulting team in 1976 that worked with a corporate-staffed race relations advisory group. A combination of factors—similar to those arising at other organizations that would launch diversity drives—led to the change effort. First, civil rights protest and polarization came into the corporation with the formation of the Black Managers Association (without opposition from management—in contrast to the situation at Xerox). Second, a white male CEO was dedicated to establishing "progressive race relations." Third, and most important, race relations were being soured by the operation of a vigorous affirmative action program that bred resentment and dissatisfaction among both white and black employees. (As we shall see in many other organizational settings, allegedly broader diversity programs are designed to rationalize affirmative action and are often evaluated in the same head-counting formats.)

After an initial study found that race and gender heavily influenced perceptions of organizational problems, Alderfer and his associates launched a series of three-day educational race relations competence workshops in 1982 and an "upward mobility intervention" program, open to both blacks and whites.

The workshops bore results: "A significant proportion of managers who worked to improve upward mobility decisions participated in the race relations competence workshop." A major function of the workshops evidently was to justify affirmative action and squelch white males' complaints: "White men were able to acknowledge that they often found it easier to tell other white men that 'quotas' took a recommendation for promotion out of their hands than to say that they found a black person to be more qualified than a white person." And Alderfer was pleased that workshoppers discovered that "a significant proportion of the variance in any upward mobility decision is highly subjective."[50] Subsequent evaluations of the workshops were largely positive or neutral, with blacks being more enthusiastic than whites, especially white males.

The mobility interventions were designed to pierce the invisible glass ceilings of institutional racism and sexism. The percentage of black managers in middle and upper management rose from 0 percent in 1973 to 7 percent in 1986; the percentage of white women jumped from 2.2 percent to 15.2 percent. The percentage of blacks and women in lower management remained constant.

Other social forces were at work, however, and Alderfer admitted that XYZ Corporation likely eliminated the race relations task force in 1986 to reduce overall stress resulting from downsizing, corporate mission, and the changing composition of top leadership. And, not unlike many other diversity consultants, Alderfer could not resist closing his analysis with some political parting shots at the Reagan and Bush administrations: "I have noted . . . that the kinds of changes attempted and achieved at XYZ were decidedly not in accord with the Reagan administration polices and practices. . . . Serious work to effect progressive race relations is not easy. Although the current national political leadership is not as regressive as its predecessors, it is not as progressive either. Perhaps the fairest characterization is that they are less regressive."[51]

Digital Equipment Corporation

"Valuing differences" was a concept first coined by Digital's Barbara Walker, who became the first vice president for diversity in the 1980s.[52] Digital's philosophy was to cultivate and capitalize on a range of individual differences, not just race and gender. According to Walker and Vice President William Hanson:

> Digital's Valuing Differences philosophy focuses employees on their differences. Employees are encouraged to pay attention to their differences as unique individuals and as members of groups, to raise their level of comfort with differences and to capitalize on differences as a major asset to the company's productivity.
>
> The philosophy is anchored in the conviction that the broader the spectrum of differences in the workplace, the richer the synergy among the employees and the more excellent the organization's performance. It is a belief in the constructive potential of all people. It assumes that each person's differences bring unique and special gifts to the organization. . . . It goes beyond traditional protected-class issues of equal employment opportunity (EEO) and addresses issues created by all kinds of differences among people in the workplace.[53]

The valuing differences philosophy arose in the mid-1970s to counter negative perceptions of affirmative action. Specifically, the learning experience that led to valuing differences came out of Hanson's experience in managing production plants in Puerto Rico and a heavily minority-staffed plant in Springfield, Massachusetts. Previous managers had resisted affirmative action as detrimental to productivity and quality, but Hanson and others were determined to "do the right thing" on affirmative action and sought to identify obstacles that blocked senior managers from working effectively with black and Hispanic employees.

In 1977, Hanson employed consultant-psychologist Price Cobbs to conduct two-day workshops for small groups of top-level management: "These sessions became intense and deeply meaningful. . . . These dialogues helped senior managers get in touch with a fundamental obstacle to their ability to provide the necessary leadership in AA/EEO. They had regarded open and candid conversation about race and gender issues as taboo."[54] Walker and Hanson believed efforts to see one another as individuals had overlooked (and undervalued) group-based differences.

Core groups arose throughout Digital to discuss differences. The groups, which met on company time, were led by employees trained at Digital's two-day training seminar, known as the Affirmative Action University. Core groups were designed to strip away stereotypes, probe for differences in others' assumptions, build relationships, raise levels of personal empowerment, and identify and explore group differences. The publication of *Workforce 2000* shifted diversity outlooks to the future, and diversity came to represent three separate kinds of work: affirmative action, multiculturalism (usually geographically specific cultures, such as those of foreign nations), and values and empowerment work emphasizing "differences in lifestyles and learning."[55] The initial work was slow, and some managers complained that the sessions were "forced guilt trips" designed to help only women and minorities.

By 1984, valuing differences became official company policy. Walker and Hanson argued that the policies had made Digital a better place to work, empowered managers and employees, promoted innovation, and encouraged higher productivity. Digital's valuing differences themes—and some of its personnel—were featured in Lewis Griggs and Lennie Copeland's seminal "Valuing Diversity" video series, which provided one of several emerging program statements for a far more organized policy movement.

Higher Education and the Diversity Machine

A major theme of this book is that the underlying ideas for business and government diversity programs originated in the transformation of elite wisdom in university and intellectual circles, in conjunction with the growing crisis in affirmative action. However, I shall spend little time here recounting PC and multicultural battles on campuses, amply dealt with within a growing number of books and a torrent of articles analyzing the curriculum battles, free speech, affirmative action, and other aspects of ethnic and gender politics on campus.[56] Education-oriented journals and newsletters, especially the PC-titled *Chronicle of Higher Education,* report on these events frequently.

Universities and colleges moved more quickly on such issues as curricular change and in alternately fomenting and mitigating radical feminism and racial separatism. Affirmative action preferences may have been applied more swiftly and zealously in academic settings, especially in the liberal arts and schools of education.

In the actual implementation of diversity management, however—permanently changing the organization's structure and general cultural climate—it becomes difficult to separate rhetoric from reality. Like business and government, colleges and universities may be having trouble moving beyond rhetoric and proportional personnel appointments because they have encountered many of the same problems: the recession, downsizing, and demands for "quality" and "accountability." (Indeed, just as the academy's politically correct and multicultural vocabulary has penetrated business, so now does the business vocabulary of efficiency and customer service penetrate the halls of ivy.) I shall focus in detail on the evolution of diversity management in two very different academic organizations later in the book: the California Community Colleges System and the University of Michigan.

By way of instructive preview and contrast, however, one California liberal arts college moved somewhat ahead of others in launching an aggressive multicultural makeover. According to English professor Eric Newhall, a self-described "tactician for institutional change," Occidental's drive toward multiculturalism began in earnest in 1983 when Dean of Faculty Jim England packed several key selection committees in order to obtain a more diversified faculty. A forty-page document supplied four reasons for doing so: (1) minority students were isolated, (2) women and minority faculty were isolated, (3) diversity was morally and socially just, and (4) the demographics of the city, state, and nation were rapidly shifting.[57]

Occidental's president was friendly but relatively indifferent. "We had to be willing to rough up administrators," said Newhall. In 1984, the faculty overwhelmingly voted to speed recruitment of minority faculty by revising the college's equal opportunity statement to make minority status "one of various factors to be considered in determining which candidate was best qualified." Searches that did not produce an adequate number of minority candidates would be disqualified. And rank and salary were to be more flexible to compete better for minority talent.[58]

Newhall and other faculty also lobbied the college trustees in selecting a new president: African American John Slaughter, former president of the University of Maryland. Slaughter immediately declared Occidental a school dedicated to "excellence and diversity," and minority student enrollment doubled by 1995; the minority faculty percentage rose from 13 to 22 percent.

As many other organizations have discovered, changing the numbers of minorities and women does not automatically produce peaceful multiculturalism. A December 2, 1992, *Wall Street Journal* front-page story and a later 1995 documentary by Los Angeles's Public Broadcasting Service affiliate found an unsettled campus. Although some minority students and faculty thought the campus climate had improved, other minorities and whites testified to a climate of stereotypes, ethnic separatism, and censorship. In the documentary, a Chicana student who joined a sorority was called a sellout by liberal Hispanics. PC was so strong, she said, that people kept their true opinions to others like themselves—if they disclosed them at all. Members of a ten-member conservative coalition claimed that prejudice against conservatives at Occidental was very strong. A black student felt that he and other blacks were stigmatized as less-than-qualified by affirmative action. But Slaughter and others defended the college's new direction and insisted that excellence was fully compatible with "equity, justice, and fairness." Ethnic separateness, some argued, was a natural development as students from oppressed backgrounds came together in a multicultural setting.

Eric Newhall continued to claim that "a fully inclusive, democratic system can work," but it was "naive" to think that students coming from a variety of separate backgrounds would mix without tension. "No pain, no gain," he said. But in 1995 the pain became financial when Occidental ran a $3 million budget deficit. Some alumni groused that the source of the deficit in part was the large number of scholarships awarded to increase minority enrollment. Nor was the proclaimed mission of unifying "excellence and diversity" effectively demonstrated when, in 1994, Occidental fell out of the first-tier institutions to forty-first place in the widely watched annual survey of colleges by *U.S. News and World Report.*

The architects of the diversity machine were prepared for such disappointments. The linking of excellence, productivity, and diversity was so strongly etched in the policy movement's founding manifestos that evidence for the link was not yet required.

Chapter 2

The Evangelist and the Business Professor

The Early Diversity Manifestos

Wearing a tie but less often a coat, golden-haired, blue-eyed, jogger-thin Lewis Griggs has more the manner and appearance of a smooth, successful California businessman than a self-described evangelist for workforce diversity. In fact, he is both. In 1987 he and his first wife, Lennie Copeland, produced the first and best-selling videotape training series "Valuing Diversity," which combined a pragmatic market-based sales appeal with a moralistic, New Age appeal for personal transformation in the cause of diversity.

Griggs's background was a poor predictor of future diversity stardom. Minnesota born, he graduated from Amherst College, then went to work as an aide in the Nixon White House. He next obtained a Stanford M.B.A. and went into business consulting. He confesses he became a typical suburban, San Francisco yuppie complete with a Volvo, two kids, a golden retriever, Italian shoes, a gold neck chain, and a divorce from his first wife and business partner. By way of midlife passage, he acquired a second spouse/business partner, as well as a new-found spirituality; on the gold neck chain beneath his shirt there now hangs a cross. He has taken the cause of diversity to heart and is pleased to repeat that he is a "recovering racist, classist, and sexist." He urges others to "do the inner work" to undertake similar personal change through the New Age formula of talking, sharing, confessing, and bonding.

Griggs merges spirituality, self-interest, and diversity moralism with ease. He sees himself as a "conservative in support of liberal-radical systems of free enterprise and democracy." Diversity management was simply a tool to preserve the system. It's in white males' self-interest to understand cultural differences in a world of rapidly changing demographics.

A Manifesto for Valuing Diversity

In the early 1980s, Copeland and Griggs produced "Going International," a video training series designed to help multinational corporations acclimate globe-trotting employees to international differences. The series enjoyed some success and led to hardback and paperback versions of *Going International: How to Make Friends and Deal Effectively in the Global Marketplace*.[1]

When Copeland and Griggs discovered that some corporations were attempting to adapt "Going International" to deal with domestic race and gender tensions, they raised $450,000 from thirty-two major corporations and by the end of 1987 had produced the first three installments of "Valuing Diversity." *Managing Differences* aimed at showing managers how ethnic stereotypes, cultural differences, and unwritten rules inhibit the upward mobility of women and minorities. *Diversity at Work* was designed to illustrate how workers could deal with cultural differences and "succeed without sacrificing personal cultural values and how to deal with the stress of being bicultural." And *Communicating Across Cultures* illustrated twelve situations in which cultural differences could lead to misunderstanding.

Interest and sales quickened, and four more titles were produced in 1990–1991: *You Make the Difference,* dealing with the "necessity for workers to work well with people different from themselves"; *Supervising Differences,* which demonstrates strategies for coaching, team building, and motivating culturally diverse workers; *Champions of Diversity,* which profiles executives who have implemented these policies; and *Profiles in Change,* which showcases organizations that are profiting from the multicultural workplace.

Several corporate sponsors and CEO "champions of diversity" were clients of psychologist-consultant Price Cobbs, coauthor of *Black Rage*.[2] According to Lennie Copeland, he served not only as a consultant but as a mentor in producing the three videos. By the time the second set of four videos was produced, several U.S. government officers were also on the credits roster: Valerie Clement, U.S. Postal Service; Jo Cross and Patsy Ramos, Internal Revenue Service; Sylvia Stanley, National Aeronautics and Space Administration; and Lance Yokota, U.S. Forest Service. Some San Francisco–based consultants who became associated with Copeland Griggs Productions—Frances Kendall, Herbert Wong, Steve Hanamura, and Vaporeal Sanders—helped with workshops constructed around the videos and served as cochairs or coordinators of the first through fourth National Diversity Conferences.

"Valuing Diversity" came to market just a few months after *Workforce 2000*'s publication. Copeland immediately obtained professional credibility and visibility for the series by publishing three articles in personnel journals.[3] In "Ten Steps to Making the Most of Diversity," she outlined the full change range of workforce diversity strategies:

1. Recruitment: through increased college relations programs and diverse hiring from the experienced market.
2. Career development: expose women and minority employees to the same key developmental posts that have led to senior management positions.
3. Diversity training for managers.
4. Diversity training for employees.
5. Upward mobility: break the "glass ceiling" through mentoring, executive appointment.
6. Diverse input and feedback: managers and employees should both be asked for input and direction.
7. Self-help: supportive network groups for women and minorities might be formed.
8. Accountability: managers should be held responsible for the development of diverse workforces.
9. Systems accommodations: cultural differences might be respected through recognition of religious holidays.
10. Outreach: through supporting women's and minority organizations and programs.[4]

Copeland's list illustrates the breadth and complexity of diversity programs. Simple outreach programs to local high schools require little money or organizational change. Diversity training for employees or managers introduces the possibility for moderate attitudinal and organizational change, as does mentoring. More expensive surveys and other assessments of organizational norms and values open the door to more complete overhaul, as does the formation of minority support groups and accountability, the practice of rewarding managers in terms of their minority and female hiring and promotion records. (Cross-cultural consultants, such as Sondra Thiederman and Tom Kochman, tended to emphasize steps 1 through 4. More aggressive change masters, such as Roosevelt Thomas and Ann Morrison, saw steps 1 through 4 as preliminary; the core of diversity management would be steps 5 through 10. All the consultants varied as to how much civil rights moralism they injected into their work.)

Copeland's articles were straightforward, pragmatic, and business oriented. Griggs took up the earnest, New Age evangelist mantle, urging the gospel of personal transformation through diversity. The "Valuing Diversity" video series mixed both their views: humanistic, New Age moralism with market-based business arguments. The combination was timely. Copeland and Griggs had organized and animated ideas and practices that had been loosely developing in the academic-corporate-consultant realms. As "Valuing Diversity" caught on, the major media began to profile the new policies. In late 1988, the *New York Times* featured Griggs in a long article, as did *Newsweek* on May 14, 1989.

Five thousand partial or entire sets of "Valuing Diversity" were eventually purchased by a huge segment of corporate America as well as by numerous government agencies and universities. (Corporate rate prices range from $695 to $995 per tape, the entire series at $4,500; prices for nonprofit institutions are slightly lower.) Conference keynote addresses and train-the-trainer seminars (at $1,500 per person) have augmented these profits, which Lewis Griggs insisted were rather modest. "I could have made more money doing other things," he avers. Copeland was more satisfied to note in a 1993 interview that "the product has run its course—everybody has them."

"Valuing Diversity"'s special significance is that its video format gave the producers the chance to breathe multimodal life into their concepts. "Media is the most powerful agent of change," said Copeland. "We wanted to get the message out and video was the way to go." The printed page could be read and quickly forgotten. The images, facial expressions, tone of voice, and body language contained in videotaped interviews and vignettes achieve greater emotional impact and linger far longer in the mind, especially when the tapes are combined with lengthy discussion sessions led by talented trainers. By the same token, the multimodal communication in the tapes makes more salient the underlying assumptions, sentiments, ideology, and moralistic leanings of the producers and their consultants.

"Valuing Diversity" both teaches and preaches.

The Major Themes of "Valuing Diversity"

1. The Democratic Imperative Provides Diversity's "Competitive Edge"

Every videotape in the series begins with the assertion that current and predicted demographic changes mandate changes in workplace cultures. In the first and sixth videos, a fusillade of statistics reinforces this thesis: white males are already a minority in the workforce (46 percent); in the 1990s, 75 percent of those entering the workplace will be women and minorities; by 2010, whites will be only 48 percent of California's population, and in the next century, blacks, Asians, and Hispanics will outnumber whites in the Golden State. The opening narration of the fourth video tried to sustain these projections even in the face of downsizing and layoffs. The narrator still insists that there is an "oncoming scarcity of labor . . . the baby bust, too few people entering the work force to replace the aging baby boomers." In any case, downsizing necessitates increased teamwork, and "the ability to work with people of difference will become a key competence. Quite simply, organizations who manage diversity well are more productive."

2. Equal Treatment Is Unfair Treatment: Invisible Rules of White-Male Culture Must Change

African American consultant Gerry Adolph introduces a central tenet in most workforce diversity perspectives: equal treatment under values and rules made by and for white males is not truly equal. On the contrary, "the problem with maintaining a white male standard as the norm and measuring everyone against it is that you set up a sizeable portion of your workforce for failure. There's no way I will be perceived as a white male," Adolph explains.

Daisy Chin-Lor, Avon Products' director of multicultural planning and design, argues that treatment must be color and gender coded. Women and minorities must be treated differently from white males: "Equal treatment is not fair treatment. I have been rewarded for managing everybody the same, getting the same results, giving them the same performance appraisal, giving them the same kind of feedback." Chin-Lor invokes one of the most famous metaphors in managing diversity: "If I were planting a garden and I wanted to have a number of flowers, I would never think of giving every flower the same amount of sun, the same amount of water and the same soil. I'd be sure to groom and cultivate each individual breed of flower differently."

Scripted dramas illustrate culturally adjusted fair treatment and the need to renegotiate the unwritten rules of white male culture. A white female junior executive cannot negotiate—and is not taught—the taken-for-granted rules of the "white male club," and she leaves to join another corporation. A Hispanic midlevel executive makes a clumsy presentation to his colleagues because he was not provided proper insight and coaching by his superior. *(Narrator: "Was Ricardo Ortiz unprepared or was he judged differently because of his looks, manner, or accent? In fact, this presentation is almost identical to one made by a white male who did get his $12 million budget. But we sometimes let unimportant differences in style obscure the quality of content.")** Cultural in-

---

*Italicized portions indicate voice-overs.

sensitivity leads to misjudgment during a promotion interview in which a shy Asian, following Asian cultural tradition, insists on crediting his coworkers rather than himself for his accomplishments. A Native American woman is embarrassed by her supervisor's public praise; he did not understand that such behavior violates Native American norms of modesty. *(Concludes Avon's Daisy Chin-Lor: "That, to me, was clearly a fact of not being able to understand, nor having the curiosity to find out about, what makes her feel good. As a manager, our task is to motivate, and if we are arrogant enough to think that the same carrot works for everybody, our head is in the sand.")*

3. Valuing Diversity Enhances Productivity, Creativity, and Teamwork

Throughout the series, corporate CEOs, such as Xerox's David Kearns, assert that valuing diversity produces business advantages. "The company that gets out in front of managing diversity will have a competitive edge," states Kearns. "Recruiting women and minorities will bring a whole new set of ideas." Hewlett-Packard's King Ming Young explains that when management teams have similar social backgrounds, they produce a similar solution to a problem. "When you bring people with diverse kinds of perspectives into the picture, it may take longer to get a consensus, but you will have a very rich, a much more complete type of solution to the problem." John Simms, vice president at Digital, employs a sports metaphor: "Whether it's on the athletic field or in the workplace, the same rules apply: the teams that win are teams that play together, the teams that complement one another, and wherever you find a situation where people who are of a different sex, or a different color can't play together on a team, that team doesn't win." States Digital's Barbara Walker: "We will find ways in which we can become interdependent and work together more productively. We will be more synergistic, we will share power, we will be more collaborative and we will be more creative and at that point we'll make more money."

In a scripted diversity drama, a black female tries to present a new scheduling system to her white manager but fails to convince him. *(Intones the narrator: "Some managers doubt their minority employees and need to learn to trust people different from themselves. On the other hand, many employees, in their haste to do well, take on too much too fast and fail to complete all the necessary steps.")* A second vignette concerns homogeneous clustering of Hispanics and Anglos in the company cafeteria. An argument breaks out over the Hispanics' use of Spanish language. *("When people speak Spanish . . . work relationships may suffer," advises the narrator. "Those who speak only English should learn to accept other people's need to speak their own language, but it also makes sense for all employees to either use the dominant language or to let others know what is being discussed.")* A third drama finds a quiet, unassertive Asian male not participating in a brainstorming session; he participates more actively after the manager explains the taken-for-granted assumptions and unwritten expectations. *(Says King Ming Young of Hewlett-Packard: "In order to manage a diverse work team well, a supervisor has to first get to know the employees as individuals, spend some time with each individual, get some information on the person's cultural heritage.")*

The Asians-avoid-arguments theme is repeated in a new vignette in which a black supervisor scolds an Asian female worker for repeating a mistake. The Asian worker had acknowledged a prior admonition and explanation with a quiet "yes." The supervisor did not understand the multiple meaning of "yes" in Asian cultures. *(Explains Daisy Chin-Lor: "Asian cultures, to save face, will say 'yes,' and it isn't necessarily a lie as much as it is 'I will try' . . . but to say 'no' blatantly is an insult.")* There is a happy ending as the supervisor and her employee discuss this and other cultural differences over coffee.

Lack of cultural sensitivity can lead to decreased production and costly litigation. An argument over an airline reservation between an assertive and angry East Indian client and a strained but polite black ticket agent points out culturally different conventions for courtesy and assumptions about authority relations. A vignette on "phasing" illustrates how Hispanics often wish to take their time "getting to know the whole person" before discussing business matters, while Anglos tend to discuss business much more quickly and directly. A disagreement between a black and white man illustrates the more reserved, objective style of whites compared to the more emphatic, emotional styles of blacks. Another segment warns against cultural hot buttons such as ethnic jokes and phrases such as, "He throws the ball like a girl," or "Women are emotional," or "Some of my best friends are black," or "My children are acting like wild Indians."

4. *Reverse Discrimination Is a Myth: The System and Stereotypes Contribute to Minority and Female Failures*

In *You Make a Difference,* the fourth video produced in 1991, Copeland–Griggs set out to debunk rising complaints about affirmative action and reverse discrimination. In a carefully scripted scene, an older white male complains about reverse discrimination in losing a promotion to a black female; his younger colleague reminds him it was only a five-point difference on an "interview exam." An angry black male also claims discrimination on the same promotion: "Ten years I've been the wrong color. Now I'm the wrong sex." In a women's restroom, two white females discuss the same promotion, agreeing that the winner got the job because she is both black and female. All are surprised when the new supervisor turns out to be disabled as well. *(Lynn Brickhouse counsels that "you have to recognize that any promotion is controversial. . . . We can't think in terms of minority/non-minority issues. We have to think in terms of the value that people have to offer, no matter what color you are, no matter where you come from."* A discussion note in the text suggests that "feelings of injustice may be compounded when there seems to be 'evidence' of promoting a 'less qualified' candidate. Some people fail to recognize the inadequacy of test scores to precisely measure many job skills and the inherent biases of any testing procedure.")

In another vignette, a group of white-collar machine operators withholds vital information from a female Hispanic maintenance worker called in to repair a malfunctioning machine—information they offer freely to her white supervisor. The supervisor compounds this silent sabotage by telling her to "go make coffee" when she tries to explain. In another scripted minidrama, a new female Native American employee improperly operates a drill press after receiving vague operating instructions from an African American foreman. The message: Another minority has been set up to fail. *(Fred Jacoby, an administrator at Weyerhauser Inc., states: "What happens, basically, is it gives diversity a black eye because the co-workers . . . say, 'Well, here we go, diversity again, and look what happened, we basically have put an individual in there that hasn't done the job." Eastman Kodak production manager Jackie Hill states, "It's been my experience that when people fail it's because we as supervisors did not do our job.")*

The worst stereotypes were reserved for whites. In one scene, a nerdy-looking white male wanders through his office building repeatedly offending minority and female coworkers. He asks a black security guard, "Hey, my man! How about that game last night?" The reply: "Hey, my man! I went to the symphony last night!" To a Chinese woman, "Hey, Rose—so what do you think is the best Chinese restaurant in town?" He sees black men exchanging money in the men's restroom and assumes it's a drug deal; it is actually a football pool payoff. (In the fifth video, a white female tours her office, muttering to herself stereotypical criticisms about minority and female workers; all are subsequently contradicted.)

5. Corporate "Champions of Diversity" Undergo Personal Conversion

An entire video, *Champions of Diversity,* is devoted to a favorite Griggs theme: the conversion experiences of (mostly white) corporate executives. Digital vice president Bill Hanson recalls being in high school during the 1950s with Japanese students who had been in internment camps but never talked about the experience. Jack Macallister, president of U.S. West, recalls the divergent career paths of whites and blacks on his college football team. San Francisco State president Robert Corrigan was asked to start an African American program at the University of Iowa and realized he knew little about black history. He waxes happy about current efforts to incorporate San Francisco State's rich student cultural diversity into the curriculum. Larry Waller, director of pluralism at U.S. West, tells of seeing his daughters suffer oppression. Digital Equipment's valuing diversity pioneer Barbara Walker speaks rhapsodically on the "personal journey, working beyond race and gender, to sexual orientation, disability, even styles of bonding, intimacy, love, forgiveness, taking risks."

6. Leading Corporations Value Diversity

The final and longest video demonstrates "how leading organizations are valuing and managing the richness that diversity brings." Opening statements emphasize the importance of commitment from the top, the role modeling of diversity by managers. "Strength is in diversity at Security Pacific," states the bank's CEO, Bob Smith. He is shown hosting a dinner for the company's minority support groups and presents awards to those who have done the most in fostering diversity. Senior executives, Smith warns, are "going to be judged on how well they get with the program."

Kim Breese, a chief administrative officer for Dow Jones, argues that the *Wall Street Journal* benefits from having a "female view in the newsroom" in covering such issues as day care. In groups of new employees called "quads," a senior executive mentors one female, one person of color, and one white male. Breese sweeps aside any questions about costs or problems of managing diversity: "Is managing diversity going to create morale problems? Is it going to be expensive? We don't know right now. We just know that we've got to deal with these issues of diversity."

Robert Corrigan, president of San Francisco State University, had no qualms about hiring a faculty that "represents the population." In 1991, 42 percent of the new faculty were minorities and 65 percent were women—in spite of faculty resistance. Black studies professor Mary Hoover instructs sensitivity workshop participants to monitor all aspects of campus behavior: "I want you to join me in a conspiracy to change the attitudes of this whole school."

A meeting of the pluralism council at U.S. West demonstrates employee involvement. In response to U.S. West's periodic celebration of various ethnic groups, the committee responds to an anonymous note suggesting a "white males month." This hint of backlash triggers a cascade of contempt. A black man dubs the idea "extreme" and "ridiculous." A white female condescendingly remarks that "there is a lot of frustration that the white male is experiencing." Larry Waller, a white male and director of pluralism, states that the last thing they need to do is facilitate white men getting together. "We're born to power and privilege no matter how poor economically we're born." Added another black male: "As soon as some minority groups or protected groups or whatever you want to call them begin to carve out a small piece of the pie, again, the folks who have the pie don't want to give it up."

The pluralism council then turns to changing language. A black man complains that "white paper connotes good paper." Larry Waller shouts that "this is a passionate issue." CEO Jack Macallister notes that "we're ridding ourselves of the roadblocks which include bias and prejudice in the workplace that left employees with less than a fair opportunity to show their full potential."

The scene shifts to a meeting of representatives from U.S. West's employee resource groups (groups formed on the basis of ethnicity, gender, and sexual orientation). The director of public relations admits getting hate mail regarding a company magazine story on the resource groups. Craig, a gay male, laments that "many" gay and lesbian managers will not come out of the closet; Margo, a Native American, states that her people will "not be victims any longer. We must continue to introduce our cultures into the corporate culture, so that I don't have to act like a white European male to be successful in this corporation." Paul, an Asian male, whines that "we've been the silent, invisible minority." Craig speaks emotionally about his experience at a diversity workshop. During a stereotyping exercise, participants were to paste one-word reactions to wall posters containing the name of a minority group. When someone put a "sick" sticker on the gay-lesbian poster, Craig went home and "cried for two hours."

"You're never done with this work," admits Larry Waller.

"All I'll ever be is a recovering racist," sighs Darlene Siedshlaw.

The scene shifts to a pregnant woman working at home: GTE is valuing health and disability differences. At Hewlett-Packard, employees are seen gaining insights into disabilities by pretending to be disabled for a day. Corporate outreach programs are illustrated by Eastman Kodak's attempts to work with public schools to "fill the pipeline" with minority and female talent. Kodak executives act as visiting teachers in classrooms as part of Kodak's PRISM (Program to Interest Students in Science and Math) program. Allstate

Insurance employees are shown at a recruiting booth in a Chinatown festival. *(Intones the narrator, "Companies that value their diverse workforce also honor the diversity of their customers and vice versa. These companies are realizing the power of diverse advertising.")*

The public sector workforce is especially close to the public. Jim Nixon, director of affirmative action at New York City's Metropolitan Transportation Authority, observes that "being responsive is easier when you understand the customer because the customer is you. . . . You need to have a work force that's got a sufficient mix of people that someone with credibility to this [diverse] audience is there. . . . White males assume that when they say something it has credibility . . . but in some contexts, no matter what they say, how truthful, no matter how sincere, it will be suspect."

Indeed, as I later observed at diversity conventions, many minority consultants were ambivalent or suspicious toward white male Lewis Griggs. We shall see Griggs struggle with this and other problems—and reassess "Valuing Diversity"—later in the book.

Moving "Managing Diversity" Beyond Race and Gender

Though it rankles his rivals, R. Roosevelt Thomas, Jr. put workforce diversity policies on the professional map with a specific variation he termed "managing diversity." Poised, self-assured, conservatively dressed, Thomas fits the image of a consummate business-oriented pragmatist; he deliberately, and with great controversy, severed managing diversity from affirmative action by arguing it was a new set of policies that *followed* affirmative action. Managing diversity would be a long-term, management-led transformation of white male corporate culture to accommodate changing demographics and increased pluralism. His 1991 book, *Beyond Race and Gender*, emphatically established his desire to expand diversity into other dimensions of difference: age, disability, sexual orientation, and work and family issues.[5]

Thomas lent professional stature to diversity policies in part through his Harvard Business School affiliations: he obtained a doctorate there, was on the faculty for five years, and then published "From Affirmative Action to Affirming Diversity" in the flagship *Harvard Business Review* in 1990.[6] Thomas established a research- and education-oriented, nonprofit business, the American Institute for Managing Diversity, located at Atlanta's Morehouse College, where he became college secretary. The institute gathered an impressive roster of corporate clients, and in 1992 Thomas sold the consulting arm of the institute to the giant Towers Perrin group. Though Thomas would later return to consulting work, he was also delivering highly polished lectures for up to $10,000 per engagement.

In "From Affirmative Action to Affirming Diversity," Thomas decisively distanced managing diversity from affirmative action, which he termed a temporary, "artificial" recruitment tool. Demographic change would supplement and then supplant "artificial" affirmative action: "Sooner or later affirmative action will die a natural death. Its achievements have been stupendous, but if we look at the premises that underlie it, we find assumptions and priorities that look increasingly shopworn."[7] One by one, Thomas debunked the original rationales for affirmative action:

- Prejudice is not dead but it is not the problem it once was; prejudices are too deeply suppressed to interfere with recruitment.
- Demographic change is decreasing the need for legal, coercive measures to hire more minorities.
- U.S. business is no longer a solid, unchanging edifice; instead, they are scrambling to become more flexible and attract all the talent they can find in order to increase productivity and profitability.
- Women and minorities no longer need a boarding pass; they need an upgrade. The problem is not getting them in at the entry level; the problem is making better use of their potential at every level, especially in middle-management and leadership positions.
- White males no longer make up the U.S. business mainstream; half the U.S. work force now consists of minorities, immigrants and women.[8]

Adding insult to injury, Thomas scorned affirmative action's claim to furnish "role models":

> I doubt very much that individuals who reach top positions through affirmative action are effective models for younger members of their race or sex. What, after all, do they model? A black vice president who got her job through affirmative action is not necessarily a model of how to rise through the corporate meritocracy. She may be a model of how affirmative action can work for the people who find or put themselves in the right place at the right time.[9]

Nevertheless, Thomas argued that assimilation is dead and today's immigrants, women, and minorities wish to maintain their own cultural identities. This "unassimilated diversity" leads to organizational inefficiencies and conflict. Thomas offered one of his most famous metaphors: a changing mixture of fuel (people) requires the reconstruction of the engine (the organization):

> Unless we rebuild the engine, it will no longer burn the fuel we're feeding it.
> . . . Affirmative action gets blamed for failing to do things it never could do.
> Affirmative action gets the new fuel into the tank, the new people through the
> front door. Something else will have to get them into the driver's seat. That
> something else consists of enabling people, in this case minorities and
> women, to perform to their potential. *This is now what we call managing di-*
> *versity . . . to get from a heterogeneous workforce the same productivity, commit-*
> *ment, quality, and profit that we got from the old homogeneous workforce.*[10]

Without changing the organizational environment, Thomas contended, a cycle of crisis, action, realization, and disappointment sets in. Organizations recognize a problem in ethnic relations either on their own or through legal action; affirmative action is implemented, and there are great expectations. Frustration follows when minorities and women do not move up the ladder or remain with the company. Dormancy and inaction are followed by a crisis flowing from interest group and legal pressures and failure to align workforce diversity with that of emerging customer bases. The cycle begins anew.

Thomas expanded these concepts and specific policy recommendations in his landmark 1991 book, *Beyond Race and Gender.*

The Major Themes of *Beyond Race and Gender*

1. Pluralism Replaces Assimilation

Like most other diversity theories, Thomas's policies were premised on the axiom that demography is destiny. But unlike many other proponents, Thomas refused to exaggerate the projected decline of white males. He corrected the *Workforce 2000* misprint that only 15 percent of new workers in the 1990s will be white males: "In 1985 . . . white males composed 49 percent of the labor force; by 2000, they will constitute approximately 45 percent."[11] Thomas noted that the seemingly spectacular growth rate for some minorities (such as Asians) is the result of their growing from a much smaller base.

In any case, the numbers were less important than the cultural and psychological change away from assimilation to white male norms. The growing number of immigrants and minorities wish to maintain their cultural identities at home and in the workplace: "They want to be themselves."

2. Managing Diversity Empowers Everyone: Diversity Is More Than Race and Gender

Thomas responded to criticisms that "managing diversity" implies "managing minorities" by emphasizing an expanded definition of diversity: "It is not about white males managing women and minorities; it is about all managers empowering whoever is in their work force."[12] Ideally, managing diversity will create an environment in which "every single employee will do his or her best work."[13] Thomas was the first author to emphasize that managing diversity should include white males. Indeed, he cited management accounts that one of the most pressing areas of difference is age and generational: between senior- and junior-level white male managers: "They simply don't understand each other."[14]

3. Managing Diversity Is Not Affirmative Action or Valuing Differences

Thomas again turned to the difficult task of trying to prove to skeptical businessmen that managing diversity was not just "warmed-over" or "back-doored" affirmative action, while refuting denunciations by militant blacks and women that he was abandoning the moral crusades against racism and sexism. Thomas advised the latter audience that refusing to expand the concept of diversity reflects traditional, zero-sum thinking where one group gains at another's loss. Managing diversity "calls for recognizing that people are different without condemning them for those differences."[15]

Thomas unconvincingly argued that "managing diversity is congruent with true notions of color-blind and gender-blind." As for arguments that diversity agendas compromise merit, Thomas challenged the pure meritocratic notion that "cream rises to the top." Promotions, he argued, have three dimensions: task merit, cultural merit, and political merit. People who are culturally different, he claimed, may not be able to meet the second two criteria. The concept of meritocracy also ignored real-life, political "assists" and mentoring.[16] Thomas did not state whether any sort of standardized personnel tests might truly measure merit.

Thomas also tried to distance managing diversity from Copeland-Griggs's concept of valuing diversity. Thomas and his disciples at the American Institute for Managing Diversity viewed valuing diversity as concerned with deeper, more difficult changes in interpersonal attitudes. At the Second Annual Diversity Conference in 1992, Thomas suggested that a better term might be "understanding differences," a useful step toward managing diversity but one that might also be more difficult and unending. But Thomas had no time for a Lewis Griggs–style campaign for personal transformation. He wanted to get on with the job of getting managers to recognize and deal with demographic and cultural changes, regardless of whether they deeply believed in these changes.

4. Managing Diversity Involves Long-Term Cultural Change

Thomas correctly observed that campaigns for cultural diversity in American organizations have usually been the result of some sort of crisis or deliberate initiatives by CEOs, often beginning with a "vision statement." (Copeland-Griggs also vigorously emphasized the importance of CEOs as role models and champions of diversity.)

After top commitment to long-term cultural change has been established, a systematic "cultural audit" should follow. This involves interviewing or surveying employees concerning their perceptions of organizational norms, values, practices, procedures, levels of satisfaction, formal and informal feedback, and so forth. Thomas provides a sample survey form containing seventy-six items—for example:[17]

- What makes [organization name] good at what it does?
- What kinds of things have encouraged you to stay with [organization name]?
- What two or three experiences have contributed to your success?
- How many mentors or coaches have you had?
- How did these relationships come about?
- To be successful in your work, are there any *unwritten* rules that you are expected to follow?
- What are some of these unwritten rules?
- What have been the *weaknesses* of the career development attention you have received?
- What does your immediate management really pay attention to?
- What, if anything, needs to be done to help minorities to do their jobs better and advance?
- Is it acceptable for you to discuss with your supervisor issues of racism, sexism, or other biases held by other employees?
- How optimistic (positive) or pessimistic (negative) are you about progress being made at the [organization name] in providing equal opportunity for all employees?

Thomas warned that subsequent efforts to change organizational culture may challenge deeply held "root concepts" that guide an entire enterprise: for example, that the organization is a melting pot, that the "cream rises to the top," that the organization is "like a family," or that the organization is like a team. According to Thomas, all of these concepts deny the validity of individual and group cultural differences and how such differences can impede worker satisfaction, productivity, and upward mobility.

Thomas targets monocultural management styles such as the "doer"—the get-things-done manager who assumes that employees are followers and will imitate what he does. Such managers are an impediment to managing diversity. The doer tends to scorn people issues in an organization, preferring to focus on economic nuts and bolts, such as accounting. Doer managers tend to see employees as an extension of themselves "so that their ability to do is enlarged."[18] Thomas favors the empowerment model of management, which focuses on motivating employees to "behave in ways required to achieve business objectives."[19]

5. Managing Diversity Is Effective

Of the three case studies provided in the book, the approach of Avon Products is the most comprehensive and forthright. Thomas describes Avon as an aggressive affirmative action employer in the 1970s and into the 1980s. The company then began to consider the need to match the demographics of its workforce with those in its customer base. "In retrospect, management realized that if the company had better used the women in its workforce, it could have avoided some of the business problems it encountered in the late 1970s and early 1980s."[20]

The Multicultural Planning Research Project was formed to evaluate how managers and employees saw promotion practices, review company systems and policies, and identify barriers to promotion. A cultural audit found that informality still characterized the recruitment and promotion processes and that there were weaknesses in development and training systems as well as appraisal and feedback. There were no social support systems for women, who complained of largely unconscious stereotyping, though prejudice toward minorities was somewhat more open. Many of those interviewed did not understand the meaning of multiculturalism.

In early 1990, Avon renewed its commitment to diversity with new procedures for monitoring multiculturalism. A task force on diversity was formed that immediately broadened the concept of diversity to include sexual orientation, religious minorities, and employees over age forty. Additional interviewing of employees found a major workforce issue was caretaker-related benefits, such as maternity leave and flextime. The company developed a five-year plan for implementing diversity through a partnership between line management and human resources. The goals included "getting the right people in the right place," reinforcing and rewarding performance, enhancing career planning and development, integrating work and family policies and offering flexible benefits, and implementing more programs such as mentoring and accountability for managers. With a bow to Thomas's influence, the plan divorces itself from preferential treatment and identifies diversity as a business issue.[21]

6. Managing Diversity Is Compatible with Total Quality Management

Thomas knew that managing diversity would have to compete with other management trends. One of the hottest topics of the 1980s was total quality management (TQM), so Thomas offered ideas on how to merge managing diversity with total quality management.

The two management philosophies do have a surprising number of elements in common. Both emphasize the centrality of social systems, teamwork, customer service and satisfaction, the creation of a fear-free and harmonious workplace atmosphere, and, especially, the substitution of a more cooperative win-win philosophy in favor of the competitive, zero-sum win-lose outlook. (Ironically, TQM's conceptualization of teamwork and win-win optimism has its roots in the barn raisings and quilting bees of the lily-white, turn-of-the-century, Iowa farm country of TQM's late founder, W. Edwards Deming.)

TQM emphasizes the commitment and involvement of all employees to making change and innovation in all aspects of organizational life to improve product quality. Much of this involves human relations work, such as creating an atmosphere where workers are less fearful to ask questions and raise criticisms in teams or "quality circles." Traditional hierarchies of authority are downplayed in favor of flattened organizational structures made up of "empowered," more entrepreneurial workers, who assume more responsibility and accountability for themselves. TQM was so influential that in 1987 the Congress authorized the Malcolm Baldrige Award, named after President Reagan's secretary of commerce. Many of the corporations that have won this award for quality management have been active in experimenting with workforce diversity strategies: Xerox, Motorola, AT&T, and Eastman Chemical Company.[22]

Thomas quickly linked managing diversity and TQM as complementary strategies for long-term organizational change. He emphasized the common themes of greater employee empowerment and a more open workplace atmosphere. TQM proponents had much to learn from managing diversity, said Thomas, because changing demographics mean that the employees to be empowered are culturally diverse. Managers can effectively implement TQM only if they can manage a range of culturally different employees.[23] (Alas, these overtures, by and large, have not been returned. While diversity management advocates often bring up their policies' links to TQM, the latter rarely returns the favor.)

Thomas would continue to adjust and broaden his managing diversity framework into the 1990s, but he would not cease efforts to avoid moralism and to emphasize that he was simply educating managers to make them more effective in dealing with dramatic, new demographic and cultural realities.

Thomas built a research-and-consulting empire at the American Institute for Managing Diversity. Although the institute did much to spread the word and to refine managing diversity policies, it was the evangelistic Griggs who began to cobble together a social policy movement through a series of annual national diversity conferences beginning in the spring of 1991. With registration fees at $800 to $1,000, these relatively pricey meetings, strongly oriented toward business and government, would provide valuable networking sites and forums to showcase and debate emerging theories and techniques. The diversity machine was getting ready to roll.

Cross-Cultural Consultant Profile I: Lillian Roybal Rose

Lillian Roybal Rose, a self-described consultant in cross-cultural awareness, doesn't advertise. People hear of her by word of mouth. Most of her clients have been in the nonprofit and public sector, especially the sprawling California State University and California Community Colleges systems. Her fees are $3,000 plus travel for a one-day workshop or $5,000 for a two-day workshop. Her corporate rate is slightly higher, but she rarely gets it: "I can't break into the private sector. They want bottom line, cost effectiveness, and all that, and I can't figure out how to transfer what I do to the bottom line."[1]

Rose's radical politics have mellowed somewhat, but she still wants to change hearts and minds. She's a humanist and civil rights moralist committed to teaching people about cultural relativism and institutional oppression: "I teach cross-cultural communication skills. I raise consciousness. That's all I can do. I teach how to shift frames of reference—from one of dualism to one of committed relativism. To be able to shift into someone else's frame of reference and understand where they're coming from. I teach process, not answers."

Rose uses experiential, emotional, and sometimes confrontational techniques to raise awareness about personal harm caused by the "isms": racism, sexism, heterosexism, ageism, and others. She has learned to keep some of her civil rights moralism under control, though her interests and background are rooted in those struggles: "I don't come from the rage any more. It isn't that I don't have rage. I work on rage all the time. I can put rage aside and keep thinking."

She sees her mission as helping organizations cope with the emotional upheavals caused by the "transition from the old Anglo-dominated status quo to a new multicultural order." Movement away from the status quo provokes fear, anxiety, loss, and misunderstanding. Intercultural communication can help calm the waters of ethnic change. "It's one thing to have a multicultural education," Rose told a California Community Colleges conference. "It's another thing to experience it." Change rattles the emotions. She should know.

The daughter of East Los Angeles political activist Ed Roybal, Lillian was tutored in political outrage by a crusader against police brutality and other forms of urban-ethnic discrimination. The senior Roybal's rise to a city council position was so tumultuous and drew such serious threats that his children were closely guarded by family and friends. Lillian was a political activist at California State University, Los Angeles, where she earned a B.A. in sociology in 1967, and at the University of Southern California, where she earned a master's in education in 1970. She became a teacher, then an exhausted political dropout. She married, moved to beautiful but isolated Santa Cruz, and had children. Eventually she returned to part-time teaching and became involved as an education counselor for migrant children for six years. She began conducting workshops for Latina groups and conferences on bilingual education. Her transition from teaching to conducting workshops on cultural issues was also facilitated when she attended Stanford Institute of Intercultural Communication in 1981.

Rose fused cross-cultural interests with the theory of "internalized oppression," which she learned from Erika Marcuse, the wife of Marxist philosopher Herbert Marcuse. Drawing deeply on the radical reformist heritage, the theory's first assumption is that individuals are basically good and basically equal but are corrupted by social institutions. Basically decent individuals are socialized from childhood to be perpetrators or victims of many forms of inequality and oppression: racism and sexism, class prejudice, adultism, heterosexism, antisemitism, ageism, ableism. The internalization of negative societal stereotypes causes individual psychological pain, rage, distortion, and self-destruction, made manifest in grim health statistics among oppressed minorities.

To revive memories and promote self-awareness of social-psychological injuries, Rose utilizes a silent group exercise she terms "target, nontarget." Workshop participants are divided into different subgroups according to whether they are men or women, white or people of color, from college-educated or not-college-educated families, have had alcohol abuse in family or no abuse in family, and so on. They are asked to stand and eye one another across the room. The groups shift in composition as the criteria change. "People of color," claims Rose, "may be blown away when they are in the nontarget group and looking across at blond blue-eyed whites who are in the target group for, say, alcohol abuse." After the exercise, Rose "debriefs" them and they talk about what they felt—as targets or nontargets. "Nontargets become dehumanized to some extent and get numb." Emotional outbursts are expected.

"I think one reason for my popularity is that I deal frankly with fears about cultural and transitional change. I work with affect, emotions—not just the cognitive aspects. My workshops can be very emotional. I try to create a setting where people can feel safe to be real, honest and express their fears about change."

I saw no emotional displays at the 1990 half-day lecture-seminar I attended at California State University, Los Angeles. It was an uneventful lecture. (Lack of time to do "emotional work" has led Rose to refuse shortened workshops.) But Itabari Njeri, a former feature writer on diversity issues for the *Los Angeles Times,* described how Rose stimulated whites' confused sense of cultural identity during a longer workshop:

> A fragile-looking woman with blond hair and delicate, pale skin, flushed pink with emotion is biting her lip. The setting is a conference room on the UCLA campus. . . .
>
> "This is the only place you are going to be able to say this and not be called a racist because of the imbalance of power in our society," says Lillian Roybal Rose. . . . "I want you to pull back your shoulders and say, 'I'm proud to be white.'"
>
> "I'm proud to be white," Cindy Nulty says quietly.
>
> "What goes through your mind?" Rose asks,
>
> "That it's okay to be proud to be white," says Nulty.
>
> "Uh, huh. Say it once more time."
>
> [Rose] then places them in a circle that represents the essential goodness of all human beings, and she urges them to say: "I want to come home."
>
> The woman, in tears, can barely mumble it. "I want to come home."
>
> "What is it you're thinking?" asks Rose.
>
> "I want a place to belong," says Nulty.[2]

Many diversity management books contain admonitions that trainers must continually work on their own biases and hidden interests. A good many harbor covert or overt hostility toward white males. Rose was no exception. She admitted that her East Los Angeles background led her to be somewhat hostile toward white males, whom she subconsciously associated with her father's police enemies. In 1987, however, a training workshop trauma produced a more tolerant trainer.

One of the worst experiences I have ever had—but one of the most growing ones, those stretches you must do—was with a major police department in 1987. I did seven workshops with them. The workshops were mandatory. Four went okay. I had an ethnic mix of participants and results were good. Then two policemen were killed on the streets. Emotional anxiety soared. At the fifth workshop, I found myself dealing with about forty-five people, nearly all of them white males, many of whom had been written up for racism or sexism infractions.

Within the first ten minutes, the back row burst out laughing at a sexual joke—it worked its way through the room as I tried to teach. I got nervous and stammered. So they mimicked that, my hand gestures, movements, made sarcastic remarks just beyond my hearing, ridiculed my examples. It went on throughout the whole five-hour workshop.

I survived. But I felt physically battered. Initially, I was furious. If I had had an Uzi, I would have killed them. On the long drive back to Santa Cruz, though, I remembered that Erika Marcuse had told me that a great test would be to see the humanness in people whose behavior you hate. And then I remembered their responses in the target, nontarget exercises. Three-fourths of the men had been targets of class prejudice. Most were Vietnam vets. Most were alcoholics or children of alcoholics. Some had been divorced three or four times. Some had been suicidal. Today, they might not pass preliminary psychological screening. At the end of day, I asked them to hold hands. They laughed, but they did it. And so, while driving home, my visions met my emotions. I realized that these men had been acting out the pain of their internalized oppression. I felt the pain of classism. I now affectively understood the acting out of hurt from class issues. It was a physical shift in my frame of reference—I felt it move in my head and heart. I had compassion. And, now that I think about it, I'd been scared since childhood of white male cops.

When I went back to finish the series, the quality of the workshops was so much better. You can't work with people for whom you have contempt.

Rose claims she has learned to control her own emotions while trying to get whites to connect with the pain of racism by comparing their own victimization under one of the other isms (sexism, classism, alcohol abuse, etc.). She also tries to communicate the "costs of being privileged. . . . Nobody talks about the dehumanization of the nontarget group. What white males feel is their dehumanization, the walking on eggshells, the rationalization, the apologies, the guilt. That's the price of a nontarget. . . . It's hard to be white male."

Getting white males to vent their feelings is a major satisfaction for Rose.

The best workshops have been where white males have burst out crying for being let off the hook for being the bad guy. Mostly it happens in academic settings. I'm always amazed. One of the most moving was my workshop at a major nuclear laboratory—with scientists who do not deal with affect at all and are resistant. A white male nuclear engineer came up to me and burst out crying. I literally felt for him—all of his pain. He told me, "I've been holding in so many years of guilt and shame; this is the first time someone has given me permission to be okay as a white male. When I came into this field I was a hero; now I'm a baby killer."

But Rose shares no pain with white males on the topic of reverse discrimination. Like most other diversity consultants, she defines it away: "I set up the basic requirements for oppression: (1) It must be in the national consciousness, (2) it must be rewarded in the institutions, and (3) there must be an imbalance of power. Though you cannot have racism in reverse until the balance of power shifts, prejudice and discrimination still feels bad. So I validate the fact that white males do feel that it's unfair and that is a personal experience—though it is not racism in reverse . . . but feeling bad and having institutionalized oppression are two different things."

The debate over expanding diversity's scope beyond race and gender troubles her: "I don't want to have a fight over whether race, class, or gender is most important. People of color have never had a forum to vent their rage. But we can't blame others." She's also aware that her workshops may be used as window dressing, as a hollow good-faith effort by organizations beset by legal or public relations crises. "It's difficult to not collude with the mandated requirements—to become another notch on the organizational belt." She's now doubly suspicious when clients request two-hour workshops: "I feel used by that and won't do it any more."

Rose is puzzled by the emergence of minority conservatives: "We're seeing a conservative interpretation from people of color themselves: Clarence Thomas, Shelby Steele [author of *The Content of Our Character*] and Richard Rodriguez [author of *Hunger of Memory: The Education of Richard Rodriguez*].[3] I'm not sure where it comes from. Rodriguez has never resolved his pain. He never got over the pain—internalized oppression. You don't have to give up your cultural identity." Rose also experiences pangs of self-doubt: "Every once in a while I get overwhelmed by this and think, 'What am I doing this for?' It's too big. Nothing's going to change. But it's not a place where I can stay. You have to come from the frame of reference where you say, 'you can do it all.'"

Chapter 3

Demography Is Destiny

The Diversity Machine Takes Off

Two long lines of well-dressed people nearly blocked my exit from the elevator on the mezzanine of the huge San Francisco Hilton. I'd expected to register quickly for the First Annual National Diversity Conference in May 1991, but the sponsors were overwhelmed and understaffed.

The First, Second, and Third Annual National Diversity Conferences were wonderful windows through which to observe the building of the diversity machine, as were smaller conferences and professional activities I observed in southern California, a prime staging area for the diversity management movement. Consultant gatherings on the national and regional levels reflected growing consensus, concerns, and types of conflict within the increasingly powerful policy movement. The conferences and workshops also provided forums where diversity management advocates answered mounting public criticism of their programs.

"Valuing Diversity" producer Lewis Griggs and psychologists Price Cobbs and Herbert Wong were the organizers of the high-profile First Annual Diversity Conference. It attracted a sell-out crowd of three hundred people whose $800 (nonprofit) to $1,000 (corporate) fee had been paid by a who's who of fifty-two corporations, twenty-three federal government agencies, eighteen state and city agencies, and an assortment of nonprofit organizations. Boise Cascade alone supplied eleven conventioneers; AT&T and Battelle Pacific Northwest Labs each sent ten; Du Pont fielded a team of seven; Hughes Aircraft, six. Corporate presence tilted heavily toward high tech, aerospace, financial services, and utilities, but such consumer product firms as Pillsbury, General Mills, Miller Brewing, Procter and Gamble, Gillette,

Nordstrom's, Reese, and Kinney Shoes were also represented. The Central Intelligence Agency sent the largest federal delegation: six people. Other agencies included the Internal Revenue Service, the Department of Defense, NASA, the Food and Drug Administration, the General Accounting Office, the Secret Service, the Environmental Protection Agency, the Department of Agriculture, the United States Postal Service, the Bureau of Indian Affairs, and the Smithsonian. Despite a recent affirmative action lawsuit, the Federal Bureau of Investigation registered no one. (Three G-men would attend the following year.) The high registration fees excluded the usual multicultural conference crowd of professors and community activists, though many panelists and consultants had backgrounds in higher education—usually in student services or affirmative action administration.

Upon registering, conference participants were given hefty packets consisting of a conference schedule, background material on speakers and panelists, and reprints of articles on diversity management, most of it sandwiched into a five-pound loose-leaf binder. More brochures, books, and tapes awaited in the nearby exhibition area, to be hauled about in a complimentary tote bag emblazoned with the Copeland-Griggs "Valuing Diversity" logo.

I carried this unwieldy bundle into the main ballroom and inadvertently confirmed a diversity management truism: in a sea of minority faces, I gravitated to a chair next to someone of my own ethnicity. Thus did I meet blond-haired, blue-eyed Sondra Thiederman, an up-and-coming author and diversity consultant (profiled in this book). We cheerily exchanged introductions. Thiederman expressed polite interest that I was writing a book on emerging diversity policies, then turned away to cultivate more potentially lucrative relationships with a team of managers from Boise Cascade.

"Let's get the cards going, guys," said Thiederman crisply, distributing her professional cards and accepting theirs. (Other consultants were also working the crowd.) Later Thiederman admitted one regret: that she hadn't bought an exhibition booth to showcase her new books—as had Julie O'Mara, coauthor with David Jamieson of the newly published *Managing Workforce 2000*.[1] "Julie O'Mara seems to be selling tons of books," Thiederman sighed. (She was.)

But Sondra Thiederman was doing well and would do better. The recipient of a UCLA doctorate in cross-cultural anthropology, Thiederman already received $2,500 per day (plus expenses) for keynote addresses and $3,000 for a full-day keynote and workshop. She had published *Bridging Cultural Barriers for Corporate Success,* with a second on the way, *Profiting in America's Mul-*

ticultural Workplace.[2] She would soon produce a commercial training video-tape, *Bridging Cultural Barriers for Corporate Success,* with Barr Films. Through such efforts, she was expanding her client base. (At the Second and Fourth Annual National Diversity Conferences she would be featured as a "famous diversity author.")

The conference belatedly commenced when San Francisco's mayor, Art Agnos, was introduced. He boomed that he was pleased to preside at the opening ceremonies of such a significant event, then plugged his city as well as the conference by noting that the convention was convening in the city that best "recognizes and celebrates diversity." Conference cosponsor Price Cobbs, an imposing African American psychiatrist and author of *Black Rage,* keyed the twin themes of moral mission and organizational change.[3] He saluted the mushrooming interest in diversity management and immodestly compared the conference to the founding of the United Nations: "We have spawned a business, a movement, an industry," intoned Cobbs, "but we must slow down and try and separate reality from the myths." In so doing, he cautioned participants to beware of excesses of political correctness and to consider in candid, "nonjudgmental" fashion the increasing white hostility and unease, as well as other evidence of "resistance."

Cobbs was gently prodding the militant moralists of affirmative action. His challenge was immediately answered during the opening panel discussion when NASA affirmative action officer Harriet Jenkins rumbled that she was not about to uncouple the aims of managing diversity from those of affirmative action. She insisted that affirmative action's ultimate goal *is* workforce diversity. Her remarks were greeted by murmurs of approval from dozens of current and former affirmative action officers in the audience.

The second panelist, Jean Kim, a Stanford University administrator and consultant, more gently spelled out her preference for deep, moralistic reform by describing various "models of diversity management." Kim favored least those conservative models that tried merely to "help people do better what they did already." She said she would work with only those organizations that accept the "multicultural model" of valuing ethnic differences, empowering employees, and decreasing white male dominance in corporate culture. Kim also articulated the "equal-treatment-is-not-fair treatment" theme. Echoing the Copeland-Griggs "Valuing Diversity" themes, Kim argued that evaluating women and minorities according to qualifications established by white males is ipso facto unfair. Each person should be evaluated according to his or her cultural background. Kim gave no hint as to how to circumvent legal mandates to the contrary. (Nor did an African American panelist who subsequently endorsed culturally adjusted treatment by comparing it to his mother's philosophy of child rearing: "I love each of you as much as you need it.")

Digital Equipment vice president William Hanson (a "champion of diversity" profiled in the "Valuing Diversity" video series) chronicled his conversion to diversity management. Hanson recalled his problems managing Digital's ethnically mixed plants in the early 1970s. He sought out Price Cobbs, who introduced him to the idea of institutional racism. This "cornerstone diversity concept" posits that discrimination is "in the air," invisibly built into taken-for-granted, white male organizational attitudes and practices. To convince his white male subordinates that they were silently privileged, Hanson sent them to intensive, small-scale sensitivity workshops in Cobbs's San Francisco offices. Digital's diversity efforts have since expanded into numerous focus groups that discuss all manner of differences.

Pacific Bell lawyer Michael Rodriguez addressed the growing dilemma of increasing workforce diversity during the downsizing era. Rodriguez claimed Pacific Bell's workforce had become 70 percent female and minority, despite vigorous downsizing ("rightsizing") campaigns. Rodriguez also previewed two emerging conference themes: that managers must make efforts to legitimate workplace discussions of ethnic and cultural differences and that white males must be brought into the process.

Panel chair Ann Morrison, consultant and author of *Breaking the Glass Ceiling,* returned to the issue of how closely diversity management should be tied to affirmative action.[4] On the one hand, she criticized Harriet Jenkins's attempt to portray workforce diversity as an extension of affirmative action. Emerging white male backlash, Morrison suggested, required rethinking and more complex approaches. (Jenkins returned the standard bureaucratic line: cultural diversity goals are fully compatible with Equal Employment Opportunity Commission principles. Managing diversity, she said, simply looks at resultant workplace problems and addresses subtler issues like informal norms.) But Morrison then took a U-turn back toward endorsing goals and timetables (which she would heartily recommend in her forthcoming book, *The New Leaders*).[5] Morrison polled the audience: Should there be goals and timetables for retention and promotion as well as recruitment? Should managers be rewarded explicitly for meeting such goals? More than 80 percent of the conventioneers agreed. Only three people raised hands to oppose the measure. Knowing laughter rippled through the ballroom. The lopsided vote confirmed the clout of civil rights moralists and their tightly focused war against entrenched racism and sexism; Price Cobbs's opening call to break free from political correctness seemed doomed.

Cracking PC Moralism

To break PC conformity and inhibitions, Cobbs, Griggs, and the convention organizers had randomly assigned conventioneers into small discussion groups with preselected leaders who were provided with questions to probe taboo issues. The groups were basically brainstorming sessions designed to raise quickly and briefly react to a range of questions supplied by the leaders. Among relative strangers, no one wanted to risk stumbling over politically correct landmines. Tantalizing statements were offered but only occasionally explored. Yet sensitive issues were at least raised, previewing simmering problems that would be used to set the agenda for the Second and Third Annual Diversity Conferences.

My group contained about twenty people from corporations such as AT&T, Boise Cascade, du Pont, Electronic Data Systems (EDS), the CIA, the Defense Communications Agency, and three consultants. As instructed, we began by listing current workforce diversity issues, among them, non-managerial white males, problems in classifying "minorities," breaking the glass ceilings, the limits of awareness training, problems of trust, dealing with white males, dilution of the movement by power holders, and fraud and credentialing problems with diversity trainers.

Trial balloons were lofted—usually to be shot down. Opening discussions of "equalizing the playing field" were suddenly squelched when a Romanian-born woman from the CIA wondered aloud if the reverse discrimination complaints of nonmanagerial white males were justified. This was a huge taboo within the diversity movement. Reverse discrimination was assumed to be a "myth." After a pause, a few people mumbled that this was a problem. Then we moved on.

Another paradox in the diversity movement quickly surfaced. A Hispanic female consultant complained about "replacing one stereotype with another" in some forms of diversity training. Several people briefly agreed but admitted they did not know to avoid this risk if general cultural differences were to be discussed at all.

The increasingly open clash between radical moralists and more conservative pragmatists arose. Our designated leader, a white female consultant, seized the initiative and waxed happily radical, insisting that the "best models for change are revolution." An Asian Indian from Du Pont responded warmly that there were "many revolutions" ongoing at that corporation. But a tough-minded Hispanic engineer from EDS cut short this drift into radical chic and civil rights moralism. "We must get accountability for individual actions," he demanded. "Get beyond victimization. It's hard to get someone to accept responsibility when they've been conditioned not to do so." Sketching graphs on a large flip-pad at the center of our group, he argued that diversity must be seen as a strictly business and efficiency utilization issue. His minilecture was politely received. But his presentation was dry, other ideas were percolating, and attention spans were short.

A white female consultant brought up New Age themes of trust and communication. Diversity efforts, she insisted, would not get very far without interpersonal trust. But two other group members squelched warmth and trust by raising the unhappy specter of mounting restructuring and layoffs: How could trust, loyalty, and even diversity be furthered under such difficult circumstances? The curtain fell on New Age optimism.

The delicate issue of mandated versus voluntary diversity training for employees was raised by a white male captain from the Glendale Police Department. Mandated training had not gone down well with the Glendale cops. Again heads nodded, but no one had any answers. (I did overhear an uncharacteristically blunt response to this dilemma during a convention coffee break the next day: "But if it weren't mandatory, no one would come. We wouldn't get any work.")

The day's proceedings closed in the grand ballroom with a warm, multicultural benediction. Elizabeth Parent, chair of American Indian studies at San Francisco State University, welcomed us "to our liberating, productive, and profit-making journey." She not unexpectedly put in a plug for Indian history and customs. Indians value the aged, Parent informed the audience, and Iroquois Indian laws contained provisions for gender balance, a feature omitted when writers of the U.S. Constitution "plagiarized" much of the Iroquois system. (Not everyone bought such revisionism. "Was that stuff about the Iroquois true?" a personnel administrator from the Smithsonian Institution whispered to me at the following hosted reception.)

Tough Apple for Hard Times

Cobbs, Griggs, and the other convention planners were willing to tolerate Elizabeth Parent's San Francisco PC silliness, but they were determined to emphasize the tough, business-oriented side of selling diversity programs. Parent's soothing multicultural rambling the prior evening would be followed the next morning with a shower of cold data and prickly predictions provided by Apple Computer vice president Kevin Sullivan. In a cordial but firm keynote, Sullivan shattered the optimistic glow of *Workforce 2000* and accompanying assumptions of diversity management's inevitable triumph. Sullivan previewed other changes in the workplace and society that would complicate the diversity machine's drive to become the 1990s hot-track policy.

Sullivan made quite clear that civil rights moralism and race and gender militancy would not sell diversity management to CEOs. He forecast a Darwinian business landscape. Global competition, he said, had raised pressures for cost cutting and instant analyses. Job growth and revenue growth will continue to be primarily offshore. Corporations were scrambling to subcontract lower-level administrative work overseas or to local "white-collar sweatshops" of temporary workers. The jobs that had traditionally been the first rungs up the corporate ladder would no longer be there for increasing numbers of minorities and women. These and other traditional sources of social mobility were closing. Meanwhile, fundamental institutions—family and education—were decaying. Polarization between rich and poor was being accompanied by a move to bare-bones government. Society was fragmenting into numerous subsocieties based on ethnicity and class. White males, like everyone else, would be denied upward mobility as corporations downsized and restructured. In this environment, Sullivan warned, diversity management must be sold as "business, not social work." A rational and positive approach was a must in order to satisfy bottom-line demands in tough times. Avoid the punitive and preachy, he warned. "Progress in hard times," Sullivan glumly admitted, "may simply mean not losing ground."

Surprisingly, the conventioneers gave Sullivan a huge ovation. The largely business-based crowd had sensed the onset of these harsh trends in their own workplaces. Sullivan's talk was years ahead of the business journal cover stories on these grim topics. His stern realism and candor were a bracing challenge to the gushing demography-is-destiny optimism.

Nevertheless, civil rights moralists discovered yet another champion in Gail Snowden, an African American director at First Boston Bank who dominated a panel discussion on breaking the glass ceiling. She bluntly described the glass ceiling as a "glass-bottomed elevator moved by the pulleys of racism and sexism." The people being groomed for leadership are still white male, she grumbled. She warned the audience not to assume that a glowing "vision statement" on diversity would be put into effect by middle managers when "the front-burner issue today is cost-cutting." A questioner asked Snowden, "How do you track progress on diversity?" Her answer was tart: "When you see more women and minorities."

Lewis Griggs Has a Bad Day

Sullivan's and Snowden's tough talk clashed with the softer exhortation for personal transformation and conversion advocated by the conference co-convener, Lewis Griggs. More than forty people crowded into a conference room to hear his mid-morning workshop, "Working with White Male Power Structures."

Rasping through a bad cold, Griggs said he would present approaches he had found successful in reaching white male senior management, followed by a preview of executive testimonials contained in his latest "Valuing Diversity" installment, *Champions of Diversity.* Some minority consultants chafed at the specter of an upper-middle-class white male making so much money off the diversity boom. On the other hand, even among diversity moralists, nothing succeeded like success. If anyone held the keys to CEO inner sanctums, Griggs seemed to have them. But he didn't.

Instead Griggs droned on in an introductory fashion about valuing differences. People may be mostly alike, he indicated, but it is not the similarities that cause problems. Differences cause problems. Diversity management involves recognizing, discussing, and valuing differences. Individual differences ("differences are assets") get lost in group stereotyping. To illustrate this, Griggs invited us to stereotype him. We did: as an upper-middle-class yuppie. Griggs admitted that in many ways he was superficially a "demographic cliché." But the inner Griggs was different. The transition through midlife, he explained, had given him a new spirituality and reinforced his diversity work.

Griggs claimed his confessions of being a "recovering racist, classist, and sexist" provided a bond with other white male managers. Admitting one's own ethnocentrism established interpersonal trust, a must in getting corporate types and others to undergo the personal transformation vital to diversity training: "Establish trust, then set them up," he counseled.

An almost palpable level of frustration and impatience had been building in the conference room. Many in the workshop were themselves consultants or human resources officers who already knew and practiced the introductory diversity catechism through which Griggs was taking the workshop. They had expected Griggs to reveal major secrets of getting inside the power structure, but he wasn't. Some walked out, slamming the conference room door behind them. Others began interrupting with questions. "What if they tell you to take your 'personal work' and shove it? Then what?"

"Then talk dollars and demographics," advised Griggs, shifting to business-based pragmatism. "Talk about EEOC complaints, lawsuits, recruitment and retention problems, training expenses lost when people leave. Focus on the changing demographics in terms of workforce and customer bases. You have to get individual buy-in from the power structure. . . . I want to try and use the white male senior management language. . . . You have to understand where white male managers are."

Griggs talked more about Griggs. He was a "conservative in support of liberal-radical systems of free enterprise and democracy." It's in the self-interest of white males to get on board: "As a white male, I'm not going to be able to maintain my power if I can't learn to work with people different from myself—given the changing demographics. I won't be able to compete with people who have bicultural skills."

A white female diversity officer from a liberal arts college protested, "I've been working for the same liberal arts college for five years. The president still doesn't understand why I'm there. He doesn't know about pluralism. How do I get through his office door?"

Griggs responded that selling diversity means a balance of talk about demographic and money-saving benefits and deft use of his videotapes. The latter takes managers "away from themselves," allowing them to look at familiar situations anew.

Still struggling with the workshop participants' growing dissatisfaction, Griggs stumbled toward saying that the key to working with white male power structures is to be a white male. "I speak their language. I'm weaned on it. It's my culture," he explained. This version of identity politics was met with stunned silence.

Griggs then asked if we still wanted to see his videotape.

"No."

More people stalked out, and the workshop limped to a conclusion. Afterward, I asked Griggs about the diversity argument that a workforce should be ethnically matched to its clientele. Wasn't suggesting that Hispanics sell to Hispanics rather like the pre-1960s segregationist rationale that white clients would accept only white salespeople? The weary Griggs answered that it was a good question but reflected too much white male, linear, critical thinking. Nonlinear sympathy for Griggs's ordeal led me to drop the matter. (Later I would recall the words of Griggs's ex-wife: "Fortunately Lewis doesn't have the gene that causes embarrassment.")

In addition to the workshop on white male power structures, seven other sessions were offered on: creating corporate cultural changes, networking and coalition building, developing career development programs, and developing a successful diversity consultant practice. I attended the last with about ten others. The seminar leader, Sylvia Gerst, had been an EEO specialist with two computer corporations for thirty-five years. When she left—voluntarily or downsized (this is never quite clear with consultants)—she bought a friend's consulting firm. Although the core of her business was still affirmative action consulting with firms that could not afford full-time EEO staff, she was branching out into workforce diversity. Affirmative action was still her bread and butter because the programs were mandated and corporations had to do them. But Gerst felt that workforce diversity would be moving from more voluntary to more mandated form—and more business for consultants. (Fellow workshopper Sondra Thiederman was a bit disappointed: "So I guess that's how you build a successful consultant practice: buy one.")

Later I watched Thiederman enter the San Francisco Hilton's cocktail lounge. She looked about slowly—and came over to the table where most of the whites were clustered.

"The Future Is Now in L.A!" The Diversity Machine Expands in Southern California

Southern California would be closely identified with the diversity management movement. As the nation's immigration magnet, local and national consultants looked toward Los Angeles as a multicultural mecca, an early fulfillment of the *Workforce 2000* prophecies: "The Future Is Now in L.A!" became a popular diversity slogan before the April 1992 riots sullied both the slogan and the city.

A southern California preview of the more expensive and nationally based First Annual National Diversity Conference was offered in Los Angeles in early February 1991. UCLA's School of Industrial Relations and a steering committee of professional human resources associations organized a conference, "HR2000: Strategies for Managing the Multicultural Workforce." The registration fee was a mere $150, permitting more people from public and educational institutions to be among the 250 in attendance. As would typically be the case with diversity conferences, about two-thirds were women and perhaps 40 percent were minorities; there were few Asians or white males.

Oakland diversity consultant Benjamin Harrison who keynoted the conference opened with the lighthearted observations that the U.S. workforce has always been culturally diverse and that, to some extent, we've always known how to manage diversity. But now, he wryly observed, consultants can be paid well for doing so.

Harrison synthesized key diversity management rationales that were emerging in conferences and literature, especially the Big Two: demographic change and the threat of economic and educational polarization.

Two major changes, declared Harrison, will make diversity management both more difficult and necessary: demographic changes, fueled by surging immigration, will mean that diversity management will be linked more closely to productivity and profit, and a mounting crisis in the quality of education means that graduating high school seniors are ill prepared to assume jobs in an increasingly technologically sophisticated workplace. Therefore, because of labor shortages and shifting ethnic worker and customer bases, employers will have to train and more carefully retrain the people they get, especially women and minorities. There will be fewer white males.

Establishing managing diversity as a serious policy science, warned Harrison, means challenging several myths:

- Increased utilization of women and minorities means lowering standards.
- Women and people of color are less qualified.
- Diversity is a "soft," low-priority goal.
- There is no accountability or reward for making a good effort.

Harrison had obviously studied R. Roosevelt Thomas's *Harvard Business Review* article on diversity management. Harrison repeated what was becoming a diversity mantra. The United States has passed through two "paradigms" of employee relations and is entering a third. The first paradigm was that everyone would be treated the same in a colorblind fashion; differences were not recognized, much less valued. The second stage was that of equal economic opportunity and "leveling the playing field"; this involved "righting past wrongs" for targeted minorities and the recognition of group oppression and differences. The new third stage is that of valuing and managing diversity: recognizing that all manner of differences are assets to be appreciated and harnessed for greater market competitiveness. Diversity moves beyond race and gender to issues like work and family tensions and day care needs.

Corporations will assume the lead, predicted Harrison. They will incorporate diversity into their vision statements, and activist CEOs will have to drive the diversity process through "vision and mission." Staff will be added. Many corporations, he correctly noted, have been appointing vice presidents to head up diversity efforts.

But HR2000 also gave evidence that California's public sector organizations were leading the drive to change the white male workplace. Just how ambitious and how expensive such diversity efforts might become was previewed by Daniel Scarborough, a personnel administrator with the city of San Diego—one of two full-time people in charge of putting the entire 10,000-member municipal workforce through diversity training during the next three years. They had already developed a slogan, "Diversity brings us all together," and a multicolored logo. The Cincinnati firm of Kaleel Jamieson Associates had picked up the consultant contract of more than $137,000. Preliminary planning had begun with surveys and more than sixty focus groups in various departments along various diversity dimensions: there were groups for disabled, Middle Easterners, and gays and lesbians. Training had begun at the top with six days of off-site training for the city manager's office. Other employees would receive one to two days of training. (The $200,000 estimated expenses did not include employee released time.)

California's health care industry, already feeling the impact of demographic and cultural change, would be a prime target for diversity trainers. At the conference, Kurt Schusterich and M. Jean Gilbert discussed the beginnings of their valuing diversity research for the huge, 2.2-million member Kaiser Permanente health maintenance organization. Valuing diversity had just become part of Kaiser's corporate vision statement. Schusterich and Gilbert's specific research location was Kaiser's big West Los Angeles facility, where more than half of the workforce was African American, 20 percent was Asian, 12 percent Hispanic, 15 percent white, and 2 percent "other"; the workforce served a client base that was 53 percent African American, 28 percent Anglo, 11 percent Hispanic, 7 percent Asian, and 2 percent "other." Schusterich and Gilbert had been working on "breaking down barriers" in dialogue groups, which gathered to discuss cultural differences. One major sore point was language differences. English speakers were annoyed that foreign-born coworkers spoke other languages on the job. Male-female differences sometimes eclipsed ethnic differences, for example, in terms of assertiveness. Despite some social strains and awkwardness, Schusterich and Gilbert were pleased to report that dialogue group members were becoming personally committed and wanted to stay involved.

The delicate task of charting diversity management's course away from civil rights moralism to business-based pragmatism was the subject of a workshop conducted by consultants Sunny Bradford and Ginger Lapid-Bogda. They described the 1960s racial change efforts as characterized by "pain, suffering, guilt, purging, and self-flagellation." Affirmative action was propelled by "do-goodism" and legal mandates. Earlier efforts at awareness training were simplistic and "with no real idea of what we were doing." On the other hand, demography and business concerns would drive diversity in the 1990s. That there would be less concern with social, moral, and legal matters called for an explicit organizational change strategy: (1) start at the top, (2) assess the organization, (3) link the diversity effort to real business issues, such as customer demographics, (3) develop sponsors and "evangelists" through a diversity steering committee, (4) nourish strong pro-change networks, (5) educate everyone on the shared vision of valuing diversity, (6) tailor programs to specific organizational situations, and (7) get continuous feedback. Commitment of senior management is crucial. Diversity management, they emphasized, must be seen as more than mere repackaging of affirmative action and EEO.

The two consultants' presentation was so smooth and compelling that there were no objections from moralists fearing displacement of affirmative action's race and gender focus.

Catching Southern California's Diversity Training Wave

Bradford and Lapid-Bogda's presentation had been so impressive that I wanted to know more about them and other L.A. consultants. Sunny Bradford remained somewhat standoffish, but two weeks later I pursued the pair's visionary but pragmatic thoughts on diversity when I met with Ginger Lapid-Bogda over a lunch of matzoh ball soup at Junior's a popular West Los Angeles delicatessen. Lapid-Bogda was more of a feminist and civil rights moralist than she seemed. Her interests in diversity stemmed from her student days in the early 1970s at the University of California at Santa Barbara. There, while working on a bachelor's degree in political science, she became active in the feminist movement, an ardent worldview she has not relinquished in spite of her formal presentation of diversity's basis in business interests. She completed a doctoral dissertation on sex role behavior at the University of Pennsylvania and went to work as an organizational development specialist with Kaiser Permanente. She married in 1986 and became a freelance consultant, signing on as a "core white woman" with a consulting firm in San Francisco headed by Ron Brown. She also worked on diversity projects with Price Cobbs. Like cross-cultural consultant Lillian Roybal

Rose, Lapid-Bogda had been nourished by Erika Marcuse's teachings on internalized oppression. From Marcuse, Lapid-Bogda learned that everyone is born color-blind; racism, sexism, and the other isms were learned; and through deep self-awareness training, such prejudices can be changed.

Lapid-Bogda considered herself fairly new to diversity training but was confident that "the more I do, the better I get." She acknowledged that contacts and networking were crucial in getting diversity consulting contracts. Once on the job, her greatest frustrations involved getting white male managers to perceive and understand group-based differences; they wanted to value only individual differences. For example, said Lapid-Bogda, a white male executive told her that he'd refused a promotion to a woman employee because "she might get pregnant." Lapid-Bogda had difficulty explaining to the man that his actions were based on a sexist stereotype.

Ironically, I learned toward the end of the interview that Lapid-Bogda herself planned a pause in building her career: she was about to become an adoptive mother. Within the week she anticipated driving the birth mother to the hospital. (Indeed, I did not see or hear of Ginger Lapid-Bogda for some years after that, until I saw her name on a panel discussion at a regional diversity conference.)

Other Los Angeles consultants had been getting into diversity training through a variety of paths and contacts. African American social worker Helen Mendes traced the origins of her diversity consulting firm to her early 1970s experience in writing an international cookbook. Interests kindled there matured into more formal academic study: a Ph.D. social work dissertation completed at UCLA in 1975 on how cultural backgrounds, especially religion, influence the practice of psychiatric social work. Her cross-cultural slant carried into a teaching career at the University of Southern California and a subsequent independent practice. Mendes's first venture as a diversity consultant occurred in 1985 when she was asked to provide cultural awareness training to senior management at a local radio station.

Other diversity work came Mendes's way through contacts at the Los Angeles Human Relations Commission, through which she gained a contract to design a diversity training curriculum for local police departments. She found the police somewhat difficult to work with because they'd been conditioned by the worst elements of society—and therefore with the worst of minority group members. She expanded a similar style of training for courts and mediators. Her fee was $1,000 for a typical one-day seminar. But her biggest prize was a 1990 contract to conduct a series of diversity classes at Hughes Aircraft, a firm wracked by discrimination complaints.

Another independent social worker, Fanda Bender, was one of Mendes's trainers, but Bender was not impressed by what she saw: "The training at Hughes was superficial—like a beginning sociology or race and ethnic relations course—and most participants were white male engineers and scientists who sat passively through most of the presentations." Bender ventured into her own diversity training. She led a couple of weekend workshops for a California state university-affiliated religious group on human dignity that focused on diversity. Bender used more experiential tools such as psychodrama and reading poetry from diverse cultures. She also had participants bring with them an ethnic cultural artifact from their family (a photo, a serape, an eagle feather, a yarmulke) and discuss the significance of these objects with the group. She later used these same exercises to train campus dormitory resident advisers.

But Bender was primarily a dabbler in diversity, performing a wide range of social work services for a varied clientele—"whoever can pay," she admitted. She taught part-time in the California state university system and had also been trying to get a piece of the action in the burgeoning cases of child abuse being reported.

Uvaldo Palomares was another southern California consultant who tapped temporarily into diversity consulting by way of lecturing on his patented LATS program—Leadership Attributes Training Series. The former California state university professor, who held a doctorate in educational psychology, specialized in teaching career enhancement skills: self-promotion, self-advocacy, and learning the informal organizational rules and networks. By and large, he found the teaching of such skills to minorities to be gratifying, though there were occasional frustrations. Palmares had been particularly discouraged by the response from Asian males and females who persisted in believing that dogged, hard work alone would lead to automatic advancement. Palomares had not caught the optimism about diversity training surging through the early conventions. On the contrary, he was pessimistic about the future of affirmative action and diversity efforts. The momentum, he felt, was already fading, and diversity programs were being encapsulated in human resources departments. He had just returned from lecturing public school teachers who worked in the Bronx and was horrified by the conditions they faced.

"I don't stand back very often, but in my darker moments I'm scared. They did a study in World War I about those who left the front lines. They discovered that they really needed to try to understand those who stayed, not those who left. I feel the same way about the teachers who are staying on the front line in the Bronx, not the ones who are leaving for the South or the Midwest. Why do they stay?" (Palomares himself did not stay long in the diversity movement; his name never surfaced in any of the conventions or professional activities I observed nationally or in southern California.)

Internal Corporate Advocates

I'd heard about Uvaldo Palomares from Jackie Hempstead, Security Pacific Bank's first African American female senior vice president for human resources and the bank's equal employment opportunity officer. Diversity management advocates inside the corporate world were invaluable as sources of employment for external consultants and for spreading the ideology and practice of diversity management from within the organization.

Jackie Hempstead was a low-key diversity evangelist who was also keenly aware of the practical realities of corporate life and Los Angeles's changing demographics. The poised, affable Hempstead was among the generation of women with children who had worked their way up from middle management to break the glass ceiling. Hempstead saw a typical corporate pattern in Security Pacific's handling of ethnic and gender relations: the bank had passed through numbers-driven affirmative action in the 1970s and then into more qualitative cultural changes in the 1980s. (Indeed, 70 percent of the bank's workforce was female by 1990 when I first interviewed Hempstead.) Much of this had been made possible, Hempstead noted, by the progressive CEO of that period; she sighed that a new Security Pacific CEO was more interested in the bottom line than softer human resources topics. Still, she was pleased with progress.

Security Pacific had been host to a number of diversity consultants and techniques. Price Cobbs had conducted seminars as early as 1978. Security Pacific was one of the corporations that provided funding for the Copeland–Griggs "Valuing Diversity" series and the bank's diversity awards ceremonies were profiled in the series; in turn, "Valuing Diversity" was standard training fare at the bank. Security Pacific's Seattle offices had contracted for diversity training with B'nai B'rith's Workplace of Difference team. All this was good for consciousness raising and encouraging networking, Hempstead felt, but now the bank was getting down to more extensive in-house efforts to encourage networking and support groups for minorities and women. Hempstead herself had been a member of Black Officers of Security Pacific, and other groups for Hispanics and Asians were woven into an overall minority officers network. A formal mentoring program for women and minorities had been instituted. Hempstead maintained contacts with the external consultant community through the Los Angeles Organizational Development Network, an association dedicated to planned organizational change.

Security Pacific's emphasis on diversity management apparently did little to strengthen the bank's position sufficiently to prevent a takeover by Bank of America in 1992. Thousands lost jobs in the merger, but not Hempstead. She maintained a similar position in the newly merged enterprise, becoming Bank of America's vice president and manager of diversity development. Though her department was smaller—"I'm it, plus a couple of secretaries"— she nurtured the bank's diversity network, geographically based groups designed to encourage career development through workshops, mentoring, and other educational activities. However, she admitted the new organization was not as progressive and "advanced" as her former employer. The merged organization was definitely more traditional, conservative, hierarchical—and assimilationist. There were no minority support groups, and the message was that "we are all Bank of America." Diversity consultants were still coming in from time to time. The bank had continued outreach programs in the wake of the 1992 riots, a civic disaster that saddened Hempstead but one that she also felt had been useful as a wake-up call.

June Jones was Hempstead's analogue at Los Angeles's giant First Inter-State Bank. In a pattern similar to that described by Hempstead, Jones had gone through a conversion from being a more aggressive proponent of numbers-oriented affirmative action to trying to integrate affirmative action and diversity goals into other programs more directly tied to productivity and quality control. (Indeed Jones was ahead of the curve: the desire to merge diversity with other management initiatives would become more pronounced in the mid-1990s.)

Another well-known L.A. corporate insider and affirmative action–diversity activist was Dave Barclay, appointed Hughes Aircraft's vice president for workforce diversity in 1990. Barclay had a background in civil rights activism and during the 1960s had worked for the California Fair Housing and Employment Department, the state counterpart to the federal EEOC. Barclay went with Hughes in 1970 and rose through the ranks of Hughes's EEO division. In October 1987 he testified before the U.S. House Subcommittee on Employment Opportunities as a result of Hughes's being the target of several discrimination complaints and court cases. (Hughes boosted its minority employment percentage from 10 to 30 percent before the layoffs of the 1990s. Barclay was responsible for Hughes's considering racial and ethnic balances during the layoffs.)

The discrimination complaints and court cases helped focus the attention of top management to diversity issues, as did Hughes's growing number of minority and women's support groups. Growing overt racism, increased polarization among ethnic groups, language differences, and management resistance to change were all problems to be solved under the new managing diversity umbrella. One bright spot for Barclay was Hughes's many outreach programs to black high schools and colleges, especially to black engineering colleges in the South, including Morgan State and Jackson State. Barclay was profiled in several minority-oriented business magazines and became a star speaker on the conference circuit. He had made the acquaintance of several people in the external consulting business when he brought them to Hughes, notably Price Cobbs, Helen Mendes, and two UCLA faculty members.

Hughes and the big banks were not the only corporations hosting diversity seminars. Utilities such as Southern California Edison, Pacific Bell, and the Los Angeles Department of Water and Power hosted several diversity consultants. Hughes went further and developed its own internal trainers and consultants, one of whom was Pam Fomalont.

Networking in a Troubled Multicultural Mecca

Like the suave Lewis Griggs, charming, blond, blue-eyed Pam Fomalont hardly resembled the stereotype of a typical PC diversity monger, nor was she the product of a multicultural background. On the contrary, Fomalont grew up in the 1960s in rural, poor-to-working class, all-white Oregon. She worked long hours in the fields during summers before graduating high school and then joining the U.S. Air Force. The air force helped pay her way through the University of Oregon, where she acquired a B.A. in sociology in 1981, an M.A. in public administration in 1983, and a strong civil rights ideology. Shortly after, she was hired by Dave Barclay as an affirmative action officer for Hughes Aircraft in 1986. Fomalont had been conducting diversity training for Hughes employees shortly before she fell victim to the downsizing scythes in 1991.

Fomalont bounced back and quickly joined the American Society for Training and Development's Los Angeles chapter and became chair of its Cultural Diversity Division within a year. The division, formed in 1990, had been headed by Devra Korwin, a former drama teacher who was transferring her skills to business as a communications consultant and "just getting into diversity." (Korwin departed in 1992 when she obtained a human resources position at a health maintenance organization.) About 110 people eventually joined the division.

Fomalont brought great zeal to the job, and the campaign to build a strong diversity network began with high expectations. By 1991, southern California's rapid demographic transformation was displayed to *Workforce 2000* skeptics as proof that an imminent Third World America was indeed at hand. The L.A. area seemed a laboratory for diversity management theory and practice. One-third of all new immigrants settled in California, more than half of them in the Los Angeles area. There are more Laotians and Cambodians in Los Angeles than anyplace else outside of Laos and Cambodia; the same is true for Koreans and Filipinos; and there is likely a greater concentration of persons of Mexican descent in East Los Angeles than any place other than Mexico City. By the early 1990s, *Time* magazine characterized Los Angeles as the "New Ellis Island," and David Rieff titled his book about the city *Los Angeles: Capital of the Third World.*[6]

By 1991, the entire Golden State, especially southern California, was ripe for diversity management recipes. State and local government, along with the state's massive higher education system, were awash with affirmative action mandates and parity goals for workforce and student body proportional representation. Then came the 1992 "Rainbow Riots" and a long, deep recession.

Instead of happily proclaiming "The Future Is Now in L.A!" southern California's diversity consultants had to build their policy movement within a simmering ethnic cauldron that made discussion of diversity policies both more urgent and more difficult than on the national level. There were the unending broadcasts of the videotaped beating of Rodney King and the subsequent civil disturbance that followed the initial acquittal of the accused police officers; next ensued ethnically polarized local and state political contests, rising crime, strained social services, rapidly increasing white flight, and the passage of proposition 187 (which denied public benefits to illegal immigrants), capped by the polarizing O. J. Simpson double-murder trial.

The prolonged recession and the financial near-collapse of several counties and other public agencies sharply curtailed business and government abilities to retain or hire minorities, women, diversity consultants—or anyone else. Worse, California's steep slide from boom to bust mocked diversity consultants' boasts concerning the alleged economic benefits of immigration and multiethnic workforces. These fractures tested nearly every aspect of diversity theory and practice and made both policy crusaders and potential clients deeply anxious.

Southern California is a fascinating vantage point from which to watch the birth and halting progress of the diversity machine. The demographic imperative remained strong, but economic, political, and cultural factors combined in unpredictable ways to stall—temporarily?—the progress of diversity management in the greater L.A. area. The riots and the Simpson trial, for example, exerted powerful, contradictory desires to talk—or not talk—about race relations. Could the diversity machine triumph over all these obstacles?

Paradoxically, however, downsizing and mergers furnished leaders for the local diversity industry by providing a bumper crop of unemployed human resources and affirmative action officers. They attempted to carry on the workforce diversity crusades as external consultants.

A central focus for such efforts was the American Society for Training and Development's (ASTD) Los Angeles chapter, a networking and educational organization for many current and ex–human resources personnel. At ASTD seminars and conferences, independent consultants mingled with current or former corporate and government training officers. Many also searched for new contacts, new jobs, or entirely new careers. Graduate and professional students occasionally checked out ASTD gatherings to preview career possibilities. The 1,100-member ASTD-LA is a branch of the fifty-year-old ASTD National, headquartered in Alexandria, Virginia, which bills itself as the world's largest full-service professional association for human resources specialists with some 25,000 members. An additional 25,000 are dues-paying members of local chapters but do not hold concurrent membership in ASTD National. ASTD National publishes *Training and Development Magazine,* a journal devoted to human resources studies, as well as other books; the organization maintains a Washington lobbyist. The much smaller ASTD-LA chapter publishes a monthly newsletter, *InterChange,* which advertises various ASTD-sponsored workshops and educational and speaker events.

ASTD-LA diversity division launched a somewhat awkward first session on managing the multicultural workforce in February 1991, when about thirty-five people convened over breakfast at a Studio City restaurant to hear four panelists briefly define the field, then take questions and answers. Consultant Ann Kusomoto, a former EEO consultant at Atlantic Richfield, gave the standard introductory definition: diversity management is not simply affirmative action or "managing minorities"; it's an inclusive "relationship issue" that promotes productivity and enhances an organization's competitive position. Consultant Catherine Lawrence cheered the goal of moving from denying differences to more actively recognizing one's own prejudices, but she simultaneously warned against promoting new stereotypes and called groupthink "powerful stuff." Occidental Petroleum vice president Terry Owens complained that "we ask people to meet white male standards and this causes stress." As evidence he cited a study on African American executives' high blood pressure. Not unexpectedly, the *Los Angeles Times* spokesperson was the most radical. Gerald Alcantar, the *Times's* staffing and communications manager, urged the most aggressive diversity management rationale: the call for "accountability" by tying executives' bonuses to affirmative action and "minority development." He also insisted that "trainable" or "qualifiable" minorities—not just those fully qualified—should be considered for advancement.

Unlike many other diversity management forums, this panel was not preaching to the choir. The first question from the audience was refreshingly politically incorrect. A manager of a large medical facility stated, "I have a U.N. workforce. No two people are alike. I see a fundamental division: those who have the work ethic and those who do not. Some, especially the younger ones, are sloppy, slow. When they get written up and fired, they bring suit and claim harassment. Is this a diversity problem?" This was the wrong thing to say: she had blamed the victims, not the system.

Reeducation commenced. Kusomoto suggested this was not a diversity problem, but that the questioner should reconsider the different needs and motivations of her employees. Alcantar warned that some work standards are inappropriate. The *Times* stopped "losing good people" when it dropped spelling and typing tests for customer service applicants. Another audience member reminded everyone that "training doesn't end after the worker is hired."

Another questioner seconded consultant Lawrence's concern about promoting stereotypes through diversity training. This produced an amusing gaffe from the white male Occidental executive: "We put people in categories," said the vice president. "Stereotypes are true for some people." There was a nervous ripple of nervous laughter: even most of those in the audience knew that stereotypes could only be denounced in public. The two consultants on the panel looked mortified. They popped the problem of "understanding" stereotypes into the all-purpose blame-the-system framework: oppressive stereotypes have been created when organizational culture "feeds people's images of themselves" or when people "do what they can to survive economically."

Kusomoto then closed the morning meeting by urging patience: "Everyone's struggling with this. No one or no organization has arrived. It's a long-term process." The breakfast adjourned amid a flurry of business cards being exchanged.

A month later, a more formal, even somber, gathering of some seventy people convened at UCLA for a second ASTD panel on cultural conflict in the workplace. The session was given added urgency and salience by the recent police beating of Rodney King and the constant broadcast of the amateur videotape of that event. Indeed, the first panelist, African American sociologist Michael Woodard, invoked the incident to explain individual and institutional racism ("inequality resulting from routine operations of the system"). "You are agents of social change to develop positive evaluations of diversity," Woodard told us.

The doctrine of identity politics obviously dictated the composition of the panelists and what they would discuss. Buddy Takata, a retired Hughes Aircraft training and development manager, was the Asian who discussed Asians in the workplace. He maintained that Asians have few problems getting hired; the problem is the glass ceiling on promotions. Asians get pigeonholed, he said, as meticulous technologists with poor personnel skills. And the "model minority" myth had masked economic and social problems among new, poorer immigrants who were not well educated.

Jack Beal, an Atlantic Richfield Corporation vice president, provoked nervous laughter by joking about the absence of white males at the gathering. "I'm the minority," he observed. ARCO, he confessed, faced a typical problem. It was stuck in affirmative action's emphasis on the numbers and had not moved into more sweeping culture change, though he was pleased to point to significant numbers of promotions for women and minorities.

Latino issues went unaddressed because the Latino panelist, Blanco Barrera, an executive with Pacific Bell, didn't show up.

As at the first ASTD gathering, the first question from the audience was politically incorrect. American Red Cross trainer Paul McGuane had botched a diversity seminar when white males "felt attacked," and he asked how to avoid this. Naturally any resentment felt by white males could not be validated, so McGuane was treated to a series of patronizing prescriptions. Panelist Michael Woodard admitted that "this is a very different society than the one white males were raised in." Takata urged that "these people should be honest with themselves." Consultant Ann Kusomoto counseled that such workshops must "be set up to make each participant feel safe. But there will be levels of discomfort." Others suggested using a multicultural training team, balancing group discussions and exercises, and repeated an oft-cited diversity trainer motto: the consultant should do his or her own "inner work" and "know thyself."

This question ignited the moralism-pragmatism conflict. The issue of white males triggered a surge of civil rights moralism from Takata, who began grumbling about waning support of affirmative action. "The quota issue is a lot of garbage!" he snorted. Consultant Mark Strunin, active in the National Conference of Christians and Jews, sympathized but shifted the focus back to pragmatic business concerns. Strunin urged those present to consider business angles in promoting diversity and what "corporations really want: how to avoid lawsuits, serve customers, break into new ethnic markets, achieve smoother personnel functions and interpersonal relations." As the session adjourned amid the usual chatter and card exchanges, I met Pam Fomalont and her still-employed Hughes associate Dave Wagemaker. We would see more of one another as ASTD-LA, like the national diversity machine, struggled with more complex issues as the mid-1990s evolved.

Diversity Management Literature Takes Off

Any fledgling field must generate a critical mass of books, articles, and other media that attest to its subject matter's validity and importance. Diversity management has generated such a professional library. The gathering volume of books and articles has set the major themes for many of the diversity machine's conferences and workshops. Displays and sales of these books provide feedback on how managing diversity is being received by the public.

In the take-off year of 1991, diversity management books fairly exploded onto bookstore and library shelves. Among the several seminal diversity management books published were R. Roosevelt Thomas's *Beyond Race and Gender;* Marilyn Loden and Judith Rosener's *Workforce America!* David Jamieson and Julie O'Mara's *Managing Workforce 2000: Gaining the Diversity Advantage;* John Hernandez's *Managing a Diverse Workforce;* and Sondra Thiederman's two books, *Bridging Barriers for Corporate Success* and *Profiting in American's Multicultural Workforce.* Susan Jackson's compendium of analyses, *Diversity in the Workplace,* followed in 1992, as did Ann Morrison's landmark study of diversity policies in sixteen organizations, *The New Leaders.* In 1993 consultant John Hernandez published his second book, *The Diversity Advantage,* and Lee Gardenswartz and Anita Rowe published their massive *Managing Diversity: A Complete Desk Reference and Planning Guide,* followed in 1994 by their *Managing Diversity Survival Guide* and the expensive ($350) package, *The Diversity Tool Kit.*[7]

A trickle of more academic books and articles on the theory and impact of these policies began to appear. Academics appeared wary of the topic for political reasons. Dutch scholar Geert Hofstede had long been studying the impact of national cultures on corporations since the 1980s; he published *Culture's Consequences* in 1980 and *Cultures and Organizations* in 1991.[8] An academic association, the Academy of Management, had "The Management of Diversity" as the theme of its 1992 annual meetings. University of Michigan business professor Taylor Cox, Jr., published *Cultural Diversity in Organizations* in 1993.[9] In 1994, a compendium of conference-based papers was published in *Cultural Diversity in Organizations.*[10]

Two major newsletters provided articles, advertising, and a calendar-training bulletin of various diversity-related activities. The Seattle-based GilDeane Group began publishing *Training and Culture Newsletter* in 1988. In tune with the times, the publication's title changed to *Cultural Diversity at Work* in 1991. Subscriptions leveled out in the mid-1990s to about 2,000. The periodical covered a range of topics, from "Does Media Sabotage Diversity Efforts?" (November 1990), "Interviewing Candidates from Diverse Backgrounds" (January 1991), and "Resistance Is Part of the Change Process" (September 1992) to "Diversity Management: Putting Ideas into Practice" (January 1993) and "Beyond the White Male Paradigm" (1995). The editors also ran surveys of consultant concerns.

Managing Diversity began monthly publication in October 1991. Lee Gardenswartz and Anita Rowe, Harris Sussman, and other consultants contributed short articles and training tips as well as book reviews. It has a circulation of 8,000, though 4,000 are "multiple subscribers"—corporations, state, and federal government agencies (including the U.S. Postal Service and Social Security) that may purchase up to 500 issues for mass distribution. The articles were similar to those in other publications: "O.K. We've Raised Awareness: Now What?" (March 1993), "The Case for Hiring 'Diversity Professionals'" (December 1993), and "Managing Diversity in Stressful Times" (March 1994).

Most significant, the *Wall Street Journal* in 1993 began to run diversity-related themes on the front page of its second section, notably the columns by Leon Wynter on "Business and Race" and by Sue Shellenbarger on work and family issues.

Lewis Griggs's "Valuing Diversity" video training series soon had strong competition, most notably from Washington, D.C.–based BNA, *Bridges* and *A Winning Balance.* Several smaller firms entered the market with single-video training tapes, including two in 1993 by the same name: *The Power of Diversity.* Just as there were beginning to be too many training tapes, leading consultants grumbled that there were too many consultants, especially in view of the continuing recession and the building backlash among white males.

Cross-Cultural Consultant Profile II:
Sondra Thiederman

Sondra Thiederman exemplifies the business-oriented, pragmatic approach to cross-cultural training. She states flatly in her first book, *Bridging Cultural Barriers for Corporate Success,* that "cross-cultural management training must be marketed as something that will provide managers with practical knowledge and techniques that will make their jobs easier. Social work and conversion are secondary. The other goals—improving teamwork, promoting harmony, reducing racism—will happen but only if the manager sees a person benefit in the training."[1]

Thiederman was the most ideologically neutral diversity consultant whom I met or observed in action. Her UCLA doctoral training, coupled with a primary focus on immigrants rather than race, inhibits any drift into race and gender political correctness, especially the sloppy assumption that skin color is linked to individual or group viewpoints. Thiederman does not advocate organizational change nor does she attack corporate culture. She's sensitive to white males' interests and admits without hesitation that reverse discrimination has occurred.

By 1993, Thiederman was asking and receiving $2,500 per day (plus expenses) for keynote addresses and $3,000 for a full-day keynote and workshop. She had a second book, *Profiting in America's Multicultural Workplace,* and had made her first book into a commercial training videotape for Barr Films, *Bridging Cultural Barriers for Corporate Success.*[2] Through such efforts, she was expanding her client base.

Thiederman avoids shocking readers or clients with exaggerated, dire demographic forecasts. She rarely mentions the Hudson Institute's *Work-*

force 2000. Instead, she invokes more reassuring parallels with the past. History is simply repeating itself: early in the twentieth century, one out of five Americans was an immigrant or the child of immigrants, and that is again true today. Her brisk message: We've been through this before. Deal with it.

What's called for is not changing American culture but acquiring a little knowledge and sensitivity in interpreting and motivating a new mix of workers. Cultures vary in terms of linguistic rules concerning pauses, interruptions, volume, degree of directness, spontaneity, and type of ritualistic phrases that may be invoked. American society is a low-context culture, meaning that there are relatively few rules of proper behavior. While American culture places great emphasis on individual identity, freedom, and accomplishments, most Third World immigrants bring with them a more group-centered culture that mandates loyalty to family and community over individual aspirations.

Thiederman cites traditional American proverbs to illustrate how taken-for-granted, go-getter values of American society might baffle tradition and family-oriented immigrants from Third World lands: "There's no fool like an old fool," "God helps those who help themselves," "Busy hands are happy hands," and "Take the bull by the horns" embody American emphases on youth, individual initiative, activity, and ambition. She contrasts this with non-Western themes of harmony and balance, maintained by avoiding direct or negative confrontations, minimizing embarrassment to all participants and saving face; not calling attention to the individual at the expense of the group ("the nail that sticks out gets hammered down"), and the primacy of the group, especially family, over the individual ("managers might also notice a tendency for workers not to seek promotions if to do so would separate them from the cultural group that generates their identity"). Authority figures are often regarded with much more deference in Third World lands. Therefore, "Be sensitive to the fact that participative management and an informal relationship with the boss can make immigrant and ethnic workers uncomfortable."

Much of her advice on communication and language is practical common sense: speak slowly and clearly, avoid slang, organize your thoughts, check for understanding frequently, keep it simple. Thiederman's books are full of basic explanations, examples, and tips for communicating with immigrants.

Some of this information is imparted by way of what might be seen as an individualized version of R. Roosevelt Thomas' cultural audit. A "Cultural-Diversity Quiz" opens her second book:

1. On average, how long do native-born Americans maintain eye contact?
   a. 1 second
   b. 15 seconds
   c. 30 seconds
2. True or False: One of the few universal ways to motivate workers, regardless of cultural background, is through the prospect of a promotion.
3. When an Asian client begins to give you vague answers before closing a deal, saying things like, "It will take time to decide" or "We'll see," the best thing to do is:
   a. Back off a bit, he or she may be trying to say "no" without offending you.
   b. Supply more information and data about your service or product, especially in writing.
   c. Push for a "close," his or her vagueness is probably a manipulative tactic.
   d. State clearly and strongly that you are dissatisfied with his or her reaction so as to avoid any misunderstanding.
4. True or False: One of the few universals in etiquette is that everyone likes to be complimented in front of others.
5. Which of the following statements is (are) true?
   a. It is inappropriate to touch Asians on the hand.
   b. Middle Eastern men stand very close as a means of dominating the conversation.
   c. Mexican men will hold another man's lapel during conversation as a sign of good communication.
6. Building relationships slowly when doing business with Hispanics is generally:
   a. A bad idea; if you don't move things along, they will go elsewhere.
   b. A bad idea; they expect native-born professionals to move quickly, so will be disoriented if you do not.
   c. A good idea; it may take longer, but the trust you build will be well worth the effort.

   (Answers: 1a, 2f, 3a, 4f, 5c, 6c)[3]

By 1993, health care organizations made up about 40 percent of her client base; another 10 percent are hotels and restaurants, and the rest are other service-oriented organizations such as banks and in-flight food providers. The recession dampened business somewhat. Like Lillian Roybal Rose, Thiederman suspects that about 20 percent of the workshops she conducts are mandated by employers who may be "running scared" about discrimination lawsuit possibilities; another 10 percent may be the product of trendy flavor-of-the-month motives. Whatever the case, Thiederman maintained, her efforts can still promote awareness and change. Her major complaint is that of all diversity consultants: "People want things quick and quantitative; this is a soft-skill *process.*" Like everyone else in the diversity business, she regrets that there are no studies offering quantitative proof that the policies work.

Thiederman has lately broadened her focus to include gender, sexual orientation, and disabilities. She has also followed a trend in some diversity circles by shying away from her earlier emphasis on detailed descriptions of ethnic cultures out of fear of reinforcing stereotypes.

Though her influence has spread through her books and her new video, Thiederman has noticed that being white in a heavily nonwhite industry can have drawbacks—but also advantages. "I think white audiences might be more at ease with me." Again, like Griggs, she's especially pleased when she draws praise for her expertise from minorities, who are sometimes suspicious of white female consultants.

Though it has not happened to her, Thiederman has heard about confrontational blow-ups in diversity training. She acknowledges that multiculturalism and diversity training can cause conflict and polarization. Thiederman avoids this by going easy on discussions of racism and sexism. She also emphasizes consensus: "We need to emphasize commonalities as well as respecting differences." She acknowledges that the late 1980s' forecasts of drastic demographic change in the workforce may have been premature, but the ethnic mix of the customer base is changing rapidly. That is what is catching CEO attention on cultural diversity training.

The Consultant in Action

For her October 1993 afternoon workshop "Managing the Multicultural Staff" for Palm Haven Health Care Network (a pseudonym), Sondra Thiederman is dressed with professional aplomb in a beige knit business suit with a colorful scarf around her neck. She also sports her trademark plastic badge: "Just because we're equal does not mean we're the same." While some forty, mostly female employees finish a furnished lunch of salad and sandwiches, Thiederman moves through the room mingling informally and distributing a seventeen-page background book and manual.

Everyone knows that Palm Haven's personnel manager has scheduled all employees to receive four hours of cross-cultural training (during morning or afternoon sessions) because of increased friction among the increasingly multicultural members of the staff, as well as misunderstandings between staff and an expanding multicultural mix of patients (and patients' families).

At one o'clock, Thiederman moves to the front of the room, attaches a microphone to her collar, and begins. She seeks to put participants at ease by poking fun at diversity trainer stereotypes. "Some people, especially outside of California, think: 'Oh, oh, here comes the California diversity trainer. This is going to be touchy-feely or confrontational.' Well, we're not going to do anything weird or confrontational—like the trainer I recently saw who 'sensed tension' in the room and had participants massage one another's necks. The only way that this embarrassing exercise relieved tension was because people were glad it was over!" A ripple of laughter moves around the room. People seem at ease.

Moving from humor to business, Thiederman briskly outlines the goals of her training: "The idea is to sustain teamwork and productivity, minimize stereotypical thinking (which everyone does), make you more aware of how to interpret behavior of others, to provide skills to motivate others who are different, and communicate across cultural lines."

Like other diversity consultants, Thiederman tries to create an atmosphere for candid discussion by providing ground rules of "mutual responsibilities": (1) really listen, (2) be cautious with generalizations (if someone feels a generalization does not apply, speak up), (3) responses should be free and open, with no straining to be politically correct, and (4) participation may inevitably involve taking chances with "ethnographic dynamite."

Thiederman jests about her own limits: "If you raise a problem and I don't know how to deal with it, I'll say, 'I haven't the foggiest idea how to solve your problem' or I'll use a typical trainer's trick. I'll say, 'Isn't that an interesting point. Does anyone else have anything to say about it?' Then I'll take your answer and make it mine."

Thiederman then asks participants to name the author of a harsh quotation about immigration: "Immigrants negatively influence America, by infusing it with their spirit, warping its directions, turning it into a heterogeneous, incoherent, distracted mass."

"Rush Limbaugh," says a woman on the front row. Everyone laughs.

"No, it isn't Rush, it isn't David Duke, and it isn't Archie Bunker," states Thiederman.

"Ross Perot?"

"Jessie Jackson?"

"Pete Wilson?"

"Diane Feinstein?"

Someone finally names the author: "Thomas Jefferson."

With a mock flourish, Thiederman rewards the respondent with one of her buttons. Everyone laughs.

"Good. Now, how many of you have German ancestry?" asks Thiederman. "Well, Jefferson was talking about Germans. He was worried about 'Germanization.' . . . I do not put this up to denigrate the founding fathers, but because it has a familiar ring. You hear this today. We have a history of looking at people who are new as threatening and strange. What are the problems some of you might have with immigrants?"

A middle-aged white woman quickly volunteers, "It's the language. Speaking a foreign language in the workplace."

This would be the dominant issue of the day. Palm Haven had an official "English-only" policy, but it was not enforced. Immigrant workers lapsed into their native language both at work and during breaks.

Thiederman admits that this is a common problem. "Why is it so hard to enforce?"

The head of the nursing staff proffers, "It varies by department. The housekeeping staff has the highest number of Hispanics, and they speak Spanish a lot. I don't feel it's my place to tell the housekeeping staff to speak English. And some of the nurses speak Togali." Another person complains about Asian medical consultants who spoke in their native tongue.

"It's divisive to teamwork," agrees Thiederman. "People may feel they're being talked about or excluded. . . . But sometimes jokes or other phrases lose meaning when translated into English." Thiederman suggests asking people politely to speak in English.

Several members in the workshop disagree, saying that different immigrant groups have different standards of "sophistication" and "courtesy."

Thiederman asks them to rethink such ideas. "Sometimes people slip into their native language without thinking about it or because they're lonely. Another source of this problem is when someone from a new group gets a promotion; it is easier and keeps bonds up to use the native language. . . . There's the problem of they're thinking they have to give up their culture and heritage if they are asked to speak English only."

A related series of complaints surfaces about immigrant workers' clustering together, coolly excluding outsiders. Thiederman responds that it is natural for people to congregate with others like themselves, observing wryly that such clustering occurs even at diversity conferences. She asks, "If you were in a foreign nation, would you struggle with language and customs of the natives or would you go with people like yourself?"

"But they're cliquish," complains a head nurse. "They especially exclude new people."

Thiederman admonishes workshoppers to take more initiative and break the ice with such groups: "Perhaps these should be almost forced at times to get things to open up."

"But people who move here should try to learn about American culture and language," protests the same head nurse. "And I don't see that on the part of a lot of people."

This comment produces a discussion of "American culture" and to what extent there should be pressures to assimilate. Finally, though, Thiederman wearies with continued complaining about clustering and in-group, out-group problems: "What I'm trying to distinguish here is between small stuff and the stuff that matters. Don't sweat the small stuff—things like eye contact. You can handle it."

The head nurse responds that explaining such differences could be difficult: "Some of the Filipino nurses are kind of cool and reserved. The patients like it, but the families think they're too detached. It's hard to explain that it's simply their cultural style."

"During the civil rights movement, we were not supposed to notice cultural differences," counsels Thiederman. "We were all to be considered alike. Now that's changing."

Cultural insensitivity can create unplanned problems in promotions, explains Thiederman. A local aerospace firm with a large number of Asian employees promoted an especially able, young worker who had been with the company a long time. In doing so, they bypassed an older Asian man who, largely because of his age, was an informal leader. Feeling humiliated, he quit, taking ten other workers with him. He felt he had no choice. "What could this organization have done to keep this from happening?"

The group initially decides that it is important to recognize subcultures and informal leaders. Thiederman seizes the opportunity to warn about an affirmative action dilemma. "But," cautioned Thiederman, "it doesn't mean that you promote the informal leader. *You don't lower standards.*" Thiederman suggests that supervisors might have informally discussed the situation with the older man.

The self-promoting individualism and outspokenness that many Americans take for granted may be viewed with distaste in other cultures, Thiederman explains. She contrasts the meaning of American and Japanese versions of the saying, "A rolling stone gathers no moss." To Americans, the phrase means, "Keep moving, or you will acquire the moss of lethargy, passivity, decay, and laziness." But the same phrase has the opposite meaning to Japanese: "If you move too much, you will fail to accumulate the moss of commitment, involvement, connections, and experience."

Thiederman adds that some cultures prize group harmony, and individual disruption of that harmony, including questioning of authority, is frowned on. And even when American norms and values are explained, newcomers may find them so strange as to be unbelievable—for a while.

Thiederman now comes to the delicate issue of racial discrimination. She admits that political correctness has led to hypersensitivity but that there are real problems of racism, such as the patient who complained about an African American nurse, "I don't want her, I want a real nurse." Some workshop participants shared similar stories.

The solution, says Thiederman, is to discuss differences more openly but also to stress the commonalities that everyone has beneath "the cloak of cultural differences."

"We need to find connections," instructs Thiederman. "For example, I was looking for a magazine to read on an airplane. I eyed *People* magazine. (I'm letting you in on the big secret that Ph.D.s read *People!*) The cover story was about Nick Nolte being the sexiest man alive. I was appalled—everyone knows it's Tom Cruise!—and I had to vent. There was a young woman in East Indian dress behind the counter, so completely on impulse, I said to her, 'Isn't this disgusting.' And she said, 'Yes it is—it should have been Tom Cruise!'"

Thiederman now confronts the key danger in diversity discussions: that talking about general cultural differences might seem like stereotyping. But stereotypes, she held, are rigid, negative, and limiting, and they do not allow for variations within the group. Careful discussion of general cultural differences should allow for the fact that not everyone in the group acts in accordance with his or her group culture. Spending time around these groups, Thiederman confidently insists, usually ends stereotypes.

To illustrate the inaccuracy of stereotypes, workshoppers discuss how they've been incorrectly stereotyped or mistakenly stereotyped others. (This proceeds good-naturedly, especially when a large Anglo woman recounts the misperceptions and surprises she and her short, Thai husband often encounter together in public settings.)

Thiederman returns to the difficulties of language and the perils of cross-cultural communication. English is not an easy language, even for those who speak it, says Thiederman, reciting a sign she saw in an English hotel: "Guests are encouraged to take advantage of the chambermaid."

The workshop comes to a close with some quick tips on "cross-cultural motivation":

- Provide cultural and psychological safety for employees.
- Interpret behavior correctly and provide proper feedback.
- Explain your perspective carefully.
- Communicate respect.
- Reinforce desired behavior with positive reinforcements.
- Acknowledge differences, recognize commonalities.

It is four-thirty, and most people leave quickly, trying to get out ahead of the worst of the five o'clock freeway rush hour. A few people come up to greet Thiederman with positive remarks, though Thiederman herself must get on the freeway in order to conduct an evening workshop for still another group of health care professionals.

Chapter 4

Recession, Rebellion, Riot

The Diversity Machine at Bay

The diversity machine shifted gears at the Second Annual National Diversity Conference, held at Washington, D.C.'s Sheraton Hotel in early May 1992. The initial take-off period of expansion and euphoria was waning. Consultants still had confidence that demography was destiny and that diversity management was the wave of the future, theories and techniques of diversity management were proliferating and being explored, and largely positive press attention continued to buoy public interest. But the problems raised or only partially explored at the First Annual National Diversity Conference had come home to roost.

Corporate downsizing showed no signs of easing, and human resources departments (which usually housed affirmative action and diversity functions) were being hit hard. The 1991 recession had lingered longer than anyone expected and was deepening sharply in the diversity laboratory of southern California. Worse, the riots over the Rodney King verdict only two weeks before were so recent and searing that they were rarely referenced. And the increasing white male rebellion against diversity programs had become so obvious that it could not be dismissed or denied.

Conference registration, sold out at more than 450 people, would never be higher. Corporate participation reached its zenith with ninety corporations (some with several representatives), among them: Aetna, Allstate, Amoco (three), AT&T (fifteen), American Express (fourteen), B.F. Goodrich (three), Coca-Cola (three), Digital Equipment (ten), Eastman Kodak (seventeen), Florida Power and Light (two), Gillette (two), Johnson and Johnson, Lockheed Missiles (four), Motorola Codex (six), Pacific Gas and Electric

104

(three), Polaroid (four), Prudential Insurance, Shearson Lehman (five), TRW (two), Walt Disney Company, and Xerox (two). Heavy industry was largely absent; consumer-oriented companies, utilities, high-tech, and defense contractors predominated. Since the site was Washington, the gathering drew the attention of several federal agencies, including the Army Corps of Engineers (four), CIA (seven), Environmental Protection Agency (two), Federal Aviation Authority, Naval Surface Warfare Center (two), Office of Personnel Management, NASA (five), Secret Service (two), U.S. Army (four), U.S. Department of Agriculture (eight), U.S. Department of Agriculture, Forest Service (four), and U.S. Postal Service (four). There were also a host of state and local government units as well as nonprofit groups, including several health care organizations, the American Association of Retired Persons, and the National Education Association.

The presence of star keynoter R. Roosevelt Thomas, Jr., signaled both the significance of the Griggs-sponsored gathering and the increased emphasis on business-based pragmatism. Thomas also pushed his call for an expanded definition of diversity beyond race and gender. Interestingly, he offered the audience a tactical reason not published in his writing: an expanded definition of diversity would serve to prevent accusations, such as those originally leveled at Thomas, that "diversity" was just another code word for advancing black issues. Thomas amused the crowd with his distinctive metaphors. A jar of jellybeans described genuine diversity as a unique, collective mixture of all differences and similarities in each organization. Such mixtures included race and gender but also other variables, such as sexual orientation, age, and work and family issues. Affirmative action was basically flawed because it emphasized minority recruitment and white male assimilation. This would not work because it was like "grafting limbs from a Georgia peach tree onto an old oak tree." The "root concepts" of this white male corporate culture tree would have to be challenged and transformed. And when you try to change the roots, Thomas warned, look out! That's when the defensive "root guards" emerge.

Thomas predicted that total quality management and diversity techniques would merge in a shared emphasis on empowerment, employee commitment, and efficiency in a downsized environment. Globalization would reinforce the need for diverse perspectives. With a nod to the terminology of the conference producer, Lewis Griggs, Thomas suggested that asking managers to truly appreciate and really value diversity might be asking too much; mere understanding of differences might be a better goal. In any case, said Thomas imperiously, in the long run, managing diversity will render obsolete the concepts of affirmative action and valuing differences.

The market-savvy Griggs, however, was already moving beyond both valuing or managing diversity. He was producing a new video training series, "Valuing Relationships," in which valuing diversity was merely one factor in obtaining "synergy" from human relationships. In a luncheon keynote on the second day of the conference, Griggs blended diversity into his newer and wider vision. He restated his diversity evangelism and insisted that corporate and government leaders must undergo a similar, personal conversion and "start at their own center and do their own work." Leaders, not workers, must change. They must abandon demands that workers assimilate to the dominant culture and the assumption that "equal opportunity is designed to make me comfortable with you." Leaders, like everyone else, must "let go, quit studying and do diversity." The only way they can keep their cherished control is by changing. As leaders realize the importance of relationships and trust in capitalistic enterprise, declared Griggs, then valuing differences must be seen as a resource in globalizing markets. People must be nicer to one another. Concluded Griggs, "We must learn to treat clients and coworkers as we treat siblings and parents."

Griggs's preaching fell flat according to several persons in the new discussion group to which I'd been assigned (a practice continued from the first conference); on the other hand, reaction to Thomas was largely favorable. Like the previous year's group, this one was supposed to raise and assess sensitive topics in rapid-fire fashion. The new group contained a mix of twenty-two people from Digital, AT&T, American Express, Chase Manhattan, Pacific Gas and Light, NYNEX, Bell Atlantic, and Associated Press, plus government entities such as the Tennessee Valley Authority, U.S Department of Agriculture, and Lawrence Livermore Labs. Compared to the general convention, we had a hugely disproportionate number of white males: five.

One white male from the Associated Press immediately challenged Griggs's authenticity: "Where does *he* live? What's *his* lifestyle? How integrated is *his* life?" A woman from AT&T complained Griggs "had nothing new to say. He was patronizing. He provided basic information that most of us are beyond." A man from the American Psychological Association jeered that Griggs's materials "were a lot of pabulum. He was a white person. What validity could he have?" a remark that cracked open a ticklish topic that was immediately seized on by our preassigned group facilitator, a Hispanic consultant from the Bay Area: Could white males authentically discuss diversity? There was ambivalence. One or two people delicately suggested that whites had credibility problems in this profession. Others argued that white males needed to be included to legitimate the field lest diversity departments turn out to be yet another corporate minority ghetto.

"People of difference are being relegated to certain departments," grumbled a black man from Digital. "This is true of diversity work. At these conventions we have the 'same faces, different places.'" A black female from AT&T agreed: "There were no white faces at the dinner table last night."

The facilitator posed a new question: What were the chief roadblocks to promoting diversity? Responses came quickly: "rhetoric without action" and fear of change. "The organizations won't look at the deep roots," said a woman from the TVA, alluding to Roosevelt Thomas's culture-tree metaphor.

This second allusion to Thomas, though, triggered criticisms of the guru: some felt Thomas was premature in assuming that diversity was no longer confused with affirmative action and "minority interests." A white female from Mars Inc. confessed she'd been called a zealot there when, after reading Roosevelt Thomas's articles, she suggested a cultural audit. A white female from the TVA suggested a solution that worked at TVA: rename the audit a "cultural assessment." A woman from the U.S. Department of Agriculture credited Thomas's consulting with moving the department's diversity effort away from confusion with affirmative action: "Thomas broadened and defined the concept."

Talk of moving away from affirmative action stirred the moralists. The woman from the TVA insisted, "We must not abandon affirmative action and valuing diversity. You can't take up managing diversity on its own. You must get the numbers up." A white woman from Digital insisted that managers must be held accountable with goals and timetables for promotion. Several in the group complained that corporations still demand immediate, bottom-line results from diversity efforts, yet there was still no proof.

But a black man from a U.S. Postal Service center in Indiana raised a note of caution about mandatory diversity techniques: "When managers perceived they were forced to do this, they put up a wall." He was also cynical about the role of consultants, who "raise issues and offer to sell us solutions. They have two faces." No one raised any objections.

A Different Voice in a Sensible Key

It became obvious that discussion of conversations about women's issues at workforce diversity conferences, especially by women themselves, seemed far more muted and civil than at academic gatherings. Keynoter Patricia Diaz

Dennis, a vice president for corporate affairs with U.S. Sprint and United Telecom, struck this tone in a very commonsense perspective on difficulties and discrimination women face in the workplace. She artfully blended competing ideological themes of equity feminism (law and workplace policies should treat men and women alike) and gender feminism (women have different, needs, talents, and leadership styles).

"Women are more prepared than they think," said Dennis. "They must seize opportunities." They must also define themselves lest others do it for them. She gave full credit to her husband for encouraging her to attend law school in the 1970s. She'd begun her career as the only Latina at an L.A. law firm and was then appointed to the National Labor Relations Board in 1983 which she regarded as an "overwhelming experience." She next moved onto the Federal Communications Commission, then another law firm, and then became a lobbyist for U.S. Sprint. "Discrimination increases as you move higher," she warned referring to the so-called glass ceiling of subtle discrimination. Having done and said all that, Dennis was nonetheless forced to concede, "Women are different. Jobs are not a first priority." And "life changes when you have a child."

I listened for rumbles of dissent, looks of dismay, even boos or hisses—reactions not unlikely at academic gatherings. But at the Second Annual Diversity Conference, I could detect no protest. She got a warm round of applause, and her comments went unremarked in my discussion group.

When the topic turned to white males, however, corporate and university responses were much more alike.

Confronting the White Male Rebellion

So important was the problem of white male backlash that the 1992 conference featured both a panel discussion and a workshop on the hot topic. Diversity consultants had found themselves on the front lines of a gathering white male rebellion against reverse discrimination and political correctness. Consultants had become what journalist Tom Wolfe wryly termed "flak catchers": they took the heat for policies implemented by elites without open discussion or debate. Consultants often found themselves rationalizing or defending affirmative action. Diversity consultants became the visible targets for passively or actively antagonistic white males increasingly emboldened by the soaring popularity of talk radio, especially Rush Limbaugh.

Real or perceived reverse discrimination was the primary source of white male protest, along with so-called white male bashing on talk television and within some feminist and multicultural circles. But like social scientists and the elite press, political correctness blinded most diversity consultants to recognizing any validity in white men's complaints. I was surprised to discover that few consultants—most with human resources and affirmative action backgrounds—were aware of extensive race norming of employment exams; fewer still knew that the 1991 Civil Rights Act had declared such practices illegal. And few had any idea of grossly disparate standards that universities and professional schools were using in preferential admissions and hiring.[1] Even when faced with such data, however, most fell back on arguments of cultural relativism: test scores and grades were biased tools used to maintain white male domination.

Discussion of white male resistance was somewhat risky inasmuch as the topic triggered the tensions between civil rights moralists and business-based pragmatists. Moralists rushed to defend affirmative action. They wished to confront charges of reverse discrimination head-on with denials and counter-arguments of white male privilege. This sometimes led to white male bashing and gave diversity training a bad name. The cooler, business-oriented pragmatists, on the other hand, wished to distance diversity efforts from affirmative action entanglements. They were willing to acknowledge whites' feelings—if not fully accepting the reality—about reverse discrimination and try to include whites as a category in diversity training.

Key Articles on White-Male Backlash

White male backlash ("defensiveness, resistance, backlash, scapegoating, blame") emerged as the dominant concern in a 1992 survey of consultants by the editor of *Cultural Diversity at Work*. Nearly every other survey would come to the same conclusion. "The biggest challenge facing diversity trainers today is how to handle backlash," stated Michael Mobley and Tamara Payne in a late 1992 *Training and Development* article titled "Backlash!"[2] The problem would break into national headlines by cover stories: "White Male Paranoia" in *Newsweek* (March 29, 1993); "White, Male, and Worried," in *BusinessWeek* (January 31, 1994); and "No White Men Need Apply?" in *U.S. News and World Report* (February 13, 1995).

Some professional writers tried to maintain a fairly neutral and analytical approach to the problem. Mobley and Payne's long *Training and Development Magazine* article provided a list of backlash's complex causes: deep-seated biases and prejudices; lack of jobs and increased competition for resources; race and gender as political football issues; sensationalist journalism that can create scapegoats and highlight stereotypes; that people are comfortable with those similar to them and uncomfortable with others who are different; political correctness as direct threat to First Amendment rights; confusion of political correctness with diversity, multiculturalism, pluralism, equal opportunity, and affirmative action; poor implementation of affirmative action and EEO programs; and whites and males tired of feeling guilty—the Demonic White Male Syndrome.[3]

Mobley and Payne admitted that affirmative action efforts and some diversity training had sowed seeds of discord by putting the burden of change on white males. The relative absence of white male diversity trainers had given diversity consulting the appearance of interest group lobbying. They wrote, "Many existing programs may foster backlash. And backlash can eventually kill a program."[4] Mobley and Payne were almost alone among writers and consultants in suggesting that targeted or set-aside positions create backlash. They were also nearly alone in pointing out the seeming clash between antidiscrimination laws emphasizing equal treatment for all individuals and personnel policies treating people on the basis of cultural differences. Diversity training with the best of intentions can lead to discriminatory practices.

To avoid backlash, Mobley and Payne suggested several strategies: (1) get management aboard before a diversity training program is implemented, (2) involve employees before the design of the program, (3) use an inclusive definition of diversity, (4) use well-qualified professionals (including white males), (5) acknowledge resistance, (6) use experiential activities, (7) affirm each person's experience, (8) value sameness as well as differences, (9) put an end to the PC police—don't encourage people to pay lip-service to a politically correct agenda, (10) communicate management's expectations and business connections, (11) "laugh, smile and enjoy," (12), follow up and reward those who incorporate a diversity mind-set into their jobs, and (13) create an open atmosphere.

Most other books and articles, however, took a strong ideological stance. The most popular theme was that diversity challenged the silent system of white male privilege, a concept popularized in the radical classic, "White Privilege: Unpacking the Invisible Knapsack," by Peggy McIntosh, a Wellesley College women's studies professor.[5] Deemed the "Pol Pot of Education" by opponents of her public school reforms, McIntosh, in politically correct fashion, transferred Marx's class conflict model to race and gender relations.[6] She argued that white males, like Marx's bourgeoisie, were all "privileged" people who took for granted some forty-six advantages—for example:

- I can, if I wish, arrange to be in the company of people of my race most of the time.
- If I should need to move, I can be pretty sure of renting or purchasing housing in an area which I can afford and in which I would want to live.
- I can go shopping alone most of the time, fairly well assured that I will not be followed or harassed by store detectives.
- I can turn on the television or open to the front page of the paper and see people of my race widely and positively represented.
- Whether I use checks, credit cards, or cash, I can count on my skin color not to work against the appearance that I am financially reliable.
- I am never asked to speak for all the people of my racial group.[7]

University of Massachusetts Education School dean Baily Jackson used McIntosh's "white privilege" concept to articulate a common written and oral standard diversity response to white male rebellion against reverse discrimination: "For many folks who are critical of affirmative action, the issue is how to regain their former privileged status; they don't like the increased competition. Life would be much easier if they could shrink the competition back to where it used to be, particularly in a time when there's so much volatility in the workplace."[8]

PC or Psychology? Two Conference Responses to White Male Backlash

McIntosh's theories were in the background of a panel discussion at the Second Annual National Diversity Conference, "White Male Reactions and Work Force Diversity." Consultant David Tulin warmed up the audience by asking what they hoped to hear. Answers were eagerly returned:
"Understanding!
"Why white males react!"
"What are their fears?"
"How does diversity benefit them?"
"Ditto!" (laughter)
"Overcoming denial!"
"Twelve-step recovery programs for white males!"
"Candid and hard-hitting analysis!"
The panelists, in fact, delivered little candid and hard-hitting analysis. What the audience got instead was an elaborate rationalization of white males' complaints. Consultant Marion Gindes outlined white males' fears of losing power, majority status, taken-for-granted privileges, and the benefits

gained through informal rules of the old-boy network. David Tulin observed that white men did not understand the concept or reality of institutional discrimination. He suggested some pithy putdowns of reverse discrimination complaints: "There's been an affirmative action program for white males for 200 years." As for any grumbling about ethnic support groups, "the Chamber of Commerce is basically 1,000 white men." Tulin offered more varied causes of white male discontent in his handout, "Resistance to Diversity Programming." Among them:

- Assimilation as the national and organizational role-model instead of pluralism.
- Shrinking economic pie increases competition for the slices.
- Affirmative Action implementers use quotas as the quick-fix, setting up minorities and women for failure, frustration and hostility.
- A slow, incremental "with all deliberate speed" Affirmative Action process undermines the ability to achieve the "critical mass" necessary to change relationships and break down stereotypes.
- Subconscious belief by many white men that their success was not based on competence but on "old boy" Affirmative Action, and concomitant fear that they will be "exposed" as incompetent and/or displaced.

Digital vice president Bill Hanson edged closer to acknowledging the legitimacy of white males' complaints. Their seemingly hostile silence, said Hanson, stemmed from politically correct pressure to "say the right thing" and from lack of involvement with affirmative action and diversity issues. Hanson thought backlash was a symptom of three developments: a widening gap between public and private views, that whites' problems were being ignored, and that "affirmative action is going too far." Rather than follow through, Hanson quickly sat down.

The question-and-answer session was tepid. In response to practical questions about dealing with backlash, fear, resentment, and "denial," general bromides were offered. Panelists advised being "patient and nonconfrontational" and to take more time to talk and increase communication. Responding to downsizing queries, Marion Gindes answered that white males no longer have an extra measure of security provided by their privileged status as white males; they have to live with the same insecurity as everyone else. Hanson pointed out an irony: most white males were unconcerned about affirmative action issues until the specter of downsizing loomed.

A more crowd-pleasing performance on the topic was turned in by Denver psychologist-consultant Anthony Ipsaro, who offered an illuminating social-psychological portrait of white males laced with tension-breaking humor. "White males are feeling like White Ignored Male Personnel: WIMPs," quipped Ipsaro. Not all white males are the same, he observed. Some wield considerable power; some do not. Hard work alone gets anyone only so far; "even white males hit glass ceilings."

Ipsaro emphasized the "male" in "white male." Affirmative action and diversity efforts could rightly or wrongly be perceived as a threat to a male's primary source of identity: his job. Men get little satisfaction or sense of identity outside their job. And "middle-management white males are getting killed by downsizing." Hence, the backlash.

Ipsaro was one of the few presenters I heard at any diversity conference who praised the core values of American society, emphasizing that the United States is one of the few countries that strives for equal access regardless of race, color, or creed. He pleased workshoppers by arguing that these traits could be combined with diversity, empowerment, and collaborative efforts, and that less competition could bring about a "renaissance of American capitalism." But Ipsaro's criticisms of hard-line affirmative action and the potentially polarizing aspects of emphasizing differences brought a sharp response from a corporate patron, Motorola vice president Roberta Gutman, who had employed him as a consultant at Motorola. Although she chuckled good-naturedly throughout his talk, Gutman took issue with Ipsaro's warnings about coercive forms of diversity in the form of goals and timetables. Despite his recommendations, she said, Motorola nonetheless had a strong top-down push for ethnic and gender diversity. Managers had been told, "If you don't do this, we will move you out'—Anthony doesn't like me to talk about this," Gutman added.

Herbert Wong's Wish List: "Total Diversity" and Unwelcome Survey Surprises

Herbert Z. Wong, conference co-organizer and recipient of a University of Michigan Ph.D. in psychology, gave an all-too-detailed keynote lecture describing a "total organizational systems approach." Some audience members began to doze during an excruciatingly detailed and dull oral presentation. But Wong's handout laid out the breathtaking scope of what sophisticated diversity merchants would like to do if their clients provided free rein and a blank check. Wong's "total organizational" approach included these components:

Diversity climate surveys and organizational cultural scans

Strategic planning and organizational development design

Organizational diagnosis and assessment

Executive briefings and seminars

Diversity survey feedback

Diversity process consultation

Culture-specific training programs

Career development seminars

Diversity training seminars

Training-for-trainers programs

Coaching and mentoring programs

Employee involvement, empowerment, and team building

Continuous diversity improvement process programs

Diversity leadership skills seminars

Equal employment opportunity and affirmative action update programs

Sexual harassment prevention seminars

Workplace accommodation programs

Sales and marketing to diversity programs

The price of all this was never mentioned, but other consultants had sold similar packages at $250,000 and above. Wong did list the usual "factors for success": commitment from the top; strategic planning; employee involvement and empowerment; employee-defined (i.e., ethnic and women's) support groups; outreach, recruitment, and retention monitoring; mentoring; and accountability (evaluating or rewarding managers based on goals and timetables performance).

Yet even the first steps of Wong's total diversity approach could be fraught with peril. During a subsequent conference workshop, NYNEX's diversity director Joseph Anderson and Frank D. Wilson, the company's external consultant, focused on how to conduct a cultural audit, the first step of Wong's comprehensive strategy. The NYNEX audit was broad in demographic focus, inclusive, and designed to expand organizational culture and foster diversity initiatives.

An initial task, both speakers admitted, was getting through the CEO's door. Anderson recommended an external consultant, perhaps a white male, to avoid the appearance of interest group advocacy or "black packing" and to give some appearance of neutrality—especially if the audit results contained any bad news. Even if the CEO agreed, however, the danger was that the audit would be as far as diversity change would get; the audit would be politely received, acknowledged, and used as "eyewash." Not only did top management have to back the process, they warned, but CEOs must be treated with great care—briefed in advance of any controversial developments or findings.

NYNEX's massive audit did indeed come up with some surprising and somewhat unwelcome surprises, especially for those at the Second National Annual Diversity Conference. It turned out that white male craftsmen, not women or minorities, were the most alienated, demoralized group in the NYNEX survey. (The possible reasons for this, including the reputation of phone companies' aggressive use of affirmative action, went unmentioned.) But what set off a cry of anguish from the packed workshop were data indicating that whites were consistently better educated than minorities and were widening the gap even further by disproportionately using company-sponsored educational benefits (such as tuition reimbursement) at two to three times the rate of minorities. Data like these were dangerous, some immediately insisted, because they perpetuated negative stereotypes of minorities as unmotivated. Anderson and Wilson looked somewhat surprised and perplexed.

The keynotes, topics, and workshops at the Second Annual National Diversity Conference reflected a continuing shift toward business-based pragmatisism, a trend that would accelerate in the mid-1990s. The more militant moralists nourished their views elsewhere.

In the Radicals' Red Glare: Homecoming for Campus and Consultant Moralists

The diversity machine was hardly sealed off from its more radical campus roots. Several consultants shuttled among corporate, public sector, and academic clients, attending and making presentations at both corporate-oriented conferences and higher education gatherings. The key topics were often the same: recession, downsizing, white male rebellion. But these issues were addressed and responded to far differently. Consultants, especially the civil rights moralists, seemed far more candid and at home in more liberal educational settings. The ideological building blocks of more aggressive diversity management—cultural relativism, proportionalism, and identity politics—were more prominently displayed for academic audiences.

The interchange of consultants among academic, government, and business institutions raised questions as to how far removed the new diversity management movement was from campus race and gender radicalism. I thought it would be revealing to sample a setting in which those in higher education mingled with diversity consultants. It was.

I attended the Fifth Annual Conference on Race and Ethnic Relations in Higher Education, a gathering recommended to me the previous autumn by Zaida Giraldo, the University of Michigan's affirmative action officer. "They're cutting edge," she said. This was not an understatement.

The June 1992 conference was held at the posh San Francisco St. Francis Westin Hotel two months after the Los Angeles riots. In contrast to the very muted response to those events at the Second Annual National Diversity Conference one month before, the mood in San Francisco waxed angry and apocalyptic. Response to white male backlash and criticism of American society in general were far more intense.

Entering the "Post–Rodney King Era"

Dueling radicals Michael Meyers and Julianne Malveaux set the tone for the conference in a preliminary workshop, "Collision in the Academy: Afrocentric vs. Multicultural Education—Visions of Political Correctness." Meyers, executive director of the New York Civil Rights Coalition, declared that whites needed to be put on notice that higher education was no longer the preserve of the privileged and so-called meritocracy. Norms of "dispassionate inquiry" masked indifference toward minorities. A true multiculturalism, he charged, does not leave unexamined the prejudices and biases of the oppressors. Political correctness was really "paternalistic curriculum." Ethnic studies programs focused on the victims and, in any case, were largely bypassed by white students and faculty. A more aggressive multiculturalism should educate whites about their oppressor status. Meyers railed against white hypocrisy: whites attacked admissions preferences for minorities but not children of alumni; reporters videotaped whites looting Frederick's of Hollywood in the Los Angeles riots, then turned to discussions about the pathology of black family structures. He warned, however, that race and culture were being confused. There is but one human race, Meyers said, and many cultures.

Economist and commentator Julianne Malveaux defended the centrality of race in American life and, therefore, the curriculum. White reporters and academics are still hopelessly biased. The media associates blacks and whites with different social problems: whites are interviewed on the subject of unemployment; blacks are profiled on studies of welfare. White men are largely "studying their navels," while white sociology focuses on black pathology. Malveaux scorned interpretations on race by Andrew Hacker ("He says very little but that some people should be honorary whites") and Shelby Steele ("He does not often look in the mirror"). The "decade of the immigrant" behind white academics' celebration of the new multiculturalism ignored that new immigrants all too readily assimilated white racism from white culture. Said Malveaux bluntly: "I want equality of outcomes, not equal opportunity." She dismissed affirmative action as mere counting and playing games, tinkering that, combined with declining urban aid, produced the L.A. riots, "a long overdue insurrection."

"We are not ethnic cheer-leading," Malveaux concluded. "Racism is as American as the Constitution." (Cheers of "That's right!" were returned from the audience.) Meyers and Malveaux jousted about whether blacks could be racists. Meyers insisted they could and cited the case of blacks targeting a Jewish man for murder in Crown Heights, Brooklyn; Malveaux countered that blacks could not be racist because they had little power to enforce their views. She trumped Meyers by noting that the "fools on the Simi Valley jury in the Rodney King case were permitted to exercise legal violence while protesting blacks were not." (Obviously neither the content nor the tone of this entire discussion would have played well or long in a mainstream business setting—or even at the National Annual Diversity Conferences.)

Maggie Abudu, the head of Oklahoma University's Southwest Human Relations Center, which organized these annual events, opened the conference on an urgent theme: "New racial and ethnic divisiveness has surfaced, though long ignored. . . . In the aftermath of domestic unraveling, superficial media analysis has shifted away from deeper structural issues. The triggering event and tardy [law enforcement] response was not the issue. Alienation, hopelessness, and exclusion of people was." Abudu introduced Berkeley historian Ronald Takaki, who solemnly intoned that this was a "momentous time." Events in Los Angeles had made it imperative to redefine America along multicultural lines. The fires in Los Angeles made Takaki think of the burning oil fields in the recent war in Iraq. We had entered, he said, the "post–Rodney King Era."

Feminist Sensibilities and Diversity's Demographic Imperative

The standard diversity rationales of demographic change combined with growing economic polarization were keyed with interesting details over lunch on the second day of the conference. Harold Hodgkinson, a Washington, D.C., demographer, used slides and lecture to emphasize "increases at the margins, declines in the middle." There would be more low- and high-end jobs, more rich and more poor, more single parents and nontraditional families, more older people and more youth. Today's kids, said Hodgkinson, do not have it easy: 24 percent live below the poverty line, 28 percent would not be vaccinated for polio until school registration, and 30 percent would likely never make it as far as high school. And education has a crucial impact on life expectancy: while the average white man lives four years longer than the average black man, there is no difference in the life span of black and white male college graduates. Hodgkinson believed in preventive programs but pointed out that funding for them was relatively low.

Hodgkinson noted that the world now contains five billion people. Can the West lead the world in 2025 with only 9 percent of the total world population? Nine out of ten people born on the planet are in developing nations; only 19 percent of the world's population is white.

Immigration into the United States during the nineteenth century was basically "more of the same" in terms of ethnicity and culture, explained Hodgkinson. During the twentieth century, immigration became "more of different" ethnicities and cultures. Economic polarization is increasing. High-wage blue-collar jobs are disappearing, especially in California, and the vast majority of new jobs created do not require a college degree. The prison population grew 139 percent from 1980 to 1990. The rise in single-parent families compounds the situation. In the next census, Hodgkinson predicted, there would be one nonstandard household for every standard one (two parents and children). Educated middle-class women were delaying or not having children: 35 percent of today's children have no brother or sister. Hodgkinson attempted a moment of light humor when he flashed on the slide screen a reprint of a cartoon showing a distraught white woman with the caption, "I can't believe I forgot to have children."

I thought Hodgkinson's performance was fairly standard stuff until the next day's lunch. I was seated at a table with two African American college administrators when four women came up. "Do you mind if we sit with you?" asked one, as the others were already taking their seats. After some introductions, the discussion turned to Hodgkinson's analysis.

"What did you think of Hodgkinson's talk?" demanded Claire,* a director of a women's action center at a Big Ten University. She clothed her enormous frame in loose slacks and a top, which resembled billowing black pajamas. A

---

*Indicates pseudonym.

self-proclaimed radical-lesbian-feminist, she seemed an imposing, formidable figure. The two African American administrators at the table glanced apprehensively at one another and then at me and said nothing.

I tried to be noncommittal. "I thought it was interesting."

"You mean you didn't think it was racist and sexist?" said Claire.

"Well, no, not necessarily," I replied. The women looked disgusted.

Sarah,* a well-dressed black dean from a Seven Sisters school, politely instructed me on the error of my ways. She did not appreciate the tone of his talk or his humor, especially the cartoon about white women forgetting to have babies. Furthermore, he discussed the growth of nonwhite populations in a menacing fashion, and he omitted the role of poverty in causing many of these problems. Sonia,* a slim Asian Indian woman dressed in a sari who taught ethnic studies at the same school with which Claire was affiliated, said that she "as a woman of color" resented being described as "being at the margins."

I asked Sonia about her course in ethnic relations, assuming she had her doctorate in social sciences. Again, I was corrected: her degree was in English literature. Evidently I looked surprised.

"What's wrong with that?" asked Claire, glaring intently.

I suggested that, as a sociologist, I'd found it was useful to have training in statistics and comparative social science research to teach such a course.

Claire scoffed that she had an M.A. in sociology and it had done her little good. "Oh," was all I could say.

Ending Racial Classifications? A Different Sort of Radical Goes Too Far

Fortunately, at that conversational juncture, the new luncheon keynoter was introduced: Itibari Njeri, a contributing editor to the *Los Angeles Times Magazine*. The iconoclastic Njeri injected into the proceedings a strong dose of doubt and complexity not often considered aloud at diversity conferences: the growing rifts over racial identity within the black community and the sloppy and ill-advised system of racial classifications.

Slavery is dead, Njeri declared, but internalized oppression of whites' negative stereotypes of minorities has made the mind the "last plantation." Njeri argued that internalized oppression was the source of light-versus-dark skin divisions within the African American community. The new category of "mixed race" threatens racial solidarity even more. By considering this category for use in the year 2000 census, the U.S. government is considering

*Indicates pseudonym.

what has already become a reality: an increasing number of racially mixed people who do not identify with any of the major racial groups. Blacks and other "communities of color," Njeri claimed, have been most guilty of treating mixed-race individuals badly while refusing to recognize their separate identity. Civil rights leaders want mixed-race people classified as black and fear that should the U.S. Census permit a mixed-race category (which it is considering), millions of mixed-race persons will flee from any sort of black identity. Sadly and ironically, noted Njeri, in demanding that mixed-race people be classified as black and not mixed, black leaders are applying southern segregationist one-drop-of-blood theory of identity: one drop of black blood, and you must be considered black.

Njeri mourned the "deadly conflicts" between Koreans and blacks. Koreans, she declared, are the foot soldiers of white capitalists. They shielded whites from black discontent. "White people aren't going to let anyone riot on Rodeo Drive."

Njeri proposed two solutions. For individuals, she hailed "reevaluation" psychotherapy for "liberating" internalized oppression. In terms of social policy, she proposed a startling course: get rid of all racial categories by the year 2000. "The demographic handwriting is on the wall," said Njeri, "and blacks are a shrinking minority." Rather than arguing about new racial categories, people should consider larger issues of social and economic justice.

Though she received a long ovation, I never heard anyone take Njeri's proposals seriously—at this or any other conference. Psychotherapy was not a call to social action, nor did blacks like to hear that they were a dwindling minority. And the abolition of racial categories, or even the addition of a mixed-race category, would sink both affirmative action and the diversity machine. It was more convenient to reinforce categories and help everyone, including white males, explore their racial identity.

Raising White Awareness and Identity, PC-Style

The Fifth Annual Conference on Race and Ethnic Relations in Higher Education sponsored several workshops or panels on white males and diversity. The two I attended were taught by highly regarded consultants who conducted training in corporate settings. The focus in both workshops was how to raise white males' racial consciousness in hopes of fostering multicultural understanding, leadership, and greater participation in antiracism efforts.

"Do you think of yourself as a white male when you look in the mirror?"

asked San Francisco consultant Ronald Brown as he opened his workshop, "New Models for White Male Leadership in a Culturally Diverse World."

Brown, an African American, answered his own question: No. White males do not think of themselves as white males. They are unaware of their own survivalist, individual-against-the-world culture, which grew out of Europe and the Western military experience. White male culture is very organized, rational, and mechanistic, designed to dominate and conquer nature, not live with it. Acknowledging his intellectual debt to consultant Tom Kochman's "archetype theories" (a controversial system of qualified, empirical generalizations about ethnic cultures), Brown argued that white men are control oriented and analytical, and they leave little room for chance. They insist that there is one best way to do things. They favor hierarchy, functional efficiency, and carefully defined roles. They love to plan and don't like anyone to deviate from the plan. Competition yields quality and efficiency.

I could not resist challenging Brown's grab-bag of stereotypes and broke my social science role of being the passive observer. I asked, "Aren't you describing the traits of capitalism and bureaucracy described by sociologist Max Weber? Don't these traits transcend ethnic cultures?"

A deep silence ensued. Then someone in the audience sneered that Weber was a white male, and a German at that. What could he know? A ripple of laughter moved through the room. Brown first responded with the usual diversity management rhetoric: "But who created these systems?" There were murmurs of approval from the audience. Then Brown tried to be professional and scholarly, drawing on Weber's observation that Chinese bureaucracy is different—more tradition oriented. Still, this was an evasive answer. Brown and other diversity consultants constantly confused white male culture with capitalism and bureaucracy and just plain formal organization. It was useless to argue in this type of environment. I let it ride.

My heresy, however, triggered another gesture of dissent. One of the few other white men in the room asked, "What about the '60s generation? They were different." The general response from Brown and others was that such people—like Tom Hayden—had moved back into the system. Someone brought up Bill Bennett: "William Bennett epitomizes white male culture." White males were all alike. And that was the end of that.

Brown continued to invoke Tom Kochman's archetypes in contrasting white male culture to African American cultural expression. African American culture favors adaptation to nature rather than mastery of it; blacks place a high value on improvisation and spontaneity, but within a team context.

Black jazz bands illustrated this. A questioner asked whether Colin Powell had denied his identity in order to move up. Brown responded that Powell is good with blacks but that he has been "adaptable" and good at mastering the system. So have many Asians, noted Brown. They're even better at controlling emotions than white males. Hispanic culture, maintained Banks, is strongly family oriented, and great emphasis is placed on the group and bonding. That Hispanics are not openly aggressive or individualistic promotes clashes with white male corporate culture.

Brown concluded by declaring that white males must help one another understand their own culture in terms of an increasingly diverse society. He received a warm round of applause. He was never seriously challenged or criticized.

Brown's smug attitude toward white males was mild compared to the antiracism anger of Frances Kendall, a consultant who helped Lewis Griggs organize the National Annual Diversity Conferences. Her workshop, "Working Effectively with White Administrators and Faculty," meant understanding the invisible system of "white male privilege" and, if possible, helping white men fight racism by promoting their self-awareness as members of an oppressive racial group.

Kendall explained how she came to understand her own "whiteness." She grew up in Waco, Texas, and internalized southern stereotypes about blacks, which she later found not to be true. She discovered a vast institutional racism and whites' complicity in the system. She obtained a Ph.D. at the University of North Carolina, taught at Tufts University, and then left "to help people talk about racism, sexism, and homophobia." She was doing a great deal of work with professional schools at the University of Michigan and spoke highly of the university's president, James Duderstadt.

After distributing copies of Peggy McIntosh's "White Privilege: Unpacking the Invisible Knapsack," Kendall explained that being white means never thinking about race and having privileges whether you want them or not. Even to struggle against racism, whites must realize that it is difficult to work in nonracist ways because racism is so deeply embedded. Whites have difficulty seeing their own culture, said Kendall. For example, when white students ask, "Why don't we have a white student union?" Kendall responds, "You do—it's called the student union." Similarly, white lawyers don't need a White Bar Association; they dominate the American Bar Association.

The individualism of American culture also inhibits understanding of racism, Kendall complained. So does the decentralized nature of the university and the general antiauthority attitudes. Other hang-ups include fear of affirmative action issues and overt homophobia. Additional problems are the core of long-time faculty who will not change and the administrators of color who behave like white males, failing to appreciate affirmative action and minority cultures. The same people show up for all the change seminars; it's like preaching to the choir. Working with corporations is easier, she felt, because there is strong, top-down decision making and less resistance.

Whites have no reason to complain of reverse discrimination; it doesn't exist. "Someone has even written a book on white victims of discrimination," Kendall snorted with contempt. (One of the book distributors had kindly displayed my book, *Invisible Victims: White Males and the Crisis of Affirmative Action.* To my surprise, I'd seen two or three people carrying copies. I stretched my coat lapel over my name tag.) Kendall also denounced protests against "political correctness" as the rage of whites who'd been used to saying what they'd wanted to for years and now could not. The anti-PC movement, she declared, is fueled by right-wing foundations.

A white female university administrator said that cutbacks on her campus were raising the reverse discrimination issue. Should she have a workshop on that?

"I'd be careful about advertising anything on reverse discrimination," bristled Kendall. "You may have to say things that they don't want to hear. Besides," Kendall's voice rose, "I know there's no such thing as reverse racism! I don't want to hear those fools! This experience is in their heads and their gut!"

Kendall scoffed about whites' fears of being called racist. She mentioned that Andy Rooney had made racist remarks on *60 Minutes* and was returned to the air "in three minutes." Kendall also expressed skepticism for diversity consultants, such as Roosevelt Thomas, who wanted to move beyond race and gender. "I care about racism and sexism," she declared.

Indeed, Kendall declared racism more important than sexism, classism, or gay and lesbian issues. She never talked about gender without race because white women are too quick to identify themselves as women rather than white, which lets them "skate" over their oppressor status. Jewish women are quick to emphasize their Jewishness, glossing their status as a white oppressor. The same holds for white gays who say, "I'm gay, not white." Kandell's response is that they must see themselves as oppressor *and* oppressed. Nor can class be used as an escape to avoid issues of racial oppression. That way opens the door into the "I'm more oppressed than you," admitted Kendall.

We participated in a personal checklist exercise, drawn from Judith Katz's book, *White Awareness: An Anti-Racism Handbook.*[9] Each of us was to select five words from a list of one hundred that best described us as an individual, then as a member of a cultural-racial category. Among the choices were these: *adaptive, arrogant, average, beautiful, blamed, Christian, conservative, controller, emotional, exploited, friendly, good, humble, individual, leader, liberal, nice, normal, oppressed, oppressive, outraged, paternal, powerful, privileged, rich, right, schizophrenic, scientific, soft, soulful, strong, tokenized, undereducated, unemotional, uptight, victimized,* and *worthy.* The exercise turned out as planned: attributes assigned to individuals were more favorable than those assigned to racial categories. Americans were uncomfortable thinking about race. Indeed, stated Kendall, this sort of exercise may be the first time whites have been asked to think of themselves explicitly as a member of a racial group.

Questions continued to percolate. A university administrator asked about training uncooperative people: "I work with people who are angry because they've been told to go [to the workshop] by their managers." Kendall recommended building alliances with people in power: "Start working with people at the top. To get into the business and law schools, talk about fully educating students to deal with a changing world." She continued, "Try to get how well one deals with diversity into tenure and promotion policies. The University of Michigan School of Social Work faculty are evaluated by faculty and students on how they deal with diversity." (This was true.)

An associate director of admissions from an Ivy League school grumbled that "people have told me this is 'bullshit' and they won't deal with it." One of the most uncooperative was an Asian male: "We hire Asian men to avoid hiring blacks or browns." Kendall counseled restraint and acknowledged assimilationist pressures on Asians. (As an example, she cited an article in *Focus* magazine, "Race Without Face," on an Asian man who had plastic surgery to fashion a more European look to his eyes.). "Get his manager to manage him," she advised.

Time was running out, and it was time to turn to antiracism action strategies. First, we scanned a "power inventory" sheet that forced assessment of the range of institutions one might influence (from employer to grocer), the extent to which one had control over money, physical property, and the ability to introduce new ideas. There was another worksheet of "Questions to Ponder," such as these:

- Do I think of myself as a prejudiced person?
- What price am I paying for my stereotypes?
- How am I benefitting from my stereotypes?
- What are three fears that I have about dealing with my prejudices?

The workshop drew to a close with a brief discussion of a list of "Possible Action Strategies—Commitment to Combat Racism," including these:

- Have I aggressively sought out more information in an effort to enhance my own awareness and understanding of racism?
- Have I re-evaluated my use of terms or phrases that may be perceived as degrading or harmful by others?
- Have I realized that white Americans are trapped by their own school, homes, media, government, etc.? Even when they choose openly not to be racists?
- Have I suggested and taken steps to implement discussions or workshops aimed at understanding racism with friends, colleagues, social clubs, or church groups?
- Have I been investigating political candidates at all levels in terms of their stance and activity against racist government practices?
- Have I investigated curricula of local schools in terms of their treatment of the issue of racism? (Also textbooks, assemblies, faculty, staff and administration?)
- Is my school or place of employment a target for my educational efforts in responding to racism?

There was almost no time left for interaction on these points. However, as the workshop dissolved, most people seemed fairly pleased. One white male, a regent from Oklahoma Teacher's College, declared that the workshop had been a revelation and that his conversion to antiracism was complete.

Brown and Kendall were partly correct in assuming that many white men (and many white women) have not often consciously considered the visible and invisible norms of society, nor do they think of themselves in racial terms. On the other hand, many younger white men, especially those in education and the public sector, are all too aware of their membership in a racial category forged by thirty years of affirmative action and real or suspected reverse discrimination. In this context, forcing "white privilege" racial awareness on white males, especially during mandatory training, could be a most alienating and disruptive enterprise. Peggy McIntosh-inspired lectures and exercises might stimulate guilt and reexamination among white academics, but among rank-and-file white workers, such stereotyping and guilt-tripping is more likely to fuel contempt and backlash and help build the "angry white male" voting bloc that so stunned and perplexed the diversity machine and its liberal and politically correct allies. Despite Kendall's downgrading of the importance of class factors, working-class and middle-class white males hardly feel privileged after thirty years of layoffs, covert and overt reverse discrimination, and white male bashing in the media and on television talk shows.

Ideology and denial were used to confront the "Myths and Illusions of Affirmative Action" workshop, conducted by Florida State presidential assistant Freddie Lang, which was essentially one long rationalization for the policies ("whites must share the burdens; they are not 'punished,'" "affirmative action helps bring qualified people who will bring in 'something special' because of their race and gender"). She did reveal that the university had begun layoffs using race and gender as criteria, agreed to by the unions and as yet unchallenged in court.

There were dozens of other workshops and panel discussions on building multicultural curriculums, multicultural campuses, mentoring programs, accommodating demographic change, and multicultural teaching—for examples, "Bridge Building Through Dramatic Skits as a Way of Promoting Education for Human Understanding in Racial and Ethnic Relations," "Multicultural Education vs. the Rhetoric of Neo-Racism," "Responding to the Unique Needs of Southeast Asian Students," "Defending the Multicultural Curriculum from Charges of Political Correctness," "Welcome to Campus, Now Go Home," "When the Professional Becomes Personal: A Commitment to Pluralism," and "Ethnoviolence on Campus: The Victims and Victimizers, the Individual and Social Effects, and Future Prospects."

I was not able to sample subsequent Conferences on Race and Ethnic Relations in Higher Education, but an increasing number of people did: attendance almost doubled from 1992's 800 to an anticipated 1,500 by 1996. Conference organizer Maggie Abudu told me in April 1996 that more recent conferences had featured themes of alliance building, "curricular infusion," and change. She was pleased to be part of a "social movement for access and success for underrepresented groups." The confidence and optimism of those involved in the conferences, she felt, was stronger than ever in the face of mounting societal and political opposition. Indeed, the sessions listed in the 1996 convention announcement included "Building a Statewide Network of Allies," "White Women, Women of Color and Multiracial Women: Dynamics and Strategies for Becoming Effective Allies (conducted by Frances Kendall and Patricia Waters), "The Anger Shop," "Helping Students from Privileged Groups Understand Their Self-Interest in Eliminating Oppression," "Staying in the Fray: How Do We Continue Doing Anti-racism Work?" (conducted by Frances Kendall and Rosselle Wilson), "Exploring and Improving Interracial Relations on Campus Through Social Action Theatre," and "Strategies for Institutional Change in an Era of Backlash." The last topic begged the question that no one dared ask at such politically correct gatherings: did the "strategies for institutional change" have anything to do with *creating* "an era of backlash"?

White Males in a Fishbowl: The Researcher Becomes a Panelist

When I began my studies of the diversity machine, I intended to follow good social science practice and be as unobtrusive an observer and interviewer as possible. But I also wanted to avoid reactive measurement—possible negative reactions to my previous research. When I had authored *Invisible Victims,* a critical study of the impact of affirmative action on white males, I had no idea white male backlash would subsequently become a prominent issue among consultants, much less society at large.

My cover of relative obscurity began to evaporate in 1991 when a paperback edition of *Invisible Victims* appeared as well as several articles about me or by me that were critical of diversity management.[10] Surprisingly, all this proved more boon than bane. The response to me in diversity circles continued much the same as it had always been: a mix of friendly and guarded curiosity. Unfolding publicity no doubt raised suspicion and wariness, but it also coincided with recognition of backlash. Simply as a white male, I was an unusual specimen in a policy movement where there were few such people; as the only sociologist with a book on the white males, I became a resource and moved from being a passive observer to a more visible, active one. (To their credit, diversity consultants provided the few forums in the nation where white males' perceptions of diversity issues could be discussed—however nervously.)

In October 1992 I was asked to participate in a panel discussion, "White Male Issues," hosted by the Los Angeles chapter's American Society for Training and Development's Cultural Diversity Division (see Chapter 5). The initial planning session was not auspicious. Civil rights moralism and business-based pragmatism clashed almost immediately. The cultural diversity division chair, Devra Korwin, feared even bringing up reverse discrimination; former Hughes Aircraft affirmative action officer Pam Fomalont grumbled that she was "tired of hearing white males whine." Others, however, insisted the issue had to be vented. The proposed panel moderator, David Jamieson, suggested a compromise of having the panel discuss "why some white males adapt to change and some don't." Consultant Angela Airall wanted to illustrate author Peggy McIntosh's concept of "white male privilege" using a group discussion exercise called the "fishbowl." Glaring at me, she also growled that she would also like to talk about "collaborators."

Nonetheless, we persevered, and on the first day of December, about forty people packed a classroom at Antioch College West for brief presentations by the panelists followed by the fishbowl exercise. Dave Jamieson opened the session with a broad definition of diversity: "Our real challenge tonight is to recognize that diversity means everyone."

Consultant-author Anita Rowe gave the standard frustration–aggression explanation of white male backlash: whites feared "uncomfortable" change and loss from shifting demographics and women's liberation, but negotiations and happy endings were possible; white men could lose graciously. Rowe cited the case of an older, more experienced white male who had been passed over for promotion in favor of a younger, less experienced white female: "They talked about it openly to each other. They shared how they felt . . . they both made a commitment to make this work. . . . The man said, 'I'd made my mark. I'd probably never get an opportunity to get a promotion like that again. I'd had my chance and now it was her turn.'"

Panelist David Wagemaker, a management development specialist at Hughes Aircraft, first made it clear he spoke only for himself, not his corporation. A white male, he was obviously weary of his corporate duties of defending political correctness and reverse discrimination. He became our angry white male. Wagemaker hinted that some reverse discrimination complaints concerning layoffs might be valid. (Indeed, Wagemaker later informed me that he'd been denied at least one promotion to a position that had been reserved for a female or minority.) He sarcastically observed that he didn't feel like a "privileged white male" when visiting corporations headquartered in Hawaii, Haiti, and Puerto Rico, nor were white males privileged when working for Japanese firms. "I would like to see your Japanese males talk about sharing power—or whether Mary Kay of Mary Kay Cosmetics talks about power sharing."

African American consultant Bill White was the jovial, business-oriented pragmatist. He lightly criticized affirmative action for creating an us-versus-them atmosphere. The latter, he said, puts white males on the defensive, as did exaggerations of *Workforce 2000*'s demographic predictions. White observed that younger white males appeared more at ease with diversity training than older whites worried about forced retirements and downsizing. (Privately White claimed to be making big money in consulting. He was especially proud of being asked to "mop up" other consultants' botched diversity training efforts, one of which occurred at a nuclear weapons facility.)

As a white male who had studied white males, I was received with a mixture of curiosity and politeness. I emphasized variations within the white male category—by occupation, education, ethnicity, religious affiliation, public or private sector employment. Ethnic and religious differences could be important. I could not resist pointing out variations within the presidential family: Bill Clinton, from a lower-middle-class southern background, was in the White House, but his brother was a recovering substance abuser. I thought this a fascinating contrast; no one else seemed impressed.

The fishbowl exercise was supposed to feature six to eight white males responding to questions about white maleness while seated in a circle, surrounded by silent white females and minorities. Since there were few white males in the audience—as was usually the case at ASTD diversity division functions—panelists David Jamieson and David Wagemaker volunteered to do double duty. The rest of us watched from outside the circle.

Newly installed division chair Pam Fomalont was the designated questioner: "What is life like for you as a white person?" Most admitted they hadn't thought about it much. "I've thought about my Dutchness more than whiteness," returned Wagemaker. Other questions followed: What do you like most about being a white male? What advantages have you experienced? How do you feel now, in this group, talking about this issue? Some gave politically correct responses indicating white culpability and guilt. Two mentioned feeling badly about the riots. But Vince Kates, an iconoclastic white male salesman, ventured politically incorrect potshots: "I have a twelve-year-old boy who will have to move from La Cañada if he is to get a job."

David Wagemaker grew testy. "I'm supposed to feel guilty? My child should pay? Do I owe somebody?"

The female and minority audience responded with varying one-word judgments: "Disappointing," "avoidance," "interesting," "surprised," and— several times—"denial."

"Denial of what?" Wagemaker demanded.

"Responsibility for hurting others."

"No acknowledgment of collusion in an oppressive system."

"Privilege! Going jogging is a white male privilege!"

On that note, the fishbowl exercise was declared ended. We rearranged the chairs once again to restructure the room to the panel audience format. Returning to his moderator role, Jamieson tried to fashion a politically correct happy ending: "We must have a more level playing field before we can have true diversity."

Most of those present judged the presentation a success. There was a flurry of friendly chatter and networking after the presentation. Later I suggested to the other panelists that we take our action to the road—to the Third Annual Diversity Conference in Chicago. They readily agreed, and so did the conference organizers.

In Chicago, the panel was scheduled for ninety-minute afternoon and evening time slots. The format was much the same, but two of the panelists had slightly changed their ideological tunes. Anita Rowe was more moderate; she had picked up on my remarks about class differences—white elite's imposing affirmative action on rank-and-file white males. Wagemaker, on the other hand, was an angrier white male. He contemptuously waved a recent *Newsweek* cover story on white male "paranoia" at the audience and quoted a feminist's remark that she looked forward to watching white males die.

The two fishbowl exercises varied remarkably. Participants in the morning exercise were milder and less confrontational. Most admitted they'd not thought much about what it meant to be a white male; one considered out loud that "society is geared toward me." They protested being stereotyped as a unitary group, but most responded that it "felt good to lay out feelings" on the matter. The audience responded in kind with one-word comments of "fabulous," "hopeful," "good-natured," and "candid." (The only awkward moment was when a black consultant in the audience rose to denounce one of my *Wall Street Journal* articles. "Despite what Fred Lynch wrote, there are affirmative action officers doing a good job!" he indignantly declared. He claimed proof that affirmative action and diversity practices improved the bottom line and offered to send the materials to me. [They never arrived.] He glared at us from the back of the room during both sessions.)

The second session netted more feisty white males for the fishbowl. One participant criticized perceptions that "everything comes automatically for whites" and contended that "whites are hardest on one another." A southern white male complained about prejudice toward white southerners, while a Vietnam vet drew a hushed response describing the awkward silence accorded him and other working-class vets for twenty years, until the Vietnam Memorial. One took potshots at the exaggerations of *Workforce 2000:* "By the year 2000 we're going to be gone. We'll work hard, play hard while we can." The audience response was more varied: "surprised," "vulnerable," and "relieved," but several "disappointed" and "denials." Toward the end of a brief question-and-answer period, a large black man commandeered the microphone and began a harangue: "We're here for diversity. This is White Male Anger 101. What we need to do is train these people as change agents!" Those already drifting out of the conference room quickened their pace.

The L.A. Riots: A Tarnished Multicultural Mecca

The 1992 Los Angeles riots were possibly the single most searing, traumatic event endured by the diversity machine, largely because the urban violence had to be suffered in relative silence. Consultants could not "explain" the events as they might have liked to outsiders. However tempted many consultants may have been to wax radically indignant over L.A.'s "long-overdue insurrection" (in Julianne Malveaux's terms), such radical war dancing was simply impermissible in front of potential corporate or government clients. The "Rainbow Riots" were so profoundly painful, embarrassing, and, above all, threatening to the cause of multicultural engineering that consultants largely remained silent, even with one another. In public settings, by and large, even the civil rights moralists knew to keep their mouths shut. (The 1995 O. J. Simpson verdict and polarized response was painful and also embarrassing, but it had been foreshadowed, in part, by the 1992 "civil disturbance.")

Hence, the eerie silence on the topic at both the Second and Third National Annual Diversity conferences as well as in diversity management newsletters, books, and journals. In the official, public realms of diversity management, it was as if the "civil disturbance" hadn't happened at all.

The riots were especially embarrassing since they exploded in the city that consultants celebrated as the model multicultural mecca forecast in *Wokforce 2000:* "The Future Is Now in L.A.!" Exhortations about the glories of diversity and multiculturalism clashed with news footage of burning, looting, and the obviously racist beating of white truck driver Reginald Denny. In addition, as Itabari Njeri observed at the Fifth Annual Conference of Racial and Ethnic Relations, the riots deepened hostility levels among blacks and Koreans. Business-oriented pragmatists knew that the riots would quicken the pace of white flight out of southern California, already spurred by the recession, massive aerospace layoffs, crime, poor schools, and other problems.

Even in Los Angeles, consultants tried to put the disturbance behind them as quickly as possible. (This was not easy to do. Backstage tensions remained high throughout the region, as evidenced by a riot-inspired minor panic that ensued some eighteen months later when false rumors began circulating that the jury had reached a verdict on federal charges against the police officers accused of beating Rodney King. As downtown offices emptied quickly, freeways became jammed in a manner one commentator likened to populations fleeing invading Martians or alien monsters in 1950s science-fiction movies.)

Paradoxically, the immediate aftermath of the riot gave temporary lift to the mission of civil rights moralists who felt that the riots confirmed their worst visions of institutional racism and oppression. The violence was taken as an indicator that even more talking, communicating, and understanding of differences was necessary to restore domestic tranquility.

Indeed, the riots triggered a flurry of anxious calls from local businesses and government agencies to organizations known for preaching tolerance and prejudice reduction, such as the Los Angeles chapter of the National Conference of Christians and Jews, recently renamed the National Conference). Most inquiries were referred to veteran trainer Lucky Altman, an amiable, talkative, dedicated civil rights moralist who came to NCCJ in the late 1970s after obtaining a master's degree in religious studies from Mount Saint Mary's College in Los Angeles. Altman's family had long been involved in civil rights protests. The official NCCJ director of "interreligious and administration of justice" touted the work on "white privilege" by Peggy McIntosh (as well as books by Ann Morrison, Roosevelt Thomas, and antiracism activist Judith Katz) and was committed to helping white men and women recognize and ameliorate institutional racism. Altman admitted that she became so emotionally involved in training sessions that she sometimes cried, leading her parish priest to chide that "your bladder is behind your eyes." She had worked as a trainer with local police departments, government and civic organizations, church groups, and youth groups (NCCJ operated an intercultural youth camp). NCCJ charged $1,200 to $1,300 per day (with two trainers) for diversity or prejudice reduction training, substantially less than many independent, professional diversity consultants. But, Altman claimed, NCCJ was choosy and selective. Clients had to be sincere and interested in long-term change.

The Anti-Defamation League's Workplace of Difference training program and the NCCJ's Dialogue program were tied into the diversity machine primarily through links to the civil rights moralists who shared the ADL's and, especially, the NCCJ's emphasis on moral change and overcoming institutional racism.

A hallmark NCCJ program was the Interracial Dialogue Series, five workshops designed "to create a more respectful inclusive community by increasing sensitivity to the issues of prejudice, stereotyping, and racism and their effects. To improve communication and cooperation among group members by addressing the personal and interpersonal dynamics that create misunderstanding and fear. To address the institutional dynamics that divide and discriminate." The series largely emphasized "sharing-and-talking" formats and utilized minilectures, experiential exercises and debriefing, role plays, readings, and "the uses of images to evoke reactions."

Six weeks after the riots, an "ASTD-LA Town Meeting" was called for "putting our skills to work to rebuild Los Angeles." Altman was on a brief but forgettable panel discussion. A primary reason for her attending was to recruit for a jointly sponsored ASTD-NCCJ version of an upcoming Dialogue series. Over a period of several weekends, ASTD and NCCJ members would train volunteers to be dialogue-style facilitators. The newly trained facilitators would then work (on a pro bono basis) with the seventy nonprofit agencies, youth groups, law enforcement agencies, and others that had requested postriot diversity training from NCCJ.

Forty people signed up for the training. NCCJ subsequently discovered that many organizations requesting cross-cultural help simply wanted a quick fix just to calm things down. They were not ready to make a commitment to long-term cultural change. Therefore, only ten to twelve persons who emerged from the NCCJ-ASTD training were engaged with any regularity. Los Angeles was learning to live with the legacy of the riots.

The riots, recession, and white flight haunted a preliminary planning session for a subsequent ASTD-LA panel discussion, "Diversity Training: Where Have We Been, Where Are We Going?" Consultant-author Anita Rowe complained that the long recession was hurting reception of diversity training. "No one cares about anyone else," she complained. "All anyone cares about is their job security. They don't want to be bothered with anything else." Nearly everyone was worried about another round of riots resulting from the second trial of the police who beat Rodney King. All agreed that diversity's continued entanglement with affirmative action caused problems, but African American consultant Bill White still insisted that race and gender should remain the paramount concerns of the new policies.

As the meeting adjourned, when only whites remained, the seen but officially unnoticed topic of white flight arose. Cultural division chair Pam Fomalont revealed that she and her husband were pondering a return to her native Oregon within a year. She felt guilty but was not pleased with the declining quality of their Santa Monica neighborhood with its "dirty beach and dirty people." Others agreed that L.A. was going downhill fast. Consultant Joan Clark observed that the upper middle class could get out of L.A., but the middle classes were stuck. She and her husband planned to abscond to San Diego or northern California. (In a slightly deflected exit the following year, Clark subsequently took a job in largely white Irvine, on the coast of Orange County.)

A week later, at the formal presentation, star panelist, UCLA demographer Leo Estrada, was not optimistic. A new member of the much-heralded official reconstruction committee Rebuild L.A., he reflected on his efforts to foster cross-cultural communication among the city's many groups. Estrada was dumbfounded at how little awareness most people had of other cultures. More frustrating, in cross-cultural dialogue, he saw people try to reestablish boundaries as fast as they dissolve. Consultant Bill White argued that hiring underrepresented groups was good for business because minority customers favored companies with strong reputations for hiring and promoting minorities. (He cited no evidence for this, nor did anyone bother to ask.) Others talked about remaining committed to diversity, the "pain of discomfort and unfamiliarity," and the keeping in mind the "five D's of difference: denial, distancing, devaluation, defensiveness, and discovery."

Audience members rose to give minispeeches on random topics. A white female civil rights worker talked about the need to carry on that tradition. A white woman from Interfaith discussed the need for "communication." Another white women made some useful points about how diversity awareness could foster networking in a global economy. A speech therapist testified that diversity skills help him minister to a ward of "diverse brain-damaged people." Book dealer Vince Kates fired off a tough question as to how "fixable" Los Angeles was in the wake of the riots. (Panelists agreed the situation was fixable.)

Cross-Cultural Consultant Profile III:
Tom Kochman and Associates

Like Sondra Thiederman, Tom Kochman is a business-oriented, pragmatic Ph.D. whose stated mission is to "promote multicultural flexibility." Unlike Thiederman, however, Kochman takes four days of seminars to focus in depth on the "cultural archetypes" of Anglos, African Americans, women, Hispanics, and Asians. He has resisted expanding the definition of diversity beyond ethnicity and gender. (Like many other diversity consultants, Kochman dodges the topic of how gay and lesbian culture differs from the heterosexual mainstream. "I'm ready to plead ignorance on that aspect," he shrugged. "I don't have any information on gay-straight cultural differences.") Like Lewis Griggs, Kochman notes that ethnic groups in America share similarities, but it is patterns of cultural differences that cause problems. Good management focuses on minimizing culturally induced conflicts and "tapping into differences."

A child of German-Jewish parents, Kochman claims lifelong sensitivity on issues of discrimination and prejudice. He obtained his Ph.D. from New York University in 1966, studied black-white communication patterns, and authored a well-regarded book on the topic, *Black and White Styles in Conflict*.[1] He incorporated his consulting firm in 1986, then moved from part-time to full-time involvement in 1991 when he took early retirement from his position as professor of communications and theater at the University of Illinois, Chicago Circle. Academe served as a recruitment base for other culture-keyed Kochman associates. Ilya Adler, an associate professor of communications at the University of Illinois, Chicago Circle, conducts the seminar on Hispanic-Anglo differences. Adrian Chan, assistant vice chancellor for minority affairs and educational psychology professor at the University of Wisconsin, Milwaukee, and consultant Celia Young handle the seminar on Asian-Anglo cultural styles. And consultant Jean Marvelis does a day on male-female cultural styles.

Kochman Communication Associates offers its four-day seminar series on cultural differences four or five times a year in cities around the nation: San Francisco, Houston, Chicago, Washington, D.C., and Atlanta. The sessions are approximately $415 per participant per day. Based on price, Kochman's complete course is probably the Mercedes-Benz of multicultural training. The settings are equally deluxe. The three sessions I attended began on March 30, 1992, at the posh Madison Hotel in Washington, D.C. (Seminar participants got a hefty room discount, though the tony surroundings were a novel experience for more budget-oriented public and nonprofit sector employees. "This isn't my usual Motel 6," quipped one.)

The evening before our seminar series, Kochman advertised via an open house. Potential clients viewed some of the videotapes used in the seminars, browsed through the brochures, and met Tom Kochman and his instructor-associates. Kochman also spread word of his services by speaking at conferences, attending conventions (such as the American Bankers Association), advertising in professional newsletters, and using word of mouth. Through such methods, Kochman had obtained a client roster featuring the U.S. Forest Service, AT&T, Michigan Bell, Edison Electric Institute, units of the University of Michigan, Banc One, University of Cincinnati, U.S. Postal Service, the Chicago Police and Fire Departments, and Exxon.

Our sessions averaged about ten participants per day. Those there for the entire four days included Steve Schmidt, a director of education and training at a major federal security agency; Buzz Cook, Schmidt's colleague and an EEO officer from the same agency; Alex Owen and Sam Brown, two African American men from a Midwest church federation; Sue Holden, an EEO officer with the U.S. Postal Service; André Kerchoff, a personnel manager with a major airline; Tom Hoffman, another airline executive; Belinda Bernardo, a recruiter and multicultural program manager with a federal intelligence agency; and Andrea Steiner, an EEO director with a major advertising agency. Several one-day participants were especially active: Margaret Bronson, another cross-cultural consultant; Cheri Doyle, shipping division manager with a major airline; and Raj Aggarwal and Max Hartman, human resources directors for a major hotel chain. Two graduate students from local universities maintained a relatively quite presence for two days. (The names of individuals are pseudonyms.)

Each day's format was basically the same: a university-style lecture-seminar, punctuated by videotapes of actors portraying problematic cross-cultural situations. Each seminar participant was provided a thick, three-ring workbook. (Kochman avoids simulation or role-playing formats as too time-consuming. "I'm interested in getting basic information across," he said during a separate interview. "The videos get to problematic points much quicker and with equal effectiveness.")

Day One: Diversity and "Archetypes"

Kochman began with the standard diversity management spiel. Changing demographics will propel the United States from the old "melting pot," based on assimilation to Anglo-male standards, toward a new "salad bowl," based on two-way social accommodation. The melting pot, Kochman argued, had been unilaterally proposed and did not include "proportional input" from America's expanding range of minority groups. After the 1960s civil rights battles, minority groups began to reject assimilation and to demand reciprocal cultural accommodations.

The demand for mutual, cultural accommodation created two major problems: how to talk openly and candidly about cultural differences and the concept of equal treatment. The old melting pot ideal was to treat everyone the same, but according to white male, Anglo cultural standards. The new salad bowl ideal is to be sensitive to individual needs, accommodate many cultural differences, and dispense with a one-size-fits all white male standard.

Talkative Alex Owen tossed Kochman a multicultural hot potato: "What about the Detroit school controversy—you know, where they're trying to establish some public schools just for black males?" Kochman deflected the question with observations of how black male students work better with a coach-student model than with a more formal teacher-student relationship. But then he used it to press a point often made by diversity consultants, though with little supportive evidence: organizations that permit minorities to retain their identities at work will win greater loyalty and productivity. Yet Kochman insisted that culturally sensitive treatment of employees does not mean preferential treatment. He used Daisy Chin-Lor's "Valuing Diversity" metaphor of the flower garden. Every flower in the garden cannot be treated exactly the same. Some need more water, others, less; some may require one kind of fertilizer, while others require different nutrients. A less fragrant example was that of restroom science, which had recognized the unequal effects of having an equal number of stalls in each facility: women need more minutes per use.

Kochman was the only consultant I observed who carefully tried to distinguish between general cultural patterns and stereotypes. Kochman claimed to be probing "archetypes." Stereotypes are often used in an accusatory fashion and contain negative evaluations, distort and exaggerate, and are done from an outsider perspective. Archetypes, on the other hand, are nonaccusatory, nonmoralistic, and nonrestrictive (allow for individual variations); offered from an insider perspective; and are descriptively accurate and representative of a significant number of group members—what anthropologists term the "salient patterns" within a group. (Usually a cultural pattern has to be true for at least 30 percent of a group to be considered valid as a generalization or archetype.)

Kochman was also among the very few writer-consultants who pointed out sociological findings that ethnically based cultural differences have usually been most distinct for poor and newly arrived groups. Second and third generations tend to assimilate, especially if they are upwardly mobile. Blacks were a partial exception. According to Kochman, middle-class blacks may have two cultures: a more Anglicized one at work and a more African one in their private worlds.

Black-White Culture Clashes

Three videotapes keyed discussion of Anglo American and African American behavioral traits and communication styles. The videos showed different greeting patterns between a black male and female, on the one hand, and a white male and female, on the other; a black couple and a white couple socializing and debating the issue of euthanasia; and an African American secretary asking her white supervisor for time for medical reasons but refusing to be more specific.

In discussions, we connected the video vignettes with the archetypes outlined in the workbooks. Anglo males tend to be aggressive, independent, dominant, self-confident, self-directed, pragmatic, and controlled emotionally. Females tend to be passive, dependent, nurturing, conforming, focusing on harmonious relationships, expressive of emotions, people oriented, and harboring feelings of inadequacy. African American male and female traits were combined: aggressive, independent, nurturing, self-confident, sexually assertive, emotionally expressive, focusing on personal relationships, and nonconformist. "African Americans say it's better to have a sincere argument than an insincere peace," observed Kochman. The presence of emotionally heated confrontation is an inevitable consequence of truth seeking around issues that people care about. "Commitment to truth seeking and social progress requires that people continue to struggle with the issue, notwithstanding the emotional heat that is present." Levels of verbal intensity or aggression that would be seen as fighting in Anglo realms are simply seen as "woofing" in African American culture.

Black-white communication conflicts arise from the clash of more personal, expressive styles of African American culture with the more detached, dispassionate Anglo culture. Discussion styles of African Americans have tended to emphasize expression of personal conviction and readiness to act on that conviction. Strong beliefs should be stated with strong emotions. Within the Anglo cultural framework, truth should be debated in abstract, transpersonal, and objective terms. Flexibility in the face of changing circumstances is a virtue. "If a topic is likely to be volatile and controversial, it's better not to talk about it. It might lead to divisions and antagonisms. If things are becoming emotionally heated, it's time to withdraw from the truth-creating process." African American culture, on the other hand, tends to see high-intensity debates as clarifying. Truth is personal, and conviction is demonstrated by willingness to "walk that talk," do what you say, and pay a price if need be. Integrity and credibility mean taking and holding fixed positions. Obviously, continued Kochman, someone who is trying to gain credibility among whites may appear cool and uncommitted to blacks. Conversely, someone who is trying to prove credibility with blacks may appear extreme, overaggressive, and hostile to whites.

Workplace misunderstandings can also arise over black-white cultural differences concerning task and time management. Anglos are clock watchers and future oriented, and they tend to be highly rationalized in shaping tasks to time slots. They tend to focus on one task at a time and plan their work by the rules. But African Americans are not clock oriented and tend to be inventive, spontaneous, and creative in getting the job done. African Americans are more likely to improvise and may work at many projects at once.

Alex Owen, the African American head of the midwestern church federation, heartily agreed: "I've seen so many colleagues and friends get fired for just this reason!" Their work, Owen argued, was fine; their bosses didn't like how they went about doing it.

Whites will also rush a meeting to its conclusion because of external time constraints, Kochman observed. Blacks may wish to continue a meeting until everyone has had his or her say and there is a sense of completeness.

Again, Alex Owen thundered agreement: "This is exactly what happens at some of the general community meetings we hold! The whites all show up on time, while the blacks may come in late. The blacks want to talk things out, tell personal stories about general points. They want to stay late, but the whites get up and leave when the meeting is set to adjourn."

Anglo American and Hispanic Cultural Differences

On the second day, Ilya Adler outlined the three basic Hispanic subgroups: Caribbean (Cubans, Puerto Ricans, Dominicans, Venezuelans), meso-American (Central Americans), and Latin American. Class rather than color, Adler informed us, has been basis of status in Latin America. Though there is much variation within and between groups, Hispanics do possess a common culture based on Catholicism, the Spanish language, and—in this country— their status as immigrants and/or a minority. (New immigrants tend to be less critical of an Anglo status quo, whereas their children or grandchildren may become more restive.)

A videotape, *Eddie's Quitting,* portrayed a Hispanic employee who ceased coming to a small factory setting after an Anglo colleague asked for and received a pay raise. Adler explained that the Hispanic worker felt that he too deserved a raise but that self-promotion and seeking attention are considered unseemly by many Hispanics. One should wait to be recognized and let work speak for itself. Confrontation with authority is also to be avoided. There is greater respect for hierarchy among Hispanics than among Anglos.

"These are not the types of Hispanics I've seen in corrections work," said Alex Owen. "Gang members are quite assertive."

"For themselves or for the group?" asked Kochman.

This exchange sparked discussion among the seminar group that evolved into general agreement that Hispanic culture did not emphasize individual assertiveness *as much as* Anglo or African American cultures did. Kochman cited an interesting experiment that had been done in which schoolchildren were given boxes of crayons with the green crayon missing. African American children immediately protested, Anglos demurely asked about the situation, and Hispanics said nothing. Emphasis on the individual is an English idea, said Adler.

Other videotapes and lectures showed that Hispanic culture emphasizes family and *sympatia,* an emphasis on building and maintaining warm, personal relationships. Hispanics personalize business dealings; family and friends are also sources of funds and of employers or employees. Anglos tend to separate business and friendship, remaining cool and neutral. "Hispanics rely on friends so as not to have to rely on institutions; Anglos rely on institutions so as not to have to rely on friends." To some extent, African Americans and Hispanics mix personal and business dealings in the same settings and may try to do many things at one time. But Hispanics and blacks may clash over the degree of intimacy and information transmitted early in a friendship.

"What about Hispanics who exclude other Hispanics?" asked Margaret Bronson, another consultant who had joined us for the day.

Adler explained that ethnic solidarity among Hispanics is not as strong as with other groups. But subgroups will form around friendship networks. Thus, Cubans hire other Cubans not necessarily because they are Cuban but because they are friends. There are distinctions between foreign-born Hispanics and U.S.-born Hispanics.

Bronson began to object to the lack of discussion of sex roles. She was told, much to her dismay, that gender was singled out for examination on the last day. She was disappointed but continued to raise questions, often about gender.

"At what point do we accommodate nations that do not accept women in positions of authority in business?" she wanted to know.

Kochman counseled inclusion when possible. But flexibility may be required. He quoted a line from a favorite book, *Love in the Time of Cholera*: "When you're buying, you need one language; when you're selling, you need many."

More than Kochman realized, this line foreshadowed the next day's events.

An On-Site Cultural Conflict: What Is Asian Culture?

At the beginning of a third seminar, on Asian-Anglo cultural differences, Kochman associates Celia Young and Adrian Chan stumbled over a major problem in cultural anthropology and cultural diversity: How do you define a culture? Which subgroups are included in that culture, and which are not?

Young and Chan explained that Asian cultural groups have a common geographical origin: Asia. Then they turned to the values and outlook underpinning Confucianism. Max Hartman and Raj Aggarwal, two hotel chain executives, had enrolled hoping to learn more about an increasing number of employees from India and Pakistan. The argument illustrated the conceptual confusion as well as group dynamics that had evolved during the previous two days.

Adrian: Asian society is a very hierarchical type of society, position-based society. One of the more common philosophies that permeates Asian society is Confucianism. We can talk about certain types of well-defined relationships: parent-child, employer-employee. Duties and responsibilities all well defined. You rule with justice, wisdom, benevolence, kindness.

Within this worldview, all things are in a harmonious balance. Another is this issue of order. There is both harmony and order.

Max: How different is this from southwest Asian culture? Is this the same?

Adrian: I'm not sure of that. Probably more eastern.

Max: Is it significantly different from what you have here?

Adrian: I'm not sure.

Raj: There are a lot of countries in Asia, but the focus here is on the southeast, the Far Eastern cultures. If we're talking about Asian Americans in general, then this should be a lot more balanced. There are a million Asian Indians in this country. Okay? It's a powerful group in this country. You don't have anything on that.

Tom: We have some materials in the manual.

Celia: Are there harmony and order in Indian culture?

Raj: Yes.

Max: Because of the employees we're managing, our stronger interest is more in the southwest Asians.

Tom: Our usual emphasis is on southeast Asian cultures. East Asian and Indian groups tend to get together to form support groups in corporations.

Celia: We can't talk about regional differences. There isn't time.

Raj: But there is a tremendous focus on east and southeast . . .

Celia: If we took the east and southeast out, would you feel better?

Raj: Yes, because you're trying to talk about Asian Americans in general. There are a million Asian Indians in this country. What about Hindu theory? It's very sophisticated. This is very, very bad.

Steve: If you look at the chart that he's looking at, it goes immediately to Chinese culture and confucianism . . .

Adrian: But the values are shared beyond China.

Raj: What you should do is evaluate Hindu and Confucian cultures, and get a common order. This is not right.

Tom: You don't feel included?

Raj: We're not included here. You're looking at a million plus group, a powerful group.

Adrian: In terms of the workshops we deal with, most of our clients work with a broad work base of Chinese, Japanese, and Koreans.

Steve: But the workshop is advertised as an Asian workshop.

Celia: If it is not true for you, Raj, then let's talk about what you believe.

Tom: If we promised to remedy this part of the program, would you agree to discussing this particular way of describing you, and we can invite you to add other pieces as we go on? I would hate to think you would shut off the process.

Steve: I don't think he's shutting off the education process for us, Tom. This is an education—that there are such differences. I understand where he's coming from. I think he's expanding the education process instead of shutting it down. It must be disconcerting for you on your materials . . .

Raj: This is so Far Eastern driven. Chinese, Chinese. San Francisco, UC-Berkeley. All Chinese. The highest per capita income in this country is Asian Indians. There are a million Asian Indians. Lots of doctors, engineers. They follow Hindu values.

Alex: I'm hearing something else. If I were to take Raj's perspective. What I'm hearing here is us against them. I'm an African American. I don't claim to be an expert on Asian philosophy or religion. But Christianity and Judaism and Hinduism and Buddhahism . . .

Raj: Buddhism.

Alex: Excuse me! Maybe I don't pronounce it right, but I'm trying to communicate with you. . . . We're trying to share and understand about one another. We're not trying to separate out differences about one another. This is to be inclusive. We have to agree to disagree. We got to get to that. I want to go on and get some of this information.

What I'm hearing from you I heard from African American revolutionaries back in the sixties. You know, "I got to be better. I got to be recognized." All that does is lead to divisiveness. You've got a sound point. I think they heard you. But I came here to learn as much as I could in a short span of time, and I want to be able to share that experience with everyone here. I don't understand all the issues you're raising. . . . East Indians are making more money. That's great to hear. But that's not what we're processing on.

Raj: But you're here to learn Asian American culture, and this is Far Eastern driven.

Alex: We understand that. So we're not going to learn as much as we might have. So let's accept that and move on.

Raj: So we should redefine this whole project for today as Far Eastern Asian studies.

Tom: Raj, can I ask you to hold some of this until the end of the day? One of the characteristics of Indian culture is honor and the defense of honor, and being excluded is an important piece. That's why I was asking Raj what form of acknowledgment we could make at this point to move along with the information to get past this thing. But I don't want to get past this . . . what's here is important . . . we will certainly add to this . . . but I hope this doesn't increase the resistance.

Raj: I want to redefine this part as Far Eastern culture study.

Tom: For the moment, okay?

Raj: For the moment.

This disruptive exchange lasted nearly an hour and was, as Steve Schmidt indicated, something of an education in and of itself. First, it illustrated that by the third day of the seminar series, a certain degree of affection and bonding had built up among the continuing participants in the group. We were somewhat protective toward Kochman, though Steve Schmidt continued his role as the primary questioner and challenger; Alex Owen and his colleague Sam Brown had become smitten with Kochman and his work (during breaks and in the evenings, they recorded long, copious notes on a laptop computer). And the up-front nature of their defenses confirmed Kochman's lectures on the sometimes emphatic nature of African American cultural styles.

Most important, however, the vigorous disagreement pointed up what sociologists have known for some time: that ethnic and cultural boundaries can be maddeningly inexact and difficult to map. Though Kochman and his associates were more careful than most other diversity consultants to point out such imprecision and other, cross-cutting group boundaries (such as class), the entire industry of diversity consulting rests on the presumption of some degree of homogeneity within cultural groups. But both "Asians" and "Hispanics" are such general, vague concepts that the degree of individual and subgroup variation within each category makes even broad generalizations risky. *Which* Hispanics? *Which* Asians? (Indeed, *which* white males?)

Kochman's work illustrated a growing dilemma within both the diversity machine and American society: to what extent are ethnic and gender cultures recognizable, and to what extent do they endure? And what if they even partly confirm, or seem to confirm, less-than-flattering stereotypes?

Kochman on His Work and the "Diversity Paradox"

In a 1993 interview, Kochman remained pleased with his work and its reception. His most satisfying moments were when people "sang and danced" over recognition of cultural differences, as Alex Owen had with regard to black-white issues. Kochman agreed with several other consultants that public sector employees are often more amenable to cross-cultural training because, in part, there is less mobility and employees have known one another longer.

On the other hand, Kochman echoed common consultant complaints. He was annoyed that both corporations and public sector organizations are short of funding for training and that they were anxious to get to bottom-line benefits. And he admitted he was having to devote increasing amounts of time to "resistance," most of it from white males. White conservatives were not necessarily the worst, said Kochman; academics and white liberals were sometimes the most trying. Anxious liberals repeatedly tried to demonstrate their lack of prejudice, yet they remained wedded to the "we-are-all-the-same" assimilationist model and were defensive about discussions of cultural differences. Liberal academics and medical doctors sometimes considered Kochman's training an infringement on their professional autonomy. Kochman also observed a variable often ignored by other consultants: regional differences. In training sessions, African Americans were more vocal in the East and the Midwest, less vocal in the South and the West. Discussions of gender differences were more difficult in the South and Southwest, which Kochman attributed to the influence of more traditional sex role cultures.

But Kochman's archetype approach was controversial even among his peers. He was caught in the middle of a great "diversity paradox." On the one hand, consultants constantly chattered about the need to "talk about differences" in order to "capitalize on differences." On the other hand, when consultants such as Tom Kochman or Lewis Griggs tried to illustrate specific ethnic group differences, they stumbled into accusations of purveying "stereotypes."

Generalists like R. Roosevelt Thomas remained rather vague about just what specific differences needed to be managed. Other cross-cultural consultants like Lillian Roybal Rose talked about the general "isms" (racism, sexism, heterosexism, adultism), and Sondra Thiederman was pulling away from her earlier emphases on the specifics of immigrant cultures.

Despite his careful explanations and repeated qualifications about archetypes, Kochman was using a culture-specific approach that was becoming increasingly controversial, even among diversity consultants. Proof has been largely based on relatively few qualitative and impressionistic field studies both here and abroad. To ardent conservative and liberal assimilationists, Kochman's views would appear as the worst sort of difference mongering and stereotyping. Assimilationists would argue that such group differences melt away over generations. (Kochman would partially agree, noting that upward mobility and social class hasten a degree of assimilation.)

The most passionate professional and public debate concerns the depth and breadth of black-white differences, especially in the wake of the 1995 O. J. Simpson trial. The May 1996 issue of the *New Yorker* magazine and a concurrent *New Yorker*–sponsored Harvard symposium, "African-Americans in the Media," made plain a range of contradictory viewpoints about black-white differences among black academics and reporters.

"There is a risk to what we do," Kochman admitted in a May 1996 reinterview. "No pain, no gain, as they say." At the start of his seminars, he sometimes gets complaints that he is propagating stereotypes, but such concerns usually vanish by the end of the sessions—though not always. After doing a workshop for journalists, Kochman recalled overhearing two African American participants vigorously arguing with one another over the stereotype issue. Even if they feel the information is accurate, Kochman noted, African Americans are extremely sensitive about the use that may be made of such views. Nevertheless, discussion of culturally specific differences is once again gaining respectability, as is suggested by the prominence given to Kochman and his associates' work, along with citations of some supportive evidence, in Antony Carnevale and Susan Stone's recent massive survey of workforce diversity, *The American Mosaic: An In-Depth Report on the Future of Diversity at Work.*[2]

Kochman now opens his seminars with a question about what qualities participants feel their employer does not appreciate. He finds repeatedly that black participants in his seminar feel that their cultural style—more direct, candid, and sometimes confrontational—is suppressed in cooler, "risk-averse" white male conversational cultures. Asians, on the other hand, complain about lack of loyalty and reciprocity.

I countered that, during the contemporary period of downsizing, white males were also greatly concerned about reciprocity and corporate loyalty.

"But whites put opportunity first," responded Kochman. "They do not hesitate to go into the boss and state, 'I've got a better offer; can you match it?' But do that in, say, a more traditional Hispanic organization and you're through. Loyalty comes first."

As is almost always the case in diversity management, the lasting impact of such training is difficult to assess. When I tried to contact others in the Kochman seminar series I attended, I discovered that many had since moved on to other corporate positions or left altogether. Steve Schmidt saw the training as generally useful but was not overly enthusiastic. On the other hand, Alex Owen called me. He was so taken with Kochman's work that he had become a part-time trainer and consultant.

Chapter 5

Frustration and Stall

Confronting Awkward Cultural and Political Differences

By the mid-1990s, workplace and economic changes had severely undercut diversity management's major sales rationale: the *Workforce 2000* prophecies that labor shortages and declining numbers of white males would compel employers to change their cultures to compete for talented women and minorities who wished to "be themselves." On the contrary, downsizing and the newer management trend of reengineering had forced hordes of middle-aged white men (and women) back onto the labor market; job prospects for new college graduates were bleak. The first half of the 1990s was an employers' market. Nor was there much hope that these conditions would change. As Apple Computer's Kevin Sullivan had predicted, diversity management would be a hard sell in a tough world.

Leading diversity authors and consultants became more concerned about the policy movement's public image as criticism began to surface in the press.[1] Media and scholarly attacks on political correctness intensified, and the political and cultural climate began to change, culminating with the 1994 publication *The Bell Curve* and its controversial analysis of unwelcome ethnic differences in IQ. Then came the 1994 Republican congressional landslide.

These frustrations fueled tensions between the moralists and the pragmatists. Moralists considered the worsening environment further evidence of America's deep-seated racism and sexism, requiring even more vigorous condemnation. Business-oriented pragmatists worried that moralists' shrill rhetoric simply confirmed public suspicions that diversity management was really just a front for race and gender radicalism.

By and large, however, the business-oriented pragmatists were gaining control of the diversity machine. The drift in newsletters and convention keynotes was unquestionably toward a more complex, business-based pragmatism with an expanded beyond-race-and-gender diversity definition, largely mirroring the views of Roosevelt Thomas. But more aggressive change masters, notably Ann Morrison, continued to demand that middle- and upper-level managers should be held accountable for their retention and promotion records of minorities and women (through performance evaluations and financial bonuses). Advocacy of these tactics led diversity management into a major quagmire in terms of movement building, public image, and actual implementation in organizations. Arguments over the worth of the broader aims of diversity management kept sliding back into numbers wars about the percentages of women and minorities hired, promoted, and retained. Such squabbles reinforced suspicion that diversity management was merely "backdooring affirmative action" (in Roosevelt Thomas's words).

Leading consultants and writers sensed the stall and frustration. Just before the 1994 elections, *Cultural Diversity at Work* editor Barbara Deane outlined "Critical Choices at the Crossroads" that consultants must overcome to move beyond the quick-fix diversity training solutions into which consultants and clients seemed to be sinking. First, Deane pleaded that it was time to get beyond moralist-pragmatist battle over whether diversity should emphasize race and gender or be expanded. As a compromise, Deane quoted the Society for Human Resource Management's new diversity director Patricia Digh's recommendation that the definition vary with each organizational client. The second dilemma was an old nemesis: the continuing lack of proof that diversity policies delivered welcome changes. There had been some progress on a third problem: getting strong leadership backing and buy-in from the top. The fourth task was to integrate diversity throughout the organization—breaking diversity programs out of the affirmative action–human resources ghetto. The fifth critical choice was to shift from the moralistic rhetoric to the more business-based argument of diversity management's "competitive advantage." And Deane's sixth dilemma was to "get beyond backlash and fear."[2]

All of these problems were being churned in other books and articles and at the National Annual Diversity conferences, yet no one seemed closer to solving them. Indeed, a sense of formula repetition and drift was setting in. The conferences were becoming a peculiar combination of collective complaints (especially in the discussion sessions) and public testimonials (especially during the keynotes). Worse, attendance and enthusiasm were fading.

Trying to Maintain Momentum

The 1993 Third Annual Diversity Conference was held in Chicago, five years after *Workforce 2000* had launched diversity management policies. The recession was receding in many parts of the nation, but corporate downsizing continued unabated. Consultants still grumbled about superficial corporate commitment and "being stuck in the training mode" of one-day, quick-fix solutions. Fears were being voiced that diversity management was being labeled as a faddish "flavor of the month" rather than being recognized as a major policy trend.

A Lockheed diversity director summed up the frustration in my new discussion group. "We did all of the same things in the 1960s and the 1970s—sensitivity, training, and so on. We followed all the legal mandates. We're no closer. In this room there is diversity. But when we go back to our offices, it's not there." Our group leader, an Amdahl personnel director, mechanically responded with the familiar mantra: "EEO and diversity aren't the same. We must deal with glass ceiling issues. Changing demographics, diversity is a resource, helps you compete. Diversity still means putting qualified people in jobs—but making sure they have training."

Conference attendance had backed down to about 280, and the number of participating corporations had dropped to about 70. There were far fewer corporations with multiple representatives, though one, Chicago-based Amoco, set a conference record by sending thirty people; the federal government attendance record was topped by the U.S. Postal Service, which sent twenty-four.

The fourteen workshops and twelve panels had an all-too-familiar ring: balancing work and family; being a change agent; the challenge of men and women working together; using games and simulations in diversity training; staying motivated in initiating, developing, implementing, and maintaining diversity programs; developing diversity programs for state and local agencies; diversity management in health care; diversity and the business connection; how to make diversity teams work.

Although most events came off as scheduled, there were signs of disorganization behind the scenes. Rumors spread that some of the previous year's panelists had their expenses reimbursed late or not at all. Indeed, I had experienced problems communicating with the conference's chief coordinator,

Herbert Wong, regarding the scheduled ASTD-LA panel—the "fishbowl" on white males. More evidence of last-minute scrambling surfaced as I checked into the hotel. Associate conference coordinator, consultant Frances Kendall, spotted me near the elevators and urgently asked if I would be a discussion group leader. (I pleaded lack of hands-on experience with diversity policies and declined. Had I not been so surprised—had she forgotten about my book on affirmative action and white males?—I might have accepted.)

Another omen of declining enthusiasm occurred on the first day when Chicago's mayor failed to show up for the scheduled official welcome. There were fewer well-known diversity stars and corporate notables and far more independent consultants. (Ominously, some of those attending the conference with nominal corporate affiliations were competing with the independent consultants for business and contacts. Digital and Prudential had spun off diversity units. The new units would have to stand on their own budgets, in part, by selling their services to outside clients.)

Still, conference organizers gamely accommodated both moralists and pragmatists with a combined agenda of "moral significance" and "what works." With a nod toward current events, conference cochair Percy Thomas, provost of Montgomery College, raised the specter of Bosnia-style conflicts if the United States could not learn to merge diversity with harmony. He invoked the more peaceful but worn-out flowers-in-the-garden metaphor that people with different types of cultural background should be treated accordingly.

Diversity's High Rollers

By the Third Annual Diversity Conference, it was becoming apparent to those inside and outside the diversity machine that the policies were being driven, or at least accommodated, primarily by large corporations and government agencies, which could afford the time and personnel for the more elaborate total diversity programs outlined by Herbert Wong at the 1992 conference.

June Hanson of Prudential Insurance described how her company had organized an expensive "holistic" approach to workforce diversity. Launched in 1990, diversity awareness training was provided to 15,000 managers and executives, and plans were in place to train all employees. A new diversity council and a business unit diversity action process used opinion surveys, homogeneous and mixed focus groups, a cultural audit, and a study of employee grievances to track diversity concerns and integrate them into business strategy, other training programs, and the company's core values. According to Hanson, diversity goals had been incorporated in personnel policies, performance appraisal, and management compensation. A company-wide "critical issues survey" included questions on diversity issues. Other means of assessing Prudential's diversity programs included follow-up surveys; discussions in company newsletters; "organized advocacy groups" for women, African Americans, and gays and lesbians; increasing diversity on the board of directors; and being recognized for diversity efforts by *Hispanic Magazine, Working Mother's Magazine, Personnel Journal,* and the Urban League. The major problems were not being able to quantify results and relate all these efforts to the bottom line. And then there was the white male revolt: "a huge backlash in our organization to affirmative action." Active CEO commitment to diversity had been crucial on such matters.

The Tennessee Valley Authority's diversity managers, Frank Robinson and JoAnn Howell, explained that backlash had also erupted among the mostly white male 19,000-person TVA workforce. Following Roosevelt Thomas's lead, diversity at TVA had been broadly defined. Personality styles, military or nonmilitary background, and even smoking and nonsmoking were under the diversity umbrella. TVA, the largest power distributor in the world, demanded that its contractors—even giant General Electric—also institute workforce diversity programs. TVA had goals in place for increasing the number of minority and female contracting firms. Unions and white employees had been brought into the diversity process through diversity awareness education. Executive bonuses had been tied to diversity goals. Out of thirty-five vice presidents, minority vice presidents had jumped from one to six; females, from one to five. In spite of downsizing, Howell claimed that the percentage of minority employees is rising. Robinson and Howell were trying to link diversity to increased productivity and reduced turnover and absenteeism. Alas, the purported bottom-line savings from all this "have yet to be validated by research."

There was no other corporate name more associated with employee training and education than Motorola. That corporation's vice president for diversity, Roberta Gutman, had been in the audience for the first two conferences. Now a keynoter, she told the assembled convention how Motorola had created a "welcoming organization" for minorities and women—one, it turned out, built on ethnic and gender goals and timetables imposed by a strong CEO. Motorola board chair George Fisher, a mathematician, was impressed by the skilled labor shortages forecast in *Workforce 2000* and became convinced that having minorities and women in senior management would indicate a "welcoming environment" for prospective minority talent. Thus, it was decreed that by 1996, the ethnic and gender composition of Motorola's labor force would reflect the national labor pools of appropriately skilled workers. The heads of Motorola's business units were put on notice and instructed to do the same with all employees through training. Invisible barriers to women and minorities should be identified and surmounted. Backlash from white males was allegedly being controlled by careful education and explicitly linking diversity to business needs. Motorola's managers submitted "parity progress" reports five days prior to their annual meeting with the chairman. Changes at the top had been impressive. In 1989 there were two female vice presidents; by 1993, sixteen vice presidents were women (two of them minority). In 1989 there were six minority vice presidents; by 1993 there were twenty-six (one-third each Asian, Hispanic, and African American).

Backsliding into Affirmative Action and the Numbers

The huge ovation for Gutman had just died away when the first questioner asked a question no one at the conference—or in the entire field—wanted to hear: Wasn't Motorola's diversity plan really just affirmative action—more goals and numbers? Gutman weakly responded that managers weren't *specifically* evaluated on pure numbers, but that diversity achievements were incorporated into an overall package of quality, productivity, and so on. But the downhill slide back into numbers controversies deepened during a follow-up panel of several "champions of diversity." Charles Reid, director of diversity for Kraft General Foods, freely blended affirmative action and diversity management: "Numerical activities are critical." Like Motorola, each business unit of Kraft had ethnic and gender targets reported monthly up through the hierarchy to Philip Morris, which owned Kraft. "Diversity will not exist without affirmative action throughout the company," declared Reid. "My job," he joked, "is to meddle in everyone else's business."

Chicago Tribune vice president and legal counsel David Hiller talked about his original aims to promote diversity at the newspaper beyond the common misconception of "quotas, numbers, compromises in quality, and P.C. orthodoxy." Hiller's main accomplishment, besides pushing the numbers—as it turned out—was appointing a black lawyer who later became a vice president for business relations. Hiller confessed that the organization had a long way to go and broached the "problem of balancing equity for experienced white males with the need to change the organization." The *Tribune,* he insisted, would set an example for Chicago as a "good citizen."

Sense and Sensitivity

If confusion with increasingly disreputable affirmative action was a primary roadblock in the path of the diversity machine, there were emerging openings as well. By 1993 and 1994, most consultants with whom I spoke were increasingly aware that appeals to change the white male workplace per se were not a strong selling point, even as a form of lawsuit protection. Instead, the route to CEO cash and commitment lay in pointing out changing customer bases. Immigration was unquestionably transforming customer bases in New York, Los Angeles, Houston, Miami, and—via 800 service and developing electronic networks—throughout the rest of the nation. The case for some sort of cultural sensitivity training for corporations with international customer bases was increasingly obvious.

Thus, the strong spot of the 1993 National Annual Diversity Conference was a sensible description of cross-cultural sensitivity training presented by Rebecca Chou, director of customer service for Northwest Airlines. The arrival of the service and global economies, said Chou, made culturally sensitive workers imperative. Chou deftly linked awareness of customer cultural differences to total quality management's emphasis on customer satisfaction and the feedback process between customer and employee. In today's fast-paced world, Chou said, every employee is an "individual marketer" for the organization. Employee attitude, trust, communication, and problem-solving abilities were crucial to obtaining customer satisfaction, loyalty, and smooth, error-free transactions. "For a smooth process," said Chou, "we must learn to deal with one another's differences." Intercultural understanding was also essential to building trust and empathy among employees and between workers and customers.

Chou's mention of trust and empathy had a more realistic ring than when such terms turned up on the conference's final day when moralism and New Age themes flowered briefly. In a morning keynote, Frances Kendall appealed to waning civil rights moralism. She mourned the contradictions sometimes involved in "doing good and doing well." Progressive practices may not always pay off. Stride-Rite Shoes, she noted, was closing its New England plant. Apostles of workforce diversity, she said, must have "courage to open our hearts and minds to people who are the 'other.' Go back on Monday and bring others into our effort."

Lewis Griggs used his afternoon keynote address to push new his new "Valuing Relationships" training series. Griggs, too, talked about the necessity for trust and building relationships. "We need to get beyond polarization," he urged. "We need to enhance complementary differences." Diversity in workplace and other relationships, he insisted, could release "unpredictable creativity and logarithmic productivity." To free such energy and creativity, people would have to "own their relationships . . . get past the isms." To understand and utilize all the ways we are different, explained Griggs, would take deeply personal, patient work.

Few minorities in the audience had patience with Griggs's New Age focus on building trust and relationships. Many walked out before he was finished. Several had departing planes to catch, but an exasperated Digital consultant muttered as she walked by me, "I've heard all this from Lewis before."

The sense of wheel spinning was marked, as at previous conferences, by what was not stated as well as what was. A representative from the American Association of Retired Persons (AARP) voiced proper frustration with the entire proceedings' paying little heed to age. Sexual orientation issues once again fell flat, if they were raised at all. Court cases and legal issues (with the exception of the Americans with Disabilities Act) were rarely mentioned. Although ethnic warfare in Bosnia was publicly noted, the L.A. riots were rarely referenced. And, incredibly, there was little public or private mention of the new presidency of Bill Clinton and how his "look-like-America" administration might move to sustain or expand workforce diversity initiatives. (When I later mentioned this to author-consultant Julie O'Mara, she grumbled about the lack of depth and sophistication among many consultants.)

I did not attend the fourth conference, nor did many other stalwarts. New York consultant-author Sibyl Evans felt the conferences had become a forum for external consultants' selling their wares. Internal consultants, she felt, were more cutting edge. Too few new ideas and approaches were being showcased. California consultants Anita Rowe and Sondra Thiederman felt the freshness had gone out of the conferences. "Same old, same old," said Thiederman, who was present for the fourth conference. The ever-ebullient conference organizer, Lewis Griggs, claimed satisfaction with a smaller but wiser fourth conference. "There were fewer people," he admitted, but more of them "got it," sensing the need to do the "inner work" on diversity.

Consultants Get Couch Time with Gardenswartz and Rowe

The National Annual Diversity conferences had served their purpose in getting diversity management off the ground by exposing potential clients and new consultants to the basics of the new field. There were also lessons in new and developing concepts and techniques. Yet the small group discussion sessions raised issues but did not solve them. Thus, consultants who encouraged others to talk about cultural differences and to do Griggs-style inner work on diversity were themselves tired. They needed "couch time" of their own, to vent and discuss problems at greater lengths in a friendly environment.

Group therapy was called for and delivered in Los Angeles by two up-and-coming consultant-authors, Lee Gardenswartz and Anita Rowe, both former Los Angeles school teachers who had worked diligently to become rising diversity stars. They had gotten into diversity training in the 1970s through civil rights and conflict-resolution work in their schools. Although there were elements of civil rights moralism in their work, their approach was primarily pragmatic and business oriented. They stressed an expanded and complex definition of diversity. They were emerging as national spokespersons through their books, *Managing Diversity: A Complete Desk Reference* and *The Diversity Tool Kit,* their frequent contributions to diversity-oriented newsletters, especially *Managing Diversity,* and their even more frequent professional workshops. They reduced their presence in ASTD-LA as they became major consultants to the even more respected and powerful business-professional association, the Society for Human Resource Management. Like R. Roosevelt Thomas, Gardenswartz and Rowe would seek to merge diversity with other management trends, most notably with team building in their 1995 book, *Diverse Teams at Work.* In spite of their prodigious efforts, however, their client list was modest by the mid-1990s, not yet in the same all-star league with Roosevelt Thomas and Price Cobbs: AT&T, Nissan Motor Corporation, California State Department of Health Services, the Government of Canada, Southern California Gas Company, and Prudential Insurance Company.

In July 1994, sixty people paid sixty dollars apiece to attend an ASTD-LA workshop to examine Gardenswartz and Rowe's new venture, *The Diversity Tool Kit,* a $300, ten-section file folder brimming with data sheets and exercises on cultural awareness, communication styles and skills, team building, interviewing and recruiting people from different backgrounds, mentoring and coaching, "warm-ups, mixers, and energizers," diversity resources (books and movies), and sample training agendas.

Selling the tool kit was an obvious goal of the session, but there were also a series of self-assessment techniques that, when focused on, turned the workshop into a therapy session. Consultants opened themselves up for self-assessment, exploration, and criticism—sometimes quite inadvertently. The workshop emphasized business-based pragmatism and an expanded definition of diversity; conversely, a related message was to tone down civil rights moralism and political correctness—neither easy nor entirely successful.

As usual, there were thirty or so faithful members of the Cultural Diversity Division: a majority of white women, several black and Hispanic women, with a sprinkling of "others." There were, however, almost as many outsiders and newcomers, especially several human resources personnel who had been, or were about to be, retired or downsized (two from Pacific Telephone and one from Southern California Gas Company). A Los Angeles Police Department psychologist was present (she was quiet most of the time and left early).

In addition to thick workbooks, people entering the conference room were handed forms to complete on "Similarities and Differences" before the formal start of the program. Simple questions asked about make of car, favorite movie, television show, foreign country to visit, and so forth. After completing the form, we were instructed to seek out others whose responses matched ours.

Having previewed the tool kit, Gardenswartz and Rowe then began the workshop by tapping a volcano of consultant frustrations. When asked what were the current "challenges" facing diversity consultants, workshop participants erupted:

"Unreasonable expectations!"

"Flavor-of-the-month fad!"

"Difficulty of linking diversity to business needs!"

" 'Entitled' persons believe there is no problem!"

"Mandatory training leads to lack of 'buy-in'!"

"The desire for quick-fix recipes!"

"The need for practical tools beyond conceptual foundations!"

"Closed-mindedness and denial among participants!"

"Resistance!"

"Conflict and polarization!"

"Trainer problems in dealing with their own 'isms'!"

"Confusion with affirmative action issues!"

"Continued 'we are all the same' assimilationism!"

Gardenswartz and Rowe dutifully absorbed all this and then began to counsel in a low-key style. Diversity management, they said, involves knowledge of three overlapping spheres: individual attitudes, organizational values and policies, and management skills and practices. They summarized four lessons they'd learned in their reassessment of workforce diversity training:

1. Diversity starts from within.
2. Everyone is involved—no white male bashing.

3. Learning takes place through interaction in groups.
4. Diversity training's effectiveness is hugely dependent on the trainer's abilities.

Everyone seemed to think this was reasonable. (It was.) Therefore, we opened up the tool kit and went to work on self-diagnosis.

Getting in Touch with Touchy Topics

To check out our inner diversity aptitude, we filled out the tool kit's "Diversity Trainer Self-Assessment." We were asked to rate ourselves as "almost always," "sometimes," or "almost never" to twenty-five questions—for example:

- I am able to present complex ideas simply and make them understood.
- My own assumptions and stereotypes surprise me.
- It is stimulating to work with someone who does not have my values.
- I can talk knowledgeably about the civil rights and other liberation movements.
- I value a wide range of views and attitudes.
- I am in tune with my own biases.
- I'm not carrying a banner for any group or viewpoint.
- Diversity works when all sides make adaptations.

Civil rights moralism and political correctness flared as we discussed the meaning of several questions. A white women objected to the question about carrying a banner and suggested (enthusiastically) that promoting diversity is (and should be) tantamount to flying diversity's flag. A black female raised an objection to the next question, grumbling that the privileged, not the non-privileged, should adapt. Other criticisms were more reasonable. Several people nodded when a white male suggested modifying one of the statements to read, "It is *sometimes* more stimulating to work with someone who does not have my values."

Another exercise was designed to push consultants out of race and gender thinking and to confront more complex realities. We were asked how we would personally rank the importance of key diversity variables—among them, race, gender, marital status, religious affiliation, work experience, educational background, and sexual orientation. This list was to be compared to how these factors had been ranked in two organizations with which we were familiar.

In subsequent analyses of the lists, several people immediately noted the clash between their personal high ranking of sexual orientation versus some client organizations' concern with religious affiliation. Specifically, two or three consultants in the room were conducting diversity training with a government agency (reported over lunch to be the Federal Aviation Administration). In trying to broach gay-lesbian cultural differences, they'd run into opposition from religious fundamentalists, who strongly objected to the issue's even being raised. What to do?

An African American consultant described how he had dealt with the homosexuality-Christianity clash in a recent training session. When a fundamentalist objected to even mentioning the gay-lesbian issue, he asked, "What if your child were gay?" The fundamentalist evidently struggled with the question but finally admitted that he would have to think differently about the issue if he had a gay child.

But the consultant had stumbled over a politically correct landmine among his ASTD-LA colleagues. A white female consultant angrily objected to this "what-if-your-child-were-gay?" technique. She charged that it sounded apologetic and negative—suggesting "I wouldn't wish this on anyone." The African American consultant looked somewhat chagrined and surprised, stammering that although the negative connotations were unintentional, the technique nonetheless had been effective. Still, he would reconsider such tactics. (Others in the room evidently considered the testy exchange; gay-lesbian issues were rarely referenced for the duration of the workshop.)

In other activities, we looked at leadership and management styles and how those might affect management of diversity. We compared individual and group rankings of essential traits of leadership behavior and completed a form comparing individual communication styles (directness, eye contact, loudness, impersonal or personal topics, etc.). Diversity concerns were thought to be addressed through more personable and informal styles of management.

The morning agenda had been fairly full and brisk. By late afternoon, half the participants had drifted out the door. Ironically, though the workshop was designed to promote a more complex and pragmatic business-oriented view of diversity, the moralists inherited the workshop by outlasting everyone else. This became obvious during the day's final exercise: each discussion group was asked to design a diversity logo and slogan. Piety and political correctness surged to saccharine levels. The therapeutic nature of the session was symbolized in one group's drawing of a huge globe with Gardenswartz and

Rowe leading people out of the center and human figures ringing the globe with hands joined—rather like the United Auto Workers seal. "Leading Us to the Light" was the slogan. Another group had four different-colored hands joined below the words "Diversity Works." A third group portrayed an hourglass with the sand running upward to illustrate the "old order expiring on the bottom and the new order emerging on top" with the words "Information Age." (This brought gleeful applause from the remaining participants.)

The workshop had illustrated—perhaps provoked—a new diversity among diversity consultants. The heretofore iron curtain of political correctness had cracked several times. One trainer described to the workshop how she'd arrived early at the home of a prospective client, who was not there. Two men of color were removing items from the house. The consultant tried to purge stereotypical thoughts about the men being criminals, only later to discover she had indeed been watching a burglary. A white female consultant admitted enjoying aspects of the "Rush Limbaugh Show," and cultural diversity division head Pam Fomalont admitted that she listened appreciatively and regularly to L.A. radio neoconservative commentator Dennis Praeger.

Fomalont had remained an active force in the ASTD-LA cultural diversity division but—like Gardenswartz and Rowe—would begin drifting away gradually as she became more successful. She had formed her own consulting firm and claimed that she had more business than she could handle from both the public and private sectors. She dismissed the 1994 Republican electoral sweep. Diversity was inevitable. Affirmative action would remain institutionalized. People were used to it and still viewed it as "the right thing to do." (Nevertheless, by the fall of 1995, Fomalont had changed the name of her diversity consulting business to Partners in Synergy. The "D-word," she admitted, had acquired negative connotations.)

Fomalont and others in the L.A. area claimed two sources of consulting activity: organizations that had not done any diversity training at all and now felt "behind the curve" and organizations that had completed basic awareness training and workshops and wished to move into more extensive cultural change.

Fomalont felt that diversity training was moving through one of the "critical crossroads" cited by *Cultural Diversity at Work* editor Barbara Deane: diversity policies were slowly being integrated into other new consulting trends, especially team building and empowerment. "Organizations are flattening out," said Fomalont. "People have to know more and have more self esteem. Things are changing fast."

The more successful Anita Rowe was more modest about prospects for diversity management and its practitioners: "You won't get rich doing this work. There are too many consultants and not enough clients."

Trying to Defuse the Gay-Lesbian Time Bomb

The gay-lesbian issue was a time-bomb topic not only in American society but within the diversity machine. "It's the most difficult area of difference we face," observed Julie O'Mara in a 1996 interview. R. Roosevelt Thomas and the more business-based pragmatists barely mentioned the topic, if at all. Cross-cultural trainers such as Tom Kochman and Sondra Thiederman generally avoided the issue. At the First Annual National Diversity Conference, the topic was almost entirely ignored—even though the host city was San Francisco. Workshops on the topic at the Second National Annual Diversity Conference were sparsely attended.

Like the wiring of a complex explosive device, there were a host of reasons why gay-lesbian issues were avoided. In an article in *Personnel Journal*, "Opening the Corporate Closet to Sexual Orientation Issues," Shari Caudron noted that gays and lesbians may comprise anywhere from 6 to 12 percent of the workforce, a percentage equal to or above that of Asians and Hispanics and perhaps equal to that of blacks. She cited a *Newswire* estimate that a hostile work environment for gays and lesbians may cost as much as $1.4 billion in lost output per year and admitted that there had been "an enormous shift in the last five years in the general level of awareness of gays and lesbians in the workplace."[3] But the topic continues to be ignored in diversity training and management largely because employers "don't realize how unsupportive the environment is to begin with" and because gay and lesbian employees don't push the issue. Backlash from religious fundamentalists inside and outside a company also lends pressure to ignore sexual orientation differences.

Caudron did not mention what I heard backstage among consultants: discussion of gay and lesbian cultural differences was clearly seen as offputting to conservative corporate CEOs. In diversity training workshops the topic could trigger explosive exchanges with religious fundamentalists. Even in backstage conversations, however, few recognized that active discussion of gay and lesbian claims vibrated deep intergroup fault lines in both society and within the diversity machine itself. Gay and lesbian claims to minority status threatened fractious arguments over the victimization pecking order. Talk of "sexual minorities" generated skepticism and suspicion among those who considered themselves to be the "real" oppressed minorities: African Americans and Latinos. In addition to purely political rivalry, African American response to homosexuality was negatively filtered by religious fundamentalists' relatively lower levels of education; Hispanic responses to the issue were similarly conditioned by Catholicism and educational level. Nor were Asian consultants more likely to press the topic. Furthermore, gay and lesbian proponents could be among the most dogmatic and politically correct of all the civil rights moralists. Other civil rights moralists appeared uneasy with some of gay and lesbian activists' more controversial assertions yet simultaneously felt compelled to defend them.

A window on this tangle of problems was opened during a 1991 ASTD-LA Cultural Diversity Division workshop, "Sexual Orientation in the Workplace." Fifty members and guests packed a classroom designed for forty at Antioch College West on a July evening (in contrast to a previous workshop on ageism, which attracted a mere ten people).

An introductory ten-minute video portrayed what it might be like to be heterosexual in a homosexual world: there would be self-hatred, secrecy, an inability to connect with others, being called a "breeder" (but not wanting to be a breeder), discovering a girl at a heterosexual bar, finding a heterosexual magazine and sneaking it home, and so forth.

The initial responses were sympathetic. "I felt isolated and lonely," said a white woman. "I felt sympathy for a brother who I discovered was gay," said a white man.

American Red Cross trainer Paul McGuane struck a sour note. "It didn't work for me. I found it hard to empathize. The narrator told me how to feel."

There was a long silence. Panelist Carol Anderson, an L.A. attorney, suggested that not all gay and lesbian people were alike. She compared sexual orientation to being left-handed.

Dottie Wine, founder and president of the South Bay Lesbian/Gay Community Organization, conducted a stereotyping exercise. We were asked to list traits associated with four categories. "Masculine" was identified with being macho, strong, man, ego, emotionless, stoic, brave. "Feminine" was typified as weak, soft, pretty, devious, gentle, flighty, sensitive, small, mother. Traits for "gay man" were sensitive, fluff, artistic, creative, effeminate, matching china, designer, sissy, wimpy, bitchy. "Promiscuous," added Paul McGuane daringly. He also contributed "tennis player" to the list of traits others offered for the lesbian stereotype: butch, aggressive, strong, militant, undesirable, man hater, and PC. Wine pointed out the obvious: that men's aggressive traits were viewed positively but lesbians' were not; that women's weak, sensitive, delicate traits were viewed positively but those of gay men were not. Gay and lesbian differences were not appreciated.

Vince Kates, a book distributor for several diversity consultants, joined McGuane in cracking the politically correct veneer: "I think white males are harder on one another than on members of other groups."

This was greeted with shock and ripples of laughter.

"How?" said panelist Carol Anderson.

"Physically, mentally, in every other way . . ."

"You mean you expect more from other white males?"

"No, we'll kick their ass harder. I'm talking about methods of selection in the dominant group, if you will. Something as simplistic as a fraternity. Some guys trying to get in get selected out. Some who do get in get killed. It's boot camp."

Glenda Madrid, acting ASTD Cultural Division chair, intervened: "I'm going to interject here because I think this is a whole different topic worth exploring later. So thank you for raising the issue." She then introduced Ron Smebye, a Xerox field programs manager. Smebye, in turn, introduced his wife and daughter and then sought to surprise the gathering by revealing that he was gay. Smebye maintained that corporations lose money and productivity and could face large lawsuit settlements by not valuing gay and lesbian employees. He suggested that 10 to 30 percent of all employees were gay or lesbian and that perhaps 10,000 of Xerox's 55,000 employees were. Younger employees, he alleged, were less willing to hide their sexual orientation.

The third panelist, Phil Sheley, a trainer and PWA (person with AIDS), discussed the need to educate managers and employees about the legal and medical aspects of the illness. Lawyer Carol Anderson briefly outlined discrimination issues and lamented the fact that twenty-four states still had sodomy statutes on the books and that California had not enacted antidiscrimination statutes protecting gays and lesbians.

The division chair moved to wrap up the evening by asking, "What do we do now?" The suggestions were predictable: antidiscrimination and partner benefits policies, gay and lesbian support groups, encouraging gays and lesbians to come out, and inclusion of the topic in cultural diversity training. I mentioned that professional consultants—such as those at the First Annual Diversity Conference in San Francisco—appeared leery of the gay and lesbian issue out of fear of scaring off corporate clients. There were several nodding heads, and another white male quickly seconded this "tough problem." My follow-up mention of the brewing conflict between religious fundamentalists and gay and lesbian issues was not as well received.

Fundamentalist Christianity was *not* a cultural difference to be valued. Dottie Wine frostily dismissed the importance of religious fundamentalists:

"The reality is that they are not as strongly represented in the workforce as [newspaper] letters to Pete Wilson might suggest. . . . Fundamentalist women tend to stay home and have babies because that is what God told them to do. They are not department heads or producers in corporate America. There is a much higher percentage of gay and lesbian people in corporate America than there are fundamentalist born-again Christians."

This was too much for Paul McGuane, who later admitted he was becoming fed up with excessive political correctness and reverse stereotyping. He suggested that it was his experience that white males were more likely to be more tolerant of homosexuality than males from other cultural backgrounds. Michael Woodard, the African American sociologist from UCLA, archly asked if there were any scientific data to support such views. (No one had questioned the evidence regarding statements that 10 to 30 percent of the workforce were gay or lesbian or that there were more gay and lesbian executives than fundamentalist Christians.) Two other audience members indicated that Asians and Filipinos were very accepting of homosexuality. Dottie Wine helpfully explained that perceptions may clash with expectations: we expect oppressed ethnic minorities to be more sympathetic to gays and lesbians, but if minorities' acceptance is no better than the general society, we feel let down. Pam Fomalont mentioned that nearly half the people in her diversity classes did not want to be there. In that context, introducing gay and lesbian issues would simply be one more initial obstacle to overcome. "You may not like to do it, but you do it."

To judge by recent feedback, however, most consultants still do not.

Simulations and Games: Participatory Diversity Training

In a Conference Board survey, *Diversity Training: A Research Report* (1994), participative exercises emphasizing interaction and group involvement were deemed the most effective approach. Simulations and games were part of the consultant repertoire to get people more self-involved in diversity training and to learn by doing. Simulations were supposed to foster a sense of what it was like to be culturally different and were popular among the more "touchy-feely" consultants who favored "experiential" exercises. The aim was to stimulate lasting, "Aha!" moments of inner realizations about cultural differences.

Lawrence Flores, who designed the Multicultural Promotion Track Simulation Game, argued that "simulation games speak to the fact that there are some things in life that cannot be explained—they must be experienced."[4] He and others hold that games permit trainees to process information that is more conventionally presented. There are also more conventional formats featuring game boards or card decks that have a less experiential emphasis but draw on Americans' desire to be entertained as well as informed.

I participated in abbreviated demonstrations of a popular simulation and, some months later, a new Monopoly-style game through the American Society for Training and Development's Los Angeles Cultural Diversity Division. The goofy-sounding simulation, BaFa, BaFa, had nonetheless become a classic exercise for cross-cultural trainers. Originally formulated in the early 1970s to help acclimate U.S. troops to overseas settings, the new version (which normally required at least a half-day) had been honed and refined in corporations such as Procter and Gamble.

The simulation's creator, Garry Shirts, divided us into Alpha and Beta cultures. Betans went to another room, while we Alphans remained to learn the rules of our new culture. Alphans were basically a warm and fuzzy, traditional Third World tribe. We smiled a lot, exchanged boisterous greetings and hugs upon meeting each other, showed and exchanged various cards, and exchanged toy coins willingly and easily. Subtribes were identified by wearing different colored armbands: orange banded peasants, who could not talk directly to high-status blues; greens were the intermediaries. Strangers were not permitted to approach oranges; if they did so, strangers were asked to leave by a blue-banded person.

The Betans were an acquisitive, class-structured, capitalist First World culture where status was determined by possession of cards of various value (e.g., money). They had to speak in code centering around *Ba, Fa,* and *Wa* sounds—hence the name of the game. Visitors and ambassadors were exchanged between the cultures and reported back to their home tribes. Game monitors gave visitors coming into the Betan culture a few cards to bargain with—if they could figure out how to do it.

The aim of the exercise was to generate culture shock, to impart the feeling of confusion, frustration, and even foolishness that comes from trying to figure out the unwritten rules of a new society—as presumably minorities, women, and immigrants must learn to negotiate the invisible white male rules of corporate America. Indeed, this was brought out in the debriefing of all players following the game that asked various questions: What did I learn about others? What did I learn about organizations? What are the obstacles to newcomers? Are people who are different denied access or power?

Supposedly such discussions in actual organizational settings lead to the advertised results of helping "participants identify the obstacles to managing diversity effectively" and "understanding how cultural diversity within the

workforce can be a tremendous asset." Just how this happens was not speci-
fied. (Shirts later told me the game was basically a sensitizing device.)

Then came the sales pitch. A license and trainer kit cost $750; to certify
additional trainers from the same organization cost $250; a set of thirty-six
workbooks for players costs $432. (Despite Shirts's follow-up calls to work-
shop participants, there were only two major sales—to consultants who
worked for medical and hospital groups.)

In a later interview, Shirts confessed he'd been frustrated by the compressed
time span and even more by lack of sales. He observed, with some accuracy,
that "I got the idea that most of the people there were looking for jobs." Shirts
also was aware that diversity training could be a game in more than one way: "A
Fortune 500 executive told me that they view such training as a 'check-off'—
it's something they do, but they don't want to spend much time doing it.")

The chief risk with BaFa, BaFa was the potential for participants to feel
thoroughly embarrassed, childish, or foolish. Extroverts, people with a sense
of humor, and those who were flexible and adaptable had least to lose in these
situations. But those who were shy and not good at improvising in new situations could look stupid—which might lead to their discounting and disparaging the game and its lessons. Indeed, some consultants were wary that
such games were especially risky with upper-level managers because of the
potential to demean managers' sense of importance and self-esteem: there
was too much possibility to lose face. All of these difficulties led George Simons to market a more content-based contest patterned after a comfortable
American family game, Monopoly.

The ASTD-LA tried out George Simons's Diversophy ten months later.
Diversophy was a hybrid of Trivial Pursuit question-answer cards grafted to a
Monopoly-style format with dice, cards, and game board (which we did
without). Simons, a consultant who holds a doctorate in psychology and the-
ology, directed the activities. He introduced the game with a humor-spiced
reappraisal of the standard workforce diversity rationale. Showing a cartoon
of a balkanized "Bosnia, U.S.A.," he admitted that diversity had acquired the
same negative connotations of affirmative action—causing more conflict and
divisions than it cured. He criticized simple proportionalism, the rush to victimization, and urged that diversity move beyond tired clichés like "leveling
the playing field." (Simons provocatively joked that he had solved all his
"quota problems" by hiring one multiethnic office assistant. Yet PC was melting. There were smiles. A year before, jests about "Bosnia, U.S.A.," or use of
the term "quotas" would have been unthinkable.)

Significantly, Simons was one of the first writers and lecturers to signal a retreat from the Griggs-Thomas scenario of inevitable ethnic pluralism. Some corporate cultures, Simons observed, would continue to emphasize assimilation and uniformity. Elements of IBM's culture would be the same worldwide. A balance between assimilation and pluralism would evolve.

Then the "tournament" commenced with the sixty participants grouped at tables seating about seven people each. We rolled dice and chose, more or less randomly, from three stacks of cards.

"diversiSMARTS" cards asked questions about data or information (with answers on the back):

Women tend to define and esteem themselves through their:
    A. Ability to produce results
    B. The high quality of their relationships to others
    C. Their independence from others
    (Answer: B)
When faced with a complaint, women are more likely to offer:
    A. Empathy
    B. Solutions
    C. A complaint in return
    (Answer: A)
One of the chief reasons why Mexican-Americans are gaining better recognition is:
    A. Their increasing numbers, particularly in the Southwest
    B. The militancy of the 1960s generation of Chicano activists
    C. Women's suffrage
    (Answer: B)
Of those choosing to take parental leave, child care and flex-time benefits:
    A. Women comprise 90% and men 10%
    B. Women comprise 60% and men 40%
    (Answer: B)

"diversiRISK" or "diversiCHOICE" cards posed tasks or problematic situations:

- In the next 30 seconds, name as many famous lesbian or gay persons as you can, politicians, scientists, artists or entertainers, scholars or writers.
- Celebrate Black History Month by naming 5 famous African-Americans.
- You lose the best mentor you ever had after rumors linked the two of you as romantically involved.

- Your "man bashing" and "cheap shots" at men have kept you on the outside of decision-making in your organization. You become even more self-righteous and negative about men. (Cardholder was instructed to "give this card to a man in the group.")

- Actions that seem common sense to you may be strange and uncomfortable for immigrants. Speaking up, saying no, disagreeing with a manager may be unacceptable in their culture. To help immigrants acculturate, you might:

  1. Speak up for them until they "get the hang of it."
  2. Explain the reason for the preferred behavior and how it works in this culture.
  3. Warn them that "old country" habits will get them in trouble here.
     (Answer: B)

"diversiSHARE" cards were self-explanatory:

- Tell the group one or more of the things that would make you want to avoid working with someone of the other gender.
- Demonstrate two non-verbal ways in which people in your culture say "No!" (Pause to share)
- Think of a stereotype you once held about a person or a group of people. Describe what made you drop that stereotype. (Pause to share)

Simons was cooler than Garry Shirts in pressing for sales; we were simply given printed order forms along with the other hand-out materials. The more sets of the game you bought, the less they cost: one to three games cost $375 each; for ten or more, each game set was $295. There was an 800 number, and VISA and Mastercard were accepted.

Obviously, the appeal of Diversophy was the same as Trivial Pursuit and Monopoly. It was a competitive learning situation, with elements of risk and fun. It was group-based learning so one got to know other people playing the game. In this sense, Diversophy might serve dual functions: providing information about diversity while acquainting workers in a mildly competitive situation. There were also risks: those with people-oriented skills (and those who were up on news and current events) were likely to perform better than those who were sociologically inept. One could still lose face, though not nearly to the degree as in BaFa, BaFa.

The other problem with some of the Diversophy questions, such as the diversiSmarts questions about women, was confirming stereotypes. (As seen in the profile of cross-cultural consultant Tom Kochman, this diversity paradox—the desire to discuss cultural differences but not trigger negative stereotypes—was at the heart of diversity training.) But it was interesting to observe that none of the many politically correct people present at the ASTD session objected to these question-and-answer cards.

Apart from the high price and the possibility of creating too lighthearted an atmosphere for what some considered a serious subject, the primary problem with these simulations and games was running up against the most important variable mentioned in the Conference Board's study of diversity training: time. Setting up simulations and games—distributing the props, then explaining the rules—could take more than an hour, and conducting the actual simulation or game could take a day or two.

Yet in June 1996, George Simons reported to me that sales and interest in Diversophy had suddenly surged at recent conventions. The price had been steeply cut, and he also found that purchasers were streamlining the game, reducing the time required to play it by dispensing with the game board and dice (just as at the ASTD-LA simulation). He was preparing a new individualized computerized version of the game but was convinced of the benefits of group learning. Simons maintained that competition and elements of risk and testing produce excitement and involvement. Pam Fomalont thought such aspects were especially attractive to white males, but Julie O'Mara disagreed. She insisted that the key variable with games—and any other training in general—was institutional commitment.

Fomalont and Simons were impressed with the keen interest in a variety of new games and simulations they observed at the March 1996 International Society for Intercultural Education, Training, and Research (SIETAR) in Munich. Fomalont, Simons, and many other consultants felt intercultural or global diversity was the coming wave in diversity management. The turn to global issues was partly driven by rising public skepticism and hostility to race and gender engineering in the United States, as seen in a remarkable shift in the intellectual and political climate.

Under Siege: Battling the Bell Curve and the Changing Political Landscape

The 1994 elections decisively signaled a swift shift in the intellectual and political climate, which further dimmed diversity management's aura of a hot trend, and its inevitability as routine business practice. The Republican congressional landslide demonstrated that the fledgling field was still dependent on uncertain political trends.

On the one hand, rising conservative tides had slowed, if not reversed, multicultural momentum. Supreme Court decisions had severely restricted the scope of public sector affirmative action, diversity management's disreputable twin. And despite frantic efforts to separate the two fields, diversity management is being tarred along with affirmative action in the post-1994 explosion of criticism against all things politically correct.

On the other hand, President Clinton's allegiance to affirmative action and diversity "look-like-America" lingo remained steadfast. Feminist and civil rights groups were already gearing up opposition research in preparation for the California Civil Rights Initiative, a proposed 1996 voter referendum that would prohibit state use of ethnic and gender preferences. Gingrich-Kemp Republicans continued to run from the topic. Best of all, the White House and allied lawyers were actively pondering how to use workforce diversity as the "compelling interest" rationale for continuing ethnic and gender preferences in federal programs—to try to satisfy "strict scrutiny" requirements contained in the 1994 Supreme Court decision, *Adarand Constructors, Inc. v. Pena* (in which the Court held that broadly drawn policies of federal ethnic favoritism for minority companies were unconstitutional).

These new developments were anxiously pondered by four hundred consultants, human resources managers, and others interested in multicultural management at the June National Multicultural Institute Conference in Washington, D.C. This was the tenth such conference sponsored by a private, nonprofit organization founded in 1983 "to improve understanding and respect among people of different racial, ethnic, and cultural backgrounds." NMCI offers diversity training and consulting, develops educational resource materials, and maintains a multilingual mental health counseling and referral service. The institute publishes a range of publications, including a multicultural trainers' guide ($149).

The registration fees were about half those at the National Annual Diversity conferences. Therefore, although many consultant faces were the same (Gardenswartz and Rowe were there to conduct a workshop on team building) the paying audience was more downscale. The vast majority appeared to be from public and nonprofit institutions.

Several sessions emphasized measuring results, but there were no findings worthy of salvaging the field. Instead, the tone of the meetings waxed defensive and indignant with regard to ideological threats, especially renewed public discussion of unwelcome ethnic IQ differences raised in the late Richard Herrnstein and Charles Murray's best-selling *The Bell Curve*.

NMCI president Elizabeth Salett opened the conference with a conciliatory call for more rational dialogue and debate on multiculturalism—in vain. Her speech was followed by a thoroughly intemperate panel discussion of *The Bell Curve* by several PC luminaries. Wellesley College's Peggy McIntosh urged more white people to debate (attack) *The Bell Curve* and offered her stern "common sense critique of what these men have done." The book was "shoddy social science," especially since Herrnstein and Murray had ignored gender bias and McIntosh's own pet theory of ubiquitous "white skin privilege." Although Herrnstein and Murray might acknowledge "environmental factors" in IQ equations, McIntosh nonetheless divined racist imagery of "safe streets versus crime and disorder." Asked if the book was part of "genocide against black people," McIntosh answered without hesitation: "Yes, it is. . . . This furthers the right wing's unannounced policy against people of color."

University of California, Berkeley, sociologist Martin Sanchez-Jankowski tried reason and moderation, acknowledging that race and ethnicity were the focus of only two chapters of *The Bell Curve*. And Sanchez-Jankowski refused to go along with test-bashing remarks of other panelists' and audience members: "If you don't like tests—get over it. They're here to stay." This was not well received.

Alvin Pouissant's impassioned, rambling critique brought down the house. The panel moderator could scarcely stop the Harvard psychologist. Pouissant charged that *The Bell Curve* contained "nothing new" and was written for "political power purposes." He scorned standardized testing as biased and drew laughter by mocking test questions such as, "What does a policeman do?" and by jeering Dan Quayle ("If we had a meritocracy, then Dan Quayle would be a dishwasher"). Blacks, he declared, are only thirty years away from the heritage of slavery and if Herrnstein and Murray could find and test a comparable sample of whites with the same history, "we'll win that one." (Pouissant was in such a tizzy over *The Bell Curve* that he seized on arguments used by affirmative action opponents: that race and ethnic identities are bogus categories and that within-group variations may override seeming differences between groups.)

Worries about rebellious "angry white males" rumbled throughout the conference. With California's pending antipreference California Civil Rights Initiative on the horizon, "white male resistance," once thought to be amenable to suppression or patronizing, was turning into an open revolt. What was going wrong?

During a packed workshop on white men in the workplace, a white female consultant played the politically correct audience like a piano: white men feared losing unearned privilege through competition with equally capable women and minorities; white males were scapegoating affirmative action and diversity for their own declining economic status in the changing global order; and such anxieties were being fanned by the mass media, especially talk radio and the demonic Rush Limbaugh. The primary source of white male discontent—reverse discrimination—was rarely referenced and was quickly dispatched as a myth.

The few white males attending the workshop said little except during coffee breaks when some whispered that much was being left unsaid. Indeed, although conference participants often threw verbal darts at "white male privilege" and "monoculturalism," the gathering pulsed with its own PC race and gender dogma. The multicultural veneer seemed exceedingly thin in view of the dominance of black-white issues and the convention's composition. An overwhelming majority of 400 conventioneers were women; blacks far outnumbered a sprinkling of other ethnic minorities. There were a handful of middle-aged white males, and I saw only three Asian men. (It is one of the ironies of the diversity industry that it is not very diverse.)

Indeed, the composition of the NMCI convention confirmed a continuing, nettlesome image problem: diversity management still appears to be and largely is a human resources ghetto for victim-mongering blacks and women, humored and patronized by savvy CEOs who were obviously using diversity training as a talisman against discrimination lawsuits.

In view of these problems, multicultural merchants have been on the lookout for other sure-bet trends to which they can hitch their professional wagon. Some have noticed the surge in alternative forms of dispute mediation and arbitration as replacements for overcrowded, costly court procedures. Ergo: NMCI offered a two-day workshop on multicultural conflict resolution.

Seeing Conflict Through the Lenses of Race, Class, and Gender

Conflict resolution has long been an established branch of applied academic social science, with both humanistic and highly mathematical branches. The potential for group conflict to intensify when ethnic or racial divisions are superimposed on previously existing conflict groups based on class, religion, or other variables was mapped brilliantly in the modern sociological classic, *Class and Class Conflict in Industrial Society* (1959) by German sociologist Ralf Dahrendorf.[5]

As Lewis Griggs frequently noted, it was cultural differences, not similarities, that generated problems, including misunderstanding, tension, and possibly outright conflict. The attraction to team building and conflict resolution among diversity consultants was fairly natural, not contrived, though it may have been financially strategic. Conflict resolution was a more established policy domain.

There is some intelligent, perceptive writing on conflict management by diversity management authors. Diversity consultants Lee Gardenswartz and Anita Rowe outlined several normative orientations that can affect conflict and conflict resolution:

1. Conflict is seen as disruptive to harmony: such norms can range across a variety of cultures but is more pronounced in Asian cultures.
2. Conflict presents a risk of loss of face. Gardenswartz and Rowe suggest that Latino and Middle Eastern groups are sensitive to such chances.
3. Different communication styles can make resolution more difficult. Gardenswartz and Rowe cite an example of an African American and a Filipino woman whose disagreement is compounded by the African American's more direct and confrontational style as opposed to the more reticent and retiring type of behavior dictated by Filipino culture.
4. A history of intergroup discrimination may lead to an interpretation of conflict or criticism as discrimination or prejudice—"they're only doing this because I'm . . . "[6]

And in their more recent book, *Diverse Teams at Work,* they noted several "diversity variables" that affect both teamwork and conflict resolution:

1. Egalitarian culture versus hierarchical or authoritarian culture.
2. Direct communication style versus indirect style.
3. Individualistic culture versus group or collectivistic culture.
4. Task-oriented focus versus more social or relationship oriented focus.
5. Change-oriented culture versus traditional culture.[7]

At the NMCI workshop, these subtleties surfaced but were largely overwhelmed by a heavy PC emphasis on race, class, and gender. Michelle LeBaron, an adjunct professor at nearby George Mason University, and Rosemary Romero Morris, a New Mexico dispute resolution consultant, directed about thirty people through a series of small group exercises designed to demonstrate how the lenses of race, gender, and class affect our abilities to see and deal with conflict.

The die was cast when, in the fashion of identity politics, we were asked to sort ourselves into self-selected "primary identity" groups to discuss how group viewpoints affect interpersonal strengths and weaknesses. Predictably, given the nature of the conference, the largest groups formed around tables for ethnicity and gender. Those who identified with gender decided that women had greater empathy, understanding, patience, and tolerance and were more willing to compromise; stout-hearted men were more rational, calm, and goal oriented. Those sitting at the ethnicity table thought that those in the "dominant culture" (white males) tended to be optimistic, trust in the system, and had faith that they could actively master situations; members of "subordinate cultures" (minorities) had "active listening skills" (a favorite phrase of our instructors) and more fully understood all sides of the conflict because many minorities were "bicultural." Such responses were very much in line with Deborah Tannen's *You-Just-Don't-Understand* multiculturalism. Our instructors were delighted, suggesting other self-awareness workouts, such as, "Think about the way you have privilege."[8]

The next small group exercise was trickier—and an invitation to activate stereotypes. After counting off to form new groups, we were given lists describing five hypothetical candidates for kidney dialysis, which had to be rationed because there were only two available machines. The candidates varied along every conceivable ethnic, gender, and class dimensions, and one was gay. Whom would we choose?

Less sensitive folk might have stumbled over obvious class, ethnic, or "contribution to society" land mines embedded in the candidates' biographical sketches. (Clearly the gay candidate was a sitting duck for homophobia.) But nearly everyone in the workshop was on PC autopilot, and we quickly arrived at a set of fairly neutral criteria: the number of dependents and the financial hardship placed on them should the candidate die. (At one point in our group's discussion, I prodded a PC trip-wire by suggesting that one dialysis candidate, an immigrant, might be ruled out on the basis of citizenship, especially if he were here illegally. A social worker hotly objected, suggesting that such this would be "antiforeigner" and had ominous overtones of California's successful ballot proposition to deny public services to illegal immigrants. She was seconded by a black personnel consultant who proclaimed that if immigrants paid taxes, citizenship was irrelevant. I dropped the issue.)

We engaged in simulated class struggle between a landlord group versus those chosen to represent a tenants' association group. This was a study in stacked-deck bargaining—familiar to some group members who had poverty backgrounds. In negotiations the effective landlord negotiators used calming language, mourned any previous miscommunications, and effectively staved off badly needed repairs by saying they would have to check with other authorities. Tenant negotiators who became emotional, interrupted, overreacted, or were too confrontational were less persuasive than those who calmly appealed to compromise and landlords' better instincts.

It became clear that many in the workshop robustly enjoyed talking, arguing, and engaging in the drama of disputes; some did not or could not. Thus came the question of how to resolve conflicts with those who would not or could not openly argue. Instructor Rosemary Romero Morris offered a cross-cultural illustration of subtle and indirect tactics. On an Indian reservation where verbal disputes were repressed, a dog that constantly barked was building tensions. A tribal elder began repeatedly visiting the offending dog's owner but only indirectly referred to the dog. The dog owner surmised the reason for the increased visits and took greater care of the dog. ("A happy ending, I suppose, but it wouldn't work in business," muttered a woman near me.)

As people began to drift away about halfway through the second day, the instructors stooped to using one of the oldest training tools in the book. They passed out bags of Tinker Toys and asked groups of us to compete in trying to build the tallest toy structures. Like the other ethnic and gender aerobics, the real goal was to illustrate how gender, personality, and other differences emerged. (True to form, men tended to dominate and manifest greater construction skills.)

Politically correct thought and speech were a given throughout the workshop, but there were occasional blunders. Instructor Michelle LeBaron needlessly and effusively apologized at the beginning of the second day's workshop for prior offhand use of the phrase "black sheep." In an ensuing discussion of subtle and institutional biases, an exasperated white male NASA computer specialist protested vigorously about "walking on eggshells" at his workplace. Use of the term "ladies," he said, had been derided for its association with "ladies of the night." He no longer felt like talking there at all.

This complaint produced patronizing sympathy from minority and female workshoppers. There was ready agreement that there had been PC zealousness, but the instructors bade us consider the "inner ouches" that careless remarks might cause others. Sensitivity overkill, the instructors counseled, alienated whites and other potential allies in building a more multicultural workplace. Indeed, it already had.

During the next coffee break, the NASA engineer grumbled that he'd be glad to get back to his computers; the machines didn't complain about discrimination or sexual harassment. Indeed, he departed forthwith, missing a concluding segment fusing PC conciliation with New Age oneness. In the final half-hour, the remaining fifteen workshoppers formed a circle to reflect on our workshop experiences. Given the tone of the workshop—and that the dissatisfied had already left—this was a safe strategy: all experiences were positive. A black postal worker from Michigan declared she'd not only learned a great deal but had developed great affection for the friends she'd made in the workshop. A white woman consoled the three remaining white males that she'd found out what it was like to watch white men as a minority group. Michelle LeBaron burbled that the outcome of the workshop was "like clear water." With that, came two minutes of hushed meditation. This gave the two instructors a brief pause before they dashed for the airport to catch a plane for Switzerland, where they would latch onto another hot trend being developed by the diversity machine: applying cross-cultural training in international or global settings.

Conference Burnout

The tenth NMCI conference provided a much-needed pep rally for civil rights moralists and served as an introductory bazaar for the new and curious interested in sampling basic concepts and techniques, or shopping for anything from a new career to diversity books, literature, t-shirts, and jewelry. Still, seasoned conference junkies confessed a sense of weariness. (As mentioned previously, attendance at Griggs's Fourth Annual National Diversity Conference was down by almost 50 percent.)

"I'm not coming to these things any more," grumbled Los Angeles consultant Pam Fomalont. "We need to move on and build a whole new vision of the world that stresses win-win, instead of the competitive win-lose." A consultant from the high-powered Kaleel Jamieson firm sniffed that she could have taught the workshop she attended.

In spite of stall, frustration, and the changing political and cultural climate, by 1994 the diversity machine was acquiring increased allegiance from two powerhouse professional associations: the Conference Board and the Society for Human Resource Management. But what was really needed was systematic proof that diversity policies delivered. That would be difficult.

Chapter 6

Strong New Allies, Weak Policy Proof

Griggs and Thomas Reformulate Diversity

B y the mid-1990s, two premiere business-based professional associations, along with the American Society for Training and Development, were poised to become primary powerplants in the diversity machine. Strong diversity initiatives were launched in 1993 by the Society for Human Resource Management (SHRM) and in 1994 by the influential New York–based Conference Board. Several big corporations and external consultants associated with the National Annual Diversity conferences became associated with one or both of the new efforts.

Lewis Griggs was a prime beneficiary of both organizations' relatively new-found faith in diversity management. He became a consultant to the Conference Board's Workforce Diversity Council and, in 1996, SHRM asked to partner with Griggs on a rejuvenated National Annual Diversity Conference, which would be publicized, marketed, and heavily organized by SHRM's experienced staff. Though there would be traces of civil rights moralism, especially at SHRM, the emphasis there and at the Conference Board would be overwhelmingly on pragmatic business appeal, with an expanded definition of diversity and a broad change master focus on changing corporate culture and structure.

More than two years before bonding with Lewis Griggs, SHRM began a major initiative aimed at educating its staff about the benefits of diversity management as well as the wider membership of 52,000 professionals and student members. It formed a workplace diversity committee, began diversity sessions at its annual conference, inaugurated diversity training at SHRM leadership conferences, and sponsored diversity speeches to SHRM chapters and state conferences. (Despite efforts to separate affirmative action and diversity management, however, the SHRM board inadvertently revealed the two policies' kinship by voting to rename its Equal Employment Opportunity Committee as the Workplace Diversity Committee.)

SHRM commissioned cross-cultural consultant Sondra Thiederman to author a booklet, *Ten Strategies for Achieving a More Diverse Membership.* In 1994 SHRM began working with California consultants Lee Gardenswartz and Anita Rowe to launch a SHRM Managing Diversity Forum Certificate Program (budgeted for thirty-five people, the forum has been a sell-out). By 1995, the association had begun publishing *Diversity Reference Guide* and *Mosaics,* a bimonthly newsletter on diversity issues. Creating a World of Difference was the theme of the 1995 SHRM Annual Conference in Orlando, Florida. Keynote speakers included San Francisco consultant Lee Brown, and William Brooks, General Motors vice president of corporate relations and an emerging national figure in the diversity machine. Barbara Bush spoke on the need for literacy programs.

SHRM Diversity Initiative chair, Patricia Digh, was generally optimistic about the new programs but admitted that the term "diversity" had become tagged by the public as a civil rights issue; diversity policies were still stuck in the human resources department and had not yet been woven throughout corporate culture. The policy movement's internal fault line, she readily recognized, was the strong disagreement over expanding the definition of diversity beyond race and gender. Digh had worked on SHRM's international diversity conference and seen that national cultures were the focus there; race was regarded as a minor factor. When international and domestic consultants had gathered at last year's diversity forum, there had been a big "blow-up" over the issue, she said. Digh herself seemed ambivalent: "Look at the O. J. Simpson verdict. People feared workplace riots as a result of the verdict. How can you talk about going beyond race and gender?" On the other hand, she felt there were other issues with which to deal, while "racism will never be solved in my lifetime." Digh clearly favored the business-pragmatist approach to diversity broadly defined. She obviously had the civil rights moralists in mind when she criticized some consultants for using diversity consulting as a platform for politics. "For them," she said, "everything is about race."

Digh was refreshingly candid about diversity management's ideological underpinnings. She was distraught about the conservative revival of the mid-1990s and was one of the first diversity professionals I'd spoken with who was frank about the role politics would play in the future of the diversity machine. She conceded that a Clinton victory would be crucial in continuing diversity momentum. "It's one of the more important presidential elections in my lifetime because of the antidiversity, anti-immigration feelings. Pat Buchanan can publicly say he won't hire gays!" She felt that the public's general fear and anxiety, creating hostility against diversity programs, were being whipped up by the news media, which painted an exaggerated picture of affirmative action. It was "irresponsible behavior . . . Hispanic and black reporters must say something," she felt.

Digh saw big changes in the coming years. The dimensions of diversity would expand even further, and "a whole generation of managers is going to die off." The upcoming generation of managers would focus more on empowerment and more flexible styles. Digh sounded Griggsian notes as she talked about how "people will recognize themselves as part of a system" and will "look for spirituality at work."

Digh admitted that proof of the effectiveness of diversity strategies was skimpy and that the policies had to be accepted on faith and "a value judgment that diversity is good." When I noted that several business magazines, such as *Fortune,* had paid little attention to diversity management, she happily corrected me by pointing out a thick segment in the April 15, 1996, issue of *Fortune,* "Diversity, a Global Business Issue." Satisfaction, however, quickly turned to chagrin. "Oh, shoot," sighed Digh, "it's an ad."

Yet in terms of mapping growing corporate support for diversity, the glossy forty-six-page "special advertisement" was intriguing. The ad resembled a standard magazine article showcasing a series of profiles of the diversity chiefs and several well-known corporations: Chase Manhattan Bank, Chrysler Corporation, Coca-Cola, Ford, General Mills, General Motors, IBM, Chubb Insurance Companies, Owens-Corning, Quaker Oats, Philip Morris, Prudential Insurance, Rockwell International, Salomon Brothers, Sara Lee Corporation, and Sears Roebuck. Although the corporate profiles were generally smooth appeals to business-based pragmatism, the race and gender focus of civil rights moralism was occasionally apparent, especially in the advertisement's origin and partial funding by two African American executives' associations: the Executive Leadership Council and the Executive Leadership Foundation.

A different set of corporations participated in projects by the Conference Board, a well-known education and research association located in New York City. From its 2,500 member companies (including 75 percent of the Fortune 500 corporations) the Conference Board turned to diversity directors from Procter and Gamble, Digital Equipment, General Electric, du Pont,

General Telephone, Kraft General Foods, Kaiser Permanente Health Mainte- nance Organization, Levi-Strauss, Pillsbury, 3M, Pacific Bell, Los Angeles Department of Water and Power, Bank of America, Girl Scouts of America, RJR Nabisco, and Sara Lee Corporation, and joined with external consul- tants (and National Annual Diversity Conference veterans). They were joined by consultants such as Lewis Griggs, David Tulin, and Sybil Evans and representatives from the Anti-Defamation League's World of Difference Institute. Yet the Conference Board was slower than most such professional associations to get aboard the diversity machine.

Bob Falcey, vice president of conferences, admitted that the Conference Board was "slow to get off the line" on diversity management. But he felt the "subject was on its way up" thanks to the work of Conference Board research associate Michael Wheeler, who was organizing the organization's first major diversity conference for the spring of 1997, to be sponsored by du Pont, General Motors, and Deloitte and Touche.

In November 1995, Wheeler released a Conference Board task force re- search report, *Diversity: Business Rationale and Strategies*. Fifty-one organiza- tions had participated in the survey. Yet the report was not so much a research document as an advocacy brief. Indeed, one of the first chapters was addressed to building a business case for diversity and advised that "diverse markets and a global economy are the strongest arguments for diversity ini- tiatives."[1] The report featured testimonials from corporations that had al- ready converted to the cause of diversity based largely on the faith of determined CEOs and legal compliance with affirmative action. The report was a grab bag of corporate diversity statements and consultant rationales and prescriptions. It echoed much of what had been said—again and again— at the National Annual Diversity conferences.

Despite the advocacy tone, however, the report was notable for its strict business-pragmatism emphasis; civil rights moralism was almost totally ab- sent. The race and gender theme nearly vanished under an expanded defini- tion of diversity pushed to cover almost too many dimensions. The report cited Kaiser Permanente's "broad range of human differences": ethnicity, resi- dence, age and generation, race, tenure, gender, birth order, family structure, education, sexual orientation, religion, marital status, disability, politics, parental status, education, sexual orientation, religion, marital status, disability, politics, parental status, shift and work site, personal history, profession or discipline, socioeconomic status, and level in organization.[2]

The report also summarized received wisdom for trying to infuse diversity throughout all organizational processes. Suggested steps included these:

1. Having organizational mission statements that emphasize the importance of diversity as a business issue
2. Annual reports that push the diversity theme
3. Handbooks and action plans for more detailed behaviors and systematic monitoring of policy
4. Accountability in objectives (evaluation reports and bonuses to reflect managers' affirmative action records)
5. Employee involvement through networking and support groups, focus groups, employee surveys
6. Community involvement and outreach
7. Career planning and development programs
8. Creation of a diversity leadership position
9. Emphasis on long-term culture change[3]

Though nicely illustrated with examples of each step from participating organizational leaders in the diversity management realm, the list also suggested that diversity management hadn't come very far since Lennie Copeland's similar list, "Ten Steps to Making the Most of Diversity," published in 1988.

Michael Wheeler felt that diversity management "was not going to go away" and was more than a fad. Yet there were notes of ambivalence as he discussed how domestic political and economic changes created roadblocks for the diversity machine. He acknowledged that the moralistic tone of several diversity advocates made the policies appear more as a social movement than a bottom-line necessity. Wheeler said the topic had been discussed by internal councils devoted to other issues; they seemed unsure whether diversity programs were just another "flavor of the month." Like many other shrewd diversity advocates, Wheeler increasingly pinned hopes for the field on expanding interest in international and global diversity issues.

There were many ambivalent voices in the Conference Board with regard to diversity management. On the one hand, Bob Parent, an external consultant who organized Conference Board symposiums, was enthusiastic: "We are just now seeing this topic [diversity management] come to the fore," especially through culture change. But Ron Cowan, another Conference Board independent consultant, took a different view. He almost never incorporated diversity management under such obviously related topics as "The 1996 Conference on Managing Change." Asked why, Cowan echoed Wheeler's fears that diversity management was seen as a social or political movement. Specifically, Cowan thought that diversity management was viewed as "an

agenda" (political) and remained a lower-ranked issue behind more dominant bottom-line concerns, such as reducing costs, reengineering, and restructuring. Cowan confirmed observations of many diversity consultants in
acknowledging that affirmative action and diversity had already been worked
into the culture of Fortune 500 firms: "It's old hat to them." He also agreed
with the findings of recent surveys that such programs were still legally and
defensively driven. The labor shortages on which diversity had depended had
disappeared. Corporations were "after the best service at lowest cost regardless of diversity."

A third independent Conference Board coordinator, Lee Hornich, did
feature sections on diversity management—for example, at a 1996 West
Coast Corporate Communications Conference, where Lewis Griggs would
join with General Motors's William Brooks and Xerox's Glegg Watson.
When I interviewed him in 1995, Hornich initially burbled with diversity
platitudes: "The workforce is changing. Better get on the boat." Within a few
minutes, however, his ambivalence also came through. "It's seen as a soft
issue," he acknowledged. "It's confused with affirmative action. People are
sick of hearing about it."

One business-based educational association that had cooled on diversity
management was the American Management Association. The organization
had sponsored diversity seminars for years, but by 1995 its August 1995–
April 1996 catalog of seminars contained not a single diversity entry. Nina
Weber, executive director of the association, told me in August 1995 that the
topic was "no longer a big public seminar draw." She felt diversity training
had shifted to on-site locations at specific companies and was becoming
more of a module in general management. She discounted the role that the
1996 presidential campaign would play and instead insisted that what happened in Congress would be more important, especially with regard to affirmative action legislation.

In early 1996, Ken Boughrum, director of Towers Perrin's Diversity Consultants Division in Atlanta, told me that the controversy over affirmative action
"has taken us a step backward." Consultants had not done a good job in classifying the purpose of affirmative action, that it was more than race and gender.
"We're trying to move beyond the numbers," he said, "trying to get beyond
legally driven mandates." But he felt the policies had a solid future. Echoing
many consultants and the Conference Board report, he noted that changing
demographics in the United States and global markets meant that corporations
had a huge cultural variety in their customer base. Boughrum felt that employers would eventually see that effectively "managing differences adds richness to

problem solving." Towers Perrin was trying to conduct research to establish this as fact, as had many others—with disappointing results.

Elusive Proof

In most of the popular books and articles on diversity management, the policy's effectiveness in specific organizations has simply been asserted or described by enthusiastic CEOs or, more often, officers of human resources departments. Some books and surveys, however, have more systematically and scientifically assessed the spread, depth, and effectiveness of diversity management policies, though the results of some surveys have been compromised by very low response rates. And there are other problems.

First, optimistic case study or survey data gathered before or during the recession and massive economic restructurings of the 1990s may now be obsolete. Second, social science studies of ethnic and gender attitudes have long been problematic. Interview subjects may knowingly or unknowingly tailor their responses to presumed views of the social scientist; refusal or noncooperation can also taint results. There is a notorious "words versus deeds" gap on matters of race; people may or may not act out their attitudes. (For example, whites who are prejudiced toward blacks may, under pressures of public opinion or law, curb discriminatory behavior; conversely, managers who respond enthusiastically about their diversity policies may not actually put them into action. In the lingo of diversity moralists, executives may not be "walking the talk.")

Third, as Paul Sniderman and Thomas Piaza have recently explained in *The Scar of Race,* attitudes about race and ethnic policies are embedded in more complex beliefs about politics and economics. In their surveys, for example, opposition to affirmative action programs was more a reflection of political opposition to government programs in general rather than specific ethnic bias. Hence, opposition to or criticism of affirmative action or diversity policies cannot necessarily be taken as evidence of racism or sexism, as some of the more ideological authors explicitly or implicitly imply.[4]

Fourth, as I emphasize in the methodological appendix of this study, there is a formidable amount of fear and cognitive dissonance about affirmative action and diversity management. When positive, hopeful attitudes about these policies clash with dissonant experiences, there may be a tendency to hang onto the happy attitude and deny the bad news. And there are legal and public relations problems in making public pronouncements on diversity issues. As *New York Times* reporter Judith H. Dobrzynski discovered in her assessment of corporate diversity policies, "While many of the more than two dozen company and industry association executives contacted spoke privately about affirmative action, almost none would comment for the record."[5]

Nevertheless, consistent findings about managing diversity programs have begun to register in several reputable studies. Generally, surveys and other case studies confirm the course of events described in the previous three chapters: the policies have gained a measure of superficial acceptance in large corporations and government agencies. However, in all but several pacesetter corporations, such policies, on closer examination, turn out to be affirmative action–style programs still driven by government regulation and fear of possible lawsuits. More advanced and aggressive diversity policies still face a range of barriers.

The Extent of Diversity Management Programs

In 1992, the giant Towers-Perrin firm published *Workforce 2000 Today,* a replication of a 1990 survey of more than 200 human resources executives that showed accelerating support for diversity policies. Like the Hudson Institute's original *Workforce 2000,* the Towers-Perrin study was enthusiastically touted by diversity consultants that their programs were indeed a major management trend. More than 54 percent of these human resources officers reported that management support for workforce-related programs had increased over the previous two years in spite of recession and downsizing problems; only 4 percent reported a drop in support. More than 92 percent thought that managers felt that cultural diversity and other human resources policies are directly connected to profitability: "management now sees the connection between the bottom line and those on the line."[6]

Nearly 75 percent indicated that their companies have or are planning diversity training from managers and supervisors (up from 47 percent two years before). Another 75 percent believe that their companies also "take cultural diversity (specifically, minority hiring and promotion) into account in management decision-making and strategic planning, up from 58 percent nearly two years ago."[7] Two-thirds considered the needs of working women, a jump from 45 percent two years before.

A June 1991 survey of 404 senior corporation executives by Lou Harris and Associates for *Businessweek* produced somewhat similar results. Harris and his colleagues found that 88 percent thought that the "changing makeup of the labor supply" would drive affirmative action efforts regardless of government action. Another 86 percent cited the "benefit of having different types of people in the workforce" as a reason to continue affirmative action. For these reasons, 65 percent of executives didn't think affirmative action laws were needed. (Yet 71 percent admitted that "worry about government enforcement action" was "very important" or "somewhat important" in driving the programs.)[8]

Still, a majority of executives had woven government-initiated affirmative action programs into their own corporate cultures and were fairly content with the results. Eighty-six percent thought they were doing an "excellent" or "pretty good" job of hiring women and minorities into entry-level jobs, and 68 percent felt the same way about promoting women and minorities into middle management; however, only 30 percent rated promotion of women and minorities into top management as "excellent" or "pretty good." And about 45 percent thought affirmative action was "a lot" or "some, but not a lot" of trouble.[9]

By 1994, *Training* Magazine reported that 56 percent of organizations with 100 or more employees provided diversity training. But what was diversity training: just warmed-over affirmative action compliance?[10]

Still Entangled with Affirmative Action

The complaints that riddled conferences and workshops about confusion of diversity policies with narrower affirmative action mandates were confirmed repeatedly in case studies and surveys. Nor were more extensive diversity measures, favored by the change master consultants, being implemented at more than a handful of large corporations and government agencies.

Ann Morrison and her colleagues were disappointed to find in their otherwise optimistic studies of sixteen organizations at the forefront of diversity management that the new policies were, perhaps deliberately, being blurred or substituted for affirmative action. "Diversity has become an alternative to affirmative action because of the negative connotations of 'quotas.'"[11]

A 1993 SHRM survey of 785 of its members revealed a disappointing portrait of diversity initiatives. Diversity was not a high priority in respondents' organizations, especially when compared to business issues like profitability, productivity, and market share. Diversity was often "narrowly defined" synonymously with affirmative action in both theory and practice. Thirty percent of the human resources officers in the survey defined diversity as "managing minorities and women."[12]

Only 32 percent of organizations included in the SHRM survey were conducting diversity training of any sort. About 70 percent of those were sessions lasting one day or less. There was little follow-up, and only a third of the respondents felt the training was successful. About 20 percent of organizations "somewhat" rewarded managers for increasing diversity of their work groups.

The survey's authors were sadly surprised by their own findings. "The jury is still out on diversity training," they concluded. "Too often diversity training is conducted for the public relations value it will provide rather than with the intent of making any real changes in how people work with each other."[13]

Two other surveys published in 1994 also revealed frustrating findings. Sixty-four percent of 490 companies employing at least 250 workers in the New York–New Jersey–Connecticut area responded to a survey directed by Joanne Miller at the Queens College Center for the New American Workforce. Legal compliance with affirmative action appeared to dictate the vast majority of diversity efforts: "Most companies that initiate programs or provide benefits to specific groups direct their initiatives primarily to those covered by employment legislation . . . or groups long associated with affirmative action." Nearly 80 percent have programs for the disabled, 46 percent have recruitment or promotion programs in place for minorities, 34 percent have targets in place for women, and 46 percent have policies on the books for family caregivers. Only 29 percent had provided sensitivity training to managers and 26.9 percent to workers. Center director Joanne Miller had to conclude that "companies are reactive rather than proactive in dealing with diversity issues."[14]

Conference Board researcher Michael Wheeler also published his survey results on diversity training in 1994. Although his results largely reflected those of Miller's study, Wheeler's work illustrated the problems of nonresponse that afflict evaluation of diversity policies. Of survey forms mailed to 219 organizations identified by the Conference Board as "leaders in diversity," only 20 percent responded. Twenty-five telephone interviews were used to supplement the survey findings.[15]

Although there was lofty rhetoric about diversity training for "business need" and "competitiveness," Wheeler confirmed again the familiar finding that most diversity training was geared to affirmative action legal compliance, focused on race and gender issues. Indeed, one diversity manager largely judged the effectiveness of diversity training by how well it boosted affirmative action numbers. Even among this survey of diversity leaders, there was surprisingly little current activity. Only 33 percent offered diversity training to managers, though 47 percent offered such training to employees.[16]

By 1995, the executive search firm of A. T. Kearney found that 72 percent of the top fifty U.S. corporations have diversity programs in place. Another 8 percent were developing such programs, and another 8 percent had more scattered programs operating; only 12 percent had no such programs in place. The problem was in how deeply these programs were embedded. But diversity was very broadly and vaguely defined, and "companies that do provide diversity management programs are increasingly bypassing traditional affirmative action approaches and regard them as nonproductive or counterproductive."

Barriers to Diversity Management Programs

In her study of sixteen diversity pacesetter organizations, Ann Morrison identified "barriers to opportunity" for "nontraditional" employees. By and large, these are the same barriers for implementation of diversity management programs:

1. Prejudice: treating differences as weaknesses.
2. Poor career planning.
3. A lonely, hostile, unsupportive working environment for nontraditional managers.
4. Lack of organizational savvy on the part of nontraditional managers.
5. Greater comfort in dealing with one's own kind.
6. Difficulty in balancing career and family.[17]

In other words, the barriers to upward mobility for women and minorities were the targets of the diversity programs recommended by Morrison and others throughout this book: emphasizing diversity in corporate literature, mentoring and career development programs, support groups, training and work and family programs, and managerial accountability for meeting goals and timetables.

Lack of top-level commitment, lack of funding, and lack of time were obvious and common complaints at conventions and in the literature. The mounting consultant frustration against white males was mirrored in the survey studies: white male backlash was the number one barrier to advancing the workforce diversity agenda.

The 1993 SHRM survey found the major roadblock in diversity management's momentum was the "resistance" of white males: "The increased focus on diversity has led to growing alienation of white males within many organizations."[18] The SHRM study's authors rationalized backlash by the "narrow definition of diversity" around affirmative action's us-versus-them focus on race and gender. The following year, Michael Wheeler of the Conference

Board found that 61 percent of his respondents felt that fear of backlash from white males is among the three most serious barriers to implementing diversity initiatives. Wheeler rationalized white male backlash as "not so much a barrier as a sign of change." One precaution taken by companies against backlash was in "making programs inclusive and seeking legal counsel."[19]

The *New York Times*'s Judith B. Dobrzynski also saw white male backlash as the primary source of opposition to affirmative action and diversity. She argued that corporations embraced diversity policies on the assumption of *Workforce 2000*'s prediction of a shortage of white male workers, coupled with an eye toward ethnic markets. But the predicted bust in white males turned into a surplus. "But thanks to an unprecedented wave of corporate restructuring, white men looking for jobs turned out to be plentiful. Many of them began to see affirmative action as a personal threat."[20]

Although downsizing may have exacerbated white male rebellion, backlash was present before the recession. Gathering data in the early 1990s, *New Leaders* author Ann Morrison discovered that "managers in our study mentioned backlash more than any other problem as the weakness in their diversity efforts and some managers cited backlash as a barrier in itself to the advancement of nontraditional managers." Backlash may have been the result of reverse discrimination: thirteen of sixteen organizations she studied used such exclusionary practices as targeted training, mentorship, set-aside positions, and higher salaries or bonuses for minorities. (Such programs had also been misused as when the white wife of a university psychology department chair was hired as a "diversity" candidate.) Thus, managers recognized backlash and legal and morale dangers. Subsequent Supreme Court decisions against ethnic gender preferences—as well as ballot and legislative efforts to repeal such formulas—would obviously sharpen these issues.

The Effectiveness of Diversity Management Programs

Although her data were gathered just prior to the early 1990s recession, Ann Morrison's *The New Leaders* remains the most optimistic book-length study of workforce diversity policies. Like R. Roosevelt Thomas, Jr., Morrison retained faith that oncoming labor shortages would make employers heed employee demands for cultural change. She also concurred that workforce diversity proponents should emphasize business performance rather than the moral imperative of affirmative action.

Through surveys and interviews, Morrison and her colleagues studied diversity policy practices in sixteen organizations (twelve private sector, two government agencies, and two educational institutions). She found widespread use of a variety of initiatives. In all sixteen organizations, Morrison and her associates confirmed favorite consultant recommendations: strong and interventionist top management and some sort of accountability for diversity results. Thirteen organizations targeted recruitment of women and people of color for nonmanagerial positions; ten used such targets for managers. Another ten had internal advocacy groups or ethnic task forces, nine had a strong emphasis on equal opportunity statistics, and twelve had diversity statistics as criteria for performance evaluation ratings (six tied diversity goals to financial rewards such as merit increases or bonuses).

Some of Morrison's subjects expressed reservations about diversity strategies. Out of two organizations came objections that hiring and promotion goals fostered shortsightedness. Most top managers were wary that female and minority support groups could "become the unions of the future."[21] Lawsuits from minorities or women were sometimes cited in fears of giving minority or female employees negative feedback or evaluations.

Morrison discovered and articulated the strongest rationale for diversity management policies: "changes in the consumer market and political arena seem to capture the attention of executives more than do changes in the labor force per se."[22] Morrison also raised an urban political pressure issue not often examined in diversity management literature: "Some managers have attributed some of the progress made on diversity within their organizations to the growing number of nontraditional politicians in their areas, especially in cities where the political fiber is dominated by people of color."[23]

As indicated previously, Morrison was alarmed to find that some of her subject organizations were substituting more palatable diversity policies for more vigorous affirmative action. Morrison thus became famous for advancing both a business-based pragmatist and civil rights moralist arguments. As was seen in Chapter 3, her statements at the First National Annual Diversity Conference anticipated a major theme of her forthcoming *New Leaders:* diversity management must not displace affirmative action's emphasis on numerical results. Since her surveys identified prejudice ("treating differences as weaknesses") as a top problem, remedying ethnic and gender inequalities must remain primary; other diversity efforts must be seen as secondary. Indeed, Morrison argued that affirmative action methods, such as goals and timetables, needed to be expanded, not abandoned or ignored. A measure of "mild coercion" was still necessary:

The most frightening aspect of moving too hurriedly from affirmative action for targeted groups to promoting the diversity in everyone is that this becomes an excuse for avoiding the continuing problems in achieving equity for people of color and white women. These issues cannot be postponed any longer. . . . Affirmative action practices should not be limited to recruitment; they should also be used to achieve the goals of multiculturalism.[24]

Morrison argued that diversity policies increased productivity, competitiveness, and workplace harmony. Eleven of the twelve private sector firms in her study had been ranked by *Fortune* magazine among its "most admired corporations" (the twelfth was not ranked because it was privately held). Three of them had won the Malcolm Baldrige Award for total quality management. But Morrison ultimately admitted that such awards did not "prove" the case for diversity and that probably no definitive data ever would: "The argument that diversity increases productivity and profitability is still based more on faith than on statistics. . . . Although diversity activities may indeed improve managers' skill in supervising and developing their people and consequently improve their productivity, we probably will not be able to prove it."[25]

In a telephone interview in 1993, Morrison admitted the recession had stalled, though not reversed, diversity management's momentum. "Things really would have taken off if it hadn't been for the recession." On the other hand, the recession and its aftermath produced financial turmoil for many corporate diversity champions: Apple Computer, IBM, General Motors, Digital, and much of the banking industry.

Other Studies on the Effectiveness of Diversity Management Programs

When Catherine Ellis and Jeffrey Sonnenfeld attempted to measure the impact of cultural diversity training in two organizations, they found that exposure to cultural diversity increased employees' perceptions of managerial concern about the issue, decreased their perceptions that minorities receive too much attention, and confirmed that the company is concerned with their individual growth. The vehicle of exposure could be a magazine or a newspaper article or a one-day workshop; the form of exposure made no difference. Still, the authors recommended the training as providing three benefits: giving voice to historically underrepresented segments of the workforce, providing facts and knowledge to dispel affirmative action fallout, and indicating a shift in corporate philosophy.[26]

Carolyn Jew analyzed a ten-year follow-up study of diversity efforts at a large (unnamed) southern corporation. Survey data were combined with more in-depth study of five focus groups (with five to thirteen persons each), as well as five personal interviews with middle managers. Although "tremendous progress" was noted, there were complaints of the continued existence of influential, informal ("old boy") networks. Belief persisted that one had to fit a certain mold or image (partly based on race and gender characteristics) to get promoted. Minorities complained about "institutional racism" and that "white males were highly concerned with 'perceived' minority quotas, which were assumed to lower the quality of production in general." Overseas, in international branches, lack of understanding and respect for local cultures still fostered problems. Finally, a corporate culture emphasizing conformity and nonconfrontation seemed to stifle creativity, individual initiative, and enthusiasm.[27]

Anne Tsui and Lyman Porter's findings on the effects of workforce diversity efforts at fifty-five Orange County, California, companies was compromised by an 11 percent response rate. Still, their findings both confirmed and negated diversity consultants' claims. Tsui and Porter's respondents reported that the benefits of workforce diversity were increased understanding of the needs of diverse customers, increased creativity and commitment to the organization, and better retention and attendance. But the training backfired by creating more difficulties in recruiting, supervision, motivation, training, and communication.[28]

Tsui and Porter's highly qualified findings confirmed those in a limited number of experimental social-psychological studies: "There is good evidence that heterogeneous groups have both benefits and costs. . . . They are beneficial for tasks requiring creativity and judgement, but they can also decrease cohesiveness and increase turnover. Thus, managers face a difficult balancing act, paying attention to the negative effects of diversity on individual attachment and turnover while simultaneously attempting to capture the benefits of heterogeneity."[29]

In more recent work, however, Tsui faulted experimental studies for relying almost exclusively on college students. As such, the studies did not control for two of the most important variables in more large-scale studies of organizational turnover, communication, and cohesion: age or tenure (length of group membership). Tsui also criticized diversity management research "as focusing on one or at most two attributes. A man is not only a man, he may be a white man, an old man, a well-educated man, a man of certain religious beliefs, or a man of distinguished family background."[30]

Many of Tsui's criticisms concerning restricted diversity dimensions and college student data apply to Taylor Cox's recent book, *Diversity in Organi-*

zations, a disappointing venture offering several introductory-sociology-style chapters on prejudice, discrimination, ethnocentrism, and stereotyping. Theoretical models and propositions were supported with admittedly skimpy data on the effects of diversity (mainly race and gender) on group organizational performance. Cox himself authored a few small group studies (involving college student subjects) that suggest that ethnic and gender diversity enhances creativity and decreases intragroup competitiveness. But he was also candid in admitting that "the limited amount of research on creative performance has rarely defined group diversity along the specific dimensions of gender, nationality, and racioethnic identity, which are points of emphasis in this book."[31]

Like other researchers, Cox found that white male backlash "against affirmative action and similar practices are among the most serious forms of intergroup conflict in organizations."[32] But he feebly attempted to resolve the confusion of affirmative action with other forms of workforce diversity by redefining affirmative action as a means of gaining organizational "value-in-diversity": "Organizational leaders who believe there is direct positive value in diversity for the organization's economic mission may consider the use of affirmative action as a way to foster diverse perspectives for finding high-quality, creative solutions to organizational challenges."[33]

(Cox recently contradicted his own emphasis on "racioethnicity" and gender when he discovered that educational background and occupational identity eclipsed the importance of race and gender in generating conflict in two organizations. Subjects perceived intergroup conflict in their departments more in terms of "work function" [63 percent] and "background and training" [32 percent] than race [29 percent] or gender [19 percent]. Work function was also the primary source of stereotyping. Tensions were especially strong between engineers and those with liberal arts backgrounds.)[34]

In 1994, *New York Times* reporter Judith H. Dobrzynski found "some action, little talk" on corporate diversity policies. She concluded that the promises of diversity strategies were not proven: "So far, the evidence for such a 'diversity payoff' is largely anecdotal."[35]

In 1995, Kara Swisher of the *Washington Post* surmised that diversity consultants were "learning from past mistakes." She found that confrontational white- or male-bashing diversity training has been counterproductive and that leading consultants worry about the bad name such training gives the entire field. She reported that some diversity consultants had begun to specialize in cleaning up after others' botched diversity efforts, such as the notorious training sessions for many Chicago employees of the Federal Aviation Administration:

> Last year . . . the Federal Aviation Administration agreed to settle an unfair labor practice complaint by the National Air Traffic Controllers Association over training sessions that took place in June, 1992.
>
> In one session, men were asked to walk through a gauntlet of women. After touching and looking at the men who were clothed, women rated their masculinity on a scale of 1 to 10. In other exercises, participants were asked to discuss their feelings about sexually explicit pictures and urged to recall traumatic events in their personal lives.
>
> "It turned out to be such a debacle," says Jeff Bedlow, spokesman for the air traffic controllers group. "We have never had anything against diversity training, but this went to such an absurd extreme that we think it's more important than ever to pay more attention to what is out there."[36]

Other employees told Swisher about childish summer camp–style exercises in which everyone formed a large circle, only to have some individuals kicked out of the circle based on their ethnic heritage, age, or geographical origin. Others were asked when they'd first had sex, whether they'd been abused as children, or whether they had had an abortion. Corporations, concluded Swisher, are now more carefully scrutinizing potential consultants and trying to work on changing people's behavior, not their hearts and minds.

A ten-thousand-word article in the American Society for Training and Development's *Training and Development Journal* in 1994 began the giant literature view that became the 527-page *The American Mosaic: An In-Depth Report on the Future of Diversity at Work* (1995). The conclusions to both the article and the book were identical: "The jury is not in with regard to the effectiveness of diversity programs, or on ways to cope with resistance to them."[37]

In a related policy arena, the jury of professional opinion is now more certain of the impact of race and gender determinism on—as it happens—jury decisions. And the data are not auspicious for workforce diversity merchants. Their consultant cousins specializing in jury selection also claim great abilities to sway jury outcomes using demographic variables. But, according to *Wall Street Journal* reporter Andrea Gerlin, "After reviewing numerous studies comparing trial outcomes with race, gender, income and occupation, Shari Diamond, a senior research fellow at the American Bar Foundation, concluded that demographics account for no more than 15 percent of the variation in jury-verdict preferences."[38]

Employees' Views of Diversity Training

Most studies of workforce diversity's results emphasize managers' or human resources officers' perceptions. Except for noting white male resistance, the rank-and-file employees' views are rarely solicited. Workers may be more satisfied with current workplace cultures than many diversity proponents think.

Indeed, a recent study by the International Survey Research Corporation found that minority employee dissatisfaction cannot be easily assumed. Hispanic, black, and Asian American workers were more positive about corporate career advancement programs—and their companies in general—than their white coworkers. Minorities did detect more supervisory and pay bias than did whites, but they felt more positive about the performance appraisal process, quality efforts, the competitive position of the company, and, especially, their promotion prospects. Whereas only 32 percent of whites described their promotion prospects as "good," 35 percent of African Americans did so, as did 40 percent of Asians and 43 percent of Hispanics.[39]

A *Los Angeles Times* study specifically focused on employee response to diversity training. A survey of 987 working Americans found that 62 percent felt diversity training sessions were "worthwhile" in raising sensitivities to race and gender differences. On the other hand, 87 percent of whites felt "race relations at their workplace are good or excellent," as did 52 percent of blacks. Nineteen percent of whites and 66 percent of blacks felt that "more effort is needed to guarantee racial minorities fairness in the workplace." Twenty-six percent of men and 38 percent of women thought that "more effort is needed these days to guarantee that women get fair treatment in the workplace." Eleven percent of whites and 46 percent of blacks felt they'd been discriminated against in the workplace.[40]

There remain tendencies for self-segregation. A 1993 study by the Families and Work Institute on changing workforce found that more than half of 2,953 workers surveyed would prefer working with people of the same race, sex, gender, and education. Most workers agreed that minority workers' chances of advancement were less favorable than those of nonminorities. (White males and white females rated minorities' mobility chances higher than minorities did.) This resulted in reported feelings of burnout and loss of initiative. Male managers were half as likely as women managers to rate their chances of advancement as "poor" or "fair." (Most of those surveyed saw little difference in the way men and women managed, exploding the popular notion that women are more nurturing or sympathetic.)[41]

From the perspective of employees, then, diversity training seems partly a sop to majorities of black employees who feel such training is needed—and who also want even greater efforts. Other minority workers may already be quite satisfied in several aspects of their work and even more positive in outlook than whites. That workforce diversity consultants are "stuck in the training mode"—and cannot enact extensive organizational change—evidently reflects the will of the people.

The Costs of Workforce Diversity

Just as the alleged benefits of workforce diversity programs are difficult to assess, especially with quantitative measures, so are the costs. In 1995, U.S. employers budgeted $52.2 billion for formal employee training. Diversity training was one of the hotter topics provided by 53 percent of firms with over 100 persons.[42]

As we have seen, however, most diversity training (when such training really *is* diversity training and not more legal updating on affirmative action rules) is of the one-shot variety and is not an especially big ticket item. It is, however, like paying insurance. A bit of such diversity training can help ward off expensive lawsuits, settlements, and adverse regulatory actions. Indeed tax-cutting proponent Steve Frates, executive director of the San Diego Taxpayers' Association, told me how he justifies that city's massive million-dollar diversity training program: "If it stops one sexual harassment suit, it's worth the investment." (On the other hand, such defensive training could backfire. Based on a court case involving California's Lucky's Supermarkets, seemingly racist or sexist statements made in diversity training sessions can be subpoenaed as evidence in subsequent discrimination cases.)

Permitting the formation of various cultural support groups is likely a negligible expense—if these activities are conducted after hours. (Executive listening time may be more costly.) On the other hand, the creation of full-time diversity managers in larger organizations suggests that the tasks are becoming too time-consuming to be added on to other responsibilities.

The most potentially expensive workforce diversity policy is the one urged most fervently by its most radical proponents: rewarding mangers for proportional promotion and retention of women and minorities. A recent *Wall Street Journal* assessment found that only a handful of corporations do this; it is not yet a trend, largely because "measuring the bottom-line benefits of diversity has been especially difficult for many U.S. corporations."[43] Insofar as such practices mimic the costs of affirmative action hiring, there is a general quantitative benchmark: Peter Brimelow and Leslie Spencer's *Forbes* magazine study. The direct and indirect costs of the visible part of the "quota iceberg," as they describe the programs, is approximately $113 to $116 billion. The below-the-waterline, hidden costs of bad hiring and misallocation of financial resources they estimate at $236 billion—and that does not include the likely huge expense of "effect on morale." Affirmative action preferences, they conservatively conclude, have a total cost of more than 4 percent of the gross national product.[44] Should the full range of spreading workforce diversity programs equal the costs of affirmative action, then the drag on the GNP may approach 10 percent—a development to delight the nation's international competitors.

As with affirmative action, academic researchers—and many independent ones—sense that diversity management is a subject best not closely studied. A university professor who threw cold water on such policies, especially if he or she were in the liberal arts or softer social sciences, would likely be subjected to isolation, if not direct retribution. A researcher close to the heart of the diversity machine let the cat out of the bag: "People are afraid to find out that these programs don't work. There is a lot of money being made."

"Valuing Relationship" and Other Metamorphoses: Lewis Griggs and His Associates Keep the Faith

Lewis Griggs never stops evolving. He has personally journeyed from international cross-cultural communications, to producing and defending "Valuing Diversity," and on to a more general, sociological view of how interpersonal relationships, properly understood and developed, are the core of modern organizational enterprise and "synergy." In a 1993 interview, Griggs addressed several criticisms of his work and of himself. He admitted that being a prominent white male in a largely female and minority field had been a major hurdle. On the other hand, Griggs felt that having minorities and women come forward and admit that they finally trusted him had provided "some of my most enriching moments."

He regretted the simplistic fashion in which white men were portrayed in "Valuing Diversity." But he dismissed rising white male backlash as "nothing more than pent-up anger caused by repression of discussion of differences. We don't like to look at our own racism or other cultures." Unlike many other consultants, Griggs readily admitted that there was reverse discrimination; he just didn't see it as a problem. "I think we should have reverse discrimination," Griggs explained, partly because "a culturally different individual is of measurable value." Employment and discrimination law, he added in a 1994 conversation, should allow for "cross-cultural competence" as a factor in hiring and promotion. (Somehow the image of white males does not come to mind when Griggs talks about "cross-cultural competence.")

Griggs rejected frequent criticisms that "Valuing Diversity" promoted ethnic stereotypes. "To talk about generalities in groups is dangerous. It's a state which we must go through. . . . Academics criticized the videos for being too general, simple and popular. But my niche is to take all the statistics and details and communicate the essence of cultural differences—popularize it so that ordinary people can understand."

In a 1995 interview, Griggs admitted that the diversity movement had stalled. He was losing money on the "Valuing Diversity" series; there was too much competition. "Everyone is getting in." Like other consultants, he felt that the rising white backlash meant that the policies were "striking the bone where it hurts." He was not yet concerned about the changing political environment. "It's not overwhelming to me—to some others, maybe. . . . The reactionaries won't win. They're dinosaurs." He conceded that the law that had once helped propel diversity initiatives may now be changing and so hurt the movement—for a time. But Griggs remained certain that the "whole philosophical underpinnings of democracy and capitalism are dependent upon inclusion." He was taken with his "Valuing Relationship" concept of three overlapping circles: culture, relationships, and diversity.

So sure was Griggs of the continuing importance of his old and new human relationship themes that in 1995 he and his second wife, Lente-Louise Louw, edited a new compendium of essays by colleagues, *Valuing Diversity: New Tools for a New Reality.* In his own contribution, "Valuing Relationships," Griggs outlined in written form some of the materials in his new video training series by the same title. Today, declared Griggs, awareness of cross-cultural differences was insufficient; changing demographics, organizational structures, and new technologies necessitate new ways of learning to relate. "Relationships are the information and communication networks of the organization, creating its real structure and its texture," states Griggs.[45] In an era of teamwork, effective managers must foster productive, creative relationships. They must not be too controlling or too lacking in control. To build effective relationships in the workplace, counseled Griggs, identify commonalities and build trust; "decrease energy-depleting patterns (control,manipulation, lying) and increase energy enhancing patterns (honesty, understanding, commitment)."[46] Successfully building relationships across individual and cultural differences is at the heart of creating interpersonal creativity and "synergy" in modern organizations.

In essence, Griggs videos, writings, and my conversations made it clear that he had basically undergone another conversion—this time to the discipline that silently underpins much thought about valuing and managing diversity: sociology. In particular, Griggs seems to be harkening back to sociological functionalism. A theoretical perspective constructed in the 1950s and 1960s, sociological functionalism emphasizes that social systems are made up of interdependent, different parts whose operation contributes to the functioning of the whole. Functionalism also holds that social order is premised on a consensus of values, which Griggs now agrees is needed. Multiculturalism, he feels, has led to too much group separatism and inhibits the all-important communication across group boundaries.

Griggs's new *Valuing Diversity* book, however, also furnished a brief peek behind the consultant curtain in the form of a "Dialogue on Diversity" among Griggs and several of the consultants who helped organize the National Annual Diversity conferences: Lente-Louise Louw, Shelly Lieberman, Percy Thomas, Rafael Gonzales, Frances Kendall, and Steve Hanamura. The consultants voiced many of the same complaints heard at those gatherings: diversity training was confused with EEO training; diversity training was often a short-term, one-shot affair with no follow-up procedures or efforts to build it into business culture; diversity training was seen as something negative that an organization has been forced into by a lawsuit or other crisis; white male backlash was occurring because "white men are continually being told by films, by articles, that they are being replaced and that they are not useful anymore";[47] that concerns about job loss and "being treated like" dirt complicated the training picture.

On the other hand, the consultants were undaunted and boldly enthusiastic about their work. They were more convinced than ever of diversity training's transforming—even subversive—power. The mood grew evangelical. Percy Thomas testified: "One of the things that the training does is foster relationship, and in many organizations they really don't want others to know what they are doing. So when you come in and start talking about valuing diversity and fostering relationship across ethnic, cultural, and organizational divisions and departments, and you get people to talk, this stuff becomes so effective that they don't want you to do it."[48] Added Lewis Griggs: "Once the door is open, it is hard to close." Frances Kendall declared, "This is really about organizational change." Percy Thomas added even greater vision: "It's about world change."[49] Rafael Gonzalez regretted they were often termed "trainer," which implies someone who merely sells a program. Gonzalez considered himself a more comprehensive consultant for organizational change. Adding a bit of the revolutionary "top-down, bottom-up" formula for change, Lente-Louise Louw reminded her colleagues to drive organizational change not only from the top but by building a "groundswell of support" from "people from the bottom."[50]

By 1996, Griggs realized that the "Valuing Relationship" video was not taking off and that it was "too soft." He launched another six-part video series, "Human Energy at Work." In the summer of 1996, Griggs themes moved from video into a computer-learning product, a set of three CD-ROMs entitled "No Potential Lost." The themes remained largely the same: how "cultural dynamics, relationship, and diversity" affect personal effectiveness, competitive advantage, and high-performance work relationships and teams. Although this would seem to be old wine in new, computerized bottles, the series did place second in the CINDY awards (Cinema in Industry), topping, among others, "The Interactive Manager," by the Harvard Business School.

More important, Griggs's sponsorship of the National Annual Diversity conferences and his evangelistic enthusiasm for diversity issues attracted the attention of the prestigious and powerful SHRM, which had been slow to climb aboard the diversity machine. They approached Griggs with an offer to cosponsor the conference. He agreed, and the joint conference was held with the full prestige and advertising backup of SHRM in October 1996.

R. Roosevelt Thomas, Jr.: Resurrection Through Reinvention

Six years after launching the concept of managing diversity in the seminal *Harvard Business School* article, "From Affirmative Action to Affirming Diversity," R. Roosevelt Thomas, Jr., declared temporary defeat. In opening his 1996 *Redefining Diversity,* Thomas mourned that in spite of the enthusiastic reception to his managing diversity manifesto, "no miracles occurred. In spite of the best efforts of people of goodwill, American business organizations are little better equipped today to deal with the fragile threads of a multicultural workforce. . . . We have changed our vocabulary, but not our behavior."[51] Thomas admits that "diversity" is now a "buzz word." What went wrong?

In *Redefining Diversity,* Thomas would not concede that his beloved managing diversity concept had been thoroughly blended in the diversity machine with the cause of affirmative action—especially by civil rights moralists who had *not* moved their focus beyond race and gender. Indeed, still trying to make amends for early criticism of affirmative action, Thomas pointedly reaffirmed his belief in those policies and declared firmly in *Redefining Diversity* that "race matters." But he would not admit in the book that the growing battle over affirmative action would further confuse the distinction with managing diversity. (He did acknowledge this to me during a telephone interview in May 1996.)

Thomas largely blamed the "lack of progress" in managing a multicultural workforce on the stubborn persistence of the assimilationist model: "Managers continue to talk about *facilitating the assimilation of minorities and women.*"[52] Progress in hiring, retaining, and promoting has been through the same old "targeted recruitment efforts." Managers "persist in pursuing their pet theories—striving to fix minorities and women, relieve white males of their biases and facilitate harmonious communications and understanding."[53] Serious organizational and cultural change was still being avoided. Thomas reluctantly concluded that there was much similarity in current diversity efforts and the old consciousness-raising and recruitment efforts of the 1960s. What to do?

In *Redefining Diversity,* Thomas tried to redefine and expand diversity further than in his *Beyond Race and Gender.* Thomas told me during an interview that he thinks Diversity Management (his capitalization) should now focus on matters other than race and gender—returning to those two volatile issues at a later date. But the race and gender specters of affirmative action and identity politics linger subtly or more blatantly in various sections of the book.

Basically, Thomas redefines diversity to the point where the term now encompasses almost any conceivable mix of difference and similarity. The metaphor of the jelly bean jar is continued: managers must learn to deal with the distinctive mix of the entire jar of different jelly beans, not just the last few that are added. Thomas separately defines Diversity Management and Managing Diversity. The former is the broader of the two and encompasses all manner of diversity mixtures. At its core is the Diversity Paradigm, with "eight action options": (1) exclusion, (2) denial or mitigation of differences—"we are all the same," (3) assimilation—minorities conform to majority standards, (4) suppression of differences, (5) isolation or compartmentalization of differences—such as a Catholic church holding English and Spanish masses at different hours, or a corporation permitting clustering of minorities in certain departments, (6) toleration—a "live and let live" atmosphere promoting superficial interaction, (7) building relationships—which may encourage dialogue about cultural differences or minimize them through emphasis on "similarities," and (8) mutual adaptation, that is, everyone accommodates changes.[54] Thomas clearly prefers mutual cultural accommodation. But he holds that any strategy may be "appropriate" to an organization's specific circumstances or managerial style. The latter may be heavily influenced by race and gender and, more important, by tolerance and comfort with complexity. "Diversity creates complexity which, in turn, presents challenges for all individuals and creates resentments within those with limited capacity for complexity."[55]

Managing Diversity now refers only to managing workforce diversity through the single choice of mutual adaptation; it is subsumed under the more general domain and many strategies of Diversity Management. A new concept is "diversity tension"—the conflict, stress, and strain associated with the interaction of the elements in the mixture."[56]

Thomas applies Diversity Management and the paradigm's eight modes to a variety of organizational situations: the evolution of BellSouth's work-family policies, functional diversity and reengineering at Hallmark Cards, managing a mixture of national cultures at globally oriented Electronic Data Systems, and Goodyear Tire and Rubber's multistrategy approach to change (total quality culture, managing diversity, succession planning, and the learning company). The final case study, that of General Motors, is more of a throwback to Thomas's older paradigm. Under Managing Diversity, GM incorporates valuing diversity and affirmative action with regard to its own workforce, its suppliers, and winning a satisfied, diverse customer base. The company's new brochure, *Diversity: A Competitive Advantage,* contains concepts, slogans, and charts directly out of Thomas's works.

Indeed, GM values diversity so much that it became a patron of Thomas's American Institute for Managing Diversity (AIMD). In 1995 GM awarded the AIMD a grant of $300,000 to help further a series of research projects and conferences.[57] John Smith, Jr., General Motors's chairman and CEO, wrote the foreword to Thomas's *Redefining Diversity.*

Thomas repeated many of his new book's themes in an April 17, 1996, interview. Diversity, he assured me, is not a choice. It is there. The problem is how to manage this mix. Managing diversity, he said, is basically an aspect of general management—rather like leadership. Thomas, however, had a rather low opinion of management as practiced. Too much management, he said, is either "no management or bad management." Much modern management is short term; "one manager told him that stress was so great, he could only make sure that the top twenty percent of his employees were working up to full potential." This, said Thomas—in Lewis Griggsian terminology—meant losing much potential.

Correcting some of the hype spewing from the diversity machine, Thomas cautioned that a diverse workforce per se does not mean more creativity and productivity; managing it does. However plausible, Thomas's qualified statements still begged for proof; one could reasonably argue that a well-managed relatively homogeneous team can be creative and productive. Ask the Japanese. Ask the Germans. Ask the Swedes.

Ann Morrison Calls "Time Out"

Though Griggs and Thomas were willing to stay the course by further reforms, the upsurge in societal criticism and skepticism has taken a greater toll on other veteran commanders of diversity's long march through the institutions. Indeed, some were beginning to show signs of burnout. When I spoke with star consultant Ann Morrison in mid-June 1996, the author of *The Glass Ceiling* and *The New Leaders* informed me that she had taken a one-year sabbatical from her recently established New Leaders Institute.

"I get discouraged," she sighed. "Same old, same old." Morrison had not spoken to other diversity consultants for some time. She was clearly dejected by the attacks on affirmative action, which she saw more than ever as the key to subsequent successful diversity management. The California Civil Rights Initiative had qualified for the November ballot, substantially boosting the level of controversy over diversity policies. "It used to be considered a good thing, a do-good, moral thing. Now it's seen as hurting and stigmatizing covered groups. The business case still hasn't been made." Court setbacks for affirmative action reflected rising controversies. She echoed the others' bitter complaints that "things are being undone that many considered done. We have to keep fighting to stay in place."

There was simply too great a sense of treading water. Too many business schools, she felt, still regarded diversity management as "touchy-feely" at best, "threatening" at worst. Although her influence as a consulting expert on the 1995 Glass Ceiling Commission's fact-finding reports and recommendations had been obvious, Morrison grumbled that the final recommendations were too timid—and largely ignored. Women, she felt, were still fighting skepticism, still having to prove themselves, still "hitting the wall." Others had become burned out and discovered the "I-have-a-life movement."

As for further projects, Morrison was "awaiting inspiration."

The Fate of the Field

Other consultants and writers were also reassessing diversity management by the mid-1990s. The new policies were changing America, but they were also being changed by economic and developments in the wider society.

Before dealing with those broader changes in the book's concluding chapter, I will examine how different versions of these policies operated—or did not operate—when implemented in three different organizations: the Los Angeles Sheriff's Department, the California Community Colleges system, and the University of Michigan. Through extensive interviewing, fieldwork, and sometimes participant observation, I have studied how the same path of euphoria-exploration-frustration-reassessment that the broader diversity machine traveled was reenacted in each of these organizations.

Chapter 7

Defensive Diversity Training

The Los Angeles Sheriff's Department

The University of Michigan, the California Community Colleges, and the Los Angeles County Sheriff's Department are nominally very different types of public sector organizations. Yet in many respects, their experiences with workforce diversity programs appear to have been similar to that of many private and other public sector organizations engaged in diversity initiatives. Most have had diversity directives either externally imposed or internally initiated by strong, future-oriented CEOs, most of whom were also responding to past and present legal or public relations crises. And as elsewhere, diversity efforts were complicated by the recession, downsizing, the rebellion against political correctness, continued confusion with affirmative action, and threatened eclipse by other organizational needs.

The three organizational chieftains who became workforce diversity evangelists offered both sunny and somber rationales for such policies, as did many private and public executives. As optimists, they wanted to be in tune better to serve and capitalize on the emerging multicultural mix. On the other hand, they waxed apocalyptic about possible societal polarization. They feared the formation of a two-tiered society of largely white haves and a swelling minority underclass of have nots. "If those people aren't in community colleges," warned California Community Colleges chancellor David Mertes in an interview, "they're going to be on welfare, in prisons, dependent upon society." Michigan's president Duderstadt and L.A. sheriff Sherman Block were attuned to similar concerns about widening societal divisions. Diversity programs in all three organizations were, to varying degrees, "customer driven" by existing and anticipated demographics.

In many respects, the public sector institutions profiled here represent the best chance for diversity theory and practice. The University of Michigan has been at the forefront of multicultural scholarship; it would seem an ideal environment for multicultural workforce policies. And the two California institutions would seem to be natural test sites for diversity policies that respond to that state's huge population transformation.

Each of the organizations represents a different approach in range, scope, and success of diversity management. The Los Angeles County Sheriff's Department took only the first steps in diversity management: basic sensitivity and educational training about cultural differences among "customers" and workplace colleagues; there was no attempt to change official organizational culture. The strength of affirmative action efforts appeared to be moderately strong, but the department was not under a legal quota system.

The California Community Colleges system might have gone much further down the road of multicultural makeover in terms of changing the composition of its personnel and organizational culture and procedures. Though broadly successful in terms of obtaining greater proportional representation in "access" (college admissions), more ambitious plans to expand beyond affirmative action and promote "student equity" (proportional graduation and transfer to four-year universities) were thwarted by the recession, political and legal changes, and growing reconsideration of the complexity of diversity issues. Progress toward achieving a legal mandate that faculty composition mirror the adult population of California was similarly stymied by economic and legal difficulties.

The University of Michigan has more aggressively promoted its own multicultural transformation than most other organizations in the nation. There was far more top-down motivation and money available to obtain an undergraduate and graduate student enrollment and faculty that "looks like America" rather than just the state of Michigan. Student speech codes were instituted but declared illegal; affirmative action efforts were pushed to, and perhaps beyond, legal limits; there have been extensive programs to promote cultural change. Yet the institution's relentlessly competitive, individualistic, decentralized, and achievement-oriented culture considerably moderated and fragmented the multicultural drive, as did the inevitable entanglement with faculty and campus politics.

These three organizations differ hugely in terms of size, purpose, organizational structure, and clienteles. Michigan is a giant education and research engine, epitomizing what sociologist Robert Nisbet once termed the "higher capitalism" of modern academe. More and more, the institution blurs public-private boundaries, mixing modest state support with a swelling endowment and an "entrepreneurial" faculty scrambling (quite successfully) for federal, foundation, and corporate dollars. Its ambitious president and faculty do more than study and forecast social change; they aspire to manage and control it.

Two thousand miles away, the much more pragmatic and proletarian 106-campus California Community Colleges (CCC) system is far closer to the demographic changes from which Michigan is more insulated. Amid the worst budget crises in its history, the CCC system is struggling to maintain basic literacy of U.S. citizens, begin English literacy training of California's immigrant tidal wave, train and retrain workers to help keep and lure more employers with high-tech "good" jobs to a state reeling from the decline of cold war industries, and offer the last hope of lawful employment to California's burgeoning underclass.

Management of those whom life and the educational system fails will fall to the L.A. Sheriff's Department, which is policing one of the most ethnically diverse areas of the nation. The LASD is a law enforcement cum social work agency sworn to provide a tradition of service while dealing with the downside of diversity tensions in its own workplace and among a client base increasingly fearful of crime and vying with each other for jobs in a declining economy. LASD's "customers" offer up everything from ethnic riots to runaways and sidewalk psychotics, to drug empires and schoolchildren with guns, to monumental traffic jams and domestic violence—all in dozens of languages.

Sensitively Policing the New Ellis Island: The Los Angeles Sheriff's Department

The demographic transformation of Los Angeles County has been one of the largest and swiftest in peacetime human history. Nearly one-third of all new immigrants to the United States in the 1980s—most from the Third World—located in California and about half of those in the Los Angeles area. A special issue of *Time* asked if surging immigration levels made California the "endangered dream," and David Rieff titled his 1992 sociological profile of the area *Los Angeles: Capital of the Third World.*[1] By 1990, the percentage of Hispanic residents nearly equaled that of Anglos: 37.8 percent and 40.8 percent, respectively. By 1993, the recession and white flight had produced a Hispanic plurality. African Americans remained about 10.5 percent of the population, barely ahead of the most rapidly growing minority group: Asian and Asian–Pacific Islanders, at 10.2 percent. The jump in the number of Asian groups had been especially dramatic. In 1970, there were fewer than

50,000 people of Chinese ancestry in the county; by 1990, there were nearly 250,000. The 1970–1990 jump for Filipinos was from about 25,000 to above 210,000; Koreans shot up from only a few thousand to nearly 150,000. The Los Angeles metropolitan area has the largest concentration of Cambodians outside Cambodia, the largest concentration of Vietnamese outside Vietnam, the greatest number of Armenians outside Armenia, and the largest number of people of Mexican ancestry outside of Mexico City. At least 1 million of L.A.'s 7 million residents are not citizens.

Along with the Los Angeles Police Department (LAPD) and several smaller municipal forces, the county sheriff's department is responsible for maintenance of law and order over a territory of 3,182 square miles, populated by 2.5 million persons. The department also contracts with nearly half (forty-one) of the smaller municipalities in the county that do not have their own police departments, ranging from relatively poor areas such as Pico Rivera to some of the wealthiest residential areas of the nation: Rolling Hills, Rolling Hills Estates, and Rancho Palos Verdes. The LASD is the third largest urban police force in the United States, ranking just behind New York City and Chicago.

From 1980 to 1992, the department grew rapidly, from 5,800 budgeted positions in 1980 to 8,500 budgeted positions in 1992. (These positions are for sworn personnel: uniformed members who have had police academy and other appropriate training. By 1992, there were an additional 4,000 budgeted civilian positions, making the LASD about 2,000 persons larger than the Los Angeles Police Department.) Although L.A. County continued to grow during the 1990s, budget freezes and cutbacks thwarted any LASD expansion during the early 1990s. Indeed, four jails were closed. The LASD pay scale, however, remained quite good. Beginning deputies earn more than $40,000 annually; sergeants earn a minimum of about $54,500; lieutenants start at about $69,000; commanders are paid about $84,000. (These figures do not include overtime pay.) Indeed, LASD pay raises ate up what budget increases the department received. (The *Los Angeles Times* reported on May 20, 1996, that most of the department's $240 million budget increase since 1990–1991 has been consumed by the salary increases and employee benefits granted by the county board. Since January 1990 sheriff's employees have received six salary increases totalling 24 percent.)[2]

The LASD's demographic profile changed more slowly than the county's. In 1992, the composition of the department was 87.5 percent male and nearly 73 percent were white, though these figures varied considerably by rank. Of the ninety-one top officials, eighty-four were male and seventy-eight were white, whereas 70 percent of the entry-level deputies were white (18 percent were Hispanic, 9.4 percent African American, 2.2 percent Asian, and the rest Native American or Filipino). A commission that launched a county-sponsored investigation into LASD problems in 1992 noted that "it appears that the Sheriff's Department serves areas in which Hispanics are the largest single minority. As is also apparent . . . the racial and ethnic make-up of the area police does not often correspond to the racial and ethnic make-up of the sworn personnel in the area."[3] The LASD has been even more demographically dissimilar to the jail population that it oversees: the overwhelming percentage of those in custody have been Latino and African American, while their sheriff custodians are still heavily white. (All new graduates of the sheriff's academy must spend their first two years staffing the jails, a rough, tough chore most leave behind as quickly as possible.) Most LASD members are in their mid-thirties, but the charismatic sheriff, Sherman Block, is over seventy and has been reelected to three four-year terms of office since 1982.

The LASD is a paramilitary, hence somewhat "masculine," organization that is strongly rule oriented and hierarchical. Promotions are based on written and oral exams. Police have often been called the "garbagemen of society" since they may routinely see aspects of the human condition and behavior that most other citizens don't—or don't want to—see. Divorce and high levels of personal stress are relatively common occupational hazards. (Intervention in domestic violence was once the riskiest situation for a peace officer; today merely pulling over a motor vehicle to the side of the road tops the danger list.) Most police prefer deference and respect from citizens, and the commission investigating the LASD criticized rough or violent behavior by some LASD members that evidently resulted from "contempt of cop"—disrespectful language or gestures from citizens.[4] On the other hand, the LASD's gang control unit, Operation Safe Streets, is regarded as a model of its kind and is reputedly less confrontational and more community friendly than the Los Angeles Police Department's gang unit.

The LASD has tried to moderate the influence of an inevitably cynical and tough us-versus-them, know-it-all cop culture by drafting a high-minded Core Values Statement in March 1992. The document dedicates the department to be a service-oriented organization with "the highest possible degree of personal and professional integrity." Among its key elements are these:

- Protecting life and property
- Preventing crime
- Apprehending criminals

- Always acting lawfully
- Being fair and impartial and treating people with dignity
- Assisting the community and its citizens in solving problems and maintaining the peace
- We shall treat every member of the Department, both sworn and civilian as we would expect to be treated if the positions were reversed
- We shall not knowingly break the law to enforce the law
- We shall be fully accountable for our own actions or failures and, where appropriate, for the actions or failures of our subordinates
- In considering the use of deadly force, we shall be guided by reverence for human life
- Individuals promoted or selected for special assignments shall have a history of practicing these values

By and large, this official culture of the LASD has been strongly Eurocentric, favoring universalistic standards, equal treatment and equal opportunity, impartial treatment, and the Golden Rule. As it launched a massive diversity training effort in 1991, the department's leaders would strive to be culturally sensitive but resist sliding toward cultural relativism, militant pluralism, and different standards of treatment for various ethnic groups, whether within or outside the LASD.

"A Need for Doing Something Different Out There": Sources of the LASD's Cultural Awareness Training Program

L.A. County's dramatic demographic changes alone might have sparked diversity training initiatives in the Los Angeles Sheriff's Department, but other ingredients typical of diversity management campaigns were present as well.

First, there was strong leadership from Sheriff Block. Nearly everyone interviewed for this book noted Block's clear, constant backing of diversity initiatives. In the summer of 1994, the seventy-year-old lawman recalled, in plain-spoken Gary Cooper style, the moment when he realized diversity initiatives were needed: "There comes a time when you look around and you see a need for doing something different out there."

"Years ago," he explained, "protection and apprehension of criminals were primary duties. What has changed is the environment." Block echoed a favorite diversity slogan when he added, "We must change in how we approach the job—we can no longer use the 'one size fits all' mentality." Block and many other LASD administrators saw cultural awareness training as a component of their drive for more community-based policing. As in the private sector, cultural awareness training, they thought, would ensure better customer service.

Second, there were diversity mandates pending in the form of state directives. A 1989 state law, AB 2680, required the California Peace Officers Standards and Training Commission (POST) to develop training and guidelines for law enforcement officers on racial and cultural differences among state residents. Sherman Block was a prominent member of POST.

Legal disputes and public relations problems constituted a third major factor behind LASD diversity initiatives. A well-planned cultural diversity program in the department would have considerable value in defusing public relations embarrassments, such as the 1991 press exposé of an informal fraternity of mostly white sheriff's deputies known as the Vikings. Among their other exploits, Vikings had driven squad cars at dawn through a large minority housing project blaring Richard Wagner's "Ride of the Valkyries," imitating U.S. Army Air Cavalry tactics portrayed in the Vietnam War epic *Apocalypse Now.*[5] Media accounts of the Vikings led Pasadena Rose Parade officials to rebuke the LASD publicly. They briefly considered ending their long-standing contract with the LASD for policing the huge New Year's Day spectacle. An angry Sherman Block settled the matter by threatening to sever the contract himself. Parade officials knew they could not come up with an alternative peacekeeping force on short notice, so the controversy faded. (Block must have been grimly amused the following year when the Rose Parade Committee was blasted by local minorities as being a racist, all-white-male bastion. The committee hurriedly added minority representatives.)

Past, present, and future legal disputes were also on the minds of the LASD brass. In department lingo, the training was a good, defensive "cover your ass" strategy. Training deputies in cultural awareness might actually reduce intercultural misunderstandings, thereby reducing the probability of future discrimination lawsuits from either citizens or LASD employees. And even if the training was not effective, the fact that it was provided would nonetheless look good in dispute resolutions.

As for past and present legal hassles—and in a pattern familiar in many other corporate and government settings—the LASD was moving one step ahead of coming court decisions and external investigations that would likely recommend or mandate diversity training. Indeed, as the Cultural Awareness Advisory Committee (CAAC) was being launched, the LASD was working out a court agreement ending a twelve-year sexual discrimination and harassment lawsuit—the so-called *Bouman* decision. Among other things, the *Bouman* decision stipulated that the department provide mandatory sexual harassment and cultural diversity training for all members of the department.[6] The latter, of course, had already begun, as Sheriff Block proudly observed in public discussions of the settlement.

The Los Angeles Sheriff's Department (LASD) also anticipated a major public investigation modeled after the Christopher Commission that studied the LAPD in the wake of the Rodney King beating. In early meetings of the Cutural Awareness Advisory Committee (CAAC), LASD commander Bill Stonich openly stated that the LASD was carefully studying the Christopher Reports' recommendation with an eye toward its own problems. The sheriff's department had been the target of rising complaints after a series of controversial shootings. And since 1988, the county had paid out over $32 million in settlements of alleged LASD excessive use of force against minority citizens.

In early 1992, the Los Angeles County Board of Supervisors formed the Kolts Commission, a panel headed by Superior Court Judge James Kolts, a conservative Republican, to study several problems within the sheriff's department, especially an increase in officer-related shootings. The commission issued its findings in a 359-page report on July 21, 1992. The report's authors acknowledged—but did not agree with—"the perception . . . within various communities that racism, discourtesy, excessive force and outright violence by the LASD not only happens, but is commonplace." (The commission was chagrined to discover that policing Los Angeles did not increase deputies' ethnic tolerance. They cited the LASD's own survey of 3,764 sworn and civilian employees, which had found that 26 percent reported decreasing levels of ethnic tolerance since joining the department.)

The commission did concur with the popular perception that the department "takes care of its own" when responding to citizen complaints. The commission also found that there were problems with lax discipline and the tracking of problem officers.

With regard to diversity, "language barriers and insensitivity," the commission's researchers recommended increasing diversity in hiring better to reflect the changing demographics of Los Angeles County. The commission noted, for example, that in the Firestone Station area, there were only 19 Spanish-speaking officers out of 116 who dealt with a heavily Hispanic population.

The Kolts Commission made some criticisms of the fledgling diversity training program that were either inaccurate or out of date by the time the report was published, largely because the training programs were still in a state of flux and being continuously modified. Indeed, the LASD's training was moving through a modified version of the stages outlined in previous chapters: (1) demographic and crises-inspired programs to enhance affirmative action and change organizational culture, which almost immediately collided with (2) prolonged, severe budget constraints, (3) somewhat futile attempts to divert rising anger concerning real and alleged reverse discrimination, (4) the transformation of seemingly voluntary efforts into mandated programs by political and legal events, and (5) the inability to deal with inconvenient facts of complex urban problems.

It was the LASD's bad luck that the rush to launch diversity training coincided with the worst local economic downturn since the Great Depression. Like other L.A. County agencies, the department suffered repeated budget and personnel freezes. Although the first round of diversity training was designed for new LASD recruits, there were effectively no LASD recruits to train during 1993. (Budget battles in 1994 were so intense that Sherman Block threatened to close several county jail facilities, giving the inmates a de facto furlough.) The January 17, 1994, earthquake, which collapsed sections of some major freeways, also strained departmental resources.

Nevertheless, the Cultural Awareness Advisory Committee having been established in 1991, community and LASD volunteers were recruited, subcommittees were formed, and two competing diversity training agendas were developed.

The Cultural Awareness Advisory Committee: Sounding Board and Public Relations Forum

"I kind of admire the way the Sheriff's Department does things, their 'we-can-do-it' attitude," said psychologist-consultant Victoria Havessy in a 1994 interview. "Word is put out that 'we have to build a house.' So one group shows up with nails, another arrives with the lumber, a third group does the roof, and so on." Havessy's metaphor was an apt summary of how the LASD devised its diversity training programs by relying heavily on its own members' resources, talents, and ambitions. This strategy also reflected wariness toward external consultants. Late in 1990, Sherman Block attended POST's first diversity training demonstration. "It was done by academics," he recalled, "and it was a disaster." In 1991, a captain at the LASD's Walnut Station initiated his own diversity training session with a team of outside consultants from the National Conference of Christians and Jews (NCCJ).

The politically correct presentation turned confrontational, and the deputies baited the trainers. (Veteran NCCJ trainer Lucky Altman remembered the session with alarm: "It was my worst training experience ever. I feared for my life." Another NCCJ consultant, a Hispanic university professor, claimed he'd been insulted and sent a bitter letter of complaint to the sheriff.)

Thus, the LASD's do-it-yourself approach avoided the explosive potential of mixing outside, politically correct trainers who might be incompatible with or insensitive to us-versus-them cop culture. But this somewhat ad hoc approach also inadvertently produced two competing diversity training formats. Tony Argott and Gil Jurado formulated their recipe for cross-cultural education and valuing differences. But another group of officers and psychologists vigorously urged a more experiential, prejudice-reduction training. Both were later awkwardly combined.

The formal umbrella vehicle for discussing diversity training was the CAAC, overseen with other diversity efforts by fifty-one-year-old commander Bill Stonich. Stonich initially knew next to nothing about cultural diversity training but was a skilled administrator then in charge of all of the LASD's training programs. Stonich was also an agile thinker and a poised spokesman. (Like several others in the department, the hard-working, ambitious Stonich had labored at obtaining a college education in his off-hours, completing a bachelor's degree nearly fifteen years after he'd joined the LASD in 1969.) Stonich immediately attended a train-the-trainer course conducted by POST. There, even among relatively high-level law enforcement administrators, he was surprised at the explosiveness of the reactions that could be elicited by discussion of race and gender issues. He would be wary of such deep emotions in implementing diversity training in his own department.

Word of the committee's formation spread throughout the department. And true to the do-it-yourself approach, LASD personnel began to volunteer for the CAAC, bringing along various skills, interests, and motives.

Soldiers and Citizens Together—Uneasily

The CAAC and its related subcommittees proved to be a major undertaking requiring enormous amounts of time and energy both on and off the clock. For most LASD members, CAAC duties were yet another add-on responsibility—one of many in the tough economic climate. But no one saw the strained budgets coming when the monthly CAAC meetings began with an ambitious agenda in the spring of 1991. There were two distinct categories of members. The larger group consisted of department members formally trained and sworn into LASD (the sworn personnel) and a few LASD or county civilian employees. The thankless task of recruiting citizen members fell to amiable, fifty-two-year-old Alabama native Lieutenant Clyde French, who had a difficult enough job as the department's affirmative action officer.

Stonich and French repeatedly contacted some of the major ethnic organizations in the L.A. area, such as the Urban League, the Council of Black Ministers, NAACP, and various Hispanic and Asian groups—usually to no avail. Ironically, African American Clyde French had little success in recruiting African Americans. Long-standing suspicion of the sheriff's department undoubtedly was a factor, but French was frustrated by irresponsibility and interest in financial gain. "Some people who agreed to be on the committee never showed up. I never got a response from the Black Ministers Association, even after repeated calls." The city's most celebrated black ministers were busy with other activities. The more average black ministers "wanted a quid pro quo. They were disappointed there would be no pay." (French finally did get several ministers to attend one committee meeting. They did not return.)

Several diversity consultants called to offer their services—provided there might be the possibility of remuneration or if the department could be listed as a "client" on consultants' advertising brochures. (French refused such offers.)

French was more successful in obtaining Asian and Hispanic involvement. Most faithful in attending were Bobbie Molina, a Native American who worked as a community liaison employee of county social services; Louis Herrera, a Hispanic car dealer and businessman; Rudy De Leon, a consultant and retired LAPD officer; Bernita Walker-Moss, a retired African American LASD officer and manager of an inner-city women's shelter; Charles Park, a Korean businessman; Mimi Nguyen, director of the Indo-Chinese Youth Center; René Flores, a personnel manager at Southern California Edison; Eleanor Montano, active in neighborhood gang control projects; and myself.

The monthly CAAC meetings were businesslike and usually well run, with a formal agenda and minutes of the previous meetings always distributed at the beginning of each session. Press and journal articles about minority relations and diversity matters were often appended to the handouts. CAAC meetings during 1991 and 1992 were, as might be expected, devoted primarily to the task of getting the diversity training up and running for recruits, patrol officers, and veteran field officers. Locales for these CAAC gatherings were rotated from one section of the county to another. The Sheriff's Training Academy Regional Service Center (STARS Center) was the CAAC's nominal focal point, but there were frequent rotations to meeting rooms at various LASD stations and, once, one of the county's custodial centers.

By 1993, the CAAC shifted to a quarterly schedule and a more educational and ceremonial agenda. The meetings sometimes became primarily field trips to several ethnic and cultural community cultural centers. In May 1993 the CAAC toured L.A.'s new Beit Hashoah Museum of Tolerance. In the fall of 1994 the meeting was held at the American Indian Museum. The June 1994 gathering at the Hsi Lai Temple combined a lecture on Asian culture and police relations by three Asian American members of the department, plus a tour of the largest Buddhist temple-monastery in the Western hemisphere. A heavily attended February 1994 meeting at the Korean Cultural Center provided a lecture on Korean American culture and history by two community leaders, a public relations forum for Sherman Block to announce the arrest of several members of a troublesome local Asian gang, and a series of ceremonial dances by schoolchildren.

Citizens Teaching Soldiers?

In obtaining citizen involvement in the CAAC, the LASD had a combination of public relations and political-instructional interests in mind. Citizen oversight of police was a touchy issue in Los Angeles and had been vigorously resisted. Citizen participation on the CAAC therefore was a gesture (but not much more) toward reducing such tensions. And citizen involvement would provide an aura of community legitimation for diversity efforts. Citizens would provide oral and written input into the program, and it was hoped that some would represent their cultures as volunteer classroom instructors.

The assumption that skin color, rather than training or educational credentials, qualified someone to talk about an entire ethnic culture was one of the few politically correct dictates of the LASD's training: that Hispanics should lecture about Hispanic culture, African Americans about African American culture, and so forth. The use of ethnically appropriate LASD and community instructors was part of the identity politics trend sweeping universities and the general culture. This sort of thinking was taken as a given by some top LASD brass and many minority group members of the CAAC. The practice was also strongly encouraged by POST curriculum guides and later urged by the Kolts Commission. (Most of the instructors, especially Paul Harman and Tony Argott, disagreed with this ideology, but they were overruled.)

And, again, there was public relations. The imagery of minority citizens counseling LASD recruits and deputies on ethnic cultures had good public relations value. As Lee Baca later stated, the offer to let CAAC citizen members instruct the cadets was something of an unpaid quid pro quo: it was felt that the department could not ask for citizen input without permitting some form of participation.

Although some members of the department may have intended otherwise, citizen participation in the CAAC turned out to be superficial and something of a sham. A few civilian members made significant contributions, but most of the real work and all of the supervision was done by two core subcommittees of deputies. The citizen-members "were used and sometimes lied to," said one anonymous department source. When the 1992 decision in the *Bouman* case—mandating sexual harassment training—was announced by Bill Stonich, an active civilian committee member, Bobbie Molina, was profoundly disillusioned. The LASD's interest in cultural diversity, she realized, was as much compelled as voluntary.

Civilian participation in the actual training was tried but quickly phased out of recruit training. Some did not or could not show up on the appropriate day and time; others could not get time away from their regular work. A few were simply deemed unsuitable or problematic. Retired sheriff and civilian member Bernita Walker-Moss was "fired"—her words—because of what everyone acknowledged was her strong personality and Afrocentric views. Although Moss nonetheless continued to play an active role on the committee (and probably did reflect the views of a segment of South Central Los Angeles), the episode illustrated a common problem for corporate and public administrators who assemble diversity committees: fending off highly motivated, but politically inspired members who wished to use such a committee as a platform. (This was reportedly an infrequent problem for the LASD but evidently led to complaints vented in the Kolts Commission by disgruntled minority police association members.)

Citizen involvement also came to naught in an ill-fated attempt to avoid a permanent training staff by building a pool of cultural diversity facilitators from the CAAC and elsewhere in the LASD. The goal was to train some fifty people (mostly department personnel but with a sprinkling of community members) to guide discussions about prejudice and stereotyping. These facilitators would assist the more seasoned staff in training sessions at various stations. The department signed a $4,800 contract with the Anti-Defamation League's Workplace of Difference unit to assist in training the facilitators over two weekend periods. Although the training was carried out, budget and logistics problems quickly sank further implementation. As happened with community volunteers in the recruit training, the deputy-facilitators had trouble obtaining released time from supervisors. After Lieutenant Harman had to cancel two training sessions for field deputies when his newly trained assistants did not show up, diversity activists on the CAAC pressed hard for funding a permanent training staff at the academy. Such a staff was assembled in late 1993.

The CAAC presented three formal recommendations to Sheriff Block on June 8, 1992. The first was that the public "is fully aware of the significant programs that are being used by the Department to train, educate, and enhance the level of service and positive interaction our personnel provide to our citizens and communities." Second, the committee recommended the possibility of mandating that "all personnel attend and take an active role in specific community cultural events, performing in a non-traditional police function." (Most members of the committee had in mind the various cultural festivals held around Los Angeles.) The third was to provide "each specific cultural group" with immediate access and communication to "express their thoughts and concerns to an established station representative." Such community liaison officers were already on duty at some stations.

CAAC's two most important and interesting meetings concerned the committee's primary purpose: the November 1991 evaluation of the proposed diversity training for recruits and the November 1992 CAAC participation in an abbreviated version of diversity training for the more seasoned in-service field deputies.

The Perils of Cross-Cultural Education

Lieutenant Tony Argott did not have positive early contacts with the LASD. During his childhood, he had watched his older brother repeatedly clash with law enforcement officers. Sheriff's deputies once chased the oldest sibling through the Argott house, with Mrs. Argott in hot pursuit of the deputies with her broom. Mr. and Mrs. Argott were Mexican immigrants whose eleven children would achieve a variety of destinies. Young Tony was a wannabe gang aspirant for a time, but strong family and neighborhood controls, as well as the influence of a football coach who would later become a scholar on gangs, pulled Argott back on a path so straight and narrow that he graduated from college and joined the LASD in 1980. (Ironically, one of Argott's first calls as a field deputy was to go to the scene of a drug overdose. The deceased victim was Tony's wayward older brother.)

In 1988, Argott teamed up with Sergeant Gil Jurado during off-duty hours to teach a community college course on Los Angeles gangs. The success of the course led to their developing another class, this one on cultural diversity in policing. They taught the course off-campus at the Santa Monica Police Department, where their instruction served as part of a court settlement of a discrimination complaint. Next stop was the City of Rialto Police Department, also in the process of settling a federal discrimination lawsuit. The City of Alhambra was becoming heavily Asian, so Argott and Jurado offered to provide cultural diversity training to that police force, with the aim of forestalling possible cultural misunderstanding and lawsuits.

Argott obtained a certificate in management and quality improvement in multicultural work environments offered by the continuing-education program at California State University, Fullerton. He also sought data and professional advice on ethnic group cultures from a wide variety of sources—university professors, the National Conference of Christians and Jews, and the Anti-Defamation League's new Workplace of Difference program.

Argott and Jurado developed a cross-cultural approach of lectures on general cultural differences, spiced with humor and videotapes. Since they'd already conducted cultural diversity training for other police departments, they became the leaders of the CAAC subcommittee tasked with formulating cultural diversity training for new recruits.

Cultural diversity advocates in the LASD were successful in scheduling a full twenty-two hours for recruit training in cultural awareness apportioned accordingly: general overview (four hours), Hispanics (three hours), African Americans (three hours), Asian–Pacific Islanders (four hours), "other ethnic minorities" (Native American, Middle Eastern, religious minorities—two hours), people management skills (two hours), and formal testing and role playing (four hours). (A second subcommittee devised an eight-hour "prejudice-reduction" course that would be given to both recruits and field officers.) Argott would conduct the general overview and lectures on Hispanic culture. An LASD instructor and CAAC civilian volunteer were to be ethnically matched to the African American and Asian sections of the training. Gil Jurado would lecture on "tactical communication" skills, and Sergeant Rufus Tamayo, on the academy's instructional staff, took charge of role playing and formal tests.

On November 21, 1991, Argott and Jurado presented to the full CAAC a highly condensed preview of the recruit training to begin the following month with academy class 279. Argott was one of the more able trainers I observed in the course of this research, but his presentation to the heavily minority and female CAAC proved a difficult task. He and Jurado were used to force-feeding cultural diversity to heavily right-of-center, largely unfriendly white policemen. Argott now had to present sensitive concepts and data to his LASD superiors and to heavily left-of-center colleagues and community activists.

Argott began his presentation as he would with the recruits: with demographic and customer service rationale. L.A.'s population transformation complicated community policing. By keeping prejudice out of the workplace and by becoming more aware of the cultural and sociological traits of the many ethnic minorities in Los Angeles, the LASD would provide far better community service and help avoid legal entanglements for both the department and individual deputies.

Argott explicitly disavowed white male bashing or department bashing. He also tried to preempt any disunity set in motion by the course by emphasizing LASD solidarity. On the job, members of the LASD were "a single class of green and tan" (the departmental colors). Argott reiterated department policy to "treat everyone fairly and equally once in uniform." The basic mission of the LASD was "to protect life and property, to prevent crime, to apprehend criminals, to act lawfully, to be fair and impartial and to assist citizens in solving problems and maintaining the peace."

The most ideologically loaded section was a brief discussion of "kinds and levels of racism," drawn from the theory of institutional racism promoted in the Cal State certificate program and by the National Conference of Christians and Jews. Although Argott did not dwell on this section in the CAAC presentation, this racism-is-everywhere perspective has become standard fare in diversity training and was detailed in his handout materials. According to these sources, racism can be manifested at the cultural, institutional, and individual level. It can also be conscious or unconscious, as well as manifested in mental attitude or actual behavior.

As cited in the written materials Argott had distributed, examples of conscious, institutional, racist attitudes were beliefs that affirmative action is reverse racism and that minority children have limited intellectual abilities; examples of conscious institutional, racist behaviors would be busing of black children to white schools, and not vice versa, and discrimination against minority home buyers for fear of panic selling by whites. Conscious, individual racist attitudes were beliefs that blacks are genetically inferior or that all Native Americans are alcoholics; conscious, individual racist behaviors include the refusal to integrate or bus white children or the use of racial epithets. Instances of unconscious, institutional racist attitudes include disregarding minority cultural perspectives in developing standardized tests and assuming that white personnel can meet the needs of all the people in the institution, but that minority staff can deal only with their own kind; examples of unconscious, institutional racist behaviors were the teaching of white American history and the destruction of minority housing in urban renewal to make way for commercial

or upper-income housing. Unconscious, individual racist attitudes were belief
in the melting pot theory or the denial of racism; unconscious, individual racist
behaviors included laughing at racist jokes or dealing with racist businesses.

Argott covered these materials in very abbreviated form, preferring to illustrate these rather abstract distinctions by running a videotape on hate
groups narrated by Bill Moyers. He spent the remainder of his two-and-a-
half hour presentation describing the major ethnic cultural groups in Los Angeles, aptly noting at the outset that second-and third-generation groups
differ from those newly arrived and that new immigrants' attitudes toward
U.S. police may have been shaped by considerable contempt and fear of law
enforcement in homelands.

In the condensed CAAC presentation, Argott narrowed his focus to a tight
summary of the demographics, trends, values, and stereotypes associated with
Hispanics and African Americans. (In the regular training schedule, two to
three hours would be allocated for similar analyses of Asians–Pacific Islanders,
Native Americans, and "other minorities.")

Nomenclature was briskly reviewed (Hispanics, Latinos, Chicanos, Mexican-Americans, etc.), as were stereotypes, (lazy, sleepy, "Frito Bandito," welfare oriented, "all Hispanics are alike"). Hispanics' general values have
included a strong family orientation, strong religious influence (Roman
Catholic), relative isolation in ethnic enclaves, and low priority on education
(Hispanics have the highest dropout rate). Trends among Hispanics, according to Argott's handouts, were very high birthrates and very young median
age, continued strong immigration (legal and illegal), and the legacy of the
bracero program. (In full session, Mexicans, Cubans, and Nicaraguans were
separately examined.) Argot ran a videotape of Mexican American comedian
Paul Rodriguez, who satirized outsiders' views of Chicanos.

African Americans received similar attention. African Americans were
once termed colored or Negro. The history of racism has led to powerful
stereotypes of inferiority. Today's trends have emerged from the civil rights
movement under Dr. Martin Luther King and the urban riots of the 1960s,
which produced a wide range of groups from the Black Panthers to the Nation of Islam. Many African Americans have been understandably suspicious
of police. Argott pointed out steadily rising educational levels of blacks and
that middle-class blacks perform academically on a par with middle-class
whites. However, "progress and regression have occurred simultaneously."
Over half of black youngsters live at or below the poverty level, and female-
headed families are the largest growing segment. Argott broke his lectures
with two videotapes. Rap group Public Enemy pumped out a message

against "self destruction," and Eddie Murphy, dressed as Buckwheat from the "Little Rascals," attempted to mock black stereotypes.

When Argott finished and the group was asked for feedback, there was a long silence that crackled with tension. Argott had stumbled into two hornets' nests very familiar to seasoned diversity consultants. First, general data on group cultural traits and behaviors can reinforce—or seem to reinforce—stereotypes. Such data have been clouded with politically correct taboos. Argott's mention of the single-parent family "problem" among black inner-city poor was still taboo in 1991 and raised eyebrows. Second, Argott had tried to engage the audience with comic videos and a few humorous asides, such as "a rap tape does not a culture make." Again, taboos against ethnic or gender humor were stronger in 1991 than today.

Sensing the uneasiness in the lecture hall, affirmative action officer Lieutenant Clyde French suggested that Argott "be careful to avoid stereotyping ethnic groups in his handouts." After two other CAAC civilian members seconded this, French also suggested that "people from the community advise us on what to say in the lecture and the handout." Bernita Walker-Moss more firmly emphasized that people from the community need to be involved in the lectures themselves.

Sergeant Tessa Cruse, an African American LASD community liaison officer, took strong exception to the Eddie Murphy video skit. "It took everything positive away," she began to explain, and then broke down sobbing.

The lecture hall again fell silent. Tony Argott looked lonely, confused, and chagrined. A second deputy then questioned the purpose of the Eddie Murphy tape, and a third offered the observation that it was not educational. Commander Bill Stonich, anxious to avoid any more emotional eruptions, closed the discussion by observing that there was still time to offer changes to the curriculum.

Gil Jurado followed up with a lecture on "people skills," basically communication skills and acquiring a "command presence." (One does this, we were told, by having the right data, voice, and body language simultaneously.) Voice is one's "verbal personality," but much interpersonal communication also involves body language. Such things varied enormously by ethnic and gender cultures. Tension and interest had already been spent on Argott. The afternoon was growing late, and those remaining seemed relieved to adjourn.

Prejudice Reduction: Changing Hearts and Minds?

When he joined the LASD in 1978, no one would have thought that Sergeant Bill Corrette would become a champion of cultural diversity, least of all Corrette himself. By his own admission, Corrette had been a typical tough cop who "judged people by appearances" and regarded cultural differences with doubt, if not suspicion or scorn. Corrette had been interested in training recruits and deputies, but only in the manly arts of survival and defensive tactics. He wearied of that but, after working at one of the LASD stations, managed to get returned to the Academy Recruit Training Bureau in 1991, largely because it was a good launching pad for promotions. Corrette resumed teaching defensive and physical defense skills. Shortly after his arrival in early 1991, however, his supervisor, Lieutenant Steve Selby, told Corrette there was "heat from the top" to develop curriculum materials for cultural diversity training. He gave a less-than-pleased Corrette the job. Corrette assumed the assignment would be one of short duration; instead, he became an architect of a second diversity training curriculum.

Corrette obtained materials and advice from the National Conference of Christians and Jews and the B'nai B'rith Anti-Defamation League. He then assembled a committee including the LASD's chief psychologist, Nancy Baker; an external police psychologist consultant, Victoria Havessy; and two members of the County Human Relations Committee.

Brainstorming commenced. Corrette was determined to teach the psychologists the deeper realities of cop culture, and they were bent on convincing Corrette of the value of diversity training. Cultural differences flared among the participants. "The dialogue and discovery processes on the committee were similar to the training itself," remembered Havessy. "There were cultural clashes among us, too. For example, Nancy Baker wanted to include gay and lesbian culture in the training. A Hispanic member of the committee snorted, 'Where were those guys in Selma, Alabama?' And Nancy shot back, 'Where were the Hispanics?'"

Corrette's group met about once a month during the next year and a half. They designed the prejudice-reduction class for new recruits and became integrated into the CAAC subcommittee on diversity training for field deputies. In 1992, they merged again, this time with Argott and Jurado's group, to form a single "cultural curriculum committee."

With two psychologists on board—and occasional participation by diversity trainers from the NCCJ and the ADL—Corrette's group not surprisingly wanted to foster deeper attitude change, not just modify on-the-job behavior. They favored a deeper, more experiential, discussion-oriented style of probing and reducing individual prejudices and stereotypes. Perception puzzles and videotaped vignettes on race relations would be used to stimulate introspection and "Aha!" moments of inner recognition of deep prejudices and stereotypes. This was in contrast to Argott and Jurado's more information-oriented cross-cultural lectures.

Surprisingly, the committee's first convert was Bill Corrette. In part, Corrette claims to have changed because he became a born-again Christian and began to reexamine his own assumptions. This dual conversion produced profound moments of discovery, such as the realization that those who remain neutral toward prejudice and discrimination may not be neutral at all.

Working with people on the committee caused me to grow. One experiential exercise that they tried with me (that didn't work in later classroom settings) really made an impact. They told me to close my eyes and try to imagine a time when I had been bullied. Then they told me to remember who else was present, who took the bully's side, who tried to help me and who remained neutral? I remembered my anger at those who'd been neutral—they were just as guilty as those who sided with the bully.

Corrette became recognized as a highly effective instructor in the cadet prejudice-reduction course, but his prior reputation in the department hampered his effectiveness as a policy spokesperson. Cynics suspected that Corrette's new devotion to diversity was feigned and that the long hours of personal time he spent on committee activities were simply career motivated.

In 1992, Lieutenant Paul Harman, who was writing a master's thesis on cultural diversity, joined the curriculum development committee. Harman quickly merged his own research with that of the committee and organized two trial runs of a field deputy training format at two troublesome LASD stations in the fall of 1992. These experimental sessions, even with a largely self-selected group, demonstrated the need to refine techniques.

Suddenly, however, Bill Stonich announced to Sherman Block that cultural awareness training of the field deputies was ready to begin. A surprised Harman and his colleagues hurriedly prepared a one-day preview-participation session for the CAAC.

On November 5, 1992, exactly a year after Argott and Jurado previewed their proposed cultural diversity training for cadets, the CAAC and several of the LASD top brass gathered at one of the LASD training centers to participate in a one-day condensed version of cultural diversity training being readied for field deputies. About sixty people attended—three times the number preferred by the trainers. Harman and his multicultural training team, the nonjudgmental facilitators of discussion, distributed a workbook containing a restatement of department values, policies, and definitions and reading materials, many of which were drawn from the NCCJ or ADL.

Harman introduced the session with the standard diversity rationale. Drastic demographic changes in L.A., he explained, had produced a complex "stained-glass window" of distinct cultures, replacing the more assimilationist melting pot. Following NCCJ and ADL formats, Bill Corrette outlined ground rules similar to those used by the NCCJ and ADL trainers: questions and comments were welcomed, as were "honest self-examination and sharing of feelings, experiences, judgments," though comments made during the session should not be discussed outside the classroom. Free speech, active participation, and sharing of emotions were encouraged.

Instruction began with two perception-discussion exercises. The object of these exercises was that perception of a single situation depends on an individual's frame of reference; that is, an individual's background influences what he or she sees. We were shown the familiar ambiguous line drawing designed to elicit at least two responses: Was the drawing of a vase or of two human profiles facing one another? We were then asked to estimate the number of squares in a second ambiguous drawing—of either a grid or a number of larger squares.

Next came a stereotyping exercise of various racial and ethnic groups. Two of Harman's assistants collected the sheets and read the responses, while another recorded them on a flip chart. We were asked which stereotypes were negative or positive, stimulating comments about whether "good at math" was a positive or negative stereotype of Asians. The point of the exercise was that stereotypes lead to self-fulfilling prophecies and affect police responses toward citizens.

The remainder of the day was devoted to discussion of several video vignettes that portrayed problematic ethnic and gender tensions in two types of settings: "within-the-family" situations dealing with workplace interaction among deputies and "outside-the-family" situations dealing with deputy-citizen encounters. In the first video, a scene from the film *House Party,* an African American male adult, clad in a jogging suit and moving swiftly along a neighborhood street, becomes hostile toward two police officers who stop and question him. The facilitators stopped the video and asked how both the citizen and the police should have behaved. Some anticipated the film's preceding scene, which we saw next, making clear the motivation for the midnight jaunt: the man was searching for his son who had not come home as instructed. But we had seen how stereotyped perceptions can affect deputies' interaction with minorities.

The next video scene was a within-the-family dilemma. A female sergeant walked into a roll-call room with a blackboard on which a derogatory ethnic cartoon had been sketched. She muttered, "Oh, you guys," erased the cartoon, and got on with business. This vignette triggered a wide range of responses, with African Americans and Hispanics arguing for strict condemnation of the cartoon and a search-and-destroy effort to find the cartoonist. One person advanced the argument of prejudice by omission: that silence equals guilt in such matters. Others agreed that such inappropriate workplace behavior should be sternly condemned, not brushed off. But tempers flared when one white officer urged lenient treatment for offenders, confessing that he'd had moments of indiscretion in his younger days. This comment was met with a stern rebuke by two minority officers, one of whom suggested that the white officer's parents hadn't properly raised him.

Paul Harman intervened to suggest we break for lunch, which was served on the medium-security premises by silent county jail inmates. In small groups, we talked over the morning's training. Men as a rule were more blasé about ethnic and gender workplace rules. A white LASD officer thought rules should be more flexible. Another minority officer admitted that he and his partner said things to one another they wouldn't say in a wider public setting. Another officer talked about the frequency with which New York City police exchange ethnic remarks.

Within-the-workplace use of ethnic remarks was the subject of our first after-lunch video. In an ethnically mixed police station, officers banter, and one Asian American uses the term "slopehead" to josh an Asian American officer along with comments about eating fishheads and dogs. Then an African American officer enters the room and causes consternation by innocently using the "slopehead" term, which he'd overheard. In subsequent group discussion, opinion was again divided though not along ethnic lines. A black female took a hard line, insisting that such banter was never appropriate; a black male responded that he had exchanged ethnic and gender jokes with colleagues, such as a sexist jest that sheriff stations should only have urinals. (There were ripples of shock and laughter, but the facilitators held fast to their nonjudgmental duties.)

Ethnic solidarity clashed with police instincts after a video vignette showing white police patrolling a wealthy neighborhood. The only car on the street was an old Toyota containing two black males. The police stopped, asked the young men if there was anything wrong, asked for identification, and checked to see if the car was stolen. Some minority officers and civilians perceived unnecessary discrimination and harassment in the video; others saw the behavior as prudent policework and community protection. A minority female officer admitted she had engaged in behavior similar to the officers in the video, and another minority female officer said she'd seen such police behavior in her neighborhood—and appreciated it.

A scene showing black police officers brutally treating a black adolescent in the movie *Boyz 'n' the Hood* provoked a discussion over whether minority police officers treat minorities more stringently than whites. An officer from a heavily minority station noted that some communities ask for same-race cops, only to complain later about how tough they are. A minority male said he'd once been treated exactly like the events in the movie. A minority female said she'd been pulled over by a minority officer while giving a ride to a younger man. The officer suggestively remarked that he liked older women too. She reported him.

A final vignette was the most simplistic: police treat a white male driving a Corvette far more politely than they do an African American male driving the same car.

The training demonstration closed with a restatement of department policy to treat everyone as individuals and with equal courtesy and respect. A public service spot featuring actors Judd Hirsch, Edward Asner, and Linda Lavin echoed this same message.

The two-thirds of those attending who filled out evaluations gave the facilitators and the videos overwhelming approval, though the stereotype exercise was favorably viewed by only 78 percent. The majority of complaints were in the "not enough time" category. Of course, this venture was preaching to the choir. The true test would come over the next two years as the field deputies trooped through the training schedule.

Impact of the LASD's Training

By the end of March 1994, the LASD was again training new recruits and had completed cultural awareness training for 3,230 sworn personnel and 108 civilians. Under terms of the *Bouman* agreement, the department is scheduled to complete cultural awareness and sexual harassment education for the entire department by August 1997.

Time and resources for cultural awareness and sexual harassment training have expanded significantly. In three years, LASD went from a largely volunteer committee to a full-time instructional staff devoted to cultural awareness and sexual harassment training. The unit has a annual budget of $4 million, though half that amount is allocated to a third specialty, use of force. While this would seem to be an impressive funding feat, no one knows—or is willing to state—how much money was spent on diversity training before 1993, in part, because the expenses were largely in the form of released time and overtime for officers taken away from other duties. As is the case in many other organizations, this ignorance seems quite sincere and has the added benefit of deflecting critics who think the department might have spent too much or too little. One bottom-line financial figure that was cited for cultural diversity and sexual harassment training at the time of the *Bouman* sexual discrimination settlement was $2.5 to $4 million. (This does not cover the costs of training recruits.)

The thirty-two hours of prejudice-reduction and cultural awareness education for recruits also accommodated a half-day field trip to L.A.'s Beit Hashoah Museum of Tolerance, which, to judge by recruits' evaluations, leaves a major impression. As originally intended, the field deputy curriculum provided eight hours for the experiential, prejudice-reduction course, and another eight hours for the cross-cultural education lectures. Some of the same video vignettes presented to the 1992 CAAC evaluation were still used, but new ones were substituted. One new instructor used a long segment from the movie *Mississippi Burning* for the section on African Americans, a segment of the training that has never broken free from backward-looking "oppression studies." And instructors were still ethnically matched to course materials: Asians teach Asian awareness, Hispanics teach the section on Hispanics, and so on. Only passing mention was made of gay and lesbian issues, which drew the ire of Kolts Commission researchers, who monitored the department through 1995. (More emphasis on gay and lesbian issues has since been added.)

How effective was the instruction? Course evaluations were hard to assess because at least half the deputies reportedly don't bother to fill them out— perhaps a judgment in itself. Of those who do, about half do so perfunctorily. As of the summer of 1994, no one in the LASD or on the Kolts Commission had tabulated the results, and few seemed to have scanned the raw forms. I did.

As expected, the recruits were an easier and more enthusiastic audience. Their ratings of the course were quite high. As for the in-service deputies, the results were surprisingly, mildly favorable. On a 1-to-5 scale, the instructors usually earned a 4 or 5, and several of the presentations were rated 3 or higher. *A Class Divided,* a video showing Jane Elliot's experiment dividing Iowa schoolchildren into blue-eyed privileged and brown-eyed oppressed groups, was very highly rated. Women and minorities responded more favorably, especially in written comments. White males, on the other hand, furnished many unfavorable comments, often disparaging the amount of time and money the department was spending. (Some instructors were coming to a similar conclusion.)

By the summer of 1994, Tony Argott had decided that there was too much overkill in the time allotted to the cultural awareness. Although he thought white males needed to know about cultural diversity, he was wary of the training's polarizing tendencies. Some sources within the department estimated that perhaps 20 to 30 percent of the training sessions for field deputies became tense or fractious at times; these problems became public during a meeting of the CAAC in the fall of 1995 when Lieutenant Nancy Reid complained that her instructors were suffering from "wear and tear" after deputies had "taken on" the instructors in a number of training sessions. The complaint was also aired that some in the custody division of the LASD were also needlessly alarming people by sarcastically referring to the cultural awareness training sessions as "reeducation camps."

Complicating Factors

Instructor Turnover and Burnout

Mobility up and throughout the LASD was considered an attractive organizational feature, but constant instructor and supervisor turnover hurt quality and consistency in cultural awareness training. In 1994, a new training administrator, psychologist John Chamberlin, was dismayed by the lack of planning and absence of a permanent register or tracking system indicating which deputies had taken the training and which had not.

Constant mobility also meant considerable loss of talent and experience. Nearly all of those originally involved in the planning and enactment of this new policy—and who cared deeply about these efforts—were no longer involved by summer 1994. Bill Stonich missed being promoted to chief and instead became commander of another LASD unit. Paul Harman took early retirement at age fifty and moved to Sacramento to take a position with POST, though he would have been interested in being head of the new diversity training unit. Both Harman and Bill Corrette admittedly suffered burnout from trying to perform regularly assigned duties as well as the add-on burden of building the cultural diversity program. Corrette claimed he resigned in 1993 in part to force establishment of a full-time cultural diversity staff, which wound up being supervised by an old rival, Rufus Tamayo.

Tamayo's performance dazzled a Kolts Commission monitor, especially his hard-line approach to "inappropriate" remarks made during the training.

In the *Second Semiannual Report,* published in April 1994, the Commission observed: "Sgt. Tamayo explained that when a trainee makes an inappropriate comment or confronts the instructor with a racist, sexist, or other discriminatory statement, whether verbally or in a written question, the Training Bureau now follows a procedure to isolate that individual and focus the class's attention on the inappropriateness of the trainee's comment or action." Other trainers strongly objected to this sort of targeting. They thought it sabotaged the educational process of self-awareness through open discussion and threatened the rule of confidentiality promised during the sessions. (One sergeant in the LASD told me that deputies feared that comments made during the training were being relayed to commanding officers. For a time, word spread that the safest policy was to remain silent during these sessions, lest future promotion opportunities be jeopardized.)

Nevertheless, Tamayo, too, moved on to other duties within a year. Burnout was one factor. Two other complaints were familiar to diversity trainers: Tamayo saw few career rewards for this sort of work and feared long-term career damage: "If I get painted as the 'ethnic guy,' I'm dead. My career is dead."

Yet Tamayo's fears were not entirely borne out. Some people involved in the cultural awareness effort were promoted, including Tamayo, Argott, and Jurado. On the other hand, several whites involved in the training were not—Bill Stonich, Steve Selby, and Bill Corrette—and Paul Harman retired at the same rank. His African American assistants, Beauchamp Hyde and Regggie Gautt, won promotion but nonetheless left their work as cultural diversity trainers by the summer of 1994. Diversity training in the LASD was hard work, and trainers had to absorb a fair amount of passive and active aggression from their students.

Argott became very frustrated with the department's handling of the diversity effort. Although he and Jurado were leaders in implementing cultural diversity training, he was miffed that their efforts were not officially recognized, while Bill Corrette, Paul Harman, and Steve Selby received ceremonial recognition and commemorative plaques. Argott much preferred his cross-cultural education approach and reported that the experiential discussion techniques favored by Corrette, Havessy, and Harman had produced blow-ups and hard feelings. The most puzzling development of all was the LASD's choice of Nancy Reid instead of Argott to head the expanded diversity training staff. Argott had applied for the job, wanted it, and had considerable training and background in the field. Reid, who had liked working in the homicide division, had no background in cultural diversity or harassment training, had never attended a meeting of the CAAC, and did not apply for the job until asked to by a supervisor. Argott began attending law school during off-hours.

Confusion with Affirmative Action and the "White Male Problem"

Nearly everyone interviewed for this book admitted that ethnic and gender preferences were the source of much, if not most, of the department's internal ethnic and gender tensions. But the topic was declared off-limits in the LASD training programs. Nevertheless, arguments over the policies erupted—or threatened to erupt—throughout the training.

Although the department officially claimed to have no quotas, the new, future-oriented workforce diversity scenarios that the department should mirror the population were weighing on the minds of the top brass. (So was a U.S. Justice Department inquiry into the department's affirmative action practices.) The department had no true quotas in recruiting, but the LASD was mindful to adjust (lower) the minimal pass score in order to have more minorities from which to choose. Thus, as Clyde French explained, an Asian female might be admitted to the LASD with a lower (but still passing) score while a white male with a higher score might be excluded. These delicate distinctions were lost on white recruits, some of whom ruptured the taboo on the topic in a cultural awareness seminar when they sparked a fierce debate with the ill-fated civilian instructor, Bernita Moss. Chief Lee Baca pondered the possibility that cultural diversity training might be seen as rationalizing affirmative action "as a way of softening people up for accepting minorities who aren't worthy of promotion and coveted assignments—so that 'when you stick us with these less qualified people, we won't be as hostile towards them.'"

Similar strategies were employed in promotions. Within a broad band of applicant scores, the department felt free to give women and minorities an edge. Thus, upon his reelection in 1994, Sherman Block immediately demonstrated his sensitivity by appointing three new captains: an African American male, a white male, and a Hispanic male. When ten promotions to lieutenants in 1994 had the carefully balanced look of affirmative action (four minorities and two females), a white officer scorned the "affirmative action" promotions within earshot of the new Lieutenant Rufus Tamayo, who claims he received one of the highest exam scores.

A retired-sheriff-turned-diversity-consultant, Lucinda Freeman, noted generational tensions among whites over preferential promotions. Freeman stated, "The younger whites are more white conscious because the minorities have banded together and don't care about whites." The top brass appeared to listen to female and minority complaints but told white males "to stop whining." (Indeed, when asked about charges of reverse discrimination, Sherman Block immediately retorted that such charges were a way of "rationalizing one's own inadequacies.")

In November 1995, a veteran LASD sergeant, Ed Kirste, sought to provide LASD white males with an official forum. He announced at a press conference that he was organizing the Association of White Male Peace Officers. He claimed that "white guys are getting shafted," though (as Lucinda Freeman observed) his anger was directed not at minorities but at the white male brass who enforced affirmative action and diversity policies. Kirste could point to no specific instances of obvious reverse discrimination, though broad banding of test scores implied it.

Area newspapers picked up on Kirste's conference, as did local and nationwide talk radio shows. The LASD brass were publicly silent but highly displeased; Kirste claims he was subjected to considerable pressure to drop his plans. In March 1996, he appealed to Sherman Block, who put out a memo indicating that Kirste's new association should be accorded the same rights and privileges as similar associations for blacks, Hispanics, women, and others. Kirste obtained about seventy dues-paying members (at twenty-five dollars each), twenty from outside the LASD (a few from as far away as Florida). While he claimed much informal support ("lots of people told me, 'it's about time'"), only seventeen people showed up for two meetings in the spring of 1996, and no one wanted to assume leadership, fund-raising duties, or other roles where their names might appear on rosters or letterhead. "Almost everyone is still afraid of retribution" in the form of damage to their careers. Only eighteen months away from retirement, Kirste admitted he was somewhat immune from intimidation. (Ironically, Kirste went through the cultural awareness training after he'd formed the Association of White Male Peace Officers; the instructors did not target him, and he claimed to be "Joe Good-Guy." He did feel the training was too general to be of much practical use. He reported that his colleagues sat through the training rather passively.)

In the LASD and other organizations, real or suspected affirmative action preferences mingled with preexisting suspicions of friendship links and political pull in the promotion process. No group seemed satisfied. Whites quietly pondered reverse discrimination, and there were reports that some cultural awareness instructors sent the message that whites "had to apologize for being white." Hispanics, blacks, and women claimed that politics and the old-boy networks hindered promotion. And yet nearly everyone interviewed thought race and gender relations were better today than twenty years ago for a prime, paradoxical reason: more opportunities for women and minorities.

Some deputies—almost always white males—thought that the cultural awareness training was a waste of time or that the community should be more sensitive and respectful toward law enforcement, not the other way around. Investigators from the Kolts Commission found that

> several deputies were quick to express their hostility towards this "*career* survival class." One deputy argued that "the *community* is the one that's disrespectful. They should learn our culture." Another complained that the Department wants them to transform themselves into "humorless robots." Another deputy stated, "I'm worried about cuts in our health insurance. Why are they spending money on this?" When instructors counseled deputies not to fight change, one deputy responded, "It's not just this class we're objecting to. It's the whole *spectrum* of changes. We're making the wrong adaptations. As the streets get wilder, they're asking us to be softer."[7]

Inconvenient Facts

The beating of Rodney King, the trial of his police assailants, and the subsequent L.A. riots shattered illusions of L.A. as a multicultural model. As few others did, the LASD directly confronted the complex realities of the riots and their aftermath. The riots, protracted recession, white flight, rising gang warfare, and strain on social services posed by unending legal and illegal immigration suggested far more dangerous but unmentionable realities just outside the door of the cultural awareness classroom.

In the LASD, as in many other organizations, cultural diversity training sometimes veered toward simplistic race and gender rationales, concealing complex problems: the LASD's internal affirmative action dilemmas and the multiple causes of troublesome urban street realities that many recruits would soon discover and many deputies already knew. There was a tendency to avoid or rationalize what Max Weber, the founder of German sociology, termed "inconvenient facts." For example, a local television station annoyed the LASD with its weekly broadcasts of gun-related deaths, comparing Los Angeles County with surrounding counties. Especially embarrassing were comparisons of Los Angeles and Orange counties: through November 1, 1994, there had been nearly 1,224 gun-related deaths in Los Angeles compared to 88 in Orange. LASD personnel deftly and quickly attributed the difference to L.A. County's larger population. (This was a weak rebuttal: L.A. County had approximately 3.6 times the population of Orange County; the number of homicides was about 14 times that of Orange County.)

These data reflected deeper social forces relevant and obvious for law enforcement but lightly glossed over or rationalized in LASD diversity training. The roles of class and poverty were perfunctorily acknowledged in careful discussion of the disproportionate number of young black men involved in violent crime. But an equally potent factor has been soaring incidence of teenage single motherhood. Tony Argott quickly mentioned the "problem" of black, inner-city single parents, but avoided the full gravity of the situation by omitting the numbers: 68 percent of African American births are to single mothers. Precise data on black male crime were avoided too: black males are 3 percent of the California population but more than 40 percent of imprisoned felons and prison inmates. New recruits would see this soon enough in their compulsory tour of duty in county custodial facilities.

Inconvenient ethnic crime data still figure in police probability-based profiling of criminals, which is useful in deciding whether there might be legal probable cause to stop or arrest someone. "I know what a hype [addict] in a certain area is going to look like—and it is ethnically related," said one anonymous source. Alas, collective criminal profiles often resemble stereotypes. But there was no mention, no honest acknowledgment of inconvenient facts on black crime and how such data might figure in legitimate use of profiling. Instead, the litany of oppression history was tolled in long lectures on slavery, the 1960s civil rights movement, and videos such as *Mississippi Burning*.

"We got this in college," a white male recruit politely informed me— which raises a valid point: If university professors substitute guilt-ridden history for inconvenient data, as they have for twenty years, then how can the LASD hope to present neutral analyses of tough urban realities? Indeed, with activist members of the Kolts Commission pressuring for more dictatorial, top-down, politically correct indoctrination, the LASD trainers would have been foolish to focus on inconvenient facts.

The Training Transformed

Sheriff Sherman Block worried that the intrusion of Los Angeles's increasingly fierce racial politics may have partly undermined the LASD's official, customer-service, demographic rationale for workforce diversity initiatives. "The deputies now think this training is because of Rodney King, the Kolts Commission, and the discrimination suit settlement," he sighed. The Kolts Commission monitors sounded the same theme: "It is important to acknowledge that these efforts, especially in the area of cultural diversity, are widely perceived by the trainees as a sop to outside political pressures. . . . This training will have an impact only if the Department's top management shows that they believe in it and are not merely offering it to propitiate outside critics."[8] Several instructors also voiced a common complaint of diversity consultants: that their work was being dismissed as a flavor-of-the-month fad.

Thus, by the summer of 1994, Clyde French was asking Sherman Block for another forceful, official restatement of the need and purpose for such training. Privately, Block saw L.A.'s ethnic tensions as rooted in deeper, changing economic class divisions. Overwhelming immigration, combined with the ravaged post–cold war economy, said Block, was pushing ethnic antagonisms beyond traditional black-white lines to conflicts among minority groups. Like every CEO interviewed for this book, Block worried about the emergence of a socially unstable, two-tiered economy, with many people trapped in low-wage jobs. But Block sounded conservative themes in noting the rising sense of entitlement, the search for conspiracies and deprivation, and the lack of individual responsibility and accountability. He worried about the reduced pull of assimilation yet had no inkling that cultural awareness training had the potential to fragment American society further.

The man likely to succeed Block, Chief Lee Baca, also sees poverty as generating crime and ethnic antagonism. But Baca is more upbeat about Los Angeles's prospects. Although the 1992 riots "brought out an awful lot of negative feelings that are still around," he thinks that California is more tolerant and culturally diverse than at any other time in its history. He sees much cross-cultural cooperation in the city's marketplaces. But he bristles when talking about one major consequence of L.A.'s diversity: white flight.

> We've seen the City of L.A. go minority as the result of busing orders. We've seen neighborhoods change over completely—just based on undesirability on the part of whites to integrate.
>
> Let's be fair: the white community has voiced itself with its feet, by moving out because they don't want their children raised with these renegade, rebel, crime-infested minorities. It's clear. But those whites who have stayed, those whites who have not run are a better quality white. . . .
>
> White flight is true in the sheriff's department as well—but you can't judge by the police point of view; because we deal with the worst, we're over-reactive. Emotionally, cops are battered, battered professionals; their nerves are

frayed. They're going to try and go find peaceful havens—burned-out teachers [do this] too.

Indeed, within the LASD, even "better-quality" whites and minorities were considering an exit from L.A. Ironically, some eyeing the exits were those most deeply involved in the cultural awareness effort. Even while rationalizing diversity's problems, they feared for the area's future and their own children's safety in the public schools. Paul Harmon has already left, and a nonwhite instructor worried out loud, "I'm not saying we've lost L.A., it's just that . . . that . . ." He decided to say no more.

In the fall of 1994, the *Los Angeles Times* headlined a rising exodus of mostly white LAPD and LASD officers.[9] The chief causes cited were overwork, the polarized social environment, and a common perception of "not having a future" in the LASD. The number of sheriff's officers departing for jobs with other police agencies rose from twenty-four in fiscal 1991–1992 to seventy-five in 1993–1994. A personnel administrator informed me that he also noted stepped-up white flight among newly retired personnel. "They used to stay. But many are heading for Idaho," he said. "They're looking for Paradise Lost." (Officially the department disputes such claims and argues that dissatisfaction among younger whites stems from the hiring freeze and their inability to move quickly out of entry-level duties in the country correctional facilities.) On the other hand, the LASD was criticized in a February 1996 semiannual Kolts Commission report for failing to boost the numbers of women, African Americans, Asians, and gays and lesbians.[10]

Though educating its employees to understand the cultural differences among its clientele, within its own workplace LASD still sounds the call for universal norms, equal treatment, and equal opportunity. More proportional themes of equity and diversity are not yet core values. The department's core values statement still emphasizes "being fair and impartial and treating people with dignity," and treating "every member of the Department, both sworn and civilian, as we would expect to be treated if the positions were reversed." The Golden Rule, then, has not been replaced by diversity management's more relativistic Platinum Rule: treat other people as they would wish to be treated. Nor has the department officially adopted the more aggressive diversity management policy of accountability—tying managers' raises to their affirmative action record.

A recent U.S. Justice Department probe does raise the specter of more quota-style procedures. But everyone interviewed for this study, including women and minorities, dreaded the likelihood of coercive goals and timetables. LASD members of minority police officers associations (which include other southern California police departments) have not been especially active. Ironically, spreading ethnic and gender divisiveness outside the department may be checked inside the department in part by the allegedly recalcitrant cop culture, which bonds most police personnel with shared training, experience, and—especially today—a shared sense of being misunderstood by the media and community activists.

The lasting impact of the LASD's cultural awareness education remains unknown. In all probability, the training raised interest, salience, and cultural diversity topics temporarily. Lieutenant Steve Selby hopes the cultural awareness education will be remembered and will promote useful mental shifts among those who encounter difficult situations in the field. Chief Lee Baca is more pragmatic:

> There's no long-term impact to be found in this sort of training. But the department has declared that this is important. . . . Once you've planted the seeds, this is a priority, everyone is on notice, this is worth your time, don't ignore it. When a person identifies themselves with LASD, someone may say, "Oh, yeah, you guys are pretty up to speed on diversity."
>
> I see this as a positive way of leading people to become more, knowing full well that if you left it to their own resources, they wouldn't do a damn thing about it. I'm one of those people who say that you can force benevolence into people. . . . I think you can train people to be more ethical, sensitive. This is teaching people about how to have sensitivity for one another. . . . If minorities are willing to do it, the majority should. This is a win-win situation.

By the fall of 1994, LASD psychologist John Chamberlin echoed Sherman Block's worry that the court settlement decree, coming on top of the L.A. riots, had placed the contaminating stigma of "mandated" on the department's diversity training program. The training would be done, and "that's it." A planned follow-up survey on the training's effectiveness had become bogged down in negotiations with the unions. At LASD and elsewhere, Chamberlin mused, there may be reluctance to do follow-up studies for fear of finding out that more training is needed and there is no budget for it. Ownership of diversity theory and practice, said Chamberlin, would vary enormously from one station to another. In the department's decentralized structure, station captains had a good bit of autonomy. Some would champion diversity; some would not.

As in the larger workforce diversity movement, Chamberlin saw diversity being woven as a subtheme into other forms of decision making. For example, said Chamberlin, diversity sensitivities should be fused with renewed clamors for station security, recently revived when a civilian walked into the Carson station and shot a deputy. The deputies now wanted bullet-proof glass in the lobby. Rather than risk alienating members of the community by installing cheap, translucent, bar-and-plexiglass designs, suggested Chamberlin, the department should consider more expensive, tasteful, clear glass shielding, such as that found at some banks.

Psychologist-consultant Victoria Havessy was more hopeful about the prospects for long-term attitudinal change: "There are two major changes I have seen in police attitudes. The first is declining tolerance of alcohol abuse. Second, now cops will hug."

Chapter 8

From Diversity Dreams to Budget Nightmares

The California Community Colleges System

The California Community Colleges system bills itself as the largest higher education system in the world, though the vast majority of its 1.4 million students are part time and have an average age of twenty-seven. Under California's Master Plan for Higher Education, the CCC's 71 community college districts and 107 campuses form the base of the state's higher education pyramid. The CCC system was originally free of charge, open to all high school graduates, and had balanced, dual missions of offering vocational education or a more academic curriculum for students who wished to transfer to four-year institutions. Today there is a $150-per-semester fee and a pronounced trend toward vocationalism as students increasingly seek training and certification in more practical fields, such as cosmetology, culinary arts, computer science, dental hygiene, nursing, drug and alcohol studies, radiologic technology, real estate, criminal justice, and fire science. Officially only 3 percent eventually transfer to four-year institutions, most frequently the twenty-campus California State University system.

With the 1978 passage of property-tax-cutting Proposition Thirteen, funding began to flow toward the state and away from strapped local districts. Today more than 50 percent of community college funding comes from the state. With mushrooming growth and increased state funding came greater state control through a comprehensive reorganization in 1988: the Community College Reform Act (Assembly Bill (AB) 1725).

Managing California's demographic diversity was much on the minds of the reformers, and affirmative action ethnic proportionalism was woven into AB 1725 as well into rules added to Title V of the California Administrative

238

Code. AB 1725 provided two specific mandates for affirmative action. A short-term goal was to achieve a 30 percent ethnic minority faculty by the academic year 1992–1993. A long-term mandate was that the workforce of the CCC system should mirror the ethnic diversity of California's adult population by 2005. In 1992, the board of governors, in coordination with the CCC academic senate, also mandated proportional graduation and transfer rates to universities through "student equity plans" to be drafted by every campus.

Although there would be much happy talk about the value of cultural diversity, AB 1725 also painted a darker, more urgent rationale for this vast administrative crusade: social control and societal stability. Integrating minorities into the CCC would help prevent "what has been called a 'permanent underclass,' mostly minority, and a semi-permanent, semi-employable stratum of low-skilled workers. The consequence of this development would be dire: the permanent underutilization of the energies and talents of our people, the deepening of racial resentments and fears, and the constant anxiety among more and more of us that the future has no place for us" (AB 1725, sect. 1g).

"Foster diversity" thus became one of the seven goals of the newly established basic agenda of the board of governors. A state chancellor's office was established for coordinating the CCC system and achieving the diversity mandates. David Mertes, a long-time administrator at several community college campuses, articulated the diversity theme often. In his introduction to the system's 1990 slick promotional brochure, *California Community Colleges: A Partnership of Opportunities,* Mertes wrote:

As the numbers and diversity of our population increase, the value systems and needs of both the workers and the workplace are in transition. California's economy, as sophisticated as it is, must develop an international perspective if we are to compete successfully in a rapidly expanding, global marketplace. The future of our state is highly dependent on the strengths and abilities of a multicultural citizenry to rapidly adapt to social, technical, and economic change.

The same brochure stressed the importance of the CCC as an avenue for minorities' upward mobility: "More than three-quarters of all minority college students in California attend Community Colleges. The largest segments of our future work-force, women, Blacks, and immigrants of Asian and Hispanic origin, will be educated at a Community College."

The CCC system, then, had state-imposed diversity mandates and officials committed to championing them, but the means to obtain these ends were in legal and political flux. Competing conservative and radical strategies for implementing affirmative action and diversity policies developed. In addition, as in the case of the Los Angeles Sheriff's Department, the CCC's diversity initiatives had barely been launched when California tumbled into a grinding five-year recession. The course of workforce diversity initiatives moved through the community colleges in stages typical of diversity campaigns elsewhere: (1) an enthusiastic affirmative action revival wrought by demographic predictions, (2) explorations of theories and techniques to change organizational cultures, (3) frustration produced by the deep recession, backlash and resistance, and tightening legal discretion, and (4) realization that simple race and gender formulas did not address complex realities and that diversity initiatives would be subordinated to more pressing needs of organizational survival.

I observed the progression of themes and diversity strategies through a series of annual conferences beginning in 1990. I attended keynote speeches and workshops that reflected changing policy perspectives and mingled with participants over lunch and after hours. (Indeed, my faithful attendance at workshops and panel discussions was noted. People seemed pleased that someone outside the CCC system was sufficiently interested to study their organization for a book.)

Although a few individual campuses and districts were reported to have active diversity drives (at least before the budget crunch), the centralized conferences were hardly models of revolutionary discipline. The conference participants—upper- and middle-level administrators—seemed generally amiable, mildly liberal people, naive about discrimination law, with a sprinkling of those motivated to "do good." Roaming among them, however, were ethnic and feminist civil rights moralists who pushed a more radical interpretation of the law. They defined diversity as proportional representation and critiqued the dominant white male culture. With the aid of small grants from the chancellor's office in Sacramento, they constructed pilot projects on their campuses and then reported results at the conferences. A dedicated few were openly cynical about legal procedures, especially the rights of white males. For the moralists, the ends generally justified the means in a contest against a racist and sexist system.

Among the most militant moralists were some district chancellors—most of them white—who were determined to demonstrate their diversity commitment to internal and external ethnic constituencies, as well tacking with the prevailing winds from Sacramento. With intense rhetoric, they tried to show they meant business about diversity—sometimes above and beyond the law. They may also have had in mind the replacement of the older, more expensive white male faculty. Any of the latter who ignored or resisted diversity initiatives were contemptuously portrayed as dinosaurs who would have to die off. Said Chaffey College's administrative activist Inge Pelzer, "We'll just have to wait for them to retire."

The official representatives of law and methodological order at these gatherings were the chancellor's legal and statistics experts, (respectively) Ralph Black and John Madden. As the pragmatists in this setting, they tried to ensure that affirmative action and diversity plans were crafted according to the latest legislation and court cases and with attention to proper statistics, fairness, and common sense.

Demography Is Destiny: An Affirmative Action Revival

The first three-day faculty-staff Unity Through Diversity conference attracted a sell-out crowd of 300 people to San Diego's Omni Hotel in late March 1990. It would be the most lavishly appointed and festive of these gatherings, held in the twilight of California's seemingly unstoppable postwar expansion and before the long recession, riots, and immigration controversies. Nearly $140 million had been appropriated to help campuses convert many part-time positions into full-time slots. It was assumed that hundreds of new positions would open up throughout the decade.

An indicator of enthusiasm was a standing-room-only crowd of eighty people who arrived for a preconference affirmative action workshop held in a room seating fifty. A massive workbook provided legal background and guidelines for mapping out hiring goals, but the speakers articulated conflicting radical and conservative interpretations.

Rod Patterson, a seasoned affirmative action officer for the Los Angeles Community District, provided a workman-like introduction, explaining the difference between voluntary goals and court-imposed quotas. Goals were a product of a college's "underutilization" of women and minorities, calculated by comparing the ethnic and gender composition of various categories of the campus workforce to at least three other labor pools: the state population, the civilian labor force, and the percentage of population who possessed skills required for the job. Quotas could be imposed only by a court after specific findings of discrimination. Data were important to prevent such actions, especially by disgruntled whites: "If you have problematic data and you get a backlash suit, you're in trouble," Patterson warned.

A more legally daring 50 percent minority and female hiring goal was unveiled by Charlene McMahan, director of affirmative action and personnel recruitment for the San Diego Community College District. The district chancellor had unilaterally set and achieved such a goal for sixty-five faculty hired in 1989–1990, a bounty wrought by cleaning out older white male faculty with "golden handshake" retirements. (No one in the workshop raised legal questions about a strategy that even top community college officials in Sacramento later admitted was dubious.) The 50 percent goal had caused "a great deal of fear—especially among older, conservative faculty." But district leadership remained resolute and opened-up lines had gone even further, launching a minority faculty intern program, designed to put them in line for upcoming full-time positions.

"How many of you would give race or gender preference if you could, if it were legal?" asked José Peralez, assistant superintendent for human resources at Santa Monica City Community District. "Well, you must if you are an affirmative action officer." Peralez offered his expansive view of affirmative action. The 1964 Civil Rights Act, Title VII, he said, legitimated race and gender preferences. And Peralez argued that the Supreme Court would not use the Fourteenth Amendment's equal protection clause to block affirmative action efforts. "It would be stupid if a law which was designed to encourage integration was used to block it." (The Supreme Court did exactly this in *Richmond v. Croson*, handed down six months earlier.)

Peralez preached the PC gospel of cultural relativism. "Standards" were arbitrary. "What's 'fair' is in the eye of the beholder." He recited the parable of the fox and the stork. The fox invited the stork to dinner and served the stork a meal on a plate—at which the stork could only nibble. The stork returned the favor by inviting the fox over for a meal served in narrow, long-necked jars.

Peralez urged workshop participants not to get bogged down in process and procedure, but to "get results" and "adjust attitudes." "We're the people deciding these things. Now we have the force of law on our side . . . and money."

Peralez's remarks thoroughly annoyed John Madden, a former math professor at Pasadena City College and the CCC coordinator of research and regulation on faculty/staff diversity, Madden, a strict constructionist, sparred briefly but politely with Peralez over interpretation of Supreme Court cases. Madden then went on to tell workshop participants to focus on obtaining legal and proper behavior. "If you are going to be a career affirmative action person, take employment law," Madden warned. "Do some of your own paralegal work and be intelligently conversant with lawyers." Affirmative action, he counseled, is a temporary remedy. "The goal of every affirmative action officer is to do away with his/her own job." Only a few people smiled. Madden silently vowed to bring in a top-flight lawyer for next year's gathering.

Diversity with Gusto: The Moralists Rule

Madden's caution was one small voice in a convention keynoted by increasingly aggressive sermons and stem-winders. Speakers trumpeted themes of urgency, righteousness, great expectations, and calls for more aggressive tactics. The main conference was vintage civil rights moralism.

Dan Grady, head of the San Diego Community College District's Board of Trustees, vigorously defended his district's 50 percent minority and female hiring goal as "necessary, and the right thing to do!" University of California, Berkeley mathematician Uri Treisman gave hope to social engineers by describing his pilot project for minority undergraduates. The problem for Hispanic and black student underachievement, Treisman found, was that they were isolated and studied alone. By fostering more student interaction and group study outside the classroom, minority academic performance improved.

Peter Espinosa, chair of a CCC committee on student equal opportunity, warned about continuing "pipeline dangers." Too many students lacked proper training for community colleges, and the more remedial courses they took, the lower were their chances of graduating.

The American Council on Education's Reginald Wilson wanted more decisive action. He argued that the pipeline must be totally "recreated" with measures far more aggressive than the CCC's AB 1725. Wilson was weary of the rhetoric he'd heard at fifteen diversity conferences since January. More than talk would be needed to counter the Reagan-era neglect that had produced a 35 percent decline in black enrollment in higher education from 1976 to 1988 and a 22 percent decline in the production of black Ph.D.s. As examples of more aggressive action, Wilson cited vigorous, fast-track hiring of minority faculty at Miami University of Ohio. The University of Michigan, he said, had used 1 percent of its total 1987 budget for minority initiatives, including hiring its own minority doctoral candidates, and recruiting ex-military minority teachers.

"You are not going to achieve your goal on AB 1725! There's a feeling of being besieged on American campuses," thundered Wilson. "It's time we stopped bullshitting each other and tried to do something serious!" (Wilson got a huge ovation, but had trouble afterward advising an earnest white male instructor who could not get his students to accept what appeared to be reverse discrimination. "Tell them their future depends upon it," counseled Wilson.)

"Denying minority people an education is immoral and criminal!" declared the next day's keynoter, Tomas Arciniega, president of California State University, Bakersfield. Arciniega grumbled that "academic excellence has replaced equality of opportunity" but was pleased to point out that the CSU system was fighting this trend by blurring the distinction between "best qualified" and "qualified." CSU campus presidents were demanding that they be given unranked lists of finalists for new faculty positions, permitting greater administrative latitude to choose minority candidates. Indeed, some campus presidents were rejecting such lists altogether if there were no minority names. Arciniega shocked some in the audience by describing how Cal State presidents could set aside special "opportunity hire" positions—bonus slots available only to departments that found minority candidates. The "two-for-one" approach may be used to hire both a top-ranked white candidate and a "qualified" minority person from the same applicant pool. After recruitment, Arciniega warned, there is the task of retention. "Don't expect minority faculty to know how to [computer] access the library."

A panel of tough-talking CCC district presidents discussed "What Every Good CEO Should Know and *Do* About Effectively Enhancing Diversity Within the College Milieu." Allan Brooks, a self-described FYM (fiftyish white male) and president of the San Diego Community College District's Mesa College, was especially hard-line. Brooks was proud to state that he and other administrators overrode faculty objections to "quotas" and "lower standards" by taking their case to community organizations and using endowment and state funds to recruit out-of-state candidates. Ernest Martinez, president of Cerritos College, claimed to have put older, recalcitrant faculty in their place by reminding them that many had been hired twenty-five years ago without a master's degree. Ron Kong, president of Alameda College, strongly recommended multicultural workshops for faculty. Others considered expanding recruitment efforts, setting "reasonable qualifications" (not using Ph.D. requirements to exclude women and minorities), mentoring, and changing attitudes.

Other conference discussion sessions and workshops reflected concern with basic affirmative action definitions, measurements, and techniques. Session titles included "Cross-Cultural Mentoring," "Action for Diversity," "Impact of Staff Diversity on Curriculum, and "What Is Reasonable Accommodation for Disabled Faculty and Staff?" John Madden conducted a sophisticated numbers crunching workshop on how to measure campus "utilization" of ethnic minorities and women by comparing the college workforce with other data such as the general population, general labor force statistics, and others. Many in Madden's workshop appeared bored or uncomprehending. One or two dozed. Not even the euphoria of demographic destiny could keep them awake.

The Diversity Machine Meets the Community Colleges

The 1991 diversity conference, held at the San Francisco Airport Hilton, had as its theme "Beyond Parity to Managing Diversity," billed in honor of star speaker R. Roosevelt Thomas. But the organizers supplemented Thomas with other well-known diversity keynoters to move the conference beyond affirmative action's civil rights moralism and on to the more pragmatic techniques of overhauling white male workplace culture and oppression.

Before the main conference, there was another preconference workshop on affirmative action, twice as crowded as the year before. Again the legal pragmatists and moralists jousted, but John Madden made good on his 1990 silent vow to bring professional, pragmatic legal instruction to the 1991 preconference affirmative action workshop. Lynn Thompson, an attorney with a high-powered L.A. law firm, warned the sixty participants that affirmative action was a changing, dangerous area of the law. Race-conscious or set-aside measures were controversial and risky, and minorities-only hiring was illegal. Faculty hiring goals could be set only by comparing current faculty composition with applicant or labor pools that have M.A. degrees, not with the general population. Thompson gave a careful summary of the 1987 Supreme Court *Johnson v. Santa Clara* case: all job candidates in that case were equally qualified, but the female candidate with a slightly lower score got the nod because of a gross statistical gender imbalance in that workforce. Be "realistic," she urged. Court decisions have been inconsistent, and there are a lot of competing forces at work—"and more affirmative action complaints are headed your way."

José Peralez appeared unfazed by Thompson's talk. He discussed getting minorities into and through personnel screening processes. "Over the years," he said, "I've tended to recognize the value of flexibility. We tend to be inflexible, fearful of lawsuits. Exercise a lot of flexibility in implementing rules and law. . . . You must fight smarter, not harder." Peralez described how he became involved in faculty searches, helping to decide what positions to staff, sometimes asking whether a retiring faculty member's exact specialties needed to be replaced or whether others could teach what he taught. "It's psychological warfare. There is a lot of discretion."

Peralez was openly cynical about the rising dilemma throughout the community college system posed by balancing diversity goals in the face of large numbers of white part-time faculty who had patiently waited for full-time slots. Peralez admitted, "I talk out of both sides of my mouth. When there is a strong adjunct minority faculty member, I'll stress that 'you know them.' I also try to find good minorities to get in as part-timers, especially if I know there's a full-time position coming up." On the other hand, long-term, white part-time faculty were owed nothing. "When underrepresentation is an issue, then the part-time problem is not important." (After the workshop, I asked him if he thought that screening out long-time white part-timers from full-time positions was fair, even in the name of diversity. He was curt: "As far as I'm concerned, we've paid them, and that's the end of it.")

Roosevelt Thomas, Jr., gave a masterful keynote presentation complete with color slides filled with key points and supportive data from his books and articles. Many for the first time heard Thomas explain that diversity refers to the collective mixture of the workforce, including white males and people of different age, educational background, sexual orientation, functional position, and geographical origin. It was more than race and gender. But Thomas quickly bonded with the audience when he lightly criticized the inflexibility of white male culture with his favorite metaphor: the inability to graft a branch from a Georgia pecan tree (minority culture) onto an old oak tree (white male organizational culture). In other words, the white male organizational tree must be freed from its basic assimilationist, deep-root assumptions ("we're like a family," or "cream rises to the top") to its branches. Mutual adjustment would be the new order of the day, though managing diversity would require vision, mission, and long-term commitment.

Thomas was the first—and one of the only—conference speakers deliberately to deflate demography-is-destiny exaggerations. He sharply corrected the errors in *Workforce 2000* by telling the convention that by the year 2000, the workforce will still be 40 to 43 percent white male, only slightly down from 49 percent in 1985. Minorities are growing faster, but their numbers are still small. Thomas stated careful criticisms of affirmative action: the policies have been a forced, temporary, artificial corrective action, premised on the individual's adjusting to organizational culture. Thomas also risked moralists' ire by noting that affirmative action now carries a lot of "negative baggage." This did not endear him to the moralists, but he was well received (though one questioner seemed to think Thomas's views were better suited to business than education, a distinction that would blur as community college budgets dramatically worsened.)

Lillian Roybal Rose offered her view of diversity training as requiring deep social-psychological change. She warmed the crowd by discussing her childhood in East L.A. as the daughter of famous Mexican-American activist Ed Roybal. Individuals needed to "shift frames of reference" mentally and emotionally and endure the emotional trauma of change. "Everyone wants to have a multicultural educational system," she said. "But no one wants to experience it." Internalized rage and undischarged anger inhibit and damage people, especially minorities. The triumph over emotions, especially fear, releases beneficial emotions and produces change and clarity.

Milton Bennett, a Portland State University professor and head of the Intercultural Communication Institute (an occasional intellectual watering hole for Rose and several other consultants), outlined the necessary path toward cultural relativism from "ethnocentric" to "ethnorelative" states. The typical pattern begins with "denial of difference" and a tendency to dehumanize outsiders. The "defense against difference" tends to devalue other cultures as "underdeveloped." A third "minimization of difference" stage involves recognizing and accepting superficial cultural differences, such as eating customs. But especially in the United States, everyone is defined as alike—in terms of white male norms. Cultural relativism begins with an appreciation of cultural differences and cultural relativity. "Adaptation to difference" involves deeper intercultural understanding, while "integration of difference" sees internalization of bicultural or multicultural frames of reference as natural.

Workshops and smaller panel discussions carried the new diversity management and valuing differences themes: "Diversity and Valuing Differences," "Diversifying the Faculty (An Intersegmental Approach)," "Creating a College Vision of Diversity (Not Just a CEO Responsibility)," "Toward an Understanding of Campus Climate," "Faculty Intern Program for Diversity," and "Developing Intercultural Sensitivity." The mood was still enthusiastic, exploratory, and experimental. Ralph Black, assistant general counsel for the chancellor's office, in "A Civil Rights Update," tried to ground more grandiose utopian visions by reinforcing Lynn Thompson's discussion of legal do's and don'ts of affirmative action.

As at many other diversity gatherings, gay and lesbian differences were rarely addressed and were met with ambivalence when they were. Indeed, the most embarrassing conference note was a comedy routine performed at the reception buffet by Tom Ammiano, a gay entertainer, who was a new member of the San Francisco School Board (and subsequently elected to the San Francisco Board of Supervisors). He cracked one-liners such as:

"Nice to know we have a strong man in the White House—Barbara Bush."

"When I was in Texas, I was asked if I wanted to get hung—boy did I!"

"Dianne Feinstein got in an elevator with a lesbian. When asked if she was 'going down,' Di hastily said 'oh, no!'"

"Dan Quayle is so dumb that when he saw a sign 'wet floor,' he did."

Several people, especially blacks and Hispanics, looked pained or disgusted. There were a few ripples of laughter mingled with groans. People started leaving. Diversity was not yet as inclusive as many at the conference professed. This dimension of difference was definitely regarded as a luxury, especially as the CCC campuses became increasingly preoccupied with basic economic survival.

California's Economic Debacle Stalls the Diversity Drive

Beginning in 1992, the faculty-staff diversity conference was merged with the chancellor's megaconference of several types of community college administrators. The official reason was to mainstream diversity themes into the more general agenda. (An unofficial reason was to curb the expense and ideological excesses at the separate diversity conferences.)

The 1993 megaconference was held in Irvine in April, a year after the L.A. riots protesting the Rodney King case verdict. Through Irvine was a lush enclave, the conference occurred in the wider context of California's worst economic crisis since the Great Depression. Befitting the times, the chancellor intended to provide shock therapy, furnished in the form of a grim demographic-economic forecast by Thomas Nagle, director of the state's Employment Development Department. Nagle's analysis had been honed and crafted many times before other audiences and was so impressive that it had become known throughout the state bureaucracies simply as "The Speech."

Nagle forecast a burgeoning, illiterate, crime-ridden, dependent underclass that had already begun to gobble up an increasing share of public expenditures, leaving less and less for higher education. Tax-paying, middle-class whites were fleeing the state. The immigrant-driven diversity seen by activists as the dawn of a multicultural dream was instead becoming a fiscal nightmare threatening bankruptcy. Using both wide-screen projections and a handout folder packed with data, Nagle showed that California's population growth would come from foreign immigration and the high birthrates of new arrivals. The state was adding two to three thousand people per day, the equivalent of a City of San Francisco every year. Only 1 percent of California's growth stemmed from immigration from other parts of the United States. By the year 2000, minorities will be 50 percent of the state population and 50 percent of its workers. Nearly 80 percent of future workers will be Asian or Hispanic. The younger age group is rapidly expanding, while the 45–65 age group is fleeing. Crime and the prison population are ballooning, as are the number of single parents dependent on public welfare. With 12 to 13 percent of the population, California accounts for 26 percent of the entire nation's expenditures on welfare.

The most ominous development, said Nagle, was the dwindling ratio of taxpayers to tax receivers. In 1960, there were 6.9 taxpayers for each tax receiver; by 2000, not seven years off, there would be 2.9 taxpayers to each tax receiver. The growth industries of the new Third World state would be services and retail trade, which pay minimum wage. And the 20 percent and growing share of the population that is functionally illiterate would likely have trouble holding even those jobs.

Nagle provoked uneasy laughter with a lame jest about white flight: "I have only a few more years until I retire and I, too, can move to Oregon or Washington. People are thinking, 'I've got to get out before all this collapses.' But the problems will follow them."

The 800 people in the hotel ballroom appeared too stunned to boo Nagle, and he was given polite applause. But anger built during the break. "He made it sound like the barbarians are at the gate!" snorted a white male administrator from northern California.

Chancellor David Mertes caught the anger and the boos at his luncheon address built on Nagle's hard-time themes, as he talked about budget tightening and the need to measure results. Uneasy affirmative action officers felt that Mertes was threatening to withdraw program funds distributed from the chancellor's office, though Mertes claimed he was misunderstood.

In a workshop following Mertes's speech, Ralph Black, assistant general counsel for the chancellor's office, continued the grim era-of-limits theme by presenting "the new legal environment" created by Supreme Court curbs on affirmative action and the subsequent revisions of the state Title V regulations. There has been a "narrowing of permissible techniques," Black emphasized. Set-asides were impermissible. Hiring goals based on 1980 general population data must be abandoned. Black ticked off the new list of rules:

- Goals must be set based on the qualified applicant pool.
- Goals cannot last longer than necessary and cannot become rigid quotas.
- Affirmative action focus should be on recruitment and outreach.
- Recruiters should avoid asking for qualifications higher than state minimum qualifications, unless they are certain it won't have an adverse impact on underrepresented groups.
- Screening and selection processes should be monitored to detect adverse impact.
- Factor in the new requirement that applicants must demonstrate sensitivity and understanding of diversity (this will likely favor minority candidates).
- The 1989 Supreme Court decision in *Johnson v. Santa Clara* (1987)—that underrepresented group status may be taken into account in the final selection process—is permissible "if you want to be aggressive."

A battle-weary vice chancellor for diversity, Maria Sheehan, admitted the phrase "affirmative action" made "eyes glaze over" and was commonly misunderstood as "hiring the unqualified." She much preferred the term "diversity," which she defined as "preparing for the future."

In a more upbeat workshop, Chaffey College administrator Inge Pelzer discussed her efforts to induce culture change at Chaffey. Pelzer had obtained permission from the chancellor's office to use half her salary time to build a Chaffey College President's Equity Council. As was often the case with diversity initiatives, external pressure had been applied. Chaffey had received eighteen diversity-related recommendations from a recent reaccreditation report. The report had emphasized sensitizing faculty and staff selection committees to the needs of affirmative action, emphasizing and improving the representation of underrepresented groups in recruiting and hiring staff, creating an "affirmative" learning environment, and expanding sensitivity training.

Chaffey's president decided that diversity would primarily refer to color and all individuals from underrepresented groups. (Issues of gender equity would be set aside for the first year.) Pelzer met with activist groups on campus and in the community, eventually establishing a council of forty members: thirty-five from the college and five from the community. The purpose of the committee was "to design and implement an integrated equity program that brings together the various interests, activities, and mandates related to diversity." Subcommittees were formed to deal with three major areas: student equity, faculty and staff affirmative action, and the Americans with Disabilities Act. A sensitivity training session had been scheduled for May 20. By June, the committee hoped to report to the president "what is wrong at Chaffey College."

There were other several seminars reporting on projects funded with diversity money from the chancellor's office. Many described minority mentoring programs for faculty or staff positions. Most had mixed results, often due to budgetary difficulties. Margot Greever of Chaffey College, however, reported that nine out of ten of their counseling interns got full-time positions.

There was more attention paid to the rising dilemma of how to balance diversity needs with justice for the huge, heavily white pool of part-time faculty. CCC campuses had exploited the huge oversupply of white Ph.D.s produced during the 1970s and 1980s by hiring them as near-permanent temporary or adjunct faculty at very low hourly rates. In 1989, CCC campuses came under a state mandate to reduce the percentage of credit courses taught by part-time faculty to 25 percent. (Part-time faculty had reportedly been up to 80 percent at some campuses.) "This is the last of the old-boys' network," said the chancellor's statistics expert, John Madden, whose studies indicated that nearly half of new full-time faculty jobs were going to these part-timers.

Dora Valenzuela, compliance officer of San Diego Community College District, was more direct: "This has to stop!" And stop it her district fully intended to do. At a workshop demonstration, the San Diego Community College district showcased its new computerized hiring system, partly designed to curb perceived tendencies of white deans to hire white part-timers. Standardized part-time applications were screened by a department chairperson or a designate, the affirmative action officer, and the dean of classroom instruction. This was fed into the central computer pool. Ideally, when an opening appeared, the dean would access the computer, which would furnish a list of eligible candidates containing the individual's name, brief committee comments, and whether he or she was from a "historically underrepresented group" (HUG). No other data appeared. Insofar as they met the minimum hiring criteria, all candidates were equally ranked. If a dean wanted more specific information, an individual's entire application could be viewed. The problem was getting deans to use this system for each of the 1,500 to 2,000 annual, part-time faculty appointments. "Resistance has been incredible," complained Charlene McMahan.

Economic Survival and Diversity Reconsidered

By 1994, the state's deep recession, especially in aerospace-dependent southern California, had taken a severe toll on the low-tuition community college system. "Many of California's community colleges are financially sick," stated a McClatchy News Service report on October 30, 1994. "Nearly half of the state's 71 college districts overspent their general fund budgets in the 1993–94 fiscal year." The report quoted a state official: "Even the healthy districts are questioning how much more they can hang on. It has become a 'can you keep the place going?' conversation." The mandate to increase the proportion of full-time faculty was being ignored by most community college campuses.

At the 1994 megaconference, Building Partnerships and Empowering Communities, Governor Pete Wilson's higher education aide, Maureen Di-Marco, bluntly sounded the alarm. "Wake up!" she warned. "Time is running out for public education unless something changes." She informed the eight hundred conference members that California had "lost one-third of our income" and that the vast majority of those who actively vote do not have children in the schools. Crime control is voters' top priority, and passage of the pending "three strikes and you're out" ballot proposition would send criminal justice and prison expenses soaring. Nonetheless, DiMarco called on educators not to underestimate nor battle the shift in public mood but rather to be positive and pull together rather than fragmenting. (Indeed, conventioneers were only dimly aware of the tidal wave of anger building against both illegal immigration and affirmative action preferences, which would surface in ballot initiatives in 1994 and 1996.)

The ascent of economic priorities became obvious when Chancellor David Mertes unveiled the "number one goal" of a new Community College Foundation: building partnerships with the private sector. (Yet diversity was woven into such efforts. Southern California Edison was providing scholarships and intern programs for minority students, and IBM was considering computer labs for disabled students and hardware and software for campus day care centers. Compacts had been formed with the University of California, Cal State, and more distant institutions. Rensselaer Polytechnic Institute offered three scholarships for community college transfer students: two open to everyone and one to minorities only).

Mertes discussed the new Community Colleges' Commission on Innovation, which posed growth as its number one issue. There would be development of "distance learning"; using computer technology, the CCC system hoped to deliver more educational services to homes and workplaces. Quality control—of student learning and student success—was essential. Another goal was "diversity broadly defined—age and preparation as well as ethnicity."

Diversity issues were still on the agenda, but the lone convention keynoter on the topic urged major reconsideration of diversity's simplistic race and gender identity politics. Santiago Rodriguez, Apple Computer vice president for multicultural programs, discussed the multifaceted nature of the "multi-cultural conversation." The term "diversity," Rodriguez feared, had become too trendy, the sure sign of a fad. Diversity had also become a buzzword for other terms that have become sullied. Equal opportunity failed, declared Rodriguez, because it meant treating everyone the same according to white male norms. Affirmative action served a recruitment and outreach function but generated little passion or follow-through by the "nonprotected classes." Current diversity efforts were hampered by the growing recognition that promoting group differences revived or created new stereotypes, while ignoring individual variations. Drawing on his own complex biography, Rodriguez closed by exhorting the crowd to embrace a new spirit of *E Pluribus Unum:* "We can reinvent ourselves, because there is so much creativity, so many ideas." He received a thunderous ovation.

A Defensive Diversity Is Folded into the Mix

A multiethnic student singing group opened the initial ballroom gathering of the 1996 Fifth Annual Chancellor's Megaconference in San Jose, but the conventioneers heard little else about ethnic diversity or multiculturalism from general session speakers for the first day and a half. The 1995 conference was billed as "Working Together for Student Success." The salad days of public funding would never return, but the nearly 800 people attending the conference (mostly women, minorities, and a distinct minority of older white males) were obviously relieved to welcome the first state budget increase in five years. Talk of crisis and deteriorating budgets could be replaced by a guarded optimism and planning for the future.

In the initial general convention sessions, affirmative action and diversity issues were initially mentioned perfunctorily, if at all. Race and gender diversity was generally folded into an emerging new mix of issues. One sensed that ethnic and gender diversity was a nagging, old issue, a squeaky wheel associated with the horrid years of budget slashing. Diversity had become something of a downer, even for diversity advocates, because the political world had turned upside down. This was the first megaconference held since a series of shattering setbacks for the diversity machine: the University of California Regents had voted to abolish affirmative action preferences the previous July; the California civil rights initiative, which would end state-sponsored ethnic and gender preferences, had just qualified for the November general election, and ten days before the convention, the federal Fifth Circuit Appeals Court ruled against the use of ethnic preferences by the University of Texas Law School. Diversity issues simmered quietly on the first day of the general sessions, burst through occasionally on the second day, and surfaced somberly in the final day's keynote.

Terry O'Banion, author of *Placing Learning First*, kicked off the conference with a bouncy discussion of his vision of a future "learning college"—a more flexible environment with self-guided small groups, stand-alone video training, student-based schedules, and far less emphasis on grades ("inaccurate judgment of a biased and variable judge"). The future learning college would not be time or place bound. He mentioned the word "diversity" just once.

Kathleen Connell, the conservative Republican state controller, sounded a more down-to-earth theme of the 1994 Republican revolution as she spoke happily about California's potential as an "engine of growth." Rebuilding California's economic base and infrastructure would depend on a supply of educated, technologically skilled workers, and the community colleges were the key providers of both skilled workers and university graduates: 75 percent of California State University graduates began at the community colleges, as did 66 percent of the University of California graduates. (Connell ingratiated herself with the convention through a bit of reverse snobbery. Her neighbor's daughter had obtained an English degree from Berkeley and had been without a steady job for three years, yet graduates of a local community college computer design program quickly received multiple job offers.)

But Connell did not promise funding increases; indeed, she had just finished salvaging half a billion dollars of "waste" by auditing the huge medical program and was moving on to audit the giant California correctional system. ("Are we next?" growled a white woman near me.) Connell sternly warned the crowd: "California government would have to change the way it does business." She too made only a passing reference to diversity. But she made strong reference to the kindred issue of class and ethnic polarization, referring to the colleges' mission to promote social stability through employment: "Our best hope of employing the unemployed is through the community colleges." Connell received polite applause.

The keynoters were on target. California's higher education enrollments had remained steady or declined, instead of slowly rising as expected. All three systems of higher education—the University of California, California State University, and the community colleges system—had been battered financially. Classes were cut; tuition rose. In the early 1990s, enrollment in California's public colleges fell 210,000. In 1993, the community colleges' enrollment fell 7 percent after a fee hike. The Cal State system lost $200 million in funding and 50,000 students from 1990 to 1994. Rising fees coupled with reduced course offerings were popular explanations. Some noted that the percentage of California high school graduates seeking higher education in other states rose slightly, from 3.2 to 4.6 percent. But the primary factor—an embarrassing one, not often acknowledged in public—appeared to be a court order barring illegal immigrants from enrolling in the community colleges and from paying much lower in-state tuition for university educations.[1]

The substantially higher fees and tuition at the universities had resulted in an increasing number of reverse transfers into the community colleges as Cal State, the University of California, and other university students began taking more courses at the far less expensive community colleges. This added a glaring new dimension of academic and socioeconomic "diversity" on the two-year campuses: well-prepared, bright university students, sometimes from middle-and upper-middle-class backgrounds, now mingled in classes with inadequately or barely prepared first-generation college students.

In addition, more and more higher educational officials were publicly worrying about "tidal wave II," the anticipated surge of nearly half a million more students created by the maturating of baby boomer and immigrant children. Tight-fisted taxpayers (most of whom did not have school-age children) were not about to shell out an additional $5.2 billion to pay for new campuses and classrooms.[2]

Terry O'Banion's dreamy keynote about new types of learning colleges no longer seemed so farfetched during a nuts-and-bolts panel discussion on "Approaching the New Millennium." Community colleges would soon see—some already were witnessing—widening gaps between remedial and advanced students; more students from homes and schools with little discipline or support; more gang members; some students would be computer literate, some not literate at anything; there would be a multitude of learning styles, as well as teaching styles, which increasingly would emphasize "not sage on the stage, but guide on the side." There would be more flexible scheduling and more use of "distance learning" (through televised, videotaped course instruction); choices would have to be made between "high tech or high touch." Students would be even more torn among school, family, and job commitments. There would be more dropping in and dropping out, more transfers in and out.

The alternative to doing things differently would be rationing of higher education. Who would be educated? Should standards be raised? The end of affirmative action might reduce minority enrollment, but what would be the societal consequences? What was fair? Thus did the question of race and gender diversity arise once again. Years ago, however, many at the conference would have assumed that race and gender were the heart of the issue. In 1996. the picture seemed far more complex.

Diversity Advocates on the Defensive

Diversity and affirmative action began gaining more attention at noon on the second day of the conference from Rose Tseng, chancellor of West-Valley Mission Community College District. In a thick accent, she rambled briefly about how the community colleges served the thriving immigrant populations and how "diversity is our secret weapon: everyone wants to come here." She then introduced Vishwas More, president of the Community Colleges Board of Governors. A native of India and a Republican appointee of Pete Wilson, he nonetheless defied Wilson's antiquota stance. More pledged that the board of trustees would not cave into political pressures as had the University of California Regents in voting to end affirmative action preferences. (This was greeted with heavy applause and scattered cheers.) On the contrary, More declared that his board was dedicated to increasing the ethnic and gender diversity of community colleges staff and faculty so that they would "better reflect the communities we serve."

The third day's keynoter, Stanford University's provost, Condoleezza Rice, an African American, finally offered a sustained, though qualified, defense of affirmative action and valuing diversity. Rice began with old-fashioned rhetoric:

> Our complicated journey to appreciate and accept the value of diversity and really value it, not just tolerate it, is not done. Two hundred plus years ago when the Framers said "we the people," they did not mean me. But little by little by little, step by step, we struggled with this and we continue to struggle with this concern and we have remained open to people of other cultures, too. . . .
>
> We should not lose track in these hot and heated political days of these two pillars of strength of the USA: that to value diversity and strengthen diversity and to have it really be something in which we all participate is an active process. *Affirmative* action meant exactly that, an active process. It did not, in my mind; this does not mean admitting or hiring people who were unqualified. It simply meant that, yes, if we wanted to wait three hundred years to get to the Founders' vision, it might all happen naturally. But that was too long. We wanted to do it actively, now; we wanted to go aggressively after an America in which diversity really was a fact, not just a dream. And that's what it meant to be affirmative in our desire to act.

Similarly, if this country ever loses sight of how important immigration has been to us, then we shall surely be lost. [Applause]

But then Rice began to raise problems that affirmative action wouldn't solve or that it exacerbated. The Stanford provost cautioned that affirmative action must be defended as a privilege, not a right—and without rancor. Nor could affirmative action be used as an excuse to bypass the growing drive for individual accountability. Nor would the policies substitute for hard work. Rice had asked several black Stanford undergraduates how many intended to obtain Ph.D.s; when they responded that such credentials required too much time, she told them not to blame administrators when no blacks could be found in academic job searches. "I can't create faculty out of whole cloth," she told them.

Most emphatically, Rice warned of cultural and ethnic separatism: "We've been pulling apart from the larger society," she noted. "We have to reintegrate diversity into pluralism . . . make ourselves one society again. . . . We have to make clear, especially to ethnic minorities, that we're committed to one America, not several." (One could not help but think that Rice had in mind not only Stanford's own notorious faculty and student separatists, but the specter of Mexican flags being waved in the streets of Los Angeles prior to the 1994 vote on Proposition 187, the ban on public services to illegal aliens.) The applause was appreciative but not overwhelming.

Rallying to Confront or Circumvent the Antipreference Mood

Another somewhat chastened champion of affirmative action was activist and civil rights moralist José Peralez. A twenty-year veteran of struggles for affirmative action with three community college districts, Peralez had suddenly become the new vice chancellor for equity and diversity when Maria Sheehan departed for the presidency of a community college district. At the second day's convention luncheon, he presented awards for outstanding diversity achievements to college districts and individuals, including an appreciative plaque for Sheehan.

In the hotel's smaller conference rooms, Peralez led three different panel discussions on changes in affirmative action and equity issues: the University of California ban on affirmative action preferences, the California Civil Rights Initiative, and the one-week-old decision by the federal Fifth Circuit Appeals Court against the use of ethnic preferences by the University of Texas Law School. Attendance at the sessions was, as usual, ghettoized with mostly blacks and Hispanics, some Asians and white women, and a few—often relatively quiet—white males (including me).

In the first panel, "How Changes in Affirmative Action Will Impact Access to Higher Education," the heretofore cocky Peralez seemed somewhat dazed and disorganized, vacillating between conciliation and frustration. He was perplexed by the sudden, organized opposition to what he saw as simple access and integration issues. "Access is an issue of how to share," pleaded Peralez. "Integration," he explained, "is uncomfortable."

Like most other diversity consultants, Peralez rationalized the rebellion against ethnic and gender preferences through the frustration-aggression model. Integration was working—and that was the problem. "We're getting administrative and teaching jobs. Ethnic minorities are now more than 50 percent of community colleges' students." But the "dominant groups" try to control access. The "powers that be" were "playing on divisiveness." Opponents of affirmative action weren't thinking of the collective good. Peralez claimed that even physicist Albert Einstein recognized we must transcend our individuality:

> A human being is part of the larger whole. . . . He experiences himself, his thoughts and feelings, as something separated from the rest . . . a kind of optical delusion of his consciousness. This delusion is a kind of prison for us, restricting us to our personal desires and to affection for a few persons nearest us. Our task must be to free ourselves from this prison by widening our circle of compassion to embrace all living creatures and the whole of nature in its beauty.

Felix de la Torre was a more nuts-and-bolts tactician, as befitted a political analyst with the Mexican-American Legal Defense Fund (MALDEF). He offered a primer on how to argue against the civil rights initiative. The ballot measure would destroy outreach and faculty hiring, especially crippling the community colleges as a "haven for minorities." He questioned the concept of merit and grade-point averages as indicators (unfair to many minorities because they have no home support group). Besides, "grades capture student ability about as well as a high school yearbook." Minorities needed higher education degrees because they would return to serve their communities. (I bit my tongue; most low-income black and Hispanic undergraduates I'd encountered during twenty years of college teaching wanted upward mobility *out* of low-income communities; in any case, talented minorities with technical and scientific degrees would likely be caught up in alluring bidding wars, regardless of any desires to return to their community of origin.) Finally, de la Torre waxed ultraradical. Why fight over positions at the University of California, Berkeley? Why not make *every* UC campus equal in stature to Berkeley?

John Matsui, a biologist from Berkeley, mourned the changes on campus that he described as "deeply shaken." People were "mobilizing" and talking to one another. He rued the change in campus climate. "Comfort levels have shifted. Majority students feel vindicated. Minority students won't use targeted services" out of fear of being stigmatized. He warned that using socioeconomic hardship instead of ethnicity as an admissions criterion would still decrease the numbers of Latino and African Americans.

The most touching, effective, and animated plea for programs targeted at minorities came during a workshop on encouraging minority students to transfer to four-year universities. Isaac Guzman headed Rancho Santiago College's minority transfer program. Yet Guzman's problems were as much or more related to poverty and poor academic preparation as ethnicity. His district was located in Santa Ana, now home to huge numbers of poor immigrants. When he took over the program in 1990, there were 7,000 Latino students at the school; none transferred to the University of California. "We weren't transferring anybody." By 1996, thirty-five transferred. Guzman thought that a success.

Guzman worked with what he had. "A kid with a high school algebra class is University of California material to me!" he exclaimed, provoking warm laughter in the room. Few of the students who came through his door had ever been told they were four-year college material. "They've been told repeatedly that they're no good," said Guzman. When such students first meet him, Guzman asks if they're tired of hearing gunfire in their neighborhoods. Then he shows them a postcard of University of California, Santa Cruz. "Do you want to go there?" he asks. With Ford Foundation funding, Guzman organized a summer institute for 100 at-risk kids, which, he claimed, was a modest success. He was devastated by the UC regents' decision against preferences as well as the recent federal appeals court decision against the use of preferences by the University of Texas Law School. His response was that students and their mentors would have to be clever about completing admissions essays, taking care to use the right "code words" in order to signal "disadvantaged."

Unless opened to all students, Guzman's program might be jeopardized under the changing rules of affirmative action. The community colleges system had taken heed of changes in the political climate beginning with the regents' decision against ethnic and gender preferences. As early as September 14, 1995, Tom Nussbaum, the board's vice chancellor for legal affairs, warned that "our regulations or policies could be problematic under the most recent U.S. Supreme Court decisions." Indeed, Governor Wilson had already sued his own state to cease using preferences. One target in the lawsuit (which ultimately was denied a hearing) was the community colleges provision in AB 1725 to require a faculty and staff that reflected the adult population of California by 2005. (This clearly violated the Court's 1989 *Ward's Cove v. Antonio* decision, which insisted that "relevant labor pools" be used in assessing discrimination or imbalance. A low percentage of California's population had a master's degree or better, yet the law remains in the California Education Code as this book goes to press.)

Echoing the early warnings of John Madden that affirmative action officers are destined to go out of business, Nussbaum indicated that the colleges should no longer require or maintain ethnic and gender balance unless districts demonstrate underrepresentation compared to relevant labor pools. Once such underrepresentation is remedied, the plan should be ended. But Nussbaum fudged the line between using preferences or goals and timetables. The former would be forbidden; the latter acceptable.

Nussbaum also warned that the system's programs guaranteeing a portion of college business contracting to women and minority-owned firms would have to "change significantly." Ethnically targeted student programs were suspect. The Pacific Legal Foundation was suing San Bernardino Valley Community College on behalf of a student who was denied admission to a class for black students and then denied admission to a Latino-oriented English-language program. Reverse discrimination complaints or lawsuits regarding faculty or staff positions were still relatively rare. However, in 1992, four white part-time instructors won promotion to full-time slots in San Francisco Community College District after charging they'd been excluded from such jobs on the basis of race.[3] (That district had earlier been the source of a federal lawsuit that a white male claimed he'd been racially excluded from obtaining a dean's position.)

The Diversity Machine and the CCC: What Might Have Been, What Is, What Still Might Be

The CCC diversity programs might have been more effective—and far more radical—had not the long recession severely stymied the ability to implement and expand workforce diversity initiatives. Although California's substantial demographic changes gave affirmative action and visions of diversity management a huge and enthusiastic start, stagnating student enrollments and massive falloffs in full-time faculty hiring limited diversity efforts from going beyond affirmative action–style recruitment and monitoring the numbers.

More expensive, expansive efforts to change the basic campus climate and "white male workplace" culture collapsed in the midst of more basic struggles to keep campuses open and provide basic services. Although budgetary conditions were severe in the CCC, trends in that system reflected national trends. As survey data in Chapter Six indicate, many diversity efforts in other organizations stalled, remaining wedded to affirmative action compliance with some occasional diversity training, and workforce diversity in other organizations was usually assigned lower-priority levels than advocates would have liked.

Some California community colleges established and maintained community and student outreach programs, but they too were stunted by the funding crisis. Besides, it was clear from the chancellor's conference agendas that a new kind of outreach had far higher priority: tapping the coffers of private industry to assist with funding or training.

As severe budget constraints and cutbacks began to lift by 1996, ethnic and gender hiring preferences and workplace diversity initiatives had become yesterday's issues, taken for granted, and now tainted by a changing political climate. As elsewhere, workforce diversity issues moved from being viewed as simple and moralistic to more complex and complicated. The recession and the 1994 Republican revolution ushered in tougher, more achievement-oriented priorities for student success, individual accountability, efficiency, and partnerships with private enterprise. These themes ran counter to the key doctrines of the diversity machine: cultural relativism, identity politics, and proportional representation. Affirmative action and diversity issues had to be folded into a mix of looming new problems. Again as on the national level, efforts in the CCC to change the "white male workplace" were being eclipsed by even more drastic workplace and organizational changes in anticipation of projected enrollment surges with corresponding budget increases.

By 1994, the vice chancellor for diversity, Maria Sheehan, was discouraged: "We had looked at the 1990s as a window of opportunity stretching into 2005 with many, many jobs. Now I hear that, in terms of the national workforce, 80 percent of workers who will be aboard in 2005 have already been hired." Symbolic of the shift of priorities, the chancellor's diversity staff had been slashed from seven to fewer than three positions. Still, Sheehan acknowledged the presence of all-important support from the top. David Mertes had been steadfast, in part, because of pressure early in his tenure from the *Sacramento Bee*. (Interestingly, an African American chancellor who had served a brief term prior to Mertes provided little leadership on diversity issues.)

The board of governors, which had an equity and diversity subcommittee, had wavered in its support of diversity mandates. Sheehan and others reported initial enthusiasm, followed by something of a lull, followed by a swift recent return of interest with the appointment of more minority board members. But, as with the system as a whole, that interest appears to have been swamped by other concerns.

Besides the recession and the relative halt in hiring, Sheehan blamed conservative court decisions and "backlash" for slowing the California Community Colleges' diversity march. California's tarnished public image (riots, earthquakes, gangs, crumbling schools, crime) had also hindered national recruitment of faculty.

In a darker moment, Sheehan pondered whether slow progress in changing the faces of faculty and staff might ignite protests from relentlessly rising numbers of minority students. Indeed, in 1994 Hispanic students at Fullerton College engaged in diversity-inspired demonstrations, arguing that although 70 percent of the district population is Hispanic, there are "few people who look like us" on the faculty. Black students at Palomar College also demonstrated for more faculty diversity, though that district as yet contains few minorities. Yet race and gender concerns were not mentioned at all in studies of dissatisfied students; the major complaints were impersonal atmosphere, unavailability of key courses, parking problems, and increased fees.[4]

Despite the severe budget reductions, however, funds were available to reward financially and symbolically those districts with the best minority hiring records. The system did practice a small measure of accountability. Plaques were presented at the annual conferences to districts with outstanding records. Financial awards ranging from $4,000 to $60,000 flowed from the Faculty Staff Diversity Fund, authorized under Title V of the California Administrative Code. (Twenty-five percent of the $1.5 million fund goes to technical assistance, service monitoring for diversity compliance functions, and several small campus diversity projects; the rest goes to district awards.) This fund, as well as faculty and staff development program grants, provided small research grants for mentoring projects, campus climate surveys, and other projects to foster diversity.

As in other organizations (including the case studies for this book), personnel changes blunted policy continuity and stability. In January 1996, Chancellor David Mertes announced his decision to retire in June. Vice Chancellor for Diversity Maria Sheehan departed even more abruptly in December 1995 when a district chancellor's job was suddenly offered to her. Her replacement, José Peralez, noted at the 1996 megaconference that some high-level officials suggested not replacing Sheehan at all, but Chancellor Mertes selected Peralez and gave him a modified new title: vice chancellor for diversity and equity.

Stuck in the Numbers Wars

By the mid-1990s, rank-and-file faculty and staff were quietly reconsidering theoretical and day-to-day difficulties and contradictions associated with affirmative action and diversity management. R. Roosevelt Thomas, Santiago Rodriguez, and Condoleezza Rice stimulated and confirmed reconsideration of diversity policies in the CCC system. Ironically, as thinking about affirmative action and diversity management became more complex and mature, the older, proportional ethnic and gender formulas have become an obsolete legal straitjacket. "Many administrators are wondering how we get out of this," said John Madden by late 1994. Some were already trying.

Administrative Fatigue and Passive Revolt

The CCC remained stuck with legally mandated ethnic and gender proportionalism not only in hiring but in student recruitment, retention, and graduation. With regard to enforcing the last, however, there appeared to be a form of massive, passive disobedience. District administrators struggling to keep basic programs alive simply had their backs to the wall on more urgent matters.

In 1992, the board of trustees, in cooperation with the CCC Academic Senate, had added requirements to the California administrative code that each community college had to develop "student equity plans." Based on the proportion of women, ethnic groups, and disabled in the general population goals were to be set throughout all levels of the college experience, goals for student admission course completion, ESL (English-as-a-Second Language) and basic skills completion, and transfer to four-year institutions.

Only half of the districts had met the July 1993 filing deadline, subsequently extended to September 1994. A sample survey of district and campus CEOs by Vice Chancellor for Diversity Sheehan found that spirits were willing, but the budget was not. She found broad understanding and support for student equity and faculty and staff diversity. Forty-two percent of district and campus CEOs were making student equity a high priority. Seventy percent

were satisfied with current progress. The greatest obstacles reported were negative attitudes (mostly from faculty) and inadequate resources. (But even the
spirit of compliance was fading; by 1996 more than half the campuses had not
complied at all or had filed inadequate student equity reports.)

Sheehan told me that Long Beach Community College District had submitted an exemplary student educational equity plan. I obtained a copy. It
was a typical diversity management document: lack of proportional representation was blamed on biases or faults in the system. The task force members
who authored the report hailed student equity as "the principle that drives all
decisions and policies related to curriculum, support services, human resources, and the institutional planning and governance of the District." The
group was pleased to note that the district's enrollment ("access") generally
mirrored the population. Among males, 39 percent were white, 11 percent
were black, 24 percent were Hispanic, and 22 percent were Asian–Pacific Islander; among women, 44 percent were white, 15 percent black, 20 percent
Hispanic, and 17 percent Asian–Pacific Islander.

Incredibly, the report played down the positive. Although the number of
graduates was small, the report failed to note that graduation percentages
roughly approximated parity with the district's adult population: in the most
numerous 21–25 age group category, 44 percent of male graduates were
whites, 7 percent were black, 16 percent Hispanic, and 21 percent Asian.
Among women, 43 percent were white, 7.6 percent were black, 11 percent
were Hispanic, and 20 percent were Asian. Instead, in the style of the Labor
Department's "glass ceiling reports," the task force turned to rooting out "barriers to increasing student success." As in nearly every other CCC district, the
task force was frustrated by lack of expensive hardware and software to track
proportionalism in greater detail, but the available data did indicate significant disparities. Sixty-five percent of African Americans and 50 percent of
Hispanics (as compared to 30 percent of whites and Asians) needed remedial
math courses; the task force therefore sensibly recommended increased course
offerings, more tutoring, more day care, and better scheduling. As with everything else in the CCC, though, the problem was where to find funds.

Other data indicated deep disparities that might not be remedied by
strengthened tutorial and remedial efforts. Forty-seven percent of whites intended to transfer to four-year institutions but only 15 percent of blacks, 14
percent of Hispanics, and 12 percent of Asians. Partly as a result of these differing aspirations, 55 percent of white students and 19 percent of Asians
were on the dean's list, but only 5 percent of blacks and 11 percent of Hispanics. (Academic probation was more of a level playing field: 20 percent of

blacks, whites, and Hispanics were on probation.)

The Long Beach task force officially ignored the likelihood that most of these disparities were produced by socioeconomic factors, poor high school preparation, family structure, lifestyle and aspirations, and other cultural factors—not to mention the mysterious role of individual motivation. Instead, the system was to blame. The lack of ethnic and gender proportionalism mandated changing the system: (1) hire more "diverse" role model faculty and staff through minority faculty internships, formalizing part-time appointments, and similar other avenues; (2) "infuse the curriculum with multiculturalism" by implementing multicultural course requirements and encouraging additional ethnic studies courses; (3) encourage faculty to develop "innovative instructional methods," and (4) train staff in greater multicultural understanding.

Behind these reports, in informal, conversational settings, an increasing number of CCC administrators to whom I spoke understood that a host of factors beyond race and gender were at work in producing lack of ethnic and gender "equity," especially social class (parents' income, educational level, aspirations, etc.), changes in the workforce and occupational structure, the immigrant history and level of acculturation of various groups and subgroups, and individual motivation and talents.

Those who worked with minority classifications on a daily basis recognized that the porous categories masked considerable variations within and between groups of students and faculty. As at the four-year universities, Asian students were consistently "overrepresented," often double their proportion in the population. With constrained student enrollments and budgetary limitations, the prospect of expanding the proportion of blacks and Hispanics by reducing the shares of whites and Asians, as has happened at University of California, Berkeley, made CCC administrators squirm.

That most districts refused to submit anything like the Long Beach report vexed Sheehan and one or two minority members of the board of trustees, but no major sanctions were brought to bear.

Ironically, even without enactment of "equity reports," the CCC student enrollment continued to mirror closely the shifts in the California general population: in 1992–1993, 54 percent of students were white, 21 percent were Hispanic, 12 percent were Asian, 8 percent were black, and 5 percent were "other"; 55 percent were women and 45 percent were men. By 1996, more than 50 percent of community colleges students were minorities. A "majority minority" student body had come to pass; few at the conference seemed to take much notice.

Faculty Hiring

The CCC's diversity efforts remain legally locked into the simplistic two-factor race and gender emphasis of early workforce diversity: race and gender proportionalism was cemented into AB 1725 and the state administrative code. By 1994, chancellor's counsel Ralph Black admitted that several U.S. Supreme Court decisions put the CCC system on the horns of a legal dilemma. In particular, the Court's 1989 *Richmond v. Croson* decision held that public agencies must have a proved record of discrimination before implementing any preferential programs. Any such plan would have to meet these criteria of strict scrutiny under the U.S. Constitution's Fourteenth Amendment and Title VII. On the other hand, the California legislature had incorporated more activist language into the State Education Code section 87100 "legislative findings and declarations":

> Generally, the California Community Colleges employ a "disproportionately low" number of racial and ethnic minorities classified employees and faculty and a disproportionately low number of women and . . . minorities in administrative positions.
>
> It is educationally sound for the minority student . . . to have available the positive image provided by minority classified and academic employees. It is likewise educationally sound for the student from the majority group to have positive experiences with minority people . . . by having minority classified and academic employees at schools where the enrollment is largely made up of majority group students. . . .
>
> Past employment practices created artificial barriers and past efforts to promote additional action in recruitment employment and promotion of women and minorities have not resulted in a substantial increase in employment opportunities for such persons.
>
> Lessons concerning democratic principles and the richness which racial diversity brings to our national heritage can be best taught by the presence of staffs of mixed races and ethnic groups working toward a common goal.

. And AB 1725 defined affirmative action in terms of proportional representation:

> "'Affirmative action employment program' means planned activities designed to seek, hire, and promote persons who are underrepresented in the work force compared to their number in the population. . . . Affirmative action requires imaginative, energetic, and sustained action by each employer to devise recruiting, training and career advancement opportunities which will result in

an equitable representation of women and minorities in relation to all employees of the employer.

Even worse, no one challenged continued chanting of the illegal diversity mantra that the community colleges faculty should look like the student body or the surrounding community, especially when the chanting was done by the president of the board of trustees.

The computerized faculty and staff job applicant registry, established in 1989, was the system's single greatest accomplishment, according to Maria Sheehan. The more than 2,000 names on the registry symbolized the proper, legal function of affirmative action as a recruitment tool for enlarging the applicant pool and "put to bed forever the excuse that 'there's nobody out there,' you know, the administrators who say, 'we'd hire these people, but they don't exist.' Well, now they do." Paradoxically, the promise of the applicant registry has been a primary source of disappointment. "I get calls from people of color with master's or doctorate degrees who can't get hired and think we're kidding and that they're being used. All I can tell them is 'keep trying.'"

The computerized faculty and staff job applicant registry evolved concurrently with annual job fairs in southern and northern California. The first southern CCC job fair was pronounced a disappointment by Gary Plaque of the chancellor's office because it drew "too many white males," most of them members of the surplus Ph.D. population of baby boomers. Shifting the location of fairs in subsequent years began to draw more women and minorities, though exact numbers were difficult to tally. The recession and the dwindling number of available jobs also compromised results. Chancellor David Mertes saw the fairs as at least a symbolic gesture of the CCC's commitment to diversity, and the gatherings had the more practical result of obtaining applicants for the faculty and staff diversity registry.

During the banner hiring year of 1991, approximately two-thirds of those hired for new, full-time faculty positions were women and minorities. But hopes for swiftly changing faculty ethnic composition were dashed by the recession and continued reliance on part-time faculty.

Emphasis on minority faculty hiring appears to be increasing, rather than reducing, ethnic and gender polarization among academic fields. Data from the CCC faculty and staff diversity registry and data on new faculty actually hired for 1991—one of the two banner hiring years—suggest continued domination of the physical sciences and engineering by white males and Asians, where there have been few minority candidates. Women are making inroads in the sciences but are well on their way toward totally "feminizing" the already heavily female humanities and the softer social sciences such as interdisciplinary studies and psychology (Table 1).

At first glance, data for the faculty registry show a surprisingly large proportion of minority applicants for scientific fields. But recalculating the percentages by specific ethnic group changes the picture. Asians were sometimes more than 50 percent of the "minority" figure in the suspected fields of engineering and the sciences. These data help in interpreting those actually hired for full-time positions in the CCC system for 1991. The top six fields for minority hiring are shown in Table 2. Given the data in the registry, it is likely that many, if not most, of the minorities hired in mathematics and the physical sciences were Asians.

Women constituted over half of all new faculty hired (52.7 percent). Most were hired in already "feminized" fields (Table 3). However, women were more than half those hired in the biological sciences (53 percent) and as strongly represented in physical sciences hires (45 percent) as in social sciences (43 percent). They were also 39 percent of the new mathematics instructors, and the two architectural and environmental design faculty were both females. (The data do not indicate what percentage of women scientists were Asian, but a 50 percent figure is a reasonable guess.)

The data also strongly suggest reverse discrimination against white males in the softer social sciences and in the humanities. Again, the categories of "minority" and "female" overlap. Assuming an equal male-female split in minori-

TABLE 1

California Community Colleges Registry: Participation by Discipline Area
(Ranked by Proportion of Minorities)

Field	% Total Minority	% Asian	% Hispanic or Black
Agricultural management	43.8	19	19
Agricultural science	44.1	29.4	12.5
Science	37.9	20.4	16.8
Engineering	37.2	26.5	9.1
Health technology	32.8	16.3	16.3
Mathematics	34.7	22.3	11.6
Physical sciences	24.5	15.3	8.8
Science technology	28.6	28.6	0.0

Source: Chancellor's Office, California Community Colleges, 1993.

TABLE 2

Top Fields for CCC Minority Faculty Hired, 1991

Field	% Minorities Hired
Foreign language	62.0
Social sciences	34.7
Commercial services	33.3
Mathematics	31.5
Humanities	29.0
Physical sciences	28.8

Source: *Affirmative Action Programs in the California Community Colleges, 1991–1992: An Annual Report to the Board of Governors and the Legislature,* January 14, 1993, p. 6.

ties hired, then all but 2 or 3 of 16 of the psychologists hired by the CCC system in 1991 were women or minorities; 77 percent of the 238 humanities positions were filled by women or minorities; 82.3 percent of the 116 interdisciplinary studies positions were filled by women or minorities; 60.5 percent of the 95 social sciences positions went to women or minorities (Table 4).

Chancellor David Mertes was concerned with reverse discrimination problems, but Maria Sheehan offered a common neutralization: "We still hire mostly white males and females." This common perception is not quite

TABLE 3

Top Fields for CCC Female Faculty Hires, 1991

Field	% Females Hired
Commercial services	88.8
Consumer education/home economics	86.0
Health	80.2
Psychology	75.0
Interdisciplinary studies	68.0
Foreign languages	68.0
Humanities	62.0

Source: *Affirmative Action Programs in the California Community Colleges, 1991–1992: An Annual Report to the Board of Governors and the Legislature,* January 14, 1993, p. 6.

TABLE 4

Full-Time Faculty Hired, by Gender, Ethnicity, and Discipline, Fall 1991

Discipline	Total	Female	White	Minority	Minority (%)
Agriculture and natural resources	6	0	5	1	16.7
Architecture and environmental design	2	2	2	0	0.0
Biological science	39	21	30	9	23.1
Business and management	83	38	60	23	27.7
Communications	7	3	5	2	28.6
Computer/information science	50	22	37	13	26.0
Education	76	34	66	10	13.2
Engineering and related technical fields	86	15	70	16	18.6
Fine and applied art	111	50	91	20	18.0
Foreign language	50	34	19	31	62.0
Health	91	73	74	17	18.7
Consumer education/ home economics	37	32	28	9	24.3
Law	4	2	4	0	0.0
Humanities	238	149	169	69	29.0
Library science	-	-	-	-	-
Mathematics	130	51	89	41	31.5
Physical science	59	27	42	17	28.8
Psychology	16	12	13	3	18.8
Public affairs/services	30	10	24	6	20.0
Social science	95	41	62	33	34.7
Commerical Services	9	8	6	3	33.3
Interdisciplinary studies	116	30	85	31	26.7
Totals	**1,335**	**704**	**981**	**354**	**26.5**

Note: Total does not equal reported sum of parts because of miscodes and unknowns.

Source: *Affirmative Action Programs in the California Community Colleges, 1991–1992.* Chancellor's Office, 1993.

true. If half of the minorities category were also women, then nearly two-thirds of all CCC faculty hired in 1991 were women and male minorities. (In other workforce categories, the CCC reported that although the number of positions increased by only 17.9 percent, there was an overall increase of 60.5 percent for Asians, 43.2 percent for Hispanics, 11 percent for blacks, and a 20 percent increase for women.)

Complicating demands for new minority faculty was the strong pressure for justice for hundreds of mostly white part-time faculty exploited during the baby boom Ph.D. surplus and the lean community colleges' budgets of the 1980s. That nearly half of the full-time positions were being filled with such part-timers indicated considerable sympathy for this time-honored principle—and a quiet revolt against diversity dictates. The faculty union favored preference for well-qualified part-timers. And, just as clearly, the administrative pressure was on to stop such practices.

Budget problems, growing awareness of the complexity and limits of workforce diversity strategies, and rising revolts against political correctness and reverse discrimination were problems common to all organizations implementing diversity policies. One strategy not available to the CCC, but apparently used by some corporations and government agencies, was to replace older white workers with younger, less expensive minorities and women. To the obvious dismay of several administrators and ethnic radicals, tenure protected older white faculty.

The tension between activists who wanted maximum flexibility and the strict legal constructionists lent credence to widespread suspicion that affirmative action and workforce diversity initiatives could be potent sources of corruption and a spoils system mentality. There were flashes of an us-versus-them mentality and ugly flashes of vindictiveness against white males. CCC administrations openly expressed their desire to replace retiring white faculty with minorities to mirror the ethnic composition of their student bodies better:

> The Los Angeles Community College District is nearing agreement with union officials on an early retirement package that could spur the departure of up to 20% of its full-time faculty. . . . If enough older, full-time teachers opt for the incentive, officials said, the result would be an opportunity to reinvigorate the district's academic programs and diversify its faculty through the mass replacement hiring that would occur. Currently, about 70% of the full-time faculty is white, even though the district's college-age population is about 70% minority.[5]

White males who challenged this imperative were in for a difficult time. Leon

Waszak, who recently won a reverse discrimination lawsuit against Pasadena City College, was appalled at the level of duplicity and lying during the hiring process and in the courtroom itself.

Admittedly the raw ends-justifies-the-means thinking was less obvious in the CCC than in the California State University system, which (as CSU Bakersfield president Tomas Arciniega told the 1990 conference) openly used minority set-aside positions for faculty, female-or-minority administrative interns, and hundreds of minorities- or females-only scholarships and loans. (The flagship University of California system also advertises "targets of diversity" positions; the University of California Law School at Berkeley was caught using a quota-style admissions system by the Department of Education.) Nevertheless, as the above data suggest, *sotto voce* talk in academic circles was rife that certain fields in California higher education were largely closed to white males.

Officially, the CCC's diversity machine is carefully reconsidering its affirmative action and diversity programs in the light of recent Supreme Court decisions, the federal Fifth Circuit Court of Appeals decision against preferences at the University of Texas Law School, and an eye towards the fate of the antipreference California civil rights initiative, as well as the likely outcome of the 1996 presidential election.

Vice Chancellor for Equity and Diversity José Peralez was conciliatory and reflective about the nature and fate of diversity programs when I spoke with him in early June 1996. The problem of equal student access to the CCC system, he admitted, had been largely solved, though Hispanics were still slightly underrepresented. The goal of more equity in certification and transfer to four-year schools, he conceded, was beyond the scope of traditional affirmative action. He knew there were ethnic classification problems: his own children were a multiethnic mixture of Hispanic, Anglo, and Japanese. Peralez claimed to know little about more obvious and blatant abuses of affirmative action in the CSU and UC systems. The self-admitted risk taker who had worked his way up from humble beginnings to community college, then CSU, then law school knew that affirmative action would soon end; but, reciting the popular slogan, he insisted that "we're not there yet."

By the spring of 1996, CCC faculty, staff, and student activists had organized the California Community College Equal Opportunity Network (EON) to defeat the California Civil Rights Initiative. Joining with a variety of other faculty, student, and labor groups throughout the state, the EON's purpose is to (1) disseminate advocacy guidelines and suggestions to campus organizers, (2) disseminate educational materials for general distribution, (3) maintain a speakers' bureau, and (4) provide updates on statewide and national efforts to defend affirmative action. From late August through October, the organization planned a massive voter registration drive in classes and in public areas of the campuses.

To my knowledge, there were no groups or networks within the CCC system that supported the California Civil Rights Initiative. By and large, California's massive higher education system, its teachers' unions, and most of its labor unions are active or passive cogs in the wider diversity machine. With the exception of Governor Pete Wilson and a few allies, most conservative or liberal leaders do not openly challenge the diversity machine nor its doctrines of cultural relativism, identity politics, and proportional representation. A few in-house critics, such as Stanford provost Condoleezza Rice, challenge cultural relativism in the name of individual accountability and achievement. But few corporate or political leaders have openly challenged identity politics' assumption that an individual's views tend to reflect those of his or her ethnic or racial tribe.

The California Civil Rights Initiative—officially relabeled Proposition 209 on the ballot—passed by a margin of 54 to 46 percent on the night of November 5, 1996. The American Civil Liberties Union filed suit in federal court the next morning, challenging the measure's constitutionality. Simultaneously, the Pacific Legal Foundation sued to force immediate implementation of CCRI and specifically requested compliance by the California Community Colleges system. (The University of California system, already under the regents' new order to ban the use of preferences in hiring, contracting, and admissions, had postponed the advent of race-neutral admissions for a year; two days after passage of CCRI, however, UC moved to implement race-neutral admissions immediately.) The CCC system, anticipating such developments by reviewing and hedging its preference programs, appears to have joined many other state agencies in awaiting the outcome of the court contests. Should the CCRI be ruled unconstitutional, the pressures for proportionality, identity politics, and cultural relativism will likely rebound with renewed vigor.

Such sociological forces were alarmingly apparent in citizen voting on CCRI: 63 percent of whites supported the measure while 74 percent of blacks and 76 percent of Hispanics voted against it. (Sixty-one percent of Asians also voted against CCRI, as did 52 percent of all women—white females slightly favored the initiative.)

That preference policies and diversity ideology may fuel, rather than reduce, ethnic polarization may be more urgently pondered by California's elites and high-level officials. (As Newhouse News reporter Jonathan Tilove suggested to me, on the basis of such voting splits and continuing demographic changes, 1996 might have been the last opportunity to pass CCRI.) Indeed, some California leaders were considering these sociological dangers well before the CCRI vote. In the summer of 1994, I asked CCC system chancellor David Mertes if he feared that overemphasis of race and gender policies might be contributing to polarization and the retribalization of America. He answered quickly and emphatically: "Yes."

Chapter 9

Multicultural Vision Meets Multiversity Realities

The University of Michigan

To the general public, the University of Michigan at Ann Arbor is best known for its high academic reputation, its championship athletic teams, and its dazzling marching band. Annually, half a million people attend sports events in Ann Arbor, and millions more watch on television; 200,000 people attend cultural activities in the tree-shrouded, picture-book-pretty college town.

Such pizazz and pomp, however, mask the much deeper significance of Michigan and other megauniversities. They are clusters of powerful training, research, and policy centers that shape the minds of today's and tomorrow's business, political, and cultural leaders. Much scientific, legal, and social policy is crafted in places such as Michigan, including one of the most ambitious institutional diversity initiatives, the Michigan Mandate. First authored in 1988 by newly inaugurated president James Duderstadt and a group of activist administrators and faculty, this "blueprint for a multicultural university of the twenty-first century" has been implemented with varying degrees of success in a complex sprawling organization that is neither public nor private, neither corporation nor cloistered college. However classified, it is probably "the most valuable asset in the state," declared Joe Stroud, editor of the *Detroit Free Press.*

Michigan's premiere research and education engine was not the only such institution to wrestle with top-down diversity drives during the late 1980s and 1990s. The events and processes described at Michigan during the period 1988 through 1996 have many parallels elsewhere. For example, as Michigan began its diversity drive in 1988, the chancellor at the University

274

of Wisconsin, Madison, Donna Shalala, was dubbed the "Queen of PC" when she implemented speech codes and the aggressive Wisconsin Plan to boost minority enrollment, retention, and promotion. (Both the Michigan and Wisconsin speech codes were held to be illegal.) Other universities and colleges also experimented with speech codes, implemented vigorous affirmative action programs for minority students and faculty, and engaged in curricular reforms. Ethnic change and multiculturalism in California's higher education system, as we have just seen, was being more directly pushed by the dramatic demographic changes in that state. Michigan's change masters, on the other hand, were anticipating changes on a global scale; the state and the nation would wither, becoming part of a new international global and economic order.

Indeed, since James Duderstadt became president of the University of Michigan in 1988, no other multiversity has been as self-consciously loud and proud in trying to construct a "multicultural community of the twenty-first century" in the midst of a largely biracial, class-polarized midwestern state. Many other institutions, including the California Community Colleges, would like to have mounted a multicultural drive such as Michigan's, but most lacked Michigan's vast resources, combined with the vision and zeal of its top administrators, all reinforced by the one-party-state atmosphere in Ann Arbor's trendy intellectual circles. (The local school board reportedly once decreed that by the end of the century, there would be no test score differences among ethnic groups in its schools.)

More than any other organization mentioned in this book, Michigan's appears to have been the most vigorous and determined top-down drive to change its allegedly "white male" institutional climate in classrooms, research settings, and offices. More than one hundred diversity programs were deployed: aggressive outreach, awareness training, establishment of all manner of support groups, aggressive targeted hiring and promotions, constant reinforcement of the diversity mission in all publications, constant monitoring, and attempts to reward managers and departments on the basis of their diversity records. The university was not only changing its own "white male" workplace culture, but altering that of the future by producing more multi-ethnic professionals, researchers, and university faculties.

In analyzing the intended and unintended consequences of Michigan's multicultural reforms, I shall focus on the standard objectives of workplace diversity management: cultural change in order to retain and promote more women and minorities in response to the nation's changing demographics. I shall not be concerned with undergraduate curricular reforms and the ill-fated student speech codes; my focus here is with how Mandate-driven management goals meshed or collided with other university priorities in changing—or not changing—the organization's cultural climate. (This includes examination of self-censorship generated by alleged pressures of political correctness.) I have focused my interviewing primarily on administrators and an eclectic sample of faculty interested in or suspicious of the Mandate. This is by no means a comprehensive portrait. There are cultures and subcultures throughout Michigan's premiere multiversity. Generalizations can be made, but they are always tentative. ("The only generalization you can make about this place," quipped a presidential assistant, "is that you cannot generalize about it.")[1]

A Multipurpose Mandate

The Michigan Mandate was a multipurpose document with many internal and external constituencies in mind. As with many other diversity management plans described in this book, the Mandate was an affirmative action–diversity policy document crafted by white elites responding to real or perceived crises in legitimation and societal stability. Like L.A. sheriff Sherman Block and the California Community Colleges' chancellor David Mertes, Michigan's James Duderstadt was alarmed by the specter of a class and racially polarized nation.

First and foremost, the Mandate was designed to correct critically low levels of support and attachment among Michigan's growing black populations, from the relatively small numbers of black Michigan students, to the vast, simmering, alienated ghettos of Detroit, to the growing suburban black bourgeoisie, and, especially, increasingly powerful black legislators and administrators in Lansing. (The fears about black-white polarization and the sinking status of Detroit were vividly described in Ze'ev Chafets 1990 book, *Devil's Night and Other True Tales of Detroit*.)[2] The social justice, social control Mandate agenda would have some appeal in the wealthy white suburbs ringing Detroit, providing outstanding students from those high schools were not unduly excluded from the university. As we shall see, the classes ignored or injured by the Mandate's ethnic redistribution of educational and financial opportunities would be white undergraduate and graduate applicants with less-than-sterling, but still very good, credentials; they would not get the extra, sometimes crucial, consideration afforded minority applicants. No matter. Duderstadt and his allies seemed utterly convinced that greater ethnic diversity added value to the university's intellectual climate.

As in the corporate world, the Mandate was, to some extent, a strategic public relations effort—and much needed, some thought. "While others did nothing but intellectualize, Jim perceived a situation and *did something*," explained English Department chair-turned-dean, Robert Weisbuch.

Indeed, the university has long had a snobbish image and is, says *Detroit Free Press* editor Stroud, "a thing apart from the state of Michigan, more connected to Cambridge and Berkeley than the Legislature and Detroit." The place has been peopled primarily by white, upper-middle-class professionals and their student offspring. The organization's cultural traits are theirs: go-getter individualism, competitiveness, diligence, and ambition to be—as the school fight song puts it—the "leaders and best."

"Nobody ever relaxes or lets their hair down around here," grumbled Zaida Giraldo, Michigan's former affirmative action director. "They're too busy trying to be better than Harvard."

"It is *not* the University of Michigan," English professor Leo McNamara archly observed in 1992. "It is the University of Southeastern Michigan, and serves the interests of Grosse Pointe and Bloomfield Hills, and, when not those, segments of New York City, Long Island and North Shore Chicago."

Such largely apt class and ethnic cultural portraits have been a source of embarrassment for a university community that Joe Stroud characterizes as "self-consciously liberal," ardently championing affirmative action and the other egalitarian movements of the 1970s and 1980s. Ironically, the white male class-driven ambition to be the "leaders and best" in everything was tapped in some faculty and administrative quarters to fuel the campaign to be the "best" in multiculturalism (as the vice provost for academic and multicultural affairs, Lester Monts, shrewdly observed).

Yet the state of Michigan had only a small pool of blacks who were academically eligible by the university's relatively high admissions standards. (Unconfirmed reports suggested that annually, about 650 Detroit-area African Americans were U-M qualified, a figure comparable to a reported 1,000 California blacks who were annually eligible for admission to the University of California).[3] U-M had to compete for that limited population with Ivy League and other schools trying to increase *their* number of blacks. In addition, Michigan had minuscule populations of Hispanics and Asians. (Ironically, there was a sizable Arab and Middle Eastern population in the metropolitan Detroit area, but the university's administrators did not consider them minorities, and most expressed surprise or cynicism when asked about the matter.)

Therefore, the Mandate set in motion expensive and vigorous searches for out-of-state black, Hispanic, and Asian undergraduates, graduate students, and faculty. (Evidently, because of their comparative wealth, Cuban Americans were quietly excluded from the Hispanic category by the graduate school.) And it turned out there were unintended advantages to an expanded multiethnic focus. The availability of well-qualified Asian students and faculty (citizens and foreign born) allowed the university to boast about increasing its "students and faculty of color," while masking incremental increases in the percentages of African Americans. (The public and news media often assumed "color" meant "black." Therefore, unless shrewd observers asked, no one would realize that Asians had become the largest "minority" among students and faculty by the early 1990s. This was a shell game played by many other universities and corporations.)

All manner of university publications—from alumni magazines, to college catalogs, and even football souvenir programs—would be enlisted to push the multicultural agenda and portray the university as a cosmopolitan institution with people "drawn from all socioeconomic levels, representing a dazzling array of ethnic backgrounds, religions, customs, languages and ideas."

The diversity machine's "valuing diversity" rhetoric echoed throughout the Mandate and other university literature—for example, a special message on diversity from the president was placed at the beginning of many of U-M's academic catalogs and bulletins. Much of this likely flowed from or through some thirty-eight faculty and staff who identified themselves as internal consultants to the President's Commission on a Multicultural University.[4] External consultants made visits to various units of the university from time to time, but apart from influencing the internal consultants, their role was evidently minimal.

Despite the optimistic rhetoric, however, the size, scope, inertia, and decentralized nature of the multiversity presented problems for implementing any centralized crusade.

A Sprawling Research-and-Education Engine

Behind the maize and blue pageantry, the University of Michigan at Ann Arbor is a workplace for some 21,000 employees and home to 37,000 students, many of whom work part-time. It is the epitome of Clark Kerr's vision of a "multiversity," a vortex of federal, state, and corporate interests and dollars. It has been run in an increasingly corporate fashion by a president with a Cal Tech Ph.D. and a provost-finance officer who was a former business school dean. There are 19 undergraduate, graduate, and professional schools with 153 academic departments, 39 research and training centers, 18 research institutes, 2 bureaus, and 9 hospital units. Although recent downsizing campaigns throughout the university have reduced their numbers, a controversial legislative study done in Lansing once found nearly one administrator for every faculty member. (Many administrators are now housed in an office tower recently purchased by the university.)

The university's system of libraries constitutes the fifth largest research collection in the United States. There are 850,000 annual patient visits to the giant medical center–hospitals cluster, recently named Michigan's best-run corporation. The vast athletic complex houses one of college athletics most successful sports industries (topped only, perhaps and alas, by Notre Dame's). The economic trauma of the Midwest's rust belt experience in the 1970s vaulted Michigan's administrators into the vanguard of transforming "public" universities to "state-assisted" universities; there were even rumors, for a time, that Michigan might be "going private." The university has always had a constitutional guarantee of autonomy from the state. But it is becoming less and less an economic creature of its namesake; only 12 percent of its $2.5 billion budget comes from state funds (though the percentage is higher if one subtracts the nearly $1 billion medical center budget). Research grants make up an increasing share of the budget; no other university ranks higher for federal research support. Out-of-state undergraduate tuition is so high ($16,000) that such students require no state subsidy. The university recently completed an aggressive $1 billion fund-raising drive, part of which went to the $1.6 billion endowment. Such funds will unquestionably increase Michigan's look and feel as an elite, though very large, private institution. (The newer North Campus, devoted largely to music and engineering schools with neighboring high-tech companies, now boasts its own bell tower.)

As sociologist Robert Nisbet once observed, such universities have come to be peopled by high-salaried, grant-getting "higher capitalists" who analyze massive amounts of data for governments and corporations.[5] The pressure on faculty to bring in research dollars now rivals the publish-or-perish imperative. (To every grant request, the university adds a 52 percent fee for "overhead expenses.")

Sources of funding are numerous and proliferating. Faculty and administrators pursue and are pursued by directors of rich foundations, nonprofit centers, corporations, government agency directors, and occasionally the White House. Eight thousand businesspersons attend executive education courses at Michigan's business school—more than at any other. The school's deans wing their way to Hong Kong to nourish the new "Asia program." In 1995, the business school also entered into another Asian partnership with

Korea's giant Daewoo Corporation to provide management education through a package that included videoconferencing, Internet communications, short on-site classes in Korea by University of Michigan professors, and two semesters of instruction in Ann Arbor. Within the state, the business school's Business and Industrial Assistance Division (BIAD) provides management and technical assistance to some sixty-five businesses or civic organizations in forty Michigan counties.

Wall Street nervously anticipates the quarterly results of the Survey Research Center's Index of Consumer Confidence. The six-story Institute for Social Research, which takes 10 percent of the university's research budget, launches dozens of social science studies on topics from the causes and distribution of psychological depression to the nature of juvenile crime. Michigan geneticist Francis Collins now heads the Human Genome Project at the National Institutes of Health. The Center for Ultrafast Optical Science spins off new ophthalmological technology and health care procedures. The U-M Transportation Research Institute contains several subunits, such as the Office for the Study of Automotive Transportation, which conducts periodic studies of technological trends. There is a Center for Research on Learning and Teaching, a Center for the Study of Social Transformation, a Post Emancipation Studies Project, the Center for Ergonomics, the Technology Management Office, and several computer research units, such as the Center for Parallel Computing, a Center for Flat Panel Technology, and a Center for Reconfigurable Matching Systems. The university has dozens of joint research projects with private enterprise through its Industrial Affiliates Program.

The university's central administration tries to coordinate this melange of schools, institutes, and other units, each with its own priorities, subcultures, personnel, and ideologies. The decentralized structure and entrepreneurial spirit militates against order and cohesion. "How can you generate community in a place where you have trouble getting people together for committee meetings," sighed a presidential assistant. "Someone's in Washington, D.C., checking on a grant, another person is in Paris at a convention, another person is writing a book . . ."

Within the web of research centers and professional schools, Michigan has tried to preserve a reputation for high-quality undergraduate education. Seventy percent of the undergraduates are in the top 10 percent of their high school graduating class; nearly all students were in the top 20 percent of their high school class. Sixty percent receive financial aid, and more than half go on to graduate or professional school.

Tension, however, has long existed between the state and the university over the balance of in-state and out-of-state students. The university defines itself as a national institution, but the legislature watches to make sure that about 70 percent of the undergraduate students are from Michigan. In-state admission standards are very high, and admission criteria for out-of-state students are in the Ivy League range—and so is the tuition: $16,000 per year. In selecting graduate and professional students, state boundaries are ignored. Race, ethnicity, and gender became much more potent factors in admissions, hiring, and promotions after race relations crises on campus in the mid-to-late 1980s.

Crises and Call for Change: The Michigan Mandate

"The Michigan Mandate: A Strategic Linking of Academic Excellence and Social Diversity" is the consummate workforce diversity plan. The much-revised document has absorbed almost every concept, phrase, and strategy offered by the developing diversity machine. Civil rights moralism is evident with strong rededication to affirmative action and discussion of past injustices, but there is also more pragmatic appeal with references to demographic change and the emerging global society. The Mandate pulses with urgency fused with the deep personal commitment of a true CEO "champion of diversity." The document weds diversity with excellence and is infused with near-mystic devotion to "valuing differences" in a pluralistic, multicultural community for the twenty-first century.

The Michigan Mandate had its origins in escalating public relations crises. Low African American enrollments had long been a source of embarrassment at Ann Arbor. Black enrollment at Michigan hovered below 2 or 3 percent before 1970. The university then agreed to boost black enrollment to 10 percent after the first Black Action Movement (BAM) organized to protest conditions at the school. But by the late 1980s, enrollment for all minorities on the affirmative action agenda (including Hispanics, Asians, and Native Americans) was only about 10 percent. Black enrollment dipped to under 5 percent by 1983. In 1987, a series of printed and oral racial slurs were capped by a Hispanic disc jockey's accepting racial jokes on a campus radio station. Another BAM was organized and produced major demonstrations. Jesse Jackson was called in to negotiate a new series of commitments with President Harold Shapiro. He agreed to many of their demands—for example, bringing in more minority students and faculty and centers for African American studies—and instituted the first, notorious campus speech code, later struck down in federal court. Shapiro then departed for the presidency of Princeton. Retired university president Robin Fleming was recalled to serve as interim president.

Into this crisis stepped the six-foot-four provost and former engineering dean, James Duderstadt. He offered a persuasive vision that not only racial justice but demographic and global change necessited institutional change. Duderstadt claimed he'd been cued to such demographic changes in his studies of educational pipeline trends while serving on an advisory committee to the National Science Foundation. He also had been meeting quietly with an informal "change group" of activist faculty and administrators that decided that assimilation and mere affirmative action and access had failed. The University of Michigan would have to be radically changed.

Duderstadt was selected as the university's president during a series of closed meetings by the board of regents, subsequently found to be in violation of the open-meeting requirements of that body. Nonetheless, Duderstadt was installed and, after consulting with a variety of minority and community activist groups, drafted the early Mandate.

Paradoxically, the highly egalitarian Michigan Mandate also exudes another cultural trait often associated with the University of Michigan and with Jim Duderstadt himself: arrogance. The Mandate and its top-down implementation reek of a high-level hubris that social change can be planned and even micromanaged. Indeed, in late 1993 Duderstadt crowed to me that "the theory of organizational change worked here. We got buy-in from the major leadership. And we could influence that, because if people didn't buy in, we could replace them—and we replaced people. We then seeded change agents—people that had a strong commitment to the agenda—into the ranks of the faculty and empowered them, tried to get change coming from below."

Michigan's change masters would make some progress toward ethnic and gender proportional hiring, retention, and promotion, but they also unleashed a host of unpredictable consequences. "When one of these big bureaucracies begins to move," said Mandate critic and U-M regent Deane Baker, "it is an awesome thing to watch."

"Imagine the Ten Commandments, online, subject to perpetual revision," sniffed English professor Leo McNamara. "That is the Mandate. It's Duderspeak, written by a committee in the inferior prose that often comes out of the administration." Although Duderstadt explicitly rejected the aura of "Moses returning from the mountain," the early mandate is infused with both Duderstadt's personal views and admittedly fluid, "organic" outlook, as the subtitle, "Version 6.0," suggests.

The opening of the early Mandate heralded a sweeping new agenda, a vision propelled by the new demographics of the nation ("a majority of minorities") and the coming global community of the twenty-first century. As a leading higher education institution, the university must "anticipate the future direction of society" and "capitalize on racial, cultural, and ethnic diversity." This task would be the "most serious challenge facing American society today."

As was typical of diversity mission statements of the late 1980s, the overstated projections of *Workforce 2000* and other forecasts were brought in to highlight the urgency of the multicultural mission. A forward-looking university, Duderstadt claimed, must not only reflect imminent majority-minorities and build a model, cohesive organization in which pluralism is respected and valued. Michigan, he noted, is a "UNIversity, not a DIVersity." The university must meet the challenges of linking diversity with excellence, overcoming racism in all its forms, and creating a "more varied and tolerant environment."

The rest of the document outlined past and present progress toward representation and retention of minority faculty, student, and staff, coupled with strategies to boost those numbers sharply. Proposals included: (1) a Target of Opportunity program for seeking out and hiring minority faculty, (2) special support funds for minority faculty and "workload adjustments," (3) a way to meet "the full financial needs of Michigan minority students and enhance financial aid to nonresident minorities," (4) expanded minority recruiting though the admissions office and alumni networks, (5) expanded outreach programs through community colleges and K–12 schools, (6) creation of an office of minority affairs, (7) identification and support of faculty, student, and staff "change agents," (8) enhanced multicultural education, and (9) policies to "combat harassment." Affirmative action records were to be part of the evaluation criteria for department chairs, deans, and administrators— the cherished "accountability" hailed by change master diversity consultants.

How has this ambitious vision fared?

Let a Hundred Programs Bloom

In the early 1990s, the Office of Academic and Multicultural Initiatives (formerly the Office of Minority Affairs) assembled a "diversity directory" containing a bewildering array of over a hundred programs grouped under six major categories: student recruitment and retention, faculty and staff recruitment and retention, multicultural awareness, communication, interpersonal/intergroup relations, conflict management and resolution, and multicultural curriculum and pedagogy. Most programs still exist.

Programs in the U-M Diversity Directory

Office of Minority Affairs

Bilingual College Preparation Booklet: a number of King/Chavez/Parks programs: College Clubs, College Day Spring Visitation, Fellowship Program, Summer Institute, Visiting Scholars, Summer Initiative Program; Wade H. McCree Jr. Incentive Scholars Program; Hispanic Heritage Celebration; Latino Lecture Series; Martin Luther King Jr. Symposium; Association for Asian Pacific American Family & Staff; Diversity Agenda Program; Intra- and Intergroup Dialogues

Communication Interpersonal/Intergroup Relations

Business and Finance Units—Ongoing organizational change process

Career Planning and Placement—Staff development session on cultural awareness

Financial Operations—Diversity Task Force

Housing/Bursley Hall—Bursley Community Volunteers

Housing/Markley Hall—Intergroup Relations Film Series; Racism 101 Forum, video and small-group discussions; Stereotyping 101 session

Human Resource Development—Diversity Curriculum

Investment Office—Diversity program at staff meetings and other activities

Office of Development—Cross-Cultural Communications Workshop

Office of Minority Programs, U-M-Flint—Workshops: A Dialogue on Diversity–Assisting Faculty in Addressing Concerns of Ethnically Diverse Student Populations: Suggestions for Enhancing the Teaching/Learning Experience, Communication in an Era of Diversity, Responding to the Adult Learner, The Value of Cultural Diversity, Until Utopia: Established Equality Among Persons with Disabilities and the Able-Bodied

Office of Orientation—Diversity program for incoming undergraduate students

Pilot Program/College Community Program—Intergroup Relations and Conflict: formal courses linked to an extensive informal program

School of Education—Small-group diversity sessions three times per year

University Library, Cross-Cultural Communication Workshop, Peer Information Counseling Program

Women of Color Task Force—A number of programs under the theme "See beyond Today: Inspiring a Vision to Enhance the Quality of Life"

Women's Studies Program—Various programs and projects including research, a multi-media performance workshop, academic courses and a mainstreaming project

Conflict Management/Resolution

Affirmative Action Office—Consultation/workshops on racial discrimination and harassment

Department of Sociology—Teaching Students About Prejudice and Discrimination

Human Resource Development, Diversity curriculum

Pilot Program/College Community Program—Intergroup Relations and Conflict Program

Program on Conflict Management Alternatives—Report on a Retrieval Conference

Faculty/Staff Recruitment/Retention

Administrative Services Personnel Office—Minority Recruiting Information Resource Program

Center for Afroamerican and African Studies—DuBois-Mandela-Rodney Fellowship Program

College of Pharmacy, King/Chavez/Parks Visiting Scholars Program

Department of Physics—Climbing the Physics Ladder. Minorities and Women in the Physics Educational Pipeline

Information Technology Division—Annual divisionwide diversity education program, Diversity Education Committee, ITD Theatre Troupe

Institute of Gerontology, Minority Faculty Research Development in Geriatrics and Gerontology

School of Natural Resources—Committee on Diversity

School of Public Health, Paul B. Cornely Sr. Postdoctoral Fellowship Program for Minority Scholars, UMSPH Task Force on Racial and Cultural Concerns

U-M Hospitals—Medical Center Total Quality Diversity Task Force, Support Network for Affirmative Action Programs, Hospital Plant Operations/Maintenance Experimental Training Program

University Library—Managing a Culturally Diverse Workplace, Training Intern Program, Point of Intersection: The University of Michigan Library Diversity Program (10-minute videotape)

Women of Color Task Force—programs under the general theme of "See Beyond Today: Inspiring a Vision to Enhance the Quality of Life," 1991 annual Career Conference

Multicultural Awareness

Administrative Services Personnel Office—Diversity Forum

Career Planning and Placement, Staff development session on cultural awareness

Center for the Education of Women—Focus: Women of Color

Counseling Services—Programs focusing on diversity

Department of Germanic Languages & Literatures—Race and languages program with Detroit's Martin Luther King High School

Department of Physics—Climbing the Physics Ladder: Minorities and Women in the Physics Educational Pipeline presentation and discussion; Women and Minorities in Physics: The Climate in the Classroom survey and follow-up workshop

Ella Baker-Nelson Mandela Center

English Composition Board/Residential College—Mackenzie High School/University of Michigan Writing Program

Institute of Gerontology—Minority Faculty Research Development in Geriatrics and Gerontology

Housing/Bursley Hall—Bursley Community Volunteers

Housing/Mosher Jordan Library—Color of Curiosity

Human Resource Development—Diversity Curriculum

Information Technology Division—Ongoing program of creating a climate that supports multiculturalism

Lesbian-Gay Male Programs Office—Workshop on Sexual Orientation and Individual and Institutional Homophobia

LS&A/Housing—The 21st Century Program

Medical Center—Martin Luther King Commemorative Health Care Program

Office of Affirmative Action—Stares and Stairs: Achieving Attitudinal and Architectural Accessibility; Pluralism and Particularism panel; Space Is Open to All People presentation; Multiculturalism and Male/Female Relationships presentation; Reflections of Distinguished African Graduates presentation/discussion; Sexual Orientation Workshop; Workshop on Sexual Segregation: Persons with Disabilities and the Myth of Normalization

Office of Orientation—Diversity workshops for undergraduate students

Programs for Educational Opportunity—federally funded desegregation assistance center

SACUA/Senate Assembly—Committee for a Multicultural University

School of Education—Small-group diversity sessions

School of Public Health—UMSPH Task Force on Racial and Cultural Concerns

Student Activities Office, U-M-Dearborn—AIDS Awareness Week, Women's History Week

Student Organization Development Center—Winter Leadership Conference

U-M Geriatric Center—Minority Access Pilot Project

U-M Hospitals—Annual Black Managers' Forum, Martin Luther King Commemorative Health Care Program, Medical Center Total Quality Diversity Task Force, Support Network for Affirmative Action Programs

University Library—Exploring the Value of Diversity/Valuing Diversity Seminar, Managing a Culturally Diverse Workforce, Valuing Diversity in the Workplace: Sexual Orientation Session

Women of Color Task Force—Programs under general theme of "See Beyond Today: Inspiring a Vision to Enhance the Quality of Life"

Women's Studies Program—Women's studies courses

Multicultural Awareness: Films and Videos

School of Nursing—Video: "Listen to Me"

University Library—Diversity Film Festival, Point of Intersection: The University of Michigan Library Diversity Program (10-minute videotape)

Multicultural Awareness in general

Admissions Office, U-M-Dearborn—Detroit Public Schools Counselor Luncheon, Distinguished Student Leader Award

Association of Black Professionals & Administrators—Monthly Meeting

*Multicultural Awareness: Social,
Cultural/Artistic Events, and Exhibits*

Investment Office—Martin Luther King Day Celebration

Office of Minority Programs, U-M-Flint—Genesee Valley Indian Association of Native American Arts & Crafts

University Library/External Relations Office—Diversity exhibits

Division of Housing and University Unions—Project Awareness Programs

U-M-Flint—Michigan Shakespeare Festival with Buckham Alley Theatre and McCree Theatre

Minority Student Services—Hispanic Heritage Celebration; Minority Student Services/Puerto Rican Student Association, Puerto Rico Week; Minority Student Services/Socially Active Latino Student Association, Chicano History Week

Office of Minority Programs, U-M-Flint—Gospel Recital; Suzuki Strings (local classical musicians) performance; Doll for Democracy presentation

School of Music—Influences of the Harlem Renaissance (lecture and performance)

Student Activities Office, U-M-Dearborn—Arab Heritage Week, Asian American Awareness Week, Black History Month 1991: Knowledge Is Power, Ethnic Diversity Week, sponsored by Student Government Association, Middle East Lecture and Forums

Trotter House—Provides a casual environmental that enhances the social interaction among minority students, among minority students and minority faculty/staff, and among minority students and non-minority students. Minority Festival, Minority Student Picnic

School of Education, Monthly diversity event

continued...

Programs in the U-M Diversity Directory *(continued)*

Multicultural Curriculum/Pedagogy

Center for Research on Learning and Teaching—Variety of programs designed to enhance teaching and learning in a culturally diverse classroom environment

Department of English Language and Literature—English 317: Bigotry and Maturing in the Literature of Two Cultures

Department of History—History/Asian Studies 303: Diversity, Ethnicity and Conflict in Asia

Department of Humanities, U-M-Dearborn—Near and Middle East curriculum initiative

Department of Slavic Languages and Literatures—Ethnic and Cultural Diversity in Eastern Europe and the USSR via courses and lectures

Department of Sociology—Workshop: Teaching Students About Prejudice and Discrimination

English Composition Board/Residential College—Mackenzie High School/University of Michigan Writing Program

FAIR (Faculty Against Institutional Racism) Teaching Group—Project to Improve Teaching on Issues of Institutional Racism and Diversity

LS&A—TA Training Program

LS&A Dean's Office—University Course 299 Board

Office of International Programs—Summer Language Program in Spain

Pilot Program/College Community Program—Intergroup Relations and Conflict Program

School of Education, U-M-Dearborn—Child Development Training Program outreach effort, Saturday Reading Program at Woodward Elementary School, Woodward Elementary School Field Experiences

Women's Studies Program—Courses dealing with women of color, research projects and mainstreaming project

Multicultural Curriculum/Pedagogy: Research Issues and Initiatives

Center for Afroamerican and African Studies—Black History Month Symposium, CAAS Brown-bag Lunch Series, DuBois-Mandela-Rodney Fellowship Program, Graduate Student Multidisciplinary Conference

Graduate Library—Diversity Librarian Position

Program on Conflict Management Alternatives—Report on a Retrieval Conference

Student Recruitment and Retention

School of Dentistry—Pre-Doctoral Program Recruitment and Admissions of Disadvantaged Students

Career Planning and Placement—Minority Career Conference: Incentive Career Options for Incentive Scholars, Professional Improvement Program; Professional Improvement Program/Internship Opportunity Connection

Center for Afroamerican and African Studies—Graduate Student Multidisciplinary Conference

Civil Engineering—MLK Day: A Sampling of Minority Alumni (1990)

College of Engineering—Designation as a National Space Grant College by the National Aeronautics and Space Administration and leader of the Michigan Space Grant Consortium

College of Pharmacy—King/Chavez/Parks Visiting Scholars Program, Minority High School Summer Research Apprenticeship Program, Minority Student Career/Academic Information Exchange, Summer Undergraduate Research Program

Comprehensive Studies Program—Bridge Program; CSP Mentorship Program

Comprehensive Studies Program/University Course Division, Perspectives on Careers in Medicine, Dentistry and the Allied Health Care Professions

Department of Germanic Languages and Literatures—Race and languages program with Detroit's Martin Luther King High School

Department of Mathematics—Minority Affairs Committee

Department of Physics—Climbing the Physics Ladder: Minorities and Women in the Physics Educational Pipeline

English Composition Board/Residential College—Mackenzie High School/University of Michigan Writing Program

Horace H. Rackham School of Graduate Studies—Summer Research Opportunity Program

Institute for Public Policy Studies—Junior Year Summer Institute: Policy Skills for Minority Students

Institute of Gerontology—Minority Faculty Research Development in Geriatrics and Gerontology

Medical School/Office of Student and Minority Affairs—Pre-Matriculation Summer Program; Department of Pharmacology, Charles Ross Summer Research Fellowship; Office of Biomedical Research: Merck Minority Graduate Student Fellowship, Establishment of the Association of Multicultural Scientists Organization, Lilly Travel Fund, Post-Baccalaureate Pre-Medical Fellowship

Michigan Memorial-Phoenix Project—Minority and Female Intern Program, Reactor Laboratory Instruction

Minority Engineering Programs Office—Facilitated Study Group Program, Minority Engineering Program

Office of Orientation—Spring Visitation for Students of Color

School of Dentistry—Recruiting and Retaining a

Culturally Diverse Student Body, tutor-facilitated study groups, Health Careers Opportunity Program Retention Program	U-M Hospitals—Seventh Allied Health Careers Workshop for Minority Students
School of Engineering, U-M-Dearborn, Detroit Area Pre-College Engineering Program class in Computer-Aided Engineering Graphics, Engineering Society of Detroit Engineering Careers Conference and Exposition, targeted high school outreach	U-M-Dearborn Admissions, Detroit Compact Program, International Student Admissions, King/Chavez/Parks Initiative College Day Program, Wade H. McCree Jr. Incentive Scholars Program, Counseling/Support Services: Mentor Program for Special Population Students
School of Music—Academic exchange with the University of Ghana	U-M-Flint—M-Link Program; Office of Minority Affairs, Leadership Development Project-Flint Community Schools
School of Natural Resources—Committee on Diversity, Summer Research in Natural Resources	Undergraduate Admissions—Counselor Workshops, Junior Campus Visit, Minority Phone Call-Out, Minority Student Symposium, "The Pursuit of Excellence," U-M Ambassador Club, Wayne County Community College/U-M Honors Program,
School of Public Health—Facilitated study groups. Health Careers Opportunity Program Retention Program, UMSPH Task Force on Racial and Cultural Concerns, Health Services Management and Policy Summer Enrichment Program	
Student Organization Development Center—Winter Leadership Conference	University Library/Undergraduate—Peer Information Counseling Program
Trotter House—Minority Student Picnic	Women in Science Program, Center for the Education of Women, High School Internship Program

Source: The University of Michigan, *University Record,* November 18, 1991.

The student recruitment and retention programs include a number of outreach programs. Undergraduate and graduate student ambassadors visit minority high schools, a "minority phone call-out" service contacts prospective students, "college clubs" have been formed in underrepresented school districts, and the King/Chavis/Parks visitation programs bring 1,500 seventh-grade students to campus from minority school districts. Various schools of the university have their own outreach and internship programs, such as the School of Engineering's Minority Engineering Program Office's workshops and internship programs for both prospective and enrolled students. The Summer Engineering Academy takes students from grades 8–12 and provides them with classes concentrating on mathematics, engineering, and science. The university also cooperates with GM, Ford, and Chrysler to sponsor the Detroit Area Pre-College Engineering Program. The University Medical School/Office of Biomedical Research and Merck sponsor minority graduate student fellowships. The College of Pharmacy hosts King/Chavis/Parks visiting scholars and the minority high school summer research apprenticeship program. There are mentoring and internship programs throughout the university. A dormitory wing houses the "Twenty-First Century" project, modeled after Uri Treisman's successful project to retain minority students at Berkeley. The project is designed to foster multiethnic cooperative community for studying and socializing. In 1993, a new residential program began for fifty-two Women in Science and Engineering (WISE).

Financial aid became heavily skewed toward undergraduate and graduate "underrepresented minorities" in a formula that one administrator called "disproportionate by design." In response to a request about undergraduate student aid, I obtained the following data from the Office of Financial Aid in October 1994:

- 42–50 percent of gift aid (scholarships and grants) goes to underrepresented minorities.
- 80 percent of the merit scholarship dollars go to underrepresented minorities.
- 90 percent of nonresident merit scholarships to underrepresented minorities.
- From a more limited pool of funds, nonresident minorities receive a host of other financial aid packages that are harder to come by for nonresident whites.

By the 1994–95 year, the number of coveted four-year Rackham Graduate School Merit Fellowship Program fellowships had been expanded to 734. Of that number a whopping 51 percent went to African Americans and another 29 percent to Mexican Americans and Puerto Ricans. Whites, Asians, and Cuban Americans (no longer classified as Hispanic) presumably shared the rest.

The School of Business Administration became very aggressive in establishing several minority-targeted programs. Assisted by a $300,000 grant from the General Electric Fund, the business school recently launched a Faculty of the Future Program to increase diversity in its Ph.D. program and among the faculty. In addition, the business school intends to establish a graduate fellowship and forgivable loan program for minority graduate students. A Junior Faculty Coupon Program will guarantee several years of summer research funding for minorities. Finally, diversity consultant-author and faculty member Taylor Cox, Jr., will seek out minority Ph.D.s and non-Ph.D.s teaching elsewhere, inviting them to refine teaching and research skills in a new postdoctoral studies program.[6]

To enhance minority faculty and staff diversity, the university's central administration offers Target of Opportunity positions (TOP), and start-up and support money for new positions reserved for minority candidates. (About 100 had been appointed through 1995, according to President Duderstadt.) Many units have diversity task forces, such as the University Hospitals SNAPP program (Support Network for Affirmative Action Programs) to "counsel, encourage and assist employees of color at the UM Medical Center." To increase multicultural awareness, there is the Diversity Forum, which sponsors educational experiences aimed at increasing awareness levels and tolerance for persons of different ethnicity, opposite sex, or with different beliefs and lifestyles. The university library has programs on "managing a culturally diverse workforce" and "valuing diversity in the workplace: sexual orientation session." The library also offers a diversity film festival featuring the following titles: *Who Killed Vincent Chin? A Little Respect: Lesbian and Gay Students on Campus, Racism 101, Guilty by Reason of Race, Yo Soy Chicano, Maya Angelou,* and *Alice Walker: A Portrait in the First Person.* The Office of Orientation's Commitment to Diversity program sponsors a compulsory ninety-minute workshop (using two videotapes and discussion sessions) for all new students. The Office of Affirmative Action offers numerous workshops on racial discrimination and gender harassment. As part of the newly inaugurated Michigan Agenda for Women (modeled after the Mandate), the university initiated a Career Development Fund for Women Faculty, including $5,000 grants awarded to up to twenty tenured or tenure-track faculty members per term.

The Ella Baker–Nelson Mandela Center is described as a student-run "alternative resource and research facility initiated by the United Coalition Against Racism. It is the Center's goal to encourage the study of the issues of race, class, and gender as they impact upon people's lives and to begin to challenge the existing paradigms and theories which are often Euro-centric, racist, sexist and homophobic." The center sponsors the BMC Cultural Night, which brings sectors of the university and town communities "to come together and share our culture and heritage, reflect on our histories and begin to build bonds for a unified struggle."[7]

Throughout the university, Martin Luther King's birthday is annually celebrated as Diversity Day with a host of colloquia, symposiums, and lectures. (In 1994, however, the Black Student Union protested that waxing multicultural themes were diluting the proper emphasis on black social justice.)

By 1995, Michigan's School of Business Administration had a full-time M.B.A. class that is 28 percent students of color and 11 percent African American (approximately 85 percent out of state and 30 percent female). As of 1993, it had also reformulated its curriculum to emphasize practical experience, internships, and, especially, teamwork. Half of all first-year assignments are now team projects. "We don't want the students to compete with one another but help one another," stated Paul Danos, associate dean. "It's not the old-fashioned *Paper Chase* mold. We want to foster cooperation, have them help one another to achieve unit goals." (Vincent Harris, president of the graduate Black Business Student Association, acknowledged that there had been superficial acceptance of diversity but found that ethnicity and gender still structured voluntary and informal association. Efforts by the business school to promote a multicultural mix on student work teams tended to dissolve in those situations where students had the chance to pick their own team members.)

Social awareness was fostered during the first day of the M.B.A. orientation period when students are taken into inner-city areas to work on inner-city projects. There were ethnic support groups for African Americans, Hispanics, and Asians. And the school sponsored a full day of speakers during the university-wide celebration of Diversity Day. The school was less pleased that, as of the 1995 fall semester, only 26 of its 127 full-time faculty were women and 10 were minorities (most of them Asians). (The highly regarded law school experienced similar troubles: as of fall 1995, only three of approximately forty-four tenured and tenure-track faculty were minorities and seven were women. The law school has increased minority student enrollment and has several support organizations, including the newly formed Queer Law Student Association.)

The Medical Center Gives Diversity Management Comprehensive Care

The 11,000-employee Medical Center (UMMC) became involved in the most comprehensive, Roosevelt Thomas–style approach to managing diversity, spending more than half a million dollars from 1992 to 1996 to provide diversity training to all staff. That major effort was preceded by a 1989 preliminary *Report on the Multicultural Environment,* and then a UMMC Total Quality Diversity Task Force was established in 1990. In 1991 a cultural audit was conducted to assess staff perceptions of the environment. The audit found that "the culture has been white-male and task-oriented, not relation-oriented," said Sunny Roller, the UMMC's diversity coordinator, during a 1993 interview. The director of medical campus human resources, Laurita Thomas, crisply ticked off to me the core value orientations discovered in the audit: "science-oriented, research oriented, competitive (striving to be the best in everything), elite and 'supercompetent' oriented." The strong sense of individualism and competition, she felt, was "in transition" as interdisciplinary research and the team focus of total quality management asserted themselves.

Although M-Quality, U-M's version of total quality management, was viewed as the primary driver of cultural change, diversity was woven into a total quality diversity program with the following rationale, expressed in typical TQM and diversity jargon:

> In order to be the provider of choice, the employer of choice and preeminent in research and education, it is imperative that the UMMC sustains an environment in which our work processes include everyone. Implementing diversity-sensitive Total Quality teamwork helps us to continue to build a workplace environment that enables people of various culture backgrounds, ages, social classes, educational levels, physical disability and sexual orientations to be valued, feel empowered and problem solve.
>
> It is our diversity that brings to our Medical Center the richness and depth of quality that only comes from maximizing the input of the total workforce membership.[8]

Diversity education was integrated into total quality leadership courses by imparting the following skills and competencies:

- Communicate respect.
- Be nonjudgmental.
- Personalize knowledge and perceptions.
- Display empathy.
- Practice role flexibility.
- Demonstrate reciprocal concern.
- Tolerate ambiguity.

Although the Michigan Mandate focused on ethnicity, UMMC followed the trend in diversity management theory to expand efforts to build human relationships across all manner of differences: ethnic, gender, disability, gay and lesbian. UMMC developed its own diversity training manual, *What Do I Do First?* and claimed to get requests for the document from a wide range of other institutions.

A two-day managing diversity module became part of the management development curriculum in 1992. By 1995, there were over 700 graduates of the class who responded favorably to follow-up surveys: 90 percent indicated increased awareness, 83 percent felt a deepened understanding of diversity issues, and 61 percent suggested additional diversity training. Consultant Tom Kochman conducted advanced diversity skill-building workshops for managers between August 1994 and May 1995. (Kochman received very high evaluations: 94 percent of the participants rated the workshops as "excellent" or "good," and 92 percent said they would recommend the Kochman workshops to their colleagues.)

The medical center also promoted diversity awareness through brown bag lunch groups, an international flag display, an international doll exhibit, distribution of diversity calendars, posters, notepads, a multicultural day, a diversity puzzle and game, and emphasis on more multicultural holidays, including the replacement of "a traditional Christmas focus" with a more "multicultural motif" of "wintry" scenes.

A 1996 four-year progress report found that "awareness and responsiveness to diversity have increased" and that the noninstructional workforce at the medical center "closely matches the racial/ethnic mix of the communities from which it draws." But the report bemoaned an unequal distribution of employees, noting that 70 percent of African American workers hold service-maintenance or office jobs. (The same group was the most likely to file grievances.) Patient involvement was minimal, though incoming patients must now sign forms acknowledging that they'll be treated by a multicultural staff.

Layoffs of up to 1,000 people were announced in 1996. The numbers were scaled back, but, in any case, diversity coordinator Sunny Roller was certain the medical center's diversity machinery would survive. Yet indicative of the collision between diversity management and downsizing, by mid-June 1996, the center's human resources unit was sponsoring a new series of workshops on stress reduction workshops to cope with downsizing anxieties.

Committee on a Multicultural University

Composed of high-level administrators (mostly associate deans), the Committee on a Multicultural University (COMU) was created by James Duderstadt as a means to infuse multiculturalism throughout the university. Microbiologist and medical school dean Fred Neidhardt, COMU chair for 1993–1994, took great pride in the committee and the Mandate: "I came away from this past year with new pride I'd not felt since Duderstadt and the Mandate came along. Before the Mandate, the U seemed uninvolved and unconcerned." The director for the new Center for Research on Learning and Teaching, Constance Cook, was equally enthusiastic: "The committee is a place for people to get re-fueled and inspired, a place to share ideas and learn new approaches for implementation."[9]

The work of the committee took place in subgroups assigned to gather information and work on vision and measures of cultural self-assessment. The committee drafted a series of "markers and measures of success in becoming a multicultural university." The items included on organizational structure had the ring of a utopian, but rather coercive, ethnic and gender socialism:

- Inclusion of all race and ethnic groups at formal and informal work meetings.
- Playing as well as working together.
- Power is vested in working groups at all levels of the institution.
- The working groups are drawn from student bodies, staff, faculty and administration, each of which represents the population distribution of racial and ethnic groups.
- A criterion for selection of a leader is the individual's commitment to multiculturalism.
- Leaders at all levels espouse multicultural goals and are regularly evaluated for success in advancing multiculturalism.
- Participation in advisory and decision-making groups is attractive to individuals of all race and ethnic groups because their input is valued.
- Allocation of internal resources encourages activities, programs, groups, and leaders that foster multicultural goals.

These and other, similar recommendations were not intended as mere mystic idealism. COMU's new chair, David Schoem, assistant dean of the College of Literature, Science and Arts, told President Duderstadt in June 1994 that "COMU now has products that need to go to the units. Now we need to try out your ideas."[10]

That would be more difficult than anyone had realized.

Institutional Inertia and Faculty Politics

By 1993, it was becoming evident that faculty preoccupation with individual research projects and the absorption of undergraduate and graduate students with grades and career aspirations were deflecting the Mandate's early momentum. "The main problem," admitted presidential special counsel and former social work dean Harold Johnson in 1993, "is getting the Mandate on people's agenda, getting them to take it seriously." Associate graduate school dean Susan Lipshutz reluctantly agreed: "The Mandate is a distraction." In 1996, her successor, Elaine Didier, confirmed that faculty disinterest was entrenched: "The problem is to get the faculty to take anything [from the administration] seriously. Faculty see the world differently. They spend their time differently."

Furthermore, the top-down imposition of the Mandate collided with a brewing revolt among Michigan's faculty senate (the Senate Assembly Committee on University Affairs, SACUA), many of whom felt the central administration was growing too autocratic. Lack of genuine and widespread consultation with the faculty over the Mandate (and other issues) doomed widespread ownership of it by one of its most important constituencies.[11] (Reaction to imposition of diversity drives and rising faculty debates over "shared governance" were, of course, hardly unique to Michigan.)

Lack of awareness or concern about the president's "number one priority" was both a blessing and a curse for Michigan's change agents. Initially, widespread disinterest permitted them to launch programs and plant agents of change with little discussion or opposition, but, without widespread knowledge or interest, the internships, support groups, and so forth were limited in their effectiveness and were not absorbed into the organization's mainstream culture.

My direct and indirect observations suggested that the vast majority of faculty and students appeared only dimly aware of the existence of the Michigan Mandate per se. Most people interviewed for this book had not read any versions of the Mandate; graduate and undergraduate students had trouble finding a copy when they tried. On the other hand, there was widespread knowledge of the university's commitment to diversity, primarily in the form of minority preferences in admissions, financial aid, and faculty hiring, though such policies were accepted or criticized discreetly.

As for those actively aware of and interested in the Mandate, there were a small cadre of high-level supporters, a larger body of moderate or liberal skeptics, and at least two major casualties of multicultural forces set in motion by the Mandate.

Early Mandate Evangelists, Skeptics, and Casualties

Active mandate supporters often were faculty-turned-administrators who did not necessarily speak with one voice. They differed in their perceptions of how deep and long-term the mandate's remedies should be and whether increased conflict and separatism were truly troublesome developments.

Bob Weisbuch was an early convert. During an interview in the fall of 1991, the forty-seven-year-old chair of the English Department immediately winced at the term "diversity." He felt such buzzwords hid the "laudable historical and political enterprise of attempts by academic institutions to self-

consciously redress historical inequities that have intellectual consequences."
During his term as chair, Weisbuch transformed the department by hiring female and minority faculty, often, apparently, by tapping the new Target of
Opportunity positions. In combination with a large number of retirements,
Weisbuch and his colleagues were able to alter the ethnic and gender composition and curriculum of the department modestly. Over a four-year period,
twenty-five new tenure-track faculty had been hired, only six of whom were
white male; thirteen were female, including three African American women.
In doing so, Weisbuch and a minority colleague sorted hundreds of applicants into different stacks according to evident or hastily assessed ethnicity.
In anticipation of TOP funding, a position in African American literature
was advertised, though Weisbuch was worried that if a white specializing in
that area applied, "I didn't have a position for him or her."

"It was very embarrassing," Weisbuch admitted. "We're all embarrassed by
the system." He sympathized with the plight of his white male graduate students who were having trouble being hired. Like nearly everyone else interviewed, Weisbuch hadn't considered whether such procedures were legal. "I
hope so," he said.

Weisbuch had a ready response for these temporary inequities, including
complaints of higher salaries for minorities: "I would ask them if they think
being black is worth $5,000 a year." In an emotional moment, Weisbuch jus-
tified such procedures by stating that several decades ago he might have been
excluded from Yale's Ph.D. program because he was Jewish. (When I pointed
out that today he might be excluded because he is white male, his face fell. "I
hadn't thought of that," he said.) Weisbuch had chaired a 1990 report on undergraduate education that found continuing student ethnic separatism. "I
don't know what to do about that," he admitted.

Presidential assistant and Mandate enthusiast Shirley Clarkson was also
baffled by how to build "bridging mechanisms" to find "common ground"
in the multicultural university. Clarkson did feel that conflict and debates
concerning the Mandate had clarified some issues, such as forcing debate
about the curriculum and research priorities. Like many other supporters,
she had high hopes for reducing the atmosphere of "aggressive competitiveness" through new teaching and research styles, such as self-paced, nonjudgmental formats and cooperative team projects. (The head of the famed
Institute for Social Research, social psychologist Bob Zajonic, concurred
that participation in shared tasks would build cohesion.) "I'm not sure
where we're going," Clarkson sighed in May 1992. (Clarkson was more cer-

tain of her own direction; she departed for a position in the new Clinton administration in late 1992.)

The African American vice provost for multicultural affairs, Charles Moody, expressed his expansive, evangelical view of the Mandate during a 1992 interview. Achieving a multicultural organization ("parity in power and decision making") was a constant, life-long process, he explained. Moody was obviously conversant with workforce diversity literature and had written two or three unpublished papers himself. "What we're talking about is moving from desegregation toward equity-based education, social justice," he said, as well as rooting out formal and informal discrimination based on taken-for-granted policy and practice. Moody was proud of his four-dimensional model for institutional change: access (outreach and recruitment), process (producing an "equitable, fair, and humane environment"), achievement (programs to recognize and support minority achievement), and transfer ("the rate of return on college degrees must be the same for people of color as it is for white males").

Moody and several other minority administrators were unconcerned with evidence of ethnic separatism, suggesting that exclusive white cliques were not viewed as a similar "problem." Moody also scoffed at rumbles of reverse discrimination: "White males have to understand how damned privileged they've been. They get all this shit, and they don't even know how."

Moody retired and was replaced in 1993 by Lester Monts, a musicologist specializing in West Africa and a former undergraduate dean at the University of California, Santa Barbara. Monts's more modest vision was on infusing multiculturalism into the curriculum and improving multicultural teaching. He was initially baffled by the decentralized and autonomous nature of the university. He was probing the subcultures of individual schools and units. Monts was deeply involved in the provost's office, a spokesperson for multicultural matters, and took part in retention and promotion decisions. His office helped coordinate the Target of Opportunity positions. Monts worked closely with COMU and candidly admitted that "no one has the answers" to implementing multiculturalism. But a multicultural university would be inevitable, Monts maintained, because "kids in K–12 are getting multiculturalism. They'll come here. Faculty may resist, but they'll become out of step if they continue to teach monoculturally."

The left-leaning student newspaper, the *Michigan Daily,* generally supported affirmative action and the Mandate, though the editor I spoke with in 1992 objected to quota-style provisions of both the Mandate and the newer Michigan Agenda for Women. The faculty-staff weekly paper, *University*

Record, dutifully reported presidential pronouncements and celebrated any increase in minority and female hiring and enrollment. Most important of all, the university's regents voted to endorse the Mandate in spring 1993, a move that did gain widespread, temporary attention.

Skeptics: Left, Center, Right

Activist faculty and graduate and professional students echoed criticisms made by diversity consultants and advocates in other settings: that the organization had not moved much beyond preoccupation with minority admissions and hiring numbers while failing to follow through in cultural change efforts. Students urging a "do-more" perspective aired their views in a 1993 report in the right-leaning *Michigan Review*—for example, "The university encourages students to bring diversity to the school. After the minority students are here, you don't see much interaction." Activists wanted more extensive curriculum reform.

African American pharmacologist Peggy Hollingsworth in 1994 received an award for her involvement in university governance. Still, Hollingsworth and two of her colleagues complained that the Mandate's goals had not penetrated the university's reward and promotion structure, which still emphasized research and grant getting and operated through informal old-boy networks. Minorities, claimed Hollingsworth, remained isolated in a sink-or-swim climate. Hollingsworth and her colleagues criticized the university's inaction and inflexibility in more sensitively evaluating minority and female applicants and employees. They were impatient with the administration's explanation that minority faculty hiring and retention problems were largely due to "pipeline problems": inadequate supplies of black and Hispanic Ph.D.s, especially in the sciences. They cited the university's reluctance to hire its own minority Ph.D.s, engage in more active minority mentoring, or create a more diversity-friendly climate. (Indeed, Hollingsworth acted on her perceptions in 1994, filing a grievance after she, a Michigan Ph.D., was refused a promotion. A member of the promotion committee, she alleged, held racist attitudes made apparent in racist remarks.)

Social work professor Beth Reed admitted she and other active faculty had become "seething caldrons," frustrated by the emphasis on recruitment and the tendency to view multiculturalism while ignoring the underlying oppression. Sociologist Mark Chesler complained that multiculturalism had not been absorbed into the "warp and woof" of organizational culture. An anonymous department chair found many of the reform attempts to be superficial and lacking in follow-through. Her diversity efforts were never considered in her performance evaluations, nor, to her knowledge, were deans and administrators above her so evaluated. The lone Target of Opportunity position she obtained for her department consumed an inordinate amount of time and effort. (Worse, she was sued for discriminating against another female faculty member during a promotion procedure.)

Peter Steiner, retired arts and sciences dean, was a moderate, candid critic who gave voice to problems that others would make only off the record or not at all.[12] Steiner observed that Mandate-inspired programs were an add-on task that could absorb large amounts of time, resources, and management—often at the expense of other programs. Steiner and liberal critic Peggy Hollingsworth both raised the delicate issue of whether some less-than-qualified minorities had been hurriedly hired to fill the Target of Opportunity positions. (Hollingsworth took a more conspiratorial view that some such people were sometimes hired to sabotage affirmative action or to grab extra funding.) As a dean, Steiner found the TOP program led to unbalanced, unplanned departmental growth: humanities and social sciences, where minority Ph.D.s were relatively more available, grew, while physics and chemistry could not. He also suspected that reverse discrimination and political correctness fueled considerable silent hostility, as did real or alleged racial incidents.

By 1994, chemist Tom Dunn, an active faculty senate member, was annoyed at the Mandate's egalitarian excesses, including suggestions that science faculty lower the grading curve to attract more minorities and women. As an active senate member, Dunn especially objected to Duderstadt's "bulldozer" methods and lack of consultation with faculty. The administration's goals and time lines, Dunn argued, were totally unrealistic. He believed Duderstadt underestimated the difficulties of trying to build a more diverse university. For example, Dunn argued that the decision by women faculty to take time off for child rearing has far more disruptive consequences in science than in the humanities.

The insurgent, conservative *Michigan Review* criticized the Mandate and its allied programs freely. The *Review* took note of the rhetorical excesses of Diversity Day and the 1993 PC Frame-Up conference, the first national conference organized to rebut spreading media portraits of political correctness on campus; and the *Review* was the first campus publication to run a front-page article on how veteran statistician David Goldberg was being tarred as a "racist" by politically correct graduate students—as colleagues and administrators responded weakly. Former *Michigan Review* writer and Michigan graduate Jeff Muir seconded Tom Dunn's criticism of unrealistic goals by noting that if James Duderstadt wanted to achieve proportional representation for female faculty by the year 2000—a goal of the new, Mandate-allied Michigan Agenda for Women—1,000 male faculty would have to be fired. As for the effects of the Mandate, Muir argued that the university has been admitting unqualified blacks and Hispanics, which accounted for their much lower graduation rate. Muir charged that reaching for diversity contributed to Michigan's drop in student selectivity to forty-first in the *U.S. News and World Reports* and a drop in the university's overall ranking into the mid-twenties.[13]

Casualties: Center and Left

The danger in being anywhere near a politicized policy crusade is that one can be sanctioned for failing to conform *or* for enthusiastic excesses. Michigan's multicultural campaign combined both pragmatic, proportional demography-is-destiny rationales and strident, left-wing moralisms about "righting past wrongs." This was the source of centrist and conservative complaints about PC and speech restrictions. On the other hand, left-wing critics sensed that beneath the liberal rhetoric, the University of Michigan remained a conservative to moderate midwestern institution hostile to radical change and favoring smooth public relations above all else. At least two people, a faculty member and a high-level administrator, became caught in these contradictions.

In 1993, the university administration faltered when thirty-year-veteran Michigan sociologist David Goldberg became the victim of a smear campaign organized by left-wing graduate students. Goldberg was the most recent victim in a long line of social scientists, nationally and at Michigan, who confronted PC ideology with contradictory data.[14] A few years before, Goldberg's departmental colleague, renowned demographer Reynolds Farley, had made classroom remarks about Malcolm X that were misinterpreted and misquoted in the student press and later in university investigations. The most appalling aspect, according to Farley, was that colleagues were painfully slow to rise to his defense—if they did so at all. (Farley refused to teach the course for several years.)

Michigan's senior sociology faculty have been famous for their quantitative prowess. But several of the entering graduate cohort of eighteen females and two males were politically sensitized against statistics and ill prepared for the course taught by David Goldberg. During the course section on regression analysis, Goldberg chose—as he had in many previous classes—to illustrate how variables such as education, age, class, and marital status could substantially reduce apparent statistical gaps among racial groups or between men and women. Goldberg thus challenged the current popular dictum that women make only fifty-nine cents for every dollar made by a man, and he shared his consultant expertise in dissecting alleged discrimination in mortgage lending.

Some students were upset by both the data and by Goldberg's tough, nononsense approach. Classroom arguments escalated about the worth of quantitative methods and the appropriateness of classroom materials. A simple cartoon of a caveman's wife asking him about the worth of dice he was carving was taken as a slur against women's mathematical skills. After a difficult exam, a student challenged Goldberg's authority to presume "a variance of ability among students." (One graduate student later explained, "We're all smart.") Recalled Goldberg, "It was all downhill from there."

The following semester, radical students not involved in the course helped file a formal grievance while circulating an anonymous flyer charging Goldberg with racial and sexual harassment. Department chair Howard Schuman ultimately decided that the charges were unsubstantiated, but he also tried to placate the radicals by removing Goldberg from any required courses. Goldberg stood his ground and offered evidence that grades in his statistics course showed no correlation with race or gender. (Grades were best predicted by quantitative aptitude scores on the Graduate Record Exam. According to data provided by Goldberg, one student had scored in the seventh percentile and another in the fourteenth.)

An eventual compromise led to the creation of two sections of statistics: Goldberg's and a class taught by another sociologist. But this solution still impugned Goldberg's reputation. Administrators sidestepped the controversy or dismissed it as a personality clash between Goldberg and the students. "David is an SOB who can be very nasty," said one. "The students took this as racism." They were reluctant to admit that the university's vigorous promotion of affirmative action and multiculturalism might have compromised admissions standards, politicized curricula, and encouraged PC intimidation of faculty.

In September 1993, Derek Green's *Ann Arbor Observer* analysis, "The Goldberg Affair," prompted renewed concerns. A new sociology chair was suddenly appointed, and the regents began to grumble, one privately fuming that Goldberg "was left to twist in the wind" and that the university had failed a test of "institutional loyalty." One administrator reportedly tried to neutralize the case by stating that Goldberg needed psychiatric help. Parallels were increasingly drawn to the similar institutional abandonment of

Reynolds Farley. Goldberg considered a lawsuit, but ill health over the next eighteen months, including a mild heart attack, impeded his resolve. The university is trying to forget the whole thing, and the American Sociological Association has never heard of the case. (However, the Department of Sociology reportedly reassessed its graduate admissions criteria the following year.)[15]

Affirmative action officer Zaida Giraldo, on the other hand, veered too far to the left of the smooth corporate style and African American–based multiculturalism favored by Michigan's administration. Hired from the University of Wisconsin, Milwaukee, in 1989, the enthusiastic Giraldo was very conversant with the emerging theories of diversity management. She saw the university moving through stages: "We've admitted we're a racist institution, minorities have sought a comfort level in self-segregation, and now we're working on curriculum reform." A more relaxed, warmer, multicultural institution was somewhere down the road.

Giraldo quickly surmised the university's central dilemma: "A culture that reveres competitiveness will have adverse impact on groups that don't subscribe to that culture," especially Hispanics and American Indians. She observed that women too had a hard time with such a cultural climate.

In May 1992, Giraldo was sensing more organizational conflict, especially the brewing revolt of the faculty senate. The latter was annoyed by the apparent arrogance and increasing power of the central administration and its lack of consultation in initiating the corporate-style Mandate and total quality management. "Things happen quick here with Jim and Gil running the place, and there's no consultation." Giraldo debated the editor of the *Michigan Review* on the topic of affirmative action and surmised that, like everywhere else, "white males didn't realize how privileged they have been."

Giraldo's sharp perceptions and critical candor did not endear her to Duderstadt and his inner circle. "She did not fit in," one of them later confirmed. Whatever these interpersonal frictions, Giraldo's apparently fatal error was publicly and prematurely to include concerns of gays and lesbians on the multicultural agenda. The university had been quietly cooperative and supportive of gays and lesbians but, like many corporations, leery of reaction by both the right and the left. Conservative regent Deane Baker was vehemently opposed to such concerns, and ethnic minorities resented the inclusion of gays and lesbians as an oppressed class.

As seen in Chapter 5, gay and lesbian cultural differences are a potential time bomb in diversity discussions, and that was also true at the University of Michigan. In my research I found gay and lesbian issues were totally ignored unless I asked about them—and then the topic was usually briskly dismissed. "The gay and lesbian issue is an embarrassment to anyone who is not gay or lesbian," declared an African American pharmacology graduate student. The vice provost for academic and multicultural affairs, Lester Monts, carefully distanced himself from the issue: "I deal with the four basic ethnic groups— and gender."

Giraldo first stirred controversy on gay and lesbian topics in 1991 when she coauthored a public relations memo with public relations officer Walt Harrison emphasizing proper etiquette and nomenclature for gays and their companions. Demonstrations by ACT-UP that same year led to a study commissioned by Giraldo on gay and lesbian concerns. The completed study, dubbed "The Lavender Report," received no response from Duderstadt when it was sent to his office. When Giraldo subsequently released the report, it caused a minor uproar with two of the regents. When I interviewed a high-level university official in the spring of 1992 and mentioned Giraldo's name, I was sharply informed that "Zaida Giraldo does not speak for this university!"

Officially Giraldo resigned in May 1992. In reality, it was forced. In the latest corporate style, an outplacement officer was waiting for her when she left the president's office, and she was asked not to return to her own. She quickly found another position in the California State University system and was somewhat vindicated by subsequent events. The year after her departure, the regents voted to include sexual orientation in its nondiscrimination bylaws, and in 1994 the library system agreed to lending privileges for "spouses and significant others." In his 1995 political tract, *Diversity at Michigan* James Duderstadt included sexual orientation in his expanded definition of diversity.

PC or Reality?

By the mid-1990s, I saw more dramatically at Michigan what I was seeing everywhere—among diversity consultants, the L.A. Sheriff's Department, and in the California Community Colleges. The two-factor race and gender categorization of reality was too simplistic to be taken seriously for very long. More complex realities and inconvenient facts were recognized and discussed privately. As in the California Community Colleges, the clumsy, shifting affirmative action ethnic categories were proving inept, unwieldy, and fraudulent. By 1996 when I asked about apparent removal of Cubans from the Hispanic category, I was greeted with nervous laughter of embarrassment.

My final interview question regarded the possibility that other variables (class, age, region, religion) influenced social life as much as or more than race and gender. But many U-M subjects often began criticizing race and gender–restricted thinking before I ever raised the issue. Regent Shirley McFee complained that racial and gender classifications "treated everyone within those categories alike." Liberal faculty and students were most likely to raise social class as a key, perhaps *the* defining variable at Michigan. "The real issue is social class," declared a former social work dean and now special counsel to the president, Harold Johnson. When asked, even James Duderstadt acknowledged that "the students are class driven, not race driven." But Duderstadt saw race and class as intertwined and disagreed with remarks by faculty and regents that Michigan's minorities were mostly upper middle class. Friction between minority and majority students, Duderstadt felt, stemmed from their respectively segregated, homogeneous communities and environments where they'd not had to interact with other cultural groups. Hence there was a problem with resegregation on campus, although Duderstadt maintained that Michigan was not as fractured as some Ivy League campuses.

Publicly, however, race and gender PC inhibited critical thinking and analysis, the primary mission of the university. As Timur Kuran has demonstrated, with special regard to affirmative action policies, PC opened a chasm between public speech and private thought.[16] In the wake of the Goldberg case, Michigan Ph.D. and former sociologist-lecturer Mark Schneider (now at another institution) took note of Michigan's new "campus climate" with regard to discussing ethnicity in the classroom: "If you don't have anything nice to say, don't say it." (Michigan's vice provost for academic and multicultural affairs took note of this situation in a 1996 discussion; problems about hot classroom topics such as racial aspects of crime, welfare, and diversity in music were being considered in a new program on multicultural teaching and learning at the Center for Research on Learning and Teaching.)

Ironically, the Michigan Mandate never defined a key term clearly and consistently: multiculturalism. Most of those interviewed were initially stymied by one of my opening questions about how to define multiculturalism. Many recited Mandate-style diversity jargon about inclusion and valuing differences. In practice, multiculturalism on the Michigan campus usually was reduced to black-white issues. "That's where the pain has been," admitted associate graduate dean Elaine Didier. Even those who mentioned Hispanics or Asians often drifted back to black-white issues.

Critics were usually more concise. "Multiculturalism is a smokescreen," stated Leo McNamara. "No, that implies purpose. They're not sure what they're doing. 'Fog' is a better term, I think. Of course, what they want to imply is that all cultures are equal. Not true." He was not a fan of the Mandate: "The Mandate does not command intellectual respect and the source of authority isn't clear." He rejected the call to cultural relativism and for proportional representation. "Why should any institution necessarily reflect percentages of the population?"

"We equate diversity with skin color," admitted the associate dean of literature, science and the arts, John Cross. "We play these silly games." Just how cynical this game could get was illustrated in the promotion process of anthropology professor Ruth Behar, a person of mixed ethnic heritage. She was classified as Hispanic only when it benefited the university. "Officials first classified me as Latina because of my Cuban roots, then withdrew the identification because of my Jewish roots, and finally designed me as a Latina again when they granted me tenure."[17] Not surprisingly, several administrators, such as presidential assistant Shirley Clarkson, preferred that multiculturalism be left undefined.

The Dissonance, the Drama

The conflict between PC's ideological orthodoxy and the real world could generate enormous emotion and anxiety. The associate dean of business administration, Paul Danos, worked through these tensions as we talked in May 1993: "This political correctness is very pervasive. I think people don't want to deal with something controversial where you're damned if you do, damned if you don't. People are afraid. It's out of good will. There's a certain attitude, which I think is healthy, that certain types of descriptive facts won't be helpful in a societal sense." I asked Danos about the worth of doing research on affirmative action programs. At that time, I did not know about the university's strongly disproportionate distribution of financial aid to minorities. Danos likely did. Therefore, the question itself was threatening:

> I think you've got to look at history wide enough. If you open that door wide enough, affirmative action is not discrimination, it's just righting past wrongs. You've got to be logical about this. It's a name game, a damn name game and if you don't have enough wisdom to understand history, a person shouldn't be in a leadership position. . . . If you can't open the window wide enough and say oh, these people don't deserve this, they can't meet these damn standards that we've set up—then you shouldn't be a leadership position—everybody can read the damn numbers. We just do the best we can. We know that we lay opportunities. We provide education that leads to leadership. Damn it, we

have a point of view. If people want to sue us about it, let them sue us. We are open, we are affirmative, that's it.   .

I suggested the dilemma of presenting data on racial disparities in crime rates to criminology classes. Danos responded with more passion: "Open that historical window wide enough. I lived in the South. You can have all the statistics in the world. Who knows what happens when you put people under that kind of strain—four hundred years—who's wise enough to know?" David Goldberg's attempt to show how other variables reduced the earnings gap between men and women was also deemed dangerous: "You have to put it in context. That can be used for eliminating, for saying that we don't have to do anything special, that women get just as fair a shake [as men]. You go in that locker room, you go on that golf course, if you don't think women don't have a problem."

Yet as the interview progressed, Danos began to consider vigorously the importance of other major sociological variables such as class, age, personality, and appearance in determining individual success. He became especially excited about the role of personality and, secondarily, manner and appearance: "You know, you practically never see an overweight executive any more; it's taken as an outward sign of lack of discipline."[18]

Powerful party lines on race and gender could be particularly stressful for accomplished minority administrators. E. Royster Harper, dean of students, an African American with a Michigan Ph.D. in education, was especially articulate and eloquent. During a fall 1991 interview, she was generally progressive and a supporter of the Mandate's goals but noticed a distinct downside to the new emphasis on race and ethnicity.

> It used to be easier—when issues weren't framed around race and gender. Now there are increasing divisions around color. It's usually right below the surface. Who's committed and who isn't? There's constant checking, loyalty tests. There's no room for variation within or across groups. Consistency doesn't work any more.
>
> Everyone's trying to be sensitive. You wonder: Can I say "dumb stuff" and can it still be okay? Will I still be able to count on you? It undermines trust. We have to give each other permission not to be "careful." It's ironic: the very thing we're trying to do—appreciate how different we are—and I can't be different!

The new racial salience, Harper sensed, sometimes appeared to compromise her occupational status and professional credentials in the eyes of her peers and in the views of minority students:

The strength I should bring to the table as a colleague gets compromised. White colleagues see me as a representative of minority students. I'm just an older version of them. White colleagues don't allow my education and experience to frame their perception of my behavior and that thinking part of me. What they might expect of each other they don't expect of me.

On the other hand, minority students sometimes expected Harper to join them in demonstrations against the university. The new ethnic solidarity, Harper felt, had sometimes led activist faculty and staff to impute a "false maturity" to twenty-year-olds who had not worked through the same problems as people twice their age.

Another potential problem with polarization around race and gender issues involved faculty review and promotion processes. One anonymous source indicated to university officials that the racially charged climate of the university had "lowered the level of discourse" and that charges of racism and sexism could radically decrease the number of faculty willing to serve on promotion and review committees.

Although white male resentment was rising, few faculty, students, or staff mentioned evidence of open revolt. Former sociology lecturer Mark Schneider noted a sense of grievance developing among undergraduates over rumors about Michigan's "disproportionate by design" system of financial aid. Ethnic divisions were more apparent on the graduate level. The disproportionate distribution of Rackham Merit four-year fellowships to minority students created an embarrassing, highly obvious ethnic split: blacks and non-Cuban Hispanics tended to be on fellowships, while whites worked as teaching and research assistants. Several administrators and graduate students reported that minorities were thus inadvertently cut out of the informal socializing that often took place around the teaching assistant offices. There were reports that minority graduate fellows were hesitant to apply for teaching positions because that was the primary or only support for white graduate students. (Department chairs were also mindful of the situation.) Worse, lavishing four-year fellowships on blacks and Hispanics undermined cherished Mandate goals: to provide minority undergraduates with minority role models in the classroom and to expose white undergraduates to views of minority teachers.

Balkanization by specialty and discipline was a quiet worry for some faculty and administrators. Michigan mirrored national trends that were changing very slowly: minorities and women were still overrepresented in the humanities and social sciences; white males and Asians populated the sciences and engineering. There were similar splits within fields. For example, though the trend was not absolute, white males in the social sciences veered toward more quantitative specialties, while women and minorities were more likely to take up women's and minority studies. On the other hand, associate business school dean Paul Danos felt that ethnic and gender differences in specialization were moderating in those fields.

Aside from the freshman orientation diversity seminar, training for dormitory resident advisers, and the diversity programs at the medical center, there were few efforts at mandatory diversity training, and voluntary workshops were sometimes scorned by those who went to them. Bob Weisbuch was appalled at the stereotypes inadvertently put forth at a 1991 diversity training seminar for faculty. Sociologist-geographer Don Deskins attempted to please a colleague by going to another training session; he displeased the workshop leader by pointing out that at the end of the day, people still sat in segregated groups. Dean of students E. Royster Harper had been somewhat satisfied with a workshop led by consultant Frances Kendall, but she was also skeptical: "A lot of the workshops don't get below the surface. They tend to dissolve into white male bashing, or 'poor us' or 'if only you would . . . ' The drama may be more exciting than the work of it. That's where we are: the drama."

Rising External Criticism and a "Voice in the Wilderness"

The cultural and structural strains engendered by the Mandate developed in an institution increasingly defensive, stunned and angered by a rising national tide of criticism and negative court decisions directed against the "thought police" of political correctness. "Jim didn't anticipate this level of resistance," said a social science chair.

The first major controversies involved a student speech code implemented by James Duderstadt's predecessor, Harold Shapiro. Officially defined as the policy on Discrimination and Discriminatory Harassment, it provided sanctions for students who engaged in "any behavior, verbal or physical that stigmatizes or victimizes an individual on the basis of race, ethnicity religion, sex, sexual orientation, creed, national origin, ancestry, age, marital status, handicap, or Vietnam-era veteran status."[19] The American Civil Liberties Union brought suit, and a federal court decision against the code in 1989 contained a stinging rebuke that the university "had no idea what the limits of the policy were and it was essentially making up the rules as it went along."

Within two years, several magazines featured cover stories on PC, which were immediately followed by Dinesh D'Souza's unflattering portrait of Michigan and several other elite universities in *Illiberal Education*. Worse, radio host Rush Limbaugh's popularity was soaring, and late-night television comedians began to join him in mocking PC. The 1992 L.A. riots, the outbreak of ethnic slaughters in other lands, and Louis Farrakhan's antisemitism flashed new danger signals for multicultural tinkering. Then came the 1994 Republican congressional landslide, the rejection of race and gender quotas by the University of California Regents, the California Civil Rights Initiative and a similar bill in the Michigan legislature and, finally, the federal Fifth Circuit Court of Appeals decisive decision against ethnic and gender preferences by the University of Texas Law School in April 1996.

Initially U-M administrators lightly waved off criticism as the creation of extremists, if not racists. This was harder to do as the cultural and political climate on PC and affirmative action changed. A mood of wariness and defensiveness grew. Whether attempts to label critics as right-wing extremists were simply a McCarthyite debating tactic or whether such labeling reflected perceptions of the world seen through U-M's left-wing ideological lens was difficult to determine.

In the fall of 1991, presidential assistant Shirley Clarkson scoffed that protests about PC and reverse discrimination were concerns of "extremists." That same year, Bob Forman, president of the Alumni Association, quietly suggested to me that the attack on PC was, to some extent, a cover for racism. The first conference designed to rebut the "PC" label, "The PC Frame-Up," was held in Ann Arbor a year later. (Few dissenters were on the roster, though *Heterodoxy* editor David Horowitz challenged panelists from the audience.) At Ann Arbor and elsewhere, attacks on PC were portrayed as an irrational, biased "backlash" against affirmative action and minority and female gains.

Resistance meant diversity efforts must be redoubled. Multicultural themes proliferated in university and alumni-oriented publications. Whatever the damage in public relations, the attacks on PC likely stayed the course of Duderstadt and his administrators. By most accounts, Mandate-sponsored programs were spared from general budget tightening wrought in the aftermath of the early 1990s recession.[20]

Yet the twin forces of recession and political opposition were sowing increasing doubts about speech codes and preferential programs. The largest minority internship program, the Undergraduate Research Opportunity Program (UROP), was opened to whites in 1993. The university dropped a second speech code in 1992 after the U.S. Supreme Court struck down a Minnesota law restricting alleged hate speech. A proposed classroom speech harassment policy was abruptly withdrawn in the fall of 1993. And the October 21, 1993, regents' meeting featured a forum, "A Thoughtful Discussion of Political Correctness and Academic Values." According to local press accounts, the theme was still defensive and well left of center; the case of David Goldberg went publicly unmentioned. The knee-jerk response of "racist" was dropped, though closely related smears were not.

James Duderstadt reacted strongly to both the California regents' decision to drop ethnic and gender preferences and to the circuit court's decision against the University of Texas Law School. In a damn-the-appellate-court response to the latter, he told the *Chronicle of Higher Education:* "We will continue to do this until the Supreme Court says we can't any more. . . . If certain avenues are shut off, we'll try to find other ways to get the same results."[21] University officials testified against the preference-banning bill in the Michigan legislature. But Michigan philosophy professor Carl Cohen testified in favor of the measure.

Cohen had authored a stream of articles critical of affirmative action, culminating in a 1995 book, *Naked Racial Preference.*[22] The former chair of both the local and state branches of the American Civil Liberties Union then went further. Using the Michigan Freedom of Information Act, he obtained internal data on the University of Michigan's admissions processes. He published the results in a June 1996 *Commentary* article, "Race, Lies, and Hopwood." Based on the data he'd obtained, Cohen argued that race and ethnicity had become a decisive factor in admission. On a 108-cell grid defined vertically by "former school GPA" and a horizontal "best test score," the university tabulated applications and offers; separate grids were prepared for all students and a separate, though identical, grid for minority students. Cohen compared them:

> In the UM profile of 1994 (the latest available) the minority-admission rate was higher than the nonminority-admission rate in almost every cell in which there were any minority applicants at all, and in many cells the rate was *very* much higher. Thus, for applicants with GPA's between 2.80 and 2.99 (B-) and SAT scores between 1200 and 1290 (out of 1600) the nonminority-admission rate was 12 percent and the minority rate 100 percent. For applicants whose GPA was between 3.40 and 3.60 (B+), and whose SAT scores were 900—990, the nonminority rate was 13 percent and the minority rate was 98 percent. For applicants with GPA's between 3.60 and 3.79 (A-) and SAT scores 800—890, the nonminority rate was 12 percent and the minority rate was 100 percent. And so on. Similar patterns are disclosed by the reports of the University of Michigan's law and medical schools.[23]

Cohen indicated in an interview that where race seemed especially decisive was in situations where an applicant's high grades were not accompanied by equally high test scores—or vice versa. Cohen's results appeared similar to Michael Lynch's study of the University of California, Berkeley, admissions grid. Like Cohen, Lynch found that ethnicity could be a decisive factor at all but the very top and bottom range of grades and test scores.[24] (Indeed, in 1988, Michigan had hired Berkeley's admissions director, Richard Shaw, famed for increasing the number of underrepresented minorities and who, in the words of the *Detroit Free Press*, "creates, and sometimes even manipulates the criteria for admission to the university."[25] Shaw's reputation as an admissions magician spread to Yale, which spirited him away from Michigan in 1992.)

The response to Cohen on the Michigan campus was one of quiet dismay and contempt. Lester Monts was distressed by Cohen's portrait of "what we're trying to do." The response from Walt Harrison, vice president and head of the university's public relations department, was to reiterate the university's mantra that ethnicity was "a criterion" in admissions, not *the* criterion. He did not take issue with Cohen's data and had little else to say except to sniff, "I don't pay much attention to Carl Cohen." Another high-level administrator simply exclaimed, "Oh, God!" when I asked her about Cohen's article.

James Duderstadt's response to Cohen's research unveiled much more than he realized about the university's cultural climate. Asked about Cohen during a remarkably relaxed and amiable telephone conversation in June 1996, Duderstadt chuckled good-naturedly and acknowledged he'd known Cohen a long time, that he was a member of the faculty and could say what he liked. But the president characterized Cohen as "a voice in the wilderness" on campus. (A local journalist concurred. So did Cohen himself, though he claimed some privately voiced support.) Duderstadt then added that Cohen was playing to "off-campus audiences that have never accepted them [affirmative action programs] and now finds it acceptable to speak out against them. . . . He does play to, uh, Michigan has a very strong Christian right movement and pushes a number of agendas on the far right and opposition to affirmative action is one, though only one, among many. . . . They're a powerful voice in an election year."

Duderstadt's statements were revealing in two respects. First, in admitting that Cohen was alone in his highly logical and reasonable dissent from a controversial public policy, the president undermined his own and others' assertions that PC was a phony issue. Cohen's views against ethnic preferences were supported by a large majority of the American population; by late 1995, a vigorous debate on affirmative action was building in the wider society. Therefore, why didn't Cohen have some degree of support on the Michigan campus? Obviously PC pressures created a spiral of silence and pressures to support policies publicly that a substantial number of U-M personnel may have privately doubted or rejected. (Indeed, my interviews uncovered doubts about the programs most of the time.)

The reasons for this public self-censorship, in part, lay in the second half of Duderstadt's characterization of Cohen: people who criticized affirmative action would be tarred as catering to (probably bigoted) right-wing fundamentalists. I knew there was no truth to this in California or on the national level. When I spoke to the *Detroit News* reporter assigned to Lansing, Chris Christoff, he was dumbfounded that anyone would try to tie the Christian right with efforts to repeal ethnic and gender preferences. So was the Republican staff attorney, Tom Hallock, as well as a younger legislative assistant, who quickly saw the likely effects (if not intent) in Duderstadt's remarks: "On the Michigan campus, linking anyone with the Christian right is like calling them a Nazi." (As we shall see, this was not the first occasion when the university's president would associate critics of multiculturalism and affirmative action with the disreputable right.)

Backsliding into Affirmative Action's Numbers Wars

For all the money, bravado, and twisting of the law, the Michigan Mandate and its one hundred multicultural programs have produced only incremental gains and—to the horror of the administration—some recent declines in black graduate student, faculty, and staff representation. Increasing numbers of students of color come mainly from increasing numbers of Asians, now the largest "minority" among faculty, students, and staff.

Annual updates of the Mandate chronicled incremental increases and some stagnation in recruitment of minorities, especially blacks. By 1995 blacks were 8.9 percent of the undergraduate population (up from about 6 percent in 1988). Hispanic enrollment had moved up from under 2 percent in 1987 to 4.7 percent in 1995. The percentage of Asian American undergraduate enrollment nearly doubled, from 6 to 11.2 percent. The six-year graduation rate had risen for blacks to 70 percent graduated within six years compared to 87 percent of whites and Asians and 73 percent for Hispanics.[26]

Graduate school enrollment of African Americans declined from a high in 1990 of just over 8 percent to 7.3 percent in 1995. Asian enrollment rose from just over 6 percent in 1990 to 8.7 percent in 1995. Hispanic enrollment moved from just over 3 percent in 1990 to 4.8 percent in 1995, while Native American enrollment remained under 1 percent. Black and overall minority enrollments rose from late 1980s levels but began to plateau in the mid-1990s. The medical school had an enrollment of 10 percent black, and 39 percent of the entering class were students of color. The School of Business Administration brought African American participation in its full-time M.B.A. program up to 11 percent; 28 percent were students of color (slight declines from 1993, when 15 percent of the entering class were African American and 36 percent were of color). Twenty-one percent of the law school's entering class were students of color in both 1993 and 1994.

The percentage of minority tenure-track faculty improved incrementally in spite of filling one hundred Target of Opportunity positions. In 1987, African Americans were just under 3 percent of the faculty, and by 1995 they were approximately 4.9 percent; for Hispanics the corresponding figures were 0.9 and 1.9 percent; Asians went from 4.9 to 7.3 percent. Gains might have been stronger, but the university also lost minority faculty. In 1991, for example, fourteen African American faculty were hired, but seven left; in 1992, thirteen were hired, but six left. Nearly every administrator cited competitive bidding wars for talented minority faculty as a primary factor in those losses. One dean also cited Ann Arbor's semirural suburban location and largely white population.

As for professional and administrative staff, 1994 data indicated an increase of professional and administrative staff of color from 449 to 816. Duderstadt bemoaned a three-year decline in the percentage of African Americans, though he noted the number of blacks in senior management rose from 23 in 1987 to 53 in 1994; the number of Hispanics rose from 2 to 11; the number of Asians rose from 3 to 10. For all professional and administrative staff, the percentage of blacks rose from about 5.3 percent to 6.2 percent, Asian staff rose from 5 to nearly 7.5 percent, and the Hispanic staff percentage remained relatively constant at 1.3 percent.

A 1994 faculty senate subcommittee report disputed even these meager gains. Perhaps the most damning finding of the subcommittee's report was that a significant portion of tenure-track faculty of color were noncitizens: 56.1 percent of Asians, 23.3 percent of Hispanics, and 18.8 percent of blacks. (This finding confirmed long-standing rumors in academic circles that foreign nationals were being used to bolster affirmative action statistics.) The senate committee also found that nearly 80 percent of tenure-track black faculty who were at Michigan in 1982–1983 had disappeared; most of the remaining black females are still assistant professors. Compared to general population figures, blacks and Hispanics are heavily underrepresented, while Asian faculty are nearly triple their proportion in the population.

University provost Gilbert Whitaker dodged the embarrassing evidence on noncitizen minorities but systematically demolished much of the senate report in a series of press releases. The senate subcommittee, he noted, made the commonplace, politically correct argument that the proportion of minority faculty should mirror their proportion in the general population; the provost noted that the proper comparison was to the appropriately skilled labor pools—the proportion of minorities with Ph.D.s. The subcommittee report also understated the number of new minority faculty by stating their number as a percentage of the total faculty, ignoring that the total number of faculty also grew. The report also documented very general patterns of ethnic and gender pay discrimination, but the provost pointed out that important market-driven factors were omitted, such as specialty area. (Faculty in finance command higher salaries than those in women's studies.) As for minority faculty losses, the provost delicately hinted at the notorious bidding wars for minority faculty by observing that many may have been hired away.[27] Whitaker then applied the *coup de grace*: the faculty, not the administration, were the primary gatekeepers when it comes to retention and promotion. Why, then, were the faculty complaining about the administration?

This exchange did not reduce administration-faculty tensions.

Reassessment and the Recognition of Complexity

Concern with misunderstandings and the unintended consequences of the Mandate became publicly apparent in the opening pages of *Moving Forward*, the 1992 five-year assessment of the Mandate. The introductory "Conversation with the President" addressed the troublesome topics of diversity's suspected fad status, discrimination and the affirmative action stigma, separatism and segregation, polarization, and problems of cohesion and community.

Duderstadt countered diversity-as-fad charges by noting that women, minorities, and immigrants constitute 90 percent of labor force growth in the 1990s; he failed to note that white males and females will still constitute nearly three-fourths of all workers in 2000. The president also reached for the long-term prediction that during the twenty-first century "a majority of young people born in the United States will have parents not of European descent." Responding to a quotation from social work professor Edith Lewis that minorities are marginalized because of the stigma of preferential treatment, the president offered a bromide: "We cannot undo the past, but we can ensure that all who come here are regarded equally and with respect."

Duderstadt briskly tackled problems of separatism, polarization, and the need for shared values. His answers hummed with the tones of the diversity machine:

> Stressing "unity" has often in the past meant "let's all be the same." We must create a community where people's differences are valued. . . . We must recognize our differences at the same time that we celebrate our common bonds. The old paradigm of assimilation simply will not work anymore. . . . Over time our evolution should yield a co-mingling of groups, a common community that is still a place where people are allowed to retain their cultural roots and maintain their differences. This is a difficult concept.

Indeed, separatism was a danger.

> I am concerned that the perception of separation can become an excuse for splintering. I worry about the continuing ethnic violence in Eastern Europe and here at home. Ethnocentrism is a specter that has haunted our world for centuries, leading to war, injustice, and civil conflicts; and it can create tremendous tension on our campuses.

Absent from the vision of the "good community" in various versions of the Mandate was any reference to presumably outmoded concepts of Western culture: equality of opportunity, freedom of speech or association, capitalism, due process, individualism and individual rights, equal protection of the laws, the U.S. Constitution, and universal standards or truths. There is no explicit acknowledgment that Western law and culture, dynamically defined, have been and might continue to be the best foundation for a diverse society. Nor was there any mention of these ideals in the following year's report. Perhaps some of these values were implied, but Duderstadt grew testy when I asked him in late 1993 about why there were few references to equal opportunity in the Mandate. Was the concept being replaced by proportional representation, diversity, and change? The U-M president evidently felt that the obsolete concepts of equal protection and equal opportunity were best consigned to the dust bin of right-wing talk radio:

> I have never felt that equal opportunity and affirmative action have been particularly successful. It allows you to shift the responsibility to someone else. I think that the copout of the seventies was to respond to the great civil rights movement of the 1960s with bureaucracy, to pass laws and to set up organizations, affirmative action offices, equal opportunity offices and then say that's their program. We'll get on with life. And what that allowed the institution to do was to go along with the way things had always been.

[Equal opportunity and universalistic standards] are nice political ideas and they have very little relevance to what happens on a modern campus or in modern social institutions. I have very little patience and even less interest in those kinds of arguments. We'll let Rush Limbaugh and others fight about that.

Duderstadt's *Diversity at the University of Michigan,* published in the spring of 1995, linked the university's nineteenth-century efforts to provide an "uncommon education for the common man" to the "journey from this early ambition to real diversity at Michigan." He revved up rhetoric against the rising popular revolt against ethnic and gender preferences: "Our slow but continuous advancement has come from the efforts of thousands of courageous individuals and groups who followed a vision of equality in the face of great opposition."

Much of *Diversity at the University of Michigan* chronicled when Michigan first admitted blacks, women, and Asians. Their advancement, however, had been hindered by institutional racism and sexism, "a University (and national) culture still largely dictated by a white, male majority. Clearly, more was necessary. The University would have to change dramatically if it were to remain faithful to its heritage." Duderstadt did follow emerging diversity management trends and officially expanded the range of diversity beyond race and gender to age, nationality, religious belief, sexual orientation, political beliefs, economic background, and geographical background. The supporter of student speech codes hailed universities as, more than any other institutions, "striving toward a vision of tolerance and freedom."

The Committee on a Multicultural University immediately blessed the report and recommended mass distribution. COMU also issued a series of more practical recommendations concerning unintended developments of the Mandate. They found that wily department chairs were routing their "persons of color" hires through the Target of Opportunity Program (funded by the central administration) while recruiting whites for regular department-funded positions through open searches—and recommended that the practice be abated.[28] They also recommended cluster hiring of several scholars in a core academic area. In May 1996, COMU finally faced the ethnic segregation of graduate students created by the disproportionate distribution of Rackham Merit Fellowships to blacks and non-Cuban Hispanics.[29] (A source within the administration indicated that remedial action on this imbalance might have been taken sooner but for the possible interpretation by minorities that the university was caving into the changing external political climate.) COMU also recommended that the university develop "early warning systems" for students who might be encountering academic difficulties, create better exit interview processes to understand why students leave the university, and develop support systems and improved environments for students of color. Greater emphasis on recruitment was proposed for increasing staff diversity with greater emphasis on administrative accountability. By 1996, a new handbook, *Managing for Success: Strategies for Retaining Valued Staff Members,* was being readied to help chairs and hiring supervisors "understand the value of a multicultural workforce and their role in creating an environment where all staff can be successful."[30]

The university had exported multiculturalism to the wider society, and the techniques of diversity management had come back to the university.

Mandated Peace in Our Time: The Multiversity Moves On

On a recent brief trip to southeastern Michigan, I had little time to visit U-M except for a quick stroll on the main campus one moonlight night after eleven o'clock. Though the spring semester had ended, the central campus was aglow in new outdoor lighting and remarkably alive with human activity. Undergraduate and graduate students were walking, biking, or skateboarding about. The libraries were open and appeared in good use. About a third to a fourth of the seats in the relatively new Angell-Mason Hall computer center were taken. While others strolled by, perhaps a dozen students sat talking or relaxing alone on the campus square ("Diag"). A few couples sat on the grass. Graduate students or young faculty passed between the natural sciences and chemistry buildings, where some labs were brightly lit. An empty bus for North Campus waited nearby. There was ample evidence of daylight construction activity: Angell Hall was undergoing a facelift, and the landmark engineering arch was closed for reconstruction. And I noticed that there seemed to be more minority students around than in years past. The numbers had slightly changed, but the basic look and feel of the place was much the same.

When asked about the primary accomplishments of the Mandate, nearly everyone immediately mentioned the increased presence of women and minorities. When asked to name other achievements, many respondents had to think hard. One political scientist was more direct: "I can't think of any."

English professor Leo McNamara contended there was no necessary relationship between demography and culture: "There are more diverse bodies here, but the culture is still the same." Others passionately disagreed, but they were in the minority. Bob Weisbuch definitely felt the intellectual life of the university had been enriched. Jane Thorsen, assistant dean for faculty affairs at the medical school, thought the changing numbers "created a visible presence." Changing the people, she felt, changed the culture.

Some students and faculty mentioned curricular changes. New courses on women and ethnic minorities were added in several departments. Students entering in 1991 were required to take a course dealing with race and ethnicity issues, which could be met by selecting one of many fairly standard university offerings approved by the arts and sciences curriculum committee. ("The only groups in favor of required courses are those who don't have to take them," snorted Leo McNamara.) Minority, women's, and gay and lesbian support groups proliferated for students, faculty, staff, and alumni. One department chair mentioned that the university seemed more "family friendly" and willing to recognize that male and female faculty had family responsibilities as well as professional ones.

Despite the one hundred multicultural programs, Michigan's diversity management model remained assimilationist—the type R. Roosevelt Thomas recently bemoaned in *Redefining Diversity.* Despite all manner of programs, the institution's upper-middle-class, individualist, competitive, achievement-oriented culture remained strong. Minorities were heavily recruited, only to "sink or swim," as pharmacologist Peggy Hollingsworth had charged. "There's still not a critical mass for change," said associate graduate dean Elaine Didier in June 1996.

Nearly everyone interviewed for this study agreed that James Duderstadt had achieved an explicit Mandate aim: to raise ethnic and gender issues and generate discussion. "The Mandate is a challenge," said regent Shirley McFee. "We're getting things out on the table and talking about them." The problem was that such discussions were extremely constrained. Even silence in such contexts was not necessarily safe. "People take slight very easily. You can get labeled here without opening your mouth," complained Aline Soulas, director of U-M business school's Kresge Library.

The multicultural, egalitarian rhetoric still flows from the Fleming Administration Building, but the vast multiversity rumbles on pretty much as various deans and chairs would like. Indeed, the university appears to be in relatively handsome shape in terms of its finances and physical plant. In some ways, the stewardship of James Duderstadt has been a very good thing. In other ways, it has not.

The Mandate's Legal Shadowland

One of the most alarming findings throughout this book was found in intensified form at Michigan: few of those I interviewed in Ann Arbor knew or cared what legal concepts were risked in the Mandate's multicultural initiatives. Officially, Michigan is a public institution subject to the Fourteenth Amendment's equal protection clause, the basis of several recent challenges to affirmative action plans. Yet during many long interviews and reinterviews, no one raised legal issues until I did (in a question toward the end of the interview schedule). Asked if the university's programs were legal, most said quite innocently (as Bob Weisbuch did), "I don't know" or "I hope so."

Like James Duderstadt, many subjects turned cagey, or at least squeamish, at any hint of the inherent contradiction between the Mandate's drive for greater proportional representation of groups and legal guarantees of equal treatment for individuals. But given the scarce numbers of highly qualified blacks in Michigan (and the low numbers of Mexican Americans and Puerto Ricans within the state), most of those interviewed at least dimly sensed that boosting the numbers of minority students inevitably meant using different standards for different groups, subverting laws regarding equal protection and equal treatment. In terms of the relatively few blacks and Hispanics with Ph.D.s, especially in the hard sciences, the same supply-and-demand dilemma held true for faculty recruitment and retention. "I look at how far an individual has come from where he started," offered Bob Weisbuch by way of rationalization.

The university's casual, cynical attitude toward the law by "making up the rules as it goes along" (in the words of the judge who ruled the first speech code unconstitutional) bothered practically no one I interviewed except Deane Baker, a conservative regent and long the lone, outspoken critic of the Mandate, along with liberal faculty members Carl Cohen and Peggy Hollingsworth.

"We've checked with our legal department; we're covered," James Duderstadt crisply assured me in 1993. An associate dean and member of COMU stated firmly, "We're on the path we want to be on." Threats of possible *Bakke*-type reverse discrimination lawsuits mattered not. "We're not changing our policies because of that." Another associate dean responded to equal protection concerns: "Fairness has nothing to do with it. It simply depends on the social goals of institutions." He was unconcerned about the legality of Target of Opportunity Program but admitted, "I think we're in trouble on financial aid." A few other high university officials were equally cavalier. "I don't want to be quoted as saying 'the law is bullshit,'" began one high-level U-M official in explaining his view of the legal system's flexibility.

These sentiments are the most dangerous and least appealing legacy of the Mandate and its crusade for race and gender equity. As the legitimacy and effectiveness of thirty years of ethnic and gender preferences continue to collapse—and as more manipulation, abuse, and fraud are exposed—the much-recited Mandate rationalization, "It's the right thing to do," is acquiring the hollow, exculpatory ring of "I was only following orders."

Ultimately the Mandate's means undermined one of its cherished goals: the desire to link ethnic diversity with academic excellence. Though unevenly felt throughout the vast multiversity, the Mandate generally produced an atmosphere of ends-justify-the-means cynicism, duplicity and double talk, censorship, and intimidation. Such forces are the bane of intergroup trust, productivity, and creativity, much less the search for knowledge and scientific truths.

Many U-M faculty and administrators suggested that such PC pressures were overblown or the result of "cleansing conflict." Indeed, I was pleasantly surprised at how many persons I've interviewed and reinterviewed over the years who were willing to speak candidly and on the record; but there were also many others who were very guarded, and occasionally hostile. Some, of course, would not speak at all.[31]

Nevertheless, most students and faculty darkly noted that "you can't talk about these things in a public forum," as former dean Peter Steiner said. The articulate and reasonable Carl Cohen remains a campus "voice in the wilderness." At a minimum, to repeat E. Royster Harper's observation, members of the U-M community feel constrained "to give one another permission not to 'be careful.'" As elsewhere, the celebration of group differences inhibits the expression of individual differences within the group.

The Future of the Michigan Mandate

In September 1995, James Duderstadt shocked the university by suddenly submitting his resignation, effective July 1996. In November 1995, he wrote his final seven-year update on the Mandate. The "Message from the President" was a restatement of the Mandate's rationale and only slightly defensive in tone. Duderstadt was pleased to report that the university had become a national leader "in building the kind of diverse learning community necessary to serve an increasingly diverse society." The allegedly "irrelevant" concepts of "equal opportunity" and "freedom from discrimination" were revived for a final statement on the Mandate rationale:

> Sometimes people ask why the University has made this commitment to change, why diversity is the cornerstone of our efforts to achieve national excellence and leadership during the 1990s. Fundamentally, it is the morally right thing to do. Plurality, equal opportunity, and freedom from discrimination are

the foundations upon which the University is built. In an often painfully divided society, America's universities must act as leading engines of progress in our long struggle toward true equality.

But Duderstadt warned of "external forces"—challenges to affirmative action in California, Washington, D.C., and "even in our own state"—that might affect further progress.

Duderstadt's resignation and legislative or court actions against ethnic and gender preferences are among the most serious dangers to the Mandate. African American chemist Homer Neal has assumed an interim presidency. The regents have emphasized interest in multiculturalism as a criterion in selecting a new president; regent Rebecca McGowan reportedly has been especially keen on maintaining multicultural momentum.

Three looming organizational conflicts may eclipse the Mandate further: possible competition in focus and funding from a new Michigan Agenda for Women, debates over faculty governance, and the advent of a new business-style decentralized budgeting system.

First, there is the new Michigan Agenda for Women launched with some fanfare by James Duderstadt in 1995. Like the Mandate, the Agenda is designed to promote institutional change to value gender differences—and spur retention and promotion of female faculty, staff, and students. The Agenda is anchored in a flotilla of new institutions and programs: the Center for the Education of Women; a new Institute for Research on Women and Gender that annually distributes forty career development awards (at $5,000 each) for female faculty; the undergraduate WISE (Women in Science and Education) residential program; since 1992, a central-administration-funded SHARE (Senior Hiring and Recruitment Effort) program permitting departments to upgrade thirty-one junior-level faculty openings for women faculty to senior-level appointments; a three-year study of Women of Color in the Academy by the President's Advisory Commission on Women's Issues and COMU; flexible work schedules; consideration of mandatory workplace training on women's issues; and increased "efforts to educate men about the inequities women face."[32] As in the wider society, factions may develop within or between activist groups; feminist and racial agendas may collide rather than coincide; tensions could arise merely over competitive foci or be augmented additionally by a new budgeting system that could foment as much competition as cooperation.

Second, the heretofore hidden costs of diversity initiatives may emerge more fully under a new value-centered-management budget system, to be implemented in the 1996–97 academic year. Though Michigan may have learned from other organizations' use of such systems, the initial break-in period is not likely to be without wrenching organizational changes and conflict. Weisbuch and others initially feared the new corporate-style system would further increase decentralization and market-driven competition, leaving behind the quest for cultural change. While such anxieties have declined, the units and programs that push multiculturalism are, in James Duderstadt's own words, "costs"; they generate little of their own revenue in tuition or research dollars and must be supported through the central administration and indirectly through a "tax" on other units.

Third, there is the continuing antagonism toward any autocratic programs from central administration and controversies over "shared governance"—an ongoing tug of war at Michigan and other research universities. By its origin and implementation, the Mandate symbolizes growing centralization of power and funds at Michigan—and the diminution of faculty authority. Although many faculty at Michigan probably support the general goals of the Mandate, there is growing resentment about lack of consultation on this and other matters. Indeed, James Duderstadt acknowledged in a 1996 interview that the Mandate had become too closely tied to his presidency. The Mandate's impact across the university had been uneven; it had been especially ignored or resisted at the crucial middle levels of power (deans and chairs).

As in general diversity management movement, the original causes behind the University of Michigan's diversity crusades—the demographic forecasts of imminent majority minorities and race relations crises—are fading. The dire demographic projections used to justify the Mandate's proportional vision are increasingly dismissed as overblown and premature, even by diversity consultants. (As early as 1990, Harvard historian Stephan Thernstrom cautioned that "the majority-minority will never come."[33] By 1995, even New York University radical sociologist Todd Gitlin acknowledged that ideologically hyped predictions of an immanent rainbow majority were political pipe dreams.)[34]

The absence of major racial crises at Michigan, coupled with the less-than-spectacular results of recruitment of African Americans, have quelled both the Mandate's urgency and can-do optimism. In 1994, the new associate dean for the graduate school, Mandate champion Bob Weisbuch, attributed this relative campus peace to the Mandate: "The Mandate worked." James Duderstadt concurred.

Perhaps. But the relative campus peace also may have had more to do with the changing external political environment and the rising storm over PC and ethnic and gender preferences. In addition, there may be on-campus waning of what Berkeley sociologist Neil Smelser has termed the "politics of ambivalence." The increasing numbers of new minorities on campuses, Smelser argued, have experienced ambivalence over taking up the new culture of the university while leaving behind a real or imagined ethnic identity—hence the calls for multiculturalism, ethnic centers, and the demands for courses on ethnic culture, history, psychology, and so forth.[35] Whether such a transition period will result in permanent academic ghettos grafted onto the side of the mainstream university remains to be seen.

By 1994, Weisbuch and others sadly noted a "stall," a pause, and a reassessment. Departments that did not or could not harvest extra positions through the Target of Opportunity Program were complaining and "reasserting their inertia" grumbled Weisbuch. As Peter Steiner had predicted, administrators were beginning to wrestle with the problem in finding permanent financial support for unanticipated departmental growth caused by the TOP initiative.

Like diversity management policies imposed elsewhere, the Michigan Mandate has turned out to be neither a fad nor a major management trend. It promoted some changes but not Great Change. It has been neither satanic nor angelic. It fostered greater ethnic and gender awareness with the coin of political intolerance and censorship. Using admissions and hiring shell games, the Mandate warmly encouraged inclusion of some ethnic groups while coldly excluding others. It created a somewhat more multiethnic campus largely by attracting more Asian students, faculty, and staff; it has only marginally increased the number of African Americans; and the fast-paced, individualistic, aggressive, competitive upper-middle-class "white male" culture remains much the same. Faculty pursue their grants and publications; the students, their grades; the staff copes with new management and budget schemes as well as downsizing anxieties.

As in the California Community Colleges, two-factor race and gender mandates are increasingly recognized as simplistic and obsolete. Broader diversity concerns are being folded into the organizational mix of needs and priorities. Mandate excesses may continue for a time but, once exposed, will likely be worn down by the changing external political, legal, and cultural environment. Impulses for ethnic and gender engineering may also be checked by a general funding squeeze caused by an environment where "arguments about higher education's public benefits have lost their force."[36] PC excesses have damaged higher education's claim to public support, and Michigan has earned its share of public criticism and ridicule. (Some humor has been good-natured, such as Garrison Keillor's politically correct rendition of "The Victors.")[37]

Ultimately the Michigan Mandate and other race and gender formulas for changing "white male workplaces" are doomed unless it is seen that such job settings are affected by class, personality, labor markets, technology, and a host of other differences. Indeed, many white males are often unhappy and do not do well in allegedly "white male" institutions. Institutions striving to be the best in highly competitive environments for human capital and economic resources—be it the University of Michigan or the *Washington Post* (examined in the next chapter)—are social systems with their own rules and demands regardless of race or gender. They become what sociologists call "greedy institutions." Especially in capitalist systems, organizations demand all an individual has to offer, and then some. There are benefits and costs to all this. But individual and collective cultural conditioning have much to do with how well some individuals and groups adapt to such intense and organizational demanding cultures—and why others cannot or may not wish to do so.

Chapter 10

The Diversity Machine

Transformed, Transforming—and Waiting

The social policy machine that sought to transform the "white male workplace" to accommodate increasing numbers of culturally different women and minorities is itself being reshaped by rapid cultural, political, and economic changes. From its scattered, experimental origins in the 1970s and early 1980s, valuing diversity and managing diversity policies have flowered into a vast variety of theoretical schools and techniques.

This new social policy movement has nominal roots in America's noble quest to cope with an ignoble heritage of racism, sexism, and gross economic inequality. Organizational life in the United States has indeed been riddled with informal norms and understandings that have operated to exclude certain classes of people. Insofar as institutional policies violate nondiscrimination laws and principles, some diversity studies and reforms have been well advised. However corrupted they have become, diversity management and its half-parent, affirmative action, have had some positive, practical consequences. The policies have forced many institutions to reexamine formal and informal rules and procedures. "Gray flannel suit" conformity has been needless and oppressive in all too many corporate settings, and career and time schedules have not been family friendly. Testing criteria and job descriptions have been reconsidered, and sloppy or informal "good old boys" recruiting has been checked, at least somewhat. Perhaps mechanistic concepts of merit were due for challenge and rethinking. And diversity management advocates sounded a useful wake-up call in terms of the nation's demographic future: indeed, we are being forced to reconsider the very definition of what is a nation.

But the ambitious organizational change masters astride the diversity machine have far more in mind than limited reforms. They are extending affirmative action's top-down hiring campaign into a broader multicultural revolution in the American workplace and beyond. Both the ends and the means of this policy movement pose a substantial threat to the values of the generic liberalism enshrined in modern American law and culture: free speech; individualism; nondiscrimination on the basis of ethnicity, gender, or religion; equality of opportunity; equal treatment under universalistic laws, standards, and procedures; democratic process; and, above all, a sense of national unity and cohesion embodied in the spirit of *E Pluribus Unum*.

While diversity practices have been tempered by time and changing realities, their ideology continues to mold and stimulate sociological and cultural forces in the workplace and beyond. Lingering emphasis on race and gender reinforces a simplistic, two-factor, ethnic-gender focus in public discourse and policy formulation. Only recently have the machine and its allies encountered public debate and limited journalistic and social science scrutiny. Organized political opposition still sputters and stalls at both national and local levels.

The agenda of proportional fairness based on ethnic and gender cultural differences has acquired very deep structural roots—and strong support in high places. As Dinesh D'Souza, Richard Bernstein, and many others have aptly noted, multiculturalism and more radical PC egalitarian censorship first gained ground among elites in major religious, educational, philanthropic, and media-entertainment institutions. It spread quickly into teachers' unions, such as the giant National Education Association and higher education's American Council on Education. The large liberal foundations (especially the Ford, Carnegie, and MacArthur foundations and the Pew Charitable Trusts) have been instrumental in advancing the multicultural agenda in civic and community affairs, the arts, and education. As David Samuels noted in the *New Republic,* "the ideologically-driven pursuit of 'diversity' and 'inclusiveness' is perhaps the one area in which today's foundations are influencing public policy with anything like the force of their powerful predecessors of the '50s and '60s."[1]

In many universities, foundations, and government agencies, then, diversity dogma may be "in with the bricks." Although prolonged budgetary pressures may have dampened diversity drives, real rollbacks will be difficult; there are too many true believers in "equity, inclusion, access, diversity" who now have organizational clout. And they have been training others for a very long time; hence, the diversity machine's ideology of proportionalism, identity politics, and cultural relativism has spread from university curricula, to news and information services, jury selection, legislative redistricting, mortgage lending, and personnel policies in public and private sector employment.

The crucial new arena in the drive to transform Western values is the allegedly monocultural "white male workplace." When the cause of an older, backward-looking, black-white model of affirmative action began to sputter in the 1980s, savvy consultant-theoreticians fused multiculturalism with new demographic forecasts and threatened "glass ceiling" regulations to reformulate a forward-looking policy rationale for the 1990s. This new vision linking demographic change with multiculturalism energized an emerging core base of internal organizational advocates and external consultants who built a policy movement, a diversity machine. They have successfully promoted varying blends of social science and ideology through conventions, newsletters, a growing professional literature, and, more recently, mainline professional associations. Aided by powerful allies from corporate boardrooms, to major foundation directors, to White House administrators trying to build a government that "looks like America," diversity policy architects have not fully institutionalized their programs, but they have moved beyond faddish "flavor-of-the-month" status. Conceded Republican theoretician James Pinkerton in a recent *Fortune* magazine article: "Multiculturalism, as an economic and aesthetic value, seems to be permanently embedded in U.S. corporate culture."[2]

According to star author-consultant R. Roosevelt Thomas, Jr., the key question addressed by diversity management is, "How do I manage people who are not like me?" Standard white male management allegedly does not value the unique cultural competencies that women and minorities possess. Diversity management offers the paradox of seeking to remove group-based inequalities by institutionalizing collectivist countermeasures: culturally adjusted, unequal treatment ("fair treatment") and "managerial accountability" (evaluations and rewards based on proportional hiring and promotion). Formal rules and testing procedures are not merely reconsidered; they may be manipulated to attain proportional results.

The civil rights movement's original aspirations to color-blindness and its admonition to treat people equally "without regard to race, color, or creed" are regarded as laughable and delusionary in diversity circles. Like the multicultural theories nurtured in the universities (and critical race theory in law schools) diversity management proponents debunk assimilation into American liberalism as a mask for white male "one-size-fits-all" domination. Marx's class struggle between the bourgeoisie and the proletariat has been converted to identity politics' cultural war between white males and everyone else. But the alleged "monoculturalism" of the "white male workplace" has been an ill-defined concept.

One has to consider carefully the claims of many women, ethnic minorities, and well-credentialed diversity consultants who argue that there is a dominant white male culture in the workplace, especially when compared to values, norms, and behavioral styles of other groups. Asked in August 1996 to describe white male culture, Los Angeles diversity consultant Pam Fomalont readily echoed diversity management lore and literature, defining white male culture as "very goal-oriented, future-oriented, very competitive, intensely individualistic, work-centered, oriented to objective goals and measurements, affectively neutral, competitive, and they assume that the best man wins." More than anything else, felt Fomalont, white male culture lacks empathy. White males, especially the young, lack the capacity to put themselves in others' shoes. When I suggested that lack of empathy might be a trait of men in general, Fomalont countered that she saw such insensitivity in terms of taken-for-granted white privilege. The culture of Asian males, she admitted, resembles that of white males in many ways, though she felt Asian men retain more emphasis on tradition, family, and group harmony. Individuals or groups who do not fit into this cultural canopy may experience intentional and unintentional exclusion.

Yet the portrait of a modern workplace dominated by white male culture blurs when one observes that many of the cultural traits and interpersonal styles identified with white males are also those of wider cultural and social systems that transcend particular groups and individuals. As sociologists have long recognized, cultures and organizations take on a life of their own; social systems may modify and generate their own values and norms. Specifically, the cultures of both capitalism and formal bureaucracy emphasize rationality, efficiency, goal setting, careful measurement, impersonal rules, and emotional control. Characterizations of white male culture are also carelessly blended with cultural elements of the Judeo-Christian ethic in general and the work-driven Protestant ethic in particular. What is often critiqued as "white male culture" is nearly identical to the work-driven, ambitious, highly individualistic values and norms of the upwardly mobile middle classes found in many nations throughout the world. The "monocultural" label belies the incredible variations within the white male category by age, education, region, religion, occupation, and a bewildering variety of ethnic subgroups (Norwegian, Irish, English, Dutch, German, French, Italian, Polish, Greek, the various Russian subgroups, and so on). Finally, many workplaces have seen the forced exodus of millions of white males during the downsizing and reengineering waves of the 1980s and 1990s, yet their departure has been insignificant in changing workplace culture when compared to the forces of technological innovation, globalism, and new management trends.

Within these changing workplaces, diversity management policies will be further winnowed and tested in shifting job and consumer markets. Although complex and somewhat fluid, some cultural differences do exist and are made more pressing, at least temporarily, in cities with high numbers of Third World immigrants. In such areas, there is a case to be made for competent, well-trained cross-cultural educators who try to sensitize managers and workers to group-based cultural differences in order to comprehend each other or their customers better. Done properly, such cross-cultural education has potential benefits in terms of marketing research, customer service, and employee relations, especially for organizations involved in global markets.[3]

Short workshops offer a measure of protection against lawsuits and adverse government regulatory action by showing "good-faith efforts" toward overcoming discrimination, but more elaborate diversity management programs have not yet proved their bottom-line value. While some CEOs—if specifically asked—may offer testimony that diversity policies have been useful, there is little systematic proof that the programs reduce intergroup tensions and increase productivity or creativity.

The business case has yet to be established for more expansive, expensive organizational-change forms of diversity management. These more ideologically charged efforts to reform institutional racism and sexism have been more successful as a social movement than as a business-driven strategy. This can be seen in the diversity machine's response to political and societal challenges.

Mounting legal and political threats to affirmative action have redoubled the efforts of many consultants devoted to social justice and civil rights moralism. Trumpet calls for "righting past wrongs" blare more loudly than ever. Business-oriented pragmatists, such as R. Roosevelt Thomas, Jr., have renewed their support of affirmative action but have also quickened their resolve to broaden the scope of diversity policies and to prove that diversity policies improve the organizational bottom lines, reducing intergroup tensions while increasing productivity and creativity. Until such proof is at hand, newer diversity management programs will remain confused with older affirmative action controversies.

Both American society and the diversity policy movement have arrived at a crucial crossroads: will we continue efforts at race and gender engineering?

The November election results suggest that we will, though there will be planned and unanticipated changes within the diversity machine, the workplace, and society.

Growing Pains, Failed Prophecies, and the Diversity Paradox

Within the diversity machine, theoretical trends are clearly moving away from the simplistic race and gender focus toward more complex formulas. Some of this internal redefinition may have been for strategic, marketing purposes—largely in response to external attacks on radical multiculturalism, white male revolt, new trends toward globally oriented diversity, and competition from other managerial trends. Yet the turnaround is also genuine. There is a growing awareness among savvy consultants and clients that real and alleged problems of "white male workplaces" may have little to do with white males. There may still be elements of racism and sexism in contemporary organizations, but there is quiet recognition that modern workplaces are structured primarily by more impersonal, general, systemic forces: competitive capitalism and class-based cultures, globalization, demographic changes, management trends and styles, bureaucratic inflexibility, technological and organizational innovation, and globalization of markets. The risk of expanding the range of diversity issues, however, is losing coherent professional and policy identity. "What does diversity mean?" grumbled the *Wall Street Journal's* "Business and Race" columnist, Leon E. Wynter: "That's hard to pin down, except for what it isn't . . . i.e., it's not affirmative action. . . . Diversity means almost everybody."[4]

Growth in consultant numbers and ballooning policy boundaries have compounded this identity crisis and generated concerns about quality control. By 1994, *Training Magazine's* business editor, Bob Filipczak, observed that, based on training expenditures, "as a training topic, 'diversity' has spread like wildfire in the '90s . . . a 40 percent increase since 1992."[5] But he also warned, "It is also one of the most controversial training topics to gain a serious foothold in the corporate world. . . . Diversity is, to put it bluntly, a snake pit. And it keeps getting deeper all the time as more and more issues fall under its umbrella."[6] Cautioned Shari Caudron: "Ineffective training can raise the expectations of women and minorities, increase the fear and resistance among white males and harm an organization's diversity efforts."[7] Thus, the rapid spread of diversity has remained somewhat formal and superficial, "stuck in the training mode" of half- or full-day workshops. Except in a relative handful of large corporations, universities, and government agencies, grander diversity culture change designs remain on the drawing board—for now.

Yet the diversity machine is highly resilient. Those active in the fledgling field are trying to shore up quality control problems caused by the proliferation of too many hastily trained consultants flooding into a hot field; others have tried to correct the policy credibility problems caused by exaggerated demographic projections.

Though hard to measure, the surge in the number of consultants appears to have peaked. The number of consultants in the American Society for Training and Development's *Buyer's Guide and Consultant Directory* mushroomed from just fifteen in 1990 to eighty-five by 1992, but by 1996, the figure had drifted down to seventy-three. Quality control is also being addressed by credentialing programs offered by professional societies such as the Society for Human Resource Management.

The chief rationale for diversity management was that demographic change and looming labor shortages mandated cultural alterations to achieve workforces that mirrored customer bases. But this argument is now regarded as simplistic or premature even by movement faithful. Within California and other domestic demographic laboratories, a spontaneous ethnic enclave economy is emerging that is largely irrelevant to large-scale diversity management programs. Joel Kotkin has recognized that "in the Los Angeles region, there has been a proliferation of new ethnic-owned businesses, many of which tend to hire within their own ethnic groups. Whether Asian, Latino, Middle Eastern or from the former Soviet Union, the firms are among the fastest-growing job producers. In many respects, these new entrepreneurs have created a multicultural economy without the heavy hand of government or the courts."[8]

In other areas of the nation, *Workforce 2000* forecasts strain credibility; some U.S. Census Bureau projections suggest that only 25 percent of the nation's population will be nonwhite by the year 2040.[9] Even radical sociologist Todd Gitlin admits that no one knows how those in the bureaucratically created category of "Hispanic" will be regarded, or so regard themselves, sixty years hence.[10] Large areas of the nation remain relatively untouched by immigration. Although *Wall Street Journal* reporter Jonathan Kaufman recently found pockets of immigrants popping up in small cities in the midwestern farm belt, author-consultant Anita Rowe admitted, "The changes aren't happening outside of California, New York, and a few other areas."[11] Yet the old typographical error from *Workforce 2000* that only 15 percent of new workforce entrants will be white males lives on; it surfaced once again in the lead paragraph of a cover story, "Managing Diversity," in *Management Review,* the official journal of the American Management Association.[12] (Again, the figure should properly read "net new workers"—meaning those white males who will be hired *in addition to* those replacing other white males; the total number of new white male workforce entrants is more like 32.5 percent of all the newly hired.)

A third problem, which has not been solved by leading diversity authors and consultants, is the diversity paradox: the collision of the consultant mantra to talk about differences with the taboo against discussing ethnic stereotypes. Those who utilize a culture-specific or archetype approach—such as consultants Lewis Griggs, Tom Kochman, and Ronald Brown—have been caught in the diversity paradox. Part of the problem is that diversity training formats do not allow sufficient time to qualify general observations about ethnic cultures with more specific references to class, immigration cohort, and religion. There is also a relative dearth of social science research about such ethnically based cultural styles: no one is anxious to discover or verify unflattering group cultural traits. (There have been notable casualties. In the 1960s, Edward Banfield was pilloried for his portrait of urban, lower-class culture in his book *The Unheavenly City.* Most recently, Dinesh D'Souza set off a storm of controversy with his discussion of "black culture" in his massive study, *The End of Racism.*)[13]

Yet there is much truth in consultant Sondra Thiederman's slogan, "Just because we are equal does not mean we're the same." Contrary to the views of tough-minded businesspersons and conservatives who deride "soft" human resources and cultural issues, the interpersonal barriers and tensions addressed by diversity management can be quite real; left unattended, such tensions and conflicts can fester, undermining morale and productivity. Ethnic, gender, class, and other forms of discrimination do exist, but they are complicated by a host of other economic, sociological, and historical factors. For example, an individual is not only a Hispanic, middle-class male; he may also be young, a third-generation Mexican-American who grew up in California, a well-educated, ambitious, well-disciplined, highly-motivated, handsome, man with a pleasing personality and a knack for being at the right place at the right time. Conversely, another middle-class Hispanic male may be an older, second-generation Puerto Rican living in New York City, relatively uneducated, fearful of relocating lest he lose family and friendship contacts; he may be less physically attractive, have an inflexible, shy, introverted personality, with low-tech, blue-collar skills at a time when such abilities are not marketable. Likewise, organizations vary in size, structure, economic fortune, and the winds of management trends. In short, social and organizational realities are complex; policy remedies must be carefully crafted lest they increase conflict and ill will rather than soothing such tensions.

As R. Roosevelt Thomas, Jr., is quick to point out, a diverse workforce is not an asset per se, but awareness and deft management of a broad range of cultural differences among workers and customers can produce more informed decision making. For example, a recent *Wall Street Journal* case study indicated that increased cultural sensitivity might have prevented MCI Communications from making a costly mistake in moving its "brain trust" systems engineering unit to Colorado Springs from Washington, D.C. in 1991. According to the *Journal,* many minority and liberal employees were put off by Colorado Springs's less cosmopolitan, more homogeneous, "Wonder Bread" cultural climate; significant numbers quit before or after making the move; tensions arose between MCI transfers and locally hired workers who were religious fundamentalists; and creativity and productivity slowed as a result of the more relaxed regional work tempo. The relocated unit became increasingly isolated, as did the executive who engineered the move.[14]

While the case for cultural awareness in the changing workplace is strong, the future of more extensive diversity management efforts will be determined by political, sociological, and legal trends, as well as rapid changes in workplace organization, technology, and shifts in labor market conditions.

The Diversity Machine and the Changing Workplace

The grim workplace prophecies made by Apple Computer's Kevin Sullivan to the 1991 First Annual Diversity Conference have merged with Thomas Nagle's warnings of demographic and economic polarization to the 1993 California Community Colleges Chancellor's Conference. Variations of those predictions are today standard fare in countless business journals.

The lingering effects of the recession, restructuring, downsizing, outsourcing, the shift of jobs overseas, and the rise of part-time and temporary workers threatens to create a two-tiered, hourglass labor force, with a minority of educated, well-paid, technically skilled "knowledge workers" and a much larger, low-paid insecure proletariat.

The 1990s constitute a "Brave New Darwinian Workplace," warned *Fortune*'s Stratford Sherman. A "social transformation as massive and wrenching as the industrial revolution is negating old notions of advancement and loyalty. . . . People ages 50 to 60, though still energetic, are being passed over, pushed out, or shot with the silver bullet of early retirement."[15] Harvard economist James Medhoff noted that a 1993 Supreme Court decision cleared the way for corporations to take seniority and high pay into account when firing employees—without violating the federal Age Discrimination in Employment Act. As a result, Medhoff's research found that educated, middle-aged men (most of them white) were severely hurt by the 1990s recession.[16] In March 1993, a *Wall Street Journal* special series, "Down the Up Staircase," analyzed the grim results of reengineering ("Re-Engineering Gives Firms New Efficiency, Workers the Pink Slip"), part-time and contract labor ("Workers Are Forced to Take More Jobs with Few Benefits"), and shipment of white-collar jobs overseas ("Like Factory Workers, Professionals Face Loss of Jobs to Foreigners").[17] By 1995, *Wall Street Journal* reporter Fred Bleakley found that more middle-aged middle managers were unemployed for longer periods. In 1996, *Wall Street Journal* reporter Bernard Wysocki, Jr., studied some of the "million missing men" in their prime working years who, in the space of a year, disappeared from both jobs and unemployment rolls, evidence of a long-term labor force participation decline among men. Wysocki found substantial numbers were former managerial or white-collar workers loath to shift careers or accept substantially less pay.[18] Although there were many predictions that downsizing and layoffs would soon cease, the trend continued, and the June 1996 cover report on *Personnel Journal* was "Save Jobs: Strategies to Stop the Layoffs."

A no-frills, anxious workplace culture has been furthered by the rising proportion of temporary and contract workers. The temporary placement firm, Manpower Incorporated, is now the nation's largest employer; in Texas, low-wage Wal-mart has eclipsed Southwestern Bell as the largest private sector employer. *Time*'s "Temping of America" cover story mourned the arrival of the "disposable worker" and predicted a rise in the part-time workforce from the current 25 percent to 50 percent at the turn of the century.[19] *Fortune*'s report, "The Contingency Workforce," scoffed at such projections but admitted that a "growing army of temps" had risen from about half a million in 1980 to almost a 1.7 million by 1993.[20] Employer savings were substantial: "U.S. employers saved $800 million in 1992 by substituting contingent for full-time employees, out of a total $2.6 billion in payroll costs," noted an article in a magazine for pension fund investors.[21]

Economic insecurity has become a dominant global and national concern. "The lack of decently compensated jobs under decent working conditions is a global deficit so vast as to require fundamental rethinking about the global economic system itself," groaned *Harper's* Richard J. Barnet in "The End of Jobs."[22] Edward Luttwak noted the role that the new insecurity played in the 1994 U.S. elections:

> The problem in question is the unprecedented sense of personal economic insecurity that has suddenly become the central phenomenon of life in America, not only for the notoriously endangered species of corporate middle managers, prime targets of today's fashionable "downsizing" and "reengineering" but for virtually all working Americans except tenured civil servants.[23]

William Bridges, writing about "The End of the Job" in *Fortune,* was more sanguine. The job, he argued, was an artificial construct invented 200 years ago with the advent of mass production industrialism: "Today's organization is rapidly being transformed from a structure built out of jobs into a field of work needing to be done. The postjob organization will cultivate three competitive advantages: competence, coordination, and commitment. Project teams will be common."[24] But will cultural differences be valued? Will employers change their organizational cultures to attract, retain, and promote more women and minorities?

Changing workplaces and markets have generated a two-edged reality for diversity consultants. Most important, predictions of labor shortages have been undercut by increasing automation, downsizing, and the ability of employers to transfer even sophisticated white-collar work overseas. These developments have dimmed the diversity machine's scenario that employers will have to cater to scarce labor markets and more culturally different employees. Millions of middle-aged whites have been dumped onto the job markets. Although labor markets are beginning to tighten in some areas of the nation, conditions still dictate a buyers' market for most employers. The ability of job seekers or current employees to bargain for salaries or fringe benefits, much less cultural concessions, remains constricted. Indeed, employees anxious about losing jobs may not feel free to utilize or appeal to diversity policies on the books. *Wall Street Journal* work and family expert Sue Shellenbarger has found that employees, especially women, fear jeopardizing job or career opportunities by taking family leave time in workplaces that provide such policies. Another of her findings, with implications for more general diversity policies, is that "chief executives make pronouncements, companies issue new rules—and the managers on the front line ignore them."[25] SHRM's public relations director, Barry Lawrence, was even more sobered by the changing business and political climate. Clients are saying,

"Diversity is fine, but I'm concerned with shareholder value." People are disappointed that there wasn't something "more substantive" to all this.

On the other hand, downsizing and reengineering did far more to thin the ranks of white males in middle management than diversity programs likely did. In the aftermath, "What's left is more diverse," observed Julie O'Mara, echoing similar comments by Tom Kochman and Anthony Ipsaro.[26] The move to interpersonal teams does open up possibilities for diversity consultants skilled also in team building and conflict resolution. As we shall shortly see, however, the primary source for extensive managing-diversity programs is likely to remain in the political and legal realms.

Women and Work: Reappraisals of Life Priorities?

Andrew Hacker recently observed that women have been displacing men in several fields because, among other possible reasons, on average, they may still be less expensive to hire.[27] Yet there is also some evidence that women may be reappraising full-time work and careers and rebalancing work and family commitments. After climbing for three decades, the labor force participation rates for women have leveled off at 60 percent.[28] Enrollment of women in graduate schools of business has also stabilized or declined slightly.[29] Articles have appeared indicating that a combination of societal and psychological pressures may be leading both younger and older women to consider rebalancing work-family/personal life tensions in favor of the latter.[30] Although fiercely debated by feminists, part of this phenomenon may be the passage into typical midlife crisis years of the massive baby boom generation, the first generation in which careerist women tried to have it all: home, family, and high-pressure careers. Although both men and women may yearn to drop out of the rat race, cultural and social pressures are far more forgiving—even encouraging—for women who do so, as opposed to men. The fall of mortgage rates and the recent wave of mortgage refinancing may be reducing pressures for households to maintain two full-time workers. According to Richard F. Hokenson, economist-demographer for the Wall Street stock brokerage firm of Donaldson, Lufkin and Jenrette:

> What's driving the exit of young women from the work force is the reality that for an average woman who works, if she has children, 80 percent of her income goes to support her job. . . . I think until 1990, before the mortgage refinancing boom, women really didn't have a choice. You needed both incomes to service the mortgage. And it's the mortgage refinancing boom that allowed

some women . . . a choice and there are roughly two to three million women who have elected to do that.[31]

Although not that many women may exit the workforce altogether, they may feel freer to choose more flexible, alternative career paths, such as part-time or self-employment. Such reassessment of life priorities by working women might make calls for cultural overhauls of the workplace less compelling and urgent.

Diversity Management and Business Literature: Don't Ask, Don't Tell

If workforce diversity is a crucial business issue and management trend, one would expect it to be mentioned prominently and frequently in reports on new management trends and the changing workplace. It is not. The *Wall Street Journal*'s Fred Bleakley did not mention diversity management in a long article on major management trends and fads.[32] When asked why, he gave me an answer I heard from several other business reporters: "Nobody brought it up." (Evidently this was the reason that no attention was paid to the extensive diversity management systems engineered by R. Roosevelt Thomas, Jr., at Avon Products in a long 1994 profile of the company also published in the *Wall Street Journal*.)[33]

In profiles of organizations or CEOs known for their commitment to diversity programs, unless the subject is raised by researchers or interviews, the topic slides by unremarked. This suggests that, at best, diversity management remains a minor trend, or, in the words of *Cultural Diversity at Work* editor Barbara Deane: "There's still a lot of window dressing going on."[34]

Diversity management was rarely or never mentioned in the above-mentioned articles on workplace trends or in several other major articles on management trends, such as *Fortune*'s 1993 major cover story, "Managing in the Era of Change."[35] Indeed, *Fortune* has been relatively mute on the topic. Several articles on management trends or dissatisfied workers ignored diversity concerns; although several members of its list of "America's Most Admired Companies" were often associated with major managing diversity efforts (Coca-Cola, Procter and Gamble, Johnson and Johnson, Merck, and Motorola), diversity was never once mentioned. A glossy series, "Winning Companies, Winning Strategies," published by the magazine made no mention of diversity management whatsoever. The magazine finally published an article on a major multicultural sensitivity effort at Flagstar, parent company of the lawsuit-beleaguered Denny's Restaurant chain—just after the *Wall Street Journal* published a similar story.[36]

Another popular business magazine, *Businessweek,* has offered diversity-related cover stories on affirmative action and another on "White, Male, and Worried." But in stories on general management or major work trends, diversity topics all but disappeared.[37] The huge *Businessweek* cover story "Rethinking Work" in late 1994 had less than a perfunctory paragraph on diversity management.[38] Nor did the magazine mention the topic in a mid-1992 cover story, "Management's New Gurus," or—even more incredibly—in a July 1994 cover story, "The Craze for Consultants."[39]

The flagship *Harvard Business Review* sponsored a symposium on diversity strategies a year after R. Roosevelt Thomas's 1990 article on diversity management. Although there were many subsequent article titles that invited mention of the topic, the journal became largely silent on diversity management until a new article appeared in the September–October 1996 issue.

Many of the popular business books and articles (such as those by Tom Peters or Peter Drucker) fail to mention race and gender, much less affirmative action or diversity management. (In spite of a doubly suggestive title, "Service with Soul," a 1995 Tom Peters PBS special on customer service discussed teamwork, empowerment, and other trends but did not once mention diversity training or management, even in a segment on the Chicago Police Department, beset with problems over affirmative action.)[40] Although her earlier major work was on *Men and Women of the Corporation,* Rosabeth Moss Kanter et al.'s *The Challenge of Organizational Change* made practically no mention of affirmative action, race, gender, or diversity.[41] Even the highly humorous, best-selling critique of the American workplace, Scott Adams's *The Dilbert Principle,* failed to mention diversity programs, though he did offer this wry observation on the highly related topic of consultant change agents:

Consultant: So are you planning to change anything?

Manager: Well . . . yea, I suppose.

Consultant: Do you have a change management plan in place?

Manager: What's that?

Consultant: You're doomed!!! Give me money, quick![42]

California-sensitive James Flanigan, well-known business columnist for the *Los Angeles Times,* has rarely mentioned workforce diversity and, during a telephone interview in early 1995, admitted he knew little about it. (He later wrote a column about affirmative action—in response to the looming California civil rights initiative—but nothing on diversity management per se.)

Explicit diversity concerns did not register in an American Society for Training and Development survey on "four top qualities an employer wants in employees": (1) the ability to learn, (2) the ability to listen and convey information, (3) the ability to solve problems in innovative ways, and (4) knowledge of how to get things done. Diversity management is absent from many surveys of the "best companies," such as James Collins and Jerry I. Porras's *Built to Last: Successful Habits of Visionary Companies,* as well as *Time* magazine's list of "leading management trends" adopted by successful "progressive" corporations.[43]

Diversity management authors have tried to link their programs to total quality management and team building, but experts in those areas have rarely returned such overtures.

A long technical report commissioned by the California Public Employees' Retirement System did not include workforce diversity programs as an indicator of a "high performance workplace."[44] Indeed, there wasn't a single reference to any books or articles on diversity. (In some respects, it was just as well. The authors offered less than enthusiastic judgments about the ability to detect measurable gains from implementing "progressive management" trends: "it is highly unlikely that any research on workplace practices will find a robust relationship between the existence of such practices and market-based measures of performance.")[45]

Although several professional, business-oriented associations have recently climbed aboard the diversity machine, the topic seems to remain compartmentalized. Time and time again, diversity management is omitted from dozens of seminars and conferences in which it might logically be included. With the possible exception of a work and family conference, the Conference Board's "Conference Calendar and Planning Guide" for the first half of 1995 listed five programs under the category "Total Quality Management," twenty under "Human Resources and Organizational Effectiveness," and four under "Business and Society." But there wasn't a word about race, gender, or diversity.[46] Nor was the topic of diversity addressed in the American Management Association's *Catalog of Seminars* for August 1995–April 1996 or October 1996–June 1997.

If labor markets tighten, however, a greater emphasis on human resources management, including diversity programs, may result. Although the pace of layoffs at big corporations has not slackened, several experts have suggested that such trends have already run their course—or will end very soon.[47] Spot labor shortages (varying by occupational sector and region) are appearing.[48] There is growing talk about the downsizing binges producing "corporate anorexia" and concern about "hollowing out" of corporations, in the words of Stephen Roach, chief economist with Morgan Stanley Company. Though opposed to government-mandated dictates on long-term human resources efforts, the Wall Street adviser warned that corporations should be more mindful "to build for the future"—or be prepared for powerful political backlashes if they did not.[49] Business columnist Robert J. Samuelson has noted themes of new books on the bottom-line value of loyalty and stable relationships with employees and customers.[50] (Lewis Griggs's chapters, videos, and CD-ROM on "Valuing Relationships" may yet have their day in the sun.)

However the workplace trends affect the bottom-line business case for diversity management fares, there remain other powerful forces favoring both affirmative action and diversity management. Federal bureaucracies and their large corporate clients have developed a fairly stable system of law and regulation regarding discrimination issues. Large organizations resist change. Furthermore, globalization of markets and possible ethnic-class polarization continue to reinforce the interests of elites in both cross-cultural training and ethnic and gender engineering.

Unlikely Allies: The Diversity Machine and Global Capitalism

It is one of the peculiar ironies of the late twentieth century that, in exporting multicultural policies from campus to workplace, left-wing diversity merchants have found an unlikely ally: global capitalism. International capitalism, as David Rieff has shrewdly observed, has become "multiculturalism's silent partner":

> Are the multiculturalists truly unaware of how closely their treasured catch-phrases—"cultural diversity," "difference," and the need to do away with boundaries—resemble the stock phrases of the modern corporation: "product diversification," "the global marketplace," and the "boundary-less company"?
> . . .
>
> The more one reads in academic multiculturalist journals and in business publications, the more one contrasts the speeches of CEO's and the speeches of noted multiculturalist academics, the more one is struck by the similarities in the way they view the world. . . . That non-white workers will be the key to the twenty-first-century American labor market is a given in most sensible long-range corporate plans. Like the multiculturalists, the business elite is similarly aware of the crucial role of women, and of the need to change the workplace in such a way as to make it more hospitable to them. More gener-

ally, both CEO's and Ph.D.'s insist more and more that it is no longer possible to speak in terms of the United States as some fixed sovereign entity. The world has moved on; capital and labor are mobile; and with each passing year national borders, not to speak of national identities, become less relevant either to consciousness or to commerce.[51]

Globalization has likely fostered greater acceptance of diversity ideology, especially cultural relativism, among America's internationally oriented elites. Both David Rieff and the late Christopher Lasch argued that globalism has already sapped commitment to the nation-state and Western values. Rieff scoffed that "no serious player in the business world has anything but the most vestigial or sentimental interest in Western civilization."[52] Cultural relativism is more congruent with mass-market-dictated tastes and fashion. Christopher Lasch went further, arguing that many among the American professional classes have absorbed a more militant multicultural stance toward Western ideas and institutions. The nation's globally oriented wealthy elites and its professional classes

> have lost faith in the values, or what remains of them, of the West. For many people, the very term "Western civilization" now calls to mind an organized system of domination designed to enforce conformity to bourgeois values and to keep the victims of patriarchal oppression—women, children, homosexuals, people of color—in a permanent state of subjection. . . .

> It is the working and lower middle classes, after all, who favor limits on abortion, cling to the two-parent family as a source of stability in a turbulent world, resist experiments with "alternate lifestyles" and harbor deep reservations about affirmative action and other ventures in large-scale social engineering. Today, it is the masses, not the elites, who possess the highly developed sense of limits that Ortega identified with civilization.[53]

Ideological concerns aside, however, common sense and the professional literature also strongly suggest that globalizing markets do present the most rational case for some forms of diversity management, especially cross-cultural training. Language, religious, and national cultural differences can be very pronounced and strongly influence customer and organizational behavior. One of the landmark studies in this area was a comprehensive study of intercultural differences among 116,000 IBM employees in forty nations conducted by Dutch social scientist Geert Hofstede. He discovered four major dimensions along which work-related values differed across national cultures. "Power distance" measures uncovered the extent to which unequal power relations were culturally acceptable; "individualism-collectivism" referred to varying cultural emphases on independence, individual initiative, and privacy versus values of group loyalty and "fitting in." (Hofstede found that societies such as the United States, Great Britain, and Australia were least comfortable with high levels of unequal power distribution and very individualistic. Several Latin American and Asian nations, on the other hand, were more collectivistic and accepted steep inequalities in power relationships.) The two other key dimensions were "masculinity/femininity," the degree of traditional sex role dominance and segregation versus sexual equality and fluidity of sex roles, and "long-term/short-term orientation." (Hofstede found that Scandinavian nations were most flexible in sex role definitions, while Japan, Austria, Mexico, and Venezuela were the most "masculine." Asian nations tended to emphasize long-term cultural traits of persistence, thrift, perseverance, and close attention to status differences; the United States, Canada, Great Britain, Zimbabwe, and Nigeria were more short-term oriented.)[54]

Many diversity consultants are becoming more oriented to issues of global diversity. The topic has become a leading theme at conventions and in the professional literature. Since 1994, nearly every issue of the bellwether *Cultural Diversity at Work* contains an article on international topics: "Can We Export Our Diversity Approach?" (January 1994), "Royal Bank: A Canadian Diversity Leader" (May 1994), "Working Groups in Denmark" (November 1994), "Diversity in Australia" (September 1995), "Diverse Teams: Can They Work Abroad?" (July 1995), "Diversity Nudges Canadian Business" (March 1996); and "Managing Diversity, Swiss Style" (May 1996).

In addition to providing yet another policy-selling strategy, the globalization of diversity issues will likely push the entire diversity machine further away from the civil rights moralists' preoccupation with race and gender issues. In an international context, other focuses such as differences in language, national cultures, and generational issues come to the fore; emphasis on race and gender is largely seen as confined to the United States. (On the other hand, consultant-author Julie O'Mara hinted to me in 1996 that the increased respectability of globalized diversity may provide social justice crusaders with a new vehicle through which they can pursue race and gender equity concerns.)

The Inertia of the Regulatory Regime

The byzantine system of affirmative action law and regulations has, for the most part, been implemented quietly behind the scenes by courts and federal and state bureaucracies. Lawsuits and adverse regulatory reviews by government agencies can be expensive and generate terrible publicity. Thus, over the years, major corporations and federal regulatory agencies (primarily the Equal Employment Opportunity Commission and the Labor Department's Office of Federal Contract Compliance Programs) have, through informal cooperation, sought to stabilize and routinize the system. The dominant concern of employers has been to minimize the unpredictability and capriciousness of a system that is capable of abuse, if not extortion.

In explaining "Why Affirmative Action Won't Die," James Pinkerton argued that the economic appeal of "presenting a multicultural face to the outside world" will combine with fear of discrimination lawsuits to maintain less aggressive forms of outreach and affirmative action. Even if preferential policies are repealed, enough federal and state nondiscrimination laws will remain on the books to provide careers for entrepreneurial civil rights attorneys. Pinkerton cited a recent *Fortune* poll indicating that "96 percent of CEOs would not change their affirmative action efforts even if all federal enforcement was abolished."[55] Indeed, some corporations are willing to go further. There still appears to be forward motion in corporations' efforts to tie managers' bonuses to retention and promotion of women and minorities. And some are openly using set-aside positions. "Firms Designate Some Openings for Women Only," reported the *Wall Street Journal*.[56]

James Walsh, author of a widely used handbook, *Mastering Diversity: Managing for Success Under ADA and Other Anti-Discrimination Laws*, contends that most employers, especially small and medium-sized businesspersons, look at affirmative action and diversity issues as a "risk-reward situation." Their main concern is to minimize the "downside risk" with courts and regulatory agencies by spending minimal amounts of time and money in making sure their personnel activities meet legal and regulatory standards. "It's seen as a cost of doing business—a compliance matter . . . think OSHA [Occupational Safety and Health Administration]." Employers have to consider not only the people they hire, but how they deal with the people they *don't* hire— in the event the latter file a discrimination complaint or sue.

Corporate CEOs are no doubt aware of the new enforcement tone of the Clinton administration, such as Gilbert Casellas, chair of the Equal Employment Opportunity Commission: "At the end of my term, if you get a call from EEOC, I want you to worry about it."[57] Deval Patrick, head of the U.S. Justice Department's Civil Rights Division, has signaled strong support for maintaining workforce diversity through ethnic preferences in layoffs when he filed an appeals court brief supporting such practices by a New Jersey school board. James Bovard and Bob Zelnick have published accounts of the increasing aggressiveness of the Office of Federal Contract Compliance Programs. The agency obtained a record $39.5 million in financial settlements during fiscal 1994, the result of finding violations in 73 percent of the more than 4,000 reviews it conducts each year.[58] (It is a testimony to the agency's great zeal or efficiency that this has been accomplished with fewer compliance officers. OFCCP has already lost 1,000 auditors in the past fifteen years and will likely lose more of the 800 who remain.)[59]

Corporate-government détentes on race and gender engineering may become more strained over building regulatory controversies. There are looming battles over how to establish and test for "minimal qualifications" for jobs and how to measure and assess job applicant pools.[60] There is also likely to be bureaucratic and congressional wrangling over possible efforts to replace specific race and gender preferences with categories of "socially or culturally disadvantaged."[61]

And with specific regard to diversity management, a new set of "glass ceiling" proposals—first published without fanfare in November 1995—may yet acquire regulatory force.

The Glass Ceiling Commission's Diversity Policy Proposals

Policy recommendations for achieving greater upward mobility for women and minorities were formulated by the U.S. Labor Department's Glass Ceiling Commission in November 1995. The commission's policy proposals incorporated both the ideology and techniques of diversity management and strongly resemble similar recommendations made by key commission consultant Ann Morrison in her book *The New Leaders.* The commission, now officially disbanded, claimed to be bipartisan, but its membership and advisory staff were heavily liberal and activist. With the exception of the chairman, Secretary of Labor Robert B. Reich, it was also exclusively female and minority. The Glass Ceiling Commission was basically a government branch of the diversity machine.

The commission's prescriptions were largely based on its March 1995 study of top executives among *Fortune* magazine's list of the 1,000 largest corporations. The survey, "Good for Business: Making Full Use of the Nation's Human Capital," found that women and minorities made up only 5 percent of upper management ranks, though their representation was more proportionate at middle-management levels. While "Good for Business" received much comment in the press in the spring of 1995, the November 1995 report

containing the policy recommendations received practically none. The proposals contained in "A Solid Investment: Making Full Use of the Nation's
Human Capital" were likely ignored because they were published on the eve
of the federal government's late 1995 shutdown and—in all probability—because the Clinton administration was by then fully aware of the gathering
storm of criticism over affirmative action.

Nonetheless, a second Clinton administration will likely be lobbied to revive the proposals through both rhetoric and regulation. The commission's
recipe for "breaking the glass ceiling" in business included the usual diversity
management ingredients: (1) active, visible CEO commitment to diversity,
(2) company-wide policies "that actively promote diversity programs and
policies that remove artificial barriers at every level," (3) including diversity
in all strategic business plans and holding line managers accountable for
progress in achieving diversity goals, (4) using affirmative action tools and
techniques to measure progress and seek out candidates from noncustomary
backgrounds and experiences, (5) establishing formal mentoring programs
and better career development programs for women and minorities, (6) providing formal training at regular intervals to educate "all employees about the
strengths and challenges of gender, racial, ethnic and cultural differences,"
and (7) establishing work-life and family-friendly policies for all employees.
As in the earlier study of "Good for Business," the new report cited corporations that had already put many of these practices into action (Xerox, IBM,
the *Los Angeles Times,* and others).

The Glass Ceiling Commission also offered complementary prescriptions
for government and the wider society. For the former, it recommended "leading by example"; stronger enforcement of antidiscrimination laws; and better
collection, analysis, and disclosure of data pertaining to workforce diversity. Societal recommendations concerned reducing stereotyping, prejudice, and bias
(especially in the media by diversifying the ethnic and gender composition of
newsrooms) and improved educational outreach to women and minorities.

Other Regulatory Efforts

Other institutions with regulatory powers have been quietly advancing similar agendas. Top-down affirmative action–diversity regulations have entered
higher education though legislative action, as seen in the case of the California Community Colleges system, or by way of the Department of Education's Office of Civil Rights, or, more recently, via regional and public higher
education accreditation boards. Through both formal and informal pres-

sures, these accreditation agencies have attempted to impose student, faculty, and curriculum diversity requirements upon community colleges and universities. In a manner similar to these academic reviews, activist elites may be seeking to move multiculturalism more directly into business through their participation on pension fund boards of directors. What Peter Drucker once termed "pension fund socialism"—citizen ownership of much of the economy through huge pension funds—may mutate into pension fund multiculturalism.

The nation's largest private pension fund, the College Retirement Equities Fund (CREF), has made explicit diversity demands of firms in which it invests. A "Policy Statement on Corporate Governance" distributed to the fifteen hundred companies in which the fund invests included a diversity dictum: "Boards of directors should be composed of a majority of independent directors and reflect diversity of experience, gender, race, and age."[62] (When challenged by National Association of Scholars critic Barry Gross to produce evidence that diverse boards create more productive corporations, fund chairman John Biggs could offer none—except to retort that CREF and its sister, Teachers Independent Annuity Association, screened for diversity on their own boards.)[63]

The nation's largest public pension fund, the California Public Employees' Retirement System (CALPERS), is considering more active involvement in the workplace practices of corporations with lagging economic performance. Despite negligible evidence from an independent study commissioned by CALPERS, board president and California State University English professor William Crist stated that "we are now convinced there is a direct connection between workplace practices and corporate performance."[64] CALPERS will follow report recommendations not to select investments on the basis of workplace practices, but when it comes to scrutinizing investments that are lagging, CALPERS may urge "enlightened workplace practices," such as "empowering" workers to play an expanded role in business decisions and how much is spent on worker training. Though not mentioned in the independent report, given the proclivities of California's political and cultural elites, diversity policies might be read into "enlightened" and "worker training," especially if the current antiquota political climate relaxes.[65]

The Role of Corporate and Government Leaders

Workforce changes and regulatory machinery have their own dynamics, and government commissions are famous for making recommendations that receive attention and little action. What will be and has been the most important factor in the diversity machine's fortunes is continued and growing support of activist, change-oriented corporate CEOs and top government administrators.

A mixture of economic and political motivations lies behind top-down workforce diversity drives. Globalism encourages an outlook of cultural relativism and real business needs to address international cultural differences in both employment and customer bases. On the domestic side, corporate and government diversity champions are often mindful about how their organization's efforts actually or symbolically affect looming ethnic and gender strains in the wider society. Michigan's James Duderstadt, California Community Colleges' chancellor David Mertes, and L.A. sheriff Sherman Block all feared wider economic and ethnic societal polarization without diversity mandates to spur "inclusion." Such worries were implied or explicitly echoed in most profiles of corporate and government diversity champions. The urge to manage diversity in specific organizations often masks the urge to manage society itself.

As noted in Chapter 1, the urge to manage rationally and assuage morally the tensions caused by immigration, ethnic relations, and social change dates from the Progressive era's fascination with behavioral and scientific reform. Then, as now, immigration and increasingly global markets had the potential to sharpen domestic ethnic and class polarizations. Now, writers from Robert Reich to Peter Drucker to Charles Murray and Richard Herrnstein have voiced concern over the formation of a relatively small class of "knowledge workers" or "cognitive elite" and their growing distance from the masses who are not.[66] Class divisions may also be ethnic ones.

The specter of a smaller class of Asian and white well-paid knowledge workers and a heavily black and Third World underclass will continue to tempt America's top executives and administrators to reduce social tensions through affirmative action and diversity management, especially in areas of high immigration such as California. The calls for "doing the right thing" and building "a workforce that looks like America" are the cheery rationales for deeper political and sociological uses of policies of social control and societal stability. Not all diversity champions have stated the case for affirmative action and diversity programs as bluntly as former UCLA chancellor Charles Young: "I can tell you that if we hadn't done it [affirmative action], it wouldn't be an occasional uprising in South-Central Los Angeles or midtown Detroit. We'd be in a battleground."[67]

Prior to the 1994 elections, protests against top-down programs like diversity management were not greeted politely. Noted the late Christopher Lasch, "When confronted with resistance to these initiatives, members of today's elite betray the venomous hatred that lies not far beneath the smiling face of upper-middle-class benevolence."[68] Such tendencies persist. Even as taboos against criticizing affirmative action and diversity programs have fallen, American executives remain quite capable of ferociously defending diversity programs when seriously challenged.

A Final Case Study—of a Case Study:
The *Washington Post* Unloads on a Diversity Critic

The continuing controversy and newly emerging fault lines over diversity management were revealed vividly in angry exchanges between the *Washington Post* newspaper and the *New Republic* following the magazine's October 2, 1995, cover story, "The Washington Post: In Black and White." In her 14,000-word analysis, the magazine's young reporter, Ruth Shalit, charged that the *Post*'s increasing emphasis on affirmative action and diversity management had compromised its hiring and promotion standards, fostered racial divisiveness in the newsroom, undermined journalistic objectivity, and softened reporting on Washington, D.C.'s black community. Her article raised compelling questions about affirmative action's and diversity management's emphasis on cultural relativism, identity politics, and proportional representation, not only at the *Post* but elsewhere. Unfortunately, the potential for a substantive discussion was lost in the sound and fury of the *Post*'s response.

Shalit conceded at the outset of her article that the diversity concerns of the *Post* were well founded: "As the monopoly daily in a majority-black city, the paper had compelling reason to diversify what had been an overwhelmingly white newsroom." Executive editor Leonard Downie, Jr., "argues persuasively that a diverse staff is necessary to covering a diverse community."[69] *Post* editorials routinely endorsed affirmative action, and the paper practiced what it preached, nearly doubling its representation of minority journalists, in spite of national trends toward newspaper cutbacks and layoffs. Downie proudly told Shalit, "'I think you'll find we have been much more aggressive than other places.'"[70] Indeed, Shalit found that minority journalists composed 18 percent of the professional staff at the *Post*, "well above the national average and disproportionate to the pool of aspiring minority journalists."[71]

The *Post* fit the typical pattern of an organization originally pushed onto the diversity bandwagon because of racial embarrassments or crises. The paper was initially slow to hire black reporters until, in 1972, the paper settled a discrimination complaint by an informal agreement to step up minority hiring. Then came what Shalit termed two traumatic "racial psychodramas": the awarding of a Pulitzer Prize to Janet Cooke in 1980 for a story on drug addiction that turned out to be a fabrication; and a 1986 boycott of the *Post* wrought by a magazine cover story featuring a black murder suspect accompanied by columnist Richard Cohen's description of D.C. jewelry store owners who, fearful of crime by young blacks, were reluctant to admit them through security measures into the stores. In the wake of these traumatic controversies, the *Post* established newsroom hiring goals of 25 percent minority and 50 percent women.

Diversity management theory became enshrined at the *Post* via an internal study of its newsroom culture, prompted by low retention and promotion rates of women and minorities. The report indeed found considerable minority and female dissatisfaction at the *Post,* and the report recommended changing the newsroom culture—first and foremost by wedding the concepts of diversity and excellence. Officially entitled *Challenge and Change,* Shalit dubbed the study the Getler Report, so-named after the study's director, deputy managing editor Mike Getler.

Shalit described Getler as undergoing a Lewis Griggs–style personal conversion to diversity. "A friendly, approachable man who spent many years as a reporter and editor before becoming the *Post's* diversity czar, Getler now spends his days patrolling the newsroom, blasting stereotypes and preaching inclusion. 'There is racism, whether it is conscious or unconscious,' he explains."[72] Rafael Gonzales, a diversity consultant with ties to Lewis Griggs, had already done some preliminary diversity training activities with senior management, which Shalit mocked. More such training was scheduled.

The Getler Report, observed Shalit, was sympathetic to blacks' complaints about newsroom culture but derided grievances of white males as "myths" to be "corrected" through involvement in diversity training to "help them define their role in a changing newsroom."[73] (Shalit raised hackles by describing this as "reeducation.") The *Post's* director of hiring and recruiting, Jeanne Fox-Alston, was "a small reedy woman in her early 40s with a gray topknot and the tight, pursed mouth you see on the assistant principal," who openly disparaged reverse discrimination complaints. Shalit described Fox-Alston's duties as "winnowing out white males" from job applicant pools.[74]

Like many other organizations committed to diversity management,

Shalit also reported that the *Post* had set-aside or targeted positions for blacks—so-called black slots. Shalit noted that the newspaper's top-down diversity ideology brooked no dissent: "Questions about a possible trade-off between diversity and quality are received with discomfort and indignation." Asked about contradictions between pursuit of diversity and excellence, Mike Getler responded, "That is wrong. That is wrong. That is wrong."[75]

Shalit traced complaints of compromised standards and reverse discrimination to the mismatch between the *Post's* "flamboyantly unrealistic" hiring goal of 25 percent minority reporters compared to their relatively "minuscule" availability. (She noted that blacks and Hispanics were but 10.6 percent of college graduates, of which only 13 percent were communications majors.) "Many *Post* staffers allege that in playing the numbers game, the paper has been forced to hire inappropriate people, reporters who lack the skills to do daily newspaper work competently."[76] Said one anonymous source: "It's definitely a huge advantage in this business to be a minority . . . like, a giant, giant, giant advantage. There is just a different standard. White people have to knock their heads against the door and be really exceptional. Whereas, if you're black they recruit you, they plead with you, they offer you extra money."[77] And "many white reporters say they are weary of being told in interviews that they could not even be considered for particular jobs."[78] These anonymous statements infuriated *Post* higher management, as would other unattributed remarks by white reporters that some blacks on the staff were "dumb as a post." Furthermore, Shalit rubbed salt in these wounds with her own characterization of the *Post's* diversity dilemma: "If editors refuse to adjust their traditional hiring standards, they will end up with a nearly all-white staff."[79]

Concurrent with purported declines in hiring and promotion standards was the rising acceptance of "'community journalism,' a new feel-good school of newspapering which premised that editors should let their readers' comfort level dictate the boundaries of their coverage."[80] In the diversity management style, the *Post's* editors were sliding toward the assumption that black reporters were uniquely sensitized and equipped to cover black community issues, Hispanics were best suited to report on Hispanic topics, and so forth. Shalit accused the *Post* of "equal-opportunity pandering" and elevating sensitivity to community reaction above the need for aggressive reporting on painful subjects.[81] She interviewed current and former reporters who claimed controversial stories on D.C.'s black community were spiked or otherwise softened or impeded. Shalit attributed much of the pressure to

Milton Coleman, the assistant managing editor for the Metropolitan News section of the *Post*.

The *Post*'s Aggressive Response

Washington Post reporter Howard Kurtz wrote that "*The New Republic* last week launched at 13,000-word missive on race relations at *The Washington Post* that detonated with maximum force in the *Post* newsroom six blocks away."[82] The *Post* responded with massive retaliation. *Post* columnist Richard Cohen later told me he was appalled by the bullying nature of the response: "Like an aircraft carrier opening up with everything it had on a rowboat. it was sophomoric. Didn't those guys go to J-school?"

The *Post* and its defenders did not deal with Shalit's criticisms of the paper's theory and practice of diversity. Instead they attacked Shalit's character and accuracy. Shalit's critics portrayed her policy critique as an attack on the competency of black reporters or blacks in general, or they quarreled over her presentation of the facts. Some arguments were over trivial facts, while other disputes boiled down to the charges of Shalit's anonymous sources versus official *Post* denials. (Interestingly, only *Post* reporters claimed they'd been misinterpreted by Shalit; to my knowledge, no former employees or any sources not employed by the paper so complained.)

In a letter to the *New Republic*, Leonard Downie, Jr., accused Shalit of "big lie" propaganda. He denied that the *Post* was trying to mirror "precisely" the ethnic makeup of the community yet clearly implied such efforts when he declared that "Shalit's racial McCarthyism will not deter our efforts to diversify the staff of *The Washington Post* so we can report intelligently on an increasingly diverse community." Downie dodged claims of alleged "black slots" by arguing that a white reporter had originally filled one such a slot or that persons of all colors had been interviewed for other targeted positions. He further charged Shalit with two prior instances of plagiarism, which Shalit countered were the result of computerized writing and editing.[83] In another letter, *Post* publisher Donald Graham attacked not only Shalit but the *New Republic* as well: "Since she [Shalit] works at *The New Republic*, the last practitioner of de facto segregation since Mississippi changed, Ms. Shalit has little or no experience in working with black colleagues. Ms. Shalit describes a place where blacks and whites watch each other closely, where race becomes an excuse for some and a flashpoint for others. Sounds like America in 1995. Except, of course, for *The New Republic*. (Motto: Looking for a qualified black since 1914.)"[84]

The *New York Times*'s columnist Anthony Lewis also weighed in, characterizing Shalit's article as evidence of a new wave of "racist chic" based in the presumed inferiority of blacks: "Her descriptions of particular black staff members as inferior were compellingly answered by *Post* executives."[85] James Warren, Washington bureau chief of the *Chicago Tribune*, dubbed Shalit a "young journalistic Unabomber."[86]

The Battle Soberly Reconsidered

In addition to scanning printed responses, in April and May 1996 I interviewed Shalit and eight Washington-based newspersons (five at the *Post*) to get a sense of how the controversy was viewed some seven months later. Shalit was stunned by the "volcanic response" and declared the topic "toxic." On the record, she admitted no personal or professional injury; off the record, it was another matter.

Post reporter Kevin Merida, an African American, repeated previously published statements that Shalit had incorrectly tried to cast him in the same mold as the more dissatisfied blacks at the newspaper. He also felt that his rapid rise in the world of journalism wasn't as unique or extraordinary as she had made it appear. But he acknowledged that diversity policies were a topic ripe for study in spite of the attendant fears. Indeed, an anonymous white colleague was extremely nervous about discussing affirmative action or diversity issues. He thought it seemed quite natural to try to match the composition of the *Post*'s workforce with its customer base; he had "good vibes" from affirmative action. But he deferred comment on allegations that the *Post* had softened its coverage of minority issues as a subject simply "too hot to handle." Two other Washington-based journalists, also speaking under cover of "background," did state that the *Post* had reduced its critical focus on local black issues.

A former *Post* reporter now on the staff of another organization (also requesting "background" status) thought Shalit's reporting was riddled with errors, but, he admitted, "the *Washington Post* newsroom is obsessed by race, especially in hiring and promotion." He was untroubled by the paper's aggressive diversity policies, stating, "It's a bit of social engineering, really." He felt that white males' complaints were not really racism but mostly alibis by middle-aged white males who were past their prime. Asked if there weren't elements of a class struggle between older white male executives imposing a diversity agenda on younger white male staffers, he acknowledged the generational dimensions: "the older white men are from the 1960s; there's a generational clash here." (He did not appreciate my occasional observations that Shalit had reported much of what he was observing, and the conversational temperature plunged when I asked him whether he thought the *Post's* policies were legal. "I'm a liberal," he offered as an answer.)

During a long telephone interview, Mike Getler sounded just as Shalit described him: affable, mild-mannered, yet a born-again diversity convert. Getler acknowledged the dangers of identity politics and admitted that fears of being called racist curbed criticism of diversity policies. He nonetheless reeled off standard diversity management rhetoric. He complained that Shalit didn't sufficiently stress "what's exciting" about diversity management and "how diversity improves things." Both Getler and Jeanne Fox-Alston chided Shalit for not reporting on the diversity activities that had sprouted since the 1993 task force report. An in-house university had been created featuring writing seminars and other subjects, brown bag lunches on diversity topics, and expanded recruiting efforts.

As Shalit reported, Getler insisted that diversity and excellence entailed no compromise: "All the people we hire are first rate." Minorities and women, he explained, bring a different background and set of eyes to the newsroom. Their presence might provide sensitivity on reporting and editing, perhaps, noting, "This isn't how a Hispanic person would take this." Getler declared that it's impossible for whites to know what it's like to be black in certain situations: "Diversity makes us smarter about our coverage."

Getler rationalized reverse discrimination complaints with standard diversity machine phrasing: "People hire others who look like themselves. Competition is new to white males; there are a lot more women now. A lot of people who might have been hired automatically a few years ago because he looks like me or [because he] went to the same school no longer are [hired that way]." Deep down, he felt, most whites understand the value of diversity. Getler dismissed the group exercises of diversity consultant Raphael Gonzales—lampooned by Shalit—as mere demonstrations and that Gonzales did little further diversity training or "reeducation" at the *Post*. (Instead, editors and managers were being trained in management and leadership techniques, including diversity management, at the American Press Institute in nearby Reston.)

Fox-Alston conceded that there was a grain of truth amid Shalit's "sloppy" reporting—even regarding Fox-Alston's gatekeeper role with white males: white men were the largest group in the applicant pool; therefore, there were more white males to reject. Like a smooth university admissions counselor,

Fox-Alston explained that race and gender considerations might be one of many factors in determining who got a job. The importance of race or ethnicity might vary with the job. But did the *Post* use "targeted positions," restricted to minorities? Fox-Alston's slippery response echoed those at the University of Michigan and many other wary organizations: "Let me put it like this: we say we would really like a black or female for some positions and we try. For example, we wanted a woman political reporter, but wound up hiring a male. It's not absolute [but] have we made an effort?" She stated that the strength of race and gender preferences may vary as to the position. "It's not an absolute bar to someone of nonpreferred race and gender." Were the *Post*'s sliding preference practices legal? (Readers of this book can, by now, anticipate the answer.) "I don't know, I can't answer that," replied Fox-Alston. "Overall, we look for good people and balance. It may be discrimination if you refuse someone a job," she said. But not, evidently, if you award someone a job because of race or gender.

Post columnist Richard Cohen also "wasn't sure" whether the *Post*'s practices were legal. Did the *Post* use targeted positions reserved for blacks? "They say they don't." Cohen noted that the original Getler report had also stirred unease and anger in the newsroom, especially among whites. Cohen said he'd been asked to write a critical response to the task force report, tried, but could not. "The issues are clear from a distance; they get tough to write about when you're up close," he said.

"The *Post* Really Chews People Up": Beyond Race and Gender in the Getler Report

Besides the ferocity of the *Post*'s response, what was significant about the paper's attempt to reform its newsroom culture was that black-white issues at the *Post* were really a subset of—and similar to—more general employee complaints about the *Post*'s workplace culture. According to *Challenge and Change* (which Shalit termed the Getler Report), the newspaper treated a variety of employees indifferently or badly.

In reading the *Challenge and Change* report's other sections, on "Recruiting," "Hiring," "Training," and "Career Development," what emerges is a portrait of an organizational culture seen as aggressively competitive, uncaring, cold, even anonymous—where talent was not developed and supervisors might not know the names of those they supervised. The most urgent complaints concerned lack of training, career development, and, especially, promotional processes that not only overlooked in-house talent but where "senior managers often treat in-house applicants with a lack of basic courtesy and decency."[87] (The proposed solution was an "in-house job fair.") Though many of the complaints in *Challenge and Change* may have been disproportionately voiced by women or minorities, the report did not so indicate.

Race and gender topics in *Challenge and Change* were largely compartmentalized in the final twenty-five-page section, "Diversity." Many African Americans reporters felt "locked out" no matter how hard they worked; many Latinos and Asians saw the biggest obstacle to their own promotion as the "aggressiveness with which African Americans were hired and promoted";[88] white men complained that greater interest in minorities and women might block (or had blocked) their careers; some female staffers found the newsroom atmosphere intimidating and confrontational and wanted more family-friendly policies. Shalit picked up on the proposed solutions, which were largely drawn from the work of R. Roosevelt Thomas and hummed with his key themes and rhetoric: expanding the definition of diversity, linking excellence with effective diversity management, and the inclusion of white males in diversity. Diversity's demographic imperative was repeatedly invoked: dramatic population shifts required that "a diverse staff and diverse coverage, although not totally dependent on each other, are linked inexorably."[89]

Still, the overall critical theme of *Challenge and Change*, contained in a twice-cited, anonymous quotation, seemed to transcend race and gender: "The *Post* really chews people up."[90] In short, these were largely the complaints I heard at the University of Michigan—or which most social scientists would hear at many large corporations and other hard-driven organizations striving to be "the best." As at the University of Michigan, the *Post*'s diversity blueprints have provided some rhetorical balm for political crises at the expense of freedom of thought, speech, and inquiry: the bane of a free press.[91]

The situation at the *Post* illustrates once again a central theme of this book. The "white male workplaces" that diversity consultants wish to restructure may harbor varying degrees of ethnic and gender discrimination. But today's large-scale workplaces are primarily complex social systems of rules and goals that are also impersonal and insensitive to white males and quite capable of chewing them up as well—as millions of downsized white male middle managers can attest from bitter experience. Ranting about "white male workplaces" ignores the realities of class, personality differences, and poor management practices. The dissatisfaction of diversity consultants may be aimed at white males in power, but the force of diversity reprogramming and accountability schemes fall on younger working and middle-class whites.

Can or Should Ethnicity and Gender Be an Occupational Qualification?

Yet people at the *Post* and other journalists, including Ruth Shalit, raised interesting questions about whether ethnicity or gender could be viewed as quasi-legitimate qualifications for some types of reporting. As Mike Getler argued, minorities bring a different set of eyes and experiences to the newsroom. Is this a stereotype, an overstatement, or partly true? The problematics are in the phrasing.

Sociologist Christopher Jencks and, more recently, Dinesh D'Souza have discussed a form of discrimination termed "rational discrimination."[92] As opposed to purely emotionally based, irrational discrimination, this "personal probability discrimination" rests on crude calculations drawn from an individual's experience and perceptions. If, for example, an employer has found that Asian bus drivers tend to be more reliable, politer, have fewer accidents, have fewer personal problems than members of other groups, he may be inclined to hire more Asians when additional bus-driving slots open up. (The converse of such positive reinforcement is the much-discussed fear of young urban black males as potential criminals. Although most black men may be law abiding, statistically the violent crime rates for young blacks are much higher than for whites or members of other groups: hence, Jesse Jackson's surprisingly candid observation that he would feel more comfortable if, upon hearing footsteps behind him on a dark street, he discovered it was a white man. And painful though it may be, as D'Souza points out, even black cab drivers use this probability-based, rational form of discrimination when passing by other black men.)

In a somewhat similar argument, James Q. Wilson has contended that loosely defined affirmative action (selecting people based on their group membership) often occurs for a variety of reasons in real-life situations. Informally, he argues, Americans quietly judge such practices as appropriate or inappropriate. We deem it appropriate when political parties use ethnicity or gender as a criterion to select candidates, or when marketers and advertisers consider the ascribed characteristics of audiences to whom they wish to appeal. We do not deem it proper to select members of sports teams or orchestras by skin color. "We understand these distinctions intuitively," states Wilson, in part because we know that political parties and advertisers are customer driven and must please their customers' preferences; sports teams and orchestras are more concerned with merit.[93] But as diversity consultants are quick to point out, changing demographics can dictate remarkable change: all organizations are ultimately customer driven. (Ask all those out-of-work symphony musicians whose white audiences dwindled away—not to mention the major sports organizations that barred blacks for decades in deference to customer tastes.)

On the contrary, our collective intuition on the appropriateness of selecting by ethnicity and gender is not clear. In many occupational sectors, controversies rage over the appropriateness of using group-based, ascribed criteria. Should ethnicity or gender be a criterion for hiring a reporter? A firefighter? A teacher? A peace officer? A priest? A computer salesperson? Indeed, does or should Wilson's white male status affect his ability to write and publish on these matters? (Until quite recently it did.) Nor does Wilson acknowledge that it has become "intuitively known" in many higher education institutions that white males should not teach courses on ethnic relations or sex roles.

Yet social scientists have long known that the characteristics of the interviewer may influence the nature of responses given by the interview subject. Where the gathering of sensitive data in face-to-face contexts is concerned, there are occupational settings in which ethnicity or gender *is likely* to make a difference. *Other qualifications being equal,* it is not unreasonable for an editor to assume that a male Hispanic reporter investigating street crime in the barrio might be more likely to gain access to relevant situations and sources than would an Asian or Anglo male reporter. As *Chicago Tribune* Washington Bureau chief James Warren pointed out, reporters are highly dependent on their contacts in the community. Being of the same ethnicity might be—but need not be—a potent plus. The same is true in sales positions and other types of occupations emphasizing face-to-face interaction.

However, diversity management's push into greater use of ethnically weighted job assignments, whatever the grains of pragmatic truth or intuitive appropriateness, carries ugly echoes of current and past racist and sexist practices of employers who wanted only white employees or salespersons because of the preferences and biases of their customers. Ethnic and workplace trends toward matching employees and clients on the basis of ascribed characteristics have been and should be checked by nondiscrimination law. Indeed, employers can and have opened themselves to lawsuits if they "ghettoize" or make a disproportionate number of gender or "ethnically appropriate" assignments—as was the case with the Federal Bureau of Investigation when it was sued by Latino officers for basically confining them to assignments in predominantly Hispanic areas.

Ultimately, in the coming years, government regulators and the courts will likely decide the circumstances under which race and gender may be considered legitimately as job-related qualifications.

Second Thoughts on Celebrating Differences

The likely shift of the diversity machine toward a more diffuse, cross-cultural global emphasis would be a timely strategic move because an increasing number of business and government leaders are reconsidering the divisive, complex consequences of celebrating differences and ethnic and gender proportionalism within the U.S. The University of Michigan's diversity champion and retired president, James Duderstadt, expressed concerns about divisiveness and lack of common ground. In multicultural Los Angeles, Sheriff Sherman Block worried about the fading of assimilation and family values, and retiring California Community Colleges president David Mertes admitted that ethnic classifications and preferences are contributing to the retribalization of America. Even the nation's chief executive, President Bill Clinton, who allegedly wants to "mend, not end" affirmative action, has also voiced anxiety about overemphasis on "differences" at a 1996 commencement address at Pennsylvania State University: "I want an America that is no longer being driven apart by our differences, but instead is coming together around our shared values and respect for our diversity."[94]

Ironically, the diversity machine's drive to open up frank and candid discussion of race and gender issues helped crack its own protective shield of PC egalitarian censorship, which had limited the attacks on the underlying principles of cultural relativism, identity politics, and proportional representation. As seen in the conferences and workshops throughout this book, the diversity machine has had to navigate the same whirlpool of criticisms and crises that contributed to PC's decline: the rise of talk radio and other electronic media, the 1992 L.A. riots, a series of Supreme Court decisions limiting racial preferences, the 1994 Republican congressional landslide, the overwhelming passage of California's Proposition 187, which limited public benefits to illegal immigrants (now tied up in the courts), and the California Civil Rights Initiative, which would ban ethnic and gender preferences by state and local governments. Finally, there was the painful polarization of black-white opinion made obvious during and after the O. J. Simpson trial, especially by the public jubilation among some blacks after the not-guilty verdict. All these developments have unquestionably jarred what Charles Murray termed "elite wisdom" and likely provoked high-level reconsideration of policies emphasizing group differences. Noted the *Weekly Standard's* Christopher Caldwell, "Elite opinion is unusually in sync with mass opinion on the Simpson case. In virtually all polls, belief in Simpson's guilt rises steadily along with income level and education. And both white and black thinkers worry that the consequences of the O. J. trial could be 'ominous.' Whites, who now fear that the justice system is stacked against them, may be on the verge of an explosive rethinking."[95]

In the wake of such changes, people once cowed into silence or those who felt compelled to endorse publicly race and gender remedies they privately doubted (Timur Kuran's "preference falsification") have begun to raise questions and objections. As seen throughout this book, it has become more difficult for enthusiastic CEOs or mid-level government and corporate administrators to impose aggressive diversity programs on employees.

An important signal of American intellectuals' growing ambivalence toward affirmative action and diversity policies was a long article, "The End of Affirmative Action?" by a leading policy defender, Queens College sociologist Andrew Hacker. In the July 11, 1996, issue of the *New York Review of Books,* the author of the widely cited *Two Nations* admitted what critics have known for a long time: affirmative action was never seen as legitimate by a majority of the population, ethnic preferences have been hopelessly compromised by the inclusion of large numbers of immigrants, and sources of educational and occupational inequality may be far beyond the reach of social engineering. And the oft-proposed compromise to shift preferences to economic disadvantage, Hacker reluctantly conceded, "would go to lower-income Asians and whites, including immigrants from Eastern Europe."[96]

Does the value of a diverse workforce justify ethnic and gender preferences? Hacker hedged. Discussing the importance of black "representation" on the Memphis police force, he strained to link workforce effectiveness with ethnic diversity. Hacker contended that the goal of a more representative and therefore effective police force called for "deemphasizing" the disparate impact of written promotional exams.

> For the city to have effective law enforcement, it would be prudent to have a strong black presence at supervisory levels. And to obtain those officers, the department would have to reduce the importance of multiple-choice scores. This said, it can and should be argued that what was done in Memphis is not "affirmative action," but a policy designed to create a more effective police force.[97]

(Hacker did not comment on the resentment and demoralization such tactics have engendered in other police and fire departments, nor the negative "quality control" and other symbolic messages that would be sent to a public increasingly suspicious of government institutions.) Elsewhere in the article, however, Hacker confessed to difficult truths. While admitting that the world is becoming "less white," Hacker nonetheless skewered the idea that workforce diversity per se is an advantage: "It has yet to be shown that someone of, say, Puerto Rican origin would be better able to achieve rapport with distributors in Sri Lanka than a white Anglo Saxon."[98] Without explicit acknowledgment to Thomas Sowell, Hacker nonetheless applied Sowell's well-known *coup de grace*: "The Japanese are hardly multicultural, yet their firms sell successfully around the globe, largely thanks to their diligence in studying local conditions."[99] As for arguments that various forms of diversity make for an improved learning environment, Hacker expressed doubts. Describing the wide range of ethnic and international diversity in his Queens College classrooms, he observed:

> From what they say in my classes, I cannot claim that a Korean-born student has perceptions and reactions that differ from one who comes from Haiti, or that their reactions diverge from those of classmates who were born and raised here; nor should we expect much from informal conversations among students from diverse backgrounds, assuming they will involve shared experiences. While such discussions do occur, ethnic self-segregation tends to characterize most campuses, especially among black students at dominantly white institutions.[100]

Although many top executives, administrators, and intellectuals are having second thoughts about affirmative action and the benefits of workforce diversity, others are willing to stay the course. Despite diversity consultants' claims that their policies are a "business necessity," the fate of comprehensive diversity programs requiring organizational change likely rests in the realms of politics and the courts—where surprising developments are taking place.

The Diversity Machine, Politics, and the Law

Ironically, the future of the diversity machine's drive to change the "white male workplace" depends on how its policies are perceived by several different classes of white males: working- and middle-class white men, those in the executives suites, and the president of the United States.

Consultants complain that white male employees will not buy into diversity. That is because white men sense flashes of ethnic and gender vengeance and top-down totalitarianism within the diversity machine. Not without reason do rank-and-file white males often see diversity management programs as rationalizations for reverse discrimination and the inefficiencies generated by ethnic and gender preferences. Consultants confirm such suspicions with efforts to disparage such complaints with simplistic rationalizations of "white male privilege." When consultants and policymakers combine flawed demographic reports of white males' declining numbers with justifications for ethnic and gender proportionalism, white males have good reason to feel threatened. The consultants, in turn, may turn testy if asked about "inconvenient facts" concerning ethnic relations, such as urban black crime rates or problems with single-parent family structures. Thus, Michael J. Wheeler, the young, white male director of diversity efforts at the Conference Board, reluctantly admitted that "sometimes I sense hostility" in diversity meetings.

The diversity machine ignores or exacerbates the class and cultural divisions among white males. Indeed, it is rarely observed that massive downsizing as well as diversity management were authorized and implemented by—white males in the executive suites. White male CEOs and political leaders increasingly are attracted to cosmopolitan cultural relativism and to attempts at managing ethnic and gender tensions in their own organizations and in the wider society. Lesser white males who fail to fall in line with CEO visions of demographic destiny may find themselves targeted during restructuring efforts.

> How to build a diverse work force? First, realize that you'll likely encounter plenty of resistance. James Leva of General Public Utilities, for example, had to face what he calls an "entrenched culture" of mostly white male supervisors who resisted work force changes. In his case, deregulation followed by a restructuring that sliced his work force from 12,000 to 10,000 helped him shake up the shop. Leva made diversity a key goal of his reengineering effort, avoiding seniority alone as a basis for employment. "You can sometimes exploit a crisis situation as an opportunity for change," he said.[101]

Similar top-down diversity management impulses waxed strongly in the first Clinton administration, which appropriated much of the diversity machine's rhetoric and agenda, especially the concept that workforce diversity is "good business." The first Clinton administration responded to court-ordered curbs on affirmative action by mapping strategies to circumvent or soften such decisions.[102] A second Clinton administration will have even greater powers of reinterpretation and rollback. "Equity demands that we destroy the glass ceiling. Smart business demands it as well," urged former Labor Secretary Robert B. Reich.[103]

If the first Clinton administration was a strong, though increasingly discreet, ally of the diversity machine, a second Clinton administration may become a far more aggressive senior partner. During the next four years, Bill Clinton will have the opportunity to reverse or moderate recent court curbs on the uses of diversity by appointing judges more favorably inclined toward such policies. A new judicial climate and the implementation of new diversity directives, such as the unheralded 1995 Glass Ceiling Commission recommendations, may extend proportional "look-like-America" policies well into the next century. Bureaucratic pressures to circumvent the 1991 Civil Rights Act's ban on race-norming employment tests may increase, as will other efforts to push more proportional hiring and promotion results. (As James Bovard has recently argued, the affirmative action tactics of the Labor Department's Office of Federal Contract Compliance, "America's premier racial racketeering agency," remain aggressive and unbowed.[104]) Federally funded research to prove the relationship between ethnic and gender diversity and "workforce effectiveness" will receive greater White House attention.

Will Republicans and conservatives resist such efforts? Perhaps not. The rhetoric of the diversity machine has lately become bipartisan. Many political observers were not surprised when Newt Gingrich sidetracked or killed congressional efforts to end federal ethnic and gender preferences. But one of the more amazing political developments of 1996 was the Republican party leadership's enthusiastic embrace of "diversity" and "inclusion" as rhetorical themes and organizing principles for its national convention in San Diego. Although the overwhelmingly white delegates fashioned a highly conservative party platform, African Americans and women (including several who were "pro-choice" on the issue of abortion) were showcased frequently as convention speakers. There was practically no criticism of affirmative action, though a few speakers, notably retired General Colin Powell, were allowed to endorse the policies briefly. Though conservative radio host and Republican booster Rush Limbaugh claimed that Republicans' new-found fondness for diversity reflected an appreciation of diverse viewpoints, not gender or color, their convention speaker roster indicated otherwise. (So obvious were the Republicans' convention themes of diversity and inclusion that comedian Jay Leno jested that, for Republicans, diversity meant that "billionaires could mingle with millionaires.")

Though state and national Republicans quietly aided the California Civil Rights Initiative, California's business establishment remained largely para-

lyzed. Once thought to be the lightning rod for a national debate over affirmative action, the initiative remained largely a regional referendum—though
the polarized rhetoric and voting patterns will have strong national echoes.

Nearly 70 percent of white men favored CCRI while three quarters of
blacks and Hispanics voted against the measure—as did 61 percent of Asians;
minority women were solidly opposed, while white women favored the initiative. According to Claremont McKenna College government professor
Jack Pitney, similar ethnic polarization has also emerged in Congressional
elections, raising the specter of a "white elephant, black donkey": a primarily
white Republican Party and a Democratic Party peopled mostly by minorities, academics, and white feminists. As seen thoughout this book, increasing
ethnic pluralism in politics and culture has been and will be pumped into the
workplace by the diversity machine.

If the past is a guide to the future, high government and corporate officials
will likely flee the specter of sharpening ethnic-gender polarization by avoiding debate or reform of policies that would further trigger ethnic-gender divisions: abortion, affirmative action, diversity management, and immigration.
Indeed, rarely were these topics raised in post-election press and television
analyses. Instead, such forums were often filled with talk of possible bipartisan
cooperation on economic issues between the Republican Congress and the
Democratic White House.

Behind a renewed bipartisan silence and detente on affirmative action, diversity management and other "inclusion" strategies, government and corporate
leaders will continue to "manage" or ignore ethnic antagonisms. "Mending, not
ending" rhetoric will be substituted for in-depth research and criticism. Expensive "culture change" strategies in the American workplace will be maintained or
expanded for ideological and public relations reasons, rather than because such
policies have demonstrated that they are "good for business." Thus, according to
a November 11, 1996 *Wall Street Journal* report, California's corporations remain stubbornly wedded to diversity machine rhetoric and practice in spite of
recent citizen approval of the California Civil Rights Initiative.

Yet even the legal and defensive merits of massive corporate diversity programs were recently called into question. In early October 1996, Southern
California Edison Company, a leader in workplace diversity programs, settled
a racial discrimination lawsuit by awarding $11.25 million in back pay to
2,500 current and former employees and by agreeing to provide even more extensive diversity training for all of its 13,000 employees. The following month
Texaco, Inc. was embarrassed by public exposure of garbled, tape-recorded

conversations of former Texaco executives allegedly using a racial epithet and tampering with evidence in a racial discrimination case. Texaco CEO Peter Bijur repeatedly apologized to his employees and to the public; he underwent an obligatory verbal scourging by Ted Koppel on *Nightline*. Bijur promised expansion of Texaco's existing diversity programs and offered to appoint an African American to oversee expanded diversity efforts. Nor did Bijur back down after subsequent digital enhancement of the tapes by Texaco's lawyers found that the alleged racial epithet of "nigger" was actually a reference to "St. Nicholas" in the context of a conversation about African Americans' celebration of Kwanzaa. Indeed, much of the taped conversation indicated justifiable anger over excesses spawned by affirmative action and diversity programs: frustration with record-keeping on affirmative action "body counts," and perceptions of an "us-versus-them" ethnic separatism—vividly demonstrated at a Texaco meeting when blacks allegedly remained seated for the standard Star Spangled Banner but later rose for a revised, African American version. Will additional diversity training reduce, suppress, or inflame such tensions?

Worst of all, the spirit of lawlessness and duplicity engendered by unilateral imposition of ethnic and gender proportionalism will linger. Affirmative action and diversity mandates have created an ends-justifies-the-means lawlessness: widespread rigging of test scores and other selection criteria, censorship, forced employee assent to policies that are privately doubted, official deceit, lying, and twisting or evasion of regulations.

Bipartisan silence and neglect may also continue to mask a growing weakness in race and gender diversity formulas: the mounting confusion and breakdown in the ethnic classification machinery.

As seen in the case studies of the California Community Colleges and the University of Michigan (with its "non-Cuban Hispanics") even some who administer diversity machinery are exasperated, if not cynical. The problematics of classification will be further forced in preparations for the 2000 census. Indeed, it may be time to recall and consider the earlier proposal cited in this book offered by radical journalist Itabari Njeri at the 1992 Fifth Annual Conference on Race and Ethnic Relations in Higher Education: abolish racial and ethnic categories. Then abolish racial and ethnic preferences.

In a multiethnic society, discrimination by ethnicity and gender is such a volatile matter that the principle of nondiscrimination must be enshrined legally in terms as absolute as possible. On a matter of such great importance, the symbolic aspect of the law is crucial. As Carl Cohen emphasizes, the law must unequivocally send the message that ethnic and gender preferences are wrong. "Nothing—not even the most honorable motives—can justify the damage done by racial preference, or make it right to deprive individual citizens of the equal protection of the laws."[105] While it is likely that newspapers and police departments will continue to use ethnicity as a factor in making work assignments, strong laws against nondiscrimination will ensure that they do so with the greatest of care and as little as possible. The law should ensure that no one *loses* an educational or occupational opportunity because of race, color, creed, national origin, or gender. The law should not help people *obtain* a job because of race, color, creed, or national origin.

This goal may not be far off. By court decree and ballot initiative, experiments in doing without race and gender preferences are already beginning.

Beyond Race and Gender Preferences: The New Diversity Laboratories

Whether its architects are ready or not, the diversity machine is going to have to move beyond race and gender in two geographical areas of the nation. On July 1, 1996, the U.S. Supreme Court denied certiorari to an appeal from the University of Texas against the Fifth Circuit Court of Appeals' ruling forbidding the use of ethnic and gender preferences in admissions by the university's law school. By refusing to make a definitive ruling for the nation, the Court effectively created a preference-free zone for higher educational institutions within the jurisdiction of the court's decision: Texas, Mississippi, and Louisiana. Thus, public and private higher education colleges and universities within those states now have to pursue diversity goals without ethnic and gender preferences. The dismantling process began in the summer of 1996. Despite protests, the Texas Higher Education Board voted in late July to "end consideration of race in the awarding of millions of dollars in college scholarships and grants."[106]

In another region of the nation, the University of California system, by order of its regents, is also moving toward trying to achieve diversity without ethnic and gender preferences in admissions and hiring. An even larger preference-free diversity zone covering all public workplaces will be created in California by passage of the California Civil Rights Initiative, banning preferences by public agencies—provided the measure withstands challenges in the courts.

No doubt administrators will continue to circumvent the rollback of ethnic and gender preferences—to achieve ethnic and gender proportionalism by other means. (The University of California at San Diego, for example, has proposed giving preference in undergraduate admissions to students who excelled in a "disadvantaged" high school or socioeconomic environment. Computer simulations of the new admissions model indicate that it would partially reduce expected losses in numbers of black and Latino students in a post-preference environment.)

Still, regional abolition of ethnic–gender preferences will reinforce current trends within the diversity machine away from the demands of its civil rights moralists to maintain a central focus on race and gender remedies. In turn, this might move the nation as a whole away from the fixation on race and gender.

Can diversity management survive the collapse of ethnic and gender preferences? Sociologist Linda Gottfredson has formulated reasonable diversity management principles compatible with a framework free of group preferences. Above all, she calls for policy emphases on individuals, not groups: develop individuals, not groups; tailor treatment to individuals, not groups; recognize within-group variations; treat more obvious group differences as important but not special; reexamine but maintain high standards; test assumptions and support claims in situations where ethnicity or gender qualifications are assumed to be an asset; and, above all, "find the common ground."[107]

Although temptations to adjust employment and promotion exam results ethnically will persist, some employers are beginning to reconcile the use of standardized employment tests with reduced fears about "disparate impact" on minority groups by more carefully identifying the skills needed for specific jobs, using tests designed to check for those skills, and using supplemental criteria.[108]

If color-blind, gender-neutral laws are to be reinforced in a society that is more multiethnic than ever before, this legal framework will have to be informed by more open and candid theory, research, and discussion of how to identify and manage cultural differences. There *is* a bewildering variety of group-based cultural differences. *Culture counts.* It is, as Geert Hofstede aptly quips, the "software of the mind."[109]

Though some cultural and subcultural differences are transitory, those that persist should be acknowledged, accommodated, and sociologically studied *but not institutionalized in law or public policy.* The rule of law must be as fair, equal, and impartial as the founders argued that it should be. An impartial legal system requires more emphasis on shared, transcendent standards and cultural similarities instead of the dangerous push for cultural relativism and identity politics. The slick assumption of an inevitable link between demographic change and the progressive abandonment of the core values of Western society is tempting, though false, and must be resisted. As the best diversity consultants properly point out, general knowledge about cultural differences need *not* undermine Western culture, but can considerably supplement it by strengthening the ability of individuals to negotiate a changing world and, in all likelihood, manage organizations more effectively.

Methodological Appendix

Researching a topic like affirmative action or diversity management is both politically and methodologically challenging—and professionally very dangerous. Such issues are among the most deeply sensitive in American social and organizational life.

Responses to questions about these programs are fraught with legal, political, and public relations implications. Therefore, much of the meaning and significant activity regarding these policies has tended to transpire out of range of public scrutiny. How does one study such phenomena?

Related to legal and public relations hurdles, the few researchers who have ventured into these policy territories have also had to confront the twenty-year period of egalitarian censorship and rhetoric known as political correctness. This widespread pattern of individual and social self-censorship has been deeper and more extensive than the similar phenomenon known as McCarthyism. Thus, we are only now emerging from an era when "saying the wrong thing" could cost people their jobs, even their careers. Fear and intimidation are legendary in the realm of affirmative action and diversity management. There is enormous potential for professional reprisals. As Timur Kuran pointed out brilliantly in his recent book, *Private Truths, Public Lies,* under affirmative action regimes, people have felt compelled to endorse publicly policies that they privately doubt or even scorn.[1]

In this policy area more than in many others, there has been a tendency for both executives and rank-and-file subjects to try to tailor their remarks to what they believe are good public relations or what they believe the investigator wants to hear. Thus, obtaining data and interviews on these topics has been delicate and time-consuming—if such data and cooperation could be obtained at all. Many people remain hesitant to discuss these programs openly with their own colleagues, much less outside investigators.

Ideological and legal inhibitions complicate methodological approaches. The few survey and quantitative studies of diversity management, many discussed in this book, have generally proved superficial and less than satisfactory. First, typically low response rates raise strong doubts about the generalizability of whatever data are returned and analyzed. These low response rates no doubt reflect legal and political sensitivities.

Second, quantitative data reflect policy outcomes. The data only partially indicate what has happened, not why it happened or how it happened. Numbers do not get at the day-to-day operation of policy realities by human beings. Indeed, numbers can mask prodigious, but fruitless, efforts. There can be herculean affirmative action and workforce diversity efforts in the midst of much churning and turnover of personnel, yet the resulting ethnic and gender mix may remain relatively constant. (In universities, for example, outstanding minority faculty are repeatedly lured away in competitive bidding wars.)

Quantitative assessment of these controversial policies has been additionally compromised by the concurrent operation of other policies and larger societal trends, especially the restructuring of the workplace wrought by globalization, the recession, and other management techniques of reengineering. And, as Robert Nisbet conclusively demonstrated in his classic *Social Change and History,* history and social structure are shaped as much by sudden, unanticipated events as by planned programs and mathematical models.[2] The 1992 election of President Bill Clinton, the 1992 Los Angeles riots, the rising reaction against PC that contributed to the 1994 Republican election sweep, the polarized reactions to the O. J. Simpson trial, and Bill Clinton's 1996 re-election were developments forecast by practically no one, but nonetheless they have significantly affected the diversity machine and its organizational environments.

For these reasons, I have taken a largely qualitative approach to the study of workforce diversity policies. Since the fall of 1990, my primary tools have been passive and participant observation and, especially, the semistructured interview. In many settings, I simply asked people a series of questions drawn from the early workforce diversity literature. In particular, I focused on what subjects perceived as the obvious and subtle achievements and problems with diversity management policies.

In all three institutional case studies (the L.A. sheriff, the University of

Michigan, and the California Community Colleges system), I followed a pattern of strategic or "elite interviewing," questioning people in strategic or sensitive positions with regard to workforce diversity efforts. I also sought out those who were known to be strongly interested in or concerned with workforce diversity matters.

A remarkably large number of subjects in all organizational settings were highly cooperative and candid beyond my wildest expectations. To some extent I was lucky in moving into this research just as political correctness began to thaw. On the other hand, in the final few months of the study, some of those in my case studies, notably at the University of Michigan, became more guarded and defensive, in part because of the swiftly surfacing public reaction against race and gender preferences. But the integrity and candor of many subjects must also be saluted: many took risks in saying what they did when they did. I was surprised at how many were willing to speak without protection of anonymity. Writing this book took longer than anticipated, in part because I have tried to be faithful to their views while trying not to injure their careers.

These direct and indirect observations have been substantially supplemented by a growing number of books and articles on workforce diversity—though, alas, some serious analyses have sometimes been mixed with the boosterism and ideological correctness of their consultant-authors. But at least the consultants studied and wrote. As with affirmative action research (and the dearth thereof), most academics feared to look too closely.

I remain wedded to the old-fashioned ideal that social scientists can and should try to be objective and fair. In my more than five years of research on this book, I spent hundreds of hours asking questions of and listening to all manner of persons involved in diversity management. I have collected nearly one hundred files of articles and notes from professional, social science, and news media sources. Direct and secondary observations constantly grounded and guided the theories and concepts I have used. In the tradition of grounded research, I have tried to let interview subjects speak for themselves wherever space permitted. (I also remain wedded to the old-fashioned ideal that social science can be interesting, readable, and critical.)

I am very grateful to and wish to acknowledge a number of people and sources.

Consultants, corporate officials, and authors interviewed (sometimes repeatedly) include: Pam Fomalont, Anita Rowe, Lee Gardenswartz, Lewis Griggs, Tom Kochman, Sondra Thiederman, Price Cobbs, Bill White, Lewis Griggs, David Jamieson, Frances Kendall, Angela Antenore, Lillian Roybal

Rose, Jackie Hempstead, Fanda Bender, Angela Airall, Ulvaldo Palomares, Helen Mendes, Devra Korwin, Ginger Lapid-Bogda, Alex Norman, Taylor Cox, Jr., Harris Sussman, Lennie Copeland, Lucky Altman, Julie O'Mara, Jackie Hempstead, Dave Barclay, David Wagemaker, Ann Kusomoto, June Jones, and George Simons, Sybil Evans, Selma Meyers, R. Roosevelt Thomas, Ilene Wasserman, Brian Clark, Robert Lattimer, and Ken Boughrum. Consultants and officials affiliated with the American Institute for Managing Diversity include R. Roosevelt Thomas, Jr., Ann Kusomoto, and Angela Airall. At the Conference Board, Michael Wheeler, Bob Parent, and Ron Cowan gave willingly of their valuable time. Patti Digh, vice president for diversity and international programs at the Society for Human Resource Management, consented to be interviewed, as did Barry Lawrence, SHRM's public relations director.

The members of the American Society for Training and Development's Diversity Development Division were never anything less than fully professional and cooperative with me, as were those who planned the National Annual Diversity conferences. Tom Kochman, Sondra Thiederman, and the B'nai B'rith Anti-Defamation League permitted me to examine their workshops in detail—a courtesy that many other social scientists and reporters have been denied. Lewis Griggs lent me a set of "Valuing Diversity" videos for an extensive period; BNA productions was equally kind to lend me copies of their two training series, "Bridges" and "A Winning Balance"; Bill White provided me a demonstration copy of his training video, "The Power of Diversity."

The personnel of the Los Angeles Sheriff's Department were remarkably open and professional in permitting a social scientist to pry into their organization during a period when they were also being officially investigated by the Kolts Commission. Commander William Stonich and Lieutenant Clyde French deserve special thanks, as do my colleagues on the Cultural Awareness Advisory Committee, who knew that I was writing a book concerning the sensitive matters they debated. Tony Argott, Rufus Tamayo, Paul Harman, Lee Baca, Paul and Lucinda Freeman, Reggie Gautt, Bill Corrette, Victoria Havessy, Steve Selby, and numerous others gave me whatever time I asked of them. Sherman Block gave me more than an hour of extremely candid observations. Approximately eight to ten people spoke off the record. Three members of the Kolts Commission were also open and frank in their assessments of diversity training in the LASD.

I gathered most of my data on the California Community Colleges system through the four annual conventions I attended. In addition to the keynote addresses and handout materials, I obtained a wealth of data from dozens of informal conversations with people I met only fleetingly, most of whose names I cannot recall. I did conduct long interviews with those in the chancellor's office, including Maria Sheehan, Tosh Shikasado, David Mertes, and José Peralez. John Madden was especially helpful throughout this project. Several helpful people spoke off the record.

The University of Michigan is my undergraduate alma mater, and I am hoping any "Go Blue!" bias has been balanced by the special, critical insights gained from knowing that institution in a variety of roles: as an undergraduate, an alumnus, and now a visitor and a scholar conversant with the institutional strains throughout higher education. A partial listing of faculty and administrators who took time out of their busy schedule to be interviewed (and reinterviewed) includes James Duderstadt, Walter Harrison, Reynolds Farley, Leo McNamara, Joseph Adelson, Bob Weisbuch, Shirley Clarkson, John Cross, Peggy Hollingsworth, Tom Landefeld, Susan Lipshutz, Arlene Saxonhouse, Martha Feldman, Fred Neidhardt, Constance Cook, Paul Danos, Harold Johnson, Beth Reid, Peter Steiner, Nicholas and Margaret Steneck, Robert Zajonic, Charles Moody, Andrea Monroe-Fowler, Eunice Royster Harper, Ted Spenser, Don Deskins, Mark Chesler, David Goldberg, Mark Schneider, Thomas Dunn, Laurita Thomas, Sunny Roller, Ed Cooper, Bob Forman, Maurice Wheeler, Zaida Giraldo, Mary Ann Swain, Carol Hollenshead, and Jim Toy. The editors and staffers of the *Michigan Review* and the *Michigan Daily* were cooperative talkers both when I was on campus and over the telephone. Graduate, professional, and undergraduate students interviewed include William Rice, Jamie Green, Vincent Harris, Andrea Merchant, Dan Varner, Juan Battle, Alicia Lewis, Christian Calley, Ethan York, John Damoose, Brian Kight, and Anthony Woodleaf. Regents speaking on the record include Deane Baker, Larry Deitch, Rebecca McGowan, and Shirley McFee. Sue Rasmussen was both quick and gracious in providing data. As always in such terrain, several others provided useful input, but they preferred speaking off the record. In Lansing, *Detroit News* reporter Chris Christoff was helpful, as were Tom Hallock, attorney for the House Republicans, and Jim Murray, an assistant to Representative Michelle McManus.

Very special acknowledgments are due to Derek Green, a savvy reporter for the monthly *Ann Arbor Observer.* His long articles and my conversations with him were invaluable. Joe Stroud, editor of the *Detroit Free Press,* gave me more than an hour of his assessment of Michigan's statewide image.

Larry Arnn, Clint Bolick, Linda Chavez, Kenneth Cribb, Terry Eastland, Bruce Fein, Tom Fleming, C. Boyden Gray, Michael Horowitz, Charles Murray, Bradford Reynolds, William Rusher, and R. Emmett Tyrrell, Jr., were kind enough to be interviewed regarding the Reagan-Bush White Houses' responses to affirmative action.

Jonathan Tilove, the pioneering race relations reporter for the Newhouse News Service is, in my opinion, one of the best analysts of race and ethnic relations in the United States. His articles and conversations with me were a continuing source of stimulation and information on an enterprise that can get all too lonely. Columnist Linda Seebach was helpful early on. Jan Allard and Linda Gottfredson were professional social science colleagues providing useful, critical input. Diversity management author Jim Walsh provided many useful insights.

Especially after the 1994 elections, I gave dozens of interviews to journalists on affirmative action and diversity management. In turn, they often provided useful feedback to me. I have enormous respect for most print journalists. They moved in to study territory where most social scientists still fear to tread (though the elite media moved far too belatedly).

Journalists' interest was piqued by the diversity machine's moving into newsrooms; most reporters had mixed feelings about this. Journalists also spoke to me—many on "background"—about Ruth Shalit's analysis of diversity at the *Washington Post*. (Shalit gave me a valuable interview on this topic.) Jim Warren, Washington Bureau chief of the *Chicago Sun-Times,* gave me much valuable feedback on diversity matters. Kevin Merida of the *Washington Post* spoke on the record about matters there, as did Mike Getler and Richard Cohen. Other helpful journalists along the way have included James Flanigan, Jonathan Weber, Shawn Hubler, Rich Connell, and Stu Silverstein at the *Los Angeles Times,* plus one or two persons who spoke off the record. At the *Wall Street Journal,* Mike Horowitz, Hal Lancaster, Fred Bleakley, and Sue Shellenbarger provided useful input.

Finally, my debt to the *Wall Street Journal* becomes especially obvious in the concluding chapter. It is not only the premier newspaper of business and the workplace, but its front-page writers are among the most perceptive reporters in the business. My late father faithfully read that newspaper for most of his life, and if I am following in his footsteps, perhaps I have been caught in the web of "white male privilege." So be it. Perhaps Peggy McIntosh has the last word after all.[3]

Notes

INTRODUCTION

1. Dinesh D'Souza, *Illiberal Education: The Policies of Race and Gender on Campus* (New York: Free Press, 1990).

2. U.S. Department of Labor, *Report on the Glass Ceiling Initiative* (Washington, D.C.: Government Printing Office, 1991).

3. "GM: Diversity, A Competitive Advantage" (company document, 1995); *Washington Post Weekly Edition,* January 1–7, 1996, p. 21.

4. *Fortune,* April 15, 1996, special advertising section (direct quotation).

5. Ibid. (direct quotation).

6. Ibid. (direct quotation).

7. Sybil Evans, "At NYNEX, Diversity Works," *Cultural Diversity at Work* (November 1995): 8.

8. *BNA Daily Labor Report,* August 1, 1995; interview with David Barclay, October 8, 1990.

9. *BNA Daily Labor Report,* August 1, 1995.

10. Cited in "Survey Shows Many Companies Have Diversity Programs, Changes in Affirmative Action Perspective," *Mosaics* (Society for Human Resource Management Quarterly Diversity Newsletter), (March 1995): 1.

11. For example, see Jerald Greenberg and Robert A. Baron, *Behavior in Organizations,* 5th ed. (Englewood Cliffs, N.J.: Prentice-Hall, 1996).

12. The latest American Society for Training and Development's *Buyer's Guide and Consultant Directory* lists seventy-three individuals and organizations under "diversity training," down from ninety three years before.

13. See Charles Moskos, "How Do They Do It?" *New Republic,* August 3, 1991. A more extensive analysis can be found in Charles Moskos and John Sibley Butler, *All That We Can Be* (New York: Basic Books, 1996).

14. Ralph Turner and Lewis Killian, *Collective Behavior and Social Movements,* 3d ed. (Englewood Cliffs, N.J: Prentice Hall, 1987).

15. William B. Johnston and Arnold H. Packer, *Workforce 2000: Work and Workers for the 21st Century* (Indianapolis: Hudson Institute, 1987); Lennie Copeland and Lewis Griggs, "Valuing Diversity" (San Francisco: Griggs Productions, 1987); R. Roosevelt Thomas,

373

Jr., "From Affirmative Action to Affirming Diversity," *Harvard Business Review* (March–April 1990): 107–117.

16. Heather McDonald, "The 'Diversity' Industry," *New Republic*, July 5, 1993, pp. 22–26.

17. Andrew Ferguson, "Chasing Rainbows," *Washingtonian*, April 1994, pp. 35–42.

18. Richard Bernstein, *The Dictatorship of Virtue: Multiculturalism and the Battle for America's Future* (New York: Alfred A. Knopf, 1994).

19. Ibid., p. 128.

20. Timur Kuran, *Private Truths, Public Lies: The Social Consequences of Preference Falsification* (Cambridge, Mass.: Harvard University Press, 1995).

CHAPTER 1. FROM "AMERICAN DILEMMA" TO AFFIRMATIVE ACTION AND THE DIVERSITY PIONEERS

1. Gunnar Myrdal, *An American Dilemma* (New York: Alfred A. Knopf, 1944), p. xlvii.

2. Alexis de Tocqueville, *Democracy in America* vol. 1 (New York: Vintage Books, 1945), p. xlvii.

3. Robert Wiebe, *The Search for Order* (New York: Hill and Wang, 1967) .

4. Richard Hofstadter, *The Age of Reform* (New York: Vintage, 1955), p. 238.

5. Anthony M. Platt, *The Child Savers* (Chicago: University of Chicago Press, 1969).

6. Eli Ginsburg, Foreword to Susan E. Jackson et al., (eds.), *Diversity in the Workplace* (New York: Guilford Press, 1992), pp. xiii–xxii.

7. This section is drawn from Frederick R. Lynch, *Invisible Victims: White Males and the Crisis of Affirmative Action* (New York: Praeger, 1991), chap. 2. See also Steven Yates, *Civil Wrongs: What Went Wrong with Affirmative Action* (San Francisco: ICS Press, 1994); Hugh Davis Graham, *The Civil Rights Era* (New York: Oxford University Press, 1990); Jared Taylor, *Paved with Good Intentions* (New York: Carrol and Graff, 1992); Carl Cohen, *Naked Racial Preference* (New York: Madison Books, 1995); Paul Craig Roberts and Lawrence M. Stratton, *The New Color Line: How Quotas and Privilege Destroy Democracy* (New York: Regnery Gateway, 1996); Clint Bolick, *Affirmative Action Fraud* (Washington, D.C.: Cato Institute, 1996); and Terry Eastland, *Ending Affirmative Action* (New York: Basic Books, 1996).

8. Charles Murray, *Losing Ground: American Social Policy, 1950–1980* (New York: Basic Books, 1987); Christopher Lasch, "The Revolt of the Elites," *Harper's*, November 1994, pp. 39–49.

9. William Ryan, *Blaming the Victim*, rev. ed. (New York: Vintage Books, 1976).

10. Richard T. Schaefer, *Racial and Ethnic Groups*, 6th ed. (New York: HarperCollins, 1996), p. 74.

11. There is a vast literature on social mobility. For a good summary, see Dennis Gilbert and Joseph Kahl, *The American Class Structure*, 4th ed. (Belmont, Calif.: Wadsworth, 1993), chaps. 6–7.

12. *Report of the National Advisory Commission on Civil Disorders* (New York: Bantam Books, 1968), p. 2.

13. For an excellent discussion of the "overclass" and affirmative action, see Michael Lind, *The Next American Nation: The New Nationalism and the Fourth American Revolution* (New York: Free Press, 1995).

14. Shelby Steele, "How Liberals Lost Their Virtue over Race," *Newsweek*, January 9, 1995, pp. 41–42.

15. Herman Belz, *Equality Transformed* (New Brunswick, N.J.: Transaction Books, 1991); Robert Detlefsen, *Civil Rights Under Reagan* (San Francisco: Institute for Contemporary Studies, 1991); and Richard Epstein, *Forbidden Grounds* (Cambridge, Mass.: Harvard University Press, 1992).

16. Belz, *Equality Transformed,* p. 183.

17. See Gary McDowell, "Affirmative Inaction: The Brock-Meese Standoff on Federal Racial Quotas," *Policy Review* (Spring 1989): 32–37.

18. Detlefsen, *Civil Rights,* p. 152.

19. Comments quoted here were from interviews with the author in Fall 1995.

20. Ruth Shalit, "Unwhite House," *New Republic,* April 12, 1993, pp. 12–14.

21. Interview on "The Charlie Rose Show," January 14, 1994.

22. Interview with the author, March 21, 1994.

23. Interview with the author, January 25, 1994.

24. This section is heavily drawn from my book *Invisible Victims,* chap. 1

25. John David Skrentny, *The Ironies of Affirmative Action: Politics, Culture and Justice in America* (Chicago: University of Chicago Press, 1996), p. 224.

26. Harvey Mansfield, "The Underhandnesss of Affirmative Action," *National Review,* May 4, 1984, p. 26.

27. The "spiral of silence" concept, derived from Alexis de Tocqueville's "tyranny of the majority," was developed by German sociologist Elisabeth Noelle-Neumann, *The Spiral of Silence* (Chicago: University of Chicago Press, 1984).

28. For a brief summary of polling data through the 1980s, see Lynch, *Invisible Victims,* chap. 2. One of the most recent, multifaceted surveys on support, need, and effects of affirmative action is contained in a *USA Today*–Gallup–CNN poll published in *USA Today,* March 24–26, 1995, p. 3A. For a recent, excellent social science analysis of how whites' attitudes vary by the manner in which affirmative action is phrased in survey questionnaires, see Laura Stoker, "Understanding Whites' Resistance to Affirmative Action: The Role of Principled Commitments and Racial Prejudice," in Jon Hurwitz and Mark Peffley (eds.), *Perception and Prejudice: Race and Politics in the United States* (New Haven, Conn.: Yale University Press, 1997).

29. Timur Kuran, *Private Truths, Public Lies: The Social Consequences of Preference Falsification* (Cambridge, Mass.: Harvard University Press, 1995).

30. See Robert S. Lichter, Stanley Rothman, and Linda S. Lichter, *The Media Elite* (Bethesda, Adler and Adler, 1986).

31. See Lynch, *Invisible Victims,* chaps. 7 , 9.

32. Robert Holland of the *Richmond Times-Dispatch* almost single-handedly broke the scandal of race norming in 1990. See also Peter Brown, "Normin' Stormin'," *New Republic,* April 29, 1991, pp. 12–13. Top officials at the Equal Employment Opportunity Commission did not know their own agency was pressuring corporations to use race norming; see Peter Brimelow and Leslie Spencer, "When Quotas Replace Merit, Everybody Suffers," *Forbes,* February 15, 1993, pp. 80–102.

33. James Bovard, "Job Breakers: The EEOC's Assault on the Workplace," *American Spectator,* March 1994, pp. 32–37.

34. Brimelow and Spencer, "When Quotas Replace Merit."

35. "White Male Paranoia," *Newsweek,* March 29, 1993, pp. 48–54; "White Male, and Worried," *BusinessWeek,* January 31, 1994, pp. 50–55.

36. Much of the material in this section draws heavily on Clare Swanger, "Perspectives on the

History of Ameliorating Oppression and Supporting Diversity in United States Organizations," in Elsie Cross et al. (eds.), *The Promise of Diversity* (Burt Ridge, Ill.: Irwin, 1991).

37. Ibid., p. 12.
38. Marilyn Loden and Judy B. Rosener, *Workforce America! Managing Employee Diversity as a Vital Resource* (Homewood, Ill.: Business One Irwin, 1991); Marilyn Loden, *Implementing Diversity* (Burr Ridge, Ill.: Irwin, 1996).
39. Marilyn Loden quoted in Zwanger, "Perspectives," p. 14.
40. J. P. White, "Elsie Cross v. the Suits," *Los Angeles Times Magazine*, August 4, 1992, p. 38.
41. Ibid.
42. Zwanger, "Perspectives," pp. 12–13.
43. Ibid.
44. This section draws heavily on Valerie I. Sessa, "Managing Diversity at the Xerox Corporation: Balanced Workforce Goals and Caucus Groups," in Jackson et al., *Diversity in the Workplace*, pp. 37–65.
45. Ibid., p. 50.
46. Ibid., p. 63.
47. This section summarizes the extensive corporate profile by Clayton P. Alderfer, "Changing Race Relations Embedded in Organizations: Report on a Long-Term Project with the XYZ Corporation," in Jackson et al., *Diversity in the Workplace*, pp. 138–167.
48. Ibid., p. 147.
49. Ibid., p. 152.
50. Ibid., pp. 145, 146.
51. Ibid., p. 165.
52. This section is drawn from Barbara Walker and William C. Hanson, "Valuing Differences at Digital Equipment Corporation," in Jackson et al., *Diversity in the Workplace*, pp. 119–138. Also from comments made by William Hanson at the National Annual Diversity conferences.
53. Ibid., p. 120.
54. Ibid., p. 123.
55. Ibid., p. 129.
56. Dinesh D'Souza, *Illiberal Education: The Politics of Race and Sex on Campus* (New York: Free Press, 1991); Richard Bernstein, *The Dictatorship of Virtue* (New York: Alfred A. Knopf, 1994); David O. Sacks and Peter A. Thiel, *The Diversity Myth: Multiculturalism and the Politics of Intolerance at Stanford* (San Francisco: Independent Institute); Paul Berman (ed.), *Debating PC* (New York: Dell Publishing, 1992); and "The Politics of Political Correctness: A Symposium," *Partisan Review* 50 (no. 4) (1993).
57. Talk at "Affirmative Action and Beyond" workshop sponsored by the Women's Studies Program of the Claremont Colleges, September 18, 1992.
58. *Los Angeles Times*, April 22, 1984, p. A3.

CHAPTER 2. THE EVANGELIST AND THE BUSINESS PROFESSOR

1. Lennie Copeland and Lewis Griggs, *Going International: How to Make Friends and Deal Effectively in the Global Marketplace* (New York: Random House, 1978).
2. William Grier and Price Cobbs, *Black Rage* (New York: Basic Books, 1968).
3. Lennie Copeland, "Ten Steps to Making the Most of Cultural Differences at the Work-

place," *Personnel* (June 1988): 58–60; "Pioneers and Champions of Change," *Personnel* (July 1988): 44–49; "Valuing Workplace Diversity," *Personnel Administrator* (November 1988): 38–40.

4. Copeland, "Ten Steps."

5. R. Roosevelt Thomas. *Beyond Race and Gender* (New York: AMACOM Press, 1991).

6. R. Roosevelt Thomas, "From Affirmative Action to Affirming Diversity," *Harvard Business Review* (March–April 1990): 107–117.

7. Ibid., p. 107.

8. Ibid., p. 108.

9. Ibid., p. 109.

10. Ibid.

11. Thomas, *Beyond Race and Gender*, p. 5.

12. Ibid.

13. Ibid., p. 36.

14. Ibid., p. 11.

15. Ibid., pp. 168–173.

16. Ibid., p. 180.

17. Ibid., pp. 61–71.

18. Ibid., p. 46.

19. Ibid., p. 47.

20. Ibid., p. 120.

21. Ibid., pp. 120–132.

22. Ibid., pp. 159–166. See also Jerald Greenberg and Robert A. Baron, *Behavior in Organizations*, 5th ed. (Englewood Cliffs, N.J.: Prentice Hall, 1996), pp. 654–656; also see the informative 1994 PBS video, *Edwards Deming: Prophet of Quality*.

23. Thomas, *Beyond Race and Gender*, pp. 163–166.

CROSS-CULTURAL CONSULTANT PROFILE I: LILLIAN ROYBAL ROSE

1. Quotations in this profile, unless otherwise indicated, are based on an interview conducted with Lillian Roybal Rose on November 1, 1991, Claremont, California.

2. Itabara Njeri, "Facing Up to Being White," *Los Angeles Times*, December 28, 1989, pp. E1, 6.

3. Shelby Steele, *The Content of Our Character* (New York: St. Martin's Press, 1990); Richard Rodriguez, *Hunger of Memory: The Education of Richard Rodriguez* (Boston: Godine, 1982), and *Days of Oblication: An Argument with My Mexican Father* (New York: Viking, 1992).

CHAPTER 3. DEMOGRAPHY IS DESTINY

1. David Jamieson and Julie O'Mara, *Managing Workforce 2000* (San Francisco: Jossey-Bass, 1991).

2. Sondra Thiederman, *Bridging Cultural Barriers for Corporate Success* (New York: Lexington Books, 1991), and *Profiting in America's Multicultural Marketplace* (New York: Free Press, 1991.)

3. William Grier and Price Cobbs, *Black Rage* (New York: Basic Books, 1968).

4. Ann Morrison, R. P. White, E. Van Velson, and Center for Creative Leadership, *Breaking the Glass Ceiling* (Reading, Mass.: Addison-Wesley, 1987).

5. Ann Morrison, *The New Leaders: Guidelines on Leadership Diversity in America* (San Francisco: Jossey Bass, 1992).

6. David Rieff, *Los Angeles: Capital of the Third World* (New York: Simon & Schuster, 1991).

7. R. Roosevelt Thomas, *Beyond Race and Gender* (New York: AMACOM Press, 1992); Marilyn Loden and Judy B. Rosener, *Workforce America! Managing Employee Diversity as a Vital Resource* (Homewood, Ill.: Business One Irwin, 1991); Jamieson and O'Mara, *Managing Workforce 2000;* John Fernandez, *Managing a Diverse Workforce* (New York: Lexington Books, 1991); Morrison et al., *Breaking the Glass Ceiling;* John Hernandez (with Mary Barr), *The Diversity Advantage* (New York: Lexington Books, 1993); Lee Gardenswartz and Anita Rowe, *Managing Diversity: A Complete Desk Reference and Planning Guide* (Homewood, Ill.: Business One Irwin, 1993); Lee Gardenswartz and Anita Rowe, *The Managing Diversity Survival Guide* (Homewood, Ill.: Business One Irwin, 1994); Lee Gardenswartz and Anita Rowe, *Diverse Teams at Work* (Homewood, Ill.: Business One Irwin, 1995).

8. Geert Hofstede, *Culture's Consequences: International Differences in Work-related Values* (Beverly Hills: Sage, 1984); *Cultures and Organizations: Software of the Mind* (New York: McGraw-Hill, 1991).

9. Taylor Cox, Jr., *Cultural Diversity in Organizations: Theory, Research and Practice* (San Francisco: Barret-Koehler Publishers, 1993).

10. Martin M. Chemers, Stuart Oskamp, and Mark A. Costanzo (eds.), *Diversity in Organizations: New Perspectives for a Changing Workplace* (Thousand Oaks, Calif.: Sage, 1995).

CROSS-CULTURAL CONSULTANT PROFILE II: SONDRA THIEDERMAN

1. Sondra Thiederman, *Bridging Cultural Barriers for Corporate Success* (New York: Lexington Books, 1991), p. 173.

2. Sondra Thiederman, *Profiting in America's Multicultural Workplace* (New York: Lexington Books, 1991).

3. Ibid.

CHAPTER 4. RECESSION, REBELLION, RIOT

1. See, for example, Carl Cohen, "Race, Lies, and Hopwood," *Commentary*, June 1996, pp. 39–45.

2. Michael Mobley and Tamara Payne, "Backlash! The Challenge to Diversity Training," *Training and Development* (December 1992): 45–52.

3. Ibid., p. 46

4. Ibid., p. 52.

5. Peggy McIntosh, "White Privilege: Unpacking the Invisible Knapsack," *Peace and Freedom* (July–August 1989): 10–12.

6. Dennis Farney, "For Peggy McIntosh, 'Excellence' Can be a Dangerous Concept," *Wall Street Journal*, June 14, 1994, pp. A1, 4.

7. McIntosh, "White Privilege," pp. 10–12.

8. Baily Jackson, "Affirmative Action: A Half-Baked Idea," *Cultural Diversity at Work* (November 1995): 6–7.

9. Judith Katz, *White Awareness: An Anti-Racism Handbook* (Norman: University of Oklahoma Press, 1978).

10. Peter Brimelow, "Spiral of Silence," *Forbes*, May 24, 1992, pp. 76–77; Frederick R. Lynch, "Tales from an Oppressed Class," *Wall Street Journal*, November 11, 1991, p. A12; Frederick R. Lynch, "Multiculturalism Comes to the Workplace," October 26, 1992, *Wall Street Journal*, p. A10; Frederick R. Lynch, "Workforce Diversity: PC's Final Frontier?" *National Review*, February 21, 1994, pp. 32–36.

CROSS-CULTURAL CONSULTANT PROFILE III: TOM KOCHMAN AND ASSOCIATES

1. Thomas Kochman, *Black and White Styles in Conflict* (Chicago: University of Chicago Press, 1981).
2. Antony P. Carnevale and Susan C. Stone, *The American Mosaic: An In-Depth Report on the Future of Diversity at Work* (New York: McGraw-Hill, 1995).

CHAPTER 5. FRUSTRATION AND STALL

1. See especially the July 5, 1993, *New Republic* cover story, "The Diversity Industry."
2. Barbara Deane, "Critical Choices at the Crossroads," *Cultural Diversity at Work* (September 1994): 1, 10.
3. Shari Caudron, "Open the Corporate Closet to Sexual Orientation Issues," *Personnel Journal* (August 1995): 44.
4. Lawrence G. Flores, "Simulation Games: Applying a Multicultural Paradigm Shift," *Managing Diversity* (March 1995): 1–2.
5. Ralf Dahrendorf, *Class and Class Conflict in Industrial Society* (Stanford, Calif.: Stanford University Press, 1959).
6. The following points are taken from Lee Gardenswartz and Anita Rowe, *Managing Diversity: A Complete Desk Reference and Planning Guide* (Homewood, Ill.: Business One Irwin, 1993), pp. 93–94.
7. From Lee Gardenswartz and Anita Rowe, *Diverse Teams at Work: Capitalizing on the Power of Diversity* (Burr Ridge, Ill.: Business One Irwin, 1994), p. 76. Several of these variables are also discussed in terms of national culture variance by Geert Hofstede, *Culture and Organizations: Software of the Mind* (New York: McGraw-Hill, 1991).
8. I sat at a table with three others who identified with their occupation or profession: we described ourselves as analytical, rational, task-oriented folk who tended to discount emotions and social relationships. In other words, we were semiworkaholics. This was politely received by the rest of the group but was not where the action was.

CHAPTER 6. STRONG NEW ALLIES, WEAK POLICY PROOF

1. *Diversity: Business Rationale and Strategies: A Research Report* (New York: Conference Board, 1995:), cover, pp. 12–14.
2. Ibid., p. 9.
3. Ibid., pp. 30–37.
4. Paul Sniderman and Thomas Piazza, *The Scar of Race* (Cambridge: Belknap Press of Harvard University Press, 1993).
5. Judith H. Dobrzynski, "Some Action, Little Talk: Companies Embrace Diversity, But Are Reluctant to Discuss It," *New York Times*, April 20, 1995, p. C1.
6. Towers-Perrin, *Workforce 2000 Today* (March 1992), p. 2.
7. Ibid., p. 3.

8. "Does Affirmative Action Work?" *BusinessWeek*, July 8, 1991, p. 63.

9. Ibid.

10. "Who's Learning What?" *Training Magazine* (October 1994): 49.

11. Ann M. Morrison, *The New Leaders: Guidelines on Leadership Diversity in America* (San Francisco: Jossey-Bass, 1992), p. 4.

12. Society for Human Resources Management/Commerce Clearing House (SHRM/CCR), *Diversity Management Is a Culture Change, Not Just Training* (Alexandria, Va.: SHRM, 1993).

13. Ibid., 6.

14. Joanne Miller, *Corporate Responses to Diversity: A Benchmark Study* (New York: Center for the New American Workforce, Queens College, 1994), p. 2.

15. Michael J. Wheeler, *Diversity Training* (New York: Conference Board, 1994).

16. Ibid.

17. Morrison, *The New Leaders*, p. 34.

18. SHRM/CCR, *Diversity Management*, p. 4.

19. Wheeler, *Diversity Training*, p. 8.

20. Dobrzynski, "Some Action."

21. Morrison, *The New Leaders*, p. 92.

22. Ibid., p. 17.

23. Ibid.

24. Ibid., p. 9.

25. Ibid., p. 236.

26. Catherine Ellis and Jeffrey Sonnenfeld, "Diverse Approaches to Managing Diversity" (unpublished manuscript, Emory Business School, Atlanta, 1993).

27. Carolyn Jew, "Diversity and Discrimination in Corporations: A Case Study in the 1990s" (paper presented at the annual meetings of the Pacific Sociological Association, San Francisco, April 6–9, 1995).

28. Anne S. Tsui and Lyman W. Porter, "A Study of Work Force Diversity in 55 Orange County Companies" (unpublished manuscript, Graduate School of Management, University of California, Irvine, 1993).

29. Anne S. Tsui, Terri D. Egan, and Charles A. O'Reilly III, "Being Different: Relational Demography and Organizational Attachment," *Administrative Science Quarterly* 37 (1992): 549–579.

30. Ann Tsui, Terri Egan, and Katherin R. Xin, "Diversity in Organizations: Lessons from Demography Research," in Martin Chemers, Stuart Oskamp, and Mark A. Costanzo (eds.), *Diversity in Organizations: New Perspectives for a Changing Workforce* (Thousand Oaks, Calif.: Sage, 1995).

31. Taylor Cox, *Cultural Diversity in Organizations: Theory, Research, and Practice* (San Francisco: Barret-Koehler, 1993), p. 33.

32. Ibid., p. 145.

33. Ibid., p. 251.

34. Taylor Cox, Jr., "An Analysis of Work Specialization and Organization Level as Dimensions of Workforce Diversity" (paper presented at the Conference on Diversity in Organizations, Claremont McKenna College, Claremont, California, February 6, 1994).

35. Dobrzynski, "Some Action," p. C4.

36. Kara Swisher, "Learning from Past Mistakes," *Washington Post Weekly Edition*, February 13–19, 1995, p. 20.

37. Anthony P. Carnevale and Susan C. Stone, "Diversity: Beyond the Golden Rule," *Train-

ing and Development (October 1994): 22–39; Anthony P. Carnevale and Susan C. Stone, *The American Mosaic: An In-Depth Report on the Future of Diversity at Work* (New York: McGraw-Hill, 1995), p. 115.

38. Wall Street Journal, December 16, 1994, p. B1.

39. Sue Shellenbarger, "Workforce Study Finds Loyalty Is Weak, Divisions of Race and Gender Are Deep," *Wall Street Journal*, September 3, 1993, pp. B1, 5.

40. *Los Angeles Times*, November 11, 1994, p. A14.

41. Shellenbarger, "Workforce Study."

42. *BNA Communicator* (Winter 1996): 5.

43. Stephanie Mehta, "Diversity Pays," *Wall Street Journal*, April 11, 1996, p. R12.

44. Peter Brimelow and Leslie Spencer, "When Quotas Replace Merit, Everybody Suffers," *Forbes*, February 15, 1993, pp. 80–102.

45. Lewis Brown Griggs and Lente-Louise Louw (eds.), *Valuing Diversity: New Tools for a New Reality* (New York: McGraw-Hill, 1995), p. 208.

46. Ibid., p. 241.

47. Ibid., p. 246.

48. Ibid., p. 247.

49. Ibid., pp. 247–248.

50. Ibid., p. 253.

51. R. Roosevelt Thomas, Jr., *Redefining Diversity* (New York: Amacon Books, 1996), p. xii.

52. Ibid., p. 62.

53. Ibid., p. 81.

54. Ibid., p. 20.

55. Ibid., p. 84.

56. Ibid., p. 35.

57. "General Motors Funds America's Premiere Diversity Management Institute," PR Newswire Association, January 25, 1995.

CHAPTER 7. DEFENSIVE DIVERSITY TRAINING

1. "California: The Endangered Dream," *Time*, Special Issue, November 18, 1991; David Rieff, *Los Angeles: Capital of the Third World* (New York: Simon & Schuster, 1991).

2. Paul Feldman and Eric Lichtblau, "Pay Hikes Fueled Closing of 4 Jails," *Los Angeles Times*, May 20, 1996, p. A10.

3. James G. Kolts and Staff, *The Los Angeles County Sheriff's Department: A Report* (Los Angeles County, July 1992,) p. 10.

4. Ibid., p. 48; see also pp. 315–318.

5. Ibid., pp. 323–332.

6. Faye Fiore and Kenneth Reich, "Sheriff's Department Concedes on 2 Sex Bias Suits," *Los Angeles Times*, December 4, 1992, pp. A1, A36.

7. Special Counsel Bob Merrick and Staff, *The Los Angeles Sheriff's Department: 1st Semiannual Report* (Los Angeles County, October 1993), p. 55.

8. Special Counsel Bob Merrick and Staff, *The Los Angeles Sheriff's Department: 2nd Semiannual Report* (Los Angeles County, April 1994), pp. 48, 54.

9. Mack Reed, "Sheriff, LAPD Face Exodus of Officers," *Los Angeles Times*, September 19, 1994, pp. B1, B8.

10. Special Counsel Bob Merrick and Staff, *The Los Angeles Sheriff's Department: 5th Semian-nual Report* (Los Angeles County, February 1996), pp. 21–27.

CHAPTER 8. FROM DIVERSITY DREAMS TO BUDGET NIGHTMARES

1. "Pricing Opportunity Out of the Market?" *Los Angeles Times*, January 16, 1994, pp. A3, 32; Patrick M. Callan, "Equal Opportunity Disappointment," *Los Angeles Times*, October 26, 1995, p. B9; "Fewer County Students Go On to Colleges," *Los Angeles Times*, April 30, 1996, pp. A1, 20.
2. "Plan Addresses Expected College Enrollment Surge," *Los Angeles Times*, May 31, 1996, pp. A3, 29.
3. Katherine Seligman, "Tentative Pact in CCSF Reverse Bias '89 Lawsuit," *San Francisco Examiner*, June 12, 1992, p. A6.
4. "Former Students Tell Why Community College Failed Them," *Los Angeles Times*, November 24, 1995, p. B3; "Pricing Opportunity Out of the Market?" *Los Angeles Times*, January 16, 1994, pp. A3, 32.
5. *Los Angeles Times*, October 18, 1994, p. B2.

CHAPTER 9. MULTICULTURAL VISION MEETS MULTIVERSITY REALITIES

1. This chapter is based on interviews and reinterviews with more than seventy people by telephone and during my annual visits to Ann Arbor from 1991 to 1994 and briefly in 1996. Data were also gathered from campus and alumni periodicals, as well as various reports and documents kindly furnished me by the University of Michigan Medical Centers and the Committee on a Multicultural University.

      Initially my previous research on affirmative action was unknown, though I brought up the book and articles on occasion, especially if asked. By 1996, I began to suspect that, as in the old Lon Chaney epic, I was the object of a rumor that "there's a werewolf in camp." A few former talkative sources became rather taciturn. At least one negative e-mail message circulated about my work; the chair of the Sociology Department warned colleagues and graduate students not to talk to me after I began probing the David Goldberg affair. (The memo circulated after I had already obtained the needed data.) One especially timid university official, who had little to say, later requested a written note confirming confidentiality. That I had few, if any, such problems in the California Community Colleges or within the Los Angeles Sheriff's Department says much about the growing siege mentality and PC pressures at the university.
2. Ze'ev Chafets, "The Tragedy of Detroit," *New York Times Magazine*, July 20, 1990, pp. 20–26; 28, 42, 50–51, and *Devil's Night: And Other True Tales of Detroit* (New York: Random House, 1990).
3. Peter Schrag, "Don't Leave Out UC Officials When Spreading Scorn Around," *Daily Bulletin*, July 30, 1995, p. B5.
4. Council on a Multicultural University, "University of Michigan: Self Assessment Survey Information" (1993).
5. Robert Nisbet, *The Degradation of Academic Dogma* (New Brunswick, N.J.: Transaction Books, 1996).
6. "Business School Launches Program to Add Minority Faculty Nationwide," *University Record*, May 21, 1966, p. 5.
7. The center's personnel failed to come together with me and share their views of the Man-

date or anything else; repeated requests for interviews were politely accepted but never passed muster with those who grant them.

8. University of Michigan Medical Center, *Four Year Progress Report* (1996) p. 5.

9. *Moving Forward: The Michigan Mandate, A Five Year Report, 1987–92* (Ann Arbor: University of Michigan, Office of the President, 1992).

10. Ibid., p. 3.

11. See Derek Green, "SACUA Rising," *Ann Arbor Observer* (October 1994): 33–39.

12. Steiner's retirement had been hastened when he stepped on a PC landmine. He publicly mentioned that minorities not qualified to attend the University of Michigan could attend Detroit's Wayne State University. Such sentiments smacked of white male elitism and blame-the-victim thinking.

13. Jeff Muir, "Mr. Duderstadt Builds a Dream House," *Heterodoxy* (March 1993): 7.

14. Daniel Patrick Moynihan was badly mauled in the mid-1960s for his accurate, but politically incorrect, assessment of the inner-city black family in his study, *The Negro Family: The Case for National Action* (Washington, D.C.: Department of Labor, 1965), subsequently known as the Moynihan Report. University of Chicago sociology professor James Coleman was defamed and isolated when he published a series of articles in the mid-1970s indicating that school busing for desegregation was "counterproductive" and promoting white flight. For Coleman's own retrospective on this, see James S. Coleman, "Response to the Sociology of Education Award," *Sociology of Education* (Autumn 1988): 6–9.

15. The Goldberg affair at last received national attention in Lynn V. Cheney's *Telling the Truth: Why Our Culture and Country Have Stopped Making Sense—and What to Do About It* (New York: Simon & Schuster, 1995).

16. Timur Kuran, *Private Truths, Public Lies* (Cambridge, Mass.: Harvard University Press, 1995).

17. *Chronicle of Higher Education,* June 29, 1994, p. B2.

18. There is empirical evidence to support Dean Danos. "Consistent with evidence that physical attractiveness is related to obtaining employment and promotion, more attractive employees also have been found to enjoy more economic success in their careers. The research so far suggests that attractiveness is more consistently related to economic success for men than for women." Quoted in Gary Johns, *Organizational Behavior,* 4th ed. (New York: HarperCollins, 1996).

19. Quoted in Dinesh D'Souza, *Illiberal Education* (New York: Free Press, 1991), p. 142.

20. Leo McNamara complained to the president via e-mail about his paltry 1992 salary raise and received the reply that maintaining faculty salaries was the number one priority; the wily McNamara received no response when he reminded Duderstadt that the president's professed highest priority was the Mandate.

21. *Chronicle of Higher Education,* April 5, 1996, p. A29.

22. Carl Cohen, *Naked Racial Preference* (Lanham, Md.: Madison Books, 1995).

23. Carl Cohen, "Race, Lies, and Hopwood," *Commentary* (June 1995): 42.

24. Michael Lynch, *Still Choosing by Color: A Critique of the U.S. Department of Education Office for Civil Rights Investigation of Undergraduate Admissions at UC Berkeley* (Claremont, Calif.: Claremont Institute, May 6, 1996).

25. Judith Gerstel, "The Admissions Game: Who Gets into the University of Michigan?" *Detroit Free Press Magazine,* February 24, 1991, pp. 6–11, 14.

26. The 1995 enrollment figures were kindly and promptly supplied by Sue Rasmussen of the university's Affirmative Action Office. Figures in the most recent Mandate update are for 1994.

27. Other universities "target the best and brightest of our faculty and especially our minority faculty," a University of California official complained to the *Los Angeles Times*, October 21, 1994. A minority sociologist paid $70,000 at UCLA was being offered $167,000 plus other inducements by another school.

28. "There has been a great dependency on the Target of Opportunity Program as the main mechanism for recruiting faculty of color." Council on a Multicultural University (COMU) Academic Affairs Committee, Recommendations to the Full Council, April 1995. Since the TOP positions were ethnically "restricted," it had been decided that they could not be legally advertised in the usual national professional job bulletins.

29. The recommendations read:
    1. Create a Rackham Merit Fellowship (RMF) Task Force to conduct an assessment of the program over the next year.
    2. Establish a more systematic approach to the mentoring and professional development of graduate students.
    3. Establish a more comprehensive and deliberate intellectual community for graduate students.
    4. Implement more systematic means of information collection and dissemination on the politics and procedures affecting graduate students, as well as more information on graduate student life.

30. Council on a Multicultural University, *Summary of Recommendations* (May 1996).

31. I found much comfort in the comments of *American Spectator/New Republic* journalist Edward Norden who wrote a case study of the varied cultures of the University of California, San Diego, campus, not unlike my own effort. Though he tried to interview and observe a range of people and disciplines, Norden ran into occasional brick walls: "Come what may, your reporter tries to be personable. In spite of that, he wasn't made welcome by the departments of Literature, Communications, Visual Arts, Ethnic Studies, Third World Studies, and Women's Studies—i.e., those department that have either fallen into P.C. hands or were purpose-built. His telephoned requests for interviews were like pebbles down a bottomless well." Edward Norden, "A Month in Paradise," *American Spectator* (April 1992): 40.

32. "Duderstadt: Agenda for Women Is 'Everyone's Issue,'" *Michigan Alumnus* (July–August 1995): 13.

33. Stephan Thernstrom, "The Minority Majority Will Never Come," *Wall Street Journal*, July 26, 1990, p. A17.

34. Todd Gitlin, *The Twilight of Common Dreams. Why America Is Wracked by Culture Wars* (New York: Metropolitan Books, 1995).

35. Neil J. Smelser, "The Politics of Ambivalence: Diversity in the Research Universities," *Daedalus* (Fall 1993): 37–54.

36. Terry W. Hartle, "The Specter of Budget Uncertainty," *Chronicle of Higher Education*, June 28, 1996, p. B2.

37. Garrison Keillor purged "chauvinistic references" from Michigan's famous fight song, "The Victors," into a "Support Song" during an American Radio Company appearance in Ann Arbor in February 1992. The lyrics:

    We try to be supportive
    We are not ethnocentric,
    We're just from Michigan
    But you're okay too.

Your school is just as valid,
Your state has much to offer.
Though we're from Michigan
We see your point of view.

We don't dominate!
We don't discriminate
In Michigan!
No, not in Michigan!
We don't control (we don't)
Control (not we)
We try (we) try (we) try
To play holistically.

We seek to help opponents
And not to marginalize,
We try to validate
The non-Michigan.
We're into sharing power,
We want to get behind you.
Yes, yes! in Michigan,
We know that all is one.

(Copyright: Garrison Keillor. Reprinted by permission of Garrison Keillor.)

CHAPTER 10. THE DIVERSITY MACHINE

1. David Samuels, "Philanthropical Correctness," *New Republic,* September 18, pp. 25, 35; see also Althea K. Nagai, Robert Lerner, and Stanley Rothman, *Giving for Social Change: Foundations, Public Policy, and the American Political Agenda* (Westport, Conn.: Praeger, 1994).
2. James Pinkerton, "Why Affirmative Action Won't Die," *Fortune,* November 13, 1995, pp. 191–198.
3. Pascal Zachary, "Major U.S. Companies Expand Efforts to Sell to Consumers Abroad," *Wall Street Journal,* June 13, 1996, pp. A1, A6.
4. Leon E. Wynter, "Diversity Is Often All Talk and No Affirmative Action," *Wall Street Journal,* December 21, 1994, p. B1.
5. Bob Filipczak, "Looking Past the Numbers," *Training* (October 1994): 68.
6. Ibid.
7. Shari Caudron, "Training Can Damage Diversity Efforts," *Personnel Journal* (April 1993): 51.
8. Joel Kotkin, "Economic Change Is Undercutting the Rationale for Racial Preferences," *Los Angeles Times,* January 29, 1995, p. M6.
9. Gregory Spencer, *Projections of the Population of the United States by Age, Sex, and Race: 1888–2080* (Washington, D.C.: U.S. Department of Commerce, Bureau of the Census), p. 10.
10. Todd Gitlin, *Twilight of Common Dreams* (New York: Metropolitan Books, 1995), p. 112.
11. Jonathan Kaufman, "America's Heartland Turns to Hot Location for the Melting Pot," *Wall Street Journal,* October 31, 1995, A1, A15.

12. Genevieve Capowski, "Managing Diversity," *Management Review* (June 1996): 12–19.

13. Edward Banfield, *The Unheavenly City* (Boston: Little, Brown, 1970); Dinesh D'Souza, *The End of Racism* (New York: Free Press, 1995).

14. Alex Markels, "Innovative MCI Unit Finds Culture Shock in Colorado Springs," *Wall Street Journal,* June 25, 1996, p. A1.

15. Stratford Sherman, "It's a Brave, New Darwinian Workplace," *Fortune,* January 25, 1993, p. 51.

16. James Medhoff, *The Mid-Life Job Crisis,* report series (Washington, D.C.: National Study Center, May 12, 1994). See also James Medhoff, "Why Business Is Axing Older Workers," *U.S. News and World Report,* October 31, 1994, p. 78.

17. *Wall Street Journal,* March 11, 1993, pp. A1, A9; March 16, 1993, pp. A1, A9, A12. See also an earlier *Fortune* cover story, "The New Global Workforce," December 14, 1992, pp. 52–53, 58, 62, 64, 66.

18. Bernard Wysocki, Jr., "About a Million Men Have Left Work Force in the Past Year or So," *Wall Street Journal,* June 12, 1996, pp. A1, A6.

19. "The Temping of America," *Time,* March 39, 1994, pp. 40–47.

20. Jacylyn Fierman, "The Contingency Workforce," *Fortune* (January 1994): 30–36.

21. *Plan Sponsor* (October 1994): 21.

22. Richard J. Barnet, "The End of Jobs," *Harper's* (December 1993): 52.

23. Edward Luttwak, "America's Insecurity Blanket," *Washington Post Weekly,* December 5–11, 1994, p. 23.

24. William Bridges, "End of the Job," *Fortune,* September 19, 1994, pp. 62–74.

25. Sue Shellenbarger, "So Much Talk, So Little Action," in special "Work and Family" supplement, *Wall Street Journal,* June 21, 1993, pp. R1, R4; see also Lis Genasci, "Employees Resist Work-Family Options: Many Fear They'll Be Labeled Insufficiently Committed to Their Work," *Ontario Daily Bulletin,* July 2, 1995, p. E1.

26. *Black Enterprise* reporter Annette Williams challenged the thesis that white men were disproportionately downsized. She argued that blacks were disproportionately affected and that companies were "white-izing" under the guide of "rightsizing." See Annette Williams, *Black Enterprise* (March 1994): 52, 57–59.

27. Andrew Hacker, "The End of Affirmative Action?" *New York Review of Books,* July 11, 1996, pp. 21, 24–29.

28. Bernard Wysocki, Jr., "About a Million Men Have Left Work Force in the Past Year or So," *Wall Street Journal,* June 12, 1996, pp. A1, A6.

29. Eva Pomice, "The B-School Brain Drain: Why Fewer Women Want an MBA and What Business Schools Are Doing About It," *Working Woman* (August 1994): 42.

30. See the special "Work and Family" *Wall Street Journal* supplement, June 21, 1993; also, and especially, Betsy Morris, "Fed Up: Executive Women Confront a New Kind of Midlife Crisis," *Fortune,* September 18, 1995, pp. 60–86; Joann S. Lublin, "Some Adult Daughters of 'Supermoms' Plan to Take Another Path," *Wall Street Journal,* December 28, 1995, pp. A1, A4; Amanda Bennett, "Young Women May Trade Jobs for Marriage," *Wall Street Journal,* June 29, 1994, p. B1; Alecia Swasy, "Stay-at-Home Moms Are Fashionable Again in Many Communities," *Wall Street Journal,* July 23, 1993, pp. A1, A4. This last article drew heated response, and the *Journal* printed eleven letters to the editor on August 23, 1996, p. A11.

31. "Wall Street Week with Louis Rukeyser," Program 2504, July 28, 1995.

32. Fred R. Bleakley, "Many Companies Try Management Fads, Only to See Them Flop," *Wall Street Journal,* July 6, 1993, pp. A1, 6.
33. Suein L. Hwang, "Updating Avon Means Respecting History Without Repeating it," *Wall Street Journal,* April 4, 1994, pp. A1, A4.
34. Leon Wynter, "Business and Race" column, *Wall Street Journal,* July 20, 1994, B1.
35. "Managing in an Era of Change," *Fortune,* December 13, 1993.
36. Fay Rice, "Denny's Changes Its Spots," *Fortune,* May 13, 1996, pp. 133–141; see also Dorothy J. Gaiter, "How Shoney's, Belted by a Lawsuit, Found the Path to Diversity," *Wall Street Journal,* April 16, 1996, pp. A1, A9.
37. "Race in the Workplace: Does Affirmative Action Work?" *BusinessWeek,* July 8, 1991, pp. 50–63; "White, Male, and Worried," *BusinessWeek,* January 31, 1994, pp. 50–55.
38. "Rethinking Work," *BusinessWeek,* October 17, 1994.
39. "Management's New Gurus," *BusinessWeek,* August 31, 1992, pp. 44–52; "The Craze for Consultants," *BusinessWeek,* July 23, 1994, pp. 60–66. The *Wall Street Journal* also ignored diversity management in a similar account, "Downsizing's AfterMath Drives Growth for Management Consultants," *Wall Street Journal,* May 19, 1994, p. A1.
40. "Service with a Soul with Tom Peters," Public Broadcasting Service (aired on KCET Television, Los Angeles, August 25, 1995).
41. Rosabeth Moss Kanter, Barry A. Stein, and Todd D. Jick, *The Challenge of Organizational Change* (New York: Free Press, 1992). As an afterthought perhaps, Kanter did author the Foreword to Lawrence Otis Graham's, *The Best Companies for Minorities* (New York: Plume, 1993).
42. Scott Adams, *The Dilbert Principle* (New York: HarperCollins, 1996), p. 197.
43. James C. Collins and Jerry I. Porras, *Built to Last: The Successful Habits of Visionary Companies* (New York: HarperCollins, 1994); Bill Saporito, "Good for the Bottom Line," *Time,* May 20, 1996, pp. 40–43.
44. Gordon Group, *High Performance Workplaces: Implications for Investment Research and Active Investing Strategies,* report to the California Public Employees' Retirement System, May 30, 1994, pp. 10–11.
45. Ibid.
46. *Conference Calendar and Planning Guide: February–June 1995* (New York: Conference Board, 1995).
47. "This Year's Pace of Layoffs Is Fastest of Decade," *Los Angeles Times,* June 11, 1996. p. D2.
48. Some of these shortages may be due not to lack of applicants but lack of adequately trained applicants. See Raju Narisetti, "Manufacturers Decry a Shortage of Workers While Rejecting Many," *Wall Street Journal,* September 8, 1995, p. A1.
49. "The Charlie Rose Show," May 8, 1996.
50. Robert J. Samuelson, "Capitalism Under Siege," *Newsweek,* May 6, 1996, p. 51.
51. David Rieff, "Multiculturalism's Silent Partner," *Harper's,* August 1993, pp. 65–66.
52. Ibid., p. 66.
53. Christopher Lasch, "The Revolt of the Elites," *Harper's,* November 1994, pp. 39, 40.
54. See Geert Hofstede, *Cultures and Organizations: Software of the Mind* (New York: McGraw-Hill, 1991), summarized in Gary Johns, *Organizational Behavior* (New York: HarperCollins, 1996.)
55. Pinkerton, "Why Affirmative Action Will Not Die," 198.
56. *Wall Street Journal,* January 7, 1994, p. B1; Stephanie N. Mehta, "Diversity Pays," *Wall Street Journal,* April 11, 1996, p. R12.

57. *BNA Communicator* (Winter 1995): 20.

58. James Bovard, "Bureaucratic Carpet Bombing," *Wall Street Journal*, July 1, 1996, p. A12; Bob Zelnick, *Backfire: A Reporter's Look at Affirmative Action* (Washington, D.C.: Regnery Publishing, 1996).

59. *BNA Communicator* (Winter 1995): 2, 11.

60. See Zelnick, *Backfire*, pp. 67–68.

61. Writing in the *Wall Street Journal*, columnist Tim W. Ferguson asked: "Who has social disadvantage? The Small Business Administration defines it for other U.S. agencies. Right off, partiality goes to all nonwhite citizens, including those of East and South Asian heritage. Then come other openings: 'long-term residence in an environment isolated from the mainstream of American society,' 'social patterns or pressures which have discouraged the individual from pursuing a professional or business education,' 'acquisition of credit or capital under unfavorable circumstances.'" *Wall Street Journal*, March 14, 1995, p. A19.

62. "Sharing Our Views," TIAA-CREF News, *Participant* (April 1994): 8–9.

63. *Academic Questions* (Summer 1994): 87–88.

64. *Los Angeles Times*, June 6, 1994.

65. Ibid., February 3, 1995, p. D2.

66. Peter Drucker, "The Age of Social Transformation," *Atlantic Monthly* (November 1994): 53–80. Richard Herrnstein and Charles Murray, *The Bell Curve* (New York: Free Press, 1994).

67. Quoted in Frederick R. Lynch, "White Elites and Willy Loman," *Los Angeles Times*, March 17, 1995, p. B7.

68. Christopher Lasch, "Revolt of the Elites," p. 40.

69. Ruth Shalit, "The Washington Post in Black and White: Race in the Newsroom," *New Republic*, October 2, 1995, p. 20.

70. Ibid., p. 21.

71. Ibid.

72. Ibid., p. 22.

73. Ibid., p. 26.

74. Ibid., p. 23.

75. Ibid., p. 27.

76. Ibid., p. 23.

77. Ibid.

78. Ibid., p. 26.

79. Ibid.

80. Ibid., p. 31.

81. Ibid.

82. Howard Kurtz, "A Diversity of Opinions: New Republic Story on Race in Newsroom Stirs Up the Post," *Washington Post*, September 21, 1994, p. C1.

83. Letters to the Editor, *New Republic*, October 16, 1995, pp. 14–17.

84. Ibid., p. 17.

85. Anthony Lewis, "Abroad at Home: Racist Chic," *New York Times*, October 13, 1995, p. 33.

86. James Warren, "Sunday Watch: 3 Strikes, What a Coincidence," *Chicago Tribune*, October 1, 1995, p. 2.

87. *Challenge and Change: A Report by the Task Force on the Newsroom* (Washington, D.C.: Washington Post, 1993), p. 56.

88. Ibid., p. 75.

89. Ibid., p. 66.

90. Ibid., pp. 7, 66.

91. Interestingly, Shalit may have overlooked comments on Jeanne Fox-Alston in earlier sections of *Challenge and Change* that were incongruent with Shalit's aggressive portrait of the *Post* recruiter. The report noted that Fox-Alston's office lacked sufficient funds to "track and woo people" and that there were tensions between her and several senior managers, attributed to her lack of experience.

92. Christopher Jencks, *Rethinking Social Policy* (Cambridge, Mass: Harvard University Press, 1992); D'Souza, *End of Racism.*

93. James Q. Wilson, "Sins of Admission," *New Republic,* July 8, 1996, pp. 12–16.

94. "Remarks by the President," Pennsylvania State University, Graduate School Commencement. White House Virtual Library, White House Press Release, May 10, 1996.

95. Christopher Caldwell, "Why the Simpson Case Endures," *Weekly Standard,* July 29, 1996, p. 22.

96. Andrew Hacker, "The End of Affirmative Action?" *New York Review of Books,* July 11, 1996, pp. 21–29.

97. Ibid., p. 24.

98. Ibid., p. 26.

99. Ibid.

100. Ibid., p. 27.

101. Kenneth Labich, "Making Diversity Pay," *Fortune,* September 9, 1996, pp. 177–180.

102. See Abigail Thernstrom, *Don't End It, Don't Mend It, Defend It: Reviewing the Clinton Record on Racial Preferences.* (Washington, D.C.: Center for Equal Opportunity, July 1996.)

103. Quoted in Frank Swoboda, "It's Still Clear: The Glass Ceiling Exists," *Washington Post Weekly,* October 4–10, 1995, p. 34.

104. James Bovard, "Bureaucratic Carpet Bombing," *Wall Street Journal,* July 1, 1996, p. A12.

105. Carl Cohen, *Naked Racial Preference: The Case Against Affirmative Action* (Lanham, Md.: Madison Books, 1995), p. 234.

106. Terrence Stutz, "State Board Approves End to Race-Based Scholarships," *Dallas Morning News,* July 20, 1996.

107. Linda S. Gottfredson, "Dilemmas in Developing Diversity Programs," in Susan E. Jackson et al. (eds.), *Diversity in the Workplace* (New York: Guilford Press, 1992), pp. 306–319.

108. On the temptation to continue race-norming of employment exams, see Linda Gottfredson's exposé of efforts by the Department of Justice to force state and local governments to adopt a police entrance examination yielding proportional results by dropping crucially important measurements of reading, reasoning, and judgement skills: Linda Gottfredson, "Racially Gerrymandered Police Tests," *Wall Street Journal,* October 24, 1996, p. A18. For a more optimistic assessment of possible reconciliation of standardized tests with diversity goals, see Charlene Marmer Solomon, "Testing at Odds with Diversity Efforts?" *Personnel Journal* (April 1996): 131–142.

109. Geert Hofstede, *Cultures and Organizations: Software of the Mind* (New York: McGraw Hill, 1993).

METHODOLOGICAL APPENDIX

1. Timur Kuran, *Private Truths, Public Lies: The Social Consequences of Preference Falsification* (Cambridge, Mass.: Harvard University Press, 1995).
2. Robert A. Nisbet, *Social Change and History* (New York: Oxford University Press, 1968).
3. Peggy McIntosh, "White Privilege: Unpacking the Invisible Knapsack," *Peace and Freedom* (July–August 1989): 10–12.

Bibliography

Airall, Angela M. 1992. "How Whites Can Grow in Racial Identity." *Cultural Diversity at Work* (September): 6, 16.

Ansberry, Clare. 1993. "Workers Are Forced to Take More Jobs with Fewer Benefits." *Wall Street Journal* (Part One of "Down the Up Escalator" Series), March 11, pp. A1, A9.

Anthony, William P. 1992. "Managing Diversity, Then and Now." *Wall Street Journal,* July 3, p. A17.

Astin, Alexander. 1993. "Diversity and Multiculturalism on the Campus. How Are Students Affected?" *Change* (March–April): 44–49.

Aufderheide, Patricia. 1992. *Beyond P. C.* St. Paul, Minn.: Graywolf Press.

Auster, Lawrence. 1992. "The Forbidden Topic." *National Review,* April 27, pp. 42–44.

Banas, Gary E. 1992. "Nothing Prepared Me to Manage AIDS." *Harvard Business Review* (July–August): 26–33.

Barnett, Stephen R. 1992. "Who Gets In? A Troubling Policy." *Los Angeles Times,* June 11, p. B7.

Barrier, Michael. 1992. "Small Firms Put Quality First." *Nation's Business* (May): 22–32.

Beard, Henry, and Christopher Cerf. 1992. *The Politically Correct Handbook.* New York: Villard Books.

Beer, William. 1987. "Resolute Ignorance: Social Science and Affirmative Action." *Society* (May–June): 63–69.

Belz, Herman. 1991. *Equality Transformed.* New Brunswick, N.J.: Transaction Press.

Bennett, William. 1991. "A New Civil Rights Agenda." *Wall Street Journal,* April 1, p. A16.
———. 1993. "Quantifying America's Decline." *Wall Street Journal,* March 15, p. A16.

Berman, Paul (ed.). 1992. *Debating PC.* New York: Dell.

Bernstein, Richard. 1994. *The Dictatorship of Virtue.* New York: Alfred A. Knopf.

Bleakley, Fred R. 1993. "Many Companies Try Management Fads, Only to See Them Flop." *Wall Street Journal,* July 6, pp. A1, A6.

Bloom, Alan. 1987. *The Closing of the American Mind.* New York: Simon & Schuster.

Bolick, Clint. 1992. "The Great Racial Divide." (Review of Jared Taylor's *Paved with Good Intentions.*) *Wall Street Journal,* November 30, p. A10.

391

Bovard, James. 1994. "Job Breakers: The EEOC's Assault on the Workplace." *American Spectator* (March): 32–37.

———. 1996. "Here Comes the Goon Squad." *American Spectator* (July): 36–41, 83.

Bozeman, Tandy K. 1993. "A General Scouts the Soul of L.A." *Los Angeles Times*, April 20, p. B7.

Braham, Jim. 1989. "No, You Don't Manage Everyone the Same." *Industry Week*, February 6, pp. 28–35.

Brimelow, Peter. 1995. *Alien Nation: Common Sense About America's Immigration Disaster.* New York: Random House.

Brimelow, Peter, and Leslie Spencer. 1993. "When Quotas Replace Merit, Everybody Suffers." *Forbes*, February 15, pp. 80–102.

Brinton, Crane. 1938. *Anatomy of Revolution.* New York: Vintage. Rev. and exp. ed., 1965.

Brookes, Warren. 1990. "The Side Effects of Quotas." *Washington Times*, August 10, p. 20.

Brookhiser, Richard. 1993. "The Melting Pot Is Still Simmering." *Newsweek*, March 1, p. 72.

Burstein, Paul. 1994. "Affirmative Action: Big Controversy, Little Impact." Paper presented at the meetings of the American Sociological Association, Los Angeles, August 9.

Businessweek. 1991. "Does Affirmative Action Work?" July 8, pp. 50–63.

———. 1994. "Rethinking Work." October 17, pp. 74–117.

Butler, Stuart. 1989. "Razing the Liberal Plantation." *National Review*, November 10, pp. 27–30.

Capowski, Genevieve. 1996. "Cover Story: Managing Diversity." *Management Review* (June): 12–19.

Carnevale, Anthony P., and Susan C. Stone. 1994. "Diversity: Beyond the Golden Rule." *Training and Development* (October): 22–39.

———. 1995. *The American Mosaic: An In-Depth Report on the Future of Diversity at Work.* New York: McGraw-Hill.

Caudron, Shari. 1995. "Open the Corporate Closet to Sexual Orientation Issues." *Personnel Journal* (August): 42–55.

Chavez, Linda. 1991. *Out of the Barrio: Toward a New Politics of Hispanic Assimilation.* New York: Basic Books.

———. 1993. "Just Say Latino." *New Republic*, March 22, pp. 18–19.

Chemers, Martin M., Stuart Oskamp, and Mark A. Costanzo (eds.). 1995. *Diversity in Organizations: New Perspectives for a Changing Workplace.* Thousand Oaks, Calif.: Sage.

Chen, Chris. 1992. "The Diversity Paradox." *Personnel Journal* (January): 32–36.

Cohen, Carl. 1995. *Naked Racial Preference.* Lanham, Md.: Madison Books.

———. 1996. "Race, Lies, and 'Hopwood.'" *Commentary* (June): 39–45.

Cook, William J. 1993. "Engineering Diversity." *U.S. News and World Report*, March 22, pp. 65–66.

Copeland, Lennie. 1988. "Valuing Workplace Diversity." *Personnel Administrator* (November): 38–40.

———. 1988a. "Ten Steps to Making the Most of Cultural Differences at the Workplace." *Personnel* (June): 58–60.

———. 1988b. "Pioneers and Champions of Change." *Personnel* (July): 44–49.

Corwin, Miles. 1993. "Packing Up and Going Home." *Los Angeles Times*, March 4, pp. A1, A20.

Coughlin, Ellen K. 1993. "Sociologists Examine the Complexities of Racial and Ethnic Identity in America." *Chronicle of Higher Education*, March 24, pp. A7–9.

Cox, Taylor, Jr. 1993. *Cultural Diversity in Organizations: Theory, Research, and Practice.* San Francisco: Barrett-Koehler.

Cox, Taylor, H., and Stacy Blake. 1991. "Managing Cultural Diversity: Implications for Organizational Competitiveness." *Academy of Management Executive* (August): 45–56.

————. 1994. "An Analysis of Work Specialization and Organization Level as Dimensions of Workforce Diversity." Paper presented at the Conference on Diversity in Organizations, Claremont, California, February 6..

Cox, Taylor H., Sharon Lobel, and Poppy Lauretta McLeod. 1991 . "Effects of Ethnic Group Cultural Differences on Cooperative and Competitive Behavior on a Group Task." *Academy of Management Journal* 34, no. 4:827–847.

Cox, Taylor, Jr., and Stella M. Nkomo. 1991. "Invisible Men and Women: A Status Report on Race as a Variable in Organization Behavior Research." *Journal of Organizational Behavior* 11:419–431.

Craige, Betty Jean. 1994. "Multiculturalism and the Vietnam Syndrome." *Chronicle of Higher Education,* January 12, p. B3.

Cross, Elsie, et al. 1994. *The Promise of Diversity.* Burr Ridge, Ill.: Irwin Professional Publishing and NTL Institute.

Cultural Diversity at Work. 1992. "Resistance Is Part of the Change Process," September 1, p. 10.

————. 1993. "New Survey Results." (May): 1–10, 13.

Daily Labor Report. 1993. "Texas Instruments Makes Efforts to Capitalize on Employee Diversity," p. A10.

Dembo, David, and Ward Morehouse. 1993. *The Underbelly of the U.S. Economy: Joblessness and the Pauperization of Work in America.* New York: Council on International and Public Affairs.

Detlefsen, Robert. 1991. *Civil Rights Under Reagan.* San Francisco: Institute for Contemporary Studies Press.

Deutsch, Claudia. "Diversity Bedevils M.B.A. Programs." *New York Times* (Education Life Supplement), April 4, p. 22.

Dickson, Reginald. 1992. "The Business of Equal Opportunity." *Harvard Business Review* (January–February): 46–53.

————. "Debate" (Responses to Dickson). *Harvard Business Review* (March–April): 138–157.

Dobrzynski, Judith. 1995. "Some Action, Little Talk." *New York Times,* April 20, pp. C1, C4.

Dreyfus, Joel. 1990. "The Death of Affirmative Action." *Emerge* (November): 50–55.

Drucker, Peter. 1991. "Don't Change Corporate Culture—Use It!" *Wall Street Journal,* March 28, p. A16.

————. 1994. "The Age of Social Transformation." *Atlantic Monthly* (November): 53–80.

D'Souza, Dinesh. 1991. *Illiberal Education: The Politics of Race and Sex on Campus.* New York: Free Press.

Ehrbar, Al. 1993. "Re-Engineering Gives Firms New Efficiency, Workers the Pink Slip." *Wall Street Journal* (second part of "Up the Down Escalator" series), March 16, pp. A1, A12.

Ellis, Catherine, and Jeffrey Sonnenfeld. 1993. "Diverse Approaches to Managing Diversity." Unpublished manuscript. Emory Business School, Atlanta, Georgia.

Elshut, Suzanne, and James Little. 1990. "The Case for Valuing Diversity." *HRMagazine* (June): 50–51, 183.

"Engineering Diversity: Georgia Tech Has Big Plans for Minority Students." 1993. *U.S. News and World Report,* March 22, pp. 65–66.

Epstein, Richard A. 1992. "Diversity Yes—But Without Coercion." *Wall Street Journal,* April 22, p. A17.

————. 1992. *Forbidden Grounds: The Case Against Employment Discrimination Laws.* Cambridge, Mass.: Harvard University Press.

Evans, Sybil. 1992. "Spotlight: The Prudential." *Cultural Diversity at Work* (May): 4–5.

Farney, Dennis. 1992. "Ethnic Identities Clash with Student Idealism at a California College." *Wall Street Journal,* December 2, pp. A1, A6.

"FBI Agents' Group Seeks Say in Settlement over Alleged Racial Bias." 1993. *Bakersfield Californian,* June 14, p. A17.

Fernandez, John. 1991. *Managing the Diverse Workforce: Regaining the Competitive Advantage.* New York: Lexington Books.

————. 1993. *The Diversity Advantage.* New York: Lexington Books.

Fierman, Jacylyn. 1994. "The Contingency Work Force." *Fortune,* January 24, pp. 30–36.

Fillipczak, Bob. 1994. "Looking Past the Numbers." *Training* (October): 67–74.

Finn, Chester. 1991. "Quotas and the Bush Administration." *Commentary* (November): 17–23.

Friedman, Norman, and Susan Friedman. 1992. "Diversity Management: An Emerging Employment/Consulting Opportunity for Sociological Practitioners." Paper presented at the meetings of the American Sociological Association, August.

Fuchsberg, Gilbert. 1992. "Managing: Business Schools Address Limited Black Presence; Working with Others Matters for Big Kids." *Wall Street Journal,* December 11, p. B1.

Fukuyama, Francis. 1993. "Making It." (Review of Joel Kotkin's *Tribes.*) *New Republic,* April 19, pp. 41–43.

Galinsky, Ellen, James T. Bond, and Dana Friendman. 1993. *The Changing Workforce: Highlights of the National Study.* New York: Families and Work Institute.

Gardenswartz, Lee, and Anita Rowe. 1993. *Managing Diversity: A Complete Desk Reference and Planning Guide.* San Francisco: Business One Irwin.

————. 1995. *Diverse Teams at Work.* Burr Ridge, Ill.: Business One Irwin.

Gaiter, Dorothy. 1996. "How Shoney's, Belted by a Lawsuit, Found the Path to Diversity." *Wall Street Journal,* April 16, pp. A1, A9.

Gerlin, Andrea. 1994. "Jury Pickers May Rely Too Much on Demographics." *Wall Street Journal,* December 16, p. B1.

Gerstenzang. James. 1993. "Limited AIDS Impact on U.S. Seen by Panel." *Los Angeles Times,* January 5, p. A1.

Glynn, Patrick. 1993. "The Age of Balkanization." *Commentary* (July): 21–24.

"GM to Minority Contractors: No More Special Treatment, Improve Quality and Cut Prices." WWDB Radio, December 8, 1992.

Goldstein, Jeffrey, and Marjorie Leopold. 1990. "Corporate Culture vs. Ethnic Culture." *Personnel Journal* (November): 83–92.

Gordon Group. 1994. *High Performance Workplaces: Implications for Investment Research and Active Investing Strategies.* Report to the California Public Employees' Retirement System, May 30.

Gordon, Jack. 1992. "Rethinking Diversity." *Training* (January): 23–30.

Gottfredson, Linda. 1992. "Dilemmas in Developing Diversity Programs." In Susan Jackson et al. (ed.), *Diversity in the Workplace,* pp. 279–305. New York: Guilford Press.

————. 1996. "Racially Gerrymandered Police Tests." *Wall Street Journal*, October 24, p. A18.

Graham, Hugh Davis. 1990. *The Civil Rights Era*. New York: Oxford University Press.

Graham, Lawrence Otis. 1993. *The Best Companies for Minorities*. New York: Plume.

Grier, William, and Price Cobbs. 1968. *Black Rage*. New York: Basic Books.

Griggs, Lewis Brown. 1995. "Valuing Relationship: The Heart of Valuing Diversity." In Lewis Brown Griggs and Lente-Louise Louw (eds.). *Valuing Diversity: New Tools for a New Reality*, pp. 203–245. New York: McGraw-Hill.

Griggs, Lewis Brown, and Lente-Louise Louw (eds.). *Valuing Diversity: New Tools for a New Reality*. New York: McGraw-Hill.

Hacker, Andrew. 1992. "The Myths of Racial Division." *New Republic*, March 22, pp. 21–25.

————. 1996. "The End of Affirmative Action?" *New York Review of Books*, July 11, pp. 21, 24–29.

Hagerty, Bob. 1993. "Trainers Help Expatriate Employees Build Bridges to Different Cultures." *Wall Street Journal*, June 14, pp. B1, B3.

Hamilton, Martha M. 1993. "Taking Steps to Deal with Diversity in the Workplace." *Washington Post*, March 15, p. F5.

Heilman, Madeline E., Caryn J. Block, and Johnathan A. Lucas. 1992. "Presumed Incompetent? Stigmatization and Affirmative Action Efforts." *Journal of Applied Psychology* 77 (August): 538–547.

Helprin, Mark. 1994. "Diversity Is Not a Virtue." *Wall Street Journal*, November 25, p. A16.

Hernandez, John. 1991. *Managing a Diverse Workforce*. New York: Lexington Books.

Hernandez, John, with Mary Barr. 1993. *The Diversity Advantage*. New York: Lexington Books.

Hertzberg, Hendrik. 1989. "Wounds of Race." *New Republic*, July 10, pp. 4, 42.

Hofstede, Geert. 1984. *Culture's Consequences: International Differences in Work-Related Values*. Beverly Hills, Calif.: Sage.

————. 1993. *Cultures and Organizations: Software of the Mind*. New York: McGraw-Hill.

Hollander, Paul. 1994. "'Imagined Tyranny?' Political Correctness Reconsidered." *Academic Questions* (Fall): 51–74.

Hubler, Shawn, and Stuart Silverstein. 1993. "Schooling Doesn't Close Minority Earning Gap." *Los Angeles Times*, January 10, pp. A1, A16.

Ibarra, Herminia. 1993. "Personal Networks of Women and Minorities in Management: A Conceptual Framework." *Academy of Management Review* 10:58–87.

Impoco, Jim. 1993. "Working for Mr. Clean Jeans." *U.S. News and World Report*, August 2, pp. 49–50.

Institute for Corporate Diversity. *Diversity in Corporate America 1994–1995 Edition*. Minneapolis, Minn.: Institute for Corporate Diversity.

Jackson, Susan, et al. 1992. *Diversity in the Workplace*. New York: Guilford Press.

Jamieson, David, and Julie O'Mara. 1991. *Managing Workforce 2000*. San Francisco: Jossey-Bass.

Jew, Carolyn. 1995. "Diversity and Discrimination in Corporations: A Case Study in the 1990s." 1995. Paper presented at the Pacific Sociological Association meetings, San Francisco, April 6–9.

Judis, John. 1993. "The Jobless Recovery." *New Republic*, March 15, pp. 20–23.

Kanter, Rosabeth, Barry A. Stein, and Todd D. Jick. 1992. *The Challenge of Organizational Change*. New York: Free Press.

Kass, John. 1993. "Daley Pushing Class Aimed at Merchants Sensitivity Training Hit by Critics." *Chicago Tribune,* July 13, p. 3.

Katz, Judith. 1978.. *White Awareness: Handbook for Anti-Racism Training.* Norman: University of Oklahoma Press.

Kennedy, Paul. 1993. "The 'Graying' and 'Browning' of America." *Los Angeles Times,* February 28, p. M2.

Kenney, Ted. 1992. "Racial Headgames: The Downside of Diversity Training." *Eastside Week,* December 9, pp. 12–23.

Kochman, Thomas. 1981. *Black and White Styles in Conflict.* Chicago: University of Chicago Press.

Kotkin, Joel. 1993. *Tribes: How Race, Religion and Identity Determine Success in the New Global Economy.* New York: Random House.

———. 1993. "Is Clinton Falling into the Entitlement Trap?" *Washington Post National Weekly Edition,* February 15–21.

———. 1993. "The Promised Land Is Not in Our Neighboring States." *Los Angeles Times,* March 7, p. M6.

———. 1995. "Economic Change Is Undercutting the Rationale for Racial Preferences." *Los Angeles Times,* January 29, p. M6.

Kristol, Irving. 1991. "The Tragedy of Multiculturalism." *Wall Street Journal,* July 11, p. A17. (Responses, *Wall Street Journal,* August 19, p. A18.)

Kuran, Timur, 1995. *Private Truths, Public Lies: The Social Consequences of Preference Falsification.* Cambridge, Mass.: Harvard University Press.

Laabs, Jennifer. 1996. "Downshifters: Workers Are Scaling Back. Are You Ready?" *Personnel Journal* (March): 62–76.

Lakin, Martin. 1994. "Sensitivity Training, Diversity Awareness and Intergroup Conflicts on University Campuses: Some Reactions and Some Background." *Academic Questions* (Summer): 80–85.

Lambert, Wade. 1992. "Employee Pacts to Avoid Suits Sought by Firms." *Wall Street Journal,* October 22, p. B1.

Lasch, Christopher. 1994. "Revolt of the Elites." *Harper's* (November): 39–49.

Lawlor, Julia. 1992. "Study: Affirmative-Action Hires' Abilities Doubted." *USA Today,* August 31, p. 3B.

Leo, John. 1991. "The 'Us' Versus 'Them' Industry." *U.S. World and News Report,* December 16, p. 42.

———. 1992. "Bias, Bias Everywhere." *U.S. News and World Report,* March 16, p. 22.

———. 1992. "Straight Talk About Race." *U.S. News and World Report,* April 20, p. 27.

———. 1993. "The Luring of Black Students." *U.S. News and World Report,* March 15, p. 20.

———. 1993. "The Demonizing of White Men." *U.S. News and World Report,* April 26, p. 24.

Lind, Michael. 1995. *The Next American Nation: The New Nationalism and the Fourth American Revolution.* New York: Free Press.

Lipstadt, Deborah. 1993. "Academe Must Not Legitimize Denials of the Holocaust." *Chronicle of Higher Education,* July 28, pp. B1–2.

Loden, Marilyn. 1995. *Implementing Diversity.* Burr Ridge, Ill.: Irwin Professional Publishing.

Loden, Marilyn, and Judy B. Rosener. 1991. *Workforce America! Managing Employee Diversity as a Vital Resource.* Homewood, Ill.: Business One Irwin.

Lopez, Julie Amparno. 1992. "Companies Alter Layoff Policies to Keep Recently Hired Women and Minorities." *Wall Street Journal,* September 18, pp. B1, B5.

————. 1993. "Once Male Enclaves, Corporate Boards Now Comb Executive Suites for Women." *Wall Street Journal,* January 22, pp. B1, B6.

Los Angeles Times. 1990. "L.A. Police United in Attitude, Survey Says." September 2, pp. B1, B6.

————. 1991. "Activists React to Affirmative Action Losses." November 18, p. A1, A26–27.

————. 1992. "Cultural Unity Meeting Erupts into Racial Brawl," November 22, p. B1.

————. 1992. "Minorities, Citing Bias, Sue over Test of Teachers' Skills." September 24, p. A3.

————. 1993. "Study Finds Few Latinos in Top Jobs." March 5, pp. D1, 2.

————. 1993. "Workplace Diversity." Business Section Supplement, May 17.

————. 1994. "U.S. Probes Disparity Between Firing of Minorities, Whites." February 6, p. A16.

Luttwak, Edward N. 1994. "America's Insecurity Blanket." *Washington Post* (Weekly Edition), December 5–11, pp. 23–24.

Lynch, Frederick R. 1991. *Invisible Victims: White Males and the Crisis of Affirmative Action.* New York: Praeger.

————. 1991. "Tales from an Oppressed Class." *Wall Street Journal,* November 11, p. A16.

————. 1992. "Multiculturalism Comes to the Work Place." *Wall Street Journal,* October 22, p. A16.

————. 1994. "Workforce Diversity: PC's Final Frontier?" *National Review,* February 21, pp. 32–36.

————. 1995. "White Elites and Willie Loman." *Los Angeles Times,* March 17, p. B7.

Lynch, Frederick R., and William R. Beer. 1990. "'You Ain't the Right Color, Pal!' Whites' Resentment of Affirmative Action." *Policy Review* (Winter): 64–67.

Mabry, Marcus, et al. 1990. "Past Tokenism." *Newsweek,* May 14, pp. 37–43.

Malkin, Michelle. 1996. "Rodney King Republicans: Foes of Colorblind Justice." *Seattle Times,* June 25, p. 21.

Mansfield, Harvey. 1984. "The Underhandness of Affirmative Action." *National Review,* May 4, pp. 26–32, 61.

McDonald, Heather. 1993. "The Diversity Industry." *New Republic,* July 5, pp. 22–25.

McDowell, Gary. 1989. "Affirmative Inaction: The Brock-Meese Standoff on Federal Racial Quotas." *Policy Review* (Spring): 32–37.

McGowan, William. 1993. "'Affirmative Action' Gone Awry." *Los Angeles Times,* May 13, p. B7.

McLeod, Ramon G. 1993. "Young Minorities, White Women Make Pay Gains." *San Francisco Chronicle,* September 6, pp. A1, A8–9.

Mendosa, Rick. 1991. "Diverse We Stand." *Hispanic Business* (February): 20–24, 59–63.

Michaels, James W. 1993. "One Size Fits None." *National Review,* June 21, pp. 25–28.

Michaud, Ann. 1993. "Ann Morrison: She Helps Corporate Bosses See the Bottom Line." *Los Angeles Times,* May 17, p. 5.

Milbank, Dana. 1992. "Academe Gets Lessons from Big Business." *Wall Street Journal,* December 15, pp. B1, B9.

Miller, Joanne. 1994. *Corporate Responses to Diversity: A Benchmark Study.* Queens College, N.Y.: Center for the New American Workforce.

Mobley, Michael, and Tamara Payne. 1992. "Backlash! The Challenge to Diversity Training." *Training and Development* (December): 45–52.

Modern Maturity. 1992. "The Fabric of a Nation." June–July, pp. 23–32.

Morrison, Ann M. 1992. *The New Leaders.* San Francisco: Jossey-Bass.

Morrison, Ann M., R. P. White, E. Van Velson, and Center for Creative Leadership. 1987. *Breaking the Glass Ceiling.* Reading, Mass.: Addison-Wesley.

Moses, Yolanda. 1993. "The Roadblocks Confronting Minority Administrators." *Chronicle of Higher Education,* January 13, pp. B1–2.

Moskos, Charles C., and John Sibley Butler. 1996. *All That We Can Be: Black Leadership and Racial Integration in the Army.* New York: Basic Books.

"Multiculturalism in Practice: Occidental College." 1995. KCET Television, Los Angeles, June 28.

Myrdal, Gunnar. 1944. *An American Dilemma: The Negro Problem and Modern Democracy.* New York: Harper.

Nelton, Sharon. 1992. "Winning with Diversity." *Nation's Business* (September): 18–24.

Newsweek, 1993. "White Male Paranoia." March 29, pp. 48–54.

Nisbet, Robert A. 1953. *Quest for Community.* New York: Oxford University Press.

———. 1996. *The Degradation of Academic Dogma.* New Brunswick, N.J.: Transaction Press.

Njeri, Itabari. 1989. "Facing Up to Being White." *Los Angeles Times,* December 28, p. E1.

Nobile, Robert. 1991. "Can There Be Too Much Diversity?" *Personnel* 68 (August): 11.

Norden, Edward. 1992. "A Month in Paradise: Scenes from the University of California, San Diego—A Kinder, Gentler Campus, Sort of." *American Spectator* (April): 32–46.

Olson, Walter. 1993. "When Sensitivity Training Is the Law." *Wall Street Journal,* January 20, p. A13.

O'Mara, Julie. 1993. "Managing Diversity." In William R. Tracey (ed.), *Human Resources Management and Development Handbook,* pp. 103–126. New York: AMACOM.

O'Neill, Dave M., and June O'Neill. 1992. "Affirmative Action in the Labor Market." *Annals of the American Academy of Political and Social Science* (September): 88–103.

Overman, Stephanie. 1990. "Different World Brings Challenge." *HRMagazine* (June): 52–55.

Partisan Review. 1993. Special Issue on "The Politics of Political Correctness." Vol. 50, no. 4.

Personnel Journal. 1996. "Save Jobs: Strategies to Stop the Layoffs" (June): 66–89.

Pinkerton, James P. 1995. "Why Affirmative Action Won't Die." *Fortune,* November 11, pp. 191–194.

Quinn, Tony. 1993. "Triple Whammy for California's Economy." *Los Angeles Times,* February 14, p. M6.

Report of the National Advisory Commission on Civil Disorders. 1968. New York: Bantam.

Rice, Faye. 1996. "Denny's Changes Its Spots." *Fortune,* May 13, pp. 133–141.

Rieff, David. 1991. *Los Angeles: Capital of the Third World.* New York: Simon & Schuster.

———. 1993. "Multiculturalism's Silent Partner." *Harper's* (August): 62–68.

Rigdon, Joan. 1992. "Managing: Workforce Diversity Stirs Little Concern." *Wall Street Journal,* May 22, p. B1.

Rodriguez, Richard. 1991. "Mixed Blood." *Harper's* (November): 47–56.

———. 1992 "Multiculturalism with No Diversity." *Los Angeles Times,* May 10, pp. M1, M6.

———. 1992. *Days of Obligation: Arguments with My Mexican Father.* New York: Viking.

Rose, Frederick. 1993. "Moving On: Americans Who Seek a Future in California Find Others Departing." *Wall Street Journal,* January 19, pp. A1, A8.

Rosen, Benson, and Kay Lovelace. 1991. "Piecing Together the Diversity Puzzle." *HRMagazine* (June): 78–84.

Rosen, Jeffrey. 1994. "Is Affirmative Action Doomed?" *New Republic,* October 17, 1994, pp. 25–35.

Royko, Mike. 1992. "Is This Any Way to Boost Business?" *Chicago Tribune,* June 2, p. 3.

Rudolph, Susanne Hoeber, and Lloyd I. Rudolph. 1993. "Modern Hate: How Ancient Animosities Get Invented." *New Republic,* March 22, pp. 24–29.

Sacks, David O., and Peter A. Thiel. 1995. *The Diversity Myth.* San Francisco: Independent Institute.

Sanchez, Richard. 1991. "Managing Diversity: An Overview." Faculty/Staff Diversity Conference, California Community Colleges, San Francisco, March 3–5.

Schirof, Joannie. 1993. "The Gender Machine." *U.S. News and World Report,* August 2, 1993. pp. 42–44.

Schlesinger, Arthur, Jr. 1990. "When Ethnic Studies Are Un-American." *Wall Street Journal,* April 23, p. A14.

Seligman, Daniel. 1993. "PC Comes to the Newsroom." *National Review,* June 21, pp. 28–37.

Shalit, Ruth. 1993. "Unwhite House: Clinton's Diversity Record—and Bush's." *New Republic,* April 12, pp. 12–14.

———. 1995. "The Washington Post in Black and White: Race in the Newsroom." *New Republic,* October 2, pp. 20–37.

Shellenbarger, Sue. 1993. "Work and Family: So Much Talk, So Little Action." *Wall Street Journal* (Special Supplement), June 21, pp. R1–14.

———. 1993. "Workforce Study Finds Loyalty Is Weak, Divisions of Race and Gender Are Deep." *Wall Street Journal,* September 3, p. B5.

Shepard, Alicia C. 1993. "High Anxiety: The Call for Diversity in the Newsroom Has White Men Running Scared." *American Journalism Review* (November): 19–24.

Sherman, Stratford. 1993. "A Brave, New Darwinian Workplace." *Fortune,* January 25, pp. 50–56.

———. 1993. "Are You as Good as the Best in the World?" *Fortune,* December 13, pp. 93–94.

Silverstein, Stuart. 1993. "Census Finds More Women in High Jobs." *Los Angeles Times,* January 29, p. 1A.

———. 1995. "Workplace Diversity Efforts Thrive Despite Backlash." *Los Angeles Times,* May 2, pp. A1, A14.

———, and Alexei Barrionuevo. 1993. "Firms Lag in Keeping Vow to Hire More Minorities." *Los Angeles Times,* May 5, pp. A3–22.

Sims, Calvin. 1993. "The Unbreakable Glass Ceiling: Promotions Scarce in Military Industry." *New York Times,* June 7, pp. C1–5.

Skrentny, John David. 1996. *The Ironies of Affirmative Action: Politics, Culture and Justice in America.* Chicago: University of Chicago Press.

Smelser, Jeil J. 1993. "The Politics of Ambivalence: Diversity in the Research Universities." *Daedalus* 22 (Fall): 37–53.

Sniderman, Paul, and Thomas Piazza. 1993. *The Scare of Race.* Cambridge, Mass.: Belknap Press of Harvard University Press.

Society for Human Resources Management/Commerce Clearing House Survey on Diversity. 1993. *Diversity Management Is Culture Change, Not Just Training.* Alexandria, Va.: Society for Human Resource Management.

Solomon, Charlene Marmer. 1989. "The Corporate Response to Workforce Diversity." *Personnel Journal* (August):

———. 1991. "Are White Males Being Left Out?" *Personnel Journal* (November): 88–94.

———. 1995. "Affirmative Action: What You Need to Know." *Personnel Journal* (August): 56–67.

———. 1996. "Testing at Odds with Diversity Efforts?" *Personnel Journal* (April): 131–142.

Solomon, Jolie. 1990. "As Cultural Diversity of Workers Grows, Experts Urge Appreciation of Differences." *Wall Street Journal,* September 12, pp. B1, B13.

Sowell, Thomas. 1993. "Multicultural Instruction." *American Spectator* (April): 47–49.

Spayd, Liz. 1992. "Over the Hill at 40-Plus?" *Washington Post National Weekly Edition,* October 12–18, p. 22.

Steele, Shelby. 1991. *The Content of Our Character.* New York: Harper Perennial.

———. 1995. "How Liberals Lost Their Virtue over Race." *Newsweek,* January 9, pp. 41–42.

Stewart, Thomas. 1993. "Welcome to the Revolution." *Fortune,* December 13, pp. 66–77.

Stoker, Laura. 1997. "Understanding Whites' Resistance to Affirmative Action: The Role of Principled Commitments and Racial Prejudice." In John Hurwitz and Mark Peffley (eds.), *Perception and Prejudice: Race and Politics in the United States.* New Haven, CT: Yale University Press.

Stimpson, Catherine R. "It Is Time to Rethink Affirmative Action." *Chronicle of Higher Education,* January 15, p. A48.

Stoker, Laura. 1997. "Understanding Whites' Resistance to Affirmative Action: The Role of Principled Commitments and Racial Prejudice." In John Hurwitz and Mark Peffley (eds.), *Perception and Prejudice: Race and Politics in the United States.* New Haven, CT: Yale University Press.

Suro, Robert. 1992. "Poll Finds Hispanic Desire to Assimilate." *New York Times,* December 15, pp. 1, 18.

Swanger, Clare. 1994. "Perspectives on the History of Ameliorating Oppression and Supporting Diversity in United States Organizations." In Elsie Cross et al. (eds.), *The Promise of Diversity,* pp. 3–23. Burt Ridge, Ill.: Irwin Professional Publishing.

Swasy, Alecia. 1993. "Stay-at-Home Moms Are Fashionable Again in Many Communities." *Wall Street Journal,* July 23, pp. A1, A16.

Swisher, Karen. "Diversity Training: Learning from Past Mistakes." *Washington Post Weekly,* February 13–19, p. 20.

Taylor, Jared. 1992. *Paved with Good Intentions.* New York: Carroll and Graf.

Thernstrom, Abigail. 1996. *Don't End It, Don't Mend It, Defend It: Reviewing the Clinton Record on Racial Preferences.* Washington, D.C: Center for Equal Opportunity.

Thernstrom, Stephan. 1990. "The Minority Majority Will Never Come." *Wall Street Journal,* July 26, p. A17.

Thiederman, Sondra. 1991. *Bridging Cultural Barriers for Corporate Success.* New York: Lexington Books.

———. 1991. *Profiting in America's Multicultural Marketplace.* New York: Lexington Books.

Thomas, R. Roosevelt, Jr. 1990. "From Affirmative Action to Affirming Diversity." *Harvard Business Review* (March–April): 107–117.

———. 1992. *Beyond Race and Gender.* New York: AMACOM Press.

———. 1993. "Managing Diversity: A Conceptual Framework." In Susan Jackson et al. (ed.), *Diversity in the Workplace.* New York: Guilford Press.

———. 1994. "A Diversity Perspective on the Language Challenge." *Employment Relations Today* (Winter): 363–375.

———. 1994. "The Diversity Paradigm: A Framework for Practice and Inquiry." Paper presented at the Diversity in Organizations conference, Claremont, California, February 1994.

———. 1996. *Redefining Diversity.* New York: AMACOM Press.

Tilove, Jonathan. 1991. "Managing the New Diversity." *San Francisco Examiner,* July 14, 1991, pp. D1, D6–7.

————. 1991. "For Affirmative Action, 'Coke's the Real Thing.'" *San Francisco Examiner,* August 4, p. E-3.

Time. 1992. "The Cost of Quality." September 7, pp. 48–49.

————. 1993. "The Temping of America." March 29, pp. 40–47.

Triandis, Harry C. 1995. "A Theoretical Framework for the Study of Diversity." In Martin Chemers, Stuart Oskamp, and Mark Costanzo, *Diversity in Organizations: New Perspectives for a Changing Workplace.* Thousand Oaks, Calif.: Sage.

————. 1993. Review of *Cultures and Organizations: Software of the Mind* by Geert Hofstede. *Administrative Science Quarterly* (March): 132–134.

Tsui, Anne S., Terri D. Egan, and Charles A. O'Reilly III. 1992 "Being Different Relational Demography and Organizational Attachment." *Administrative Science Quarterly* 37:549–579.

Tsui, Anne S., Terri D. Egan, and Katherine R. Xin. 1995. "Diversity in Organizations: Lessons from Demography Research." In Martin M. Chemers, Stuart Oskamp, and Mark A. Costanzo (eds.), *Diversity in Organizations: New Perspectives for a Changing Workplace,* pp.191–220. Thousand Oaks, Calif.: Sage.

Tsui, Anne S., and Lyman Porter. 1993. "A Study of Work Force Diversity in 55 Orange County Companies." Unpublished manuscript. Graduate School of Management, University of California, Irvine.

U.S. News and World Report. 1992. "Race on Campus." April 19, pp. 52–65.

————. 1993. "The M.B.A. Gets Real." March 22, pp. 54–55.

————. 1993. "Where Did My Career Go? The White Collar Lament of the '90s." June 28, pp. 42–52.

Vobejda, Barbara. 1992. "A Nation in Transition: Census Reveals Striking Stratification of U.S. Society." *Washington Post,* May 29, pp. A1, A18–19.

Wall Street Journal. 1992. "They Call It 'Diversity.'" September 29, p. A14.

————. 1993. "Breaking Barriers: Work-force Diversity Faces Big Obstacles." February 2, p. A1.

————. 1993. "Campus Recruiting Plummets as Companies Target Specific Hires." February 16, p. A1.

Walters, Donna H. 1992. "Gender Gap Narrowing as Men's Pay Drops at Faster Rate Than Women's Pay." *Los Angeles Times,* September 13, p. D3.

Walsh, James. 1995. *Managing Diversity: Managing for Success Under ADA and Other Anti-Discrimination Laws.* Santa Monica, Calif.: Merritt Publishing Co.

Watson, Warren E., Kmalesh Kumar, and Larry Michaelsen. 1993. "Cultural Diversity's Impact on Interaction Process and Performance: Comparing Homogeneous and Diverse Task Groups." *Academy of Management Journal* 36:590–602.

Weiner, Annette B. 1992. "Anthropology's Lessons for Cultural Diversity." *Chronicle of Higher Education,* July 22, pp. B1–2.

Welch, John F. 1993. "A Master Class in Radical Change." *Fortune,* December 13, pp. 82–90.

Wheeler, Michael J. 1994. *Diversity Training: A Research Report.* New York: Conference Board.

————. 1996. *Diversity: Business Rationale and Strategies.* New York: Conference Board.

White, J. P. 1992. "Else Cross Versus the Suits." *Los Angeles Times Magazine,* August 9, 14–18, pp. 38–44.

Williams, Lena. 1992. "Scrambling to Manage a Diverse Workforce." *New York Times,* December 15, pp. A1, C2.

Wilson, James Q. 1996. "Sins of Admission." *New Republic,* July 8, pp. 12–16.

Winterle, Mary J. 1992. *Work Force Diversity: Corporate Challenges, Corporate Responses.* New York: Conference Board.

Wolfe, Alan. 1992. "The New American Dilemma: Understanding and Misunderstanding Race." *New Republic,* April 13, pp. 30–37.

———. 1994. "The New Class Comes Home." *Partisan Review* 50 (no. 4): 720–737.

Woodman, Richard W., John E. Sawyer, and Rickey W. Griffin. 1993. "Toward a Theory of Organizational Creativity." *Academy of Management Review* 18:293–321.

Wright, Lawrence. 1993. "One Drop of Blood." *New Yorker,* July 25, pp. 46–50.

Wysocki, Bernard, Jr. 1996. "Missing in Action: About a Million Men Have Left Work Force in the Past Year or So." *Wall Street Journal,* June 12, pp. A1, A6.

Yates, Steven. 1994. *Civil Wrongs: What Went Wrong with Affirmative Action.* San Francisco: Institute for Contemporary Studies.

Zachary, G. Pascal. 1993. "Like Factory Workers, Professionals Face Loss of Jobs to Foreigners." *Wall Street Journal,* March 17, pp. A1, A9.

———. 1996. "Major U.S. Companies Expand Efforts to Sell to Consumers Abroad." *Wall Street Journal,* June 13, pp. A1, A6.

Zelnick, Bob. 1996. *Backfire: A Reporter's Look at Affirmative Action.* Washington, D.C.: Regnery.

Index